Fodor's

WASHINGTON, D.C.

Fodor's Travel Publications   New York, Toronto, London, Sydney, Auckland

www.fodors.com

Be a Fodor's Correspondent

Your opinion matters. It matters to us. It matters to your fellow Fodor's travelers, too. And we'd like to hear it. In fact, we need to hear it.

When you share your experiences and opinions, you become an active member of the Fodor's community. That means we'll not only use your feedback to make our books better, but we'll publish your names and comments whenever possible. Throughout our guides, look for "Word of Mouth," excerpts of your unvarnished feedback.

Here's how you can help improve Fodor's for all of us.

Tell us when we're right. We rely on local writers to give you an insider's perspective. But our writers and staff editors—who are the best in the business—depend on you. Your positive feedback is a vote to renew our recommendations for the next edition.

Tell us when we're wrong. We're proud that we update most of our guides every year. But we're not perfect. Things change. Hotels cut services. Museums change hours. Charming cafés lose charm. If our writer didn't quite capture the essence of a place, tell us how you'd do it differently. If any of our descriptions are inaccurate or inadequate, we'll incorporate your changes in the next edition and will correct factual errors at fodors.com immediately.

Tell us what to include. You probably have had fantastic travel experiences that aren't yet in Fodor's. Why not share them with a community of like-minded travelers? Maybe you chanced upon a beach or bistro or B&B that you don't want to keep to yourself. Tell us why we should include it. And share your discoveries and experiences with everyone directly at fodors.com. Your input may lead us to add a new listing or highlight a place we cover with a "Highly Recommended" star or with our highest rating, "Fodor's Choice."

Give us your opinion instantly at our feedback center at www.fodors.com/feedback. You may also e-mail editors@fodors.com with the subject line "Washington, D.C. Editor." Or send your nominations, comments, and complaints by mail to Washington, D.C. Editor, Fodor's, 1745 Broadway, New York, NY 10019.

You and travelers like you are the heart of the Fodor's community. Make our community richer by sharing your experiences. Be a Fodor's correspondent.

Happy traveling!

Tim Jarrell, Publisher

FODOR'S WASHINGTON, D.C. 2011

Editor: Jess Moss

Editorial Contributors: Beth Kanter, Cathy Sharpe, Elana Schor

Production Editor: Evangelos Vasilakis

Maps & Illustrations: David Lindroth, Mark Stroud, *cartographers;* Bob Blake, Rebecca Baer, *map editors;* William Wu, *information graphics*

Design: Fabrizio La Rocca, *creative director;* Guido Caroti, Siobhan O'Hare, *art directors;* Tina Malaney, Chie Ushio, Ann McBride, Jessica Walsh, *designers;* Melanie Marin, *senior picture editor*

Cover Photo: (Smithsonian National Air & Space Museum): Alfred Wekelo/ Shutterstock

Production Manager: Angela McLean

ISBN 978-1-4000-0475-1

ISSN 0743–9741

SPECIAL SALES

This book is available at special discounts for bulk purchases for sales promotions or premiums. Special editions, including personalized covers, excerpts of existing books, and corporate imprints, can be created in large quantities for special needs. For more information, write to Special Markets/Premium Sales, 1745 Broadway, MD 6-2, New York, New York 10019, or e-mail specialmarkets@randomhouse.com.

AN IMPORTANT TIP & AN INVITATION

Although all prices, opening times, and other details in this book are based on information supplied to us at press time, changes occur all the time in the travel world, and Fodor's cannot accept responsibility for facts that become outdated or for inadvertent errors or omissions. So **always confirm information when it matters,** especially if you're making a detour to visit a specific place. Your experiences—positive and negative— matter to us. If we have missed or misstated something, **please write to us.** We follow up on all suggestions. Contact the Washington, D.C. editor at editors@fodors.com or c/o Fodor's at 1745 Broadway, New York, NY 10019.

PRINTED IN SINGAPORE

10 9 8 7 6 5 4 3 2 1

CONTENTS

MAPS

ABOUT THIS BOOK

Our Ratings

Sometimes you find terrific travel experiences and sometimes they just find you. But usually the burden is on you to select the right combination of experiences. That's where our ratings come in.

As travelers we've all discovered a place so wonderful that its worthiness is obvious. And sometimes that place is so unique that superlatives don't do it justice: you just have to be there to know. These sights, properties, and experiences get our highest rating, **Fodor's Choice**, indicated by orange stars throughout this book.

Black stars highlight sights and properties we deem **Highly Recommended,** places that our writers, editors, and readers praise again and again for consistency and excellence.

By default, there's another category: any place we include in this book is by definition worth your time, unless we say otherwise. And we will.

Disagree with any of our choices? Care to nominate a place or suggest that we rate one more highly? Visit our feedback center at www.fodors.com/feedback.

Budget Well

Hotel and restaurant price categories from ¢ to $$$$ are defined in the opening pages of the respective chapters. For attractions, we always give standard adult admission fees; reductions are usually available for children, students, and senior citizens. Want to pay with plastic? **AE, D, DC, MC, V** following restaurant and hotel listings indicate whether American Express, Discover, Diners Club, MasterCard, and Visa are accepted.

Restaurants

Unless we state otherwise, restaurants are open for lunch and dinner daily. We mention dress only when there's a specific requirement and reservations only when they're essential or not accepted—it's always best to book ahead.

Hotels

Hotels have private bath, phone, TV, and air-conditioning and operate on the European Plan (aka EP, meaning without meals), unless we specify that they use the Continental Plan (CP, with a Continental breakfast), Breakfast Plan (BP, with a full breakfast), or Modified American Plan (MAP, with breakfast and dinner), or are all-inclusive (AI, including all meals

and most activities). We always list facilities but not whether you'll be charged an extra fee to use them.

Listings	
★	Fodor's Choice
★	Highly recommended
⊠	Physical address
↔	Directions or Map coordinates
⌂	Mailing address
☎	Telephone
📠	Fax
⊕	On the Web
✎	E-mail
🎫	Admission fee
⊙	Open/closed times
Ⓜ	Metro stations
▭	Credit cards
Hotels & Restaurants	
🏨	Hotel
🛏	Number of rooms
⚴	Facilities
⍾	Meal plans
✕	Restaurant
⌖	Reservations
🔒	Dress code
⚲	Smoking
ᛩ	BYOB
Outdoors	
🏌	Golf
⛺	Camping
Other	
♻	Family-friendly
⇨	See also
⊠	Branch address
☞	Take note

Experience
Washington, D.C.

WASHINGTON, D.C. TODAY

Outwardly serene and classically beautiful, the Capitol, the White House, and the Supreme Court stand at the heart of Washington, D.C. They are powerful, steadfast symbols of the stability and strength of the nation. But the city that revolves around this axis is in a constant state of change, lived on a more human scale.

Today's D.C. . . .

. . . is obsessed with politics. The historic arrival of President Barack Obama in the White House has captivated the overwhelmingly Democratic D.C. in ways not seen in years—a dynamic only heightened by the army of new officials and other influence peddlers that accompanied the transition. Still, many local residents take a different view of national elections than the rest of the country. Given the city's measly three electoral votes and general lack of representation at the Capitol, Washingtonians may be more interested in what the outcome means for their employment than in the actual candidate-to-candidate battles.

The quest to secure the vote for D.C. continues. A bill that would pair one vote in the House for the liberal-leaning District (whose license plates read "Taxation Without Representation") with an extra House seat for conservative Utah passed the Senate in February 2009, but not before Republicans successfully attached an amendment repealing most of the District's gun control laws, which are among the strictest in the nation. As of this writing, the bill is stalled indefinitely in the House over the gun control controversy.

. . . is certifiably sports crazy. And first and foremost, it is a football town. Loyal Redskins fans are extremely passionate, selling out every home game since 1968. The 2008 season got off to a promising start, but injuries combined with a relatively inexperienced quarterback left rookie coach Jim Zorn struggling for offensive answers—and kept the team out of the play-offs. Meanwhile, the team's defense still hasn't found a replacement for sensational safety Sean Taylor, who was murdered in a botched robbery attempt in 2007. Billionaire owner Danny Snyder, a 43-year-old wunderkind in the world of business, has shelled out big bucks to attract top players and coaches, but that formula has yet to return the burgundy and gold to the Super Bowl under his watch.

D.C.: JUST THE FACTS

THE PEOPLE
Population, city: 588,292

Population, metro area: 5,306,565

Median age: 34.9

Ethnic makeup: African-American 55.2%; white 39.4%; Hispanic 8.3%; Asian 3.4%; multiracial 1.6%

Infant mortality rate: 13.6 per 1,000 births

Literacy: 63%

Crime rate: 77.1 offenses per 1,000 residents

Type of government: Limited representational democracy with no voting members of Congress; elected mayor and nine-member council

Workforce: 321,698 (66.5%)

Per capita income: $38,009

The nation's pastime has a new home in the nation's capital; the Nationals have a new sports complex on the Anacostia waterfront. The $611 million project was opposed by many residents and City Council members, who thought taxpayers contributed too much money. Salting the wounds, the new owners refused to pay the city millions in rent during the first season—a situation finally resolved at the end of 2008. Those who have wanted a baseball team in D.C. since the dawn of time have turned a blind eye to the hard numbers. They'd certainly be happier, though, if the Nationals could improve on their first-year record of 59-102.

Even soccer draws a fiercely loyal following in the District. Local team D.C. United isn't immune to stadium controversy either. At this writing, the team, which has long played at RFK Stadium, is looking for a new home, possibly in the suburbs. D.C. Council members looking to keep the team in the District are hoping to have the city subsidize a new stadium at Poplar Point, a 110-acre park along the Anacostia River, to the tune of $150 million.

D.C. is not known for being a hockey town, but locals have recently been mesmerized by their newest sports superstar, Capitals forward Alex Ovechkin. The explosive 23-year-old Moscow native was the league's MVP in 2008, drawing sellout crowds to the Verizon Center that the Caps haven't seen in years.

. . . is stuck in traffic. Spend an hour in gridlock on the Beltway—or wait 20 minutes for a Metro train to come—and you'll know why residents gripe so much about transportation. Metro initiated the largest fare increases in its history in early 2008; almost simultaneously, performance data revealed that on-time service had declined over the preceding 17-month period. The most major Metro extension is, of course, the most hotly contested. A project has been approved to build a new rail line linking the Orange Line to Tysons Corner, Dulles Airport, and other northern Virginia destinations. The 23-mi, $5.2 billion project was scheduled for completion by 2015, but arguments over whether the Tysons Corner section should be elevated or underground have held up the entire process. Given the poor public transit options from D.C. to Dulles, locals hope that someday the Metro will reach two airports—not just one.

Unemployment: 11.7% (Sept. 2009)

Major industries: Government, law, tourism, high-tech, higher education

Official motto: *Justitia omnibus (justice for all)*

Official food: The half-smoke, a large, smoked link sausage

most famously found at Ben's Chili Bowl on U Street

THE LAND
Land area: 61 square mi

Nicknames: The District, D.C., Inside the Beltway

Latitude: 38 N

Longitude: 77° W

Elevation: From sea level to 420 feet

Environmental issues: High levels of lead in the water supplies of some households; elevated arsenic levels near American University

Natural hazards: Lobbyists, motorcades, lack of congressional representation

WASHINGTON, D.C. PLANNER

Safety Tips

D.C. is a relatively safe city, but crimes do occur, even in typically "safe" neighborhoods. The best way to protect yourself is to stick to well-lighted and populated areas and avoid walking alone after dark. Many of the city's business and government districts become deserted at night, but the public transportation system is exceptionally safe, with only a few incidents of crime reported each year.

When to Go

D.C. has two delightful seasons: spring and autumn. In spring the city's ornamental fruit trees are budding, and its many gardens are in bloom. By autumn most of the summer crowds have left and you can enjoy the sights in peace. Summers can be uncomfortably hot and humid. Winter weather is mild by East Coast standards, but a handful of modest snowstorms each year bring this southern city to a standstill.

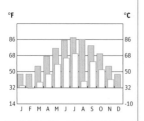

Getting Your Bearings

Four Quadrants: The address system in D.C. takes some getting used to. The city is divided into the four quadrants of a compass (NW, NE, SE, SW), with the U.S. Capitol at the center. Because the Capitol doesn't sit in the exact center of the city (the Washington Monument does), Northwest is the largest quadrant. Northwest also has most of the important landmarks, although Northeast and Southwest have their fair share. The boundaries are North Capitol Street, East Capitol Street, South Capitol Street, and the National Mall. That's where street addresses start.

Numbered Streets and Lettered Streets: Within each quadrant, numbered streets run north to south, and lettered streets run east to west (the letter J was omitted to avoid confusion with the letter I). The streets form a fairly simple grid—for instance 900 G Street NW is the intersection of 9th and G streets in the northwest quadrant of the city. Likewise, if you count the letters of the alphabet, skipping J, you can get a good sense of the location of an address on a numbered street. For instance, 1600 16th Street NW is close to Q Street, Q being the 16th letter of the alphabet if you skip J.

Avenues on the Diagonal: As if all this weren't confusing enough, Major Pierre L'Enfant, the Frenchman who originally designed the city, threw in diagonal avenues recalling those of Paris. Most of D.C.'s avenues are named after U.S. states. You can find addresses on avenues the same way you find those on numbered streets, so 1200 Connecticut Avenue NW is close to M Street, because M is the 12th letter of the alphabet when you skip J.

D.C. by Public Transit

Driving in D.C. can be a headache. Traffic is usually congested, and the road layout is designed for frustration, with one-way streets popping up at just the wrong moment. Once you've reached your destination, the real challenge begins: D.C. may be the most difficult city in America in which to find a place to park. All of this means that if you have a car you'd be wise to leave it at your hotel and use public transit whenever possible.

Metro and Bus: The Washington Metropolitan Area Transit Authority operates a network of subway lines (known locally as the Metro) and bus routes throughout D.C. Most popular tourist attractions are near Metro stops, though certain areas are only accessible by bus, most notably Georgetown and Adams Morgan.

Metro fares depend on the distance traveled. Fares range from $1.65 to $4.50 during morning and evening rush hours and after 2 AM, and from $1.35 to $2.35 at all other times. Bus fares are $1.35 (exact change only) for regular routes, and $3.10 for express routes. Since January 2009, the popular free transfers between buses are available only to holders of plastic SmarTrip cards; transfers from the Metro to the bus take 90¢ off your bus fare. One-day passes on the Metro are available for $7.80, and weekly bus tickets run $11. Both can be purchased online.

For fare information, route maps, and trip planning help, visit ⊕ *www.wmata.com* or call ☎ *202/637–7000.*

Taxi: In 2007, D.C. made the controversial switch from zone to metered taxicabs. The move was highly unpopular among taxi drivers at the time, but aside from some sporadic grumbling, the transition has been smooth. There is a $3 minimum base charge, with the rate increasing 25¢ for every sixth of a mile and for every minute either stopped in traffic or going slower than 10 mi per hour. When gas prices jumped in 2008, the city applied an additional $1 gas surcharge to each trip. That charge was removed in December 2008, but will probably return if prices at the pump rise again. For the latest information on fares, visit ⊕ *www.dctaxi.dc.gov.*

The Visitor Center

The D.C. Visitor Information Center (✉ *1300 Pennsylvania Ave. NW,* ☎ *866/324–7386* ⊕ *www.dcvisit.com*) is in the Ronald Reagan International Trade Center Building. It's open weekdays year-round and also on Saturday in spring and summer. Visitors can pick up maps and brochures, book a hotel, purchase tickets for tours or performances, and use interactive kiosks to get more information on attractions and services in D.C.

The Smoking Ban

Smoking has been banned in restaurants, bars, nightclubs, and taverns since January 2007. It is allowed outside, leading to the increased popularity of establishments with rooftop bars or back decks. The flip side of the decision is that crowds now gather on the sidewalks in front of clubs, blocking pedestrian traffic and creating noise issues for residents. Then again, if you can't handle a little noise, why live above a bar?

WHAT'S WHERE

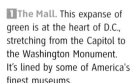

1 **The Mall.** This expanse of green is at the heart of D.C., stretching from the Capitol to the Washington Monument. It's lined by some of America's finest museums.

2 **The Monuments.** D.C.'s most famous monuments are concentrated west of the Mall and along the Tidal Basin.

3 **The White House Area and Foggy Bottom.** There's great art at the Corcoran and Renwick galleries, as well as performances at the Kennedy Center, and a whiff of scandal at the Watergate.

4 **Capitol Hill.** The Capitol itself, along with the Supreme Court and Library of Congress, dominates this area. Follow Hill staffers to find restaurants, bars, and a thriving outdoor market.

5 **Downtown.** The Federal Triangle and Penn Quarter attract visitors to Ford's Theatre, the International Spy Museum, the National Portrait Gallery, and the American Art Museum. By night, crowds head to the Verizon Center and Chinatown's bars, restaurants, and movie theaters.

6 **Georgetown.** The capital's wealthiest neighborhood is great for strolling, shopping, and partying, with the scene centering around Wisconsin and M streets. The C&O Canal provides recreation in and out of the water.

7 **Dupont Circle.** This hub of fashionable restaurants and shops is also home to the most visible segment of the gay community. The Kalorama neighborhood is an enclave of embassies, luxurious homes, and small museums.

8 **Adams Morgan.** One of D.C.'s most ethnically diverse neighborhoods has offbeat restaurants and shops and happening nightlife. Grand 19th-century apartment buildings and row houses have lured young professionals here.

9 **Upper Northwest.** This mostly residential swath of D.C. holds two must-see attractions: the National Cathedral and the National Zoo.

10 **U Street Corridor.** Revitalization has brought trendy boutiques and hip eateries to the area around 14th and U, which was a hotbed of African-American culture in the early 20th century.

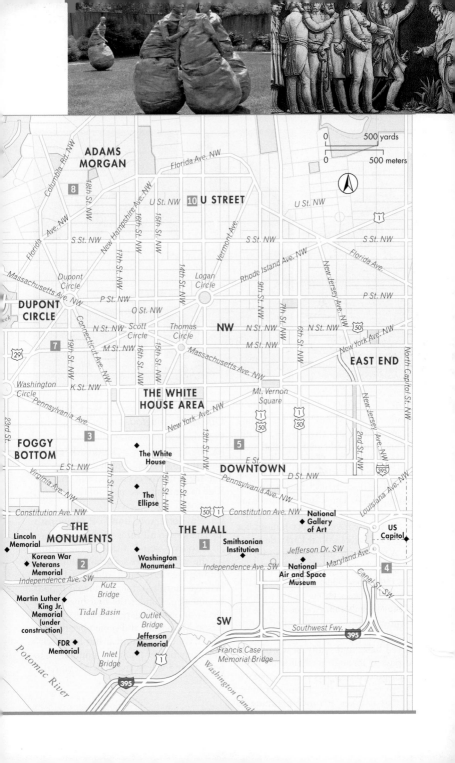

ADAMS
MORGAN

8

Columbia Rd. NW

48th St. NW

Florida Ave. NW

U St. NW 10 U STREET

U St. NW

S St. NW

S St. NW

S St. NW

New Hampshire Ave. NW

15th St. NW

16th St. NW

14th St. NW

Vermont Ave.

Florida Ave.

Florida Ave. NW

Dupont
Circle

17th St. NW

P St. NW

Logan
Circle

Rhode Island Ave. NW

9th St. NW

P St. NW

Massachusetts Ave. NW

DUPONT
CIRCLE

O St. NW

N St. NW

Scott
Circle

7th St. NW

New Jersey Ave. NW

50

N St. NW

Connecticut Ave. NW

Thomas
Circle

NW

N St. NW

6th St. NW

7

19th St. NW

M St. NW

16th St. NW

15th St. NW

Massachusetts Ave. NW

M St. NW

M St. NW

New York Ave. NW

EAST END

29

Washington
Circle

K St. NW

Pennsylvania Ave.

THE WHITE
HOUSE AREA

Mt. Vernon
Square

North Capitol St. NW

23rd St.

Virginia Ave. NW

3

E St. NW

The White
House

13th St. NW

New York Ave. NW

1
50

1
50

New Jersey Ave. NW

2nd St. NW

395

FOGGY
BOTTOM

5

DOWNTOWN

E St

D St. NW

The
Ellipse

14th St. NW

15th St. NW

Pennsylvania Ave. NW

Louisiana Ave. NW

Constitution Ave. NW

50   1

Constitution Ave. NW

National
Gallery
of Art

US
Capitol

Lincoln
Memorial

THE
MONUMENTS

THE MALL

1

Smithsonian
Institution

Jefferson Dr. SW

Korean War
Veterans
Memorial

2

Washington
Monument

Independence Ave. SW

National
Air and Space
Museum

Maryland Ave.

4

Independence Ave. SW

Kutz
Bridge

Canal St. SW

Martin Luther
King Jr.
Memorial
(under
construction)

Tidal Basin

Outlet
Bridge

SW

Southwest Fwy.

395

FDR
Memorial

Inlet
Bridge

Jefferson
Memorial

Francis Case
Memorial Bridge

Potomac River

395

Washington Canal

0   500 yards
0   500 meters

WASHINGTON, D.C. TOP ATTRACTIONS

Capitol

(A) Home of the Senate and the House of Representatives, the marble Capitol is an architectural marvel filled with frescoes and statues. Tours now begin at the new Capitol Visitor Center—a massive $621-million project that opened in December 2008. The Capitol grounds are equally stunning—Frederick Law Olmsted, the landscape architect famous for New York City's Central Park, designed them. A tour of the interior is impressive, but nothing beats attending a live debate on the House or Senate floor.

White House

(B) 1600 Pennsylvania Avenue may be the best-known address in the United States. Every president but George Washington has lived here, and many heads of state have passed through its hallowed halls. The self-guided tour lets you follow their footsteps through the historic rooms. Note that it takes advance planning to visit the White House. ⇨ *See Chapter 5, Official Washington, for details.*

Washington Monument

(C) The epitome of a landmark attraction, this 555-foot, 5-inch obelisk is visible from nearly everywhere in the city. Ride to the top to see views of the District, Maryland, and Virginia.

Lincoln, Jefferson, and FDR Memorials

(D) The key to all three of these memorials is to stop, stand, and read the writing on the walls. There's nothing quite like reading the Gettysburg Address while the massive marble statue of Lincoln broods behind you. Ponder the first lines of the Declaration of Independence at the Jefferson Memorial, and remember the line "We have nothing to fear but fear itself" as you encounter the stark monuments to poverty and war at the FDR Memorial.

National Cathedral

(E) Like its 14th-century counterparts, this 20th-century cathedral has a nave, transepts, and vaults that were built stone by stone. Unlike those historic buildings, the National Cathedral has a gargoyle in the shape of Darth Vader. For a unique experience, come for a tour and tea.

Dumbarton Oaks

(F) If you enjoy formal gardens, visit the 10-acre grounds of Dumbarton Oaks, one of the loveliest spots for a stroll.

Arlington National Cemetery

(G) The serene hills across the Potomac from the Tidal Basin are the final resting place for some 340,000 members of the armed services, from Civil War casualties to fallen soldiers of the Iraq War. A visit here can be both sobering and moving.

Smithsonian Museums

(H) Mostly flanking the National Mall, these illustrious galleries hold everything from Kermit the Frog to the *Spirit of St. Louis* and the Hope Diamond to Rodin's *Burghers of Calais*.

Vietnam Veterans, Korean War Veterans, and World War II Memorials

Touch a name on "the Wall." See your reflection alongside the statues of veterans of the Korean War. Search for the stories of those who lost their lives in WWII. These memorials are interactive, personal, and unforgettable.

National Zoo

The pandas, here through December 2010 when their loan will be renotiated, may be the zoo's most famous attraction, but they're not the only highlight. Monkeys, elephants, and lions never fail to delight, and more-exotic residents, such as sloth bears, red pandas, clouded leopards, and Japanese giant salamanders, can be found on the Asia Trail.

GREAT ITINERARIES

ONE DAY IN D.C.

If you have a day or less (and even a dollar or less!) in D.C., your sightseeing strategy is simple: take the Metro to the Smithsonian stop and explore the area around the Mall. You'll be at the undisputed heart of the city—a beautiful setting in which you'll find America's greatest collection of museums, with the city's spectacular monuments and the halls of government a stone's throw away.

Facing the Capitol, to your left are the **Museum of Natural History**, the **National Gallery of Art**, and the **National Archives**. To your right are the **Museum of African Art**, the **Hirshhorn Museum**, the **National Air and Space Museum**, and more. Head the other direction, toward the **Washington Monument**, and you're also on your way to the **World War II Memorial**, the **Lincoln Memorial**, the **Vietnam Veterans Memorial**, and more monuments to America's presidents and its past. A lover of American history and culture could spend a thoroughly happy month, much less a day, wandering the Mall and its surroundings.

If you're here first thing in the morning: You can hit monuments and memorials early. They're open 24 hours a day and staffed beginning at 8 AM. The outdoor sculpture garden at the **Hirshhorn** opens at 7:30, and the Smithsonian Institution Building ("the Castle") opens at 8:30. In the Castle you can grab a cup of coffee, watch an 18-minute film about D.C., and see examples of objects from many of the 18 Smithsonian museums.

If you only have a few hours in the evening: Experience the beauty of monuments at dusk and after dark. Many people think they're even more striking when the sun goes down. National Park Service rangers staff most monuments until midnight.

FIVE DAYS IN D.C.

Day 1

With more time at your disposal, you have a chance both to see the sights and to get to know the city. A guided bus tour is a good way to get yourself oriented; if you take one of the hop-on, hop-off tours we recommend under Day Tours and Guides in the "Travel Smart Washington, D.C." chapter at the back of this book, you'll get genuine insights without a lot of tourist hokum.

Because you can get on and off wherever you like, it's a good idea to explore **Georgetown** and the **Washington National Cathedral** while on a bus tour; neither of which is easily accessible by Metro.

Day 2

Devote your next day to the Mall, where you can check out the museums and monuments that were probably a prime motivation for your coming to D.C. in the first place. There's no way you can do it all in one day, so just play favorites and save the rest for next time. Try visiting the monuments in the evening: they remain open long after the museums are closed and are dramatically lighted after dark.

Keep in mind that the **National Museum of Natural History** is the most visited museum in the country, while the **National Air and Space Museum**, the **National Gallery of Art**, and the **Museum of American History** aren't too far behind; plan for crowds almost anytime you visit. If you visit the **U.S. Holocaust Memorial Museum**, plan on spending two to three hours. If you're with kids on the Mall, take a break by riding the carousel.

Cafés and cafeterias within the museums are your best option for lunch. Two excellent picks are the Cascade Café at the **National Gallery of Art** and the Mitsitam Café at the **National Museum of the American Indian**, where they serve creative dishes inspired by native cultures. Just north of the Mall, the newly opened **Newseum** features a food court with a menu designed by celebrity chef Wolfgang Puck. If you've got more time (and more money to spend), drop by the Source, a ritzy restaurant behind the museum.

If the weather is fine, consider a walk from the **Washington Monument** to the **Lincoln Memorial** and around the **Tidal Basin**, where you can see the **Jefferson Memorial** and the **FDR Memorial**. It's a healthy walk, however, so don't attempt it if you are already weary with museum fatigue.

Day 3

Make this your day on **Capitol Hill**, where you'll have the option of visiting the **Capitol**, the **U.S. Botanic Gardens**, the **Library of Congress**, the **Supreme Court**, and the **Folger Shakespeare Library**.

Call your senators or congressional representative in advance for passes to see Congress in session—a memorable experience. Likewise, check the Supreme Court's Web site (⊕ *www.supremecourtus.gov*) for dates of oral arguments. If you show up at court early enough, you might gain admission for either a short (three-minute) visit or the full morning session.

Day 4

Head to the **National Zoo** and say good morning to the pandas. If the weather is bad, you can still enjoy the numerous indoor animal houses. Then hop on the Metro to **Dupont Circle** for lunch. Walk west on P Street NW to **Georgetown**, where you can shop, admire the architecture, and people-watch through the afternoon.

If you got a good dose of Georgetown on your first day, consider hitting the **International Spy Museum** instead, which tends to be less crowded after 2 PM. From there you can walk over to the **Smithsonian American Art Museum** and **National Portrait Gallery**, which stay open until 7.

Day 5

Spend the morning at **Arlington National Cemetery**, one of the D.C. area's most moving experiences. While you're there, don't miss the changing of the guard at the Tomb of the Unknowns, which takes place every hour or half hour, depending on the time of year. A short detour north of the cemetery brings you to the **Marine Corps War Memorial**, a giant bronze rendering of one of the most famous images in U.S. military history.

After your quiet, contemplative morning, head across town to spend the afternoon in the neighborhoods of **Adams Morgan** and **Dupont Circle**, both of which have unusual shops, restaurants, and clubs. Lunch at one of Adams Morgan's Ethiopian, El Salvadoran, or Mexican restaurants, and take in the Dupont Circle art scene—there's an assortment of offbeat galleries, as well as the renowned **Phillips Collection**.

D.C. WITH KIDS

D.C. is filled with kid-friendly attractions. These sights are sure winners:

National Air and Space Museum

There's a good reason why this place is one of the most popular museums in the world: kids love it. The 23 galleries here tell the story of aviation and space from the earliest human attempts at flight. All three gift shops sell freeze-dried astronaut food—not as tasty as what we eat on Earth, but it doesn't melt or drip. If you've never crunched into ice cream, it's worth the experience.

American Museum of Natural History

Say hello to Henry. One of the largest elephants ever found in the wild, this stuffed beast has greeted generations of kids in the rotunda of this huge museum dedicated to natural wonders. Take your kid to the O. Orkin Insect Zoo, home to live ants, bees, centipedes, tarantulas, roaches (some as large as mice), and other critters you wouldn't want in your house.

International Spy Museum

This museum takes the art of espionage to new levels for junior James Bonds and Nancy Drews. Even the most cynical preteens and teenagers are usually enthralled with all the cool gadgetry. Note that this museum is best for older tweens and teens—if you bring along a younger sibling, you could be in for a workout: there aren't many places to sit down, and strollers aren't allowed in the museum.

National Zoo

Known more for its political animals than its real animals, D.C. nevertheless has one of the world's foremost zoos. If your child is crazy about animals, this is an absolute must—it's huge!

Washington Monument

Kids say it looks like a giant pencil, and from the top some think D.C. looks like Legoland. Older kids like to find the White House and other D.C. landmarks.

Bureau of Engraving and Printing

Any youngster who gets an allowance will enjoy watching as bills roll off the presses. Despite the lack of free samples, the self-guided, 35-minute bureau tour is one of the city's most popular attractions.

Mount Vernon

Farm animals, a hands-on discovery center, an interactive museum, and movies about the nation's first action hero make George Washington's idyllic home a place where families can explore all day.

National Museum of American History

Oh say you can see. . . the flag that inspired "The Star Spangled Banner," Oscar the Grouch, the ruby-red slippers from *The Wizard of Oz*, an impressive collection of trains, and more pieces of Americana than anyone can digest in a day.

DC Ducks

What do you get when you cross a tour bus with a boat? A duck, of course—DC Ducks, that is. Tour the city by both land and water without leaving your seats aboard these unusual amphibious vehicles: standard 2.5-ton GM trucks in watertight shells with propellers.

D.C. LIKE A LOCAL

If you want to "go native" and get a sense for D.C. as the locals know it, try these experiences.

Happy Hour on the Hill

At 6 PM on a weekday evening, bars in D.C. are hopping like a Saturday night. The happy-hour culture here is strong, as government employees, lawyers, and other city workers unwind or network over half-price beers, well drinks, and pub grub. For the quintessential D.C. happy-hour experience, throw on something business casual and head to the Hill—no one will know you're not a congressional staffer.

Shop at an Outdoor Market

Instead of sleeping in on a Saturday morning, grab your trusty canvas bag and a wad of cash and head to one of D.C.'s outdoor markets. The best-known venue, Eastern Market on Capitol Hill, underwent a modernization and restoration project after a devastating fire in 2007, and the building is gorgeous. It is *the* place to buy a quick meal or picnic ingredients and mingle with residents. On weekends there are craft, flea, and produce markets. The Dupont Circle farmers' market and Georgetown flea market are also popular with residents.

Dine on Ethiopian Food

The District's many Ethiopian expats have introduced the community to their unique African cooking. The best restaurants, such as Etete, are in the U Street neighborhood. Meat and vegetarian dishes are ladled onto a large round of spongy *injera* bread, and diners eat with their hands, ripping off pieces of bread to scoop up the delectable stews. Using your hands instead of utensils adds to the sensual appeal of this cuisine.

Go for a Bike Ride

Your typical Mall-and-monuments tourist may not know that D.C. is home to several great bike trails. The Capitol Crescent Trail and Rock Creek Trail are popular routes between D.C. and Maryland. For hard-core bikers, the Custis Trail in Arlington links D.C. to the 45-mi Washington & Old Dominion (W&OD) trail in Virginia, while the Chesapeake & Ohio (C&O) towpath runs for nearly 185 mi between D.C and western Maryland. On a warm, sunny day, expect to find the paths bustling with cyclists, rollerbladers, and strollers.

Hang Out on U Street

You won't find many tourists in the U Street neighborhood, and many locals have only recently discovered the area. During the day, browse through the unique boutiques that line 14th and U streets NW, or read the *Washington City-Paper* at one of the many cafés. In the evening, select from trendy or ethnic restaurants, hang out at a local bar like the Chi Cha Lounge, or catch live music at the 9:30 Club or Bohemian Caverns.

Catch a Flick

A typical date night's dinner and a movie gets a little more exciting in D.C. In July and August locals head to the Mall for Screen on the Green, which shows classic films alfresco.

Several movie halls around the city play host to Filmfest DC (⊕ *www.filmfestdc.org*), an increasingly popular April festival boasting an always-eclectic collection of works from amateur and professional filmmakers worldwide.

FREE IN D.C.

For the thrifty at heart, D.C. can be a dream come true. All the Smithsonian museums and national memorials are free, as are many other museums—too many, in fact, to list here. Many of the top attractions are also free, like Ford's Theatre and Dumbarton Oaks. Summertime is heaven for budget travelers, when free outdoor concerts and festivals occur every week.

Free Attractions
Anderson House
Dumbarton Oaks (free from November 1 to March 14)
Ford's Theatre
Kenilworth Aquatic Gardens
Kennedy Center tours
National Arboretum
National Zoo
Old Post Office Pavilion
Old Stone House
Rock Creek Park
Supreme Court of the United States
U.S. Botanic Garden
U.S. Capitol
Washington National Cathedral
White House

Free Performances
The **Kennedy Center** hosts performances every day at 6 PM on the Millennium Stage. Also, every September the Prelude Festival kicks off the Kennedy Center's fall performance schedule with many free events. Choral and church groups perform at the **National Cathedral**, often at no charge.

In summer, folk, pop, and rock bands perform on Monday and Thursday nights atop **Fort Reno Park**. You can also hear jazz in the **National Gallery of Art's sculpture garden** Friday in summer. The Carter Barron Amphitheatre in **Rock Creek Park** hosts performances by the **Shakespeare Theatre Company** and concerts throughout spring and summer. If you're visiting in late October, reserve your seats early for D.C.'s Free Night of Theater.

Performances of military music take place around the city. From June through August the U.S. Navy Band, U.S. Air Force Band, U.S. Marine Band, and U.S. Army Band take turns playing concerts on the grounds of the **U.S. Capitol** weekdays at 8 PM. You can also see the U.S. Marine Band every Friday night from May through August during the Evening Parade at the Marine Barracks.

Almost every day of the year, the **Politics and Prose** independent bookstore on Connecticut Avenue invites fiction and nonfiction authors to the store for book readings, talks, and Q&A sessions.

Free Festivals
D.C. is a city of festivals, many of which are free to the public (food and souvenirs cost extra). Check the **National Mall** lawn and Pennsylvania Avenue for music and dance performances, concerts, talks, cooking demonstrations, parades, and more. For a complete list of annual events, visit the Washington, DC Convention and Tourism Corporation at ⊕ *www. washington.org*.

Half-Price Tickets
TICKETPlace (⊕ *www.ticketplace.org*) sells half-price tickets to D.C.'s theater and music events.

SIGHTSEE D.C.

If ever there was a "do it yourself" city, it's D.C. The Metro system is safe and easy to navigate and most of the major sights and museums are concentrated in a single area. Armed with a Metro map, a map of the Mall, and a comfortable pair of shoes, you can do it all, all by yourself.

Nevertheless, sometimes a guided tour just makes more sense, especially when it comes to experience, insider knowledge, and a parking pass. If for no other reason, taking a guided tour can be a nice break; let someone else sweat the details for a day. Consider a guided tour if your trip matches one of the situations below. ⇨ *See the Travel Smart Washington, D.C. chapter for more information.*

If this is your first trip . . .
The Metro might be the most convenient way to get around, but it is notably lacking in city views. If you'd like to get the lay of the land, don't tax your patience (or that of your fellow drivers) by trying to navigate the District's one-way streets while looking for sights on your own. Take a guided tour and leave the driving, and the parking, to the pros.

Old Town Trolley Tours and the **Tourmobile** buses operated by the National Park Service take you to the major sites in the District and offer hop-on, hop-off convenience. It's perfect for your first day in the city.

A bike tour, with a company such as **Bike and Roll,** is also a wonderful way to take in the sights. Traversing the Mall on foot can quickly turn into a forced march; on a bike it's a gentle ride with show-stopping scenery. Visitors tempted to jump onto D.C.'s new street-side bike rentals might want to think twice. The locals-focused program requires a $40 annual membership fee. ⇨ *See Chapter 10, Sports and the Outdoors, for more information.*

If you want an insider's look . . .
Arranging constituent visits to the **White House** and to the sessions of **Congress** is one of the duties of your representative and senators. Contact their offices (⊕ *www.house.gov* and ⊕ *www.senate. gov*) in advance to arrange your visit.

Several other government buildings, like the **State Department**, require advance reservations for a tour. ⇨ *See Chapter 5, Official Washington, for more information.*

If you just can't get enough . . .
Are you mad about the movies, the political gossip, or the Civil War? Indulge your obsessions with a tour that will add fuel to your fire. Visit *The Exorcist* steps or the bar from *St. Elmo's Fire* with **On Location Tours;** hear the juicy bits from Washington's rumor mill with **Gross National Product's Scandal Tours.** Or, take a guided walking tour with **Smithsonian Associates** that focuses on Civil War history, stopping at sights like Manassas National Battlefield Park at Bull Run.

If you want a new perspective . . .
You know what the Potomac looks like from the city, but have you ever seen the monuments from the river? **Thompson Boat Center** provides the opportunity, offering hourly and daily rentals on canoes and kayaks. Pack a lunch and paddle over to Roosevelt Island for an afternoon. It's the surest way of all to beat the crowds. ⇨ *See chapter 10, Sports and the Outdoors, for more information.*

D.C. BACCHANALIA

When Washingtonians want to unwind, a drink-centered menu sometimes takes precedent. After all, the work of Washington can be a serious and frantic business, and perhaps that reason alone can explain the increasing popularity of two leisurely and sophisticated escapes: the wine bar and the Belgian beer house. Who, after all, wants to discuss the workings of government in a sports bar? ⇨ *For full reviews of the bars below, except Cork and Bardeo, see Chapter 6, Where to Eat.*

Embracing the Grape

The wine-bar craze has opened popular locations all over the city. Some of these spots are pricier than others—not to mention louder—but all of them offer oenophiles the chance to relax with their favorite glass of white or red, casually nibbling on aged cheeses, seasoned olives, and cured meats. Most also offer full menus for those hoping to make an evening of it.

The best of D.C.'s wine bars offer dozens of choices to sip from—and you don't have to be a pro to enjoy the experience: most also serve up samples and flights, so you can get a taste before splurging on that glass or bottle.

Penn Quarter's **Proof**, a pioneer of D.C.'s wine bar scene, is a posh and popular spot to impress a date. Casual newcomer **Cork** (✉ *1720 14th St. NW*), which offers 50 wines by the glass near the U Street Corridor, was an instant hit—with the crowds to prove it. Capitol Hill's **Sonoma**, a haunt for congressional staffers, boasts a sleek modern bar on the first floor and lazy sofas on the second. **Bardeo** (✉ *3311 Connecticut Ave. NW*), in Cleveland Park, has an impressive Russian art collection, while Dupont Circle's **Vidalia** wows with succulent crab cakes. **Bistrot Lepic**, a local favorite in Georgetown, offers free Wi-Fi and all things French.

Tap a Trappist

For lovers of Belgian beer in search of an experience beyond Stella Artois, D.C. is your place. From Dupont Circle in the Northwest to the up-and-coming Atlas district of the Northeast, Belgian-themed menus are moving in with the time-tested offering of *moules* (that's mussels) and long lists of wonderful Belgian brews. The mussels are offered in a range of presentations, though commonly steamed in simple sauces of wine, butter, and lemon. Some menus offer accompanying *frites*, or fries. And the beer, well, if you've never had a Corsendonk or a Brasserie des Rocs straight from the tap, let's just say you haven't truly lived.

Popular spots around town include **Granville Moore's Brickyard**, a favorite in the emerging H Street Corridor of Northeast, featuring apple-wood bacon and bleu cheese mussels and an evolving roster of Belgian beers. Capitol Hill's **Belga Café** offers traditional dark-wood elegance at the bar as well as a sidewalk café. At **Brasserie Beck** downtown, the sommelier will happily walk you through the extensive list of Belgian beer options. The friendly bar at Dupont Circle's **Bistrot du Coin** allows plenty of opportunities to mingle over enticing moules, while the roof deck at **Marvin** has become a must-visit attraction on U Street. Though the ambience in these locales might differ, the beer-and-mussels theme remains constant—and popular.

INSIDE THE SAUSAGE FACTORY: HOW LAWS ARE MADE

Amid the grand marble halls of the Capitol building, members of Congress and their aides are busy crafting the country's policies. It's not a pretty process; as congressional commentators have quipped, laws are like sausages—it's best not to know how either is made. Here's a brief tour through Washington's sausage factory.

The Lightbulb Stage

Most laws begin as mere proposals that any of Congress's 535 members may offer in the form of bills. Many are trivial, such as renaming post-office branches. Others are vital, like the funding of the federal government. Once introduced, all proposals move to congressional committee.

Congressional Committees and Committee Hearings

Thousands of proposals are introduced each year, but almost all die in committee. Congress has nowhere near enough time to entertain each bill, so committee leaders must prioritize. Many bills are dismissed for ideological reasons; for example, the conservative proposal to privatize Social Security has little chance of being considered by committees headed by liberal Democrats. Many other bills simply lack urgency. Efforts to rein in fuel costs, for instance, were popular when gas prices topped $4 a gallon, then lost steam when costs fell below $2. Special-interest money is another factor dictating the success or failure of individual bills.

More-fortunate bills continue to the committee hearing stage, where experts discuss their merits and drawbacks. These hearings—staged in the congressional office buildings adjacent to the Capitol—are usually open to the public; check ⊕ *www.house.gov* and ⊕ *www.senate. gov* under the "committee" headings for schedules. Committee members then vote on whether to move bills to the chamber floor.

Passing the House, Senate, and White House

A bill approved by committee still faces three formidable tests before becoming a law: it must pass the full House, the full Senate, and usually the White House.

Complicating matters, each legislative chamber has different rules for approving bills. In the House, proposals require a simple majority to pass whereas in the Senate opponents can block a bill simply by debating it indefinitely (watch *Mr. Smith Goes to Washington* for a dramatic example). Senate leaders can block filibusters, but to do it requires support from three-fifths of the chamber, that's 60 out of the 100 senators. The controversial $787 billion economic stimulus bill, for example, passed in February 2009 only after Democrats (who currently hold 58 seats) convinced three Republicans to support the proposal.

A bill passed by both the House and the Senate then proceeds to the White House. The president can either sign it—in which case it becomes law—or veto it, in which case it returns to Congress. Lawmakers can override the veto, but two-thirds of each chamber must support the override to transform a vetoed bill into law. When President George W. Bush twice vetoed a popular children's health care proposal, for example, House supporters couldn't rally the two-thirds majority to override it. But, the bill became law once President Barack Obama took over the White House.

If all this sounds complicated, it is. Then again, no one poking around a sausage ever said it's easy to decipher the parts.

D.C. IN THE MOVIES

Look out for these memorable movie locations around D.C.

1 *In the Line of Fire.* **A** Secret Service agent (Clint Eastwood) tries to protect the president from a psychopathic assassin (John Malkovich). Eastwood's character memorably says to Lincoln "Wish I could have been there for you, pal" at the **Lincoln Memorial.**

2 *The Day the Earth Stood Still.* **The** movie begins with a flying saucer landing on the **Ellipse** outside the White House.

3 *Nixon.* Oliver Stone's biopic depicts the life of Richard Nixon (Anthony Hopkins) from childhood to presidency to scandal, with many **White House** scenes.

4 *All the President's Men.* The real-life story of the **Watergate** scandal and the journalists at the *Washington Post* who broke the story, this movie's newsroom scenes were filmed on a soundstage; the entrance and parking lot were shot on location.

5 *Mr. Smith Goes to Washington.* James Stewart does battle with senators on **Capitol Hill.** Patriotism and faith in the people ultimately triumph over murky politics in this depiction of a corrupt government.

6 *Strangers on a Train.* Alfred Hitchcock's film noir features **Union Station,** where two strangers plot the perfect crime.

7 *The Exorcist.* The 75 steps at **Prospect and 36th streets** that lead down to M Street in **Georgetown** are second in fame only to Rocky's in Philadelphia. For a chill, see the steps from the top at night.

8 *Wedding Crashers.* Owen Wilson's character crashes the wedding of the treasury secretary's daughter. See the secretary's sumptuous mansion at ✉ **3122 P Street NW in Georgetown.**

9 *Enemy of the State.* Will Smith, playing a Washington lawyer, finds himself accidentally in possession of crucial evidence of a politically motivated murder. Jason Lee is chased through **Adams Morgan** and the **Dupont Circle underpass.**

10 *Dr. Strangelove.* A U.S. general goes insane and single-handedly launches nuclear war on the U.S.S.R. In this Cold War satire set in the **Pentagon,** Peter Sellers plays the three would-be heroes: the U.S. president, a British officer, and Dr. Strangelove.

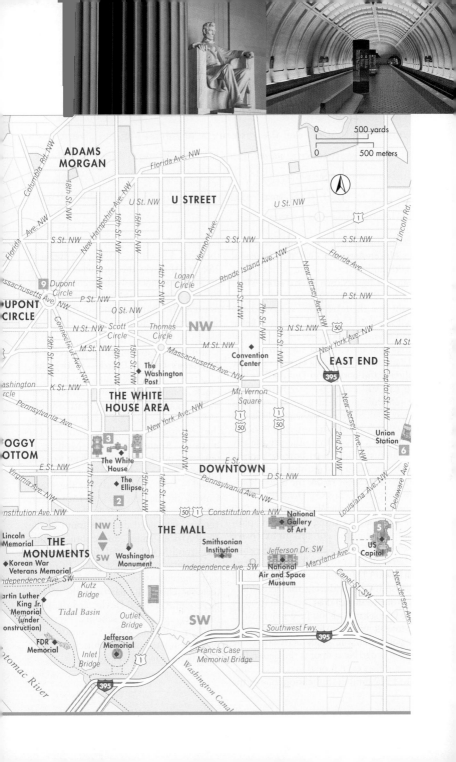

ADAMS MORGAN

Florida Ave. NW

Columbia Rd. NW

18th St. NW

U St. NW

U STREET

U St. NW

Lincoln Rd.

New Hampshire Ave. NW

16th St. NW

15th St. NW

Florida Ave. NW

S St. NW

S St. NW

S St. NW

17th St. NW

14th St. NW

Vermont Ave.

Florida Ave.

Massachusetts Ave. NW

9 Dupont Circle

Logan Circle

Rhode Island Ave. NW

9th St. NW

P St. NW

DUPONT CIRCLE

P St. NW

Connecticut Ave. NW

O St. NW

New Jersey Ave. NW

N St. NW   Scott Circle

Thomas Circle

NW

N St. NW

7th St. NW

6th St. NW

New York Ave. NW

M St.

19th St. NW

18th St. NW

16th St. NW

M St. NW

M St. NW

Massachusetts Ave. NW

Convention Center

North Capitol St. NW

EAST END

395

Washington rcle

K St. NW

15th St. NW

◆ The Washington Post

Mt. Vernon Square

New Jersey Ave. NW

2nd St. NW

Union Station

6

Pennsylvania Ave.

THE WHITE HOUSE AREA

New York Ave. NW

13th St. NW

1
50

1
50

FOGGY BOTTOM

E St. NW

3

The White House

15th St. NW

14th St. NW

E St. NW

DOWNTOWN

D St. NW

Louisiana Ave. NW

Delaware Ave.

Virginia Ave. NW

E St. NW

◆ The Ellipse

2

Pennsylvania Ave. NW

Constitution Ave. NW

nstitution Ave. NW

NW

50 **1** Constitution Ave. NW

National Gallery of Art

S

New Jersey Ave.

Lincoln Memorial

THE MONUMENTS

SW

Washington Monument

THE MALL

Smithsonian Institution

Jefferson Dr. SW

US Capitol

◆ Korean War Veterans Memorial

Independence Ave. SW

ndependence Ave. SW

Independence Ave. SW

National Air and Space Museum

Maryland Ave.

Canal St. SW

artin Luther King Jr. Memorial (under construction)

Kutz Bridge

Tidal Basin

Outlet Bridge

SW

FDR ◆ Memorial

Jefferson Memorial

Inlet Bridge

1

Francis Case Memorial Bridge

Southwest Fwy.

395

otomac River

395

Washington Canal

WASHINGTON, D.C. BLACK HISTORY WALK

A walk along U Street and the eastern rim of Adams Morgan gives a taste of D.C. that most tourists never get. This tour through "Black Broadway" bounces from lively commercial streets brimming with hip bars, cafés, and boutiques to quiet, tree-lined residential blocks and highlights African-American culture and history.

"Black Broadway"—U Street Corridor

The **African-American Civil War Memorial** at 10th and U streets is the perfect place to start; it has its own Metro stop. More than 200,000 names of black soldiers who fought for their freedom surround the small memorial. A block west sits **Bohemian Caverns**, a landmark restaurant and lounge that once hosted such jazz greats as Louis Armstrong, Ella Fitzgerald, Billie Holiday, and native son Duke Ellington. You can still catch live jazz here; check the schedule and return in the evening. Across 11th Street is **Washington Industrial Bank,** which thrived by offering African-Americans a service that others in the city wouldn't: the option to borrow money. One block south and another west you'll find the **12th Street YMCA,** the oldest black Y in the country (1853). Head back to U Street to explore the **African-American Civil War Museum,** featuring wonderful photographs from the era and an extensive on-site database for searching individual soldiers. Next, grab a half-smoke at **Ben's Chili Bowl**. A D.C. landmark, Ben's refused to close its doors during the fierce riots that followed the 1968 assassination of Dr. Martin Luther King Jr. While most of U Street was being destroyed, Ben's fed the policemen and black activists trying to keep order. Next door is the **Lincoln Theater,** another exceptional jazz venue and, from 1922 until desegregation, one of the largest and most elegant "colored-only" theaters. A few blocks west, the **corner of 15th and U** marks the spot where a party erupted spontaneously the night President Barack Obama was elected—thousands poured from bars to dance in the streets, stalling traffic for blocks.

North of U Street

Venture north one block to marvel at **St. Augustine's Catholic Church**—a gorgeous, two-tower cathedral now home to a black congregation that seceded from its segregated church (St. Matthews) in 1858. Feel free to walk inside to glimpse the striking stained-glass portrait of a black St. Augustine and St. Monica. A few steps north is **Meridian Hill (or Malcolm X) Park,** where a number of civil rights marches have originated over the years. Cutting through the park to 16th Street, you'll spot **Meridian Hill Hall,** Howard University's first coed dorm. Alumni of the elite African-American school include Thurgood Marshall and Toni Morrison. Continuing north, past some beautiful working embassies, you'll find **All Souls Unitarian Church**. Its pastor in the 1940s, Reverend A. Powell Davies, led the push to desegregate D.C. schools. President William Taft and Adlai Stevenson were once members, and the church bell was cast by the son of Paul Revere.

1

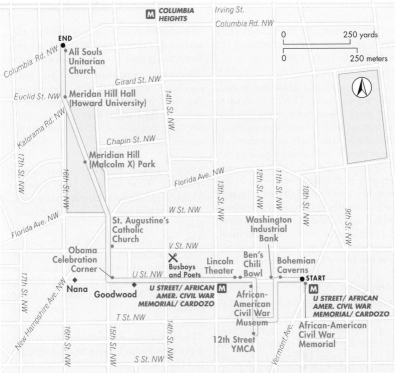

Highlights:	U Street was the center of black culture before Harlem was Harlem. See where Duke Ellington played, indulge in a half-smoke at Ben's Chili Bowl, and learn a bit about African-American history along the way.
Where to Start:	African-American Civil War Memorial on the Metro's Green or Yellow line.
Length:	About 1.5 mi; 1–2 hours, with window-shopping.
Where to Stop:	All Souls Unitarian Church. The S1, S2, or S4 bus lines on 16th Street will whisk you back downtown.
Best Time to Go:	While the sun is up, though the nightlife on U Street is an attraction in itself.
Worst Time to Go:	Avoid walking through Meridian Hill Park after dark.
Shopping Detour:	Check out **Nana** (✉ 1528 U St. NW between 15th and 16th Sts., upstairs) for new and vintage women's clothing, and browse **Goodwood** (✉ 1428 U St. NW between 14th and 15th Sts.) for antique wood furniture and estate jewelry.

D.C. TRAVEL TIPS

Travelers posting in the Travel Talk Forums at Fodors.com recommend the following D.C. travel tips.

Sights

"My advice is this: sit down and make a list of your must-sees. There is so much to see, so many monuments, museums, historic homes, and government buildings that it would take years to see them all. So most people do the major monuments (Washington, Lincoln, Jefferson, etc.) either on a night tour, or on foot or by bus during one day (it's a LOT of walking); then another day is devoted to museums, of which you should choose two to three; and a third day to the National Archives, a Congressional Tour, a White House tour (if you can score that), the Library of Congress (not all of these, just the ones of particular interest)."   —NewbE

"Christmas is a great time to visit D.C. Two of my favorite seasonal highlights: Mount Vernon decked out for the holidays and ice-skating at the National Gallery's Sculpture Garden. Temps vary widely. Average high and low are 47–32 for December, but we've had very rare 70-degrees and others that dip below zero. You can either pack for the extremes or get acquainted with Filene's downtown."   —repete

Transportation

"I went to the D.C. Metro Web site to figure out how we were going to get around town. We did not rent a car and wanted to use public transportation as much as possible. The Metro Web site not only will plan your route on the subway or the bus but will tell you how much the trip will cost."   —Texmati26

"We did a great deal of walking. Washingon is a city made for walking. The Metro is convenient and easy, but we all preferred to be outdoors enjoying the marvelous spring weather and all the flowering trees."   —cmcfong

"Don't drive anywhere unless you have no choice, get a good map, and assume that how you got there isn't how you're going to get back. There are too many one-way, one-access, or non-continuous streets [in D.C.]."   —soccr

Lodging

"This excellent Web site answers that question, 'How far is X hotel from Y Metro stop.' ⊕ *www.stationmasters.com*. Also helps first-time visitors with orientation."   —mlgb

"The Woodley Park B&B is excellent. Very clean and in a safe neighborhood with plenty of restaurant options. The owners and staff are wonderful . . . You can see the Metro stop from the front porch."   —gardendiva

Food

"There is a nice flea/crafts/artists market every Saturday at Eastern Market on Capitol Hill, and a good size farmer's market many weekdays and Saturdays. . . . Inside the market is a large veg/cheese/meat market. The Market Lunch counter is famous for its crab cakes and does great breakfasts. There are a lot of restaurants along this stretch of Pennsylvania Ave. toward the Capitol."   —Cicerone

"Take advantage of the great ethnic food offerings in D.C. and the surrounding areas. There is great Ethiopian food (Mezkerem), Vietnamese (lots in the VA suburbs), Latin (lots in Adams Morgan area), Thai (Sala Thai on P St., Haad Thai close to Chinatown), Cuban (try Banana Café near Eastern Market), Moroccan, Indian. . . Try something new, this area is a real melting pot."   —emd

Neighborhoods

WORD OF MOUTH

"I wish all Americans could go [to D.C.] at least once. It really makes you feel such a sense of pride and patriotism as you visit these wonderful symbols of our history and liberty. Take in as much as you can and enjoy it and don't worry about the things you don't have time to see—all of it is special. Have a great time!"

—texasjo

Updated by
Sarah Christie
and Cathy
Sharpe

Washington is a city of vistas—a marriage of geometry and art. Unlike other large cities, it isn't dominated by skyscrapers. The result: the world's first planned capital is also one of its most beautiful.

HOW D.C. CAME TO BE

The city that invented American politicking, back-scratching, and delicate diplomatic maneuvering is itself the result of a compromise. Tired of its nomadic existence after having set up shop in eight locations, Congress voted in 1785 to establish a permanent federal city. Northern lawmakers wanted the capital on the Delaware River, in the North; Southerners wanted it on the Potomac, in the South. A deal was struck when Virginia's Thomas Jefferson agreed to support the proposal that the federal government assume the war debts of the colonies if New York's Alexander Hamilton and other northern legislators would agree to locate the capital on the banks of the Potomac.

George Washington himself selected the site of the capital, a diamond-shape, 100-square-mi plot that encompassed the confluence of the Potomac and Anacostia rivers, not far from his estate at Mount Vernon. To give the young city a head start, Washington included the already thriving tobacco ports of Alexandria, Virginia, and Georgetown, Maryland, in the District of Columbia. In 1791 Pierre-Charles L'Enfant, a French engineer who had fought in the Revolution, created the classic plan for the city.

It took the Civil War—and every war thereafter—to energize the city, by attracting thousands of new residents and spurring building booms that extended the capital in all directions. Streets were paved in the 1870s, and the first streetcars ran in the 1880s. Memorials to famous Americans such as Lincoln and Jefferson were built in the first decades of the 20th century, along with the massive Federal Triangle, a monument to thousands of less-famous government workers.

THE MALL
AMERICA'S TOWN GREEN

It could be said that the Mall—the heart of almost every visitor's trip to Washington—has influenced life in the U.S. more than any other expanse of lawn. The Mall is a picnicking park, a jogging path, and an outdoor stage for festivals and fireworks. People come here from around the globe to tour the illustrious Smithsonian Institution museums, celebrate special events, or rally to make the world a better place.

The AIDS Memorial Quilt on the Mall in 1996.

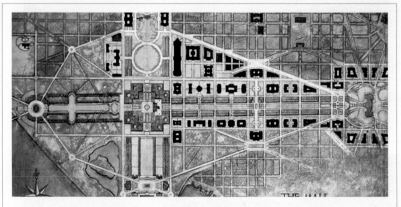

FROM TRASH HEAP TO TOURIST ATTRACTION: A BRIEF HISTORY OF THE MALL

Even before becoming the birthplace of American political protest, the Mall was a hotly contested piece of real estate. More than a century of setbacks and debate resulted not in Pierre L'Enfant's vision of a house-lined boulevard, but rather the premier green space you see today.

In 1791, Pierre Charles L'Enfant designed Washington, D.C., with a mile-long Grand Avenue running west from the Congress building. According to his plan, the boulevard would be lined with homes for statesmen and open green spaces, including a central garden bordered by a dense grove of trees.

L'Enfant's grandiose plan took more than 100 years to become a reality. By 1850, the area we now know as the Mall had not become a park, but was used instead as a storage area for lumber, firewood, and trash. With President Fillmore's permission, a group of businessmen hired landscape designer Andrew Jackson Downing to plan a national park featuring natural-style gardening. Sadly, Downing was killed in 1852, and his plan was never fully implemented.

Despite this setback, progress continued. The first Smithsonian museum on the Mall, the National Museum (now the Arts and Industries Building), opened to the public in 1881, and after 35 years of construction, the Washington Monument was completed in 1884.

A victory for the Mall occurred in 1901, when the Senate Park Commission, or McMillan Commission, was created to redesign the Mall as the city's ceremonial center. The McMillan plan embraced L'Enfant's vision of formal, public spaces and civic art, but replaced his Grand Avenue with a 300-foot expanse of grass bordered by American elms. It also called for cultural and educational institutions to line the Mall. Finally, a modified version of L'Enfant's great open space in the heart of Washington would become a reality.

The National Park Service assumed management of the Mall in 1933. In the latter half of the twentieth century, new museums and monuments opened on the Mall to create the public gathering place, tourist attraction, and tribute to our nation's heroes that we know today.

Above, McMillan Plan for the Mall, Washington, D.C., 1902.

HISTORIC RALLIES ON THE MALL

1894: Coxey's Army, a group of unemployed workers from Ohio, stage the first-ever protest march on Washington.

1939: Contralto Marian Anderson gives an Easter Sunday concert on the grounds of the Lincoln Memorial after the Daughters of the American Revolution bar her from performing at their headquarters because she's black.

1963: The Lincoln Memorial is the site of Martin Luther King Jr.'s inspirational I Have a Dream speech during the March on Washington.

1971: The Vietnam Veterans Against the War camp out on the Mall to persuade Congress to end military actions in Southeast Asia.

1972: The first Earth Day is celebrated on April 22 on the National Mall.

1987: The AIDS Memorial Quilt is displayed for the first time in its entirety. It returns to the Mall in 1988, 1989, 1992, and 1996.

1995: Nearly 400,000 African-American men fill the Mall, from the Capitol to the Washington Monument, during the Million Man March.

Top, Matin Luther King Jr. delivers his I Have a Dream speech.

Center, Vietnam War Veterans protest.

Bottom, Million Man March.

WHAT ABOUT THE MONUMENTS?

Visitors often confuse the Mall with the similarly named National Mall. The Mall is the expanse of lawn between 3rd and 14th Streets, while the National Mall is the national park that spans from the Capitol to the Potomac, including the Mall, the monuments, and the Tidal Basin. To reach the monuments, head west from the Mall or south from the White House and be prepared for a long walk. To visit all the monuments in one day requires marathon-level stamina and good walking shoes; to visit the monuments and the Mall in the same day would be the Ironman of tourism. ⇨ *For more about D.C.'s monuments and memorials, see Chapter 4.*

TOP 15 THINGS
TO DO ON THE MALL

1. Ride the old-fashioned carousel in front of the Smithsonian Castle.

2. Watch the fireworks on the Fourth of July.

3. See the original *Spirit of St. Louis,* and then learn how things fly at the National Air and Space Museum.

4. Gross out your friends at the Natural History Museum's Insect Zoo.

5. Gawk at Dorothy's ruby slippers, Kermit the Frog, Abraham Lincoln's top hat, and Lewis and Clark's compass at the American History Museum.

6. Twirl around the ice skating rink in the National Gallery of Art's sculpture garden.

7. View astonishing wooden masks at the Museum of African Art.

8. Taste North, South, and Central American dishes at the National Museum of the American Indian's Mitsitam Café.

9. Exercise your First Amendment rights by joining a rally or protest.

10. Peek at the many-armed and elephant-headed statues of Hindu gods at the Sackler Gallery.

11. Pose with sculptures by Auguste Rodin and Henry Moore at the Hirshhorn Sculpture Garden.

12. Learn how you make money—literally—at the Bureau of Engraving and Printing.

13. Follow the lives of the people who lived and died in Nazi Germany at the Holocaust Memorial Museum.

14. Eat, drink, watch, listen, and learn at an outdoor cultural festival.

15. Picnic and people-watch on the lawn after a hard day of sightseeing.

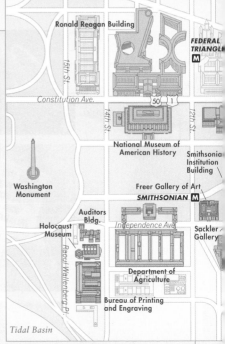

VISITING THE MUSEUMS ON THE MALL

MAKE THE MOST OF YOUR TIME

With 12 museums spread out along 11 city blocks, you can't expect to see everything in one day. Few people have the stamina for more than half a day of museum- or gallery-hopping at a time; children definitely don't. To avoid mental and physical exhaustion, try to devote at least two days to the Mall and use these itineraries (and our listings in Chapter 3) to make the best use of your time.

Historical Appeal: For a day devoted to history and culture, start with the **Holocaust Museum,** grabbing lunch at its excellent cafeteria. After refueling, the next stop is the **American History Museum,** which reopened in late 2008 after extensive renovations. Or, cross the length of the Mall to visit the **Museum of the American Indian** instead.

Art Start: To fill a day with paintings and sculptures, begin at the twin buildings of the **National Gallery of Art.** Enjoy the museum's sculpture while you dine in the garden's outdoor café. You'll find a second sculpture garden directly across the Mall at the **Hirshhorn.** If you like the avant-garde, visit the Hirshhorn's indoor galleries; for a cosmopolitan collection of Asian and African art and artifacts, head instead to the **Sackler Gallery** and **Museum of African Art.**

Taking the Kids: The most kid-friendly museum of them all, the **National Air and Space Museum** is a must-see for the young and young-at-heart. There's only fast food in the museum, but the **Museum of the American Indian** next door has healthier options. If your young bunch can handle two museums in a day, cross the lawn to the **Natural History Museum.** This itinerary works well for science buffs, too.

THE BEST IN A DAY

Got one day and want to see the best of the Smithsonian? Start at the **Air and Space Museum,** then skip to the side-by-side **Natural History** and **American History Museums.** Picnic on the Mall or hit the museum cafeterias.

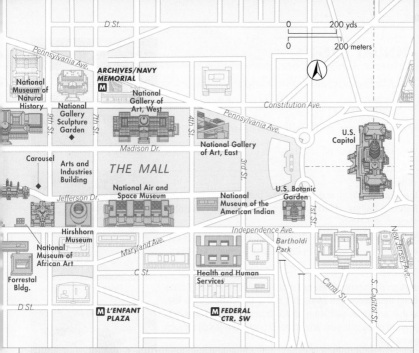

NOT ANOTHER HOT DOG! A Survival Guide to Eating Well on the Mall

Even locals wonder where to grab a decent bite to eat when touring the Smithsonian Museums. Hot dogs, soft pretzels, and ice cream from a cart don't make for a nutritious lunch, and the museum cafeterias mostly provide mediocre meals at sky-high prices. On a weekday, the streets north of Constitution Avenue offer easy-to-find lunch spots, but virtually all are closed on weekends.

Here are some places for better dining by the Mall, though several require a few blocks' walk.

Museum of the American Indian: The Mitsitam Café—the name means "let's eat" in the language of the Delaware and Piscataway people—is one of the best museum cafeterias on the Mall. Food stations serve native-inspired sandwiches, entrees, soups, and desserts from five regions of the western hemisphere.

Pavilion Café: Located in the **National Gallery's Sculpture Garden,** this eatery offers indoor and outdoor seating with views of the artwork and fountain/ice rink outside. The menu includes salads, sandwiches, and pizzas.

Pennsylvania Avenue SE: If lunchtime finds you on the east end of the Mall,

head past the Capitol to Pennsylvania Avenue SE. Between Second and Fourth Streets, you'll find plenty of pubs, cafés, and sandwich shops. It's a bit of a hike, but well worth the shoe leather.

Old Post Office Pavilion: The food court here is open seven days a week. The selection is predictable—sushi, pizza, deli, bagels, Chinese food—but they provide cheap fare for a variety of tastes.

Ronald Reagan Building and International Trade Center: The food court here is another option, but is closed on Sundays during the winter.

ANNUAL EVENTS

The Mall's spacious lawn is ideal for all kinds of outdoor festivals. These annual events are local favorites and definitely worth a stop if you're in town while they're happening.

St. Patrick's Day Parade

WINTER

Ice Skating: Whirl and twirl at the outdoor ice rink in the National Gallery of Art's Sculpture Garden. *Mid-November through mid-March*

St. Patrick's Day Parade: Dancers, bands, and bagpipes celebrate all things Irish along Constitution Avenue. *Mid-March*

SPRING

National Cherry Blossom Festival: When the cherry trees burst into bloom, you know that spring has arrived. Fly a kite, watch a parade, and learn about Japanese culture in a setting sprinkled with pink and white flowers. *Late March through early April*

Cherry Blossom Festival

SUMMER

Smithsonian Folklife Festival: Performers, cooks, farmers, and craftsmen demonstrate cultural traditions from around the world. *Around July 4*

Independence Day: What better place to celebrate the birth of our nation than in the capital city? Enjoy concerts and parades on the Mall, then watch the fireworks explode over the Washington Monument. *July 4*

Smithsonian Folklife Festival

Screen on the Green: Film favorites are shown on a gigantic movie screen on Monday nights. Bring a blanket and picnic dinner to better enjoy the warm summer evenings. *Mid-July through mid-August*

FALL

Black Family Reunion: D.C. celebrates African-American family values. Pavilions showcase businesses owned by African-Americans and events and performances feature black entertainers, celebrities, and experts. *September*

Independence Day Reenactment

National Book Festival: Meet your favorite author in person at the Library of Congress' annual literary festival. Over 70 writers and illustrators participate in readings, live interviews, and events for kids. *September*

Marine Corps Marathon: The "Marathon of the Monuments" starts in Virginia but winds its way around the entire National Mall. It's as fun to cheer as it is to run. *Late October*

Marine Corps Marathon

PLANNING YOUR VISIT

National Cherry Blossom Festival Parade

KEEP IN MIND

■ All of the museums on the Mall are free to the public.

■ Since September 11, 2001 security has increased, and visitors will need to go through screenings and bag checks, which create long lines during peak tourist season.

■ Two museums require timed-entry passes: the Holocaust Museum from March through August, and the Bureau of Printing and Engraving. If you've got a jam-packed day planned, it's best to get your tickets early in the morning or in advance.

GETTING HERE AND GETTING AROUND

Metro Travel: You can access the Mall from several Metro stations. On the Blue and Orange lines, the Federal Triangle stop is convenient to the Natural History and American History museums, and the Smithsonian stop is close to the Holocaust Memorial Museum and Sackler Gallery. On the Yellow and Green lines, Archives/Navy Memorial takes you to the National Gallery of Art. The L'Enfant Plaza stop, accessible from the Blue, Orange, Yellow, and Green lines, is the best exit for the Hirshhorn and Air and Space Museum.

Bus Travel: Walking from the Holocaust Memorial Museum to the National Gallery of Art is quite a trek. Many visitors take advantage of the hop-on, hop-off **Tourmobile** (☎ 202/554–5100 ✆ $25 per person), which stops at most major attractions on the Mall, as well as key monuments and Arlington National Cemetery.

Car Travel: Parking is hard to find along the Mall. You can find private parking garages north of the Mall in the Downtown area, where you'll have to pay to leave your car. If you're willing to walk, limited free parking is available on Ohio Drive SW near the Jefferson Memorial and East Potomac Park.

HELP, THERE'S A PROTEST ON THE MALL!

Since the 1890s, protesters have gathered on the Mall to make their opinions known. If you're not in a rallying mood, you don't have to let First Amendment activities prevent you from visiting the Smithsonian museums or enjoying a visit to the Mall.

■ **Use the back door:** All of the Smithsonian museums have entrances on Constitution or Independence Avenues, which do not border the Mall's lawn. Use these doors to gain admission without crossing the Mall itself.

■ **Know you're protected:** The Mall is a national park, just like Yosemite or Yellowstone. The National Park Service has a responsibility to visitors to make sure they can safely view park attractions. To this end, demonstrators are often required to keep main streets open.

■ **Avoid the crowds:** Even the biggest rallies don't cover the entire National Mall. If the crowd is by the Capitol, head west to visit the Lincoln Memorial. If protestors are gathered around the Washington Monument, visit the Jefferson Memorial on the opposite side of the Tidal Basin. There's plenty to see.

THE WHITE HOUSE AREA AND FOGGY BOTTOM

Sightseeing
★★★★★
Dining
★★★☆☆
Lodging
★★☆☆☆
Shopping
★☆☆☆☆
Nightlife
★★☆☆☆

Foggy Bottom includes some of D.C.'s most important and iconic attractions, the top being the White House. The home of every U.S. President but George Washington, the 132-room mansion is as impressive in real life as it is on television. It may be tough to decide what to see first with the monuments and parkland of the National Mall and Tidal Basin, as well as some of Washington's smaller museums. Adding to the variety, you'll find the Kennedy Center, the infamous Watergate complex, and George Washington University's substantial campus. Peppered among the government buildings, museums, monuments, and university buildings are also some of D.C.'s oldest houses, revealing the neighborhood's surprisingly residential character.

WHITE HOUSE AREA WALK

Seeing everything this neighborhood has to offer could easily occupy the greater part of a day, or more, so prioritize and be prepared for lots of walking. This walk takes you past the core area around the White House and then offers two ways to continue exploring the neighborhood—either checking out the monuments on the National Mall and Tidal Basin or the government buildings west of the White House. In good weather the monuments are particularly enticing, but there are interesting tours of some of the government buildings as well. Many

A statue of Andrew Jackson during the Battle of New Orleans presides over Lafayette Square.

sites require advance reservations and few are kid-friendly, but history and art buffs shouldn't miss these hidden gems.

Whether you choose to focus your time on monuments or government buildings, it's easy to wind up at the **John F. Kennedy Center for the Performing Arts** for an evening performance. Along the Potomac River, the Kennedy Center is both a memorial to the late president and a bustling cultural center with six theaters for the performance of music, dance, opera, and dramatic arts. Time your visit well, and you could catch one of the free concerts at 6 PM daily.

CORE WHITE HOUSE AREA

Arriving at either the Farragut West or McPherson Square Metro stop, you quickly reach the trees and flower beds of **Lafayette Square,** an intimate oasis amid Downtown Washington. The park was named for the Marquis de Lafayette, the young French nobleman who came to America to fight in the Revolution. His **statue** is in the southeast corner of the park. In the center, the large **statue of Andrew Jackson** is the second equestrian statue made in America.

St. John's Episcopal Church has sat across from the park since 1816. Every president since Madison has visited the church, and many have worshipped here regularly. The **Decatur House** just west of the square was the first private residence on Lafayette Square, and now houses a museum that shows the living quarters as they were in the Federal period and in the Victorian era.

Looking south, the **White House,** at 1600 Pennsylvania Avenue, is straight ahead across the park. Tops on every first-timer's D.C. to-do list should be a visit to this most famous home. Plan ahead: you must

GETTING ORIENTED

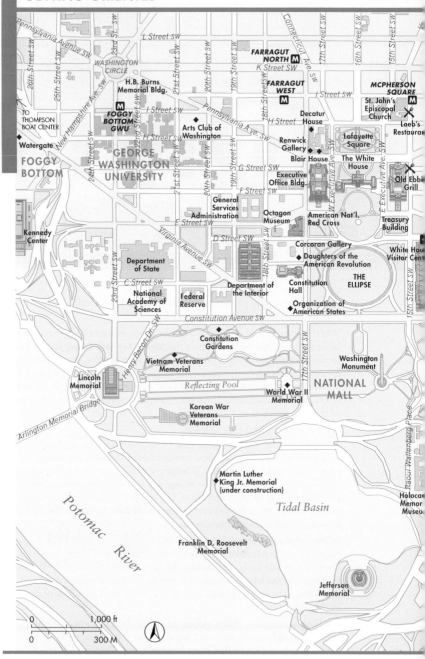

Pennsylvania Avenue SW

L Street SW

WASHINGTON CIRCLE

FARRAGUT NORTH M

K Street SW

FARRAGUT WEST M

MCPHERSON SQUARE M

H.B. Burns Memorial Bldg.

I Street SW

St. John's Episcopal Church

Loeb's Restaurant

TO THOMPSON BOAT CENTER

FOGGY BOTTOM GWU M

Arts Club of Washington

Decatur House

H Street

Watergate

Renwick Gallery

Lafayette Square

FOGGY BOTTOM

GEORGE WASHINGTON UNIVERSITY

H Street SW

Blair House

The White House

Old Ebbitt Grill

G Street SW

F Street SW

Executive Office Bldg.

Kennedy Center

General Services Administration

E Street SW

Octagon Museum

American Nat'l. Red Cross

Treasury Building

Virginia Avenue SW

D Street SW

Corcoran Gallery

Daughters of the American Revolution

White House Visitor Center

Department of State

C Street SW

Department of the Interior

Constitution Hall

THE ELLIPSE

National Academy of Sciences

Federal Reserve

Organization of American States

Constitution Avenue SW

Constitution Gardens

Henry Bacon Dr. SW

Vietnam Veterans Memorial

Washington Monument

Lincoln Memorial

Reflecting Pool

World War II Memorial

NATIONAL MALL

Korean War Veterans Memorial

Arlington Memorial Bridge

Martin Luther King Jr. Memorial (under construction)

Tidal Basin

Holocaust Memorial Museum

Potomac River

Franklin D. Roosevelt Memorial

Jefferson Memorial

0   1,000 ft

0   300 M

GREAT EXPERIENCES IN THE WHITE HOUSE AREA

Corcoran Gallery of Art: The great 19th-century American painters were inspired by the sublime majesty of the American West. See the most-definitive works—Albert Bierstadt's *Mount Corcoran* and Frederick Church's *Niagara*.

John F. Kennedy Center for the Performing Arts: See a free performance by anyone from Norah Jones to the National Symphony Orchestra here on the Millennium Stage.

The Renwick Gallery: If the White House tour doesn't satisfy your inner decorating diva, perhaps the Tiffany objets d'art, intricately carved antique tables, and opulent Victorian Grand Salon here will do the trick.

Thompson's Boat Center: Take in Washington's marble monuments, lush Roosevelt Island, and the Virginia coastline with a canoe ride down the Potomac.

The White House: You have to plan weeks, if not months, in advance, and you're only allowed into 8 of the 132 rooms, but there's no denying the kick of touring 1600 Pennsylvania Avenue—especially around Christmas.

GETTING HERE

The White House can be reached by the Red Line's Farragut North stop or the Blue and Orange lines' McPherson Square and Farragut West stops. Foggy Bottom has its own Metro stop, also on the Blue and Orange lines. A free shuttle runs from the station to the Kennedy Center. Many of the other attractions are a considerable distance from the nearest subway stop. If you don't relish long walks or time is limited, check the map to see if you need to make alternate travel arrangements to visit specific sights.

NEAREST PUBLIC RESTROOM

The Renwick Gallery, DAR Museum, Art Museum of the Americas, and the Kennedy Center all offer public restrooms. The White House Visitor Center also has facilities.

PLANNING YOUR TIME

Touring the area around the White House could easily take a day or even two, depending on how long you visit each of the museums along the way. To see Foggy Bottom's more-westerly sights will add still more time.

If you enjoy history, you may be most interested in the **Decatur House, DAR Museum,** and **State Department.** If it's art you crave, devote the hours to the **Corcoran** and **Renwick** galleries instead. Save the **Kennedy Center** and **Watergate** for the evening, when you can catch a performance or enjoy dinner in the area.

QUICK BITES

The Corcoran Gallery's On the Fly Café (✉ *500 17th St. NW* ☎ *202/639–1700*) serves light morning fare, salads, sandwiches, and small plates for sharing. It's closed Monday and Tuesday.

Loeb's Restaurant (✉ *832 15th St. NW* ☎ *202/371–1150*) makes deli-style salads and sandwiches to eat there or take with you—perfect for a picnic in Lafayette Park.

The Old Ebbitt Grill (✉ *675 15th St. NW* ☎ *202/347–4800*), once the haunt of presidents Grant, Cleveland, Harding, and Theodore Roosevelt, is still a popular watering hole for journalists and off-duty Secret Service agents.

2

make arrangements for admission months in advance with your member of Congress or embassy. For more information, stop at the **White House Visitor Center,** in the Department of Commerce building on Pennsylvania Avenue between 14th and 15th streets NW.

CITY VIEW

For a different view of the city without waiting in line, don't miss the view from the roof of the Kennedy Center. There's also a café and restaurant there.

The White House is flanked by two imposing buildings you can view but not enter. To the east, the **Treasury Building** is the largest Greek Revival edifice in Washington. Robert Mills, the architect responsible for the Washington Monument and the Patent Office (now the Smithsonian American Art Museum), designed the grand colonnade that stretches down 15th Street. The building's southern facade has a **statue of Alexander Hamilton,** the department's first secretary. To the west, the granite edifice that looks like a wedding cake is the Eisenhower **Executive Office Building,** styled after the Louvre. Built as a headquarters of the State, War, and Navy departments, it now houses offices for the vice president and other members of the executive branch. The building was the site of both the first presidential press conference in 1950 and the first televised press conference five years later.

As you go past the Executive Office Building, note the green canopy marking the entrance to **Blair House** opposite, the residence used by heads of state visiting Washington. Farther along, the **Renwick Gallery** of the Smithsonian American Art Museum exhibits American crafts and decorative arts.

Seventeenth Street leads you down to the **Corcoran Gallery of Art.** The Beaux-Arts building houses an impressive collection of American, European, and contemporary art, photography, and decorative arts. One block west, at 18th Street, the **Octagon Museum** is actually a six-, not eight-sided building. The galleries have changing exhibits on architecture, city planning, and Washington history and design.

You could detour here to the left, cut across the Ellipse and see the White House and its perfect south lawn from the other side. On the southern end stand a weather-beaten **gatehouse** that once stood on Capitol Hill and the **Boy Scouts Memorial.** By the southeast corner of the White House lawn, the **Tecumseh Sherman Monument** depicts the Civil War general mounted on his steed, surrounded by four sentries.

Otherwise, farther down 17th Street, a tour of the **Daughters of the American Revolution (DAR)** headquarters lets you peek into a few of the 32 period rooms—each decorated in a style unique to one state and one time period—and the Beaux-Arts auditorium now used as a genealogy library. The museum on the first floor hosts changing exhibitions.

Continuing south on 17th Street, the headquarters of the **Organization of American States,** which is made up of nations from North, South, and Central America, contains a patio adorned with a pre-Columbian–style fountain and lush tropical plants. This tiny rain forest is a good place to rest when Washington's summer heat is at its most oppressive.

Punctuating the skyline like an exclamation point, you can see the Washington Monument from 30 miles away.

A MONUMENTAL STROLL

At this point you probably want to make the choice between monuments and government buildings. If you choose the former, carefully cross the speeding highway that is Constitution Avenue and reach the peace and tranquility of the **National Mall,** home of D.C.'s monuments and memorials. Heading east, you can't miss the **Washington Monument.** The elegant obelisk built in memory of George Washington dominates the skyline. If you want to go to the top, go early to the nearby visitor center to reserve free timed tickets.

To the west, see the **World War II Memorial** and continue along the **Reflecting Pool,** with the imposing **Lincoln Memorial** dominating the view ahead of you. On either side are the **Korean War** and **Vietnam Veterans Memorials** and **Constitution Gardens.** If you can, make time to visit the **Tidal Basin,** home to the **Roosevelt, Jefferson** and soon-to-be **Martin Luther King Jr.** memorials. Each spring the cherry trees around the Tidal Basin burst into pink-and-white blooms, and the city celebrates the beauty of this gift from Japan with a two-week **Cherry Blossom Festival.**

GOVERNMENT BUILDINGS

If you forgo the monuments, take Constitution Avenue to the west instead. The headquarters of many government departments and national organizations reside along the blocks between E Street and Constitution Avenue west of the Ellipse. Several offer tours or exhibits for the public, but always check whether advance reservations are required, and bring photo ID.

Virginia Avenue takes you up past the **Department of the Interior,** which contains a museum with exhibits based on the work of its branches,

DID YOU KNOW?

The best views of the cherry blossoms along the Tidal Basin are from the water. You can rent a paddleboat for a romantic drift or some family fun.

such as the Bureau of Land Management, National Park Service, and U.S. Geological Survey. Turn left on C Street to the **Federal Reserve Building,** which displays special art exhibitions that are only worth visiting if you're fascinated with the subject or want to see the inside of the Fed; reserve in advance. Set back from the Fed, you'll find the **National Academy of Sciences.** It offers two galleries of science-related art. Robert Berks's sculpture of Albert Einstein outside the building has broader appeal; the creator of the theory of relativity looks—dare we say?—cuddly.

You must reserve a tour at the **State Department** months in advance, but it's worth the effort. A docent takes you to the top floor's **Department of State's Diplomatic Reception Rooms**—usually reserved for heads of state and special honorees, and the great halls and gathering spaces are furnished with American antiques and art.

Away from the White House and federal buildings, northern Foggy Bottom is the home of **George Washington University.** The university has no separate campus, but occupies many of the modern buildings and 19th-century houses between 19th and 24th streets south of Pennsylvania Avenue.

Near the Kennedy Center along the water, the **Watergate** made history on the night of June 17, 1972, but the apartment-office complex doesn't look so scandalous in person. Famous—and infamous—residents have included Attorney General John Mitchell and presidential secretary Rose Mary Woods of Nixon White House fame, as well as such D.C. insiders as Jacob Javits, Alan Cranston, Bob and Elizabeth Dole, Monica Lewinsky, and Condoleezza Rice. You'll also find shops and restaurants here.

If looking at the Potomac makes you yearn to get closer, the **Thompson's Boat Center,** at the end of Virginia Avenue, rents canoes and kayaks in the warmer months. Bike rentals are also available.

WHITE HOUSE AREA WITH KIDS

Touring the **White House** is as much of a thrill for kids as it is for adults. If you didn't plan your visit in advance, you can still get a look at White House life at the **White House Visitor Center,** where videos and photos capture first families. Unlike the actual White House, kids can roam around here and sit on the furniture.

At the **Daughters of the American Revolution Museum** kids five to seven can discover what life was like as a colonial child when they take part in the Colonial Adventure program.

In summer, give kids a break from touring the monuments with an afternoon boat ride on the **Tidal Basin.** If you're feeling a bit more intrepid, you can rent canoes from **Thompson's Boat Center** and paddle along the Potomac.

CAPITOL HILL

Sightseeing
★★★★☆

Dining
★★★☆☆

Lodging
★★★☆☆

Shopping
★★☆☆☆

Nightlife
★★☆☆☆

The people who live and work on "the Hill" do so in the shadow of the edifice that lends the neighborhood its name: the gleaming white Capitol. This is where political deals and decisions are made. Lining the streets behind these venerable buildings are some of the bars and pubs where off-duty senators, congresspersons, and lobbyists do some of their business. Beyond these grand buildings lies a vibrant and diverse group of neighborhoods with charming residential blocks lined with Victorian row houses and a fine assortment of restaurants, bars, and shops, not to mention D.C.'s favorite market and newest sporting attraction.

CAPITOL HILL WALK

Capitol Hill's exact boundaries are disputed. While most say it's bordered to the west, north, and south by the Capitol, H Street NE, and I Street SE, respectively, extending east only to 14th Street, some real estate speculators argue that the trendy neighborhood extends east to the Anacostia River. What's clear is that Capitol Hill's historic-preservation movement is hard at work, restoring more and more 19th-century houses and fighting the urban blight that creeps in around the edges of this historic part of Washington.

There's a lot to see here, but you can easily explore the streets in a couple of hours. A good place to start is **Union Station**, easily accessible on the Metro Red Line. The Beaux-Arts station, modeled after a Roman bath, dominates the northwest corner of Capitol Hill. Thanks to a restoration project completed in 1988, the city's main train station has turned into a mini mall, with shops, restaurants, and a movie theater.

In the station's front plaza sits a steely-eyed Christopher Columbus at the base of a column on the **Columbus Memorial Fountain,** designed by Lorado Taft.

Next door, the **National Postal Museum** will delight philatelists. The Smithsonian takes a playful approach to stamp collecting and the history of the U.S. Postal Service with its interactive exhibits. On the other side of Union Station the **Thurgood Marshall Federal Judiciary Building** is worth a quick peek. The atrium, designed by architect Edward Larabee Barnes, encloses a garden of bamboo five stories tall.

Following Delaware Avenue south, you come right up to the Capitol, the point from which the city is divided into quadrants: northwest, southwest, northeast, and southeast. North Capitol Street, which runs north from the Capitol, separates northeast from northwest; East Capitol Street separates northeast and southeast; South Capitol Street separates southwest and southeast; and the Mall (Independence Avenue on the south and Constitution Avenue on the north) separates northwest from southwest.

The massive **U.S. Capitol** sits majestically at the east end of the Mall, and is the foremost reason to visit Capitol Hill. Although the free tour takes you through the impressive rotunda, Statuary Hall, and Old Senate Chamber, to see your legislators at work you need to arrange in advance for (free) gallery passes—contact your senator or representative's office. The much-anticipated and oft-delayed **Capitol Visitor Center** finally opened in late 2008. Capitol tours leave from the visitor center, which is located underneath the Capitol. The imposing buildings to the north and south of the Capitol house the offices of senators and representatives.

In front of the Capitol three monuments flank a reflecting pool. In the center the **Ulysses S. Grant Memorial** is one of the largest sculpture groups in the city. To the south stands the **James A. Garfield Monument,** and to the north a **Peace Monument** commemorating sailors who died in the Civil War. Across Constitution Avenue a monolithic carillon forms the **Robert A. Taft Memorial,** dedicated to the longtime Republican senator and son of the 27th president.

Across from the Garfield Memorial the **United States Botanic Garden** is the oldest botanic garden in North America. After touring the conservatory, be sure to wander through the rose, butterfly, and regional gardens of the **National Garden.** Another lovely spot, the **Bartholdi Fountain,** was created by Frederic-Auguste Bartholdi, sculptor of the Statue of Liberty. The aquatic monsters, sea nymphs, tritons, and lighted globes all represent the elements of water and light.

Continue east on Independence Avenue, then north on 1st Street, where the Jefferson Building of the Library of Congress and the U.S. Supreme Court sit side by side. The **Library of Congress** has so many books, recordings, maps, manuscripts, and photographs that it actually takes three buildings to get the job done. The **Jefferson Building** is the most visitor-friendly. Here you can view the **Great Hall,** peek into the **Main Reading Room,** and wander through changing exhibitions related to the library's holdings. You can line up to hear oral arguments inside the **Supreme Court Building** when court is in session.

GETTING ORIENTED

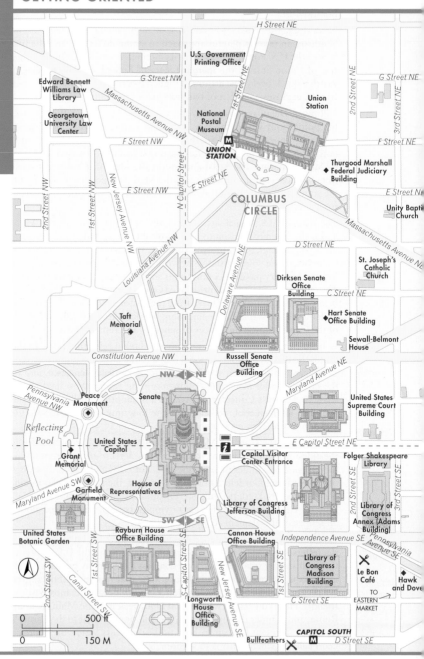

GREAT EXPERIENCES ON CAPITOL HILL

The Capitol: See democracy in action. Watch congressmen and -women debate, insult, and wrangle their way through the job of making laws in the Capitol's House and Senate chambers.

Eastern Market: One of D.C.'s most beloved weekend destinations, Eastern Market is the place to pick up fresh produce, flowers, and locally made crafts.

The Hawk and Dove: Order a pint and listen in as congressional staffers gripe about their famous bosses and locals debate the Redskins' Super Bowl chances at this quintessential D.C. bar and Capitol Hill institution.

The Library of Congress: Take a break from debate to contemplate the Gutenberg Bible, the lavishly sculpted Great Hall, and the splendor of the gilded Main Reading Room.

The Supreme Court: Round out your firsthand look at the three branches of government by watching the Supreme Court justices hear precedent-setting arguments at the highest court in the land.

United States Botanic Garden: Wrinkle your nose at the corpse flower, explore the jungle, gawk at the orchids, or stroll the paths of the new National Garden.

GETTING HERE

From the Red Line's Union Station stop, you can easily walk to most destinations on Capitol Hill. From the Blue and Orange lines, the Capitol South stop is close to the Capitol and Library of Congress, and the Eastern Market stop leads to the market and the Marine Corps Barracks. The Numbers 30, 32, 34, 35, and 36 buses run from Friendship Heights through Georgetown and Downtown to Independence Avenue, the Capitol, and Eastern Market. Street parking is available.

PLANNING YOUR TIME

Touring Capitol Hill should take you about four hours, allowing for about an hour each at the **Capitol**, the **Botanic Garden**, and the **Library of Congress**. If you want to see **Congress** in action, contact your legislator in advance, and bear in mind that the House and Senate are usually not in session in August. **Supreme Court** cases are usually heard October through April, Monday through Wednesday, two weeks out of each month.

QUICK BITES

At the **Library of Congress** there's a cafeteria serving breakfast and lunch on the sixth floor of the **Madison Building** (⊠ *Independence Ave. SE, between 1st and 2nd Sts.* ☎ *202/707–5000*).

Pennsylvania Avenue SE between 2nd and 4th streets has a large selection of restaurants. Just off the main drag, **Le Bon Café** (⊠ *210 2nd St. SE* ☎ *202/547–7200*) is a cozy bistro with excellent pastries and light lunches.

Bullfeathers (⊠ *410 1st St. SE* ☎ *202/543–5005*) has been grilling burgers for members of the House since 1980.

The food court at Union Station offers everything from pizza to sushi. Union Station notable, **America** (☎ *202/682–9555*), serves regional food from all over the country.

Bustling Union Station is a great place to grab a bite and people watch.

Behind the Library of Congress, the **Folger Shakespeare Library** holds an enormous collection of works by and about Shakespeare and his times, as well as a reproduced 16th-century theater and gallery that are open to visitors (the books are not). North of the Folger on 2nd Street, the **Sewall-Belmont House** was the headquarters of the historic National Woman's Party, and is accessible by tour.

SOUTH AND EAST OF THE CAPITOL

Away from the Capitol, you'll find some enticing attractions, including one of D.C.'s oldest communities and a thriving market. This area is well served by the Metro, though you can get around on foot.

East of 2nd Street, the neighborhood changes dramatically from large-scale government buildings to 19th-century town houses. Among them is the first Washington home of the abolitionist and writer **Frederick Douglass**, at 320 A Street NE, which you can visit by appointment.

Follow Pennsylvania Avenue south between 2nd and 4th streets to the main commercial thoroughfare. Restaurants, bars, and coffee shops frequented by those who live and work on the Hill line these blocks. Reaching Seward Square, take C Street one block to **Eastern Market** on the corner of 7th Street; it has been a feature of D.C. life since 1873. The main building, gutted by fire in 2007, has reopened after a $22 million restoration and modernization project. Here you can find an array of farmers, flower vendors, and other merchants who sell their fresh produce and crafts to locals and tourists alike. The market is open all week, but really buzzes on weekends. Seventh Street takes you back to Pennsylvania Avenue, the Eastern Market Metro station, and to the historic **Barracks Row** neighborhood. Along 8th Street, Barracks Row

A 24-foot high catwalk at the U.S. Botanic Garden offers views of the lush jungle canopy.

was the first commercial center in Washington, D.C. The Barracks were built after 1798 and rebuilt in 1901, but this neighborhood housed a diverse population even before the Civil War. On the north side of the street you'll find the barracks and opposite, a variety of shops and restaurants. The **Marine Corps Barracks and Commandant's House,** the nation's oldest continuously active marine installation, is the home of the U.S. Marine Band. On Friday evenings from May to August you can attend the hour-long ceremony given on the parade deck by the **Marine Band** (the "President's Own") and the **Drum and Bugle Corps** (the "Commandant's Own").

Right at the end of 8th Street, on the bank of the Anacostia River, you will find the 115-acre **Washington Navy Yard,** the Navy's oldest outpost on shore. On its premises are the **Navy Museum,** which chronicles the history of the U.S. Navy; the **Navy Art Gallery,** which exhibits Navy-related paintings, sketches, and drawings; and the decommissioned U.S. Navy destroyer *Barry*, which is open for touring. Find the entrance at 11th and O streets SE. It's a little farther west along M Street SE to the new **Nationals Park,** home of the Washington Nationals. Opened in spring 2008, the ballpark cost over $600 million. It offers interactive tours on non-game days and throughout the off-season. From here it's just a short walk to the Navy Yard Metro station.

CAPITOL HILL OUTSKIRTS

On the outskirts of Capitol Hill you'll find gritty neighborhoods improving at varying rates. Although there are sights worth exploring here, some of them are a long walk from the Capitol—drive or take public transportation instead. The **H Street Corridor,** also known as the **Atlas District**, after the Atlas Performing Arts Center, is a diverse, edgy, and evolving stretch of nightlife between 12th and 14th streets NE. In September the annual H Street Music Festival celebrates the developing arts, entertainment, and fashion scene here.

Following E Street east to 17th Street, you will find the **Congressional Cemetery**, established in 1807 "for all denomination of people," which was the first national cemetery created by the government. You can take a self-guided walking tour of the premises. Farther upriver, and due east from the Capitol on East Capitol Street, **RFK Stadium** is the home of the D.C. United soccer team.

CAPITOL HILL WITH KIDS

Capitol Hill offers plenty for kids to do. After they've had their fill of history, they can commune with nature, hit a home run, and sample sweet treats.

There are lots of locally made toys and games to see and touch at **Eastern Market**. Street performers entertain while kids indulge in blueberry pancakes with ice cream at the **Market Lunch** counter.

At the **United States Botanic Garden**, kids can become Junior Botanists—they receive a free adventure pack with cool tools to use during their visit and afterwards at home, as well as access to a secret Web site. There's also a family guide available.

Catch a game at **Nationals Park** or take a tour on a non-game day. You'll see the Nationals dugout, the clubhouse, and press box, plus you can throw a pitch in the bullpen and test out the batting cages.

Or take a tour with **DC Ducks**: during the 1½-hour ride in an amphibious vehicle over land and water a wise-quacking captain mixes historical anecdotes with trivia.

2

DOWNTOWN

Sightseeing
★★★★☆
Dining
★★★★☆
Lodging
★★★★☆
Shopping
★★★☆☆
Nightlife
★★★★☆

Downtown D.C. is where government, commerce, and entertainment meet. The streets are wide, the buildings as tall as they get in Washington, and it is here that D.C. feels most like a big city. It's an extensive area, encompassing some distinct districts, and packed with historic and cultural attractions, with still more development in the pipeline. Downtown is compact; you can see the main sights in an hour and a half, not counting time spent inside museums. Travel light, you'll have to have your bag screened before entering almost everywhere.

DOWNTOWN WALK

The Downtown area can be divided into several sections, each with its own personality. **Federal Triangle** is the wedge-shape area south of Pennsylvania Avenue, north of Constitution Avenue, and east of 15th Street. It's the neighborhood's serious side, with imposing gray buildings and all-business mentality. **Penn Quarter** makes up the area directly to the north of Pennsylvania Avenue. This is Downtown's party side, where restaurants and bars mix with popular museums and the burgeoning theater district. **Chinatown** gives the neighborhood an international flair, and **Judiciary Square**, immediately to the east, is like a stern older uncle frowning about the goings-on.

FEDERAL TRIANGLE AND JUDICIARY SQUARE

Begin at **Metro Center**, the core of D.C.'s Metro system and its busiest station; from here most of Downtown is a short walk away. Take 12th Street south to **Federal Triangle**. The mass of government buildings was constructed between 1929 and 1938 in order to consolidate government workers in one place, and construction continued right into the

GETTING ORIENTED

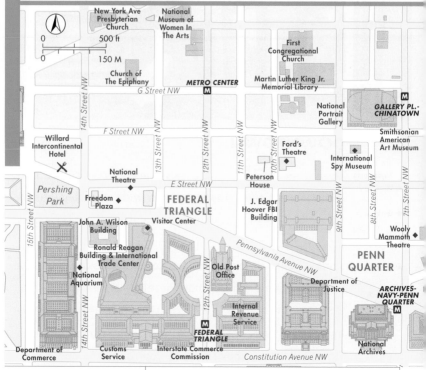

0 — 500 ft
0 — 150 M

Labels on map: New York Ave Presbyterian Church; National Museum of Women In The Arts; First Congregational Church; Church of The Epiphany; METRO CENTER; Martin Luther King Jr. Memorial Library; G Street NW; National Portrait Gallery; GALLERY PL.–CHINATOWN; Willard Intercontinental Hotel; F Street NW; Ford's Theatre; Smithsonian American Art Museum; International Spy Museum; National Theatre; E Street NW; Peterson House; Pershing Park; Freedom Plaza; FEDERAL TRIANGLE; J. Edgar Hoover FBI Building; John A. Wilson Building; Visitor Center; Pennsylvania Avenue NW; Wooly Mammoth Theatre; Ronald Reagan Building & International Trade Center; Old Post Office; PENN QUARTER; National Aquarium; Department of Justice; ARCHIVES-NAVY-PENN QUARTER; Internal Revenue Service; FEDERAL TRIANGLE; National Archives; Department of Commerce; Customs Service; Interstate Commerce Commission; Constitution Avenue NW; 14th Street NW; 13th Street NW; 12th Street NW; 11th Street NW; 10th Street NW; 9th Street NW; 8th Street NW; 7th Street NW; 15th Street NW

GETTING HERE	GREAT EXPERIENCES DOWNTOWN
Take the Metro to Federal Triangle or Archives-Navy Memorial to visit the government buildings along Pennsylvania Avenue. The Gallery Place–Chinatown stop gives direct access to the Verizon Center, Chinatown, and the American Art and Spy museums. Judiciary Square has its own stop, and Metro Center is the best choice for the National Theatre and Penn Quarter. Bus routes crisscross the area as well. Street parking is available; it's easier to find on nights and weekends away from the main Chinatown and Verizon Center area.	**Newseum:** Find out how the headlines are made, and read the front pages from all over the country, displayed in front of the building.
	International Spy Museum: Indulge your inner James Bond with a look at 007's Aston Martin from *Goldfinger*—along with more-serious toys used by the CIA, FBI, and KGB.
	The National Archives: After seeing the Declaration of Independence, Constitution, and Bill of Rights, lose yourself in the Public Vault, where you can find everything from the Emancipation Proclamation to *Mad* magazine.
	National Portrait Gallery and Smithsonian American Art Museum: These sister museums have something for everyone, from presidential portraits to old-timey "crazy quilts."
	Theater District: Catch performances ranging from Shakespeare to the avant-garde, in Penn Quarter's answer to Broadway.

2

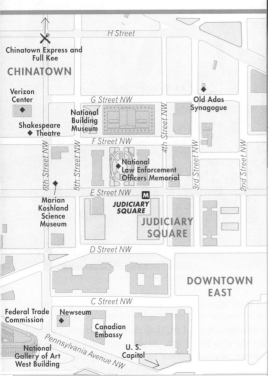

NATIONAL PORTRAIT GALLERY

CHINATOWN

Chinatown Express and Full Kee

Verizon Center

Shakespeare Theatre

National Building Museum

Old Adas Synagogue

National Law Enforcement Officers Memorial

Marian Koshland Science Museum

JUDICIARY SQUARE Ⓜ

JUDICIARY SQUARE

DOWNTOWN EAST

Federal Trade Commission

Newseum

Canadian Embassy

National Gallery of Art West Building

U. S. Capitol

H Street

G Street NW

F Street NW

E Street NW

D Street NW

C Street NW

Pennsylvania Avenue NW

6th Street NW · 5th Street NW · 4th Street NW · 3rd Street NW · 2nd Street NW

PLANNING YOUR TIME

Downtown is densely packed with major attractions—far too many to see in one day. You'll need at least an hour inside each attraction, so pick the two that appeal most and stroll past the rest. Art lovers might focus on the **National Portrait Gallery** and Smithsonian **American Art Museum**; history buffs might limit themselves to touring the **National Archives** and the **National Building Museum**; families with kids may prefer the **International Spy Museum**; and media junkies will want to visit the **Newseum** and the **Marian Koshland Science Museum**, which looks at the science behind media headlines.

SAFETY

Downtown's blocks of government and office buildings become something of a ghost town when the working day is done. You may prefer not to walk alone in this area after dark. The recently revitalized Penn Quarter still carries some vestiges of its grittier past, so stick to the main commercial areas at night.

QUICK BITES

Cheap eats abound in Chinatown. Watch the chef stretching noodles by the window before you head into **Chinatown Express** (✉ 746 6th St. NW ☎ 202/638–0424) to try some. **Full Kee** (✉ 509 H St. NW ☎ 202/371–2233) offers a large selection of Cantonese specialties.

There are back-to-back food courts in the Federal Triangle, at the **Old Post Office Pavilion** (✉ 1100 Pennsylvania Ave. NW ☎ 202/289–4224) and the **Ronald Reagan Building** (✉ 1300 Pennsylvania Ave. NW ☎ 202/312–1300) .

The historic **Willard Intercontinental Hotel** (✉ 1401 Pennsylvania Ave. NW ☎ 202/628–9100) serves breakfast and lunch at **Café du Parc**, tea in **Peacock Alley,** and drinks in the **Round Robin Bar.**

Savvy visitors skip the lines at the Washington Monument for the view from the Old Post Office Pavilion.

1990s. The neighborhood was formerly known as Murder Bay for its notorious collection of rooming houses, taverns, tattoo parlors, and brothels. When city planners moved in, they chose a uniform classical architectural style for the new buildings. As you pass by, give a nod to the **John A. Wilson Building, Internal Revenue Service Building, Department of Justice**, and Apex Building, which houses the **Federal Trade Commission**. These buildings aren't open to the public.

Ahead of you, the **Ronald Reagan Building and International Trade Center** houses the most secure tourist office and food court you'll ever see. You need to show a photo ID and go through a security checkpoint in order to collect brochures and subway schedules. It's also home to the Capitol Steps, who perform political comedy sketches on Friday and Saturday nights. Another food court and shops take up the lower levels of the Old Post Office, saved from demolition in 1973. The observation deck in the clock tower may be one of Washington's best-kept secrets. Although not as tall as the Washington Monument, it offers nearly as impressive a view. Even better, it's usually not as crowded, the windows are bigger, and—unlike the monument's windows—they're open, allowing cool breezes to waft through.

Nearby, the **Department of Commerce** houses the **National Aquarium** in its basement, a location as underwhelming as the aquarium itself. Slightly hidden across the street is a tiny and delightful shady oasis, **Pershing Park**, a pleasant area with picnic tables and a pond. Diagonally across the street the **Freedom Plaza**, named in honor of Martin Luther King Jr., is inlaid with a map from L'Enfant's original 1791 plan for the Federal City. To compare L'Enfant's vision with today's reality, stand in the

middle of the map's Pennsylvania
Avenue and look west. L'Enfant had
planned an unbroken vista from the
Capitol to the White House, but the
Treasury Building, begun in 1836,
ruined the view. Turning to the east,
you can see the U.S. Capitol sitting
on the former Jenkins Hill.

Follow Pennsylvania Avenue, the
nation's symbolic Main Street, known for inaugural and other parades
and civic demonstrations, towards the Capitol. On your left, the
J. Edgar Hoover Federal Bureau of Investigation Building has been a favorite
attraction for visitors interested in espionage and the persecution of bad
guys. Sadly, tours have been suspended indefinitely for security reasons.
The **National Archives** on the right display the original Declaration of
Independence, Constitution, and Bill of Rights. Washington's newest
museum, the **Newseum**, opened its doors in 2008. The seven-level building with 14 main galleries showcases 500 years of journalism history
with multimedia displays. The spectacular stone-and-glass edifice next
door is the Canadian Embassy.

Fourth Street takes you across Judiciary Square, where you will find city
and federal courthouses, as well as the **National Law Enforcement Officers
Memorial**. To the east, the small **Marian Koshland Science Museum** explores
and explains the science behind current news headlines. Across the street
the **National Building Museum** is known as much for its impressive interior
hall as for its exhibits on architecture and the building arts. The **Old Adas
Israel Synagogue** on 3rd Street is the oldest synagogue in D.C.

A couple of blocks to the west, new galleries, restaurants, and other
cultural hot spots have taken over much of the real estate. Look out
for the **Shakespeare Theatre Company's** new performing arts center, the
Sydney Harman Hall. The area surrounding the **Verizon Center** sports
arena has cinemas, restaurants, and shops. Expect crowds on weekend
evenings. From here, you're only a block away from the Gallery Place/
Chinatown Metro stop; continue north on 7th Street to Chinatown.

CHINATOWN AND PENN QUARTER
Chinatown begins just north of the Verizon Center. This compact neighborhood is marked by the ornate, 75-foot Friendship Arch at 7th and
H streets and Chinese characters on storefronts such as Ann Taylor and
Starbucks. Nearly every Cantonese, Szechuan, Hunan, and Mongolian
restaurant has a roast duck hanging in the window, and the shops here
sell Chinese food, arts and crafts, and newspapers. Nearby, **Martin Luther
King Jr. Memorial Library** is the only D.C. building designed by the illustrious modernist architect Ludwig Mies van der Rohe. From here detour
west on G Street and north on 13th Street to see the **National Museum
of Women in the Arts** which showcases works by female artists from the
Renaissance to the present (it has the only Frida Kahlo in the city).

South of Chinatown, below G Street, **Penn Quarter** begins. This neighborhood has blossomed into one of the hottest addresses in town for
nightlife and culture. The **National Portrait Gallery** and the **Smithsonian**

American Art Museum are the main cultural draws. The fun and interactive **International Spy Museum** across the street displays the largest collection of spy artifacts in the world.

A block west along E Street brings you out to Washington's theater district, home to the venerable **Ford's Theatre**, the **Warner Theatre** which has its own walk of fame on the sidewalk out front, and the **National Theatre**. The progressive **Woolly Mammoth Theatre Company** is nearby on 7th and D streets.

Tours of **Ford's Theatre** and the **Petersen House** take you back to the night of Lincoln's assassination. John Wilkes Booth and his coconspirators plotted out the dirty deed at **Suratt Boarding House** a few blocks away in Chinatown.

DOWNTOWN WITH KIDS

If you happen to time your visit with a monthly KidSpy workshop at the **International Spy Museum**, your junior James Bonds and young Nancy Drews can assume a new identity complete with disguise, go on a spy mission, meet real spies, and more. This is a great museum for tweens, but younger kids may not get it.

The **National Building Museum** takes building blocks to new heights as kids can strap on a tool belt and design their own cities.

At the **National Archives** kids can gawk at the Declaration of Independence, Constitution, and Bill of Rights; suddenly school history isn't so abstract.

The **Newseum** lets kids experience the stories behind the headlines, and they can even "broadcast" the news in front of the camera. Older kids can pick out big story headlines from world events they lived through.

Both the **National Portrait Gallery** and **Smithsonian American Art Museum** have something for everyone, from presidential portraits to art made from aluminum foil, bottle caps, and even television sets.

2

GEORGETOWN

Sightseeing
★★★☆☆

Dining
★★★★★

Lodging
★★★★☆

Shopping
★★★★★

Nightlife
★★★★★

At first glance, Washington's oldest and wealthiest neighborhood may look genteel and staid, but don't be fooled, this is a lively part of town. By day, Georgetown is D.C.'s top shopping destination, with everything from eclectic antiques and housewares to shoes and upscale jeans. By night, revelers along M Street and Wisconsin Avenue eat, drink, and make merry. This neighborhood was made for strolling with its historic tree-lined streets and views of the Potomac from waterfront parks. Although the coveted brick homes north of M Street are the province of Washington's high society, the rest of the neighborhood offers ample entertainment for everyone.

GEORGETOWN WALK

Georgetown can be thought of in four sections: the shopping and night-life area along **M Street**, the **university**, the **historic residential** neighborhoods, and the **waterfront**. The most popular and crowded area is the first, located mainly on M Street and Wisconsin Avenue. The C&O Canal is a sylvan spot for a bike ride, morning jog, or pleasant paddle, while the riverfront restaurants and parks at Washington Harbour let you enjoy the water views exertion-free. The neighborhood can be comfortably explored in an afternoon, though you may want to linger here.

M Street is a fitting introduction to the area that is known for its high-end clothing boutiques, antiques stores, and fancy furniture shops, now squeezing cheek-to-jowl with chain stores such as J. Crew and Banana

GETTING ORIENTED

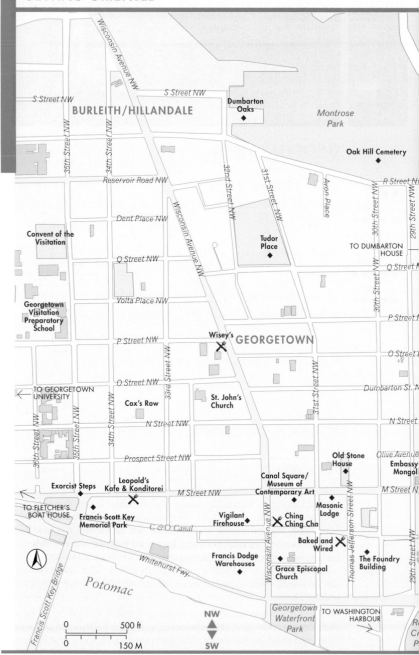

Wisconsin Avenue NW

S Street NW

S Street NW

BURLEITH/HILLANDALE

Dumbarton
Oaks
◆

Montrose
Park

35th Street NW

34th Street NW

Oak Hill Cemetery
◆

Reservoir Road NW

32nd Street NW

31st Street NW

Avon Place

R Street N

30th Street NW

29th Street NW

Dent Place NW

Wisconsin Avenue NW

TO DUMBARTON
HOUSE

Convent of the
Visitation

Tudor
Place
◆

Q Street NW

Q Street N

Georgetown
Visitation
Preparatory
School

Volta Place NW

30th Street NW

P Street N

P Street NW

Wisey's
✕ **GEORGETOWN**

O Street

33rd Street NW

O Street NW

Dumbarton St. N

31st Street NW

TO GEORGETOWN
UNIVERSITY
←

34th Street NW

Cox's Row

St. John's
Church

N Street NW

N Street

35th Street NW

Prospect Street NW

Old Stone
House
◆

Olive Avenue

Embassy
Mongol

36th Street NW

Exorcist Steps
◆

Leopold's
Kafe & Konditorei
✕

Canal Square/
Museum of
Contemporary Art
◆

M Street N

M Street NW

Masonic
Lodge
◆

TO FLETCHER'S
BOAT HOUSE
←

Francis Scott Key
Memorial Park

C & O Canal

Vigilant
Firehouse ◆

Thomas Jefferson Street NW

✕ Ching
Ching Cha

Baked and ✕
Wired

The Foundry
Building
◆

29th Street NW

Francis Dodge
Warehouses
◆

Wisconsin Avenue NW

Grace Episcopal
Church ◆

Whitehurst Fwy.

Potomac

Francis Scott Key Bridge

NW
▲
▼
SW

Georgetown
Waterfront
Park

TO WASHINGTON
HARBOUR
→

R
Cr
P

0   500 ft
0   150 M

2

GREAT EXPERIENCES IN GEORGETOWN

C&O Canal: Walk or bike along the path here, which offers bucolic scenery from the heart of Georgetown all the way to Maryland.

Dumbarton Oaks: Stroll through the 10 acres of formal gardens—Washington's loveliest oasis.

M Street: Indulge in some serious designer retail therapy (or just window-shopping). Reward your willpower or great find with a great meal afterward—all on the same street.

Tudor Place: Step into Georgetown's past with a visit to the grand home of the Custis-Peter family. On view are antiques from George and Martha Washington's home at Mount Vernon and a 1919 Pierce Arrow roadster.

Washington Harbour and Waterfront Park: Come on a warm evening to enjoy sunset drinks while overlooking the Watergate, Kennedy Center, and Potomac River.

GETTING HERE

There's no Metro stop in Georgetown, so you have to take a bus or taxi or walk to this part of Washington. It's about a 15-minute walk from Dupont Circle or the Foggy Bottom Metro station. Perhaps the best transportation deal in Georgetown is the Circulator. For a buck you can ride from Union Station along Massachusetts Avenue and K Street to the heart of Georgetown. Or try the Georgetown Metro Connection. These little white buses run along M Street to the Dupont Circle and Rosslyn metros.

Other options include the G2 Georgetown University Bus, which goes west from Dupont Circle along P Street, and the 34 and 36 Friendship Heights buses, which go south down Wisconsin Avenue and west down Pennsylvania Avenue toward Georgetown.

PLANNING YOUR TIME

You can easily spend a pleasant day in Georgetown, partly because some sights (**Tudor Place, Dumbarton Oaks, Oak Hill Cemetery,** and **Dumbarton House**) are somewhat removed from the others and partly because the street scene, with its shops and people watching, invites you to linger.

Georgetown is almost always crowded. It's not very car-friendly either, especially at night; driving and parking are usually difficult. The wise take the Metro to Foggy Bottom or Dupont Circle and then walk 15 minutes from there, or take a bus or taxi.

QUICK BITES

If the crowds of Georgetown become overwhelming, step into **Ching Ching Cha** (✉ *1063 Wisconsin Ave. NW* ☎ *202/333–8288*), a Chinese teahouse where tranquillity reigns supreme. In addition to tea, lunch and dinner may be ordered from a simple menu with light, healthful meals presented in lacquered bento boxes.

Wisey's (✉ *1440 Wisconsin Ave. NW* ☎ *202/333–4122*) is the more central outpost of university favorite **Wisemiller's Delicatessen.** There are a few tables in the small storefront. Healthy choices include panini, wraps, and salads, and smoothies and specialty teas are also available.

Known for its great window-shopping, Georgetown is a notoriously difficult place to park.

Republic or cheap and chic H&M and Zara. Slightly out of place amid the modern shops and cafés, the 18th-century **Old Stone House** and garden on M Street are thought to be the oldest in the city.

RESIDENTIAL GEORGETOWN AND GU

Leaving the throngs behind for now, 31st Street takes you north into the heart of residential Georgetown where impossibly small cottages stand side by side with rambling mansions. At Q Street, **Tudor Place** was once the home of Thomas Peter, son of Georgetown's first mayor, and his wife, Martha Custis, Martha Washington's granddaughter. A house tour lets you see many of Martha Washington's Mount Vernon possessions, as well as a 1919 Pierce Arrow roadster.

Farther up 31st Street, **Dumbarton Oaks** (no relation to Dumbarton House) can rightfully claim to be one of the loveliest spots in Washington, D.C. The 10 acres of formal gardens and English parkland may inspire a romantic proposal or a game of hide-and-seek, and the well-placed benches offer quiet nooks to rest weary feet or have a tête-à-tête. The attached museum is also well worth a visit.

To the east, **Montrose Park** entertains kids, dogs, and picnickers with wide lawns, tennis courts, and a playground. The funerary obelisks, crosses, and gravestones of **Oak Hill Cemetery** mark the final resting place for actor, playwright, and diplomat John H. Payne and William Corcoran, founder of the Corcoran Gallery of Art. A short detour east on Q Street, **Dumbarton House** is a distinctive example of Federal-era architecture and furnishings. One block farther along Q Street, **Mount Zion Cemetery** was featured in David Baldacci's novel *The Collectors*.

CLOSE UP

A History of Georgetown

The area that would come to be known as George (after George II), then George Towne, and finally Georgetown was part of Maryland when it was settled in the early 1700s by Scottish immigrants, many of whom were attracted by the region's tolerant religious climate.

Georgetown's position—at the farthest point up the Potomac that's accessible by ship—made it an ideal transit and inspection point for farmers who grew tobacco in Maryland's interior. In 1789 the state granted the town a charter, but two years later Georgetown— along with Alexandria, its counterpart in Virginia—was included by George Washington in the Territory of Columbia, site of the new capital.

While Washington struggled, Georgetown thrived. Wealthy traders built their mansions on the hills overlooking the river; merchants and the working class lived in modest homes closer to the water's edge. In 1810 a third of Georgetown's population was African-American—both free people and slaves. The Mt. Zion United Methodist Church on 29th Street is the oldest organized black congregation in the city. When the church stood at 27th and P streets, it was a stop on the Underground Railroad (the original building burned down in the mid-1800s).

Georgetown's rich history and success instilled in all its residents a feeling of pride that persists today. (When Georgetowners thought the dismal capital was dragging them down, they asked to be given back to Maryland, the way Alexandria was given back to Virginia in 1845.)

Tobacco's star eventually fell, and Georgetown became a milling center, using waterpower from the Potomac. When the Chesapeake & Ohio (C&O) Canal was completed in 1850, the city intensified its milling operations and became the eastern end of a waterway that stretched 184 mi to the west. The canal took up some of the slack when Georgetown's harbor began to fill with silt and the port lost business to Alexandria and Baltimore, but the canal never became the success it was meant to be.

In the years that followed, Georgetown was a malodorous industrial district, a far cry from the fashionable spot it is today. Clustered near the water were a foundry, a fish market, paper and cotton mills, and a power station for the city's streetcar system.

It still had its Georgian, Federal, and Victorian homes though, and when the New Deal and World War II brought a flood of newcomers to Washington, Georgetown's tree-shaded streets and handsome brick houses were rediscovered. Pushed out in the process were many of Georgetown's renters, including many of its black residents.

Today, some of Washington's most famous residents call Georgetown home, including former *Washington Post* executive editor Ben Bradlee, political pundit George Stephanopoulos, Senator (and 2004 presidential nominee) John Kerry, and *New York Times* op-ed doyenne Maureen Dowd.

2

In the nineteenth century mules pulled boats loaded with 100 tons of coal along the C&O Canal towpath.

Circling back, Wisconsin Avenue leads you downhill past a variety of small boutiques and cafés toward the intersection with M Street. Instead of following it the whole way, make a right on O Street, where you will find **St. John's Church**, one of the oldest churches in the city. Thirty-third Street brings you down to N Street to see some of the finest Federal-era architecture in D.C. **Cox's Row** is a group of five Federal houses, between 3339 and 3327 N Street, named after Colonel John Cox, a former mayor of Georgetown who built them in 1817.

N street gives way to **Georgetown University.** Founded in 1798, it is the oldest Jesuit school in the country. About 12,000 students attend the university, known now as much for its perennially successful basketball team as for its fine programs in law, medicine, foreign service, and the liberal arts.

Turn left at 36th Street to return to M Street, perhaps via the undeniably spooky 75 steps that featured prominently in the horror movie *The Exorcist*. Find them past the old brick streetcar barn at No. 3600. Down on the western end of M Street you'll find the small **Francis Scott Key Memorial Park**, honoring the Washington attorney who penned the national anthem during the War of 1812.

M STREET AND THE WATERFRONT

Walk back along M Street toward Washington Harbour, taking in the shops and restaurants along the way. The small **Museum of Contemporary Art** in **Canal Square**, a converted 1850s warehouse, is located here. You might be tempted to stop at **Leopold's Kafe & Konditorei** and linger on its shady terrace. A short detour down Wisconsin Avenue will take you to **Grace Episcopal Church** where many 19th-century residents prayed.

Georgetown's **C&O Canal** links the Potomac with the Ohio River. A sandy red path along the bank makes for a scenic walk or bike ride—look out for great blue herons and turtles lounging in the sun. Every summer the National Park Service offers rides on mule-drawn canal boats. Two miles west of the Key Bridge along the canal towpath, **Fletcher's Boat House** rents kayaks, canoes, and bikes. You can also follow the canal through the heart of Georgetown, running parallel with M Street. As you connect with Thomas Jefferson Street, note the former **Masonic Lodge** on Thomas Jefferson Street which harks back to the area's past as a working-class city populated by tradesmen, laborers, and merchants. You might want to stop for tea and cake at the fun and funky **Baked and Wired** on the same street. Head south on 31st Street toward the Potomac to take a rest on a bench under the trees in the **Georgetown Waterfront Park**.

> ## WE HAVE A SITUATION
>
> West of Wisconsin Avenue on M Street a somewhat uninspiring shopping mall, the Shops at Georgetown Park, occupies the site selected in the 1960s by the White House as the Situation Room with the first hotline to Moscow. Today's Situation Room is in the basement of the White House's West Wing; the staff of senior officers monitors and deals with world and U.S. crises.

Following the Potomac east to K Street between 30th and 31st streets you will find **Washington Harbour**, a riverfront development specializing in pricey restaurants and bars with scenic views of the river, the Watergate complex, and the Kennedy Center. Boat trips to Mount Vernon leave from here.

If you have dallied and evening approaches, you'll be in good company. By night the hungry, the thirsty, and the ready-to-party pound the pavement on this side of D.C. You'll find Vietnamese, Thai, Middle Eastern, and Ethiopian restaurants here, as well as burgers and fries at a variety of grubby pubs. After hours, college students and recent graduates overrun the bars, but a few lounges do cater to a more mature, upscale crowd.

GEORGETOWN WITH KIDS

Georgetown may not seem like the most kid-friendly part of D.C., but with nice weather the **Waterfront Park** and **C&O Canal** offer pleasant walks and picnic opportunities. If your toddlers and young children need a playground fix, north of M Street at 27th, you'll find the **Rose Park** "Tot Lot," complete with climbing frames and sandpit. **Montrose Park** to the north also has a playground.

DUPONT CIRCLE

Sightseeing
★★★★☆

Dining
★★★★★

Lodging
★★★★☆

Shopping
★★★★☆

Nightlife
★★★★☆

Dupont Circle is the grand hub of D.C., literally. This traffic circle is essentially the intersection of the main thoroughfares of Connecticut, New Hampshire, and Massachusetts avenues. More important though, the area around the circle is a vibrant center for urban and cultural life in the District.

Along with wealthy tenants and basement-dwelling twentysomethings, museums, art galleries, and embassies call this upscale neighborhood home. Offbeat shops, specialty bookstores, coffeehouses, and restaurants of all ethnicities and price ranges lend the area a funkier, more urban feel. Add to the mix stores and clubs catering to the neighborhood's large gay community and Dupont Circle becomes a big draw for nearly everyone. Perhaps that's why the fountain at the center of the traffic island is such a great spot for people watching.

DUPONT CIRCLE WALK

Two hours should be enough to walk the main sights here; longer if you want to linger in some of the neighborhood's fascinating small museums and enticing cafés.

Take the Metro to the dramatic Dupont Circle Q Street exit and you'll find yourself in the heart of it all. If you arrive on a Sunday morning you'll emerge into Dupont Circle's year-round **farmers' market** at the corner of Q and 20th streets. The large island in the middle of the traffic circle a few paces down Connecticut Avenue is a lively urban park, vibrant with rollerbladers, chess players, street performers, and a marble fountain created by Daniel Chester French. On sunny days the surrounding benches are pleasant spots for people watching, newspaper reading, or relaxing with a cup of coffee or a snack. Also nearby is the one-of-a-kind bookstore **Kramerbooks & Afterwords,** which has a broad and eclectic selection of reading material, as well as a popular café, open 24 hours on Friday and Saturday nights.

GETTING ORIENTED

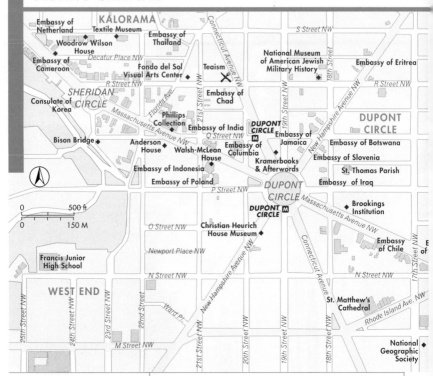

QUICK BITES	GREAT EXPERIENCES AROUND DUPONT CIRCLE
At the independent bookstore and café **Kramerbooks & Afterwords** (✉ *1517 Connecticut Ave. NW* ☏ *202/387–1400*) you can relax over dinner or a drink after browsing. For lunch or a light dinner (or just a cup of tea and an oatmeal cookie), visit **Teaism** (✉ *2009 R St. NW* ☏ *202/667–3827*). In addition to several dozen varieties of tea, there's a selection of seafood and vegetarian entrées, many available in bento boxes and seasoned with tea.	**Anderson House:** Glimpse into the life of a fabulously wealthy turn-of-the-19th-century U.S. diplomat and his glamorous, art-loving wife at their magnificent mansion. **Dupont Circle:** Grab a cup of coffee and a *CityPaper* and take in the scene around the always-buzzing fountain. **Gallery Hop:** On the first Friday of every month, D.C.'s best art scene is on display when most of Dupont Circle's art spaces are open late, free, and often with complimentary drinks. **National Geographic Society:** See *National Geographic* magazine come to life in rotating exhibits at the society's Explorers Hall. **Phillips Collection:** Admire masterpieces such as Renoir's *Luncheon of the Boating Party* and Degas's *Dancers at the Barre* at the country's first museum of modern art.

2

A GOOD WALK: KALORAMA

To see the embassies and luxurious homes that make up the Kalorama neighborhood, begin your walk at the corner of S and 23rd streets.

Head north up 23rd, keeping an eye out for the emergency call boxes now turned into public art.

At the corner of Kalorama Road, head west, but don't miss the Tudor mansion at 2221 Kalorama Road, now home to the French ambassador.

Turn right on Kalorama Circle, where you can look down over Rock Creek Park and into Adams Morgan. Kalorama means "beautiful view" in Greek, and this is the sight that inspired the name.

From here you can retrace your steps, or take Kalorama Circle back to Kalorama Road, turn right, and make a left on Wyoming to bring you back to 23rd.

GETTING HERE

Dupont Circle has its own stop on the Metro's Red Line. Exit on Q Street for the Phillips Collection, Anderson House, and Kalorama attractions. Take the Connecticut Avenue exit for the National Geographic Society, Christian Heurich House museum, or shopping between Dupont Circle and Farragut North. On-street parking is available on the residential streets away from the circle, but gets harder to find on weekend evenings.

PLANNING YOUR TIME

Visiting the Dupont Circle area takes at least half a day, although you can find things to keep you busy all day and into the evening. You'll likely spend the most time at the **Phillips Collection, Anderson House,** and **Woodrow Wilson House.** The hours will also fly if you linger over lunch or indulge in serious browsing in area shops.

NORTHWEST OF DUPONT CIRCLE

Head up the main north–south artery of Connecticut Avenue, lined with shops, restaurants, and cafés that are busy day and night. Turning left onto R Street you'll pass number 2131, an understated white-painted town house, home to FDR and Eleanor Roosevelt between 1916 and 1920. Detour a block south on 21st Street to find the **Phillips Collection**, founded as the first permanent museum of modern art in the country, with a collection including works by Renoir, Degas, Van Gogh, Picasso, Klee, and Matisse.

Along R Street lie a variety of art galleries. Nestled among them the nonprofit **Fondo Del Sol Visual Arts Center** is devoted to the cultural heritage of Latin America and the Caribbean. Detour east on R Street for the **National Museum of American Jewish Military History,** which displays weapons, uniforms, medals, recruitment posters, and other military memorabilia related to American Jews serving in the U.S. military.

SEE AND BE SCENE

Dupont's gay scene is concentrated mainly on 17th Street. A variety of gay-friendly, lively, and offbeat bars and restaurants stretch between P and R streets, many with outdoor seating perfect for people watching. JR's Bar and Grill and Cobalt are favorites. D.I.K. Bar is the place to be on the Tuesday before Halloween for the annual High Heel Drag Race down 17th Street. At the informal block party elaborately costumed drag queens strut their stuff along the route from Church to Queen streets and then race to the finish line.

At the west end of R Street, **Sheridan Circle** and Massachusetts Avenue are home to a cluster of embassies in striking villas. North on Massachusetts Avenue, you'll see some very unrestrained architecture, including the **Cameroon Embassy,** housed in a fanciful castle with a conical tower, bronze weather vane, and intricate detailing around the windows and balconies.

S Street edges into the Kalorama district. The **Woodrow Wilson House** shows the former president's home pretty much as he left it. On display are many gifts from foreign dignitaries. Next door, the **Textile Museum** hosts special exhibitions as well as its permanent collection of fabric arts, and a shop stuffed with beautiful things.

Just south of Sheridan Circle the **Bison Bridge** is guarded by four bronze statues of the shaggy mammals. Nearby, the **Anderson House** was bequeathed by Larz and Isabel Anderson to the Society of the Cincinnati, an exclusive club of the descendents of Revolutionary War officers. Next door, the **Walsh-McLean House** was once home to Evalyn Walsh-McLean, the last private owner of the Hope Diamond (now in the National Museum of Natural History). Head back to Connecticut Avenue for tempting opportunities for tea, lunch, or a snack before continuing on.

SOUTHEAST OF DUPONT CIRCLE

Past Dupont Circle, heading down Massachusetts Avenue toward Scott Circle, you'll pass the **Brookings Institution** and the **Johns Hopkins University D.C. campus** buildings. The **Christian Heurich House Museum,** once known as the Brewmaster's Castle, was the home of a German-born beer magnate and is nearby on New Hampshire Avenue. **Scott Circle** is decorated with statues of General Winfield Scott, Daniel Webster, and S. C. F. Hahnemann. If you walk to the south side of the circle and look down 16th Street, you'll get a familiar view of the columns of the White House, six blocks away. Nearby, down 17th Street, the **National Geographic Society** brings its magazines to life with interactive exhibits, photo galleries, and live shows.

> ### ART ON CALL!
>
> Throughout Dupont Circle and Kalorama you'll see obsolete police and fire call boxes that have been artistically restored. The 22 scattered around Dupont Circle and 16 in Kalorama display original art as well as historical scenes and neighborhood landmarks.

A few sights lie clustered on or near M Street south of Scott Circle, including two noteworthy religious institutions. The **Metropolitan African Methodist Episcopal Church** is one of the most influential African-American churches in the city. The Renaissance-style **St. Matthew's Cathedral** is the seat of Washington's Roman Catholic diocese, and the historic site of President Kennedy's funeral Mass. By appointment, you can tour the newsroom that broke the Watergate scandal at the **Washington Post Building.** Farther east out Vermont Avenue the **Mary McLeod Bethune Council House** features exhibits on the achievements of African-American women.

DUPONT CIRCLE WITH KIDS

Dupont Circle isn't overflowing with activities for kids. But if you're there on a Sunday morning for the **farmers' market** on the corner of Q and 20th streets, you may be able to get them excited about fruits and vegetables. If not, the homemade ice cream and cookies will certainly do the trick. The market has chef demonstrations, kids' activities, and an information table on the immense variety of foods on sale.

ADAMS MORGAN

Sightseeing
★☆☆☆☆

Dining
★★★★☆

Lodging
★☆☆☆☆

Shopping
★★★☆☆

Nightlife
★★★★★

To the urban and hip, Adams Morgan is a beacon of light in an otherwise stuffy landscape. D.C. may have a reputation for being staid and traditional, but drab suits, classical tastes, and bland food make no appearance here. Adams Morgan takes its name from two elementary schools that came together in 1958 after desegregation. It remains an ethnically diverse neighborhood with a United Nations of cuisines, offbeat shops, and funky bars and clubs. It's also the city's Latin Quarter. The area wakes up as the sun goes down, and twentysomethings in their weekend best congregate along the sidewalks, crowding the doors of this week's hot bar or nightclub. Typical tourist attractions are sparse, but the scene on a Saturday night has its own appeal.

ADAMS MORGAN WALK

This walk centers around the heart of Adams Morgan on 18th Street and its intersection with Columbia Road, where the dining and nightlife scene stretches for several blocks. You can easily see Adams Morgan in an hour or two, so you may want to combine it with a trip to Dupont Circle, or U Street, perhaps winding up here in the evening when this neighborhood gets hopping. Outside this central area, Adams Morgan starts to feel gritty at night, and most visitors never venture farther.

If you arrive here from Dupont Circle, you'll walk north up 18th Street. As soon as you reach the stretch of cheek-by-jowl restaurants, cafés, shops, and bars, you've reached Adams Morgan proper. The neighborhood's restaurant corridor lies on 18th Street south of Columbia Road

GETTING ORIENTED

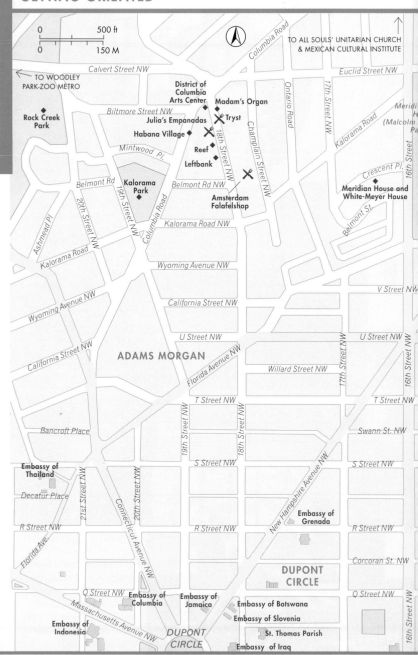

0 — 500 ft
0 — 150 M

TO WOODLEY
PARK-ZOO METRO

Calvert Street NW

District of
Columbia
Arts Center

Madam's Organ

TO ALL SOULS' UNITARIAN CHURCH
& MEXICAN CULTURAL INSTITUTE

Euclid Street NW

Columbia Road

Ontario Road

17th Street NW

Kalorama Road

Meridi
H
(Malcolm
Pa

16th Street

Biltmore Street NW

Rock Creek
Park

Julia's Empanadas

Tryst

Habana Village

Mintwood Pl.

Reef

Leftbank

18th Street NW

Champlain Street NW

Crescent Pl.

Meridian House and
White-Meyer House

Belmont Rd

Kalorama
Park

Belmont Rd NW

Amsterdam
Falafelshop

Belmont St.

19th Street NW

20th Street NW

Columbia Road

Ashmead Pl.

Kalorama Road

Kalorama Road NW

Wyoming Avenue NW

California Street NW

V Street NW

Wyoming Avenue NW

U Street NW

U Street NW

U Street NW

California Street NW

ADAMS MORGAN

Florida Avenue NW

Willard Street NW

17th Street NW

16th Street NW

T Street NW

T Street NW

T Street NW

Bancroft Place

19th Street NW

18th Street NW

Swann St. NW

Embassy of
Thailand

21st Street NW

S Street NW

S Street NW

S Street NW

Decatur Place

20th Street NW

New Hampshire Avenue NW

R Street NW

Connecticut Avenue NW

R Street NW

Embassy of
Grenada

R Street NW

Florida Ave.

Corcoran St. NW

**DUPONT
CIRCLE**

Q Street NW

Q Street NW

Q Street NW

Embassy of
Columbia

Embassy of
Jamaica

Embassy of Botswana

16th Street NW

Massachusetts Avenue NW

Embassy of
Indonesia

Embassy of Slovenia

St. Thomas Parish

**DUPONT
CIRCLE**

Embassy of Iraq

GREAT EXPERIENCES IN ADAMS MORGAN

Eat ethnic food: Adams Morgan rivals U Street with its plentiful and delicious Ethiopian restaurants. If you'd rather dine using utensils, you can choose among Japanese, Brazilian, Mexican, Indian, and other ethnic cuisines.

Hang out like a local: The residents of Adams Morgan make an art of relaxing. Follow their lead and settle into one of Tryst's overstuffed armchairs with a laptop or a copy of the *New Republic* and a coffee, or kill hours browsing the "rare and medium-rare" selections at Idle Time Books.

Stay out all night: If you want to party on until the break of dawn, this is the place to do it. Don't miss the live music at Madam's Organ, the salsa dancing at Habana Village, and the cool kids making the scene at the Leftbank.

Move to the beat: Sunday afternoon and evening in Meridian Hill Park, drummers from all walks of life form the Drum Circle, bashing out the beats while some dance and others simply sit back and watch.

GETTING HERE

Like Georgetown, Adams Morgan has no Metro stop. It's a pleasant 15-minute walk from the Woodley Park/Zoo Metro station: walk south on Connecticut, then turn left on Calvert Street, and cross over Rock Creek Park on the Duke Ellington Bridge. Or you can get off at the Dupont Circle Metro stop and walk east to (and turn left onto) 18th Street.

The heart of Adams Morgan is at the intersection of Adams Mill Road, Columbia Road, and 18th Street. Don't even dream about finding parking here on weekend evenings.

If you take the Metro, remember that stations close at 3 AM on Friday and Saturday nights and midnight other nights. If you're not ready to turn in by then, you'll need to hail a cab.

PLANNING YOUR TIME

A window-shopping wander around Adams Morgan can occupy the better part of an afternoon. And if you take advantage of the restaurants and nightlife here, there's no telling when your head will hit the pillow.

The few tourist attractions in this area aren't time-intensive, but they can be a long walk from restaurants.

QUICK BITES

Julia's Empanadas (✉ *2452 18th St. NW* ☏ *202/328–6232*) serves spicy Salvadoran snacks until 3 AM. The empanadas go well with tangy salads; all in portions you can comfortably eat standing up—a good thing, because this is mostly a to-go joint.

Everyone feels at home relaxing on the old couches and comfy chairs at **Tryst** (✉ *2459 18th St. NW* ☏ *202/232–5500*). Stop in for breakfast, sandwiches, or dessert, or sip hot chocolate or something stronger after hours.

Whether it's 1 PM or 1 AM, the **Amsterdam Falafelshop** (✉ *2425 18th St. NW* ☏ *202/234–1969*) is happy to feed you. The bargain-priced menu consists entirely of top-it-yourself falafels in pita, Dutch-style french fries, and brownies. It's open until 4 AM on weekends.

and the parts of Columbia Road and Calvert Street directly adjacent. The city's most diverse eats are served along these few blocks, a succession of Salvadoran *pupusas* (stuffed tortillas), Ethiopian *injera* (pancake-like sourdough bread), French *ratatouille* (savory vegetable stew), and West African *moi moi* (black-eyed-pea cakes) unrivaled in the city.

Adams Morgan's bar and club scene caters mostly to a young crowd in their twenties. The popular clubs often have lines out the door, and walking down 18th Street around midnight is a little like trying to drive on the Beltway at rush hour. If you're game for a drink, try the **Leftbank** for a trendy vibe amid retro furnishings or the **Reef** with its unpretentious atmosphere, colorful fish tanks, and large beer selection. The multistory **Madam's Organ** is a neighborhood institution, with live music every night, and **Habana Village** is one of the best places in the city for salsa dancing and Latin music.

The shops on 18th Street feed an appetite for the offbeat. Here you can find collectibles such as Mission furniture, Russel Wright crockery and Fiesta ware, aerodynamic art deco armchairs, Bakelite telephones, massive chromium toasters, kidney-shape coffee tables, skinny neckties, and oddball salt and pepper shakers. On the west side of 18th Street are antiques shops as well as secondhand shops set up in alleys or warehouses. Nearby is the **District of Columbia Arts Center,** a combination art gallery and performance space.

Columbia Road to the east between 16th and 18th is the area's Latin Quarter, as bilingual as it gets in Washington. At tables stretched along the street, vendors hawk watches, leather goods, knockoff perfumes, CDs, sneakers, clothes, and handmade jewelry. On Saturday morning a market springs up on the plaza at the southwest corner of 18th and Columbia, with stands selling fruits, vegetables, flowers, and fresh bread.

At the corner of 16th and Columbia, **All Souls' Unitarian Church** was a cornerstone of the civil rights movement and community activism during the 20th century. Heading south on 16th, the **Mexican Cultural Institute** promotes Mexican art, culture, and science. Farther down the street the public can explore two mansions owned by the Meridian International Center, a nonprofit promoting international understanding. The **Meridian and White-Meyer Houses** hold periodic art exhibits with an international flavor. On the opposite side of 16th Street, **Meridian Hill Park,** also known as **Malcolm X Park,** was once considered a possible location for the White House. Stop off here for shade and city views among the fountains and statues of Joan of Arc and Dante.

LOOK UP

As you walk around Adams Morgan, note the many colorful and striking murals. Champorama Mural is one of the best; it is located in a tiny park just off 18th Street on the corner of Kalorama Road and Champlain Street. Among others, Toulouse Lautrec is on 18th near Belmont Street. Find more on Columbia Road including the oldest remaining mural in the neighborhood at 17th Street.

U STREET CORRIDOR

Sightseeing
★★☆☆☆

Dining
★★★★☆

Lodging
★☆☆☆☆

Shopping
★★★★☆

Nightlife
★★★★★

Home-style Ethiopian food, offbeat boutiques, and live music are fueling the revival of the U Street area. Just a few years back this neighborhood was running on fumes, surviving on memories of its heyday of black culture and jazz music in the first half of the 20th century.

The neighborhood was especially vibrant from the 1920s to the 1950s, when it was home to jazz genius Duke Ellington, social activist Mary McLeod Bethune, and poets Langston Hughes and Georgia Douglas Johnson. The area's nightclubs hosted Louis Armstrong, Cab Calloway, and Sarah Vaughn. In the 1950s Supreme Court Justice Thurgood Marshall, then still a lawyer, organized the landmark *Brown v. Board of Education* case at the 12th Street YMCA. Now the crowds are back, and this diverse neighborhood faces the threat of yuppification.

U STREET CORRIDOR WALK

You'll need a couple of hours to explore U Street fully, especially if you want to stop in the African-American Civil War Museum. You're likely to spend most of your time along U Street itself, detouring here and there to see the sights just a couple of blocks away. Don't stray too far off the main drag, especially at night.

Beginning at the 10th Street exit of the U Street/Cardozo Metro station, you emerge right at the **African-American Civil War Memorial,** honoring the black soldiers who fought in the Union Army. For more on that story, walk two blocks west to the **African-American Civil War Museum,** which tells the tale of Africans in America from the slave trade through the civil rights movement with numerous photos and documents. The museum is housed in the former **True Reformers Building,** now the Public Welfare Foundation. Back in the day, Duke Ellington and others performed in the upstairs ballroom. Don't miss the **Duke Ellington Mural** on the western side of the building.

GETTING ORIENTED

GREAT EXPERIENCES ON U STREET CORRIDOR

African-American Civil War Memorial and Museum: Learn about the lives of slaves and freedmen, and discover whether your ancestors fought in black regiments during the Civil War.

Ben's Chili Bowl: If you can top it with chili, it's on the menu. This D.C. institution has perfected its recipe over the last 50 years and satisfies meat-eaters and vegetarians alike.

Boutiques: Whether you're after funky footwear or flashy housewares, hit the shops on U and 14th streets for trendy finds.

Ethiopian food: Nothing brings you closer to your meal than eating with your hands. Use the spongy injera bread to scoop up delectable dishes from East Africa.

Jazz and live music: Music greats like Duke Ellington made this neighborhood famous back in the 1920s. Relive the glory years at a jazz performance at Bohemian Caverns or HR 57, or rock out to today's music at the 9:30 Club or Black Cat.

GETTING HERE

The Green Line Metro stops at 13th and U, in the middle of the main business district. To get to the African-American Civil War Memorial, get out at the 10th Street exit. Parking can be found on the residential streets north and south of U Street, but as the area gets more popular, spots are getting harder to find on weekend nights.

The area is within walking distance from Dupont Circle and Adams Morgan, but at night you're better off on the bus or in a cab, especially if you're alone. The 90, 92, and 98 buses travel from Woodley Park through Adams Morgan to 14th and U, while the 52 and 54 buses travel north from several Downtown Metro stops up 14th Street.

PLANNING YOUR TIME

You'll need half a day at most to see U Street's attractions and visit its boutiques. You can also fill an evening with dinner on U Street, a show at the **9:30 Club** or **Bohemian Caverns**, and drinks afterward. If you're not driving, allow plenty of time for public transportation.

QUICK BITES

Ben's Chili Bowl (⊠ *1213 U St. NW* ☎ *202/667–0909*) has been a U Street institution since 1958. It serves cheap and filling chili (both meat and vegetarian) any which way imaginable. The quintessential meal here is the chili half-smoke, a spicy grilled hot dog covered with mustard, onions, and, of course, chili.

For a more intellectual snack, stop into **Busboys and Poets** (⊠ *1390 V St. NW* ☎ *202/387–7638*). This bookstore–cum-restaurant–cum–coffee lounge serves up a comfort-food menu of sandwiches, pizzas, and burgers. Events to liven up your meal include literary readings, open-mike nights, and musical performances.

SAFETY

The commercial district here borders a much less gentrified area. The blocks between 10th and 16th streets are well lighted and busy, but the neighborhood gets grittier to the north and east. Use your street sense, especially at night. It's wise to splurge on a cab rather than waiting for a bus late at night.

2

DID YOU KNOW?

It may sound like a bad joke, but in an effort to be more environmentally conscious, Ben's Chili Bowl switched from electric power to 100% wind power in 2007.

Once the hub of black cultural life, with first-run movies and live performances, the **Lincoln Theater** now functions as a theater and event venue. The 12th Street YMCA has been made over to the **Thurgood Marshall Center**, which houses a museum on the history of African-Americans in the U Street/Shaw neighborhood. Duke Ellington fans can find his former homes at 1805 and 1813 13th Street.

Although the neighborhood was nearly destroyed in the rioting that followed the 1968 assassination of Martin Luther King Jr., U Street has recently reclaimed some of its former pulse. **Bohemian Caverns** combines an elegant restaurant with an underground music venue and upstairs club. It's been hosting jazz greats since 1926. On V Street, the **9:30 Club** attracts big-name rock bands and lesser-known indie artists alike to one of the East Coast's coolest concert halls. South on 14th Street, the **Black Cat** rocks out with independent and alternative bands from the city and around the world. **DC9** hosts an eclectic mix of local and national bands and DJs. Find it on the corner of 9th and U.

A longtime center for African-American life in the District, U Street is now home to many of the city's East African immigrants, who've brought their culinary traditions to the neighborhood restaurants. Clubs have expanded beyond jazz to include all kinds of rock music, and new shops have popped up to bring in even more business. Standout restaurants in D.C.'s unofficial Little Ethiopia such as **Etete** tempt diners with spongy injera bread and hearty meat and vegetarian dishes. Multiculti dining is in abundance here, but the city's humble roots are not yet forgotten; the granddaddy of Washington diners, **Ben's Chili Bowl**, has been serving chili, chili dogs, chili burgers, and half-smokes, spicy sausages served in a hot-dog bun, since 1958. A sign inside used to let you know that only Bill Cosby eats at Ben's for free, until November 2008, when the Obama family was added to the list.

U Street's shopping scene has garnered attention in recent years as well. Most of the boutiques are clustered on U Street between 14th and 16th streets. Pop in and out of the little shops to find cutting-edge footwear, Asian furnishings, playful housewares, and eclectic or vintage clothing. Fourteenth Street has some rich pickings as well and you could happily detour all the way south to **Logan Circle**. On the way you'll find a variety of fun shops, unusual cafés, as well as the highly regarded **Source Theater**, part of the thriving 14th Street arts scene. East of the commercial district, the historically Black Howard University has been educating African-American men and women since 1867. Notable graduates include authors Zora Neale Hurston and Toni Morrison, opera singer Jessye Norman, and Nobel Peace Prize–winner Ralph Bunche.

U STREET CORRIDOR WITH KIDS

U Street really comes into its own at night, but tweens and teens can have a good time here during the day. Kids of any age can have a great lunch at Ben's Chili Bowl, and they're warmly welcomed in Etete as well. Teens might like browsing the eclectic shops on U Street and down 14th Street. For a sweet treat, check out the ACKC Cocoa Gallery, a bright and welcoming chocolate café on 14th Street.

UPPER NORTHWEST

The upper northwest corner of D.C. is predominantly residential and in many places practically suburban. However, there are several good reasons to visit the leafy streets, including the National Zoo and National Cathedral. If the weather is fine, spend an afternoon strolling through Hillwood Gardens or tromping through Rock Creek Park's many acres. You'll have to travel some distance to see multiple attractions in one day, but many sights are accessible on foot from local Metro stops.

UPPER NORTHWEST WALK

Upper Northwest isn't a neighborhood; it is a geographic grouping of several neighborhoods, including Cleveland Park, Woodley Park, Tenleytown, and Foxhall. The majority of attractions lie on or near Connecticut Avenue north of Woodley Park or on Massachusetts Avenue north of Georgetown. The **Kreeger Museum** is the exception, with its location in Foxhall, northwest of Georgetown. This area divides into three walks. Either focus on the zoo and surrounding area, or head up to the cluster of museums and landmarks around Cleveland Park and Massachusetts Avenue. Alternatively, Rock Creek Park offers shady walks and activities for kids, or hit the shops at the edge of D.C. Using the bus, Metro, or driving will allow you to see more of the area in a day.

ZOO AND SURROUNDINGS

The **National Zoo** is a reason in itself to head uptown; take the Metro to the Cleveland Park station. While recent attention has focused on giant pandas Tian Tian and Mei Xiang, the Smithsonian's free zoological park is full of red pandas, clouded leopards, and Japanese giant salamanders, as well as the traditional lions, tigers, and bears. The zoo makes for a picturesque stroll on warm days, but be prepared for crowds on sunny weekends.

South of the zoo lies **Woodley Park,** a residential neighborhood filled with stately apartment buildings. The stretch of Connecticut Avenue between Calvert and Woodley Road is notable for its popular array of restaurants and the **Wardman Tower,** a cross-shape tower built in 1928 as a luxury apartment building. Once known for its famous residents, it's now part of the Marriott Wardman Park Hotel. **Woodley,** a Georgian mansion that served as the summer home of four presidents, lies on Cathedral Avenue between 29th and 31st streets. At Woodley Park/Zoo Metro, the Red Line takes you back Downtown.

> ### GETTING TO THE ZOO
>
> If you're just going to the zoo, leave the Metro at Cleveland Park instead of Woodley Park/Zoo for a shorter downhill walk. At the end of your visit, return downhill to the Metro via Woodley Park/Zoo. If the zoo doesn't wipe you out, tag on a trip to Adams Morgan, easily accessible on foot from the Woodley Park/Zoo Metro stop.

CLEVELAND PARK AND MASSACHUSETTS AVENUE

These attractions are more scattered, so allow a bit more time, and plan to drive or take the bus or Metro.

A 20-minute walk uphill from the Van Ness Red Line stop or an easy drive or cab ride away, the **Hillwood Estate, Museum and Gardens** displays cereal heiress Marjorie Merriweather Post's collection of 18th- and 19th-century French and Russian decorative art. The grounds and gardens equal the art collection in beauty and size. Also in this area, **Howard University Law School** is famed for its African-American graduates, such as Oliver Hill, Thurgood Marshall, and Charles Hamilton Houston.

Farther south you could combine several attractions on Massachusetts Avenue. The **Islamic Mosque and Cultural Center,** with its 162-foot-high minaret, is the oldest Islamic house of worship in D.C. The **Khalil Gibran Memorial Garden** combines Western and Arab symbols in remembrance of the Lebanese-born poet. Opposite the garden, the **U.S. Naval Observatory** makes a stand for science. Continuing north, the Greek Orthodox **St. Sophia Cathedral** is noted for the handsome mosaic work on the interior of its dome. Dominating the skyline, the **Washington National Cathedral** is the sixth-largest cathedral in the world. Its Gothic decor features fanciful gargoyles, including one shaped like Darth Vader. Head inside for a tour or tea in the **Pilgrim Gallery.**

ROCK CREEK PARK, FOXHALL, AND OUTER D.C.

Although the 1,800 acres of **Rock Creek Park** span much of Washington and into Maryland, two of the main driving entrances are in Upper Northwest. Take Tilden Road to get to the Peirce Mill and Military Road to reach the nature center and planetarium. The park is accessible to pedestrians throughout the city.

When the weather is clear, two parks in this area are worth a visit. The 183-acre **Glover-Archbold Park** features a 3.5-mi nature trail. The highest point in the District, **Fort Reno Park** hosts free outdoor concerts in summer.

GETTING ORIENTED

GREAT EXPERIENCES IN UPPER NORTHWEST

House museums: The Hillwood Estate, Museum and Gardens showcases cereal heiress Marjorie Merriweather Post's collection of Imperial Russian art and Fabergé eggs, and 12 gorgeous acres of formal French and Japanese gardens. Chagalls, Picassos, and Monets inside contrast with the architecture at the modernist Kreeger Museum.

National Zoo: Visit the giant pandas, elephants, lions, and other members of the animal kingdom while you enjoy a stroll outdoors.

Shopping in Friendship Heights: The city's most glamorous shopping lines Wisconsin Avenue at the Maryland border. Want to actually buy something? Plenty of stores cater to shoppers on a budget, too.

U.S. Naval Observatory: View the heavens through one of the world's most powerful telescopes.

Washington National Cathedral: Look for the Darth Vader gargoyle on the soaring towers of this cathedral, then relax among the rosebushes in the Bishop's Garden. Concerts are held here, too.

GETTING HERE

Connecticut Avenue attractions, such as the zoo, are accessible from the Red Line Metro stops between Woodley Park/Zoo and Van Ness. The Friendship Heights Bus travels north from Georgetown along Wisconsin Avenue and takes you to the National Cathedral.

Parking can be tricky along Massachusetts Avenue; to see these sights, it's often more practical for good walkers to hoof it up the street or take the N2, N4, or N6 bus between Dupont Circle and Friendship Heights. For more-outlying sights, driving or cabbing it may be the best way to visit.

PLANNING YOUR TIME

The amount of time you spend at the zoo is up to you; animal enthusiasts could easily spend a full day here. You may want to plan your trip around daily programs, such as the elephant-training session or the eagle feeding.

For other itineraries, be sure to leave room in your schedule for travel between sights and, if you have a car, for parking. To maximize your time, call ahead to inquire whether on-site parking is available and when the next tour will begin.

QUICK BITES

The blocks immediately surrounding the Woodley Park and Cleveland Park Metro stations are chockablock with restaurants. If you've got the time, skip lunch at the zoo's eateries and head north or south on Connecticut to find a wealth of dining options, then head back.

FINDING A RESTROOM AT THE ZOO

At the National Zoo, unlike most everywhere else in D.C., public restrooms can be found in four convenient locations: in the Panda Plaza, next to the Zoo Police Station, inside the visitor center, and inside Amazonia.

Hillwood Estate's Japanese garden provides a tranquil spot for quiet contemplation.

Tucked away in the Foxhall neighborhood, the **Kreeger Museum** showcases the small but impressive collections of paintings, sculpture, and African art collected by wealthy businessman David Kreeger. Tour the hall where he entertained famous musicians and the dining room decorated entirely with Monets. Reserve in advance except on Saturday.

At the Maryland border, the intersection of Wisconsin and Western avenues forms **Friendship Heights**. This shopping-mall district is the place to pick up the latest finds at Tiffany, Louis Vuitton, and Neiman Marcus. Filene's Basement and Loehmann's provide designer deals.

UPPER NORTHWEST WITH KIDS

At the **National Zoo** the Kids Farm and Pizza Garden keep kids busy learning how to take care of animals and where food comes from.

Rock Creek Nature Center and Planetarium (✉ *5300 Glover Rd. NW*) offers a variety of hands-on experiences for kids in the **Discovery Room**. They can look inside beehives, create rainstorms, and crawl inside a volcano. Fish and amphibian feeding time is 4 PM. The **planetarium** has weekend shows for kids.

At the **National Cathedral**, kids can see gargoyles pulling just about every face imaginable. The **Children's Chapel** is designed to the scale of a six-year-old child, and the Space Window contains a piece of rock from the moon.

Museums

WORD OF MOUTH

"Personally, I can spend a lot of time in the museums in D.C., including some not on the Mall. You may also want to include the goofy-fun, and historically interesting Spy Museum."

—madameX

MUSEUMS PLANNER

Special Events

The Smithsonian museums regularly host an incredible spectrum of special events, from evenings of jazz to DJ'd dance nights to food and wine tastings, films, lectures, and events for families and kids. A full schedule is available at ⊕ *www.si.edu/events.* Among the most popular events are live jazz on Friday evenings in summer at the National Gallery of Art sculpture garden and in winter in the National Museum of Natural History. Both include a cash bar. Every three months the Hirshhorn Museum throws a wildly popular after-hours party with DJs, sound-and-light art installations, a cash bar, and a dance floor.

Late Hours

Corcoran Gallery of Art, Thursday until 9 PM.

International Spy Museum, April–October, daily until 8 PM.

Museum of Crime and Punishment, April–August, daily until 9 PM, September–March, daily until 8 PM.

Phillips Collection, Thursday until 8:30 PM.

The Smithsonian

Most of the 18 Smithsonian Institution museums are open between 10 and 5:30 more than 360 days a year, and all are free (though there may be charges for some special exhibits). To get oriented, start with a visit to the Smithsonian Institution building—aka the "Castle," for its swooping towers-and-turrets architecture—which has information on all the museums.

Museums with Kids

They'll need to meet a giant T. rex, see live tarantulas, and take in an IMAX movie at the Museum of Natural History. At the Museum of American History, they can build multipronged pinwheels in the **Invention at Play** workshop, conduct experiments with lively scientists in the **Spark Lab**. They can see history's most famous spaceships and fighter planes at the National Air and Space Museum's Steven F. Udvar-Hazy Center. At the Corcoran Gallery of Art exhibitions are set up with an interactive **Exploration Gallery** for younger visitors and "Conversation Starters" brochures for parents. The Freer Gallery of Art and Hirshhorn Museum offer free art workshops for kids. The National Building Museum has interactive exhibits and workshops, and at the D.A.R. Museum kids can play games and try on costumes from the time of the American Revolution.

Best Gift Shops

National Gallery of Art. Here you can find one of the country's largest selections of books on art and art history, along with beautiful posters, prints, reproductions, stationery, and gifts.

National Building Museum. With shelves filled with Philippe Starck–designed kitchenware, jewelry made out of nails and cement, and slickly photographed tomes on architecture, design lovers and modernists will be in heaven.

National Air and Space Museum. The three-story museum store is the largest of all the Smithsonian museum stores.

3

By Coral
Davenport and
Cathy Sharpe

The internationally renowned collections of the Smithsonian—137 million objects, specimens, and artworks displayed in the world's largest museum complex—make Washington one of the great museum cities. The holdings of the 18 Smithsonian museums span the depth and breadth of history, art, and science, ranging from a 65-million-year-old *Tyrannosaurus rex* skeleton to masterpieces by DaVinci and Picasso, the Hope Diamond, the original Star-Spangled Banner, and the space shuttle *Enterprise*—and all are on view for free. The city also has plenty of fascinating specialty museums, like the high-tech International Spy Museum, the design-centric National Building Museum, and the media-saturated Newseum.

JUST THE HIGHLIGHTS, PLEASE

Nowhere else can you see the Declaration of Independence and the Constitution, both displayed at the National Archives. Touch a moon rock beneath the *Spirit of St. Louis* at the National Air and Space Museum. The masterpieces of Monet and Matisse at the National Gallery of Art are must-sees, as are Thomas Jefferson's desk and Dorothy's ruby slippers at the newly renovated National Museum of American History.

For modern art, it's tough to beat the constantly changing Hirshhorn Museum, where an Alexander Calder mobile might hover over a multimedia installation by today's hottest talent. For intimately grouped masterpieces in a mansion, head to the Phillips Collection. Lovers of architecture and design shouldn't miss a pilgrimage to the National Building Museum.

CORCORAN GALLERY OF ART

⊠ *500 17th St. NW, White House area* ☎ *202/639–1700* ⊕ *www.corcoran.org* 🎫 *$10; admission for special exhibitions, $12–$35* ⊗ *Mon., Wed., Fri., and weekends 10–5; Thurs. 10–9* Ⓜ *Farragut W or Farragut N.*

The Corcoran looks like a museum and acts like a gallery, blending classic elegance and experimental edge. Washington's first art museum is housed in a Beaux-Arts marble mansion, and home to an important collection of 18th-, 19th-, and 20th-century European and American art. As the parent of the Corcoran School of Art, the museum is also devoted to showcasing cutting-edge contemporary art, from established superstars to undiscovered talents.

HIGHLIGHTS

A prize collection of masterworks by the great early American artists, including John Copley, Gilbert Stuart, Rembrandt Peale, Mary Cassatt, and John Singer Sargent, is in constant rotation, but you're always guaranteed to see a selection of the most-important pieces, displayed in gilded frames in high-ceilinged marble rooms

You're also sure to see something contemporary and fun like a neon-lighted video art installation transforming a marble-columned room or live performance art.

Photography is one of the museum's great strengths: recent exhibits of works by Richard Avedon and William Eggleston drew sold-out crowds.

The exhibition space **Gallery 31** shows work by students, faculty, and alumni of the highly reputed Corcoran School of Art.

THE FREER AND SACKLER GALLERIES

✉ *12th St. and Jefferson Dr. SW, The Mall* ☎ *202/633–1000, 202/357–1729 TDD* ⊕ *www.asia.si.edu* 🎫 *Free* ⊘ *Daily 10–5:30* Ⓜ *Smithsonian.*

3

TIPS

■ The Freer and Sackler galleries are home to the largest Asian art research library in the United States, open to the public five days a week without appointment.

■ Free highlight tours meet at the information desks at noon daily, except Wednesday and federal holidays. There are often a variety of other free tours as well; ask at the information desks.

■ The museums regularly host films, concerts, readings, and other events; check the Web site to see what's on.

■ Take advantage of the Freer's wide menu of excellent brochures on everything from Islamic art and Japanese painting to South Asian sculpture and Near Eastern ceramics.

■ At the Imaginasia workshops, held most weekends at the Arthur M. Sackler Gallery, children ages 6 to 14 work on projects such as origami and Asian board games.

Home to one of the world's finest collections of Asian art, the Smithsonian's Freer Gallery of Art was made possible by an endowment from Detroit industrialist Charles Lang Freer. Opened in 1923, the collection includes more than 27,000 works of art from the Far and Near East. When he endowed the gallery, Freer insisted on a few conditions: objects in the collection could not be lent out, nor could objects from outside the collections be put on display.

Because of the restrictions, it was necessary to build a second, complementary museum to house the Asian art collection of Arthur M. Sackler. The Sackler collection includes works from the Middle East and Southeast Asia. A lower-level exhibition gallery connects the two museums.

HIGHLIGHTS

Pick a china pattern, a favorite jade carving, or a painted silk scroll from the collections of Imperial Chinese decorative arts.

Behold the bodhisattva: a 12th-century Japanese sculpture of a Buddhist approaching Nirvana.

Ogle the undulating curves of the 10th-century Indian bronze sculptures of the dancing god Shiva and his wife, the goddess Parvati.

The museum is home to the world's largest collection of paintings by James McNeill Whistler. Be sure to see the **Peacock Room**, a jewel box of a space that Whistler designed, with gold murals on peacock-blue walls, and a peacock-feather-pattern gold leaf ceiling.

Manuscripts of 15th century Persian love poetry, in exquisite calligraphy accompanied with intricate gold and silver paintings, are a must-see in the Sackler Gallery.

HIRSHORN MUSEUM AND SCULPTURE GARDEN

✉ *Independence Ave. and 7th St. SW, The Mall* ☎ *202/633–1000, 202/633–8043 TDD* ⊕ *www.hirshorn.si.edu* 🎟 *Free* ⊙ *Museum daily 10–5:30, sculpture garden daily 7:30–dusk* Ⓜ *Smithsonian or L'Enfant Plaza (Maryland Ave. exit).*

TIPS

■ The sculpture garden makes an inspiring spot for a picnic.

■ Docents lead impromptu 30-minute tours between noon and 4. Every Friday at 12:30 there is a free gallery talk and tour focusing on a current exhibition, led by an art expert or historian.

■ Have a question? Seek out the artists and young arts professionals wearing question-mark badges around the museum.

■ There are free activities and projects for children ages 5 to 11 and their parents at the museum's drop-in **Improv Art Room** on the lower level.

■ About four times a year the museum hosts Hirshorn After Hours events: huge parties that run from 9 to midnight in the museum and sculpture garden. Check the Web site to see if one is coming up during your visit: advance tickets are essential.

■ The museum regularly screens independent and experimental films.

In 2003 the Hirshhorn made a bold addition to sculpture on the Mall: a 32-foot-tall yellow cartoon brush-stroke sculpture by pop-art iconographer Roy Lichtenstein. It became a beloved local landmark. Conceived as the nation's museum of modern and contemporary art, the Hirshhorn is home to more than 11,500 works by masters like Pablo Picasso, Piet Mondrian, and Willem de Kooning, as well as contemporary superstars like Damien Hirst and Olafur Eliasson. The art is displayed in a round 1974 poured-concrete building designed by Gordon Bunshaft. Dubbed the "Doughnut on the Mall" when it was built, it's now seen as a fitting home for contemporary art. Most of the collection was bequeathed by the museum's founder, Joseph H. Hirshhorn, a Latvian immigrant who made his fortune in uranium mines.

HIGHLIGHTS

The internationally renowned sculpture collection has masterpieces by Henry Moore, Alberto Giacometti, and Constantin Brancusi. Outside, sculptures dot a grass-and-granite garden, which, in addition to the Lichtenstein, boasts Henri Matisse's *Backs I–IV* and Auguste Rodin's *Burghers of Calais.*

Inside, the third level is the place to see masterworks from the museum's permanent collection, such as Alexander Calder's giant mobiles, Joan Miró's whimsical dreamscapes, or Andy Warhol's pop prints.

The second level has exhibits that rotate about three times a year, curated by museum staff and devoted to particular artists or themes.

The lower level houses the most-recent and experimental works, including multimedia and video installations in the Black Box Theater.

INTERNATIONAL SPY MUSEUM

✉ *800 F St. NW, East End*
☎ *202/393–7798* ⊕ *www. spymuseum.org* ✍ *Permanent exhibition only, $18;children $15; Operation Spy only, $14; combination admission $30* ☉ *Apr.–Oct., daily 9–8; Nov.– Mar., daily 10–6; hours subject to change; check Web site before visiting* Ⓜ *Gallery Pl./ Chinatown.*

TIPS

■ Advance tickets (purchased at the museum or on its Web site) are highly recommended. All tickets are date and time specific. Tickets are most likely available (and your visit less crowded) on Tuesday, Wednesday, and Thursday or daily after 2 pm.

■ Allow about two hours for a visit.

■ This is a great museum for kids age 12 and up; younger ones might not get it.

■ At the popular monthly KidSpy workshop for kids ages 10–14, participants can assume a cover identity and disguise, make a portable lie detector, crack a cipher, check out surveillance electronics, and more.

■ The museum regularly hosts films, events, and lectures by espionage experts, and more elaborate programs like a "Spy Scavenger Hunt" and a "Spy City Tour" of Washington.

■ A large gift shop, a café, and the restaurant Zola are here as well.

It's believed that there are more spies in Washington than in any other city in the world, making it a fitting home for this museum, which displays the world's largest collection of spy artifacts. Museum advisers include top cryptologists; masters of disguise; and former CIA, FBI, and KGB operatives. Exhibits range from the coded letters of Revolutionary War überspy Benedict Arnold to the KGB's lipstick pistol, to high-tech 21st-century espionage toys, showcased with theatrical panache in a five-building complex (one, the Warder-Atlas Building, held Washington's Communist party in the 1940s).

HIGHLIGHTS

Operation Spy, a one-hour "immersive experience" works like a live-action game, dropping you in the middle of a high-stakes foreign intelligence mission. Each step of the operation—which includes decrypting secret audio files, a car chase, and interrogating a suspect agent—is taken from actual intelligence operations.

The Secret History of History exhibit takes you through the espionage behind the headlines, from Moses's use of spies in Canaan to Abraham Lincoln's employment of the Pinkerton National Detective Agency as a full-scale secret service in the Civil War, to the birth of Lenin's state-run espionage ring—later known as the KGB.

There's a heavy mix of flash and fun, with toys used by actual operatives as well as James Bond's Aston Martin and tales of celebrity spies like singer Josephine Baker, chef Julia Child, and actress Marlene Dietrich.

The story of Cold War espionage is displayed in a maze of mirrors, a flashy but apt visual metaphor for the deadly game of spying and counter-spying that gripped the United States and Soviet Union.

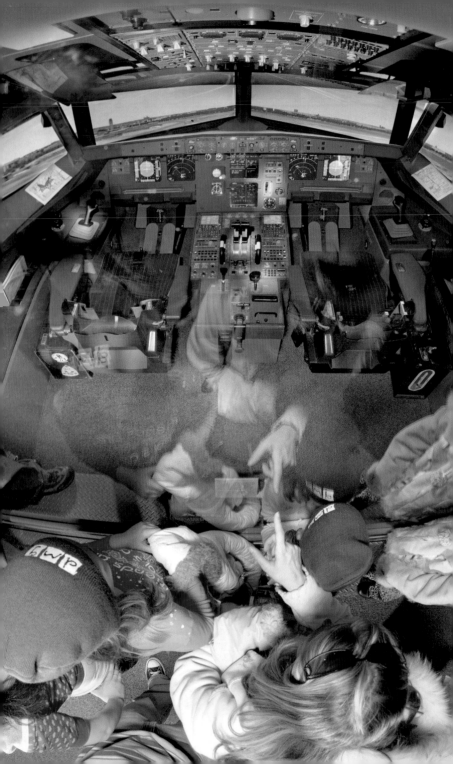

NATIONAL AIR AND SPACE MUSEUM

The country's second most-visited museum, attracting 9 million people annually to its vast and diverse collection of historic aircraft and spacecraft, is the perfect place to amaze the kids with giant rocket ships, relive the glory days of fighter jets, and even learn to fly. Its 23 galleries tell the story of humanity's quest for flight—from the Wright brothers' experiments with gliders to space exploration.

(above) Neil Armstrong and Buzz Aldrin's spacesuits.
(left) You can see into the cockpit of the Airbus A320.

PLANNING YOUR TIME

If you only have an hour take the free one-hour docent-led tour of the museum's highlights, which leaves daily at 10:30 and 1 from the Welcome Center.

To get the most from the museum, plan your must-sees in advance and allow plenty of time—at least two hours—to take everything in. The museum has three basic types of exhibits: aircraft and spacecraft; galleries of history and information; and experiences, such as IMAX films and hands-on workshops. An ideal visit would include a mix of these.

Before your visit, buy timed tickets online up to two weeks in advance for the popular IMAX films and planetarium shows to bypass the long lines and sold-out screenings.

When you arrive at the museum, consult the guides at the welcome desk; they can help you fine-tune your plan. If you didn't buy tickets for IMAX online, buy them now.

If you're traveling with kids, arrive early to avoid lines and pick up a kids' guide with games and activities at the welcome desk. Hit the wow-factor exhibits like the **Milestones of Flight** and **Space Race** first but leave time for the hands-on **How Things Fly** gallery, and IMAX and planetarium shows. Strollers are allowed through the security checkpoint; there is a family bathroom on the first floor near the food court and a baby changing station near the **Early Flight** gallery.

If you just can't get enough, the **Steven F. Udvar-Hazy Center,** a companion museum near Dulles International Airport, features a massive hangar filled with hundreds more aircraft, spacecraft, and aviation artifacts.

✉ Independence Ave. and 6th St. SW, The Mall ☎ 202/633–1000, 202/633-4629 movie information, 202/633-5285 TDD 🌐 www.nasm.si.edu 💲 Free, IMAX or Planetarium $8.75, IMAX feature film $12.50, flight simulators $7-$8 🕐 Daily 10–5:30

Albatros D.va

MUSEUM HIGHLIGHTS

AIRCRAFT AND SPACECRAFT

First stop: the **Milestones of Flight** gallery at the entrance contains museum superstars like the **Spirit of St. Louis**, in which Charles Lindbergh made the first solo transatlantic flight; **Sputnik**, the first satellite in space; and the giant **U.S. Pershing II** and **Soviet SS-20** nuclear missiles.

Sputnik replica

Next, make like Buzz Lightyear and head to infinity and beyond with a walk through the **Skylab Orbital Workshop**, the largest component of America's first space station in the **Space Race** gallery. Also on display are an arsenal of rockets and missiles, from the giant **V-2 rocket** to the devastatingly accurate **Tomahawk Cruise missile**. The **Apollo Lunar Module** is also a must-see in **Exploring the Moon**.

HISTORY AND SCIENCE

Even those who don't like history flock to the fascinating **Wright Brothers** gallery to see the first machine to achieve piloted flight, the **Wright 1903 Flyer**.

For history buffs, the **Great War in the Air**, **World War II**, and **Sea-Air Operations** galleries are essential, with legendary fighter planes such as the **Supermarine Spitfire**.

In the history of space exploration, **Apollo to the Moon** is packed with artifacts from moon missions, including **Buzz Aldrin's spacesuit**.

Is there life on Mars? Find out in the science-oriented **Explore the Universe, Looking at Earth**, and **Exploring the Planets** galleries.

IMAX AND PLANETARIUM SHOWS

Lift off with an **IMAX** film. You'll feel like you've left the ground with the swooping aerial scenes in **To Fly!** and **Fighter Pilot**. Or take a trip into deep space with **3D Sun**. In the **Albert Einstein Planetarium**, you can watch the classic tour of the nighttime sky as well as shows like **Cosmic Collisions** and **Black Holes**.

HANDS-ON

Learn to fly in the interactive **How Things Fly** exhibit geared towards kids and families. Test your top gun skills at one of the popular **Flight Simulators** where you'll get full-on fighter plane experience—barrel rolls and all.

TOURING TIPS

Avoid the Crowds: Between April and September (and on holiday weekends) the museum is slammed with visitors; it is least crowded September to March. It's always a good idea to come before noon to beat the rush.

Where to Eat: A huge food court offers McDonald's, pizza, and sandwiches, and is the most simple and practical eating option around.

Souvenirs: The three-story museum store is the largest in all the Smithsonian museums, and one of the best. Along with souvenirs, books, and collectors' items, it also displays a model of the *USS Enterprise*, used in the filming of the first *Star Trek* television series. If you have kids, don't start your tour here or you may never leave!

Flight Simulators: Tickets can be purchased at the IMAX box office or in the **Flight Simulators** gallery.

Soviet SS-20 nuclear missile.

Apollo capsule   Breitling Orbiter   Apollo 11 module   Lockheed Vega

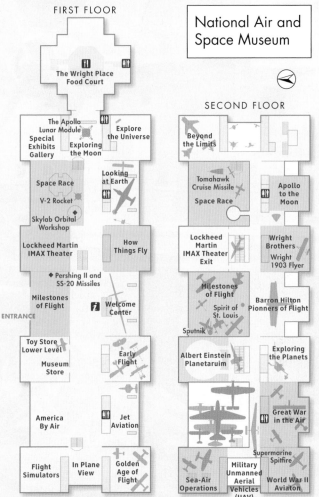

FIRST FLOOR

National Air and Space Museum

The Wright Place Food Court

The Apollo Lunar Module

Special Exhibits Gallery

Explore the Universe

Exploring the Moon

Space Race

V-2 Rocket

Skylab Orbital Workshop

Looking at Earth

Lockheed Martin IMAX Theater

How Things Fly

◆ Pershing II and SS-20 Missiles

Milestones of Flight

Welcome Center

ENTRANCE

Toy Store Lower Level

Museum Store

Early Flight

America By Air

Jet Aviation

Flight Simulators

In Plane View

Golden Age of Flight

SECOND FLOOR

Beyond the Limits

Tomahawk Cruise Missile

Space Race

Apollo to the Moon

Lockheed Martin IMAX Theater Exit

Wright Brothers

Wright 1903 Flyer

Milestones of Flight

Spirit of St. Louis

Barron Hilton Pionners of Flight

Sputnik

Albert Einstein Planetaruim

Exploring the Planets

Great War in the Air

Supermarine Spitfire

Sea-Air Operations

Military Unmanned Aerial Vehicles (UAV)

World War II Aviation

KEY

⊥ *Hanging Artifacts*

🍴 *Food court*

🚻 *Restroom*

ℹ️ *Tourist information*

0   90 feet

0   30 m

Staggerwing

NASM TALKS TO FODOR'S

The original 1903 Wright Flyer.

Boeing F4B-4

Gen. John R. Daily (USMC, Ret.), director of the National Air and Space Museum, talks to Coral Davenport about what interests him at the Air and Space Museum.

BE AMAZED
"I would like visitors to take away a better understanding of the importance of air, aviation, and space in the leadership role of this country and technology. Also, an education in the four forces of flight—gravity, lift, thrust, and drag. **How Things Fly** is a physics lab designed to be understandable for kids, but I've watched so many adults be amazed as they learn the basics of the physics of flight in that gallery."

FLY THROUGH THE AGES
"The history is extremely important—but of them all, the **Wright Brothers** gallery is probably the most important. Also, the **Golden Age of Flight** gallery, about the period when aviation was young, and people were doing crazy things—wing walking, barnstorming. The **World War II** galleries are also a big draw. I think a lot of parents and grandparents most closely relate to those galleries. They bring their families and tell stories about what it was like flying air raids over Germany."

MAKING CONNECTIONS
"This is a personal museum. There are attachments between individuals and artifacts. Sometimes families come in because Dad wants to look at his old airplane. But the designers have put together rich cross-cultural exhibits—showing the historic, but also the cultural and social impacts of aviation. They show what people were wearing, how developments in aviation led to fads and movements. It's hard to tie it all together sometimes but this museum helps people make those connections."

FAVORITE PLANE
"The **Boeing F4B-4** in **Sea-Air Operations** is my favorite plane—my father flew that exact plane the year I was born. It's a pre-World War II airplane. When you compare that to the **X-15** or the **Bell X-1**, you see the tremendous leap that aviation took in the middle of the century, as a result of World War II."

1960s flight attendant uniform

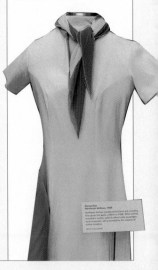

NATIONAL AIR AND SPACE MUSEUM
STEVEN F. UDVAR-HAZY CENTER

For more giant jets and spaceships, you won't want to miss the museum's **Udvar-Hazy Center** at Washington Dulles International Airport in northern Virginia. The center showcases the museum's growing collection of historic air- and spacecraft, which is much too large fit into the building on the Mall.

Unlike the museum on the Mall, the Udvar-Hazy Center focuses on one thing: planes and rockets, hung as though in flight throughout two vast multi-level hangars. This focus makes the center more appealing for families with kids too young to take in detailed historic narratives. It is also much less crowded than the Mall museum.

One giant three-level hangar is devoted to historic aircraft, such as the **Lockheed SR-71 Blackbird,** the fastest jet in the world; the sassy-looking **DeHavilland Chipmunk,** a prototype aerobatic airplane; the sleek, supersonic **Concorde,** and the **Enola Gay,** which in 1945 dropped the first atomic bomb to be used in war on Hiroshima, Japan.

A second space hangar is largely taken up by the space shuttle **Enterprise,** as well as satellites, space stations, and space missile launchers. There is also an 8-story **IMAX** theater.

✉ 14390 Air and Space Museum Parkway, Chantilly, VA ☎ 202/633–1000, 202/633-4629 movie information, 202/633-5285 TDD ⊕ www.nasm.si.edu ✈ Free, IMAX feature film $12.50, Planetarium or IMAX show $8.75, flight simulators $7-$8 ☉ Daily 10–5:30

TOURING TIPS

Getting Here: You'll need a car as there is no nearby Metro or bus stop. The drive takes about 30–40 minutes from D.C. Take I-66 West to Route 28 North (Exit 53B); drive 5 mi and exit at the Air and Space Museum Parkway, follow signs to the museum. Parking is $12.

Airport Shuttle: You can combine a morning visit with an afternoon departure flight from nearby Dulles Airport. There are 15-minute shuttles every hour between the airport and museum for 50¢. A taxi ride costs about $10.

When you arrive: Head to the welcome desk for a customized "Flight Plan" to guide you around the museum. Allow at least an hour to tour and another 45 minutes to see an **IMAX** film.

With Kids: Pick up museum guides with games and activities for kids ages 9 and up at the welcome desk.

Where to Eat: There is a McDonald's and McCafe with slightly healthier fare on the second floor.

(top) Space Shuttle Enterprise; (bottom) DeHavilland Chipmunk.

NATIONAL ARCHIVES

✉ Constitution Ave. between 7th and 9th Sts., The Mall ☎ 202/501–5000, 202/501–5205 tours ⊕ www.nara.gov ⛁ Free ⊙ Mar. 15–Labor Day, daily 10–7, Labor Day–Mar. 14, daily 10–5:30; tours weekdays at 10:15 and 1:15 Ⓜ Archives/Navy Memorial.

TIPS

■ Reservations to visit the archives are highly recommended: without one, you could wait up to an hour to get in. Reservations for guided tours, or for a self-guided visit, must be made at least six weeks in advance.

■ March, April, May, and the weekends around Thanksgiving and Christmas are the busiest.

■ Expect to spend 90 minutes here, viewing the charter documents and touring the permanent exhibit.

■ Before your tour, check out the informative introductory film at the McGowan Theater.

■ The archives are a research resource open to anyone. Family genealogists can find birth, death, military, and census records, immigrant ships' passenger lists, letters, and maps since the beginning of the nation's history. Assistants in the Archives can help you track down ancestors' records or anything else you're looking for.

The National Archives are at once monument, museum, and the nation's memory. Headquartered in a grand marble edifice on Constitution Avenue, the National Archives and Records Administration is charged with preserving and archiving the most historically important U.S. government records. Its 8 billion paper records and 4 billion electronic records date back to 1775.

HIGHLIGHTS

The star attractions, which draw millions of reverential viewers every year, are the Declaration of Independence, Constitution, and Bill of Rights. These are housed in the Archives' cathedral-like rotunda, each on a marble platform, encased in bulletproof glass, and floating in pressurized helium, which protects the irreplaceable documents. To the right of the rotunda, displayed with great majesty, is the 1297 Magna Carta, the document of English common law whose language inspired the Constitution: it's one of four remaining originals.

The permanent exhibit showcases the breadth of the Archives' holdings. You can find anything from the Emancipation Proclamation to the first issue of *Mad* magazine (used as evidence in congressional hearings on juvenile delinquency), or the rifle believed to have assassinated John F. Kennedy.

Watch films of flying saucers, used as evidence in congressional UFO hearings, listen to the Nuremberg trials, or Congress debating Prohibition—selections from the Archives' 500,000 film and audio recordings.

Many exhibits are interactive and kid-friendly. One room of letters from children to U.S. presidents includes a letter from seventh-grader Andy Smith, asking Ronald Regan for federal funds to clean up a disaster area—his room.

NATIONAL GALLERY OF ART, WEST BUILDING

⊠ *4th St. and Constitution Ave. NW, The Mall*
☎ *202/737–4215, 202/842–6176 TDD* ⊕ *www.nga.gov*
🎞 *Free* ⊙ *Mon.–Sat. 10–5, Sun. 11–6* Ⓜ *Archives/Navy Memorial.*

TIPS

■ There are many free docent-led tours every day, and a recorded tour of highlights is available for a $5 rental fee on the main floor adjacent to the rotunda. For a cheat-sheet tour, pick up the laminated "What to See in One Hour" (the same guide is available for the East Building and on the Web); it pinpoints 12 must-see masterworks.

■ The Micro Gallery near the rotunda maintains computerized information on more than 1,700 works of art from the permanent collection. Touch-screen monitors provide access to color images, text, animation, and sounds to help you better understand—and appreciate—the works on display.

■ The gallery has a full calendar of concerts, films, lectures, and other events, many free to the public. Among the most popular is the free "Jazz in the Garden" series, held Friday evenings in the sculpture garden throughout the summer.

■ Check out the outstanding museum store's books on art and art history.

The two buildings of the National Gallery hold one of the world's foremost collections of paintings, sculptures, and graphics, from the 13th to the 21st century. If you want to view the museum's holdings in (more or less) chronological order, it's best to start your exploration in the West Building. Opened in 1941, the domed West Building was a gift to the nation from industrialist and Treasury Secretary Andrew Mellon. The rotunda, with 24 marble columns surrounding a fountain topped with a statue of Mercury, sets the stage for the masterpieces on display in more than 100 galleries.

HIGHLIGHTS

The only painting by Leonardo da Vinci on display in the western hemisphere, *Ginevra de' Benci* is the centerpiece of the collection's comprehensive survey of Italian Renaissance paintings and sculpture; it also includes Raphael's *Alba Madonna* and Sandro Botticelli's *Adoration of the Magi.*

The masters of painting light, Rembrandt van Rijn and Johannes Vermeer, anchor the magnificent collection of Dutch and Flemish works.

The gallery of gorgeous French Impressionist masterworks by such superstars as Claude Monet, Auguste Renoir, and Edgar Degas, is unmissable.

Walk beneath flowering trees in the sculpture garden, on the Mall between 7th and 9th streets. Granite walkways take you through a shaded landscape and sculptures from the museum's permanent collection, including Roy Lichtenstein's playful *House I*; Miró's *Personnage Gothique, Oiseau-Eclair*; and Isamu Noguchi's *Great Rock of Inner Seeking.* The huge central fountain becomes a skating rink in winter.

NATIONAL GALLERY OF ART, EAST BUILDING

⊠ *Constitution Ave. between 3rd and 4th Sts. NW, The Mall* ☎ *202/737–4215, 202/842–6176 TDD* ⊕ *www.nga.gov* 🎟 *Free* ⊗ *Mon.–Sat. 10–5, Sun. 11–6* Ⓜ *Archives/Navy Memorial.*

TIPS

■ To reach the East Building from the West Building, you can take the underground concourse, lined with gift shops, a café, and a cafeteria, but to best appreciate the building's sleek and celebrated architecture, enter from outside rather than underground: exit the West Building through its eastern doors and cross 4th Street.

■ To protect the pigments and paper of the Matisse cutouts, the works are on view only between 10 and 2 Monday through Saturday and 11 to 3 on Sunday.

■ Free docent-led tours leave from the information desk weekdays at 11:30 and 1:30, and weekends at 11:30 and 3:30.

■ Pick up the cheat-sheet "What to See in An Hour": it pinpoints 15 highlights of the East Building.

The East Building opened in 1978 in response to the changing needs of the National Gallery, especially its growing collection of modern art. The trapezoidal shape of the site prompted architect I.M. Pei's dramatic approach: two interlocking spaces shaped like triangles provide room for galleries, auditoriums, and administrative offices. Despite its severe angularity, Pei's building is inviting. The ax-blade-like southwest corner has been darkened and polished smooth by thousands of hands irresistibly drawn to it. Inside, the sunlit atrium is dominated by a colorful 76-foot-long Alexander Calder mobile, the perfect introduction to galleries filled with masterworks of modern and contemporary art.

HIGHLIGHTS

Masterpieces from every famous name in 20th-century art—Pablo Picasso, Jackson Pollock, Piet Mondrian, Roy Lichtenstein, Joan Miró, Georgia O'Keeffe, and dozens of others—fill the galleries.

The bold shapes and brilliant teals and fuschias of Henri Matisse's giant paper cutouts make them among the most innovative, important, and purely enjoyable works of modern art. The National Gallery's collection of these is considered the world's greatest; entering the **Matisse Room** full of colorful floor-to-ceiling works is a delight.

Huge, color-drenched Mark Rothko works are a perennial favorite—the gallery owns more than 1,000 paintings by the iconic American modernist.

World-class temporary exhibitions are a big draw. Recent years have seen the collected works of Paul Cézanne, Edward Hopper, Cy Twombly, Jasper Johns, Pablo Picasso, Willem de Kooning, and Henri de Toulouse-Lautrec.

NATIONAL MUSEUM OF AMERICAN HISTORY

✉ *Constitution Ave. and 14th St. NW, The Mall* ☎ *202/633–1000, 202/633–5285 TDD* ⊕ *www.americanhistory.si.edu* 🎟 *Free* ⊙ *Daily 10–5:30* Ⓜ *Smithsonian or Federal Triangle.*

3

TIPS

■ Head to the information desk to pick up a guide to the highlights and find out if there is a free performance scheduled.

■ Expect waits of up to 20 minutes for the **Star Spangled Banner, First Ladies' Dresses,** and **Thanks for the Memories Galleries**. To see pop culture memorabilia without the wait, check out the displays in the lower-level entrance, such as C-3PO's costume from Return of the Jedi and Carrie Bradshaw's laptop from Sex and the City.

■ This is the only museum in the world with an active program of using its historical musical instruments for live performances; the Smithsonian Chamber Music Society holds regular concerts.

■ The Stars and Stripes Café on the lower level serves sandwiches, salads, pizza, and burgers. The Constitution Café on the first floor serves coffee, ice cream, and snacks.

■ The main museum store is on the first floor; a smaller best-of store is on the second.

The 3 million artifacts in the country's largest history museum explore America's cultural, political, and scientific past, with holdings as diverse and iconic as Abraham Lincoln's top hat, Thomas Edison's lightbulbs, and Judy Garland's ruby slippers from *The Wizard of Oz*. The museum's nickname, "America's attic," is apt: its 20 exhibition galleries are crammed with unexpected items and stories from every nook and cranny of American history.

HIGHLIGHTS

The new **Star-Spangled Banner** gallery is the highlight of a two-year $85 million renovation of the museum, completed in late 2008. Its centerpiece is the actual 30- x 34-foot banner that in 1814 survived 25 hours of British rocket attacks on Fort McHenry, inspiring Francis Scott Key to write the song that became the national anthem.

For political and military history, visit the **American Presidency, Abraham Lincoln, Gunboat Philadelphia,** and **Price of Freedom: Americans at War** galleries.

The **Science in American Life** gallery explores American scientific research from the invention of the lightbulb to the development of the atomic bomb. There are two hands-on workshops: in **Invention at Play,** kids can design a custom pinwheel, create a laser-generated picture of their voice, and learn about American inventors. In the **Spark Lab,** lively scientists lead daily lab explorations of a variety of subjects, such as chemical explosions and looking at DNA under microscopes.

For entertainment and sports history, line up for the **Thanks for the Memories** gallery, starring the famous ruby slippers, as well as the original Kermit the Frog and Muhammed Ali's boxing gloves.

NATIONAL MUSEUM OF THE AMERICAN INDIAN

✉ *4th St. and Independence Ave. SW, The Mall* ☎ *202/633–1000* ⊕ *www.americanindian.si.edu* 🎟 *Free* ☉ *Daily 10–5:30* Ⓜ *L'Enfant Plaza.*

TIPS

■ Visit between 10 and 2 on a sunny day to see the central atrium awash in rainbows created by the light refracted through prisms in the ceiling aligned with Earth's cardinal points.

■ The Mitsitam Native Foods Café serves a Native American–inspired menu, ranging from pulled-buffalo sandwiches and black beans to maple-roasted turkey.

■ Free timed-entrance passes are distributed beginning at 10 am from the museum's east entrance, but by midday, especially during the winter months you may find that you don't actually need one. You can also buy the passes in advance online.

■ Free tours leave from the entrance Atrium weekdays at 1:30 and 3. On weekends and in summer there are also tours at 11, except on Monday.

■ The Chesapeake Museum Store is the place to buy handcrafted jewelry, textiles, and one-of-a-kind works by Native American artisans.

The Smithsonian's newest museum stands apart visually and conceptually from the other cultural institutions on the Mall. Opened in 2004, it is the first national museum devoted to Native American artifacts, presented from a Native American perspective. The undulating exterior, clad in pinkish-gold limestone from Minnesota, evokes natural rock formations shaped by wind and water. Inside, four floors of galleries cover 10,000 years of history of the thousands of Native tribes of the western hemisphere. However, only 5% of the museum's holdings are on display at any one time, and they are arranged to showcase specific tribes and themes, rather than a chronological history. Some visitors find this approach confusing, but touring with one of the Native guides can help bring the history and legends to life.

HIGHLIGHTS

Live music, dance, theater, and storytelling are central to experiencing this museum. Tribal groups stage performances in the two theaters and sunlit ceremonial atrium.

The **Our Universe** exhibit tells the unique creation legends of eight different tribes, with carvings, costumes, and videos of tribal storytellers. The stories rotate to give exposure to the different tribes of the Americas.

Central to the Native story is the transformation that convulsed the tribes of America in 1492, the year of first contact with Europeans. The exhibits focusing on the Native world before and after "first contact" are among the most compelling.

The museum's signature film, *A Thousand Roads*, about four contemporary Native people is shown daily.

NATIONAL MUSEUM OF NATURAL HISTORY

✉ *Constitution Ave. and 10th St. NW, The Mall* ☎ *202/633–1000, 202/357–1729 TDD* ⊕ *www. mnh.si.edu* 🎫 *Free, IMAX $8.50, Butterfly Pavilion $6, but free Tuesday* ⊘ *Museum daily 10–5:30; Discovery Room Tues.–Fri. noon–2:30, weekends 10:30–3:30; free passes for Discovery Room near Discovery Room door* Ⓜ *Smithsonian or Federal Triangle.*

3

TIPS

■ The IMAX theater shows two- and three-dimensional natural history films throughout the day. Buy advance tickets at the box office when you arrive, then tour the museum.

■ The **Butterfly Pavilion** makes a great photo op. Timed tickets sell out fast—buy them in advance online or when you arrive. The Pavilion is free on Tuesday, but still requires a timed ticket.

■ The **Discovery Room** has hands-on research activities and workshops for kids.

■ Visit Friday evenings from 6:30 to 10 for the "Smithsonian Jazz Café": entertainment, food and wine, shopping, and special IMAX films.

■ Watch paleontologists at work in the glassed-in fossil labs throughout **Dinosaur Hall** and the **Life in the Ancient Seas** gallery.

This is one of the world's great natural history museums. The giant dinosaur fossils, glittering gems, creepy-crawly insects, and other natural delights—more than 126 million specimens in all—attract more than 7 million visitors annually.

HIGHLIGHTS

Get between *Tyrannosaurus rex* and his dinner, a feisty *Triceratops*. The two giant fossils are poised for action, as are the other occupants of the popular **Dinosaur Hall**, which range from a 72-foot-long *Diplodocus longus* to a tiny *Thescelosaurus neglectus* (a small dinosaur so named because its disconnected bones sat for years in a college drawer before being reassembled).

Watch out for the cheetah above you on the tree branch in **Mammal Hall**, which explains mammals' evolution, diversity, and role in the food chain with 238 taxidermy mounts.

See a perfectly preserved giant squid and the vivid ecosystem of a living coral reef in **Ocean Hall**, the museum's newest and largest exhibit. The Ocean Explorer theater simulates a dive into the depths of the sea.

Drool over the jewels in the **Janet Annenberg Hooker Hall of Geology, Gems, and Minerals**: Marie Antoinette's earrings; the Rosser Reeves ruby; and the Hope Diamond, a rare 45.52-carat blue gem donated by Harry Winston in 1958.

Walk among hundreds of brilliantly colored butterflies in the **Butterfly Pavilion**, which requires a separate admission. For a different kind of entomological experience, check out giant millipedes and furry tarantulas in the **O. Orkin Insect Zoo**, named for the pest-control magnate who donated money to modernize the exhibits. Tarantula feedings are Tuesday through Friday at 10:30, 11:30, and 1:30.

NATIONAL PORTRAIT GALLERY

✉ *8th and F Sts. NW, East End*
☎ *202/633–8300, 202/357–1729 TDD* ⊕ *www.npg.si.edu*
🎫 *Free* ⊙ *Daily 11:30–7*
Ⓜ *Gallery Pl./Chinatown.*

TIPS

■ The Portrait Gallery and American Art Museum are two different entities within the same building—the art complements the portraits, setting up a rich dialogue between the two.

■ The elegant covered courtyard has a café, free Wi-Fi, and is frequently the site of performances and special events.

■ At the "Portrait Connection" computer kiosks, you can search a database of the gallery's collections. Look up the portrait's subject, and the database can tell you where in the gallery it is and show you an image, even if it's not currently on exhibit.

■ There are free docent-led tours most weekdays at 11:45, 1, and 2:15, and most Saturdays and Sundays at 11:45, 1:30, and 3:15. Check the Web site to confirm times.

■ At the Lunder Conservation Center on the third and fourth floors, you can watch conservators preserving and restoring works.

Devoted to the intersection of art, biography, and history, this collection houses nearly 20,000 images of men and women who have shaped U.S. history. There are prints, paintings, photos, and multimedia sculptures of subjects from George Washington to Madonna. This museum shares the landmark Old Patent Office Building with the Smithsonian American Art Museum.

HIGHLIGHTS

The building itself: Built between 1836 and 1863, this gracious marble edifice is considered one of the country's finest examples of Greek Revival architecture.

The gallery has the only complete collection of presidential portraits outside the White House, starting with Gilbert Stuart's iconic "Lansdowne" portrait of George Washington. Interesting perspectives include the plaster cast of Abraham Lincoln's head and hands; political cartoonist Pat Oliphant's sculpture of George H.W. Bush bowling; and Shepard Fairey's red, white, and blue *Obama Hope* portrait of President Barack Obama.

The **American Origins** exhibit chronicles the first contact between Europeans and Native Americans, the Founding Fathers, and historic figures through the Industrial Age. Subjects include Benjamin Franklin (the painting, by Joseph Duplessis, is the basis for Franklin's likeness on the $100 bill); Native American diplomat Pocahontas; Thomas Edison in his workshop; and a full-length likeness of bushy-browed, cigarillo-smoking humorist Samuel Clemens, aka Mark Twain.

From a moving bronze sculpture of Martin Luther King Jr. to Andy Warhol's Marilyn Monroe prints, to Madonna's 1985 *Time* magazine cover, the third-floor gallery of **Twentieth-Century Americans** offers a vibrant and colorful tour of the people who shaped the country and culture of today.

NEWSEUM

✉ *555 Pennsylvania Ave. NW, East End* ☎ *888/639–7386* 🌐 *www.newseum.org* 💲 *$20* 🕐 *Daily 9–5* Ⓜ *Archives/Navy Memorial.*

TIPS

■ ABC's *This Week with George Stephanopoulos* is filmed live here every Sunday morning; museum visitors are welcome to watch.

■ Celebrity chef Wolfgang Puck designed the menu for the food court, as well as for the well-reviewed restaurant The Source, adjoining the museum.

■ The best way to tour the museum is by viewing the orientation films on the ground floor, then taking the elevator up to the top floor and working your way down.

■ Tickets for the Newseum are date specific and subject to availability; purchasing them in advance on the Web site is recommended.

■ The top-floor terrace offers one of the best public views of the Capitol and looks directly down onto Pennsylvania Avenue.

■ The museum is best for children over 12.

The Newseum opened to great fanfare in 2008, in a landmark $450 million glass-and-silver structure on Pennsylvania Avenue, set smack between the White House and the Capitol: a fitting location for a museum devoted to the First Amendment and the role of a free press in democracy. The museum has a serious purpose, but the space and exhibits are high-tech, multimedia, and sometimes shamelessly fun. Visitors enter into a 90-foot-high media-saturated atrium, overlooked by a giant breaking news screen and a news helicopter suspended overhead. From there, 14 galleries display 500 years of the history of news, including exhibits on the First Amendment; global news; the rise of multimedia; and the way radio, television, and the Internet transformed how we find out about the world. For some, though, the exhibits have a bitterly elegiac feel, documenting a profession that seems to teeter on the brink of collapse with thousands of layoffs and closures of newspapers and magazines in 2009.

HIGHLIGHTS

Live news programs are regularly filmed in the museum's central live news studio, and audiences are often welcome to watch.

The largest piece of the Berlin wall outside Germany, including a guard tower, is permanently installed in an exhibit explaining how a free press was a key contributor to the fall of the wall.

Five state-of-the art theaters, including an eye-popping "4-D" theater and another with a 90-foot-long screen, show features, news, sports, and documentaries throughout the day.

In the interactive games gallery you can create your own newscast or be a photographer in an action news event.

PHILLIPS COLLECTION

✉ *1600 21st St. NW, Dupont Circle* ☎ *202/387–2151* ⊕ *www.phillipscollection.org* 💳 *Free for permanent collection weekdays; admission varies weekends and for special exhibitions* ⊙ *Tues., Wed., Fri., and Sat. 10–5; Thurs. 10–8:30; Sun. 11–6* Ⓜ *Dupont Circle.*

TIPS

■ The Phillips employs students of art history, many of whom are artists themselves, to sit by the paintings and answer questions.

■ On the first Thursday of the month, the museum stays open late for live jazz, gallery talks, and a cash bar.

■ The museum holds a Sunday-afternoon concert in its oak-paneled music room nearly every week. Seats are unreserved and included with museum admission, but showing up early is recommended.

■ Take a break in the café, overlooking the museum courtyard.

■ There are tours of the museum and permanent collection on Saturday at 11; special-exhibitions tours are on Friday at 11. Tours are unreserved and included in the price of admission.

The first museum of modern art in the country, the masterpiece-filled Phillips Collection is unique in origin and content. It opened in 1921 in the Georgian Revival mansion of collector Duncan Phillips, who wanted to showcase his art in a museum that would stand as a memorial to his father and brother. Having no interest in a painting's market value or its faddishness, Phillips searched for pieces that impressed him as outstanding products of a particular artist's unique vision. At the heart of the collections are impressionist and modern masterpieces by Pierre-Auguste Renoir, Vincent van Gogh, Paul Cézanne, Edgar Degas, Pablo Picasso, Paul Klee, and Henri Matisse. These are grouped by theme and artist throughout the Phillips mansion, making for a museum-going experience that is as intimate as it is inspiring.

HIGHLIGHTS

The collection's most famous piece is Renoir's magnificent work of impressionism, *Luncheon of the Boating Party*. Other celebrity works include Degas's *Dancers at the Barre*, Vincent van Gogh's *Entrance to the Public Garden at Arles*, and *A Bowl of Plums* by 18th-century artist Jean-Baptiste Siméon Chardin, whom Phillips called "the first modern painter."

The glowing, chapel-like **Rothko Room** emerged from a bond between Phillips and modern master Mark Rothko. Rothko said he preferred to exhibit his paintings in smaller, more intimately scaled rooms, and Phillips designed the gallery specifically to the artist's preferences.

Cézanne's intense, piercing self-portrait was the painting Phillips said he would save first if the gallery caught fire.

PRESIDENT LINCOLN'S COTTAGE

✉ *Armed Forces Retirement Home at Rock Creek Church Rd. and Upshur St. NW., Upper Northwest* ☎ *202/829-0436* ⊕ *www.lincolncottage.org* 🎟 *$12* ⊙ *Mon.–Sat. 9:30–4:30, Sun. 11:30–5:30* Ⓜ *Georgia Ave./Petworth.*

3

TIPS

■ There are 20 spots available per tour and only scheduled tours are given; advance reservations are available on the Web site and are highly recommended. Monday–Saturday, tours every hour 10–3, Sunday, every hour noon–4.

■ Although the museum is reachable by Metro and bus, it's much easier to drive or take a cab. There is on-site parking. If arriving by Metro, take the H8 bus from the station; it will drop you at the Eagle Gate entrance.

■ There is a café in the visitor center, and a diner, the Hitching Post, across the street from the main entrance gate.

■ Visitors may also picnic on the cottage grounds, which have been landscaped to look as they did when Lincoln lived there.

In June 1862 President Lincoln moved from the White House to this Gothic Revival cottage on the grounds of the Soldiers' Home to escape the oppressive heat of wartime Washington and to grieve for the loss of his son Willie. Lincoln and his wife lived in the cottage from June to November of 1862, 1863, and 1864—a quarter of his presidency—and it was here that he became consumed with the idea of emancipation and wrote the Emancipation Proclamation. Considered the most significant historic site of Lincoln's presidency outside the White House, Lincoln's Cottage opened for public tours in 2008. The tours attempt to re-create a visit to the cottage similar to what Lincoln's many visitors in the 1860s experienced, and to take visitors inside Lincoln's mind as he anguished over the Civil War and emancipation.

HIGHLIGHTS

Audio recordings read from Lincoln's writings, and from visitors' accounts of meeting with the president at his cottage. You can hear Lincoln's own anguished words over how to end slavery in the room in which he wrote the Emancipation Proclamation. In the sitting room, you can hear General William Sherman's description of a meeting with the president, read from a letter to his wife.

Browse through period editions of the books that most influenced Lincoln, including the works of Shakespeare and Alexander Pope, in the accurate re-creation of his library.

Tours start and end at the visitor center, which has exhibitions and multimedia displays on Lincoln and the Civil War.

SMITHSONIAN AMERICAN ART MUSEUM

✉ *8th and G Sts. NW, East End* ☎ *202/633–7970, 202/633–5285 TDD* ⊕ *www.americanart.si.edu* ⊇ *Free* ⊙ *Daily 11:30–7:30* Ⓜ *Gallery Pl./Chinatown.*

TIPS

■ At any given time, more than 3,000 of the museum's holdings are in storage, but you can view them all at Luce Foundation Center's glassed-in archives on the third and fourth floors. At computer kiosks set among the archives, you can look up any work and find out exactly where it is in the exhibits or archives.

■ The third-floor Upper West Side café offers a good rest stop, with drinks, snacks, and a view into the Luce Foundation Center's glassed-in archives.

■ There are free docent-led tours every day at noon and 2.

■ The museum regularly holds lectures, films, and evenings of live jazz among the exhibits. Check the Web site for what's on during your visit.

Home to the United States' first federal art collection, the Smithsonian American Art Museum is considered the world's biggest and most diverse collection of American art. Its more than 41,000 works span three centuries, from colonial portraits to 21st-century abstractionists. Among the thousands of American artists represented are John Singleton Copley, Winslow Homer, Mary Cassatt, Georgia O'Keeffe, Edward Hopper, David Hockney, and Robert Rauschenberg. This museum is in the Old Patent Office Building along with the National Portrait Gallery.

HIGHLIGHTS

The American folk-art exhibit is fabulous, from the ceramic Elvis Presley–shape jug and the enormous intricately crafted tinfoil altarpiece, to the Coke-bottle quilt sewn by a grandmother from Yakoo County, Mississippi.

American art came into its own by the late 19th and early 20th century. The museum's collections of works from this period are among the world's biggest and best, from the light-filled neo-impressionist canvasses of Mary Cassatt and Childe Hassam to the sophisticated Gilded Age portraits of turn-of-the-20th-century high society by Winslow Homer, John Singer Sargent, and James McNeill Whistler.

An explosion of American innovation shifted the center of the 20th-century art world from Paris to New York. The museum's top floor celebrates these achievements: a hallway lined with Andy Warhol's prints, Jackson Pollock's splatter canvases, and Robert Indiana's seminal *The Figure Five* leads to rooms of quintessentially American installations, like Alexander Calder mobiles, and Nam June Paik's billboard-size neon-and-television-screen U.S. map.

UNITED STATES HOLOCAUST MEMORIAL MUSEUM

✉ *100 Raoul Wallenberg Pl. SW, enter from Raoul Wallenberg Pl. or 14th St. SW, The Mall* ☎ *202/488–0400, 800/400–9373 for tickets* ⊕ *www.ushmm.org* 🎟 *Free* ⊙ *Daily 10–5:30* Ⓜ *Smithsonian.*

TIPS

■ Like the history it covers, the museum can be profoundly disturbing; it's not recommended for children under 11, although **Daniel's Story**, in a ground-floor exhibit not requiring tickets, is designed for children ages eight and up.

■ Plan to spend two to three hours here.

■ In addition to the permanent exhibition, the museum also has a multimedia learning center, a resource center for students and teachers, a registry of Holocaust survivors, and occasional special exhibitions.

■ Timed-entry passes (distributed on a first-come, first-served basis at the 14th Street entrance starting at 10 or available in advance through the museum's Web site) are necessary for the permanent exhibition Mar.–Aug. Allow extra time to enter the building in spring and summer, when long lines can form.

Museums usually celebrate the best that humanity can achieve, but this museum instead documents the worst. A permanent exhibition tells the stories of the millions of Jews, Gypsies, Jehovah's Witnesses, homosexuals, political prisoners, the mentally ill, and others killed by the Nazis between 1933 and 1945. The exhibitions are detailed and graphic; the experiences memorable and powerful.

HIGHLIGHTS

Striving to provide a you-are-there experience, the presentation is as extraordinary as the subject matter: upon arrival, you are issued an "identity card" containing biographical information on a real person from the Holocaust. As you move through the museum, you read sequential updates on your card.

Hitler's rise to power and the spread of European anti-Semitism are thoroughly documented in the museum's early exhibits, with films of Nazi rallies, posters, newspaper articles, and recordings of Hitler's speeches immersing you in the world that led to the Holocaust.

You are confronted with the gruesome, appalling truths of the Holocaust in the deeply disturbing exhibit **The Final Solution**, which details the Nazis' execution of 6 million Jews. Exhibits include film footage of scientific experiments done on Jews, artifacts such as a freight car like those used to transport Jews from Warsaw to the Treblinka death camp, and crematoria implements. There are films and audio recordings of Holocaust survivors telling their harrowing stories.

After this powerful experience, the adjacent Hall of Remembrance, filled with candles and hand-painted tiles dedicated to children who died in the Holocaust, provides a much-needed space for quiet reflection.

3

OTHER MUSEUMS

Anacostia Community Museum. The Smithsonian's only neighborhood museum is located in Anacostia, a historically black neighborhood in southeast Washington, far off the tourist track. The museum is devoted to the rich experience of contemporary African-American culture in the nation and the capital, which has long had a majority black population. Exhibits focus on urban African-American community issues, with historic displays, fine art, crafts, and photography. The museum's facade uses traditional African design elements: brickwork patterns evoke West African kente cloth, and the concrete cylinders reference the stone towers of Zimbabwe and are ornamented with diamond patterns like those found on the adobe houses of Mali. ⊠ *1901 Fort Pl. SE, Anacostia* ☎ *202/633–4820* ⊕ *anacostia.si.edu* 🎫 *Free* ☉ *Daily 10–5* Ⓜ *Anacostia, then W2/W3 bus.*

Anderson House. A palatial home that's a mystery even to many longtime Washingtonians, Anderson House isn't an embassy, though it does have a link to that world. Larz Anderson was a diplomat from 1891 to 1913 whose career included postings to Japan and Belgium. Anderson and his heiress wife Isabel toured the world, picking up objects that struck their fancy. They filled their residence, which was constructed for them in 1905, with the booty of their travels. Visitors to Anderson House will receive a guided tour of the first and second floors, gorgeously furnished with the Andersons' eclectic collection of furniture, tapestries, paintings, sculpture, historic artifacts, and Asian art, and learn about entertaining in Gilded Age Washington. Among the highlights of the house are several floor-to-ceiling murals that reveal the splendor of the era as well as the Andersons' patriotism and pastimes. ⊠ *2118 Massachusetts Ave. NW, Dupont Circle* ☎ *202/785–2040* ⊕ *www.societyofthecincinnati. org* 🎫 *Free* ☉ *Tues.–Sat. 1–4* Ⓜ *Dupont Circle.*

Art Museum of the Americas. Changing exhibits highlight 20th-century Latin American artists in this small gallery, part of the Organization of American States. There are also documentaries on South and Central American art. A public garden connects the Art Museum and the OAS building. ⊠ *201 18th St. NW, White House area* ☎ *202/458–6016* ⊕ *www.museum.oas.org* 🎫 *Free* ☉ *Tues.–Sun. 10–5* Ⓜ *Farragut W.*

Christian Heurich House Museum. This opulent Romanesque Revival mansion, once known as the Brewmaster's Castle, was the home of Christian Heurich, a German orphan who made his fortune in the beer business. Heurich's brewery was in Foggy Bottom, where the Kennedy Center stands today. Most of the furnishings in the house were owned and used by the Heurichs. The Victorian interior is an eclectic gathering of plaster detailing, carved wooden doors, and painted ceilings. The downstairs breakfast room, in which Heurich, his wife, and their three children ate most of their meals, is decorated like a rathskeller and adorned with German sayings such as "A good drink makes old people young."

Heurich must have taken proverbs seriously. He drank beer daily, had three wives (in succession), and lived to be 102. (In 1986 Heurich's grandson Gary started brewing the family beer again, now renamed Foggy Bottom Lager. Though the beer is currently from Utica, New

York, Gary vows to someday build another brewery near Washington.) The current owners, descendants of Christian Heurich, offer guided tours and rent the house for special events. ⊠ *1307 New Hampshire Ave. NW, Dupont Circle* ☎ *202/429–1894* ⊕ *www. heurichhouse.org* ⊠ *$5* ⊙ *Tours Thurs. and Fri. at 11:30 and 1, Sat. at 11:30, 1, and 2:30* Ⓜ *Dupont Circle.*

Daughters of the American Revolution Museum (DAR). The headquarters of the Daughters of the American Revolution, the Beaux-Arts Memorial Continental Hall was the site of the DAR's annual congress until the larger Constitution Hall was built around the corner. An entrance on D Street leads to the museum. Its 30,000-item collection includes fine examples of colonial and Federal furniture, textiles, quilts, silver, china, porcelain, stoneware, earthenware, and glass. Thirty-one period rooms are decorated in styles representative of various U.S. states, ranging from an 1850 California adobe parlor to a New Hampshire attic filled with 18th- and 19th-century toys. Two galleries—one of them permanent—hold decorative arts. Docent tours are available weekdays 10–2:30 and Saturday 9–5. In the **Touch of Independence** education center for children, families can explore early American life through period games and costumes. During the Colonial Adventure tours, held the first and third Sunday of the month at 1:30 and 3 from September through May, costumed docents use the objects on display to teach children ages five to seven about day-to-day life in colonial America. Reservations are required two weeks in advance. ⊠ *1776 D St. NW, White House area* ☎ *202/879–3241* ⊕ *www.dar.org* ⊠ *Free* ⊙ *Weekdays 9:30–4, Sat. 9–5* Ⓜ *Farragut W.*

Decatur House. Designed by a celebrity architect and located across from the White House, this may have been the nation's hottest piece of real estate when it was built in 1818. The distinguished neoclassical design is the work of Benjamin Henry Latrobe, the country's first professional architect and engineer most famous for his construction of the Capitol and the design of many of that icon's most beautiful interior spaces. Today this is one of the oldest surviving homes in Washington, and one of only three remaining residential buildings designed by Latrobe. ⊠ *748 Jackson Pl. NW, White House area* ☎ *202/842–0920* ⊕ *www. decaturhouse.org* ⊠ *$5* ⊙ *Mon.–Sat. 10–5, Sun. noon–4; tours every hr at quarter past the hr* Ⓜ *Farragut W.*

Drug Enforcement Administration Museum. Just across the street from the Fashion Centre at Pentagon City—a destination in itself for shoppers—is the DEA Museum, within the U.S. Drug Enforcement Administration's headquarters. It explores the effect of drugs on American society, starting with quaint 19th-century ads for opium-laced patent medicines and "cocaine tooth drops" (opiates, cannabis, and cocaine were unregulated then). But documentation of these addictive substances' medical dangers, as well as the corrosive political effect of the opium trade, which China detested, is hard-hitting. A similar contrast is found between the period feel of artifacts from a 1970s head shop and displays on the realities of present-day drug trafficking. ✉ *700 Army Navy Dr., at Hayes St., Arlington, VA* ☎ *202/307–3463* ⊕ *www.deamuseum.org* ✆ *Free* ⊘ *Tues.–Fri. 10–4* Ⓜ *Pentagon City.*

Dumbarton Oaks. In 1944 one of the most important events of the 20th century took place here when representatives of the United States, Great Britain, China, and the Soviet Union met in the music room to lay the groundwork for the United Nations. Career diplomat Robert Woods Bliss and his wife Mildred bought the property in 1920 and tamed the sprawling grounds into acres of splendid gardens and removed later 19th-century additions that had obscured the Federal lines of the 1801 mansion. In 1940 the Blisses gave the estate to Harvard University, which maintains world-renowned collections of Byzantine and pre-Columbian art here. Both collections are small but choice, reflecting the enormous skill and creativity developed at roughly the same time in two very different parts of the world. The Byzantine collection includes beautiful examples of both religious and secular items executed in mosaic, metal, enamel, and ivory. Pre-Columbian works—artifacts and textiles from Mexico and Central and South America by peoples such as the Aztec, Maya, and Olmec—are arranged in an enclosed glass pavilion designed by Philip Johnson. Normally on public view are the lavishly decorated music room and selections from Mrs. Bliss's collection of rare illustrated garden books. ⇨ *For more information on the gardens of Dumbarton Oaks, see Chapter 10, Sports and the Outdoors.* ✉ *1703 32nd St. NW, Georgetown* ☎ *202/339–6401 or 202/339–6400* ⊕ *www.doaks.org* ✆ *Free* ⊘ *Tues.–Sun. 2–5.*

Folger Shakespeare Library. The Folger Library's collection of works by and about Shakespeare and his times is second to none. Unfortunately, the library itself is open only by appointment to academic researchers. But the white-marble art deco building, decorated with sculpted scenes from the Bard's plays, is well worth a look. Inside is a reproduction of a 16th-century inn-yard theater—the site for performances of chamber music, baroque opera, and Shakespearean plays—and a gallery, designed in the manner of an Elizabethan Great Hall, which holds rotating exhibits from the library's collection. A manicured Elizabethan garden on the grounds is open to the public. The building was designed by architect Paul Philippe Cret and dedicated in 1932. Henry Clay Folger, the library's founder, was Standard Oil's president and chairman of the board. ✉ *201 E. Capitol St. SE, Capitol Hill* ☎ *202/544–4600* ⊕ *www. folger.edu* ✆ *Free* ⊘ *Mon.–Sat. 10–5* Ⓜ *Capitol S.*

Ford's Theatre. The events that took place here on the night of April 14, 1865, shocked the nation. During a performance of *Our American Cousin,* John Wilkes Booth entered the state box and shot Abraham Lincoln in the back of the head. The stricken president was carried across the street to the house of tailor William Petersen. Charles Augustus Leale, a 23-year-old surgeon, was the first man to attend the president. To let Lincoln know that someone was nearby, Leale held his hand throughout the night. Lincoln died the next morning. In 2009, the 200th anniversary of Lincoln's birth, the Ford's Theatre Society began unveiling a multi-year, multimillion-dollar effort to transform the theater and Petersen's house into the anchors of an ambitious block-long, Lincoln-centered cultural campus commemorating the president. The theater, which stages performances throughout the year, is restored to look as it did when

CAPITAL FACTS

The federal government bought Ford's Theatre in 1866 for $100,000 and converted it into office space. It was remodeled as a Lincoln museum in 1932 and was restored to its 1865 appearance in 1968.

3

Lincoln attended, including the presidential box draped with flags as it was on the night he was shot. The portrait of George Washington on the box is the same one Lincoln sat over; its frame has a nick made by Wilkes's spur as he leapt from the box to the stage. A 5,000-square-foot exhibition area for Lincoln artifacts is planned for a space below the museum. In the restored Petersen House you can see the room where Lincoln died and the parlor where his wife, Mary Todd, waited in anguish through the night.

At this writing, construction was scheduled to begin in 2010 next door to the Petersen House on a new Center for Education and Leadership focused on Lincoln's life and presidency. Visits to Ford's Theatre National Historic Site require a free, timed-entry ticket. Same-day tickets are available at the theater box office beginning at 8:30 AM on a first-come, first-served basis. You can also reserve tickets in advance through Ticketmaster (⊕ *www.ticketmaster.com*) with a $1.50 fee per ticket. ⊠ *511 10th St. NW; Petersen House, 516 10th St. NW, East End* ☎ *202/426–6924* ⊕ *www.fordstheatre.org* 🎫 *Free* ⊗ *Daily 9–5; theater closed to visitors during rehearsals and matinees, generally Thurs. and weekends; Lincoln museum in basement will remain open at these times* Ⓜ *Metro Center or Gallery Pl.*

Frederick Douglass National Historic Site. Cedar Hill, the Anacostia home of abolitionist Frederick Douglass, was the first Black National Historic Site that Congress designated. Douglass, a former slave who delivered rousing abolitionist speeches at home and abroad, resided here from 1877 until his death in 1895. The house has a wonderful view of Washington across the Anacostia River and contains many of Douglass's personal belongings. The home has been meticulously restored to its original grandeur; you can view Douglass's hundreds of books displayed on his custom-built bookshelves, and Limoges china on the Douglass family dining table. A short film on Douglass's life is shown at a nearby visitor center. Entry to the home requires participation in a ranger-led tour. Reservations are available by phone or online. To get here, take the B2 bus from the Anacostia Metro stop. ⊠ *1411 W St. SE, Anacostia* ☎ *202/426–5961, 877/559–6777 tour reservations* ⊕ *www.nps.gov/ frdo* 🎫 *$1.50* ⊗ *Mid-Oct.–mid-Apr., daily 9–4; mid-Apr.–mid-Oct., daily 9–5; call ahead for tour times* Ⓜ *Anacostia.*

★ **Hillwood Estate, Museum and Gardens.** Long before the age of Paris Hilton, cereal heiress Marjorie Merriweather Post was the most celebrated socialite of the 20th century, famous for her fabulous wealth and beauty, as well as her passion for collecting art and creating some of the world's most lavish homes. Of these, the 25-acre Hillwood Estate, which Merriweather Post bought in 1955, is the only one now open to the public. The 40-room Georgian mansion, where she regularly hosted presidents, diplomats, and royalty, is sumptuously appointed, with a formal Louis XVI drawing room, private movie theater and ballroom, and magnificent libraries filled with portraits of the glamorous hostess and her four husbands, as well as works from her rich art collection. She was especially fascinated with Russian art, and her collection of Russian icons, tapestries, gold and silver work, and Fabergé eggs is museum-quality. She devoted equal attention to her gardens: you can wander through 13 acres of them. ⇨ *For more information about the gardens, see the Gardens section in Chapter 10, Sports and the Outdoors.* You should allow two to three hours to take in the estate and gardens. Reservations are recommended on spring weekends for tours and lunch or tea in the café. The estate is best reached by taxi or car (parking is available on the grounds). It's a 20- to 30-minute walk from the Metro. ✉ *4155 Linnean Ave. NW, Northwest* ☎ *202/686–5807 or 202/686–8500* ⊕ *www. hillwoodmuseum.org* ✉ *House and grounds $12* ⊗ *Feb.–Dec., Tues.– Sat. 10–5* Ⓜ *Van Ness/UDC.*

Kreeger Museum. The cool white domes and elegant lines of this postmodern landmark stand in stark contrast to the traditional feel of the rest of the Foxhall Road neighborhood. Designed in 1963 by iconic architect Philip Johnson, the building was once the home of GEICO insurance executive David Lloyd Kreeger and his wife Carmen. Music is a central theme of the art and the space: the Kreegers wanted a showpiece residence that would also function as a gallery and recital hall. The art collection includes works by Renoir, Degas, Cézanne, and Munch, African artifacts, and pieces with musical themes. The domed rooms also have wonderful acoustics, and serve as an excellent performance venue for the classical concerts that are regularly performed here. Information about upcoming performances is available on the museum's Web site. The museum is not reachable by Metro; you need to take a car or taxi to get here. ✉ *2401 Foxhall Rd. NW, Foxhall* ☎ *202/338–3552* ⊕ *www.kreegermuseum.org* ✉ *$10* ⊗ *Sat. 10–4; tours, reservations required, Tues.–Fri. at 10:30 and 1:30, Sat. optional tours at 10:30, noon, and 2.*

Madame Tussauds. The D.C. branch of this famous London-based waxworks franchise has a focus on local history: you can see (and pose for pictures with) uncanny likenesses of the founding fathers, as well as the Obamas, the Clintons, and the Kennedys. You can even sit in an Oval Office painstakingly re-created in wax. If you want a taste of celebrity, you can enter a "nightclub" room populated with waxen recreations of Julia Roberts, J. Lo, and Brad Pitt, among many others. There's a 10% discount on tickets purchased in advance online. ✉ *1025 F St. NW, East End* ☎ *202/942–7300* ⊕ *www.madametussaudsdc.com* ✉ *$20* ⊗ *Mon.–Thurs. 10–4, Fri.–Sun. 10–6* Ⓜ *Metro Center and Gallery Pl./Chinatown.*

3

Marian Koshland Science Museum. Sponsored by the National Academy of Sciences, this small but engaging museum explores and explains the science behind current news headlines. A permanent exhibit includes animations of groundbreaking science with interactive displays showing how these discoveries make their way into the public realm. The other exhibits illustrate the research of the academy on subjects that intersect with public policy, such as global warming and the spread of infectious diseases like SARS. You can look through microscopes at live bacteria, or play a game determining the fate of the planet based on how governments regulate human activities. Exhibits are changed and updated to reflect new discoveries and fields of research. Though the interactive exhibits are fun and educational, they are aimed at ages 13 and up. ✉ *At 6th and E Sts. NW, East End* ☎ *202/334–1201* ⊕ *www. koshland-science-museum.org* ✉ *$5* ⊘ *Sun., Mon., and Wed.–Sat. 10–6* Ⓜ *Gallery Pl./Chinatown and Judiciary Sq.*

National Aquarium. Established in 1873, this is the country's oldest public aquarium, with more than 1,200 fish and other creatures—such as eels, sharks, and alligators—representing 270 species of fresh- and saltwater life. Seekers of a transcendent aquarium experience will probably be happier visiting the Baltimore National Aquarium, which is routinely ranked among the nation's best. But the easy-to-view tanks, accessible touching pool (with crabs and sea urchins), low admission fee, and absence of crowds make this a good outing with children. There are also animal keeper talks and feedings every day at 2. ✉ *14th St. and Constitution Ave. NW, East End* ☎ *202/482–2825* ⊕ *www.nationalaquarium. com* ✉ *$7* ⊘ *Daily 9–5, last admission at 4:30; sharks fed Mon., Wed., and Sat. at 2; piranhas fed Tues., Thurs., and Sun. at 2; alligators fed Fri. at 2* Ⓜ *Federal Triangle.*

★ **National Building Museum.** Devoted to architecture, design, landscaping, and urban planning, the National Building Museum is the nation's premier cultural organization devoted to the built environment. The open interior of the mammoth redbrick edifice is one of the city's great spaces, and has been the site of many presidential inaugural balls. The eight central Corinthian columns are among the largest in the world, rising to a height of 75 feet. Although they resemble Siena marble, each is made of 70,000 bricks that have been covered with plaster and painted. For years, the annual *Christmas in Washington* TV special has been filmed in this breathtaking hall.

The permanent exhibit **Washington: Symbol and City** tells the story of the birth and evolution of the backwater that eventually became the nation's capital (beginning by debunking the myth that Washington was built on a swamp!). You can touch the perfectly scaled, intricately detailed models of the White House, the Capitol, the Washington Monument, and the Lincoln and Jefferson memorials, and look at original drawings, building plans, maps, videos, and photographs that trace the city's architectural history.

Among the most popular permanent exhibits is the **Building Zone,** where kids ages two to six can get a hands-on introduction to building by constructing a tower, exploring a kid-size playhouse, or playing with bulldozers and construction trucks.

Tours are offered daily at 11:30, 12:30, and 1:30. Interactive Discovery Cart programs for children ages five and up are offered at 10:30 and 2:30 on Saturday and 11:30 and 2:30 on Sunday. ⊠ *401 F St. NW, between 4th and 5th Sts., East End* ☎ *202/272-2448* ⊕ *www.nbm.org* 🎫 *Free* ⊙ *Mon.–Sat. 10–5, Sun. 11–5* Ⓜ *Judiciary Sq.*

☺ **National Geographic Society.** Founded in 1888, the society is best known for its magazine, but a 13,000-square-foot exhibition space gives visitors the feeling of stepping into its pages. The hall is home to a rotating display of objects from the society's permanent collections—cultural, historical, and scientific—as well as traveling exhibitions. ⊠ *17th and M Sts. NW, Dupont Circle* ☎ *202/857-7588, 202/857-7689 group tours* ⊕ *www.nationalgeographic.com* 🎫 *Free; prices for special exhibitions around $12* ⊙ *Daily 10–6* Ⓜ *Farragut N.*

☺ **National Museum of African Art.** This unique underground building houses galleries, a library, photographic archives, and educational facilities. Its rotating exhibits present African visual arts, including sculpture, textiles, photography, archaeology, and modern art. Long-term installations explore the sculpture of sub-Saharan Africa, the art of Benin, the pottery of Central Africa, the archaeology of the ancient Nubian city of Kerma, and the artistry of everyday objects. The museum's educational programs include films with contemporary perspectives on African life, storytelling programs, festivals, and hands-on workshops for families, all of which bring Africa's oral traditions, literature, and art to life. Workshops and demonstrations by African and African-American artists offer a chance to meet and talk to practicing artists. ■TIP➜ If you're traveling with children, look for the museum's free guide to the permanent Images of Power and Identity exhibition. ⊠ *950 Independence Ave. SW, The Mall* ☎ *202/633-1000, 202/357-1729 TDD* ⊕ *www.nmafa.si.edu* 🎫 *Free* ⊙ *Daily 10–5:30* Ⓜ *Smithsonian.*

National Museum of Crime and Punishment. This museum explores the history of crime and punishment in America, from pirates and Wild West outlaws to white-collar criminals and computer hackers. The museum was created in partnership with *America's Most Wanted* host John Walsh, and includes a behind-the-scenes look at the program. Exhibits range from a medieval torture chamber to the actual getaway car used by bank robbers Bonnie and Clyde. There are plenty of interactive displays: you can put your hands in pillory stocks, take a lie-detector test, and experience a simulated crime-scene investigation. The museum recommends purchasing advance tickets on the Web site: tickets are hourly with a specific date and time. ⊠ *575 7th St. NW, East End* ☎ *202/621-5550, 202/393-1099 TDD* ⊕ *www.crimemuseum.org* 🎫 *$17.95 online, $19.95 Box Office walk up* ⊙ *Sept. 1–Mar. 19, daily 10–8; Mar. 20–Aug. 31, daily 9–9* Ⓜ *Gallery Pl./Chinatown.*

National Museum of Health and Medicine. Open since the 1860s, this medical museum illustrates medicine's fight against injury and disease. It has one of the world's largest collections of microscopes. Because some exhibits are fairly graphic (the wax surgical models and the preserved organs come to mind), the museum may not be suitable for young children or the squeamish, but may be perfect for teenagers. In the presidential display you'll see one of the most famous artifacts: the bullet that killed Abraham Lincoln, as well as pieces of his skull and plaster molds of his head and hands. ■TIP→ The museum is on the campus of Walter Reed Army Medical Center, so you will be asked for identification going in. From the Silver Spring Metro station take Bus 70 or 71. From Takoma Park Metro station, take Bus 52, 53, or 54. ⊠ *Walter Reed Army Medical Center, 6900 Georgia Ave. and Elder St. NW, Upper Northwest* ☎ *202/782–2200* ⊕ *nmhm.washingtondc.museum* ☒ *Free* ⊙ *Daily 10–5:30; tours 2nd and 4th Sat. of month at 1.*

National Museum of Women in the Arts. Works by female artists from the Renaissance to the present are showcased at this museum. The beautifully restored 1907 Renaissance Revival building was designed by Waddy B. Wood; it was once a Masonic temple, for men only. In addition to displaying traveling shows, the museum has a permanent collection that includes paintings, drawings, sculpture, prints, and photographs by Georgia O'Keeffe, Mary Cassatt, Élisabeth Vigée-Lebrun, Frida Kahlo, and Camille Claudel. ⊠ *1250 New York Ave. NW, East End* ☎ *202/783–5000* ⊕ *www.nmwa.org* ☒ *$10* ⊙ *Mon.–Sat. 10–5, Sun. noon–5* Ⓜ *Metro Center.*

National Postal Museum. The Smithsonian's stamp collection, housed here, consists of a whopping 11 million stamps. Exhibits, underscoring the important part the mail has played in America's development, include horse-drawn mail coaches, railway mail cars, airmail planes, and a collection of philatelic rarities. The National Museum of Natural History has the Hope Diamond, but the National Postal Museum has the container used to mail the gem to the Smithsonian. The family-oriented museum has more than 40 interactive and touch-screen exhibits. The museum takes up only a portion of what is the old Washington City Post Office, designed by Daniel Burnham and completed in 1914. Nostalgic odes to the noble mail carrier are inscribed on the exterior of the marble building; one of them, "The Letter," eulogizes the "Messenger of sympathy and love / Servant of parted friends / Consoler of the lonely / Bond of the scattered family / Enlarger of the common life." ⊠ *2 Massachusetts Ave. NE, Capitol Hill* ☎ *202/633–5555, 202/633–9849 TDD* ⊕ *www. postalmuseum.si.edu* ☒ *Free* ⊙ *Daily 10–5:30* Ⓜ *Union Station.*

Old Stone House. What was early American life like? Here's the capital's oldest window into the past. Work on this fieldstone house, thought to be Washington's oldest surviving building, was begun in 1764 by a cabinetmaker named Christopher Layman. Now a museum, it was used as both a residence and a place of business by a succession of occupants. Five of the house's rooms are furnished with the simple, sturdy artifacts—plain tables, spinning wheels, and so forth—of 18th-century middle-class life. The National Park Service maintains the house and its lovely gardens, which are planted with fruit trees and perennials. ⊠ *3051 M St. NW, Georgetown* ☎ *202/426–6851* ⊕ *www.nps.gov/olst* ☒ *Free* ⊙ *Daily 10–5.*

Pope John Paul II Cultural Center. Part museum, part place of pilgrimage, the Pope John Paul II Cultural Center is a spectacular architectural embodiment of the Roman Catholic Church's desire to celebrate its charismatic leader and its rich artistic tradition. Themes covered include church and papal history, representations of the Virgin Mary, Polish heritage, and the Catholic tradition of community activism. These are explored through traditional displays of art and artifacts as well as with audiovisual presentations and interactive computer stations. The center is about a mile from the Metro and can easily be combined with a visit to the National Shrine of the Immaculate Conception. ⊠ *3900 Harewood Rd. NE, Catholic University* ☎ *202/635–5400* ⊕ *www.jp2cc. org* ⊠ *Free* ☉ *Tues. and Thurs.–Sat. 10–5, Sun. noon–5* Ⓜ *Brookland/ Catholic University.*

Renwick Gallery. The Renwick Gallery is a luscious French Second Empire–style mansion across the street from the White House and the Eisenhower Executive Office Building. But even with such lofty neighbors, this fancy-gingerbread house, which has the words DEDICATED TO ART engraved above the entrance, is still the most appealing architecture on the block. Designed by James Renwick in 1859 to hold the art collection of Washington merchant and banker William Wilson Corcoran, the building today is a branch of Smithsonian American Art Museum, housing the museum's collection of decorative art and crafts. The building's interior matches the architecture—much red velvet and gold trim—but the exquisitely crafted works on display have a modern and witty edge. Larry Fuente's 1988 sculpture *Game Fish* is a marlin fashioned entirely out of vintage toys—Superman and Gumby are represented, as well as dice, yo-yos, and dominoes. Best of all is Kim Schahman's 1955 *Bureau of Bureaucracy*: a beautifully crafted wooden cabinet full of cupboards to nowhere, bottomless drawers, drawers within drawers, hidden compartments, and more. This wonderful metaphor for the labyrinthine workings of government is appropriately set in a room with a view to the Executive Office Building, providing the perfect tongue-in-cheek commentary to the activities within. ⊠ *Pennsylvania Ave. at 17th St. NW, White House area* ☎ *202/633–2850, 202/633–5285 TDD* ⊕ *www. americanart.si.edu* ⊠ *Free* ☉ *Daily 10–5:30* Ⓜ *Farragut W.*

Sewall-Belmont House. Built in 1800 by Robert Sewall, this is one of the oldest homes on Capitol Hill. Today it's the headquarters of the National Woman's Party. A museum inside chronicles the early days of the women's movement and the history of the house; the museum is open for guided 30-minute tours only. There's also a library open to researchers by appointment. From 1801 to 1813 Secretary of the Treasury Albert Gallatin lived here; he finalized the details of the Louisiana Purchase in his front-parlor office. This building was the only private house in Washington that the British set on fire during their invasion of 1814. They did so after a resident fired on advancing British troops from an upper-story window (a fact later documented by the offending British general's sworn testimony, 30 years later, on behalf of the Sewalls in their attempt to secure war reparations from the U.S. government). This shot was, in fact, the only armed resistance the British met that day. The house is filled with period furniture and portraits and busts of suffragists such as Lucretia Mott, Elizabeth Cady Stanton, and longtime resident Alice Paul, who drafted the first version of the Equal Rights Amendment in 1923. ✉ *144 Constitution Ave. NE, Capitol Hill* ☎ *202/546–1210* ⊕ *www.sewallbelmont.org* ✉ *Suggested donation $5* ⊙ *Tours on the hr Wed.–Sun. noon–4* Ⓜ *Union Station.*

Smithsonian Institution Building. The first Smithsonian museum constructed, this red sandstone, Norman-style building is better known as the Castle. It was designed by James Renwick, the architect of St. Patrick's Cathedral in New York City. Although British scientist and founder James Smithson had never visited America, his will stipulated that should his nephew, Henry James Hungerford, die without an heir, Smithson's entire fortune would go to the United States, "to found at Washington, under the name of the Smithsonian Institution, an establishment for the increase and diffusion of knowledge." The museums on the Mall are the Smithsonian's most visible example of this ideal, but the organization also sponsors traveling exhibitions and maintains research posts in outside-the-Beltway locales such as the Chesapeake Bay and the tropics of Panama.

■ **TIP→** Today the Castle houses the Smithsonian Information Center, which can help you get your bearings and decide which attractions to visit. A 24-minute video gives an overview of the Smithsonian museums and the National Zoo, and monitors display information on the day's events. Interactive touch-screens provide more detailed information on the museums as well as other attractions in the capital. The center opens at 9 AM, an hour before the other museums, so you can plan your day without wasting sightseeing time. It also has a good café, offering one of the better options for lunch on the Mall, and a gift shop. ✉ *1000 Jefferson Dr. SW, The Mall* ☎ *202/633–1000, 202/357–1729 TDD* ⊕ *www.si.edu* ✉ *Free* ⊙ *Daily 9–5:30* Ⓜ *Smithsonian.*

Textile Museum. The museum showcases weavings, carpets, and tapestries from the more than 17,000 works in the collection. Rotating exhibits are taken from a permanent collection of historic and ethnographic items that include Coptic and pre-Columbian textiles, Kashmir embroidery, and Turkman tribal rugs. There's at least one show of modern textiles—such as quilts or fiber art—yearly. ✉ *2320 S St., Kalorama* ☎ *202/667–0441* ⊕ *www.textilemuseum.org* ✉ *Suggested donation $5* ⊙ *Tues.–Sat. 10–5, Sun. 1–5; highlight tours weekends at 1:30* Ⓜ *Dupont Circle.*

Tudor Place. Stop at Q Street between 31st and 32nd streets; look through the trees to the north, at the top of a sloping lawn, and you can see the neoclassical Tudor Place, designed by Capitol architect Dr. William Thornton and completed in 1816. On a house tour you can see Francis Scott Key's desk, items that belonged to George Washington, and spurs belonging to soldiers who were killed in the Civil War. You can only visit the house by guided tour (reservations are advised), but afterward you can wander freely, or picnic in the formal garden, full of roses and boxwoods, many planted in the early 19th century. ✉ *1644 31st St. NW, Georgetown* ☎ *202/965–0400* ⊕ *www.tudorplace.org* ✉ *House tour, $8, includes admission to garden; garden only, $3* ⊙ *Feb.–Dec. house tours Tues.–Sat. hourly 10–4, last tour at 3; Sun. hourly noon–4, last tour at 3. Garden Feb.–Dec. Mon.–Sat. 10–4, Sun. noon–4.*

☾ **Washington Navy Yard.** A 115-acre historic district with its own street system, the Washington Navy Yard is the Navy's oldest outpost on shore. Established in 1799 as a shipbuilding facility, it was burned during the War of 1812. Rebuilt and converted to weapons production by the mid-19th century, it gradually fell into disuse until the 1960s, when it was revived as an administrative center.

> **CAPITAL FACTS**
>
> Until the Clintons bought a house here, Wilson was the only president who stayed in D.C. after leaving the White House. He's still the only president buried in the city, inside the National Cathedral.

The **Navy Museum** (☏ *202/433–4882 Navy Museum, 202/433–4882 USS Barry* ⊕ *www.history.navy.mil*), in Building 76, chronicles the history of the U.S. Navy from the Revolution to the present. Exhibits range from the fully rigged foremast of the USS *Constitution* (better known as Old Ironsides) to a U.S. Navy Corsair fighter plane dangling from the ceiling. All around are models of fighting ships, working periscopes, displays on battles, and portraits of the sailors who fought them. The decommissioned U.S. Navy destroyer *Barry,* open weekdays 10–4, floats a few hundred yards away in the Anacostia River. In front of the museum is a collection of guns, cannons, and missiles. The museum is open weekdays 9–5 and weekends 10–5. The visitor access gate is at 6th and M streets SE. To get here, take Metro (Green line to Navy Yard station or Orange/Blue line to Eastern Market station) or the DC Circulator Union Station to Navy Yard route on weekdays. Personal vehicles are permitted into the Navy Yard on weekends only.

The **Navy Art Gallery** (☏ *202/433–3815* ⊕ *www.history.navy.mil*), in Building 67, exhibits navy-related paintings, sketches, and drawings, many created during combat by navy artists. The bulk of the collection illustrates World War II. Hours for the Navy Art Gallery are weekdays 9–3:30. ⊠ *O and 11th Sts. SE, Capitol Hill* ⛝ *Free* Ⓜ *Eastern Market.*

Woodrow Wilson House. President Wilson and his second wife, Edith Bolling Wilson, retired in 1920 to this Georgian Revival designed by Washington architect Waddy B. Wood. (Wood also designed the Department of the Interior and the National Museum of Women in the Arts.) The house was built in 1915 for a carpet merchant.

Wilson died in 1924. Edith survived him by 37 years. After she died in 1961, the house and its contents were bequeathed to the National Trust for Historic Preservation. On view inside are such items as a Gobelin tapestry, a baseball signed by King George V, and the shell casing from the first shot fired by U.S. forces in World War I. The house also contains memorabilia related to the history of the short-lived but influential League of Nations, including the colorful flag Wilson hoped would be adopted by that organization. ⊠ *2340 S St. NW, Kalorama* ☏ *202/387–4062* ⊕ *www.woodrowwilsonhouse.org* ⛝ *$7.50* ☾ *Tues.– Sun. 10–4* Ⓜ *Dupont Circle.*

Monuments and Memorials

WORD OF MOUTH

"Dusk had already settled upon the National Mall as we made our way up the steps to the magnificent Lincoln Memorial. What struck me was, that even with so many kids wandering about in the area, the mood here was surprisingly reflective. . . The imposing visage of Lincoln is hard to remove from your memory."

—maitaitom

MONUMENTS AND MEMORIALS PLANNER

Making the Most of Your Time

It takes four or five hours to tour the monuments west of the Mall, with time to relax on a park bench and grab a snack from a vendor or one of the snack bars east of the Washington Monument, near the Lincoln Memorial.

If you're visiting during the first two weeks in April, take extra time around the Tidal Basin and the Washington Monument to marvel at the cherry blossoms. From mid-April through November, you might want to spend an hour on a paddleboat in the Tidal Basin. In summer, consider taking a Tourmobile bus and travel between the monuments in air-conditioned comfort.

Across the Potomac, Arlington National Cemetery merits a few hours on its own.

In the Works

The Martin Luther King Jr. National Memorial was scheduled to open in 2009, but as of this writing construction hadn't begun. When the memorial does open, it will be the first major monument in the National Mall and Tidal Basin area devoted to a man who wasn't a president.

Ask a Ranger

You may think of park rangers as denizens of the woods, but they're a conspicuous presence at Washington's memorials—look for the olive-green and gray uniforms. Rangers lead talks about each monument and memorial run by the Park Service, with the exception of the Washington Monument, at 11, 1, 3, and 5 every day. They are an invaluable source of information; don't hesitate to ask questions of them. Kids can get Junior Park Ranger activity booklets from the ranger desks at the Lincoln, Jefferson, and World War II memorials.

Monumental Souvenirs

At **Arlington National Cemetery** there are gift shops at the visitor center, the Women in Military Service for America Memorial, and Arlington House. The National Park Service contracts with a private company that operates gift shops and bookstores at or near the **FDR Memorial** (the largest), **Jefferson Memorial, Lincoln Memorial,** and **Washington Monument.** Gift items tend to be the same at each shop. For a more eclectic selection, check out the Making History shop in Union Station.

Walking and Biking Tours

Washington Walks (⊕ www.washingtonwalks.com) has tours with witty commentary that cover most of the major monuments and memorials. They operate from April through October, and each two-hour tour costs $10. **DC by Foot** (⊕ www.dcbyfoot.com) offers free (work for tips) walking tours of the monuments. Tours meet near the Washington Monument Wednesday and Friday at 11:30 and weekends at 2 from March to November. **Bike and Roll Washington, DC** (⊕ www.bikethesites.com) conducts tours on wheels from late March through November. The cost is $40–$45 for adults, $30–$35 for children 12 and under; price includes bike rental, helmet, bottled water, and snack.

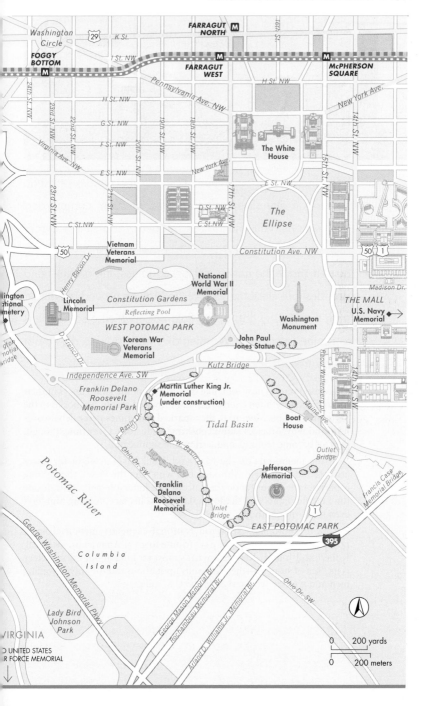

By Kathryn McKay and Cathy Sharpe

Washington is a monumental city. In the middle of traffic circles, on tiny slivers of park, and at street corners and intersections, you find statues, plaques, and simple blocks of marble honoring the generals, artists, and statesmen who helped shape the nation. Of these tributes, the greatest and grandest are clustered west of the Mall on ground reclaimed from the marshy flats of the Potomac—which also happens to be the location of Washington's most striking display of cherry trees.

These monuments now look like they're part of the landscape, but their beginnings were often controversial. From the Lincoln Memorial to the Vietnam Veterans Memorial, they sparked sometimes-fierce debate over how and why America should enshrine its history. Over time, though, they've become icons of unquestionable significance.

Visit the memorials on the Mall and Tidal Basin at night for fewer crowds and cooler air. Although you won't get the views, the lighting is particularly beautiful on the Lincoln and Jefferson memorials. Inside the Lincoln, lights and shadows play across his face, making him look even more thoughtful.

Across the Potomac, Arlington National Cemetery memorial has a power all its own. Though it pays tribute to great Americans, including Robert and John F. Kennedy, what's most striking about the cemetery is its "sea of stones"—the thousands upon thousands of graves holding men and women who served in the U.S. military.

ARLINGTON, THE NATION'S CEMETERY

The most famous, most visited cemetery in the country is the final resting place for more than 340,000 Americans, from unknown soldiers to John F. Kennedy. With its tombs, monuments, and "sea of stones," Arlington is a place of ritual and remembrance, where even the most cynical observer of Washington politics may find a lump in his throat or a tear in his eye.

EXPERIENCING THE SEA OF STONES

In 1864, a 612-acre plot directly across the Potomac from Washington, part of the former plantation home of Robert E. Lee, was designated America's national cemetery.

Today, Arlington's major monuments and memorials are impressive, but the most striking experience is simply looking out over the thousands upon thousands of headstones aligned across the cemetery's hills.

Most of those buried here served in the military—from reinterred Revolutionary War soldiers to troops killed in Iraq and Afghanistan. As you walk through the cemetery, you're likely to hear a trumpet playing taps or the report of a

gun salute. An average of 27 funerals a day are held here, Monday through Friday. There currently are some 300,000 graves in Arlington; it's projected that the cemetery will be filled by 2020.

FINDING A GRAVE

At the Visitors Center, staff members and computers can help you find the location of a specific grave. You need to provide the deceased's full name and, if possible, the branch of service and year of death.

CHARLES
ORBIE
FARRIS
RM1
US COAST GUARD
WORLD WAR II
SEP 10 1920
OCT 2 1988

4

WHO GETS BURIED WHERE

With few exceptions, interment at Arlington is limited to active-duty members of the armed forces, veterans, and their spouses and minor children. In Arlington's early years as a cemetery, burial location was determined by rank (as well as, initially, by race), with separate sections for enlisted soldiers and officers. Beginning in 1947, this distinction was abandoned. Grave sites are assigned on the day before burial; when possible, requests are honored to be buried near the graves of family members.

ABOUT THE HEADSTONES

Following the Civil War, Arlington's first graves were marked by simple whitewashed boards. When these decayed, they were replaced by cast-iron markers covered with zinc to prevent rusting. Only one iron marker remains, for the grave of Captain Daniel Keys (Section 13, Lot 13615, Grid G-29/30).

In 1873, Congress voted in the use of marble headstones, which continues to be the practice today. The government provides the standard-issue stones free of charge. Next of kin may supply their own headstones, though these can only be used if space is available in one of the sections where individualized stones already exist.

THE SAME, BUT DIFFERENT

Regulation headstones can be engraved with one of 26 symbols indicating religious affiliation. In section 60, the headstones of soldiers killed in Afghanistan and Iraq reflect the multicultural makeup of 21st-century America. Along with a variety of crosses and the Star of David, you see the nine-pointed star of the Baha'i; a tepee and three feathers representing the Native American faiths; the Muslim crescent and star; and other signs of faith. (Or lack of it. Atheism is represented by a stylized atom.)

Opposite: Sea of Stones; Upper left: Burial ceremony; Bottom left: A soldier placing flags for Memorial Day. Right: Coast Guard headstone.

PLANNING YOUR VISIT TO ARLINGTON

ARLINGTON BASICS

Getting Here: You can reach Arlington on the Metro, by foot over Arlington Memorial Bridge (southwest of the Lincoln Memorial), or by car—there's a large parking lot by the Visitors Center on Memorial Drive. Also, the Tourmobile bus (☎202/554–7950 ⊕www.tourmobile.com) and Old Town Trolley (☎202/832–9800 ⊕www.oldtowntrolley.com) both have Arlington National Cemetery stops in their loops.

🕙Apr.–Sept., daily 8–7; Oct.–Mar., daily 8–5.

🎫Cemetery free, parking $1.75 per hr for the first three hours, $2 per hr thereafter. Tourmobile Arlington Tour $7.50, Old Town Trolley $32.

☎703/607–8000 for general information and to locate a grave.

⊕www.arlingtoncemetery.org

✗No food or drink is allowed at the cemetery. There are water fountains in the Visitor Center, and from fall through spring a water fountain operates near the amphitheater at the Tomb of the Unknowns. You can also purchase bottled water at the Women's Memorial.

TOURING OPTIONS

Your first stop at the cemetery should be the Visitor Center, where you can pick up a free brochure with a detailed map. Once there you have a choice: tour by bus or walk.

Arlington by Bus. Tourmobile tour buses leave every 15 to 25 minutes from just outside the Visitor Center April through September, daily 8:30–6:30, and October through March, daily 8:30–4:30. The 45-minute tour includes stops at the Kennedy grave sites, the Tomb of the Unknowns, and Arlington House. Your bus driver will provide basic facts about the cemetery.

Arlington on Foot. Walking the cemetery requires some stamina, but it allows you to take in the thousands of graves at your own pace. On the facing page is a walking tour that includes the major points of interest.

Above: 3rd Infantry Honor Guard

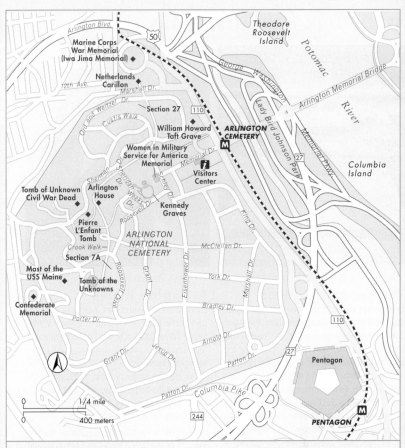

A WALKING TOUR

■ Head west from the Visitors Center on Roosevelt Drive and turn right on Weeks Drive to reach the **Kennedy graves**; just to the west is **Arlington House**. (¼ mile)

■ Take Crook Walk south, following the signs, to the **Tomb of the Unknowns**; a few steps from the tomb is **Section 7A**, where many distinguished veterans are buried. (³/₁₀ mile)

■ To visit the graves of soldiers killed in Afghanistan and Iraq, take Roosevelt Drive past Section 7 and turn right on McClellan Drive, turn right when you get to Eisenhower Drive, then go left onto York Drive. The graves will be on your right. (⁶/₁₀ mile)

■ Walk north along Eisenhower Drive, which becomes Schley Drive; turn right onto Custis Walk, which brings you to **Section 27**, where 3,800 former slaves are buried. (¾ mile)

■ Leave the cemetery through the Ord and Weitzel Gate, cross Marshall Drive carefully, and walk to the 50-bell **Netherlands Carillon**, where there's a good vista of Washington. To the north is the **United States Marine Corps War Memorial**, better known as the **Iwo Jima Memorial**. (¼ mile)

ARLINGTON'S MAIN ATTRACTIONS

The Kennedy Graves

Once while taking in the view of Washington from Arlington National Cemetery, President John F. Kennedy commented, "I could stay here forever." Seeing Kennedy's grave is a top priority for most visitors. He's buried beneath an eternal flame, next to graves of two of his children who died in infancy, and of his wife, Jacqueline Kennedy Onassis. Across from them is a low wall engraved with quotations from Kennedy's inaugural address. Nearby, marked by simple white crosses, are the graves of Robert F. Kennedy and Ted Kennedy.

The gas-fueled flame at the head of John F. Kennedy's grave was lit by Jacqueline Kennedy during his funeral. A continuously flashing electric spark reignites the gas if the flame is extinguished by rain, wind, or any other cause.

Many visitors ask where Kennedy's son John F. Kennedy Jr. is buried. His ashes were scattered in the Atlantic Ocean, near the location where his plane went down in 1999.

Arlington House

Long before Arlington was a cemetery, it was part of the 1,100-acre estate of George Washington Parke Custis, a grandchild of Martha and (by marriage) George Washington. Custis built Arlington House between 1802 and 1817. After his death, the property went to his daughter, Mary Anna Randolph Custis, who wed Robert E. Lee in 1831. The couple made Arlington House their home for the next 30 years.

In 1861 Lee turned down the position of commander of the Union forces and left Arlington House, never to return. Union troops turned the house into the Army of the Potomac's headquarters, and 200 acres were set aside as a national cemetery. By the end of the Civil War more than 16,000 headstones dotted the estate's hills.

Today the house looks much as it did in the 19th century. At this writing, most furnishings have been removed temporarily as the house undergoes renovation, but you can still take a guided tour every 20 min. or walk through. ☎ *703/235–1530* ⊕ *www.nps.gov/arho* ⊠ *Free* ☾ *Daily 9:30–4:30.*

Robert E. Lee

Tomb of the Unknowns

The first burial at the Tomb of the Unknowns, one of the cemetery's most imposing monuments, took place on November 11, 1921. In what was part of a world-wide trend to honor the dead after the unparalleled devastation of World War I, an unidentified soldier was interred under the large white-marble sarcophagus. Unknown servicemen killed in World War II and Korea joined him in 1958.

The Memorial Amphitheater west of the tomb is used for ceremonies on Veterans Day, Memorial Day, and Easter. Decorations awarded to the unknowns are displayed in an indoor trophy room.

One of the most striking activities at Arlington is the precision and pageantry of the changing of the guard at the Tomb of the Unknowns. From April through September, soldiers from the Army's U.S. Third Infantry (known as the Old Guard) change guard every half hour during the day. For the rest of the year, and at night all year long, the guard changes every hour.

The Iwo Jima Memorial

Ask the Tourmobile driver at Arlington where the Iwo Jima is, and you might get back the quip "very far away." The memorial commonly called the Iwo Jima is officially named the United States Marine Corps War Memorial, and it's actually located just north of the cemetery. Its bronze sculpture is based on one of the most famous photos in American military history, Joe Rosenthal's February 19, 1945 shot of five marines and a navy corpsman raising a flag atop Mt. Suribachi on the Japanese island of Iwo Jima. By executive order, a real flag flies 24 hours a day from the 78-foot-high memorial. ☎ *703/289–2500*

On Tuesday evening at 7 PM from late May to late August there's a Marine Corps sunset parade on the grounds of the Iwo Jima Memorial. On parade nights a free shuttle bus runs from the Arlington Cemetery visitors' parking lot.

The Old Guard are not making a fashion statement in their sunglasses—they're protecting their eyes from the sun's glare off the white marble of the tomb.

FRANKLIN DELANO ROOSEVELT MEMORIAL

✉ *West side of Tidal Basin*
☎ *202/426–6841* ⊕ *www.nps. gov/fdrm* 🖾 *Free* ⊗ *24 hrs; staffed daily 8 am–midnight* Ⓜ *Smithsonian.*

TIPS

■ If you come with a toddler, head straight to the third room. Though youngsters can't sit on Roosevelt's lap, they can pet Fala, Roosevelt's Scottish terrier. The tips of Fala's ears and his nose shine from all the attention.

■ Allow about 30 minutes at this memorial. Take your time walking through the most expansive presidential memorial in Washington and read the lines from FDR's speeches.

■ This was the first memorial designed to be wheelchair accessible. Several pillars with Braille lettering and tactile images help the visually impaired.

■ This memorial presents good opportunities for family photographs. You can strike a pose while petting Fala, joining the men in the breadline, or listening to Roosevelt's fireside chat.

■ At night the lighting over the waterfalls creates interesting shadows, and there's not as much noise from airplanes overhead.

Unveiled in 1997, this 7.5-acre memorial to the 32nd president includes waterfalls and reflecting pools, four outdoor gallery rooms—one for each of Roosevelt's presidential terms (1933 to 1945)—and 10 bronze sculptures. The granite megaliths connecting the galleries are engraved with some of Roosevelt's famous statements, including, "The only thing we have to fear is fear itself."

HIGHLIGHTS

Congress established the Franklin Delano Roosevelt Memorial Commission in 1955, and invited prospective designers to look to "the character and work of Roosevelt to give us the theme of a memorial." Several decades passed before Lawrence Halprin's design for a "walking environmental experience" was selected. It incorporates work by artists Leonard Baskin, Neil Estern, Robert Graham, Thomas Hardy, and George Segal, and master stone carver John Benson.

The statue of a wheelchair-bound Roosevelt near the entrance of the memorial was added in 2001. Originally, the memorial showed little evidence of Roosevelt's polio, which he contracted at age 39. He used a wheelchair for the last 24 years of his life, but kept his disability largely hidden from public view. The statue was added after years of debate about whether to portray Roosevelt realistically or to honor his desire not to display his disability.

A bronze statue of First Lady Eleanor Roosevelt stands in front of the United Nations symbol in the fourth room. She was a vocal spokesperson for human rights and one of the most influential women of her time.

You're encouraged to touch the handprints and Braille along the columns in the second room, which represent the working hands of the American people.

KOREAN WAR VETERANS MEMORIAL

✉ *West end of Mall at Daniel French Dr. and Independence Ave.* ☎ *202/426–6841* ⊕ *www.nps.gov/kwvm* 🎟 *Free* ⏱ *24 hrs; staffed daily 8 am–midnight* Ⓜ *Foggy Bottom.*

TIPS

■ Allow about 10 or 15 minutes at this memorial.

■ A sign at the entrance to the memorial indicates the time of the next park ranger–led interpretive talk.

■ You can get service information on the soldiers who died in the Korean War from the touch-screen computer at the memorial information booth. Further information about veterans and casualties is available at ⊕ *www.koreanwar.org.*

■ It's tempting for kids to trek through the field with the statues, but they're not allowed to. They can strike a pose next to the wall and see their reflection added to those of the 19 soldiers.

■ Visit the shop in the nearby Lincoln Memorial for books and souvenirs relating to the Korean War.

This memorial to the 1.5 million United States men and women who served in the Korean War (1950–53) highlights the high cost of freedom. Nearly 37,000 Americans were killed on the Korean peninsula, 8,000 were missing in action, and more than 103,000 were wounded. The privately funded memorial was dedicated on July 27, 1995, on the 42nd anniversary of the Korean War Armistice. Compare this memorial to the more intimate Vietnam Veterans Memorial and the grandiose World War II Memorial.

HIGHLIGHTS

In the *Field of Service,* 19 oversize stainless-steel soldiers toil through a rugged triangular terrain toward an American flag; look beneath the helmets to see their weary faces. The reflection in the polished black granite wall to their right doubles their number to 38, symbolic of the 38th parallel, the latitude established as the border between North and South Korea in 1953, as well as the 38 months of the war.

Unlike many memorials, this one contains few words, but what's here is poignant. The 164-foot-long granite wall etched with the faces of 2,400 unnamed servicemen and servicewomen says simply, "Freedom is not free." The plaque at the base of the flagpole reads, "Our nation honors her sons and daughters who answered the call to defend a country they never knew and a people they never met." The only other words are the names of 22 countries that volunteered forces or medical support, including Great Britain, France, Greece, and Turkey.

The adjacent circular Pool of Remembrance honors all who were killed, captured, wounded, or missing in action; it's a quiet spot for contemplation.

LINCOLN MEMORIAL

✉ *West end of Mall*
☎ *202/426-6841* ⊕ *www.nps.
gov/linc* 🎟 *Free* ◷ *24 hrs;
staffed daily 8 am–midnight*
Ⓜ *Foggy Bottom.*

TIPS

■ On the lower level of the memorial is a small museum financed with pennies collected by schoolchildren.

■ Lincoln's face and hands look especially lifelike because they're based on castings done while he was president. Those who know sign language might recognize that the left hand is shaped like an A and the right like an L. It's unlikely this was intentional, but the sculptor, Daniel Chester French, did have a deaf son.

■ After the 2008 election, AVAAZ erected a 24-foot message board here with the words "Congratulations President Obama—Change Won't be Easy, but…Together, As One World, Yes We Can," which gathered thousands of messages of hope and congratulations from 224 countries and territories.

■ See where Lincoln was shot (on April 14, 1865) at Ford's Theatre (✉ *511 10th St. NW*) and the bullet that killed him at the National Museum of Health and Medicine (✉ *6900 Georgia Ave. and Elder St. NW;* ⊕ nmhm.washingtondc. museum).

Many consider the Lincoln Memorial the most inspiring monument in Washington, but that hasn't always been the case: early detractors thought it inappropriate that a president known for his humility should be honored with what amounts to a grandiose Greek temple. The memorial was intended to be a symbol of national unity, but over time it has come to represent social justice and civil rights.

HIGHLIGHTS

Daniel Chester French's statue of the seated president gazes out over the Reflecting Pool. The 19-foot-high sculpture is made of 28 pieces of Georgia marble.

The surrounding white Colorado-marble memorial was designed by Henry Bacon and completed in 1922. The 36 Doric columns represent the 36 states in the Union at the time of Lincoln's death; their names appear on the frieze above the columns. Over the frieze are the names of the 48 states in existence when the memorial was dedicated. Alaska and Hawaii are represented with an inscription on the terrace leading up to the memorial. At night the memorial is illuminated, creating a striking play of light and shadow across Lincoln's face.

Two of Lincoln's great speeches—the second inaugural address and the Gettysburg Address—are carved on the north and south walls. Above each is a Jules Guerin mural: the south wall has an angel of truth freeing a slave; the unity of North and South is opposite.

The memorial's powerful symbolism makes it a popular gathering place: In its shadow Americans marched for integrated schools in 1958, rallied for an end to the Vietnam War in 1967, and laid wreaths in a ceremony honoring the Iranian hostages in 1979. It may be best known, though, as the site of Martin Luther King Jr.'s "I Have a Dream" speech.

MARTIN LUTHER KING JR. NATIONAL MEMORIAL

✉ *401 F St. NW* ☎ *202/737–5420 or 888/484–3373* ⊕ *www.buildthedream.org* 🎞 *Free* ⊗ *24 hrs; staffed daily 8 am–midnight* Ⓜ *Smithsonian.*

4

TIPS

■ Walk over to the Lincoln Memorial, where you can stand on the same step where King delivered his "I Have a Dream" speech. There's a plaque that marks the exact spot.

■ Allow about 20 to 30 minutes at this memorial, which is being designed as a place for reflection. For a look at local African-American history, visit the Frederick Douglass National Historic Site (✉ *1411 W. St. SE;* ☎ *202/426–5961 or 202/619–7222;* ⊕ *www.nps.gov/frdo*). Tours focus on Douglass's life in D.C. and his mansion.

■ Contrary to popular belief, King won't be the first African-American with a memorial in D.C. That honor goes to Mary McLeod Bethune, founder of the National Council of Negro Women and an informal adviser to FDR. Bethune is depicted in a 17-foot-tall bronze statue (✉ *Lincoln Park, East Capitol and 12th Sts. NE*). King is, however, the first African-American to be placed in Area 1 of the National Mall.

There will soon be a "King" among the presidents on the National Mall. Although the Martin Luther King Jr. National Memorial is expected to be dedicated sometime in 2011, 15 years after Congress approved it in 1996 and 82 years after the famed civil rights leader was born in 1929, don't be surprised if there are delays. At this writing, construction had not yet begun on the memorial.

HIGHLIGHTS

Located strategically between the Lincoln and Jefferson memorials and adjacent to the FDR Memorial, the crescent-shape King Memorial will sit on a 4-acre site on the curved bank of the Tidal Basin.

Visitors will enter through a center walkway cut out of a huge boulder, the Mountain of Despair. From the Mountain, the Stone of Hope will be visible. The symbolism of the mountain and stone are explained by King's words: "With this faith, we will be able to hew out of the mountain of despair a stone of hope." The centerpiece Stone will be carved by Chinese sculptor Lei Yixin; his design was chosen from more than 900 entries in an international competition. Fittingly, Yixin first read about King's "I Have a Dream" speech at age 10 while visiting the Lincoln Memorial. The 28-foot-tall granite boulder will include Lei's rendering of King, whose eyes will meet Jefferson's gaze.

The themes of democracy, justice, hope, and love will be reflected through more than a dozen quotes on the south and north walls and on the Stone of Hope. The quotes reflect speeches, sermons, and writings penned by King from 1955 through 1968. Waterfalls in the memorial will reflect King's use of the biblical quote: "Let justice roll down like waters and righteousness like a mighty stream."

NATIONAL WORLD WAR II MEMORIAL

✉ *17th St. at east side of Washington Monument* ☎ *202/426–6841* ⊕ *www.wwiimemorial.com* ✉ *Free* ⊙ *24 hrs* Ⓜ *Smithsonian.*

TIPS

■ Look for veterans. Perhaps the best part of visiting this memorial might be the last opportunities to see men and women who fought in World War II and are part of what former NBC news anchor Tom Brokaw called "The Greatest Generation."

■ Computers at the National Park Service kiosk behind the Pacific side of the memorial contain information about soldiers who lost their lives in the war.

■ Kids might be bored here. You can engage their attention by asking them to look carefully at the bas-reliefs for a dog and a radio as large as today's big-screen televisions. Then try to find Kilroy, the cartoonlike character who appears to be looking over a ledge. The image and the phrase "Kilroy was here" were popular graffiti left by U.S. soldiers during the war.

Dedicated just before Memorial Day in 2004, this symmetrically designed monument honors the 16 million Americans who served in the armed forces, the more than 400,000 who died, and all who supported the war effort at home.

HIGHLIGHTS

An imposing circle of 56 granite pillars, each bearing a bronze wreath, represents the U.S. states and territories of 1941–45. Four bronze eagles, a bronze garland, and two 43-foot-tall arches inscribed with "Atlantic" and "Pacific" surround the large circular plaza. The roar of the water comes from the Rainbow Pool, here since the 1920s but newly renovated as the centerpiece of the memorial. There are also two fountains and two waterfalls.

The Field of Stars, a wall of 4,000 gold stars, commemorates the more than 400,000 Americans who lost their lives in the war.

Although the parklike setting and the place of honor between the Washington Monument and the Lincoln Memorial may seem appropriate, some people were critical when the site for the memorial was announced, because they felt it would interrupt the landscape between the two landmarks and because it uses some of the open space that had been the site of demonstrations and protests.

Bas-relief panels tell the story of how World War II affected Americans by depicting women in the military, V-J Day, medics, the bond drive, and more activities of the time. The 24 panels are divided evenly between the Atlantic front and the Pacific front.

THOMAS JEFFERSON MEMORIAL

✉ *Tidal Basin, south bank*
☎ *202/426–6841* ⊕ *www.nps. gov/thje* ✉ *Free* ☽ *Daily 8 am–midnight* Ⓜ *Smithsonian.*

4

TIPS

■ Check out the view of the White House from the memorial's steps—it's one of the best. Jefferson was the second president to live in the White House, but the first full-term occupant.

■ Park ranger programs are offered throughout the day, and you can ask questions of the ranger on duty.

■ Learn more about Jefferson by visiting the exhibit called **Light and Liberty** on the memorial's lower level. It chronicles highlights of Jefferson's life and has a timeline of world history during his lifetime.

■ Allow 15 minutes to walk here from the Metro. The memorial is the southernmost of Washington's major monuments and memorials, and it's a full four blocks and a trip around the Tidal Basin from the nearest Metro stop, Smithsonian.

■ Limited parking is available under the 14th Street Bridge, off Ohio Drive near where it intersects with East Basin Drive.

In the 1930s Congress decided that Thomas Jefferson deserved a monument positioned as prominently as those honoring Washington and Lincoln. Workers scooped and moved tons of the river bottom to create dry land for the spot directly south of the White House where the monument was built. Jefferson had always admired the Pantheon in Rome, so the memorial's architect, John Russell Pope, drew on it for inspiration. His finished work was dedicated on the bicentennial of Jefferson's birth, April 13, 1943.

HIGHLIGHTS

Early critics weren't kind to the memorial—rumor has it that it was nicknamed "Jefferson's muffin" for its domed shape. The design was called outdated and too similar to that of the Lincoln Memorial. Indeed, both statues of Jefferson and Lincoln are 19 feet, just 6 inches shorter than the statue of Freedom atop the Capitol.

The bronze statue of Jefferson, standing on a 6-foot granite pedestal, looms larger than life. It wasn't always made of bronze. The first version was made of plaster, because bronze was too expensive and was needed for the war. The statue you see today was erected in 1947.

You can get a taste of Jefferson's keen intellect from his writings about freedom and government inscribed on the marble walls surrounding his statue.

Many people may be surprised to learn that Jefferson didn't list being president as one of his greatest accomplishments. When he appraised his own life, Jefferson wanted to be remembered as the "Author of the Declaration of American Independence, of the Statute of Virginia for religious freedom, and Father of the University of Virginia."

VIETNAM VETERANS MEMORIAL

✉ *Constitution Gardens, 23rd St. and Constitution Ave. NW* ☎ *202/426–6841* ⊕ *www.nps. gov/vive* ✉ *Free* ⊙ *24 hrs; staffed daily 8 am–midnight* Ⓜ *Foggy Bottom.*

TIPS

■ Names on the wall are ordered by date of death. To find a name, consult the alphabetical lists found at either end of the wall. You can get assistance locating a name at the white kiosk with the brown roof near the entrance. At the wall, rangers and volunteers wearing yellow caps can look up the names and supply you with paper and pencils for making rubbings.

■ Every name on the memorial is preceded (on the west wall) or followed (on the east wall) by a symbol designating status. A diamond indicates "killed, body recovered." A plus sign (found by a small percentage of names) indicates "killed, body not recovered."

■ If you're visiting with older children or teens, be prepared for questions about war and death. Sometimes children think all 58,259 soldiers are buried at the monument. They aren't, of course, but the wall is as evocative as any cemetery.

"The Wall," as it's commonly called, is one of the most visited sites in Washington. The names of more than 58,000 Americans who died in the Vietnam War are etched in its black granite panels, creating a somber, dignified, and powerful memorial. It was conceived by Jan Scruggs, a former infantry corporal who served in Vietnam, and designed by Maya Lin, then a 21-year-old architecture student at Yale.

HIGHLIGHTS

Thousands of offerings are left at the wall each year: many people leave flowers, others leave personal objects such as the clothing of soldiers or letters of thanks from schoolchildren. The National Park Service collects and stores the items. In 2007 Congress approved the establishment of a memorial center to display many of the items left near the wall. A small assortment, including wedding rings, a baseball, and photographs, is displayed at the National Museum of American History.

The statues near the wall came about in response to controversies surrounding the memorial. In 1984 Frederick Hart's statue of three soldiers and a flagpole was erected to the south of the wall, with the goal of winning over veterans who considered the memorial a "black gash of shame." A memorial plaque was added in 2004 at the statue of three servicemen to honor veterans who died after the war as a direct result of injuries suffered in Vietnam, but who fall outside Department of Defense guidelines for remembrance at the wall.

The Vietnam Women's Memorial was dedicated on Veterans Day 1993. Glenna Goodacre's bronze sculpture depicts two women caring for a wounded soldier while a third woman kneels nearby; eight trees around the plaza commemorate the eight women in the military who died in Vietnam.

WASHINGTON MONUMENT

✉ *Constitution Ave. and 15th St. NW* ☎ *202/426–6841, 877/444–6777 for advance tickets* ⊕ *www.nps.gov/ wamo; www.recreation.gov for advance tickets* 🎫 *Free; $1.50 service fee per advance ticket* ☽ *Daily 9–5* Ⓜ *Smithsonian.*

4

TIPS

■ The monument uses a free timed-ticket system for the elevator ride. A limited number of tickets are available each day beginning half an hour before the monument opens at the marble lodge on 15th Street. In spring and summer, lines are likely to start much earlier. Tickets are also available online for a $1.50 service charge. Each ticket is good for a designated half-hour period.

■ If you don't score tickets to the monument, you can still look down on D.C. at the Old Post Office Pavilion (✉ *100 Pennsylvania Ave. NW at 12th St.*) or the Washington National Cathedral's Pilgrim Observation Gallery (✉ *Massachusetts and Wisconsin Aves. NW*).

■ Maps below viewing-station windows point out some of Washington's major buildings, but you might want to bring a more detailed map (available at the monument's bookstore).

At the western end of the Mall, the 555-foot, 5-inch Washington Monument punctuates the capital like a huge exclamation point. Inside, an elevator takes you to the top for a bird's-eye view of the city.

The monument was part of Pierre L'Enfant's plan for Washington, but his intended location proved to be marshy, so it was moved 100 yards southeast to firmer ground. (A stone marker now indicates L'Enfant's original site.) Construction began in 1848 and continued, with interruptions, until 1884. The design called for an obelisk rising from a circular colonnaded building, which was to be adorned with statues of national heroes, including Washington riding in a chariot. When the Army Corps of Engineers took over construction in 1876, the building around the obelisk was abandoned. Upon its completion, the monument was the world's tallest structure.

HIGHLIGHTS

An elevator whizzes to the top of the monument in 70 seconds—a trip that in 1888 took 12 minutes via steam-powered elevator. From the viewing stations at the top you can take in most of the District of Columbia, as well as parts of Maryland and Virginia.

There's a story behind the change in color of the stone about a third of the way up the monument. In 1854, six years into construction, members of the anti-Catholic Know-Nothing Party stole and smashed a block of marble donated by Pope Pius IX. This action, combined with funding shortages and the onset of the Civil War, brought construction to a halt. After the war, building finally resumed, and though the new marble came from the same Maryland quarry as the old, it was taken from a different stratum with a slightly different shade.

DID YOU KNOW?

Each year on the 4th of July, the National Symphony Orchestra goes out with a bang, ending its performance with Tchaikovsky's "1812 Overture" and using real cannons (with blanks)!

OTHER MEMORIALS

National Law Enforcement Officers Memorial. These 3-foot-high walls bear the names of more than 18,000 American police officers killed in the line of duty since 1792. On the third line of panel 13W are the names of six officers killed by William Bonney, better known as Billy the Kid. J.D. Tippit, the Dallas policeman killed by Lee Harvey Oswald, is honored on the ninth line of panel 63E. Some of the most recent additions include the names of the 72 officers who died due to 9/11. Directories there allow you to look up officers by name, date of death, state, and department. Call to arrange for a free tour. A National Law Enforcement Museum is in the works, scheduled for completion in 2013; until then, a small visitor center (⊠ *400 7th St. NW*) has a computer for looking up names, a display on the history of law enforcement, and a small gift shop. ⊠ *400 block of E St. NW, Penn Quarter* ☏ *202/737–3400* ⊕ *www.lawmemorial.org* 🖼 *Free* ☉ *Weekdays 9–5, Sat. 10–5, Sun. noon–5* Ⓜ *Judiciary Sq.*

4

Pentagon Memorial. Washington's newest memorial, often called the 9/11 Memorial, is an outdoor tribute to the 184 people who perished when the hijacked American Airlines Flight 77 crashed into the northwest side of the Pentagon. Benches engraved with the victims' names are arranged in order by date of birth and where they were when they died. The names of the victims who were inside the Pentagon are arranged so that visitors reading their names face the Pentagon, and names of the victims on the plane are arranged so that visitors reading their names face skyward. Designed by Julie Beckman and Keith Kaseman, the memorial opened to the public on September 11, 2008, the seventh anniversary of the attacks. Staff in light blue uniforms periodically walk through and answer questions. Parking for the memorial is extremely limited and not well marked; take the Metro instead. ⊠ *Pentagon* ☏ *703/693–8287* ⊕ *www.whs.mil/Memorial* 🖼 *Free* ☉ *24 hrs; restroom facilities available 10* AM*–8* PM Ⓜ *Pentagon.*

United States Air Force Memorial. Three stainless-steel, asymmetrical spires slice through the skyline up to 270 feet, representing flight, the precision of the "bomb burst" maneuver performed by the Air Force Thunderbirds, and the three core values of the Air Force: integrity, service, and excellence. The spires are adjacent to the southern portion of Arlington National Cemetery and visible from the Tidal Basin and I–395 near Washington. At the base of the spires is an 8-foot statue of the honor guard, a glass wall engraved with the missing man formation, and granite walls inscribed with Air Force values and accomplishments. ⊠ *1 Air Force Memorial Dr., Arlington, VA* ☏ *703/979–0674* ⊕ *www. airforcememorial.org* 🖼 *Free* ☉ *Apr.–Sept., daily 8* AM*–11* PM*; Oct.– Mar., daily 8* AM*–9* PM Ⓜ *Pentagon.*

United States Navy Memorial. Although Pierre L'Enfant included a Navy Memorial in his plans for Washington, D.C., it wasn't until 1987 that one was built. The main attraction here is an 860-ton, 100-foot-in-diameter granite map of the world, known as the Granite Sea. It's surrounded by fountains, benches, and six ship masts. The *Lone Sailor,* a 7-foot-tall statue, stands on the map in the Pacific Ocean between the United States and Japan. The Naval Heritage Center, next to the memorial in the Market Square East Building, displays videos and exhibits of uniforms, medals, and other aspects of Navy life. If you've served in the Navy, you can enter your record of service into the Navy Log here. The theater shows a rotating series of Navy-related movies throughout the day. Bronze relief panels on the Pennsylvania Avenue side of the memorial depict 26 scenes commemorating events in the nation's naval history and honoring naval communities. ■ TIP➔ The panels are at a perfect height for children to look at and touch; challenge your child to find these items: a helicopter, a seagull, a U.S. flag, a sailor with binoculars, a dog, penguins, and seals. If you look carefully at the flagpole nearest the entrance to the Heritage Center, you'll see a time capsule, scheduled to be opened in 2093. ✉ *701 Pennsylvania Ave. NW, Downtown* ☎ *202/737–2300* ⊕ *www.navymemorial. org* ✉ *Free* ☉ *24 hrs; Naval Heritage Center Daily 9:30–5* Ⓜ *Archives/ Navy Memorial.*

> **WORD OF MOUTH**
>
> "I hope you did not go to Arlington in the morning. Everyone tends to go first thing. After 3 PM there is almost no one there and you get a much better view of The Changing of the Guard."
> —LaurenKahn1
>
> "While afternoon visits [to Arlington] can be better in terms of view, the sweltering heat and humidity in the summer may greatly hamper the actual time you can spend there." —travelinjo

Official Washington

WORD OF MOUTH

"The main advantage of taking a Capitol tour through the office of your Representative is that the groups they arrange are generally much smaller than those you will find on the "public" tours. The guides can take you on the subway that the Representatives take to get to the House for sessions, votes, etc."

—longhorn55

OFFICIAL WASHINGTON PLANNER

Kid Tips

Before visiting the Capitol, talk to kids about Congress's role in the government and the Capitol's place in history. Then during the tour, encourage them to move up front to see and hear better.

Kids can e-mail the president at ✎ president@whitehouse.gov or send a letter to the White House. The president and first lady even have their own zip code: 20500.

Kids get a kick out of seeing currency printed at the **Bureau of Engraving and Printing.** At the gift shop they can buy bags of shredded bills and get a postcard-size rendering of a dollar with their face in the place of George Washington's.

First Kids Facts

On their first night in the White House, while President Barack Obama and First Lady Michelle Obama were dancing at the inaugural balls, Malia, Sasha, and friends watched movies in the White House theater and went on a scavenger hunt designed to help them learn the ins and outs of their new home. Waiting for them in the East Room were pop heartthrobs the Jonas Brothers. How's that for a sleepover surprise!

December at the White House

The White House is decorated for Christmas during December every year. Even before you enter the State Dining Room, you can smell the gingerbread. The White House gingerbread-house tradition began during the Nixon administration, and has been continued by the White House pastry chefs ever since. In 2006 more than 300 pounds of chocolate and gingerbread were used to create a replica of the White House, complete with presidential pets.

Since 1961 the Christmas tree in the Blue Room has reflected themes. In 1974 the Fords' Christmas-tree ornaments emphasized thrift and recycling. In 1977 the Carters' tree had ornaments made by members of the National Association of Retarded Citizens. In 1991 the Bushes' tree featured needlepoint figurines.

■TIP→ December is far and away the most difficult time of year to secure a tour. The White House is able to accommodate fewer than 10% of the tour requests it receives.

Eggs on a Roll

Kids have been rolling Easter eggs at the White House since at least 1878. Over the years the Egg Rolls have evolved into elaborate affairs with bands and bunnies. The event is held the Monday after Easter, from 8 AM to 2 PM on the South Lawn of the White House.

The National Park Service distributes free tickets on the Saturday before Easter at 7:30 AM and at 7:30 AM the day after Easter on a first-come, first-served basis at the Ellipse Visitor Pavilion (southwest corner of 15th and E streets). Each group has to include at least one child seven years old or under and no more than two adults. Tickets are required for every attendee, including small children, to enter the White House South Lawn. No tickets are necessary for access to activities on the Ellipse.

For the most up-to-date information on the Easter Egg Roll, call the White House 24-hour information line at ☎ 202/456–7041.

Plan Ahead

You can visit many of Washington's government offices, but you have to do some advance planning in many cases—not just for the White House and Congress, but for less high-profile places as well. Here's a rundown of how far in advance you need to make arrangements. For contact information and further details, see listings within this chapter.

SITE	TIME IN ADVANCE
Capitol tour	Morning of visit–3 months
Congressional session	2 weeks–2 months
White House (spring, summer, December)	6 months
White House (other times)	1–2 months
Supreme Court	Morning of visit
American Red Cross	3 business days for Saturday tours
Department of Interior	2–4 weeks
Department of State	3 months
Federal Reserve	24 hours
Pentagon	2 weeks–3 months
Treasury Building	1–2 months

No Advance Planning Required

Two of the most impressive places in Washington don't require advance reservations. The **Library of Congress** and the **Washington National Cathedral** are architectural and artistic treasures.

The cathedral was dubbed at its creation a "House of Prayer for All People," and does indeed draw people from all over the world seeking comfort and reflection. Inside, a stained-glass window with an encapsulated moon rock celebrates the *Apollo 11* space flight, and statues of George Washington and Abraham Lincoln make it clear that this is a place where church and state are welcome to coexist. The library—the largest in the world—is adorned with mosaics, paintings, and statues, not to mention millions of books and manuscripts.

Contact Congress

To visit the White House, you have to make arrangements through your representative or senator. You can find their contact information on the Web at ⊕ www.house.gov and ⊕ www.senate.gov. (You can also find them in your local phone book.)

Don't be reluctant to contact them—it's part of their job, and they have lots of experience handling such requests. Some will even invite you to meet with them and talk about your interests and concerns.

Capitol Visitor Center

After decades of planning and numerous delays, the **Capitol Visitor Center** finally opened on December 2, 2008. The five-football-fields-size underground complex is a destination in itself, with the model of the statue of Freedom, a 530-seat dining room that serves the famous Senate bean soup, and exhibits on the Capitol. It is also the starting point for tours of the Capitol, running Monday through Saturday from 8:30 to 4:30, the last tour beginning at 3:45.

To visit the Capitol, you'll need to either reserve tickets online at ⊕ www.visitthecapitol.gov or contact your representative or senator.

5

By Kathryn McKay and Cathy Sharpe

Given the heightened security concerns of present-day Washington, it might come as a surprise to learn that most government institutions continue to welcome the general public. The Founding Fathers' mandate of a free and open government lives on—just with metal detectors and bag searches. Though security checks are no one's idea of fun, most people find them a small price to pay for the opportunity to get a firsthand look at the government in action. Being in the famous halls of the Capitol, the White House, or the Supreme Court is a heady experience. It's one part celebrity sighting and one part the world's best civics lesson.

While the Capitol, White House, and Supreme Court get the lion's share of the attention, other government institutions hold their own, sometimes-quirky appeal. The Library of Congress is the most visitor-friendly (with no lines and no reservations or tickets necessary), and it's truly impressive, even if you're not a bookworm; the free tour gives you a sense of its scope and grandeur.

If you're fascinated by finance, you'll want to plan ahead for visits to the Bureau of Engraving and Printing, the Federal Reserve, and the Department of Treasury. You need to sign up three months in advance for a tour of the Department of State, but your advance work will be rewarded with a visit to the plush Diplomatic Reception Rooms, where few sightseers tread.

ON THE HILL, UNDER THE DOME: EXPERIENCING THE CAPITOL

In Washington, the Capitol literally stands above it all: by law, no other building in the city can reach the height of the dome's peak.

Beneath its magnificent dome, the day-to-day business of American democracy takes place: senators and representatives debate, coax, and cajole, and ultimately determine the law of the land.

For many visitors, the Capitol is the most exhilarating experience Washington has to offer. It wins them over with a three-pronged appeal:

■ It's the city's most impressive work of architecture.

■ It has on display documents, art, and artifacts from 400 years of American history.

■ Its legislative chambers are open to the public. You can actually see your lawmakers at work, shaping the history of tomorrow.

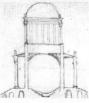

(Clockwise from top left) Moving into the new Capitol circa 1800; 19th–century print by R. Brandard; Thornton sketch circa 1797; the Capitol before the dome.

1792 - 1807 A Man with a Plan

William Thornton, a physician and amateur architect from the West Indies, wins the competition to design the Capitol. His plan, with its central rotunda and dome, draws inspiration from Rome's Pantheon. On September 18, 1793, George Washington lays the Capitol's cornerstone. In November 1800, Congress moves from Philadelphia to take up residence in the first completed section, the boxlike area between the central rotunda and today's north wing. In 1807, the House wing is completed, just to the south of the rotunda; a covered wooden walkway joins the two wings.

1814 - 1826 Washington Burns

In 1814, British troops march on Washington and set fire to the Capitol, the White House, and other government buildings. The wooden walkway is destroyed and the two wings gutted, but the walls remain standing after a violent rainstorm douses the flames. Fearful that Congress might leave Washington, residents fund a temporary "Brick Capitol" on the spot where the Supreme Court is today. By 1826, reconstruction is completed under the guidance of architects Benjamin Henry Latrobe and Charles Bulfinch; a low dome is made of wood sheathed in copper.

1850s - 1880s Domed if You Do

North and south wings are added through the 1850s and '60s to accommodate the growing government of a growing country. To maintain scale with the enlarged building, work begins in 1885 on a taller, cast-iron dome. President Lincoln would be criticized for continuing the expensive project during the Civil War, but he calls the construction "a sign we intend the Union shall go on."

(Clockwise from top left)
The east front circa 1861;
today the Capitol is a
tourist mecca with its
own visitor center;
Freedom statue.

Expanding the Capitol

1960s - Today

The east front is extended 33½ feet, creating 100 additional offices. In 1983 preservationists fight to keep the west front, the last remaining section of the Capitol's original facade, from being extended; in a compromise the facade's crumbling sandstone blocks are replaced with stronger limestone. In 2000 the ground is broken on the subterranean Capitol Visitor Center, to be located beneath the grounds to the building's east side. The extensive facility, three-fourths the size of the Capitol itself, was finally completed on December 2, 2008 to the tune of $621 million.

Freedom atop the Capitol Dome

The twin-shelled Capitol dome, a marvel of 19th-century engineering, rises 285 feet above the ground and weighs 4,500 tons. It can expand and contract as much as 4 inches in a day, depending on the outside temperature.

The allegorical figure on top of the dome is *Freedom*. Sculpted in 1857 by Thomas Crawford, *Freedom* was cast with help from Philip Reid, a slave. Crawford had first planned for the 19½-foot-tall bronze statue to wear the cloth liberty cap of a freed Roman slave, but Southern lawmakers, led by Jefferson Davis, objected. An "American" headdress composed of a star-encircled helmet surmounted with an eagle's head and feathers was substituted. A light just below the statue burns whenever Congress is in session.

Before the visitor center opened, the best way to see the details on the *Freedom* statue atop the Capitol dome was with a good set of binoculars. Now, you can see the original plaster model of this classical female figure up close. Her right hand rests on a sheathed sword, while her left carries a victory wreath and a shield of the United States with 13 stripes. She also wears a brooch with "U.S." on her chest.

THE CAPITOL VISITOR CENTER

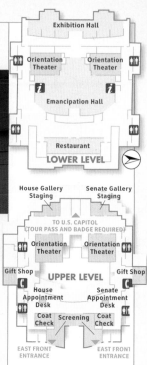

The enormous and sunlit Capitol Visitor Center (CVC) opened to much fanfare on December 2, 2008. It is the start for all Capitol tours, but it is more than just a place to begin. The center brings a new depth to the Capitol experience with orientation theaters, an interactive museum, and live video feeds from the House and Senate. It also provides weary travelers with the creature comforts—a 530-seat restaurant, ample bathrooms, air-conditioning, and two gift shops. All this and it was only $356 million over budget and three years late.

DESIGN
At 580,000 square feet, the visitor center is approximately three-quarters the size of the 775,000-square-foot Capitol. The visitor center's belowground location preserves the historic landscape and views designed by Frederick Law Olmsted in 1874. Inside, skylights provide natural light and views of the majestic Capitol dome.

EMANCIPATION HALL
The center's largest space is a gorgeous sunlit atrium called Emancipation Hall in honor of the slaves who helped to build the Capitol in the 1800s. The plaster model of the *Freedom* statue, which tops the Capitol's dome, anchors the hall. Part of the Capitol's National Statuary Hall collection is also on display here.

MUSEUM
Other attractions include exhibits about the Capitol, historical artifacts, and documents. A marble wall displays historic speeches and decisions by Congress, like President John F. Kennedy's famous 1961 "Man on the Moon" speech and a letter Thomas Jefferson wrote to Congress in 1803 urging the funding of the Lewis and Clark Expedition.

KIDS AT THE CVC

The Capitol Visitor Center is a great place for families with children who may be too young or too wiggly for a tour of the Capitol. In the Exhibition Hall, the 11-foot tall touchable model of the Capitol, touch screen computers, and architectural replicas welcome hands-on exploration.

Challenge younger kids to find statues of a person carrying a spear, a helmet, a book, and a baby.

Tweens can look for statues of the person who invented television, a king, a physician, and a representative who said, "I cannot vote for war."

PLANNING YOUR CAPITOL DAY

LOGISTICS

To tour the Capitol, you can book free, advance passes at ⊕ *www.visitthecapitol.gov* or through your representative's or senator's offices. In addition, a limited number of same-day passes are available at the CVC's Information Desk or at tour kiosks on the east and west fronts of the Capitol. Tours run every 15 minutes; the first tour begins at 8:45 and the last at 3:45, Monday through Saturday. The center is closed on Sunday.

Plan on two to four hours to tour the Capitol and see the visitor center. You should arrive at least 30 minutes before your scheduled tour to allow time to pass through security. Tours, which include a viewing of the orientation film *Out of Many, One*, last about one hour.

If you can't get a pass to tour the Capitol, the Capitol Visitor Center is still worth a visit.

To get passes to the chambers of the House and Senate, contact your representative's or senator's office. Many will also arrange for a staff member to give you a tour of the Capitol or set you up with a time for a Capitol Guide Service tour. When they're in session, some members even have time set aside to meet with constituents. You can link to the e-mail of your representative at ⊕ *www.house.gov* and of your senators at ⊕ *www.senate.gov.*

SECURITY

Expect at least a 30-minute wait going through security when you enter the Capitol Visitor Center. Bags can be no larger than 14 inches wide, 13 inches high, and 4 inches deep, and other possessions you can bring into the building are strictly limited. Take a look at the full list of prohibited items on ⊕ *www. visitthecapitol.gov*. There are no facilities for storing prohibited belongings before you pass through security, but there is a coat check inside the center. For more information, call ☎ *202/226–8000, 202/224–4049 TTY.*

BEAN SOUP AND MORE

A favorite with legislators, the Senate bean soup has been served every day for more than 100 years in the exclusive Senate Dining Room. It's available to the general public in the restaurant of the CVC (⊙ Open 7:30 AM–4 PM) on a rotating basis. You can also try making your own with the recipe on the Senate's Web site (⊕ www. senate.gov).

GETTING HERE—WITHOUT GETTING VOTED IN

The Union Station, Capitol South and Federal Center, SW Metro stops are all within walking distance of the Capitol. Follow the people wearing business suits—chances are they're headed your way. Street parking is extremely limited, but Union Station to the north of the Capitol has a public garage and there is some metered street parking along the Mall to the west of the Capitol.

IN FOCUS 5 ON THE HILL, UNDER THE DOME: EXPERIENCING THE CAPITOL

TOURING THE CAPITOL

National Statuary Hall

To see the Capitol you're required to go on a 30- to 40-minute tour conducted by the Capitol Guide Service. The first stop is the Rotunda, followed by the National Statuary Hall, the Hall of Columns, the old Supreme Court Chamber, the crypt (where there are exhibits on the history of the Capitol), and the gift shop. Note that you *don't* see the Senate or House chambers on the tour. (Turn the page to learn about visiting the chambers.) The highlights of the tour are the first two stops. . . .

THE ROTUNDA

You start off here, under the Capitol's dome. Look up and you'll see *Apotheosis of Washington*, a fresco painted in 1865 by Constantino Brumidi. The figures in the inner circle represent the 13 original states; those in the outer ring symbolize arts, sciences, and industry. Further down, around the Rotunda's rim, a frieze depicts 400 years of American history. The work was started by Brumidi in 1877 and continued by another Italian, Filippo Costaggini. American Allyn Cox added the final touches in 1953.

NATIONAL STATUARY HALL

South of the Rotunda is Statuary Hall, which was once the chamber of the House of Representatives. When the House moved out, Congress invited each state to send statues of two great deceased residents for placement in the hall. Because the weight of the statues threatened to make the floor cave in, and to keep the room from being cluttered, more than half of the sculptures have ended up in other spots in the Capitol. Ask your guide for help finding your state's statues.

ARTIST OF THE CAPITOL

Constantino Brumidi (1805-80) devoted his last 25 years to frescoing the Capitol; his work dominates the Rotunda and the Western Corridor. While painting the section depicting William Penn's treaty with the Indians for the Rotunda's frieze *(pictured above)*, a 74-year-old Brumidi slipped from the 58-foot scaffold, hanging on until help arrived. He would continue work for another four months, before succumbing to kidney failure.

TRY THIS

Because of Statuary Hall's perfectly elliptical ceiling, a whisper uttered along the wall can be heard at the point directly opposite on the other side of the room. Try it when you're there— if it's not noisy, the trick should work.

ONE BIG HAWAIIAN

With a solid granite base weighing six tons, Hawaii's Kamehameha I in Statuary Hall is among the heaviest objects in the collection. On Kamehameha Day (June 11, a state holiday in Hawai'i), the statue is draped with leis.

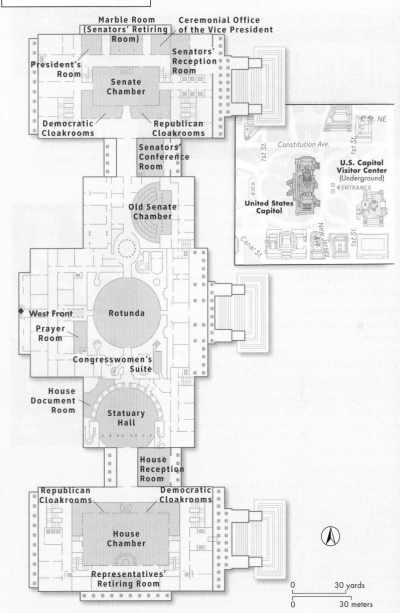

United States Capitol

Marble Room
(Senators' Retiring Room)

Ceremonial Office
of the Vice President

Senators'
Reception
Room

President's
Room

Senate
Chamber

Democratic
Cloakrooms

Republican
Cloakrooms

Senators'
Conference
Room

Old Senate
Chamber

West Front

Rotunda

Prayer
Room

Congresswomen's
Suite

House
Document
Room

Statuary
Hall

House
Reception
Room

Republican
Cloakrooms

Democratic
Cloakrooms

House
Chamber

Representatives'
Retiring Room

C St. NE

Constitution Ave.

1st St.

1st St.

U.S. Capitol
Visitor Center
(Underground)

ENTRANCE

United States
Capitol

Canal St.

New Jersey Ave.

1st St.

0   30 yards

0   30 meters

GOING TO THE FLOOR

A tour of the Capitol is impressive, but the best part of a visit for many people is witnessing the legislators in action. Free gallery passes into the House and Senate chambers have to be obtained from your representative's or senator's office. They aren't hard to come by, but getting them takes some planning ahead. Once you have a pass, it's good for any time the chambers are open to public, for as long as the current Congress is sitting. Senate chambers are closed when the Senate is not in session, but the House is open.

Judiciary Committee

HOUSE CHAMBER
The larger of two chambers may look familiar: it's here that the president delivers the annual State of the Union. When you visit, you sit in the same balcony from which the First Family and guests watch the address.

Look carefully at the panels above the platform where the Speaker of the House sits. They're blue (rather than green like the rest of the panels in the room), and when the House conducts a vote, they light up with the names of the representatives and their votes in green and red.

House session

SENATE CHAMBER
With 100 members elected to six-year terms, the Senate is the smaller and ostensibly more dignified of Congress's two houses. Desks of the senators are arranged in an arc, with Republicans and Democrats divided by the center aisle. The vice president of the United States is officially the "president of the Senate," charged with presiding over the Senate's procedures. Usually, though, the senior member of the majority party oversees day-to-day operations, and is addressed as "Mr. President" or "Madam President."

SWEET SPOT IN THE SENATE
In the sixth desk from the right in the back row of the Senate chamber, a drawer has been filled with candy since 1968. Whoever occupies the desk maintains the stash.

THE SUPREME COURT

✉ *One 1st St. NE, Capitol Hill*
☎ *202/479–3000* ⊕ *www.
supremecourtus.gov* ⌦ *Free*
⊘ *Weekdays 9–4:30; court in
session Oct.–June* Ⓜ *Union
Station or Capitol S.*

5

TIPS

■ The Washington Post carries a daily listing of what cases the court will hear.

■ The court displays its calendar of cases a month in advance on its Web site, but you won't find it on the "Visiting the Court" link. Instead, click on "Oral Arguments."

■ You can't bring your overcoat or electronics such as cameras and cell phones into the courtroom, but you can store them in a coin-operated locker.

■ When court isn't in session, you can hear lectures about the court, typically given every hour on the half hour from 9:30 to 3:30. On the ground floor you can also find revolving exhibits, a video about the court, a gift shop, an information desk, and a larger-than-life statue of John Marshall, the longest-serving chief justice in Supreme Court history.

■ Rumor has it that some lawyers visit the statue of John Marshall to rub the toe of his shoe for good luck on their way to arguing before the Supreme Court.

It wasn't until 1935 that the Supreme Court got its own building: a white-marble temple with twin rows of Corinthian columns designed by Cass Gilbert. Before then, the justices had been moved around to various rooms in the Capitol; for a while they even met in a tavern. William Howard Taft, the only man to serve as both president and chief justice, was instrumental in getting the court a home of its own, though he died before it was completed. Today you can sit in the gallery and see the court in action. Even when court isn't in session, there are still things to see.

HIGHLIGHTS

The court convenes on the first Monday in October and hears cases until April. There are usually two arguments a day at 10 and 11 in the morning, Monday through Wednesday, in two-week intervals.

On mornings when court is in session, two lines form for people wanting to attend. The "three-to-five-minute" line shuttles you through, giving you a quick impression of the court at work. The full-session line gets you in for the whole show. If you want to see a full session, it's best to be in line by at least 8:30. For the most-contentious cases, viewers have been known to queue up the night before. In May and June the court takes to the bench Monday morning at 10 to release orders and opinions. Sessions usually last 15 to 30 minutes and are open to the public.

How does a hardworking Supreme Court justice unwind? Maybe on the building's basketball court, known as "the highest court in the land." It's not open to the public, but try to imagine Antonin Scalia and Ruth Bader Ginsburg trading elbows in the lane.

THE WHITE HOUSE

✉ *1600 Pennsylvania Ave. NW* ☎ *202/208–1631, 202/456–7041 24-hr info line* ⊕ *www.whitehouse.gov* ✉ *Free; reservations required* ◯ *Tours Tues.–Sat. 7:30–12:30* Ⓜ *Federal Triangle, Metro Center, or McPherson Sq.*

TIPS

■ To see the White House you need to contact your representative or senator. To visit in spring or summer, you should make your request about six months in advance.

■ You need a group of 10 or more in order to visit, or the office of your representative or senator may be able to place you with another group.

■ You'll be asked for the names, birth dates, and social security numbers of everyone in your group, and you'll be told where to meet and what you can bring.

■ On the morning of your tour, call the White House Visitors Office information line, ☎ *202/456–7041.* Tours are subject to last-minute cancellation.

■ Arrive 15 minutes early. Your group will be asked to line up in alphabetical order. Everyone 15 years or older must present photo ID. Going through security will probably take as long as the tour itself: 20 to 25 minutes.

America's most famous house was designed in 1792 by Irishman James Hoban. It was known officially as the Executive Mansion until 1902, when President Theodore Roosevelt rechristened it the White House, long its informal name. The house has undergone many structural changes: Andrew Jackson installed running water, James Garfield put in the first elevator, and Harry Truman had the entire structure gutted and restored, adding a second-story porch to the south portico.

HIGHLIGHTS

The self-guided tour includes rooms on the ground floor, but the State Floor has the highlights. The East Room is the largest room in the White House. It's the site of ceremonies and press conferences; it's also where Theodore Roosevelt's children roller-skated and one of Abraham Lincoln's sons harnessed a pet goat to a chair and went for a ride. The portrait of George Washington that Dolley Madison saved from torch-carrying British soldiers in 1814 hangs here. The Green Room is named for the moss-green watered silk covering its walls: the place where President Monroe played cards is now known to news junkies as the site of presidential photo ops with foreign heads of state. The only president to get married in the White House, Grover Cleveland, was wed in the Blue Room. The White House Christmas tree stands in here every winter. The Red Room, decorated in early-19th-century American Empire style, has been a favorite of first ladies. Mary Todd Lincoln had her coffee and read the morning paper here. Bill Clinton's daughter, Chelsea, hosted pizza parties in the State Dining Room, which can seat 140.

The **White House Garden Tour** in mid-October provides an intimate peek at the Rose Garden and Jacqueline Kennedy Garden, among others, while a military band serenades visitors from a balcony above.

The White House

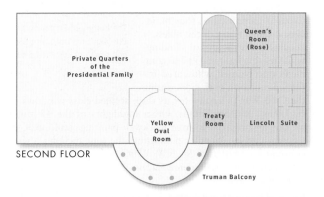

Private Quarters of the Presidential Family

Queen's Room (Rose)

Yellow Oval Room

Treaty Room

Lincoln Suite

SECOND FLOOR

Truman Balcony

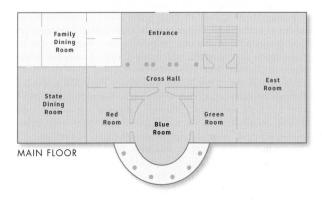

Family Dining Room

Entrance

Cross Hall

East Room

State Dining Room

Red Room

Blue Room

Green Room

MAIN FLOOR

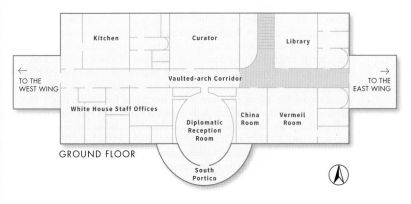

Kitchen

Curator

Library

← TO THE WEST WING

Vaulted-arch Corridor

→ TO THE EAST WING

White House Staff Offices

Diplomatic Reception Room

China Room

Vermeil Room

GROUND FLOOR

South Portico

5

OTHER GOVERNMENT OFFICES AND INSTITUTIONS

American Red Cross. The national headquarters for the American Red Cross is composed of four buildings. Guided tours of the oldest, a neoclassical structure of blinding-white marble built in 1917 to commemorate women who cared for the wounded on both sides during

the Civil War, is known for its three stained-glass windows designed by Louis Comfort Tiffany. Other highlights of the 45-minute tour include an original Norman Rockwell painting, sculptures, and two signature quilts. Weather permitting, the tour includes a visit to the courtyard. ⊠ *430 17th St. NW, White House area* ☎ *202/303–7066* ⊕ *www.redcross.org/museum* ⊠ *Free* ☉ *Tours only, Wed. and Fri. 10 and 2* Ⓜ *Farragut W.*

♻ **Bureau of Engraving and Printing.** Paper money has been printed here since 1914, when the bureau relocated from the redbrick-towered Auditors Building at the corner of 14th Street and Independence Avenue. In addition to the paper currency in the United States, military certificates and presidential invitations are printed here, too. You can only enter the bureau on the tours, which last about 35 minutes. From March through August, free same-day timed-entry tour passes are issued starting at 8 AM at the Raoul Wallenberg Place SW ticket booth. For the rest of the year, tickets aren't used. Waits to get in can be up to two hours in spring and summer, longer if a tour bus unloads just as you arrive. Tickets are not required and waits will likely be short in the off-peak months, September–February. ⊠ *14th and C Sts. SW, The Mall* ☎ *202/874–2330, 866/874–2330 tour information* ⊕ *www. moneyfactory.gov* ⊠ *Free* ☉ *Sept.–Mar., tours weekdays 9–2, visitor center weekdays 8:30–3:30; Apr.–Aug., tours weekdays 9–7, visitor center 8:30–7:30* Ⓜ *Smithsonian.*

Congressional Cemetery. Established in 1807 "for all denomination of people," this cemetery is the final resting place for such notables as U.S. Capitol architect William Thornton, Marine Corps march composer John Philip Sousa, Civil War photographer Mathew Brady, FBI director J. Edgar Hoover, and many members of Congress. Air Force veteran and gay rights activist Leonard Matlovich is also buried here under a tombstone that reads "When I was in the military, they gave me a medal for killing two men and a discharge for loving one." The cemetery is about a 20-minute walk from the Capitol. A brochure with a self-guided walking tour is available at the office and in a mailbox near the main gate. ⊠ *1801 E St. SE, Capitol Hill* ☎ *202/543–0539* ⊕ *www. congressionalcemetery.org* ☉ *Daily dawn–dusk; office weekdays 10–2, Sat. 10–1* Ⓜ *Stadium Armory or Potomac Ave.*

Department of Agriculture. Although there's not a lot to see inside, this gargantuan complex does have a one-room visitor center with displays and audio stations that highlight the nation's agricultural policies. ⊠ *Independence Ave. between 12th and 14th Sts. SW, The Mall* ☎ *202/ 720–2791* ⊕ *www.usda.gov* ✆ *Free* ⊙ *Weekdays 9–3* Ⓜ *Smithsonian.*

> ## CAPITAL FACTS
>
> The largest room in the State Department has a specially loomed carpet so heavy and large it had to be airlifted in by helicopter.

Department of State. U.S. foreign policy is administered by battalions of brainy analysts in the huge Department of State building (often referred to as the State Department). All is presided over by the secretary of state, who is fourth in line for the presidency (after the vice president, Speaker of the House, and president *pro tempore* of the Senate) should the president be unable to serve. On the top floor are the opulent Diplomatic Reception Rooms, decorated like the great halls of Europe and the rooms of wealthy colonial American plantations. Furnishings include a Philadelphia highboy, a Paul Revere bowl, and the desk on which the Treaty of Paris, which ended the Revolutionary War, was signed in 1783. ■ TIP➜ To visit the reception rooms, register online for a tour three months in advance. The tours are recommended for visitors 13 and over. ⊠ *2201 C St. NW, Foggy Bottom* ☎ *202/647–3241, 202/736–4474 TDD* ⊕ *https://receptiontours.state.gov/* ✆ *Free* ⊙ *Tours weekdays at 9:30, 10:30, and 2:45* Ⓜ *Foggy Bottom.*

Department of the Interior. The outside of the building is plain, but inside there's art that reflects the department's work. Heroic oil paintings of dam construction, gold panning, and cattle drives line the hallways. Exhibits in the **Department of the Interior Museum** outline the work of the Bureau of Land Management, the U.S. Geological Survey, the Bureau of Indian Affairs, the National Park Service, and other department branches. The Museum is currently undergoing a two-year modernization project. During this time, public programs will be offered in other parts of the main building on the first Wednesday of every month and tours of the New Deal Murals will be available by appointment. The Indian Craft Shop across the hall from the museum sells Native American pottery, dolls, carvings, jewelry, baskets, and books. ⊠ *1849 C St. NW, White House area* ☎ *202/208–4743* ⊕ *www.doi.gov/interiormuseum* ✆ *Free* ⊙ *Weekdays 8:30–4:30, 3rd Sat. 1–4* Ⓜ *Farragut W.*

Federal Reserve Building. This imposing marble edifice, its bronze entryway topped by a massive eagle, was designed by Folger Library architect Paul Cret. Its appearance seems to say, "Your money's safe with us." Even so, there's no money here (the Fed sets interest rates and thereby tries to keep the economy on track). The building's stately facade belies a friendlier interior, with a varied collection of art and two to three special art exhibitions every year. ⊠ *20th St. and Constitution Ave. NW, Foggy Bottom* ☎ *202/452–3778 self-guided art tours* ⊕ *www.federalreserve. gov/finearts* ✆ *Free* ⊙ *Weekdays 10–3:30 during art exhibitions, self-guided tours of permanent art collection by appointment only 24 hrs to 2 wks in advance* Ⓜ *Foggy Bottom.*

5

★ **Library of Congress.** The largest library in the world has more than 138 million items on approximately 650 mi of bookshelves. Only 21 million of its holdings are books—the library also has 2.9 million recordings, 12.5 million photographs, 5.3 million maps, and 61 million manuscripts. Also here is the Congressional Research Service, which, as the name implies, works on special projects for senators and representatives.

Built in 1897, the copper-domed **Thomas Jefferson Building** is the oldest of the three buildings that make up the library. Like many other structures in Washington, the library was criticized by some as being too florid, but others praised it as the "book palace of the American people," noting that it "out-Europed Europe" in its architectural splendor. The dome, topped with the gilt "Flame of Knowledge"—is certainly decorative, with busts of Dante, Goethe, Nathaniel Hawthorne, and other great writers perched above its entryway. The *Court of Neptune*, Roland Hinton Perry's fountain at the base of the front steps, rivals some of Rome's best fountains.

The Jefferson Building opens into the Great Hall, richly adorned with mosaics, paintings, and curving marble stairways. The grand, octagonal Main Reading Room, its central desk surrounded by mahogany readers' tables under a 160-foot-high domed ceiling, inspires researchers and readers alike. Computer terminals have replaced card catalogs, but books are still retrieved and dispersed the same way: readers (16 years or older) hand request slips to librarians and wait patiently for their materials to be delivered. Researchers aren't allowed in the stacks, and only members of Congress and other special borrowers can check books out. Items from the library's collection—which includes one of only three perfect Gutenberg Bibles in the world—are on display in the Jefferson Building's second-floor Southwest Gallery and Pavilion. Information about current and upcoming exhibitions, which can include oral-history projects, presidential papers, photographs, and the like, is available by phone or Web. ■TIP➔ To even begin to come to grips with the scope and grandeur of the library, taking one of the free hourly tours is highly recommended. Well-informed docents are fonts of fascinating information about the library's history and holdings; they can decode the dozens of quirky allegorical sculptures and paintings throughout the building. ✉ *Jefferson Bldg., 1st St. and Independence Ave. SE, Capitol Hill* 🕾 *202/707–9779* ⊕ *www.loc.gov* 🖪 *Free* ☉ *Mon.–Sat. 8:30–4:30; reading room hrs may extend later. Free tours Mon.–Sat. at 10:30, 11:30, 1:30, and 2:30, and weekdays at 3:30* Ⓜ *Capitol S.*

DID YOU KNOW?

In the blockbuster 2007 movie *National Treasure: Book of Secrets*, the main character played by Nicholas Cage walks through stacks of books in a public area at the Library of Congress. In reality, you can't just take books off the shelves, but you can read books at the library. Go to Room LM140 of the Madison Building with a driver's license or passport and complete a form to get registered to use the library.

5

Pentagon. This office building, the headquarters of the United States Department of Defense, is the largest low-rise office building in the world. Approximately 23,000 military and civilian workers arrive daily. Astonishingly, this mammoth office building, completed in 1943, took less than two years to construct.

Following the September 2001 crash of hijacked American Airlines Flight 77 into the northwest side of the building, the damaged area was removed in just over a month and repaired in a year. Tours of the building are given on a limited basis to educational groups by advance reservation. Tours for the general public may be booked online through the Pentagon Tour Office or through your congressperson's office at least two weeks, but no more than three months, in advance. ⊠ *I–395 at Columbia Pike and Rte. 27* ☎ *703/697–1776* ⊕ *pentagon.afis.osd.mil* Ⓜ *Pentagon.*

> **FIRST KID FACTS**
>
> Mom-in-Chief Michelle Obama set boundaries for her daughters at the White House before they even moved in. Sasha and Malia may live in the most famous house in America, but bedtime is still at 8 PM and they still have to do their chores. In an interview, Michelle Obama told Barbara Walters what she said to the White House ushers: "I said, 'You know, we're gonna have to set up some boundaries. Don't make their beds. Make mine. But skip the kids'—let 'em make their own beds.' They have to learn these things." Only after they've completed their chores do they receive their weekly $1 allowance.

Ronald Reagan Building and International Trade Center. This $818 million, 3.1-million-square-foot colossus is the largest federal building to be constructed in the Washington area since the Pentagon, and the first to be designed for use by both the government and the private sector. A blend of classical and modern architecture, the Indiana-limestone structure replaced what for 50 years had been an enormous parking lot. The Reagan Building houses the Environmental Protection Agency, the U.S. Customs Service, and the U.S. Agency for International Development. The **D.C. Visitor Information Center** (☎ *202/638–7330 or 866/324–7386* ⊕ *www.dchamber.org*), located here, is a convenient place to pick up brochures and see a free historical video. There's also a touch-screen computer kiosk with information about the city. Hours for the visitor center are weekdays 9–4:30. The building has a food court on the lower level, and a theatrical group, the Capitol Steps, performs works of political satire here on Friday and Saturday nights at 7:30. ⊠ *1300 Pennsylvania Ave. NW, East End* ⊕ *www.itcdc.com* 🖅 *Free* Ⓜ *Federal Triangle.*

Treasury Building. Once used to store currency, this is the largest Greek Revival edifice in Washington. Robert Mills, the architect responsible for the Washington Monument and the Patent Office (now the Smithsonian American Art Museum), designed the grand colonnade that stretches down 15th Street. After the death of President Lincoln, the Andrew Johnson Suite was used as the executive office by the new president while Mrs. Lincoln moved out of the White House. Other vestiges of its earlier days are the two-story marble Cash Room and the gilded west

dome. One-hour tours arranged through Congress are available most Saturdays at 9, 9:45, 10:30, and 11:15 for U.S. citizens and legal residents. ⊠ *15th St. and Pennsylvania Ave. NW, White House area* ☎ *202/622–0146 TDD* ⊕ *www.ustreas.gov/education* Ⓜ *McPherson Sq. or Metro Center.*

> ### CAPITAL FACTS
>
> Skilled stone carvers have adorned the Washington National Cathedral with fanciful gargoyles and grotesques, including one of Darth Vader.

Fodor's Choice ★ **Washington National Cathedral.** Construction of Washington National Cathedral—the sixth-largest cathedral in the world—started in 1907; it was finished and consecrated in 1990. Like its 14th-century Gothic counterparts, the stunning National Cathedral (officially the Cathedral Church of St. Peter and St. Paul) has a nave, flying buttresses, transepts, and vaults that were built stone by stone. State funerals for Presidents Eisenhower, Reagan, and Ford were held here, and the tomb of Woodrow Wilson, the only president buried in Washington, is on the nave's south side. ■ TIP➜ The expansive view of the city from the Pilgrim Gallery is exceptional. The cathedral is Episcopalian, but it's the site of frequent ecumenical and interfaith services. On the grounds of the cathedral is the compact, English-style **Bishop's Garden.** Boxwoods, ivy, tea roses, yew trees, and an assortment of arches, bas-reliefs, and stonework from European ruins provide a counterpoint to the cathedral's towers. The Cathedral's Flower Mart held annually on the first Friday and Saturday in May is one of Washington's premiere festivals. Traditionally, lobster rolls are on sale during the Friday festival. ⊠ *Wisconsin and Massachusetts Aves. NW, Upper Northwest* ☎ *202/537–6200, 202/537–6207 tour information* ⊕ *www.nationalcathedral.org* ⊠ *Suggested tour donation $5* ⊙ *Weekdays 10–5:30, Sat. 10–4:30, Sun. 8–4 (8–1 for worship only). Tours: weekdays 10–11:30 and 1–4, Sat. 10–11:30 and 12:45–3:30, Sun. 1–2:30 (tours are every 30 mins). Gardens open daily dawn–dusk* Ⓜ *Cleveland Park or Tenleytown. Take any 30 series bus.*

Washington Post Building. Although the newspaper is no longer printed here, you can see the newsroom that broke the Watergate story on a 45-minute guided tour of the building, which is otherwise not open to the public. In addition to the newsroom, there's a small museum dedicated to the history of the newspaper and old and new printing processes. ■ TIP➜ Tours are given only for organized groups of 10 to 25 people, by reservation, and children must be at least 11 years old. You can reserve up to four weeks in advance; call for further information. ⊠ *1150 15th St. NW, Downtown* ☎ *202/334–7969* ⊕ *www.washpost.com/community* ⊠ *Free* ⊙ *Tours every 3rd Mon. at 10, 11, and noon.* Ⓜ *McPherson Sq. or Metro Center.*

SEX! POWER! MONEY!

★ ★ ★

SCANDALOUS WASHINGTON

Above: New York Governor Eliot Spitzer (aka Client 9) at a March 10, 2008 news conference apologizing for his involvement in a prostitution ring at D.C.'s Mayflower Hotel. He announced his resignation two days later.

Every "gotcha!" headline since President Nixon's burglars at the Watergate has been affixed with a "-gate," but Washington's memory of kickbacks, sleaze, and dirty deeds goes back centuries further. Before there was Monica, there was Marilyn; before Marilyn, there was Carrie and Peggy and Nan. Most people are familiar with Whitewater, but what of the Star Route and Teapot Dome? The history of the United States is thick with plots, scams, and bad behavior. Herewith, selections from Washington's long and democratic history of scandal.

SEX!

Petticoat Tales

Margaret "Peggy" Eaton

Ooh la la, whispered Washington's society matrons, when President Andrew Jackson's war secretary John Henry Eaton fell for Margaret "Peggy" Timberlake, a young widow he had known for years. Pretty, charming Peggy had a fast reputation for 1829, and soon rumors flew about the circumstances of her husband's death, the paternity of her two children, and Eaton. It was all idle gossip—until Eaton married her, after which the other Cabinet wives shunned her, and the social stir of insult and offense all but shut down business at the White House for *two years.* In 1831, the Cabinet resigned en masse and Jackson was finally able to get some work done. As for Peggy? After Eaton's death, she sparked another scandal, by marrying her granddaughter's 19-year-old dance instructor. *(Location: Peggy Eaton is buried in Oak Hill Cemetery, 3001 R St. NW)*

Fanne Fox

Naked Ambition

In 1974, Wilbur Mills spent his days chairing the House Ways and Means Committee—and his nights with a stripper known as "Fanne Fox, the Argentine Firecracker." A typical Capitol romance, until his car was stopped one night by police, and his lady friend leapt from the car and into the Tidal Basin, leaving a drunken Mills to his fate. Surprisingly, Mills' political career survived—until he appeared later that year, drunk, onstage with Fox at a Boston burlesque. *(Location: Tidal Basin)*

Hail to the Cheat

Warren Harding

President Bill Clinton was hardly the first and likely not the worst of the White House philanderers. That dubious honor may go to President Warren Harding, a legendary Lothario who is purported to have carried on with paramours Carrie Phillips and Nan Britton (among others) in some unlikely places, including a White House closet. (When his wife Florence came by, a Secret Service agent warned him with a discreet knock on the door.) Relative propriety in the 1920's press meant that any blue dresses remained unreported, but Harding may have left behind a more incriminating piece of evidence—an illegitimate daughter, Elizabeth Ann. *(Location: White House)*

POWER!

Former CIA officer Valerie Plame

Reporters Bob Woodward, left, and Carl Bernstein, whose reporting of the Watergate scandal won them a Pulitzer Prize, sit in the newsroom of the *Washington Post* on May 7, 1973.

He Really Bugs Me

The Big Kahuna of Washington scandals had humble beginnings, in the discovery of a taped-open door at the Watergate Hotel one night in June of 1972. The door led to burglars, on a mission to bug the Democratic National Committee, and the burglars led through the Republican party machine straight to the White House and President Richard "Tricky Dick" Nixon. Two young reporters, Bob Woodward and Carl Bernstein, uncovered the most impossible-seeming story of the century, and their secret meetings with anonymous leaker "Deep Throat" (W. Mark Felt) are the stuff of legend. One of many fond memories of the moment when Washington lost America's trust: Nixon's immortal, and untruthful, declaration, "I am not a crook." *(Location: Watergate Hotel, Virginia Ave., near 27th St. NW)*

I Spy . . .

When Valerie Plame had her CIA cover blown in 2003—in print, by a syndicated columnist—Washington's shady nexus of journalists, politicians, and sneaky leaks was, too. Who let the cat out of the bag, to whom, and most importantly, why? Vice President Dick Cheney's chief aide, Lewis "Scooter" Libby, was convicted, but only of lying to investigators. If Plame was targeted because of her husband's slapdown to the Bush Administration over the Iraq war, whoever targeted her got away with it.

From Ronald with Love

OLIVER L NORTH
DOB 10 7 43

Oliver North

Two wrongs *can* make a right: a right-wing guerilla organization, that is. President Ronald Reagan likened Nicaragua's Contras to the Founding Fathers. Too bad funding the insurgent group was illegal. So was a secret deal the White House made to sell arms to Iran. When it was discovered in 1986 that the cash from Iran had been funneled to the Contras, the Gipper had some explaining to do. Luckily for him, National Security Council aide Oliver North had a shredder, and he wasn't afraid to use it. North's secretary, Fawn Hall, took care of the rest by smuggling out remaining suspect documents in her boots and skirt. *(Location: Old Executive Office Building, 17th & F Streets NW)*

MONEY!

William Adams Richardson

Teapot Dome scandal cartoon by Clifford Kennedy Berryman

A Cozy Deal

It may seem old hat today—access to public resources awarded in a no-bid contract to cronies of someone in the president's inner circle—but in 1922 it was front-page news. Interior Secretary Albert Fall had authority over the Teapot Dome strategic oil reserve transferred from the Department of the Navy to Interior, and once he was in charge, he leased the land to Mammoth Oil. The deal was technically legal—what *wasn't* was the $404,000 kickback he got for arranging it. Fall nearly succeeded in keeping his stake quiet, until he raised suspicions by having the office of the lead Senate investigator ransacked. *(Location: Department of Interior, 1849 C St. NW)*

Secretary of Shame

In 1872, the House of Representatives was so determined to remove War Secretary William Belknap that it voted to impeach him, even after he had already resigned. The high-living general was caught having awarded a lucrative military trading post appointment in exchange for kickbacks; the quarterly bribes he took came to ten times his official salary. The House's venom waxed poetic: legislators voted unanimously that the Secretary was "basely prostituting his high office to his lust for private gain." Belknap resigned in disgrace—and tears—and committed suicide in 1890. *(Location: House of Representatives)*

Taxman to Axman

When Treasury Secretary William Richardson hired contractor-cum-bounty hunter John Sanborn in 1872 to help the IRS collect taxes, the idea was simple. Sanborn chased down tax cheats, and was allowed to keep half of the take for his trouble. But when he ran out of tax evaders and went after honest companies, Richardson turned a blind eye—in exchange for his own cut.

The Sheik of Bribery

If Middle Eastern "businessmen" looking suspiciously like FBI agents offered *you* cash for favors, you might smell a rat—particularly if their business cards read "Abdul Enterprises." But in 1978, seven legislators gave just such men the benefit of the doubt, and had their trusting natures (and brazen avarice) rewarded with bribery convictions. Hint: Next time, guys, check the shiny shoes.

Where to Eat

WORD OF MOUTH

"We always go to the Old Ebbitt Grill. Just make a reservation. You will be glad you did. It has the best atmosphere in town. It's on 15th Street very close to the White House. . . . You will love the location near the museums and memorials."

—trillford

THE SCENE

Updated by
Elana Schor

As host to visitors and transplants from around the world, Washington benefits from the constant infusion of different cultures. Despite D.C.'s lack of true ethnic neighborhoods and the kinds of restaurant districts found in many other cities, you *can* find almost any cuisine here, from Burmese to Ethiopian. Just follow your nose.

Although most neighborhoods lack a unified culinary flavor, make no mistake: D.C. is a city of distinctive areas, each with its own style. Adams Morgan, for example, is known for its small family-run eateries. You'll find Ethiopian restaurants next to Italian trattorias and French bistros. These small ethnic spots open and close frequently; it's worth taking a stroll down the street to see what's new. The Chinatown area is often disparaged by D.C. natives for lacking the authenticity of New York's or San Francisco's, but its Asian kitchens are the finest outside the less accessible Virginia suburbs.

Downtown, you'll find many of the city's blue-chip law firms and deluxe, expense-account restaurants, as well as stylish lounges, microbrew pubs, and upscale eateries that have sprung up to serve the crowds that attend games at the Verizon Center.

Wherever you venture forth in the city, there are a few trends worth noting: Spanish tapas eateries and other restaurants serving small tasting portions are bigger than ever. You'll find this style of eating pervasive, whether you're at a Modern Greek, Asian, or American restaurant. High-end restaurants in town also have begun to add bar menus with smaller plates that are much less expensive than their entrées, but created with the same finesse.

Though Italian, French, and fusion spots continue to open at a ferocious pace, Washingtonians are always hungry to try something new, whether it's Chinese smoked lobster, fiery Indian curry, or crunchily addictive Vietnamese spring rolls.

UPPER NORTHWEST
casual neighborhood joints

ADAMS MORGAN AND U STREET CORRIDOR
ethnic eats and quirky bars

SHAW
trendy restaurants and hip lounges

GEORGETOWN
mix of white-tablecloth and no-tablecloth eateries

DUPONT CIRCLE
upscale, stylish restaurants with lively bar scene

CHINATOWN
tapas-style restaurants with eclectic cuisine

FOGGY BOTTOM
cheap cafés popular with students

DOWNTOWN
revitalized arts district with upscale eateries

CAPITOL HILL
pub grub and cafés aplenty for harried staffers

Sheridan Circle

Dupont Circle

Scott Circle

Logan Circle

Thomas Circle

Washington Circle

Columbia Rd.

Florida Ave.

Florida Ave.

16th St.

Vermont Ave.

New Hampshire Ave.

Massachusetts Ave.

Rhode Island Ave.

Connecticut Ave.

M St.

M St.

K St.

15th St.

14th St.

New York Ave.

Rock Creek

Whitehurst Fwy.

Washington Circle

Pennsylvania Ave.

23rd St.

Virginia Ave.

Constitution Ave.

Theodore Roosevelt Island

Reflecting Pool

THE MONUMENTS

THE MALL

Independence Ave.

Arlington Memorial Br.

Columbia Island

Tidal Basin

Potomac River

Francis Case Memorial Br.

Washington Canal

VIRGINIA

| 0 | | 500 yards |
| 0 | | 500 meters |

WHERE TO EAT PLANNER

Eating-Out Strategy

Where should we eat? With hundreds of D.C. eateries competing for your attention, it may seem like a daunting question. But fret not—our expert writers and editors have done most of the legwork. The 100-plus selections here represent the best this city has to offer—from hot dogs to haute cuisine. Search "Best Bets" for top recommendations by price, cuisine, and experience. Sample local flavor in the neighborhood features. Or find a review quickly in the alphabetical-by-neighborhood listings. Delve in, and enjoy!

Kid-Friendly

Though it's unusual to see children in the dining rooms of D.C.'s most elite restaurants, eating with youngsters in the nation's capital does not have to mean culinary exile. Many of the restaurants reviewed in this chapter are excellent choices for families and are marked with a ☺ symbol.

Smoking

Smoking is banned in all restaurants and bars.

Reservations

Plan ahead if you're determined to snag a sought-after reservation. Some renowned restaurants are booked weeks in advance. But you can get lucky at the last minute if you're flexible—and friendly. Most restaurants keep a few tables open for walk-ins and VIPs. Show up for dinner early (5:30 PM) or late (after 10 PM) and politely inquire about any last-minute vacancies or cancellations. If you're calling a few days ahead of time, ask if you can be put on a waiting list. Occasionally, an eatery may ask you to call the day before your scheduled meal to reconfirm: don't forget, or you could lose out.

What to Wear

As unfair as it seems, the way you look can influence how you're treated—and where you're seated. Generally speaking, jeans and a button-down shirt will suffice at most table-service restaurants in the $–$$ range. Moving up from there, some pricier restaurants require jackets, and some insist on ties. In reviews, we mention dress only when men are required to wear a jacket or a jacket and tie. But even when there's no formal dress code, we recommend wearing jackets and ties in $$$ and $$$$ restaurants. If you have doubts, call the restaurant and ask.

Hours

Washington has less of an around-the-clock mentality than other big cities, with many big-name restaurants shutting down between lunch and dinner and closing their kitchens by 11 PM. Weekend evenings spent Downtown can also be a hassle for those seeking quick bites, since many popular chain eateries cater to office workers and shut down on Friday at 6 PM. For a midnight supper, the best bets are Dupont Circle and the U Street Corridor, while families looking for late lunches should head north from the Mall to find kitchens that stay open between meals.

Tipping and Taxes

In most restaurants, tip the waiter 16%–20%. (To figure the amount quickly, just double the sales tax noted on the check—it's 10% of your bill.) Tip at least $1 per drink at the bar, and $1 for each coat checked. Never tip the maître d' unless you're out to impress your guests or expect to pay another visit soon.

If you're dining with a group, make sure not to overtip: review your check to see if a gratuity has been added, as many restaurants automatically tack on an 18% tip for groups of six or more.

Prices

If you're watching your budget, be sure to ask the price of daily specials recited by the waiter or captain. The charge for specials at some restaurants is noticeably out of line with the other prices on the menu. Beware of the $10 bottle of water; ask for tap water instead. And always review your bill.

If you eat early or late you may be able to take advantage of a prix-fixe deal not offered at peak hours. Most upscale restaurants offer great lunch deals with special menus at cut-rate prices designed to give customers a true taste of the place.

Credit cards are widely accepted, but many restaurants (particularly smaller ones Downtown) accept only cash. If you plan to use a credit card, it's a good idea to double-check its acceptability when making reservations or before sitting down to eat.

Some restaurants are marked with a price range ($$–$$$, for example). This indicates one of two things: either the average cost straddles two categories, or if you order strategically, you can get out for less than most diners spend.

In This Chapter

Restaurant Week

Almost 200 restaurants participate in **Restaurant Week** (⊕ *www.washington.org/ restaurantwk*), a popular mid-August food fest offering three-course lunches and dinners at wonderfully low fixed prices. This is the time to sample those A-list restaurants at much more affordable prices.

6

WHAT IT COSTS

	¢	$	$$	$$$	$$$$
AT DINNER	under $10	$10–$17	$18–$25	$26–$35	over $35

Price per person for an average main course or equivalent combination of smaller dishes. Note: f a restaurant offers only prix-fixe (set-price) meals, it has been given the price category that reflects the full prix-fixe price.

BEST BETS FOR D.C. DINING

With thousands of restaurants to choose from, how will you decide where to eat? Fodor's writers and editors have selected their favorite restaurants by price, cuisine, and experience in the lists below. You can also search by neighborhood for excellent eating experiences—just peruse the following pages. Or find specific details about a restaurant in the full reviews, which are listed alphabetically by neighborhood later in the chapter.

Fodor's Choice ★

2 Amys $, p. 217
2941 Restaurant $$$, p. 219
Blue Duck Tavern $$–$$$, p. 213
Central Michel Richard $$–$$$, p. 200
Citronelle $$$$, p. 208
Hank's Oyster Bar $–$$, p. 210
Inn at Little Washington $$$$, p. 220
Komi $$$$, p. 210
Nora $$–$$$, p. 211
Palena $$–$$$, p. 218
Rasika $$–$$$, p. 206
Teaism ¢, p. 203
Zaytinya $$, p. 207

Best By Price

¢

Ben's Chili Bowl, p. 215
Rocklands, p. 210

$

Etete, p. 216
Granville Moore's Brickyard, p. 197
Matchbox, p. 205

$$

Café Atlántico, p. 204
Jaleo, p. 205

$$$

Hook, p. 209

$$$$

Charlie Palmer Steak, p. 197
CityZen, p. 200
Equinox, p. 201

Best By Cuisine

AFRICAN

Etete $, p. 216

AMERICAN

2941 Restaurant $$$, p. 219
Blue Duck Tavern $$–$$$, p. 213
Cashion's Eat Place $$–$$$, p. 214
Inn at Little Washington $$$$, p. 220

ASIAN (VARIOUS)

Full Kee $–$$, p. 205
Teaism ¢, p. 203

TenPenh $$–$$$, p. 204

BELGIAN

Belga Café $–$$, p. 196
Brasserie Beck $$–$$$, p. 199
Granville Moore's Brickyard $, p. 197
Marcel's $$$, p. 214

ECLECTIC

Ardeo $–$$, p. 217
Komi $$$$, p. 210
Palena $$–$$$, p. 218

FRENCH

Bistro Bis $$–$$$, p. 196
Bistro Français $$–$$$, p. 207
Central Michel Richard $$–$$$, p. 200
Montmartre $–$$, p. 198

GREEK/TURKISH

Cafe Divan $, p. 208
Zaytinya $$, p. 207

INDIAN

Heritage India $–$$, p. 218
Rasika $$–$$$, p. 206

ITALIAN

Café Milano $$$, p. 208
Obelisk $$$$, p. 211

JAPANESE

Kaz Sushi Bistro $$,
p. 202

Sushi-Ko $–$$, p. 210

LATIN AMERICAN

Café Atlántico $$,
p. 204

Ceiba $$–$$$, p. 200

PIZZA

2 Amys $, p. 217

Matchbox $–$$,
p. 205

SEAFOOD

Black Salt $$–$$$,
p. 218

Hook $$$, p. 209

Johnny's Half Shell
$$, p. 197

Oceanaire Seafood
Room $$–$$$, p. 202

SOUTHERN

Georgia Brown's
$–$$, p. 201

Oohhs & Aahhs ¢,
p. 216

Zola $–$$, p. 207

SPANISH

Jaleo $$, p. 205

Taberna del Alabard-
ero $$–$$$, p. 203

STEAKHOUSE

Capital Grille $$$,
p. 200

Charlie Palmer Steak
$$$$, p. 197

The Palm $$$, p. 212

Best By Experience

BEST BRUNCH

Belga Café $–$$,
p. 196

Black Salt $$–$$$,
p. 218

Georgia Brown's
$–$$, p. 201

Hook $$$, p. 209

BEST FOR BUSINESS

Capital Grille $$$,
p. 200

Charlie Palmer Steak
$$$$, p. 197

The Palm $$$, p. 212

BEST HOTEL DINING

Blue Duck Tavern
$$–$$$, p. 213

Citronelle $$$$,
p. 208

CityZen $$$$, p. 200

Poste $$, p. 206

BEST POLITICO-WATCHING

Cafe Milano $$$,
p. 208

Charlie Palmer Steak
$$$$, p. 197

BEST WITH KIDS

Kramerbooks & After-
words $, p. 211

The Market Lunch
¢–$, p. 198

Rocklands ¢–$,
p. 210

CAPITAL CLASSICS

1789 Restaurant $$$,
p. 207

Ben's Chili Bowl ¢–$,
p. 215

Occidental Grill
$$–$$$, p. 202

GOOD FOR GROUPS

Heritage India $–$$,
p. 218

Malaysia Kopitiam $,
p. 211

Zaytinya $$, p. 207

GREAT VIEWS

2941 Restaurant $$$,
p. 219

Charlie Palmer Steak
$$$$, p. 197

PRETHEATER

Café Atlántico $$,
p. 204

Jaleo $$, p. 205

Rasika $$–$$$, p. 206

QUIET MEAL

Equinox $$$$, p. 201

Obelisk $$$$, p. 211

Palena $$–$$$, p. 218

Taberna del Alabard-
ero $$–$$$, p. 203

SPECIAL OCCASION

2941 Restaurant $$$,
p. 219

Citronelle $$$$,
p. 208

CityZen $$$$, p. 200

Minibar at Café
Atlántico $$$$,
p. 205

TRENDY

1905 $$, p. 215

Café Atlántico $$,
p. 204

Marvin $$, p. 216

Rasika $$–$$$,
p. 206

Westend Bistro by
Eric Ripert $$, p. 214

Zaytinya $$, p. 207

WINE BARS

Bistrot Lepic $–$$,
p. 217

Sonoma $$–$$$,
p. 198

Vidalia $$–$$$, p. 213

6

CAPITOL HILL

"The Hill," as locals know it, was once an enclave of congressional boardinghouses in the shadow of the Capitol building, but is now D.C.'s largest historic district, with an eclectic mix of restaurants.

The neighborhood's central location has kept it an integral and thriving part of D.C. from the beginning. With the House, Senate, Supreme Court, Library of Congress, and other offices nearby, government is a constant presence.

Around the Capitol South Metro station, government offices end and neighborhood dining begins. Here, along tree-lined streets, you'll find neighborhood bars and restaurants that cater to lunch and happy-hour crowds during the week and local residents on weekends. The neighborhood can turn a bit sleepy when Congress is on recesses.

New upscale restaurants have opened alongside neighborhood establishments on historic Barracks Row (⊠ *8th St. SE*), giving the Row a fresh, hip vibe.
—*Samantha Cleaver*

WORLD FLAVOR

Travel to one of Barracks Row's restaurants with international flair: **Belga Café** (⊠ *514 8th St. SE* ⊕ *2:H6*), with 84 Belgian beer varieties is "the godfather of beer," says executive chef Bart Vandaele. Pair yours with smoked foie gras or shrimp-stuffed tomatoes. Upstairs, **Banana Café** (⊠ *500 8th St. SE* ⊕ *2:H6*) is a rousing piano bar; downstairs it's a Cuban restaurant. The **Starfish Café** (⊠ *539 8th St. SE* ⊕ *2:H6*) combines Creole and Caribbean cuisines, with selections like seviche and crab cakes, while **Tortilla Café** (⊠ *210 7th St. SE* ⊕ *2:H6*) specializes in Salvadorean tamales known as pupusas.

CAPITOL HILL HOT SPOTS

NONPARTISAN PUBS

Escape politics as usual at these bars and eateries favored by lobbyists, senators, and congressional representatives.

Tune Inn (✉ *331 Pennsylvania Ave. SE ✛ 2:H5*) is Capitol Hill's last remaining dive bar. Here "you can plop down on a bar stool and be next to absolutely anybody," according to owner Lysa Nardelli. That "anybody" could be a senator or a congressional intern. The bar has a taxidermy theme, with stuffed deer heads decorating the walls. Stuffed deer backsides mark the location of restrooms.

Next door, **Hawk and Dove** (✉ *329 Pennsylvania Ave. SE ✛ 2:H5*) is the city's oldest Irish bar and a political hot spot. The atmosphere may be old Irish pub, but the daily specials venture into American cuisine. Daily after-work specials include a $3.25 "pint of the night," and sandwiches and burgers are available until 11 PM on weeknights.

The Monocle (✉ *107 D St. NE ✛ 2:G3*) has been serving up "tablecloth" dining to senators and staff since 1960. The restaurant's location, a quick dash from the Senate office at the Capitol, gives it an insider-y feel. Head to the bar for jumbo salads, roasted oysters, and fried calamari.

H IS FOR HIPSTER

Follow H Street away from the Capitol and you'll find the new Atlas District, where eclectic bars bring out politicos in heels and kids in sneakers. Live music complements the Creole bordello vibe at the **Red & the Black** (✉ *1212 H St. NE ✛ 2:H2*), where happy-hour deals last from 6 PM to 8 PM every night, while **The Pug** (✉ *1234 H St. NE ✛ 2:H2*) offers $3 beers all day long and hipster-cool games like Rock-'em Sock-'em Robots. Elsewhere, the **Palace of Wonders** (✉ *1210 H St. NE ✛ 2:H2*) boasts rotating drink specials daily—but the traveling sideshows and eye-popping circus memorabilia on the walls are the biggest draw.

HAUTE CONGRESS

Since America's founding, the Capitol has been ruled by tradition: everyone sits in assigned seats, speaks according to seniority, and expects indigestion from the congressional cafeterias. But that last custom became a thing of the past in 2007, when the nine dining spots in the House of Representatives received a classy makeover courtesy of the Manhattan catering firm Restaurant Associates. The day-old pizza was replaced with fresh grilled fish and build-your-own tacos, the limp iceberg lettuce with arugula, snap peas, and hand-tossed *panzanella* (bread and tomato) salad. Any visitor to the Capitol is free to feast at the renovated cafeterias alongside legislators and their aides. The Senate's three cafés are slated for their own posh remodeling this year—but history buffs can rest assured the bean soup that has been a menu staple since 1901 will still be available.

6

DOWNTOWN, CHINATOWN, AND WHITE HOUSE AREA

Don't let the staid steak houses and saloons fool you—the capital power brokers who dine Downtown also have a taste for the quirky and fun. The area is experiencing a boom of high-concept openings.

At the popular Latin restaurant Ceiba, above, fans rave about the seviche and caipirinhas.

Until recently, tourists who trekked north from the Mall hungry for something more than Smithsonian cafeteria food were stranded Downtown with little but high-end options. Now young Washingtonians are taking advantage of residential development and moving off Capitol Hill to Downtown, pulling trendy and affordable dining choices up north.

Chinatown and nearby Penn Quarter are the nerve center of the area, thanks to the Verizon Center and a row of popular clothing stores, but the crowds mean an inevitable wait for tables.

If you're in the mood to splurge without feeling like a stuffed shirt, perennials like **Oceanaire Seafood Room** (⊠ *1201 F St. NW* ✛ *2:C3*) and **Ceiba** (⊠ *701 14th St. NW* ✛ *2:B2*) have a more relaxed vibe on weekends.
—*Elana Schor*

MARKET SHARE

The nation's capital may be an urban jungle, but its farmers' markets are rightly revered for offering an oasis of fresh food from northern Virginia. Penn Quarter's outdoor bazaar takes over 8th Street NW between D and E streets every Thursday from 3 PM to 7 PM between April and November, transporting shoppers into the country-side with grape tomatoes from Endless Summer Harvest, and goat cheese from Blue Ridge Dairy.

D.C. FOODIES ARE BUZZING ABOUT...

FRESH FOOD FINDS

Proof (✉ 775 G St. NW ✛ 2:D2) is one of our favorite new wine-centric restaurants. Its Modern American menu spotlights locally grown ingredients and offers 30-plus choices of wines by the glass.

If you spot a strange, shockingly green pushcart while museum hopping, stop and enjoy **On the Fly** (✉ H St. and 8th St. NW ✛ 2:D2), the city's environmentally friendly route to a gourmet organic lunch.

For a quick bite on the go, visit the Californian cheese whizzes at **Cowgirl Creamery** (✉ 919 F St. NW ✛ 2:C3), where free samples of homemade cheese abound.

STARS OF THE KITCHEN

Meet three of downtown Washington's best, and enjoy their most special dishes.

Jose Andres. Since he began serving up tapas from **Jaleo's** (✉ 480 7th St. NW ✛ 2:D3) kitchen in 1993, Andres has become a capital legend. The biggest of his many talents: enticing skeptical Americans to embrace the octopus, a favorite of his native Spain. It never misses.

Alain Ducasse. The youngest chef in history to win three Michelin stars, this debonair Frenchman has chosen a worthy partner in the St. Regis hotel company. Ducasse's unifying theme at the new **Adour** (✉ 923 16th St. NW ✛ 1:G6) is "cuisine designed with wine in mind"—but with a $370 Osetra caviar on the menu, drama is also the order of the day.

Laurent Tourondel. This wizard of the grill charged south from Manhattan for his latest outpost of the lavish **BLT Steak** (✉ 1625 I St. NW ✛ 2:A2), where the free baskets of warm Gruyère-cheese popovers are so wildly in demand that you can now take a copy of the recipe home.

FOOD CHAIN

Most visitors to D.C. pack their days with as many events as possible, often leaving little time for an exciting new food experience. But even quick bites can become adventurous for those who know when to pass up McDonald's in favor of a quirky local chain. The capital's three best homegrown franchises have convenient Downtown locations. **Firehook Bakery** (✉ 912 17th St. NW ✛ 2:A2 and 555 13th St. NW ✛ 2:B3) is known for its cold salads, such as lemon orzo and curried chicken, and decadent cookies—try the Presidential Sweet, made with dried cherries. **Marvelous Market** (✉ 1800 K St. NW ✛ 1:F6) serves everything from pesto lasagna to a ham, Brie, and cornichon sandwich that would be right at home in Paris. **Wasabi** (✉ 908 17th St. NW ✛ 1:G6) is a sushi shop with kicky mod decor that wraps its tuna rolls in takeout-friendly cellophane. Raw-fish skeptics can choose chicken soup with udon noodles or teriyaki salmon.

6

GEORGETOWN

Georgetown's picturesque Victorian streetscapes make it D.C.'s most famous neighborhood, with five-star restaurants in historic row houses and casual cafés sandwiched between large national chain stores.

At its beginnings in the mid-1700s, Georgetown was a Maryland tobacco port. Today the neighborhood is D.C.'s premier shopping district, as well as a tourist and architectural attraction. The neighborhood's restaurants range from upscale Italian to down-home barbecue. Residents' resistance to opening a Metro station in the area was once a touchy subject, but more frequent bus service on the DC Circulator from Dupont Circle has eased any sense of cultural xenophobia among the well-heeled locals.

Georgetown's main thoroughfares, M Street NW and Wisconsin Avenue NW, are always bustling with university students, professionals, and tourists. On a given day you may encounter political activists on the sidewalks, wedding parties posing for photos, and gossiping teens laden with shopping bags.   —*Samantha Cleaver*

SWEET SPOT

Chocoholics go ga-ga for **Leonidas Fresh Belgian Chocolates** (✉ *1531 Wisconsin Ave. NW ✛ 1:A4*), which imports 80 varieties of chocolates from Belgium, including its popular champagne truffle. For a cool treat, stop at **Thomas Sweet Ice Cream** (✉ *3214 P St. NW ✛ 1:B4*). Before committing to a flavor, sample our favorites: tiramisu and coconut. Replacing **CakeLove** as the city's best sugar rush is **Georgetown Cupcake** (✉ *1209 Potomac St. NW ✛ 1:A5*), where two stylish sisters dish out palm-size euphoria made with Madagascar vanilla and Valhrona chocolate.

NEIGHBORHOOD FAVES

After a day of sightseeing and shopping, it's time to unwind. Here are our favorite Georgetown haunts for taking a load off.

Elegant, country inn: The **1789 Restaurant** (✉ *1226 36th St. NW ✛ 1:A5*), jacket required, is housed in a Federal building off M Street, serving American classics. Each of the restaurant's five dining rooms offers a different historical experience, from the John Carroll Room, displaying early maps of the city, to the Civil War–inspired Manassas Room.

Asian teahouse: Ching Ching Cha (✉ *1063 Wisconsin Ave. NW ✛ 1:B5*) offers 70 types of Chinese and Japanese teas, using traditional tea ware and serving techniques. Recline on thick pillows with a pot of orchid-scented Snow Dragon tea, nibbling on steamed dumplings and traditional Chinese desserts.

Bustling trattoria: Papa Razzi (✉ *1066 Wisconsin Ave. NW ✛ 1:B5*), a perennial crowd-pleaser, is located in the oldest standing firehouse in D.C. Fans rave about the thin-crust, wood-fired pizzas and the award-winning "Cesare" salad.

RIVERFRONT DINING

Dining along the Potomac River offers fresh seafood and a stunning view of D.C. From any restaurant along the riverfront boardwalk, you can see the Kennedy Center, Roosevelt Island, and the Key Bridge. **Nick's Riverside Grille** (✉ *3050 K St. NW ✛ 1:B6*) makes a mean oyster po'boy sandwich for lunch, and specializes in grilled seafood at dinner. Farther down the boardwalk at **Tony and Joe's Seafood Place** (✉ *3000 K St. NW, Suite 10 ✛ 1:B6*), don't miss the Sunday Champagne Brunch with a live jazz band. Watch the sunset while enjoying a glass of wine at **Sequoia** (✉ *3000 K St. NW, Suite 100 ✛ 1:B6*), an upscale restaurant favored by high-ranking politicians. The Asian-accented American menu features standouts like duck-and-pine nut dumplings.

FRUGAL FOODIE

Frugal foodies enviously eyeing Washington's finest kitchens may be surprised to find affordable alternatives in Georgetown. If you've been priced out of the $28 seafood at **Hook**, try its casual and beachy younger sibling, **Tackle Box** (✉ *3245 M St. NW ✛ 1:B5*), where delicate bluefish with pesto and grilled corn on the cob cost less than half the Hook price.

If you're hankering for the upscale organic aesthetic of **Restaurant Nora**, go for **SweetGreen** (✉ *3333 M St. NW ✛ 1:A5*), a takeout-only spot where the utensils are biodegradable and the "guacamole greens" salad offers an eye-popping garden of fresh vegetables for $9. The golden charms of **Brasserie Beck's** high-class beer menu are mirrored at **Birreria Paradiso** (✉ *3282 M St. NW ✛ 1:A5*), a den of Belgian brews casually hidden beneath a neighborhood pizzeria.

6

DUPONT CIRCLE AND FOGGY BOTTOM

A mixture of funky and formal, Dupont Circle and Foggy Bottom represent the progressive and the historic sides of Washington. But in the true sense of bipartisanship, dining options are as diverse as this town's political leanings.

Stop into Teaism, a café and retail shrine to tea, located in a converted town house, for more than 50 varieties of loose-leaf teas. Tea-friendly sweets and snacks are also available.

TASTY TIDBITS

The capital's reigning carbohydrate kings hold court at **Bread Line** (⊠ *1751 Pennsylvania Ave. NW* ✛ *1:F6*), where the fresh sourdough baguettes are irresistibly fluffy and the baked goods fit for Marie Antoinette.

The indoor eating area is large but no-frills, so most locals order takeout and make a picnic with their couscous, spicy lamb flat-breads, and chocolate-mascarpone Oreos.

Dupont Circle defies the staid, conservative reputation of Washington, turning D.C. Technicolor in the evening hours. The high-rent, liberal-minded neighborhood has hip art galleries, bookstores, and yoga studios that draw a mix of yuppies and activists. There's no shortage of flamboyant characters and political rallies in this always-bustling enclave. If possible, make reservations for sit-down meals, and expect crowds, especially on weekends.

The history-steeped Foggy Bottom area boasts architectural landmarks like the Watergate Hotel. Around George Washington University there's cheaper, college-friendly fare like burrito joints and coffee shops. Nearby, the Kennedy Center draws a more mature crowd with tastes that have evolved past ramen noodles and nachos.

—*Colleen Egan*

LUNCH LIKE A LOCAL

Take a break from the memorials and take in another kind of sightseeing: people-watching. See Washingtonians cavorting in their natural habitats at these popular spots.

Located near the Phillips Collection, **Firefly** (✉ *1310 New Hampshire Ave. NW ✛ 1:E4*) puts forth a hip, cozy atmosphere, and a menu of comforting fare like Waldorf salad with poached shrimp, seared-tuna club sandwich with avocado, and for dessert, caramelized banana split. The check, presented in a glass jar with holes poked into the lid, makes getting the bill almost endearing.

The Mediterranean-accented **Rosemary's Thyme Bistro** (✉ *1801 18th St. NW ✛ 1:F3*) has a fiercely loyal following that comes for sidewalk dining and stellar happy-hour specials. Grab a spot on the patio and sample fresh favorites like the spinach ravioli or the feta-meta salad.

Eschew the ubiquitous chains and get your caffeine or herbal tea fix at **Teaism** (✉ *2009 R St. NW ✛ 1:E3*). In addition to a robust variety of teas, locals come for Asian-accented fare like tea-cured salmon and smoked-turkey sandwiches with wasabi mayo. Come on weekends for cilantro-scrambled tofu and sourdough waffles. ■TIP→ Don't miss the chocolate salty oat cookie that has foodies raving.

PRETHEATER DINNER DEALS

The intimate **Notti Bianche** (✉ *824 New Hampshire Ave. NW ✛ 1:D6*) in the G.W. University Inn serves indulgent Italian cuisine. The $32 three-course prix-fixe theater menu is available from 5 PM to 7 PM every day.

The French restaurant **Marcel's** (✉ *2401 Pennsylvania Ave. NW ✛ 1:D5*) serves a $48 three-course pretheater dinner menu that includes round-trip executive car service to and from the Kennedy Center.

FRO-YO 2.0

The Hollywood-inspired craze for low-sugar, all-natural frozen yogurt (those in the know call it fro-yo) has taken hold of the District. Whether or not you're familiar with the dessert sensation first sparked by Pinkberry—think icy Dannon rather than rich Häagen-Dazs, loaded with fruit and other less healthy toppings—Dupont Circle is home to two places that will satisfy your craving for the good stuff. **TangySweet** (✉ *2029 P St. NW ✛ 1:E4*) serves plain, pomegranate, and green-tea yogurt with a plethora of toppings in an award-winning Earth-friendly setting. In snowier times, the counter brews velvet-thick *chocolat chaud* from a Parisian recipe. Its wacky competitor, **Mr. Yogato** (✉ *1515 17th St. NW ✛ 1:G4*), serves a wider range of flavors, such as caramel and strawberry, and features a rotating cast of free toppings. It is run by a former rocket scientist who gives discounts to those who stump him on *Seinfeld* trivia and features a Ghirardelli hot-chocolate bar in the winter months.

ADAMS MORGAN, U STREET CORRIDOR

Libations trump legislation in the nightlife-centric U Street/Adams Morgan area. This irreverent side of the District is characterized by bumping bars and an up-all-night attitude.

The stylish Vegetate, serves up music and art shows along with a vegetarian menu.

U Street links Shaw, centered near Howard University's campus, to Adams Morgan, and is known for indie rock clubs, edgy bars, and trendy restaurants. Although the urban hipster vibe is being threatened by skyrocketing rents and the intrusion of chain stores, you'll still find more tattoos and sneakers than pinstripes and pearls here.

In Adams Morgan legions of college kids descend on 18th Street for abundant drink specials and dance clubs. Quaint ethnic cafés (Ethiopian, French, Italian) are bustling during evening hours. But as the night wears on the crowds gravitate to greasy spoons and "jumbo slice" pizza joints. The next culinary frontier lies just east along Columbia Road, where the Salvadoran immigrant community dines on its native cuisine while young families flock to hearty local pubs for their ample portions.
—*Colleen Egan*

ERNEST CUISINE

Named for a Hemingway character with an irresistible zest for life, the chic bistro **Bar Pilar** (⊠ *1833 14th St. NW* ✢ *1:H2*) pays homage to its favorite author with simple but stunning small plates that harken back to Hemingway's Key West heyday. Think cold sugar baby watermelons and red wine braised chicken with leeks.

A NIGHT ON THE TOWN

In this town you can get drinks, eat dinner, go dancing, and listen to live music all in one venue. Paint the town red (or blue) at one of our favorite U Street or Adams Morgan spots.

Start out the night at **Café Saint-Ex** (✉ *1847 14th St. NW* ✛ *1:H3*) by dining on farm-friendly American dishes, then head downstairs to dance off dinner with the help of a rotating cast of DJs in the often crowded but always rollicking downstairs bar.

Local 16 (✉ *1602 U St. NW* ✛ *1:G2*) may have experimented with its menu (currently American with international influences), but its status as a neighborhood hot spot has never wavered. After dinner, the intimate restaurant becomes a jumping nightclub as DJs start spinning and the crowd spills out onto a balcony patio crowned by palm trees.

The multitasking **Busboys and Poets** (✉ *2021 14th St. NW* ✛ *1:H2*)—a coffee shop, restaurant, bar, performance space, and progressive bookstore—wears many hats without scrimping on taste. Try the simple yet divine peanut-butter-and-honey-on-challah sandwich for a low-key lunch, or stay for the homemade meat loaf (most entrées are in the $10 to $15 range) and a live jazz show.

The walls rattle with the echo of bumping bodies at the **Wonderland Ballroom** (✉ *1101 Kenyon St. NW* ✛ *1:H1*) during its überpopular weekend DJ sessions, while the beat slows down on Sunday with live music. The all-American menu features burgers and fries as good as Coney Island's and savory brunch salads.

The spirit of storytelling lives on, along with stellar crab cakes and mint juleps, at the Southern-themed **Eatonville** (✉ *2121 14th St. NW* ✛ *1:H2*). Here, the monthly Food and Folklore series pairs a special prix-fixe menu with a lecture on the cultural traditions of the African-American community.

BRUNCH BONANZA

Brunch is a cherished ritual on the Adams Morgan/U Street strip, where bars mop up last night's spilled beer and fire up the French toast. Some of the most unforgettable brunches can be found in otherwise unremarkable kitchens, such as **Asylum** (✉ *2471 18th St. NW* ✛ *1:F1*), a biker dive by night that turns out stellar huevos rancheros by day, and **Perry's** (✉ *1811 Columbia Rd. NW* ✛ *1:F1*), which pairs its pancakes with a rip-roaring drag queen revue. The array of up-and-coming shops in both neighborhoods makes for perfect afternoon strolling. After downing spicy sausage-and-egg sandwiches at **Bourbon** (✉ *2321 18th St. NW* ✛ *1:F1*), you can cruise nearby vintage fashion outpost **Meeps** (✉ *2104 18th St. NW* ✛ *1:F2*). Nothing helps work off the waffles of **Crème Café** (✉ *1322 U St. NW* ✛ *1:H2*) like a jaunt through **Nana** (✉ *1528 U St. NW* ✛ *1:G2*), the bohemian boutique beloved by D.C. fashionistas.

6

UPPER NORTHWEST

Lions, tigers, and lobbyists . . . oh my! After the requisite cooing over the pandas and other cuddly creatures at the National Zoo, consider wandering around this popular neighborhood to observe locals eat, drink, and play.

Many Hill staffers, journalists, and other inside-the-Beltway types live along this hilly stretch of Connecticut Avenue. Eateries and shops line the few blocks near each of the Red Line Metro stops. Restaurants in Cleveland Park range from tiny takeout spots like Vace Italian Delicatessen, one of the few places in town to get a great slice of pizza, to nearby **Ardeo** (✉ *3311 Connecticut Ave. NW* ✛ *1:D1*), an upscale Modern American restaurant where you stand a good chance of spying your favorite Sunday-morning talk-show guests at a nearby table.

Ethnic dining is also abundant here, especially in Cleveland Park. Lined up along the stately stretch of modern row houses are diverse dining options ranging from Afghan to Thai.   —*Beth Kanter*

BOOKS AND BITES

Hungry bibliophiles will want to make a lunchtime pilgrimage to **Politics & Prose** (✉ *5015 Connecticut Ave. NW* ✛ *1:D1*), one of the country's best independent bookstores. P&P boasts a full calendar of author readings, a refreshingly well-read staff, and a cozy basement café with free Internet access, dozens of tea selections, and tasty sandwiches. The café, **Modern Times**, also serves pastries and vegetarian sushi made on-site. Our favorite sandwiches are the English Roast, made with marinated roast beef, cheddar cheese, arugula, mango chutney, and plum tomatoes, and the salami and Gorgonzola panini.

DINNER AND A MOVIE

In a town teeming with monuments and memorials, Cleveland Park's **AMC Loews Uptown 1** (✉ *3426 Connecticut Ave. NW*)—known to locals simply as "The Uptown"—is a shrine to the glamour of days gone by. From the red-velvet curtain to the massive balcony to the 70-foot-long and 40-foot-high screen, this art deco movie palace is a throwback to a time when the experience of seeing a movie could be as romantic as the picture you came to see.

■TIP→ **Shows sell out quickly, and coveted balcony seats fill up fast. Avoid the dreaded sold-out sign by heading to the box office early. Then, with tickets in hand, enjoy dinner at one of the many nearby restaurants.**

Just a block away, **Indique** (✉ *3512-14 Connecticut Ave. NW ✛ 1:D1*) offers a $20 three-course pretheater menu from 5:30 to 7 PM. Choices at the attractive, upscale Indian spot might include tandoori chicken tikka, Tamilnad fish curry, and mango ice cream. A sister restaurant, **Indique Heights**, recently arrived a few miles north in suburban Maryland.

Across the street, the rustic Italian enoteca **Dino** (✉ *3435 Connecticut Ave. NW ✛ 1:D1*), is known both for its ambience and its award-winning wine list. The daily changing menu always includes a wide selection of cured meats, cheeses, and *fritti*, or fried items.

Spices Asian Restaurant & Sushi Bar (✉ *3333-A Connecticut Ave. NW ✛ 1:D1*) is a popular neighborhood pan-Asian spot offering everything from Peking duck to pad thai noodles in a bustling, bistro-esque space.

For a one-dish meal that's quick and refreshing, stop into **Nam-Viet** (✉ *3419 Connecticut Ave. NW ✛ 1:D1*). The atmosphere is minimal, but you probably won't care after tucking into juicy, salty-sweet caramelized pork chops or spicy rice-noodle soup filled with seared fish or beef.

GOLDEN GLOVER

Located just north of Georgetown and west of Cleveland Park, the Glover Park neighborhood is fast becoming Washington's home for sleeper culinary hits. You'll need a car, but any visitor eager to avoid crowds during high season should high-tail it to **Surfside** (✉ *2444 Wisconsin Ave. NW ✛ 1:A2*), where the steak burritos and mango salsa will evoke California dreaming. At **Breadsoda** (✉ *2233 Wisconsin Ave. NW ✛ 1:A2*) the pool tables, Ping-Pong, and Nintendo Wii help patrons work off the hefty spicy turkey sandwiches. "A taste of the South in your mouth" is the kitschy motto of **Kitchen** (✉ *2404 Wisconsin Ave. NW ✛ 1:A2*), where the lip-smacking "Texas caviar" is actually black-eyed peas and black beans, topped with jalapeños, tomatoes, and cilantro.

6

RESTAURANTS

Listed alphabetically within neighborhood.

CAPITOL HILL

$$$ ✕ **Art and Soul.** Best known as Oprah's longtime personal chef, Art Smith
NEW AMERICAN is now serving the Washingtonian crowd at this funky new Southern-
fried spot, located in the Liaison Capitol Hill. The signature dish here
is the hoecake, a once modest slab of fried cornmeal scarfed down by
overworked and cash-strapped field workers during the 19th century.
Smith and executive chef Ryan Morgan gussy up their hoecakes with
three sets of toppings: blue cheese and arugula, blue crab and braised
beef, and a truly decadent mélange of caviar, crème fraiche, and cured
salmon. Low Country classics such as shrimp with grits, and pork chops
served with vinegar-spiked redeye gravy are also on hand. ⊠ *415 New
Jersey Ave. NW, Capitol Hill* ☏ *202/393–7777* ⊕ *www.artandsouldc.
com* ⊟ *AE, MC, V* Ⓜ *Union Station* ✛ *2:F3.*

$–$$ ✕ **Belga Cafe.** You can go traditional with mussels and the crispiest of
BELGIAN french fries or dabble in what the chef calls Euro-fusion at this sleek
café done up with dark wood, exposed brick, and creamy chairs and
linens. Classic dishes such as *waterzooi,* the Belgian chicken stew, and a
leg of rabbit made with beer, are expertly turned out, along with newer
takes such as seared scallops with young carrots, red beets, and orange
sauce. The three-page beer list is a testament to Belgium's love of well-
made beer. Crowds at lunch and dinner sometimes mean a short wait
even with a reservation. ⊠ *514 8th St. SE, Capitol Hill* ☏ *202/544–0100*
⊕ *www.belgacafe.com* ⊟ *AE, D, MC, V* Ⓜ *Eastern Market* ✛ *2:H6.*

$$–$$$ ✕ **Bistro Bis.** A zinc bar, spacious brown-leather booths, and a glass-
FRENCH front display kitchen create great expectations at Bistro Bis, the second
restaurant from Jeffrey Buben, owner of the much-acclaimed Vidalia.
The seasonal menu seamlessly merges Modern American standards with
French bistro classics. For a first course, be sure to try the steak tartare. Main-course hits on the menu, which changes frequently to reflect
market and seasonal choices, include duck confit and grilled salmon
with porcini mushrooms, and lamb shank with sun-dried tomatoes and
polenta. ⊠ *Hotel George, 15 E St. NW, Capitol Hill* ☏ *202/661–2700*
⊕ *www.bistrobis.com/index1.html* ⌕ *Reservations essential* ⊟ *AE, D,
DC, MC, V* Ⓜ *Union Station* ✛ *2:F3.*

$$ ✕ **Cava.** Jose Andres's Zaytinya may have cornered the local market on
GREEK eclectic Mediterranean, but this modern mecca for *mezze* (small plates
for sharing) is its more conventional, equally well-bred sibling. The
entire Greek catalogue is here for the taking, from fluffy *taramosalata*
(salmon roe dip) with a touch of citrus to rich, melt-in-your-mouth
spinach pie to tender lamb shoulder topped by a puff of thick Greek
yogurt. There are few surprises on the menu, save for the grilled sliders
filled with gloriously salty halloumi cheese, but the leather-lined decor
and gallant service make the traditional dishes feel new again. There's
another location in suburban Maryland. ⊠ *527 8th St. SE, Capitol Hill*
☏ *202/543–9090* ⊕ *dc.cavamezze.com* ⌕ *Reservations not accepted*
⊟ *MC, V* ⊗ *No lunch Mon.* Ⓜ *Eastern Market* ✛ *2:H6.*

$$$$ ✕**Charlie Palmer Steak.** It's hard not to feel like a master of the universe
STEAK when ensconced in this coolly elegant dining room with a drop-dead
view of the Capitol. Oversize floral arrangements, tones of blue-gray,
a dramatic glass-enclosed wine cellar, and quasi-Danish modern furniture form a backdrop to the contemporary cuisine. Dry-aged rib
eye, marinated hanger steak, and filet mignon with roasted shallots
are the meaty choices. But soft-shell crabs and butter-steeped lobster
make a good showing, too, as do sides such as mashed Yukon Golds
and goat-cheese tubetti that seems like deluxe macaroni and cheese.
The lemon pound cake finishes things off nicely. ⊠ *101 Constitution
Ave. NW, Capitol Hill* ☎*202/547–8100* ⊕*www.charliepalmer.com/
Properties/CPSteak/DC* ⊟ *AE, D, DC, MC, V* ⊗ *Closed Sun. No lunch
Sat.* Ⓜ *Union Station* ✦ *2:F4.*

¢ ✕**Good Stuff Eatery.** Fans of Bravo's "Top Chef" will first visit this
AMERICAN brightly colored burgers-and-shakes shack hoping to spy charismatic
Ⓒ TV chef Spike Mendelsohn, but they will return for the comfort-food
favorites. The lines can be long, as it has quickly become a favorite
lunch spot of congressional aides, but Spike's inventive beef dishes—
including the "Blazin' Barn" Asian burger topped with Thai basil and
pickled radish—are worth the wait. After placing your order cafeteria-
style, remember to grab several of the fresh dipping sauces for the tasty
thyme-and-rosemary-seasoned hand-cut skinny fries. Just as important,
leave room for a toasted marshmallow or chocolate malted shake that's
as thick as the ones you remember from childhood. ⊠ *303 Pennsylvania
Ave. SE, Capitol Hill* ☎*202/543–8222* ⊕*www.goodstuffeatery.com*
⊟*MC, V* ⊗ *Closed Sun. in Aug.* Ⓜ *Eastern Market* ✦ *2:H5.*

$ ✕**Granville Moore's Brickyard.** This Belgian beer hall with a gourmet
BELGIAN soul is worth a visit despite its location in D.C.'s Atlas District, an
area that can be seedy after dark. Snag a seat at the bar or at one of
the first-come, first-served tables, and linger over unfiltered artisanal
brews that range from Chimay to the obscure, lip-smacking Brasserie
des Rocs. The food is terrific, specifically the pots of steamed mussels
served with crunchy, twice-fried frîtes paired with homemade dipping
sauces. The bison burger and prosciutto *croque monsieur* (hot ham and
cheese) sandwich are downright decadent. ⊠ *1238 H St. NE, Capitol
Hill* ☎*202/399–2546* ⊕*www.granvillemoores.com* ⌦ *No reservations*
⊟*AE, MC, V* ⊗ *No lunch* Ⓜ *Union Station* ✦ *2:H2.*

¢ ✕**Jimmy T's Place.** This D.C. institution is tucked in the first floor of an
AMERICAN old row house only five blocks from the Capitol. Sassy waiters, talk-
Ⓒ ative regulars, and this small diner's two boisterous owners, who run
the grill, pack the place daily. Soak in the local culture or read the paper
as you enjoy favorites such as grits, bacon, omelets, or the homey eggs
Benedict, made with a toasted English muffin, a huge piece of ham,
and lots of hollandaise sauce. The anything-goes atmosphere makes it
a great place for kids. Breakfast is served all day. ⊠ *501 E. Capitol St.
SE, Capitol Hill* ☎*202/546–3646* ⊟ *No credit cards* ⊗ *Closed Mon.
and Tues. No dinner* Ⓜ *Eastern Market* ✦ *2:H5.*

$$ ✕**Johnny's Half Shell.** A move from Dupont Circle to more spacious
SEAFOOD quarters on Capitol Hill may have diminished the neighborhood charm
of this seafood bar, but at least it's easier to get a table these days.

■TIP→ For a less buttoned-down vibe, head to the tiny taco joint next door, **Taqueria Nationale**, for the fish tacos that have Senate staffers raving. The Southern-tinged mid-Atlantic fare—pristine Kumamoto oysters, flavorful seafood stews, fried oyster po'boys, and a stellar pickled-onion-and-blue-cheese-topped hot dog—is still as wonderful as ever. And a new pastry chef is turning out a worthy coconut cake. Not surprisingly, the crowd is heavy on politicos drawn as much by the buzz and big-band tunes. Members of Congress can also be found downing a quick Gruyère-cheese omelet during breakfast on weekdays. ⊠ *400 N. Capitol St. NW, Capitol Hill* ☎ *202/737–0400* ⊕ *www.johnnyshalfshell.net* ═ *AE, MC, V* ⊘ *Closed Sun.* Ⓜ *Union Station* ✛ *2:F3.*

¢–$ ✕ **The Market Lunch.** For a perfect Saturday morning or afternoon on the Hill, take a walk around the Capitol, a stroll through Eastern Market, and then dig in to a hefty pile of blueberry pancakes from Market Lunch. The casual counter service and informal seating make it ideal for kids. Favorites include ham, eggs, grits, or pancakes in the morning and crab cakes, fried shrimp, or fish for lunch. Expect long lines and plan to be in line by noon on Saturday in order to ensure availability of every dish. Eastern Market was in the final phases of a renovation in early 2009, so Market Lunch is likely to have a permanent new home this year. ■TIP→ Follow convention and order quickly, eat, and give up your seat for the next customer. ⊠ *Tent hall across the street from Eastern Market, 306 7th St. SE, Capitol Hill* ☎ *202/547–8444* ⌂ *Reservations not accepted* ═ *No credit cards* ⊘ *Closed Mon. No dinner* Ⓜ *Eastern Market* ✛ *2:H6.*

AMERICAN

$–$$ ✕ **Montmartre.** With its sidewalk café, cheerful yellow walls, fresh flowers, and lusty yet chic fare, Montmartre evokes the Left Bank of Paris. Here's an unpretentious bistro that straddles classic and modern effortlessly with dishes like cream of chestnut soup, braised rabbit with olives and shiitake mushrooms, hanger steak with caramelized shallots, and cod with homemade spaetzle. It's a politicians' hangout, but you'd never know it by the cozy, rustic feel of the place. ⊠ *327 7th St. SE, Capitol Hill* ☎ *202/544–1244* ⌂ *Reservations essential* ═ *AE, DC, MC, V* ⊘ *Closed Mon.* Ⓜ *Eastern Market* ✛ *2:H6.*

FRENCH

$$–$$$ ✕ **Sonoma.** This chic multilevel wine bar has pours aplenty (in both tasting portions and full glasses) along with well-thought-out charcuterie boards piled with prosciutto, bresaola with house-made condiments like pickled ramps, and figs braised in wine. There's more-conventional fare, too, like a juicy Wagyu burger with Taleggio cheese and grilled onions. By day the crowd skews to Senate staffers, by night the place becomes a hipster scene in the bar on the second level—think low tables and sofas—while a youngish crowd shares cheese plates in the crowded street-level dining room. ⊠ *223 Pennsylvania Ave. SE, Capitol Hill* ☎ *202/544–8088* ⊕ *www.sonomadc.com* ⌂ *Reservations essential* ═ *AE, D, DC, MC, V* ⊘ *No lunch weekends* Ⓜ *Capitol S* ✛ *2:H5.*

AMERICAN

$$ ✕ **Sticky Rice.** The capital's hip young things usually begin their nights out with cocktails, not high-concept food, but this kitschy den of sushi and karaoke is a popular exception. Between the trippy wall-mounted light sculptures and the gigantic gong that rings with every order of a mind-altering "sake bomb," a night out here is always exciting. New

ASIAN

customers are thrilled to trade in those predictable California rolls for a Snap Crackle Pop, made with fresh salmon and jalapeño, or a Crazy Calamari, where cooked squid is studded with tender fish roe and piquant cilantro. Those expecting thrilling service, however, may leave frustrated. ✉ *1224 H St. NE, Capitol Hill* ☎ *202/397–7655* ⊕ *www.stickyricedc.com* ⚐ *Reservations essential* ═ *AE, MC, V* Ⓜ *Union Station* ✛ *2:H2.*

WORD OF MOUTH

"Brasserie Beck is also fantastic…French/Belgian cuisine with a killer Belgian beer menu (18 pages or so) and some really great food. The mussels are fantastic, as is the roasted monkfish."

—beanweb24

DOWNTOWN

$$$
ITALIAN
✕ **Bibiana Osteria and Enoteca.** The fingerprints of Ashok Bajaj, creator of Chinatown's überpopular Rasika, are all over this modern kitchen specializing in hearty Florence-inspired cuisine. The 120-seat dining room is decked out in Bajaj's favored spare tones and metallic accents, while servers remain uncommonly attentive and knowledgeable. And in a city where Italian spots too often hit obvious notes such as brick-oven pizzas, Bibiana's customers can try presentations such as buttery chicken liver mousse with red onion marmalade and blue crab served atop linguine colored jet-black by squid ink. The decor may be rich, but the ample portions and sensible prices make for a recession-friendly splurge. ✉ *1100 New York Ave. NW, Downtown* ☎ *202/216–9550* ⊕ *www.bibianadc.com* ═ *AE, MC, V* ☺ No lunch Sat. Closed Sun. Ⓜ *Metro Center* ✛ *2:C2.*

$-$$
INDIAN
✕ **Bombay Club.** One block from the White House, the beautiful Bombay Club tries to re-create the refined aura of British private clubs in colonial India. Potted palms and a bright blue ceiling above white plaster moldings adorn the dining room. On the menu are unusual seafood specialties and a large number of vegetarian dishes, but the real standouts are the aromatic curries. The bar, furnished with rattan chairs and dark-wood paneling, serves hot hors d'oeuvres at cocktail hour. The attire tends toward upscale business-casual. ✉ *815 Connecticut Ave. NW, Downtown* ☎ *202/659–3727* ⊕ *www.bombayclubdc.com* ⚐ *Reservations essential* ═ *AE, D, DC, MC, V* ☺ *No lunch weekends* Ⓜ *Farragut W* ✛ *1:G6.*

$$-$$$
FRENCH
✕ **Brasserie Beck.** Give in to sensory overload at this homage to the railway dining rooms that catered to the prewar European elite. Every detail of Beck's decor exudes luxury, from the vintage-accented clocks that stand above mahogany booths to the exposed stainless-steel kitchen (now rechristened the "epicurean solarium"). The food is just as rich as you'd expect: entrée-size salads with bacon and egg, *fruits de mer* platters laden with enough shellfish for a small army, and a dizzying lineup of artisanal beers. The production is impressive, and you'll remember the food fondly after returning home—but you might long for a simple sandwich afterwards. ✉ *1101 K St. NW, Downtown* ☎ *202/408–1717* ⊕ *www.beckdc.com* ═ *AE, MC, V* Ⓜ *McPherson Sq.* ✛ *2:C1.*

6

$$$ ✕ **The Capital Grille.** A few blocks from the U.S. Capitol, this New Eng-
STEAK   land–tinged steak house is a favorite among Republican congressmen.
Politics aside, the cuisine, wine list, and surroundings are all top-shelf.
Don't let the meat hanging in the window distract you from the fact
that this restaurant has a lot more to offer than fine dry-aged por-
terhouse cuts and delicious cream-based potatoes. For instance, don't
miss the panfried calamari with hot cherry peppers. A second location
in Tysons Corner has the same menu but a slightly different wine list.
✉ *601 Pennsylvania Ave. NW, Downtown* ☎ *202/737–6200* ⊕ *www.
thecapitalgrille.com* ⌖ *Reservations essential* ▭ *AE, D, DC, MC, V*
⊗ *No lunch Sun.* Ⓜ *Archives/Navy Memorial* ⊹ *2:D4.*

$$$$ ✕ **Caucus Room.** Here's the quintessential Washington political restau-
CONTINENTAL   rant. The limited partnership that owns it includes a Democratic super-
lobbyist and a former Republican National Committee chairman. The
dark wood and rich leather within make it perfect for business lunches
or dinners, and the many private dining rooms are popular for political
fund-raising events. The menu changes about three times a year, but you
can count on prime meats and seafood dishes including sea bass and
seared tuna. ✉ *401 9th St. NW, Downtown* ☎ *202/393–1300* ⊕ *www.
thecaucusroom.com* ▭ *AE, D, DC, MC, V* ⊗ *Closed Sun. No lunch
weekends* Ⓜ *Archives/Navy Memorial* ⊹ *2:D4.*

$$–$$$ ✕ **Ceiba.** At this very popular Latin restaurant you'll probably want
LATIN   to start with a mojito or a pisco sour cocktail, then taste the smoked-
AMERICAN   swordfish carpaccio or Jamaican crab fritters. This is a menu meant for
grazing, but the main courses, like rib eye with chimichurri sauce and
feijoada (stew of beans and meat) made from pork shanks, still satisfy.
Also stellar are desserts such as Mexican vanilla-bean cheesecake with
guava jelly, and cinnamon-dusted churros to dip in Mexican hot choco-
late. Island-theme murals, angular cream banquettes, an open kitchen,
and vaulted ceilings set the scene. ✉ *701 14th St. NW, Downtown*
☎ *202/393–3983* ⊕ *www.ceibarestaurant.com* ▭ *AE, D, DC, MC, V*
⊗ *Closed Sun. No lunch Sat.* Ⓜ *Metro Center* ⊹ *2:B2.*

$$–$$$ ✕ **Central Michel Richard.** French powerhouse chef Michel Richard has
FRENCH   set up camp Downtown with this semicasual bistro offering up Franco-
Fodor's Choice   American spin-offs like fried chicken, leek-and-mussel chowder, and a
★   ginger-flecked tuna burger. Rows of hams hang in a glass case. Light
fixtures are subtly stamped with the word "Central." A jazzy portrait of
Richard (think Andy Warhol) stares down from one wall. The mood is
playful and low-key; cocktails and champagne flow. And there are even
a few carryovers from Richard's more formal Citronelle in Georgetown
like "Le Kit Kat," the chef's take on a Kit Kat bar. ✉ *1001 Pennsylvania
Ave. NW, Downtown* ☎ *202/626–0015* ⊕ *www.centralmichelrichard.
com* ⌖ *Reservations essential* ▭ *AE, D, MC, V* ⊗ *No lunch weekends*
Ⓜ *Metro Center* ⊹ *2:C3.*

$$$$ ✕ **CityZen.** The Mandarin Hotel's rarefied dining room has fast become a
AMERICAN   destination for those serious about food. In a glowing space with soar-
ing ceilings, chef Eric Zeibold, formerly of Napa Valley's famed French
Laundry, creates luxe fixed-price meals from the finest ingredients.
Unexpected little treasures abound, such as scrambled eggs with white
truffles shaved at the table and buttery miniature Parker House rolls.

Main courses could include black bass over caramelized cauliflower, and braised veal shank with potato gnocchi, and desserts such as Meyer lemon soufflé seem spun out of air. A three-course meal is $75, and the tasting menus run $90–$110. ☒ *Mandarin Oriental, 1330 Maryland Ave. SW, Downtown* ☎ *202/787–6006* ⊕ *www.mandarinoriental.com/washington/dining/cityzen* ⌔ *Reservations essential* ⊟ *AE, D, DC, MC, V* ⊙ *Closed Sun. and Mon. No lunch* Ⓜ *Smithsonian* ⊹ *2:B6.*

$$-$$$ ✕ **DC Coast.** Chef Jeff Tunks's menu at this sophisticated Downtown
SEAFOOD spot brings the foods of three coasts—Atlantic, Gulf, and Pacific—to Washington. Come for lunch to try his savory version of crab cakes; if you call ahead of time, you can order them for dinner. If you're homesick for New Orleans, try the gumbo (served only at lunch). For Pacific Rim cooking, you can't beat the smoked lobster. ■ TIP➔ The bar scene is one of the liveliest in the Downtown area, kicking off as early as 2:30 PM on weekdays with the lobbyist crowd. ☒ *1401 K St. NW, Downtown* ☎ *202/216–5988* ⊕ *www.dccoast.com* ⌔ *Reservations essential* ⊟ *AE, D, DC, MC, V* ⊙ *No lunch weekends* Ⓜ *McPherson Sq.* ⊹ *2:B1.*

$$$$ ✕ **Equinox.** Virginia-born chef-owner Todd Gray looks to area purveyors
AMERICAN for hard-to-find heirloom and local foodstuffs at his low-key American eatery. The furnishings and the food are simple and elegant. The fresh ingredients speak for themselves: grilled quail with a truffle reduction, rare duck breast served on a cabbage salad, crab cakes with diced mango, and barbecued salmon with a sauce of roasted peppers and corn. There are two fixed-price five-course dinners—a market menu for $90 and a vegetarian menu for $75—as well as a six-course option for $89. Wine pairings are available for an extra fee, and an à la carte menu ($$) is available at lunch. ☒ *818 Connecticut Ave. NW, Downtown* ☎ *202/331–8118* ⊕ *www.equinoxrestaurant.com* ⌔ *Reservations essential* ⊟ *AE, DC, MC, V* ⊙ *No lunch weekends* Ⓜ *Farragut W* ⊹ *2:A2.*

$$$ ✕ **G Street Food.** Like Washington, D.C.'s layout and architecture, this
ECLECTIC upscale cafeteria takes a cue from Europe. The cosmopolitan menu echoes the best of the Continent's eclectic café scene; breakfasts range from Italian potato-and-egg panini to Norwegian lox, and lunch ups the ante with a daily sausage selection and a French-inspired "tartine of the day." Asian cuisine gets its due as well, and an Indian curry cauliflower salad packs a flavorful punch greater than its $5 price tag. Lines here can look oppressive at midday, as government workers come flocking for falafel and fresh-cut fries, but stick around and you'll be rewarded with a midday meal that's smarter, and often more affordable, than the chain spots. ☒ *1706 G St. NW, Downtown* ☎ *202/408–7474* ⊕ *www.gstreetfood.com* ⌔ *Reservations not accepted* ⊟ *AE, MC, V* ⊙ *No dinner. Closed weekends* Ⓜ ⊹ *1:F6.*

$-$$ ✕ **Georgia Brown's.** An elegant New South eatery and a favorite hang-
SOUTHERN out of local politicians, Georgia Brown's serves shrimp Carolina-style (head intact, with steaming grits on the side); thick, rich crab soup; and such specials as grilled salmon and slow-cooked green beans with bacon. Fried green tomatoes are filled with herb cream cheese, and a pecan pie is made with bourbon and imported Belgian dark chocolate. ■ TIP➔ The Sunday "jazz brunch" adds live music and a decadent chocolate fondue fountain to the mix. The airy, curving dining room has white

6

honeycomb windows and unusual ceiling ornaments of bronze ribbons. ✉ *950 15th St. NW, Downtown* ☎ *202/393–4499* ⊕ *www.gbrowns. com* ⌲ *Reservations essential* ▭ *AE, D, DC, MC, V* ⊘ *No lunch Sat.* Ⓜ *McPherson Sq.* ✣ *2:A2.*

$$ **✕ Kaz Sushi Bistro.** Traditional Japanese cookery is combined with often
JAPANESE inspired improvisations ("freestyle Japanese cuisine," in the words of chef-owner Kaz Okochi) at this serene location. For a first-rate experience, sit at the sushi bar and ask for whatever is freshest and best. The chef's years of experience preparing *fugu*—the potentially poisonous blowfish, available only in winter—means you're in good hands, though the experience is pricey at $150 per person. It's not all sushi here; innovations include sake-poached scallops with lemon-cilantro dressing. ✉ *1915 I St. NW, Downtown* ☎ *202/530–5500* ⊕ *www.kazsushibistro. com* ▭ *AE, DC, MC, V* ⊘ *Closed Sun. No lunch weekends* Ⓜ *Farragut W* ✣ *1:F6.*

$$$$ **✕ Morton's of Chicago.** Enjoy a steak on the patio at the Downtown loca-
STEAK tion of this national chain, one block from the Renaissance Mayflower, a D.C. landmark hotel. In classic steak-house tradition, the emphasis is on quantity as well as quality; the New York strip and porterhouse steaks are well over a pound each. If you have an even larger appetite (or you plan to share), there's a 48-ounce porterhouse for $88. Prime rib, lamb, veal, chicken, lobster, and grilled fish are also on the menu. ✉ *1050 Connecticut Ave. NW, Downtown* ☎ *202/955–5997* ▭ *AE, D, MC, V* Ⓜ *Farragut N* ✣ *1:F6.*

$$–$$$ **✕ Occidental Grill.** One of the most venerable restaurants in the city cov-
AMERICAN ers its walls with photos of politicians and other notables who have come here for the food and the attentive service. The standbys are best— chopped salad, grilled tuna or swordfish, lamb shank, veal meat loaf. More than half of the menu is seafood. ✉ *Willard InterContinental, 1475 Pennsylvania Ave. NW, Downtown* ☎ *202/783–1475* ⊕ *occiden- taldc.com/www* ⌲ *Reservations essential* ▭ *AE, DC, MC, V* Ⓜ *Metro Center* ✣ *2:B3.*

$$–$$$ **✕ Oceanaire Seafood Room.** This link in a Minneapolis-based chain is a
SEAFOOD beautiful throwback to another era, with dark-wood paneling, semi-circular red booths, white tablecloths, and a pink glow that makes everybody look great. Oceanaire distinguishes itself primarily with first-rate ingredients; you see it at its best by ordering simply, picking from the list of fresh fish that heads the menu—perhaps walleye pike or local rockfish. The portions are often big enough to feed a family of four. This place is a good time, and even better if you go with a group. ✉ *1201 F St. NW, Downtown* ☎ *202/347–2277* ⊕ *www.theoceanaire. com* ⌲ *Reservations essential* ▭ *AE, D, DC, MC, V* ⊘ *No lunch week- ends* Ⓜ *Metro Center* ✣ *2:C3.*

$$–$$$ **✕ Old Ebbitt Grill.** People flock here to drink at the several bars, which
AMERICAN seem to go on for miles, and to enjoy well-prepared buffalo wings, hamburgers, and Reuben sandwiches. The Old Ebbitt also has Washington's most popular raw bar, which serves farm-raised oysters. Pasta is homemade, and daily fresh fish or steak specials are served until 1 AM. Despite the crowds, the restaurant never feels cramped, thanks to its well-spaced, comfortable booths. ■TIP→ Service can be slow at lunch;

if you're in a hurry, try the café-style Ebbitt Express next door. ☒ *675 15th St. NW, Downtown* ☎ *202/347–4800* ⊕ *www.ebbitt.com* ▭ *AE, D, DC, MC, V* Ⓜ *Metro Center* ⊹ *2:B3.*

$$$
MEDITERRANEAN
✕**Olives.** Celebrity chef Todd English's D.C. outpost seems always to have a crowded dining room at lunch and dinner. The upstairs room, which overlooks the open kitchen, is where the action is, but the spacious downstairs dining room is more comfortable, albeit formal. Hearty starters include English's special butternut squash–stuffed tortelli and flat bread with goat cheese and escargots. Most plates have so much going on that there are bound to be some hits and some misses, but the spit-roasted chicken is done very well. ☒ *1600 K St. NW, Downtown* ☎ *202/452–1866* ⊕ *www.toddenglish.com* ᐧ *Reservations essential* ▭ *AE, D, DC, MC, V* ☾ *Closed Sun. No lunch Sat.* Ⓜ *Farragut N* ⊹ *1:G6.*

$$–$$$
SPANISH
✕**Taberna del Alabardero.** A lovely formal dining room, skillful service, and sophisticated cooking make this restaurant one of Washington's best. Start with tapas: piquillo peppers stuffed with *bacalao* (salt cod) or roasted leg of duck in a phyllo pastry pouch. Proceed to a hefty bowl of gazpacho or white garlic soup and venture on to authentic paella and fine Spanish country dishes. French-toast-like *torrijas* are a light ending to this rich fare. The plush interior and handsome bar make things romantic and help attract a well-heeled clientele. ☒ *1776 I St. NW, at 18th St., Downtown* ☎ *202/429–2200* ⊕ *www.alabardero.com* ᐧ *Reservations essential* ▭ *AE, D, DC, MC, V* ☾ *Closed Sun. No lunch Sat.* Ⓜ *Farragut N* ⊹ *1:F6.*

¢
JAPANESE
☺
Fodor's Choice
★
✕**Teaism.** This informal teahouse stocks more than 50 teas (black, white, and green) imported from India, Japan, and Africa, but it also serves healthful and delicious Japanese, Indian, and Thai food as well as tea-friendly sweets like ginger scones, plum muffins, and salty oat cookies. You can mix small dishes—tandoori kebabs, tea-cured salmon, Indian flat breads—to create meals or snacks. There's also a juicy ostrich burger or *ochazuke*, green tea poured over seasoned rice. The smaller Connecticut Avenue branch (enter around the corner, on H Street; closed on weekends), tucked neatly on a corner adjacent to Lafayette Park and the White House, is a perfect spot to grab lunch after touring the nation's power center. Breakfast is served daily. ☒ *400 8th St. NW, Downtown* ☎ *202/638–7740* ⊕ *www.teaism.com* ▭ *D, MC, V* Ⓜ *Archives/Navy Memorial* ⊹ *2:D3* ☒ *800 Connecticut Ave. NW, Downtown* ☎ *202/835–2233* Ⓜ *Farragut W* ⊹ *1:G6.*

$$–$$$
ITALIAN
✕**Teatro Goldoni.** Named for an 18th-century Venetian playwright, this restaurant with a colorful interior is a showcase for chef Fabrizio Aielli's modern-meets-traditional Italian cooking. For a first course, try an unusual pasta dish, such as chocolate pappardelle with a royal boar ragù. At the center of the menu is a selection of fresh fish, which may be grilled, roasted, or cooked in parchment paper Venetian-style. There's also a wide selection of vegetarian entrées. Listen to live jazz here on Friday and Saturday. ☒ *1909 K St. NW, Downtown* ☎ *202/955–9494* ⊕ *www.teatrogoldoni.com* ▭ *AE, D, DC, MC, V* ☾ *Closed Sun. No lunch Sat.* Ⓜ *Farragut N* ⊹ *1:F6.*

$$–$$$
ASIAN

✕ **TenPenh.** One of the closest restaurants to the White House, this hopping venue is always buzzing with socialites, political junkies, and politicians. Chef Jeff Tunks's menu draws from many Asian cuisines—Chinese, Thai, Vietnamese, and Filipino. Main courses range from the chef's distinctive Chinese smoked lobster to tea-rubbed beef tenderloin. A pound cake served with Yuzu huckleberries and Kaffir-lime coconut sorbet is one creation from pastry chef Norman Messer. ⊠ *10th St. and Pennsylvania Ave. NW, Downtown* ☎ *202/393–4500* ⊕ *www. tenpenh.com* ♨ *Reservations essential* ▭ *AE, D, DC, MC, V* ⊘ *Closed Sun. No lunch weekends* Ⓜ *Archives/Navy Memorial* ✢ *2:C3.*

> **THE NEW GUARD EATS**
>
> When power changes hands in Washington, the centers of culinary clout also tend to shift. So would-be White House aides took notice when Democratic honcho Rahm Emanuel chose Wolfgang Puck's The Source for his first meal after agreeing to be Barack Obama's chief of staff. No word on whether any job seekers made their move over Hong Kong salmon…

$$–$$$
ITALIAN

✕ **Tosca.** Chef Cesare Lanfranconi spent several years in the kitchen at Galileo, Washington's dearly departed favorite Italian restaurant, before starting the sleek, sophisticated Tosca with restaurateur Paolo Sacco. The food draws heavily from Lanfranconi's native Lake Como region, but isn't limited by it. Former standouts include polenta topped with wild mushrooms, and a tasty ravioli stuffed with ricotta and crushed amaretto cookies. Save room for dessert, particularly the chef's version of tiramisu, served in a martini glass. ⊠ *1112 F St. NW, Downtown* ☎ *202/367–1990* ⊕ *www.toscadc.com* ♨ *Reservations essential* ▭ *AE, D, DC, MC, V* ⊘ *Closed Sun. No lunch weekends* Ⓜ *Metro Center* ✢ *2:C3.*

$$$–$$$$
NEW AMERICAN

✕ **Wolfgang Puck's The Source.** Wolfgang Puck's first foray into Washington, D.C., provides diners with two dining experiences. The downstairs area is home to an intimate lounge where guests can order specialty cocktails, hand-rolled pizza crowned by homemade sausage, and a juicy quartet of miniature burgers with feather-light fries or tempura onion straws. Upstairs the focus is on haute cuisine: think curry red snapper with lemongrass, and suckling pig tender enough to fall off your fork. The service is so dedicated it borders on slavish. Don't miss the lacquered duck with huckleberries and the mango soufflé dessert. ⊠ *575 Pennsylvania Ave. NW, Downtown* ☎ *202/637–6100* ⊕ *www. wolfgangpuck.com* ♨ *Reservations essential* ▭ *AE, MC, V* ⊘ *Closed Sun. No lunch Sat.* Ⓜ *Archives/Navy Memorial* ✢ *2:D4.*

CHINATOWN

$$
LATIN AMERICAN

✕ **Café Atlántico.** The menu is always exciting at this *nuevo Latino* restaurant with friendly service. Conch fritters come with tiny avocado ravioli, and scallops are served with coconut rice, ginger, squid, and squid-ink oil. On weekends Atlántico offers "Latino dim sum," tapas-size portions of dishes such as duck confit with passion-fruit oil, pineapple shavings, and plantain powder. À la carte, the plates are $3 to $9, but for $35 you can get a deluxe tasting menu ($25 for a vegetarian tasting menu). The bar makes mean cocktails with *cachaça*, a liquor distilled from sugarcane juice. You are unlikely to find a more extensive selection of South American wines anywhere in the city. At **Minibar**, a six-stool bar on the second floor, you can explore a $95 tasting menu of about 30 creative morsels, such as a foie-gras "lollipop" coated with cotton candy, conjured up before your eyes. ■TIP➔ Minibar is argu-ably the most adventurous dining experience in the city, which means you have to reserve at least a week in advance. The space generally closes from mid-August to mid-September. ⊠ *405 8th St. NW, Chinatown,* ☎ *202/393–0812* ⊕ *www.cafeatlantico.com* ≜ *Reservations essential* ⊟ *AE, DC, MC, V* Ⓜ *Archives/Navy Memorial* ✛ *2:D3.*

$–$$
CHINESE

✕ **Full Kee.** Many locals swear by this standout from the slew of medio-cre local Chinese joints. Addictively salty shrimp or scallops in garlic sauce cry out for a doggie bag to enjoy again later, as do the wide assortment of Cantonese-style roasted meats. ■TIP➔ Order from the house specialties, not the tourist menu; the meal-size soups garnished with roast meats are the best in Chinatown. Tried-and-true dishes include the steamed dumplings, crispy duck, eggplant with garlic sauce, and sautéed leek flower. ⊠ *509 H St. NW, Chinatown* ☎ *202/371–2233* ⊕ *www. fullkeedc.com* ⊟ *No credit cards* Ⓜ *Gallery Pl./Chinatown* ✛ *2:D2.*

$$$
ECLECTIC

✕ **Indebleu.** Visual drama and culinary fun are the twin concepts at this restaurant where French technique meets American foodstuffs and Indian spices. Quaff mangotinis while lounging on orange futons in the noisy, high-energy bar, or head for one of the two stylish dining rooms upstairs. You can make a meal of starters such as the tower of crab and lobster spiked with curry oil, or go the more traditional route with a main course like striped bass with a mussel bouillabaisse. Leave room for the sweet "spaghetti and meatballs," made with saffron-cardamom ice cream that resembles spaghetti and warm Indian milk balls. ⊠ *707 G St. NW, Chinatown* ☎ *202/333–2538* ⊕ *www.bleu.com/indebleu* ⊟ *AE, D, MC, V* ☾ *No lunch* Ⓜ *Gallery Pl./Chinatown* ✛ *2:D2.*

$$
SPANISH

✕ **Jaleo.** You are encouraged to make a meal of the long list of tapas at this lively Spanish bistro, although entrées such as paella are just as tasty. Tapas highlights include the *gambas al ajillo* (sautéed garlic shrimp), fried potatoes with spicy tomato sauce, and the grilled chorizo. Adventurers are encouraged to sample the octopus with paprika; those with a sweet tooth should save room for the crisp apple charlotte and the chocolate hazelnut torte. ⊠ *480 7th St. NW, Chinatown* ☎ *202/628–7949* ⊕ *www.jaleo.com* ⊟ *AE, D, DC, MC, V* Ⓜ *Gallery Pl./Chinatown* ✛ *2:D3.*

$–$$
AMERICAN
☉

✕ **Matchbox.** The miniburgers, served on toasted brioche buns with a huge mound of fried onion strings, get the most press, but the main clue to what to order at this convivial triple-decker bar-restaurant is the glowing wood-burning pizza oven. The personal pizzas are "New York–style," with a thin, crisp crust. You probably won't mistake them for the very best of New York, but the pizza margherita comes close. Homey plates such as grilled filet mignon with horseradish potatoes and spicy pecan-crusted chicken add substance to the menu. There's a great lineup of draft beers and oddball martinis, and the kitchen stays open until 1 AM on weekends. ⊠ *713 H St. NW, Chinatown* ☎ *202/289–4441* ⊕ *www.matchboxdc.com* ⊟ *AE, MC, V* Ⓜ *Gallery Pl./Chinatown* ✛ *2:D2.*

6

¢–$ ✕ **Oyamel.** The specialty at this
MEXICAN Mexican stunner is *antojitos*, literally translated as "little dishes
from the street." But the high ceilings, gracious service, and gorgeous
Frida Kahlo–inspired decor are
anything but street, and even the
smallest of dishes is bigger than life
when doused with chocolatey mole
poblano sauce or piquant lime-
cilantro dressing. Standouts include
house-made margaritas topped with
a clever salt foam, the Veracruz red
snapper in a hearty olive-tomato
confit, and grasshopper tacos. Yes,
those are bugs basted in tequila and
pepper sauce—and they're delight-
ful. ✉ *401 7th St. NW, Chinatown* ☎ *202/628–1005* ⊕ *www.oyamel.
com* ⊟ *AE, D, MC, V* Ⓜ *Archives/Navy Memorial* ✛ *2:D3.*

$$ ✕ **Poste.** Inside the trendy Hotel Monaco, Poste woos diners with a
NEW AMERICAN towering skylighted space that until 1901 was the General Post Office.
Homing in on Modern American brasserie fare, chef Robert Weland
conjures up such satisfying dishes as foie-gras terrine with cognac jelly,
and pan-roasted sirloin with truffled frites. In season, panfried soft-
shell crabs are not to be missed. For dessert there's a dream of a bour-
bon pecan tart topped with caramel sauce and ice cream. In warmer
months the neoclassical courtyard is a serene spot for cocktails and light
fare. Year-round, the lively bar inside attracts scenesters with booths
on raised platforms. ✉ *Hotel Monaco, 555 8th St. NW, Chinatown*
☎ *202/783–6060* ⊕ *www.postebrasserie.com* ⊟ *AE, D, DC, MC, V*
Ⓜ *Gallery Pl./Chinatown* ✛ *2:D3.*

$$ ✕ **PS 7's.** This restaurant manages to be at once swanky yet youthful,
NEW AMERICAN and its bar scene is hip but low-key, with inventive cocktails and nibbles
like tuna tartare sliders, fried oysters with souffléd bacon mousse, and
veal "chips." In the elegant sunken dining room the menu reads like a
tasting menu and the portions are tiny. The diner calls the shots. Veal is
done three ways—a cheek, sweetbreads, the loin—all in petite portions.
And the place is not without a touch of whimsy courtesy of porthole-
like fish tanks filled with goldfish in the restrooms. ✉ *777 I St. NW,
Chinatown* ☎ *202/742–8550* ⊕ *www.ps7restaurant.com* ⊟ *AE, MC, V*
☉ *No lunch weekends* Ⓜ *Gallery Pl./Chinatown* ✛ *2:D2.*

$$–$$$ ✕ **Rasika.** This trendy Indian restaurant pairs an adventurous wine list
INDIAN with spicy fare in a supersleek setting. The chef, London export Vikram
Fodor's Choice Sunderam (from Bombay Brasserie), comes from a town where curries
★ never get short shrift. He has prepared a menu of traditional delights, like
a fiery chicken green masala, alongside newer, more inspired ones, like
lamb miniburgers, tiny crab cakes with Indian spices, and fried spinach
leaves with sweet yogurt sauce. Libations at the bar are concocted with
as much creativity as the food. Muted shades of cream, apple-green, and
cinnabar and dangling crystals evoke the subcontinent but in a stylish,

modern way. ⊠ *633 D St. NW, Chinatown* ☎ *202/637–1222* ⊕ *www.rasikarestaurant.com* ⊟ *AE, D, DC, MC, V* ☉ *Closed Sun. No lunch weekends* Ⓜ *Archives/Navy Memorial* ✚ *2:D3*.

$$
MIDDLE EASTERN
Fodor's Choice
★

✕ **Zaytinya.** This sophisticated urban dining room with soaring ceilings is a local favorite for meeting friends or dining with a group. Zaytinya, which means "olive oil" in Turkish, devotes practically its entire menu

to Turkish, Greek, and Lebanese small plates, known as *meze*. To get the full experience, make a meal of three or four of these, such as the popular braised lamb with eggplant puree and cheese, or the locally made goat cheese wrapped in grape leaves with tomato marmalade. ■ TIP→ So many options make this a great choice for vegetarians and meat lovers alike. Reservations for times after 6:30 are not accepted; come prepared to wait on Friday and Saturday nights. Belly dancers perform on Wednesday nights. ⊠ *701 9th St. NW, Chinatown* ☎ *202/638–0800* ⊕ *www.zaytinya.com* ⊟ *AE, DC, MC, V* Ⓜ *Gallery Pl./Chinatown* ✚ *2:D2*.

$–$$
SOUTHERN

✕ **Zola.** Swanky and chic, Zola channels a 1940s vibe with its snug banquettes, oval bar carts, and dramatic red flourishes. Food is fun without being over-the-top, and dishes have a Southern bent. Crisp rock shrimp spill over honeyed corn bread, a veal steak sidles up to polenta fritters, and rainbow chard gets a hit of applewood-smoked bacon. Dessert follows suit with sweets such as lemon chiffon pudding and chocolate fondue with Rice Krispies treats. Cocktail names reflect the restaurant's location inside the Spy Museum; there are daily wine flights as well. The bar menu includes a burger and a (slightly glammed-up) lobster roll. ⊠ *800 F St. NW, Chinatown* ☎ *202/654–0999* ⊕ *www.zoladc.com* ⊟ *AE, D, DC, MC, V* ☉ *No lunch weekends* Ⓜ *Gallery Pl./Chinatown* ✚ *2:D3*.

GEORGETOWN

$$$
AMERICAN

✕ **1789 Restaurant.** This dining room with Early American paintings and a fireplace could easily be a room in the White House. But all the gentility of this 19th-century town-house restaurant is offset by the down-to-earth food on the menu, which changes daily. The soups, including the seafood stew, are flavorful. Rack of lamb and fillet of beef are specialties, and the seafood dishes are excellent. Service is fluid and attentive. Try the bread pudding and crème brûlée for a sweet finish. ⊠ *1226 36th St. NW, Georgetown* ☎ *202/965–1789* ⊕ *www.1789restaurant.com* ⚬ *Reservations essential. Jacket required* ⊟ *AE, D, DC, MC, V* ☉ *No lunch* ✚ *1:A5*.

$$–$$$
FRENCH

✕ **Bistro Français.** Washington's chefs head to Bistro Français for minute steak, sirloin with black-pepper or red-wine sauce, and rotisserie chicken. Daily specials may include *suprême* of salmon with broccoli mousse and beurre blanc. In the less formal café, sandwiches and omelets are available in addition to entrées. The Bistro also has fixed-price lunches ($14.95), early and late-night dinner specials ($19.95),

6

and a champagne brunch on weekends ($21.95). ■TIP➔ It stays open until 3 am on weekdays and 4 am on weekends. ✉ *3128 M St. NW, Georgetown* ☎ *202/338–3830* ⊕ *www.bistrofrancaisdc.com* ☐ *AE, DC, MC, V* ✛ *1:B5.*

$ ✕ **Cafe Divan.** This small Turkish restaurant with walls of windows on
TURKISH three sides is a gathering spot for D.C.'s Turkish community as well as Georgetown's Euro population. You can make a meal of meze, small plates with such morsels as cigar-shape cheese-filled phyllo pastries and rice and currant–stuffed grape leaves, or pace yourself and leave room for main courses like Iskender kebab, thin slices of veal and lamb piled on crisped pita chips with drizzles of yogurt and tomato sauce. The unconventional Turkish-style pizzas from the wood oven are wonderful as well. ✉ *1834 Wisconsin Ave. NW, Georgetown* ☎ *202/338–1747* ⊕ *www.cafedivan.com* ☐ *AE, MC, V* Ⓜ *Dupont Circle* ✛ *1:A2.*

$$$ ✕ **Cafe Milano.** By night you're likely to rub shoulders with local social-
ITALIAN ites, professional sports stars, visiting celebrities, and the Euro-trendy crowd at Cafe Milano's cheek-by-jowl bar. Expect authentic, sophisticated Italian cooking and a pricey wine list. Specialties are fried stuffed olives and smelts, thin-crust pizzas, pasta dishes such as lobster with linguine and orecchiette with anchovies, air-dried ricotta, and the type of beautifully composed and dressed salads favored by ladies who lunch. ✉ *3251 Prospect St. NW, Georgetown* ☎ *202/333–6183* ⊕ *www. cafemilano.net* ☐ *AE, D, DC, MC, V* ✛ *1:A5.*

$$$$ ✕ **Citronelle.** See all the action in the glass-front kitchen at chef Michel
FRENCH Richard's flagship California-French restaurant. Appetizers might
Fodor's Choice include foie gras with lentils prepared three ways, and main courses
★ run to lobster medallions with lemongrass, saddle of lamb crusted with herbs, and breast of squab. Desserts are luscious: a crunchy napoleon with filament-like pastry and the very special "chocolate bar," Richard's dense, rich take on a Snickers candy bar. A chef's table in the kitchen gives you a ringside seat (reserve at least a month ahead). The fixed-price menu costs $155, or $230 with wine pairings. The bar menu ($$–$$$) has morsels such as mushroom "cigars" and Serrano ham. ✉ *Latham Hotel, 3000 M St. NW, Georgetown* ☎ *202/625–2150* ⊕ *www.citronelledc.com* ⌕ *Reservations essential. Jacket required* ☐ *AE, D, DC, MC, V* ⊗ *No lunch* ✛ *1:B5.*

¢ ✕ **Five Guys.** One of the quirky traditions of this homegrown fast-food
AMERICAN burger house is to note on the menu board where the potatoes for that
Ⓒ day's fries come from, be it Maine, Idaho, or elsewhere. The place gets just about everything right: from the grilled hot dogs and hand-patted burger patties—most folks get a double—to the fresh hand-cut fries with the skin on and the high-quality toppings such as sautéed onions and mushrooms. Add an eclectic jukebox to all of the above and you've got a great burger experience. There are a number of different locations around D.C. including Dupont Circle and Chinatown. ✉ *1335 Wisconsin Ave. NW, Georgetown* ☎ *202/337–0400* ⊕ *www.fiveguys. com* ☐ *MC, V* ✛ *1:B4* ✉ *1645 Connecticut Ave. NW, Dupont Circle* ☎ *202/328–3483* Ⓜ *Dupont Circle* ✛ *1:E3* ✉ *808 H St NW, Chinatown* ☎ *202/393–2900* Ⓜ *Gallery Pl./Chinatown* ✛ *2:D2.*

$$$
SEAFOOD
✗ **Hook.** Barton Seaver, the young chef who stunned Georgetown's old guard of gourmands with this ode to the "sustainable seafood" movement, is no longer cooking here—but his kitchen remains in capable hands. From weakfish to yahoo, all of the uncommon fish on the menu are caught using environmentally friendly methods that preserve overfished seafood populations like swordfish and salmon. Consciousness aside, your palate is in for a treat for lunch, brunch, or dinner. The wood-grilled calamari

> **DID YOU KNOW?**
>
> As if Washingtonians needed any more reason to cozy up to each other at Mie n Yu, pop princess Christina Aguilera confirmed its aphrodisiac powers when she told *Marie Claire* magazine that her baby was conceived the weekend she and hubby shared a plate here. Rumor has it they chose the decadent birdcage table for the best view.

with basil pesto is an unforgettable appetizer. Pastry chef Heather Chittum's fresh basil ice cream and homemade donuts stuffed with Nutella are also not to be missed. ✉ *3241 M St. NW, Georgetown* ☎ *202/625–4488* ⊕ *www.hookdc.com* ⌁ *Reservations essential* ▭ *AE, MC, V* ☾ *No lunch Mon.* ✛ *1:B5.*

$$
AUSTRIAN
✗ **Leopold's Kafe & Konditorei.** Forget all the clichés about heavy Austrian fare served by waiters in lederhosen. Leopold's is about as Euro trendy as it gets, with an all-day coffee and drinks bar, an architecturally hip dining space, and a chic little patio complete with a spewing minifountain. Food is pared-down Mitteleuropean: wine soup, crisp Wiener schnitzel paired with peppery greens, a spaetzle casserole that tastes like luxe mac 'n' cheese. In the middle of design-obsessed Cady's Alley, the café draws an artsy city crowd that's content to sit and watch the scene evolve, just as it's done in Europe. ✉ *3318 M St. NW, Georgetown* ☎ *202/965–6005* ⊕ *www.kafeleopolds.com* ▭ *AE, DC, MC, V* ✛ *1:A5.*

$$$
ASIAN
✗ **Mie n Yu.** Exotic romance abounds at this palatial retreat inspired by the Europe-to-Asia journey of explorer Marco Polo. The menu matches Polo's route along the Silk Road and takes on multiple ethnic personalities: nowhere else in the capital can you find a Thai pu-pu platter of beef satay and sugarcane pork alongside Chinese prawn toast and Indian-inspired banana hummus with naan bread. If you'd like to take your dining adventure even further, try the chef's tasting menu and take your seat inside a giant birdcage at the center of the dining room where chic couples head for special nights. ✉ *3125 M St. NW, Georgetown* ☎ *202/333–6122* ⊕ *www.mienyu.com* ▭ *AE, DC, MC, V* ☾ *No lunch Mon. and Tues.* ✛ *1:B5.*

¢–$
VIETNAMESE
✗ **Miss Saigon.** Shades of mauve and green, black art deco accents, and potted palms decorate this Vietnamese restaurant, where attention is lavished on the food and its presentation. Begin with crisp egg rolls or chilled spring rolls, and then proceed to exquisite salads of shredded green papaya topped with shrimp or beef. Daily specials include imaginative preparations of the freshest seafood. In addition, "caramel"-cooked and grilled meats are standouts. Prices are moderate, especially for lunch, but you may have to order several dishes to have your fill. ✉ *3057 M St. NW, Georgetown* ☎ *202/333–5545* ⊕ *www.ms-saigonus.com* ▭ *AE, DC, MC, V* ✛ *1:B5.*

6

¢–$ ✕ **Rocklands.** This tiny branch of the popular local barbecue chain does
BARBECUE   mostly takeout business, but even when eaten with plastic silverware,
the baby back ribs and smoked half chicken are still as tender as adver-
tised. Disposable coolers are also sold here, perfect for filling up with
corn bread and potato rolls and picnicking by the waterfront. ✉ *2418
Wisconsin Ave. NW, Georgetown* ☎ *202/333–2558* ⊕ *www.rocklands.
com* ⊟ *AE, MC, V* ✛ *1:A2.*

$–$$ ✕ **Sushi-Ko.** At one of the city's best Japanese restaurants, daily specials
JAPANESE   are always innovative: sesame oil-seasoned trout layered with crisp
wonton crackers, and a sushi special might be salmon topped with a
touch of mango sauce and a sprig of dill. You won't find the restaurant's
delicious ginger, mango, or green-tea ice cream at the local Baskin-
Robbins. ✉ *2309 Wisconsin Ave. NW, Georgetown* ☎ *202/333–4187*
⌁ *Reservations essential* ⊟ *AE, D, MC, V* ☾ *No lunch Sat.–Mon.*
✛ *1:A2.*

DUPONT CIRCLE

$–$$ ✕ **Bistrot du Coin.** An instant hit in its Dupont Circle neighborhood, this
FRENCH   moderately priced French bistro with a monumental zinc bar is noisy,
crowded, and fun. The comforting, traditional bistro fare includes
starter portions of mussels in several different preparations. Steaks, garnished with a pile of crisp fries, are the main attraction, but you might
also try the duck-leg confit or tripe *à la mode de Caen* (a beef tripe stew
with white wine, herbs, celery, and carrots). Wash it down with house
Beaujolais, Côtes du Rhône, or an Alsatian white. ✉ *1738 Connecticut
Ave. NW, Dupont Circle* ☎ *202/234–6969* ⊕ *www.bistrotducoin.com*
⊟ *AE, D, DC, MC, V* Ⓜ *Dupont Circle* ✛ *1:E3.*

$–$$ ✕ **Firefly.** The backlighted, amber bar and birch-log wall create a warm
AMERICAN   and natural look at this showcase for contemporary American bistro
food. Start with roasted beets and goat cheese or roasted turnip soup.
More-standard comfort food includes grilled pork tenderloin with Dijon
mustard, and roast chicken with bacon-braised cabbage and prunes.
The small wine list, made up mostly of California boutique labels, is
well chosen and priced fairly. ✉ *Hotel Madera, 1310 New Hampshire
Ave. NW, Dupont Circle* ☎ *202/861–1310* ⊕ *www.firefly-dc.com* ⊟ *AE,
D, DC, MC, V* Ⓜ *Dupont Circle* ✛ *1:E4.*

$–$$ ✕ **Hank's Oyster Bar.** The watchword is simplicity at this popular and
SEAFOOD   chic take on the shellfish shacks of New England. A half-dozen oyster
Fodor'sChoice   varieties are available daily on the half shell, both from the West Coast
★   and local Virginia waters, alongside another half-dozen daily fish specials. An amuse-bouche of cheddar Goldfish crackers adds a touch of
whimsy. Don't be shy about asking for seconds on the complimentary
baking chocolate presented along with your check—the kitchen doesn't
serve sweets, but it doesn't need to. ✉ *1624 Q St. NW, Dupont Circle*
☎ *202/462–4265* ⊕ *www.hanksdc.com* ⊟ *AE, MC, V* Ⓜ *Dupont Circle*
✛ *1:G3.*

$$$$ ✕ **Komi.** Johnny Monis, the young, energetic chef-owner of this small,
NEW AMERICAN   personal restaurant, offers one of the most adventurous dining expe-
Fodor'sChoice   riences in the city. The five-course prix-fixe is $74 and showcases
★   contemporary fare with a distinct Mediterranean influence. ■ TIP➔ Reservations open 30 days in advance—and the longer you wait, the smaller

your chance at a coveted table. Star plates include fresh sardines with pickled lemons, suckling pig over apples and bacon with polenta, and mascarpone-filled dates with sea salt. ⊠ *1509 17th St. NW, Dupont Circle* ☎ *202/332–9200* ⊕ *www.komirestaurant.com* ⌖ *Reservations essential* ☰ *AE, D, MC, V* ⊘ *Closed Sun. and Mon. No lunch* Ⓜ *Dupont Circle* ✢ *1:G4.*

$ ✕ **Kramerbooks & Afterwords.** This popular bookstore-cum-café is a
CAFE favorite neighborhood breakfast spot. ■ TIP➜ It's also a late-night haunt
☾ on weekends, when it's open around the clock. There's a simple menu with soups, salads, and sandwiches, but many people drop in just for cappuccino and dessert. The "dysfunctional family sundae"—a massive brownie soaked in amaretto with a plethora of divine toppings—is a local favorite, and especially popular with kids. Catch a live music performance—everything from rock to the blues—here Wednesday through Saturday from 8 PM to midnight. ⊠ *1517 Connecticut Ave. NW, Dupont Circle* ☎ *202/387–1462* ⊕ *www.kramers.com* ☰ *AE, D, MC, V* Ⓜ *Dupont Circle* ✢ *1:F4.*

$ ✕ **Malaysia Kopitiam.** The decor of this subterranean hideaway may be
MALAYSIAN Gilligan's Island meets Kon-Tiki, but the voluminous menu has Malaysian treasures to spare. Though menus with photos are usually cheesy, the binder here is quite helpful, since Malaysian cuisine is less well known than, say, Chinese or Japanese. Sticky rice with minced shrimp and chicken, okra and eggplant curry with tamarind, and crazy salads like the rojak (tofu, peanuts, egg, and shrimp fritters) are among the stars on a roster with dozens of choices. The place is a hit with groups despite its smallish size, because of its rock-bottom prices and the lively communal dining approach. ⊠ *1827 M St. NW, Dupont Circle* ☎ *202/833–6232* ⊕ *www.malaysiakopitiam.com* ☰ *AE, D, DC, MC, V* Ⓜ *Farragut N* ✢ *1:F5.*

¢–$ ✕ **Nooshi.** Always packed, with long lines waiting for tables and take-
ASIAN out, this attractive Pan-Asian noodle house has remarkably good Chinese, Japanese, Thai, Indonesian, Malaysian, and Vietnamese dishes. Try the Thai drunken noodles, which are soused in sake; gado-gado, a "cooked" Filipino salad; or the Vietnamese rice noodles with grilled chicken. After the restaurant added its extensive sushi menu, it changed its name to Nooshi (noodles plus sushi). ⊠ *1120 19th St. NW, Dupont Circle* ☎ *202/293–3138* ⊕ *www.nooshidc.com* ⌖ *Reservations essential* ☰ *AE, MC, V* ⊘ *No lunch Sun.* Ⓜ *Farragut N* ✢ *1:F5.*

$$–$$$ ✕ **Nora.** Chef and founder Nora Pouillon helped pioneer the sustainable-
AMERICAN food revolution with the first certified organic restaurant in the country,
Fodor's Choice and her seasonal, sustainable ingredients are out of this world. Settle
★ into the sophisticated and attractive quilt-decorated dining room and start with the mushroom, leek, and Brie tart or a locally grown salad. Entrées such as pepper-crusted steak and roasted salmon with parsnips emphasize the well-balanced, earthy ingredients. ⊠ *2132 Florida Ave. NW, Dupont Circle* ☎ *202/462–5143* ⊕ *www.noras.com* ⌖ *Reservations essential* ☰ *AE, D, MC, V* ⊘ *Closed Sun. No lunch* Ⓜ *Dupont Circle* ✢ *1:E3.*

$$$$ ✕ **Obelisk.** Come here for eclectic Italian cuisine. The five-course prix-
ITALIAN fixe ($65), your only option, changes every day, combining traditional

dishes with chef Peter Pastan's innovations. Representative main courses are lamb with garlic and sage, and braised grouper with artichoke and thyme. The minimally decorated dining room is tiny, with closely spaced tables. ✉ *2029 P St. NW, Dupont Circle* ☎ *202/872–1180* ⚊ *Reservations essential* ▬ *DC, MC, V* ⊗ *Closed Sun. and Mon. No lunch* Ⓜ *Dupont Circle* ✣ *1:E4.*

$$$
STEAK

✕ **The Palm.** A favorite lunchtime hangout of power brokers, the Palm has walls papered with caricatures of the famous patrons who have dined there. Main attractions include gargantuan steaks and Nova Scotia lobsters, several kinds of potatoes, and New York cheesecake. One of the Palm's best-kept secrets is that it's also a terrific old-fashioned Italian restaurant. Try the veal marsala for lunch or, on Thursday, the tasty shrimp in marinara sauce. ✉ *1225 19th St. NW, Dupont Circle* ☎ *202/293–9091* ⊕ *www.thepalm.com* ⚊ *Reservations essential* ▬ *AE, D, DC, MC, V* ⊗ *No lunch weekends* Ⓜ *Dupont Circle* ✣ *1:F5.*

$
ITALIAN
🦋

✕ **Pizzeria Paradiso.** A trompe-l'oeil ceiling adds space and light to a simple interior at the ever-popular Dupont Circle Pizzeria Paradiso. The restaurant sticks to crowd-pleasing basics: pizzas, panini, salads, and desserts. Although the standard pizza is satisfying, you can enliven it with fresh buffalo mozzarella or unusual toppings such as potatoes, capers, and mussels. Wines are well chosen and well priced. The intensely flavored gelato is a house specialty. ✉ *2003 P St. NW, Dupont Circle* ☎ *202/223–1245* ⊕ *www.eatyourpizza.com* ▬ *DC, MC, V* Ⓜ *Dupont Circle* ✣ *1:E4.*

¢–$
THAI

✕ **Sala Thai.** Who says Thai food has to be sweat inducing? Sala Thai makes the food as spicy as you wish, because this chef is interested in flavor, not fire. Among the subtly seasoned dishes are *panang goong* (shrimp in curry-peanut sauce), chicken sautéed with ginger and pineapple, and flounder with a choice of four sauces. Mirrored walls and warm lights soften this small dining room, as do the friendly service and largely local clientele. The Dupont location is the most popular, but Arlington, Bethesda, and the U Street and Upper Northwest neighborhoods all host winning Sala locations. ✉ *2016 P St. NW, Dupont Circle* ☎ *202/872–1144* ⊕ *www.salathaidc.com* ▬ *AE, D, DC, MC, V* Ⓜ *Dupont Circle* ✣ *1:E4.*

$–$$
MIDDLE EASTERN

✕ **Skewers–Café Luna.** As the name implies, the focus at Skewers is on kebabs, here served with almond-flaked rice or pasta. Lamb with eggplant and chicken with roasted peppers are the most popular variations, but vegetable kebabs and skewers of filet mignon and seasonal seafood are equally tasty. With nearly 20 choices, the appetizer selection is huge. You can enjoy the cheap eats (chicken-and-avocado salad, mozzarella-and-tomato sandwiches, vegetable lasagna, pizza) downstairs at Café Luna or in the reading room–coffeehouse upstairs at Luna

Books. ✉ *1633 P St. NW, Dupont Circle* ☎ *202/387–7400 Skewers, 202/387–4005 Café Luna* ⊕ *www.skewers-cafeluna.com* ▭ *AE, D, DC, MC, V* Ⓜ *Dupont Circle* ✛ *1:G4.*

$$–$$$
NEW AMERICAN

✕ **Tabard Inn.** Fading portraits and overstuffed furniture make the lobby lounge look like an antiques store, but this hotel restaurant's culinary sensibilities are thoroughly modern. The menu, which changes daily, consistently offers interesting seafood and vegetarian options. A popular entrée is the branzino, a flaky white fish, served with artichokes, preserved lemon, and lentils in an olive sauce. A vegetarian option might be porcini risotto with kalamata olives, Roma tomatoes, and pesto. ■**TIP**➔ **In good weather you can dine in the quaint, tranquil courtyard.** ✉ *Hotel Tabard Inn, 1739 N St. NW, Dupont Circle* ☎ *202/331–8528* ⊕ *www.tabardinn.com/rest.htm* ▭ *AE, DC, MC, V* Ⓜ *Dupont Circle* ✛ *1:F4.*

$$–$$$
SOUTHERN

✕ **Vidalia.** There's a lot more to Chef Jeffrey Buben's distinguished restaurant than the sweet Vidalia onion, which is a specialty in season. Inspired by the cooking and the ingredients of the South and the Chesapeake Bay region, Buben's version of New American cuisine revolves around the best seasonal fruits, vegetables, and seafood he can find. Try the five-onion soup made with duck broth, the shrimp on yellow grits, or the sensational lemon chess pie. The sleek modern surroundings, including a wine bar, are equal to the food. ✉ *1990 M St. NW, Dupont Circle* ☎ *202/659–1990* ⊕ *www.vidaliadc.com* ▭ *AE, D, DC, MC, V* ⊗ *Closed Sun. July and Aug. No lunch weekends* Ⓜ *Dupont Circle* ✛ *1:F5.*

FOGGY BOTTOM

$$–$$$
NEW AMERICAN
Fodor's Choice
★

✕ **Blue Duck Tavern.** Many chefs are fond of artisanal and local ingredients. Chef Brian McBride is so committed to the cause that fixings are often strewn across marble counters in the restaurant's show kitchen. By now diners have gotten used to watching pastry chefs churn ice cream to be served minutes later in glass ice buckets, but sweets—and watching for the town's biggest political names to claim their favorite tables—aren't the only pleasures. The kitchen wows with Modern American riffs like a double-cut pork chop with bourbon-glazed peaches, a marrowbone with creamy insides, and a meaty hanger steak. The dining room is stylish, done up with Shaker furniture and quilts. ✉ *1201 24th St. NW, Foggy Bottom* ☎ *202/419–6755* ⊕ *www.blueducktavern.com* ⌂ *Reservations essential* ▭ *AE, D, DC, MC, V* Ⓜ *Foggy Bottom/GWU* ✛ *1:D5.*

$$–$$$
SEAFOOD

✕ **Kinkead's.** This multichambered restaurant has a recently updated raw bar downstairs and more formal dining rooms upstairs, but the mood of quiet elegance remains. The open kitchen upstairs allows you to watch chef Bob Kinkead and company turn out an eclectic menu of mostly seafood dishes inspired by Kinkead's New England roots and by the cooking of Asia and Latin America. Don't miss the signature dish—salmon encrusted with pumpkin seeds and served with a ragout of crab, shrimp, and corn. Save room for dessert, because the chocolate and caramel sampler, which includes a chocolate-and-caramel soufflé, is a knockout. ✉ *2000 Pennsylvania Ave. NW, Foggy Bottom* ☎ *202/296–7700*

⊕ *www.kinkead.com* ⌲ *Reservations essential* ▭ *AE, D, DC, MC, V* ⊙ *No lunch weekends* Ⓜ *Foggy Bottom/GWU* ✛ *1:E6.*

$$$ ✕ **Marcel's.** Chef Robert Wiedmaier trained in the Netherlands and Bel-
BELGIAN gium, and in this, his first solo venture, his French-inspired Belgian cooking focuses on robust seafood and poultry preparations. Start with mussels, if they're available, and move on to perfectly seared diver scallops with a fennel puree. The roast chicken is a marvel, white and dark cooked separately to perfect tenderness and moistness. In season, be sure to order the fig tart with citrus crème anglaise and honey-cinnamon ice cream. ✉ *2401 Pennsylvania Ave. NW, Foggy Bottom* ☎ *202/296–1166* ⊕ *www.marcelsdc.com* ⌲ *Reservations essential* ▭ *AE, DC, MC, V* ⊙ *No lunch* Ⓜ *Foggy Bottom/GWU* ✛ *1:D5.*

$$$ ✕ **Westend Bistro by Eric Ripert.** Where else but the Ritz-Carlton Hotel
NEW AMERICAN would you find the chef of New York City's award-winning restaurant Le Bernardin? Eric Ripert is wowing the swells of Foggy Bottom with comfort food such as fish burgers with saffron aioli and a salad of local greens gussied up with truffle vinaigrette. Two caveats: side dishes must be ordered à la carte, and the handmade cocktails are a skyscraping $12 per glass. The pomegranate-spiked West End cocktail and a tangerine tequila named after the chef are particularly irresistible. ✉ *1190 22nd St. NW, Foggy Bottom* ☎ *202/974–4900* ⊕ *www.westendbistrodc. com* ⌲ *Reservations essential.* ▭ *AE, D, MC, V* ⊙ *No lunch weekends* Ⓜ *Foggy Bottom/GWU* ✛ *1:E5.*

ADAMS MORGAN

¢–$ ✕ **Bardia's New Orleans Café.** Locals swarm to this cozy café, where great
SOUTHERN food is accompanied by jazz. Seafood, whether batter-fried, blackened, or sautéed, is always a winner. The house favorite is the blackened catfish. Po'boy sandwiches (subs on French bread) are reasonably priced, fresh, and huge. Breakfast items, served all day, include traditional eggs Benedict or eggs New Orleans, with fried oysters, crabmeat, and hollandaise: they're both delicious. Don't leave without trying the outstanding beignets (fried puffs of dough sprinkled with powdered sugar). ✉ *2412 18th St. NW, Adams Morgan* ☎ *202/234–0420* ▭ *AE, MC, V* Ⓜ *Woodley Park/Zoo* ✛ *1:F1.*

$$–$$$ ✕ **Cashion's Eat Place.** Walls are hung with family photos, and tables
AMERICAN are jammed with regulars feasting on up-to-date, home-style cooking. Founder and capital cuisine superstar Ann Cashion recently sold the spot to her longtime sous chef, but the Eat Place has remained a neighborhood favorite. The menu changes daily, but roast chicken, steak, and seafood are frequent choices. Side dishes, such as garlicky mashed potatoes, sometimes upstage the main course. If it's available, order the chocolate terrine layered with walnuts, caramel, mousse, and ganache. ■TIP➜ At Sunday brunch, many entrées are a fraction of the normal price. ✉ *1819 Columbia Rd. NW, Adams Morgan* ☎ *202/797–1819* ⊕ *www. cashionseatplace.com* ⌲ *Reservations essential* ▭ *AE, MC, V* ⊙ *Closed Mon. No lunch* Ⓜ *Woodley Park/Zoo* ✛ *1:F1.*

$$ ✕ **La Fourchette.** On a block in Adams Morgan where restaurants seem to
FRENCH open and close weekly, La Fourchette has stayed in business for nearly a quarter of a century by offering good bistro food at reasonable prices. Most of the menu consists of daily specials such as venison with shallots

and pepper sauce, chicken in beurre blanc, or sweetbreads in a mushroom-cream sauce. This place looks as a bistro should, with an exposed-brick wall, a tin ceiling, bentwood chairs, and vaguely Postimpressionist murals. ⊠ *2429 18th St. NW, Adams Morgan* ☎ *202/332–3077* ▤ *AE, DC, MC, V* Ⓜ *Woodley Park/Zoo* ✛ *1:F1.*

¢–$ ╳ **Pasta Mia.** Patrons don't seem to mind waiting their turn to eat in this
ITALIAN   affordable, 40-seat trattoria, and the lines trail around the corner for a reason: Pasta Mia's southern Italian appetizers and entrées all cost around $10. Large bowls of steaming pasta are served with a generous layer of freshly grated Parmesan. Some best sellers are fusilli with broccoli and whole cloves of roasted garlic, rich spinach fettuccine, and penne *arrabbiata* (in a spicy marinara sauce with olives). Tiramisu, served in a teacup, is a civilized way to finish your meal. ⊠ *1790 Columbia Rd. NW, Adams Morgan* ☎ *202/328–9114* ▤ *No credit cards* ⊗ *Closed Sun. and Mon. No lunch* Ⓜ *Woodley Park/Zoo* ✛ *1:F1.*

U STREET CORRIDOR

$$ ╳ **1905.** This spot's logo features an antiqued key, which is the perfect
ECLECTIC   symbol for a dining experience so intimate you'll want to keep it a closely guarded secret. Young chef Jose Sanchez unites the flavors of France, Spain, and Italy for his small but satisfying menu of intelligent comfort food. Seared scallops with parsnip puree and haricot verts goes down like a buttery kiss, while the ubiquitous bistro burger gets an exotic makeover thanks to a tangy red-onion marmalade. The dining room's refurbished Victorian-era fixtures and wallpaper create a romantic buzz that recalls the Moulin Rouge—in fact, canoodling couples like to sip absinthe in the more private window booths. ⊠ *1905 9th St. NW, U Street Corridor* ☎ *202/332–1905* ⊕ *1905dc.com* ⌲ *Reservations essential* ▤ *AE, MC, V* ⊗ *No lunch. No dinner Sun. and Mon.* Ⓜ *U St./Cardozo* ✛ *1:H2.*

¢–$ ╳ **Ben's Chili Bowl.** Long before U Street became hip, Ben's was serving
AMERICAN   chili. Chili on hot dogs, chili on Polish-style sausages, chili on burgers,
Ⓒ   and just plain chili. Add cheese fries if you dare. The faux-marble bar and shiny red-vinyl stools give the impression that little has changed since the 1950s, but turkey and vegetarian burgers and meatless chili are a nod to modern times. Ben's closes at 2 AM Monday through Thursday, at 4 AM on Friday and Saturday. It opens late, at 11 AM and closes early, at 8 PM on Sunday. Southern-style breakfast is served from 6 AM weekdays and from 7 AM on Saturday. ⊠ *1213 U St. NW, U Street Corridor* ☎ *202/667–0909* ⊕ *www.benschilibowl.com* ▤ *No credit cards* Ⓜ *U St./Cardozo* ✛ *1:H2.*

$$ ╳ **Commonwealth.** Skeptics were everywhere when local superchef Jamie
ECLECTIC   Leeds, the creator of Hank's Oyster Bar, said her next project would be mastering the art of British pub food. But she has made the city a believer in cuisine never known for its taste, remixing head-scratching dishes such as frog in a puff (lamb sausage wrapped in puff pastry) and Scotch eggs (hard-boiled eggs given a coating of ground beef then deep-fried) into savory delights. The beer menu includes a rotating cast of cask-conditioned brews, which tend to be less carbonated than kegged drinks, and larger-size U.K. pint glasses. ⊠ *1400 Irving St. NW, U Street Corridor* ☎ *202/265–1400* ⊕ *www.commonwealthgastropub.*

6

com ⊟ *AE, MC, V* Ⓜ *Columbia Heights* ✢ *1:H1.*

$ ✕ **Etete.** The best of the city's Ethio-
AFRICAN   pian restaurants, Etete doesn't hold
ⓒ   back on the spices. Savory pastries known as *sambusas* are filled with fiery lentils, and ginger brightens a stew of vegetables. The sharing of dishes and the mode of eating—rather than using utensils diners tear off pieces of *injera*, a spongy pancake-like bread to scoop up stews and sautées—make for exotic and adventurous dining at this style-conscious eatery. ✉ *1942 9th St. NW, U Street Corridor* ☎ *202/232–7600* ⊟ *AE, D, DC, MC, V* Ⓜ *U St./African-American Civil War Memorial/Cardozo* ✢ *1:H2.*

$$ ✕ **Marvin.** The owner of this quirky club and restaurant named after
BELGIAN   soul singer Marvin Gaye is Eric Hilton, a D.C. local who became a national celebrity as half of the DJ supergroup Thievery Corporation. Inspired by Gaye's sojourn to Belgium in the 1980s, the menu combines soul food with traditional French classics—think chicken and waffles and steak frîtes. The food is so good it'll bust your belt. After dinner, sample a Belgian beer and shake your booty on the upstairs dance floor. Sunday brunch brings a stellar eggs Benedict and a lighter ahi tuna salad to the menu. ✉ *2007 14th St. NW, U Street Corridor* ☎ *202/797–7171* ⊕ *www.marvindc.com* ⌳ *Reservations essential* ⊟ *AE, MC, V* ☽ *No lunch* Ⓜ *U St./Cardozo* ✢ *1:H2.*

$$$ ✕ **Masa 14.** This modern lounge blends Asian and Latin American fla-
ECLECTIC   vors, with a menu of memorable small plates. The masa-panko-crusted calamari comes with a kick of Madras curry, and savory pork belly tacos are served on an Asian bun. The cocktail list, headlined by more than 100 varieties of tequila, is the star of the city's longest bar (65 feet). The only thing missing from this collaboration between raw-fish guru Kaz Okochi and fusion impresario Richard Sandoval is a full-time sushi chef—but with house music thumping and bartenders shaking fresh libations, few patrons realize their spicy tuna wasn't hand-rolled. ✉ *1825 14th St. NW, U Street Corridor* ☎ *202/328–1414* ⊕ *www.masa14.com* ⊟ *AE, MC, V* ☽ *No lunch* Ⓜ *U Street/Cardozo* ✢ *1:H3.*

¢   ✕ **Oohhs & Aahhs.** No-frills soul food is what you can find at this friendly
SOUTHERN   eat-in/take-out place where the price is right and the food is delicious. Ultrarich macaroni and cheese, perfectly fried chicken, and smoky-sweet beef ribs just beg to be devoured. Sides like collard greens have a healthy bent, cooked with vinegar and sugar rather than the traditional salt pork. Smack in the middle of the U Street area, the place is both a neighborhood hangout and destination for those missing the perennial dishes that Mama always made best. ✉ *1005 U St. NW, U Street Corridor* ☎ *202/667–7142* ⊟ *No credit cards* ☽ *Closed Sun. and Mon.* Ⓜ *U St./Cardozo* ✢ *1:H2.*

¢–$
AMERICAN

✕**Polly's Café.** Tables can be hard to come by on weekend nights at Polly's Café, a cozy oasis with a fireplace. That's when locals arrive ready to swill beer, eat better-than-average bar food such as smoked mozzarella salad, and enjoy jukebox favorites from every era. Nightly specials such as grilled tuna with ginger-sesame vinaigrette are among the more substantial plates. The hearty brunch, available every day, is one of Washington's best values. ⊠ *1342 U St. NW, U Street Corridor* ☎ *202/265–8385* ▭ *MC, V* Ⓜ *U St./Cardozo* ✛ *1:H2.*

$$$
ITALIAN

✕**Posto.** Now that the Obama administration has anointed this breezy, classic Italian kitchen its new power-dining palace, keep one eye on the door in case the attorney general or White House chief of staff comes popping in for a piece of wood-fired picante pizza. If spicy salami isn't your thing, the array of salads are convincing evidence that Italian food need not be carbohydrate-centric. The bustling aisles are often less than romantic, and service can be scattershot when a VIP is in the room, but if you're looking for a great meal with a side order of Capitol culture, there's no better place to be. ⊠ *1515 14th St. NW, U Street Corridor* ☎ *202/332–8613* ⊕ *www.postodc.com* ⌾ Reservations not accepted ▭ *MC, V* ⊘ No lunch Ⓜ *U Street/Cardozo* ✛ *1:H4.*

UPPER NORTHWEST

$
PIZZA
☺
Fodor'sChoice
★

✕**2 Amys.** Judging from the long lines here, the best pizza in D.C. is uptown. Simple recipes allow the ingredients to shine through at this Neapolitan pizzeria. You may be tempted to go for the D.O.C. pizza (it has *Denominazione di Origine Controllata* approval for Neapolitan authenticity), but don't hesitate to try the daily specials. Roasted peppers with anchovies and deviled eggs with parsley-caper sauce have by now become classics. At busy times the wait for a table can exceed an hour, and the noisy din of a packed house may discourage some diners. ⊠ *3715 Macomb St. NW, Glover Park* ☎ *202/885–5700* ⊕ *www.2amyspizza.com* ⌾ *Reservations not accepted* ▭ *MC, V* ⊘ *No lunch Mon.* ✛ *1:A2.*

$–$$
NEW AMERICAN

✕**Ardeo.** The trendy new American Ardeo and its lounge-like counterpart, the wine bar Bardeo, sit side by side in the ever-popular culinary strip of Cleveland Park. Ardeo is known for its clean design, professional and knowledgeable staff, and creative menu. Everything is skillfully prepared, from pan-roasted New Zealand rack of lamb to seared sea scallops and a loin of grilled venison. Bardeo has similar options in smaller portions, and great wine offerings, including more than 20 wines by the glass. ⊠ *3311 Connecticut Ave. NW, Cleveland Park* ☎ *202/244–6750* ⊕ *www.ardeorestaurant.com* ▭ *AE, D, MC, V* Ⓜ *Cleveland Park* ✛ *1:D1.*

$–$$
FRENCH

✕**Bistrot Lepic.** Relaxed and upbeat, with bright yellow walls and colorful paintings, this small, crowded neighborhood bistro is French in every regard—starting with the flirty servers. Traditional bistro fare has been replaced with potato-crusted salmon served with French grapes and ouzo-grape sauce. Some standards, like veal cheeks, remain. The wine is all French, with many wines available by the glass. The wine bar on the second floor has a menu of small plates such as terrine of foie gras, smoked-trout salad, and onion-bacon tart. On this level, seating is first-come, first-served, but if you reserve your spot in advance, you can order from the full menu. ⊠ *1736 Wisconsin Ave. NW, Glover Park* ☎ *202/333–0111* ⊕ *www.bistrotlepic.com* ⌕ *Reservations essential* ▭ *AE, D, MC, V* ✛ *1:A3.*

$$–$$$
SEAFOOD
✕ **Black Salt.** Just beyond Georgetown in the residential neighborhood of Palisades, Black Salt is part fish market, part gossipy neighborhood hangout, part swanky restaurant. Fish offerings dominate, and vary from classics like oyster stew and fried Ipswich clams to more-off-beat fixings like fluke with cider vinegar, lobster with Kaffir lime, and a tiramisu martini for dessert. The place can get crowded and loud, and advance reservations are a must for weekends. Regulars consider a meal at the bar a good fallback—it's one of the friendliest spots around. ⊠ *4883 MacArthur Blvd., Palisades* ☎ *202/342–9101* ⊕ *www. blacksaltrestaurant.com* ⌕ *Reservations essential* ▭ *AE, D, DC, MC, V* ⊘ *Closed Mon.* ✛ *1:A2.*

$–$$
INDIAN
✕ **Heritage India.** You feel like a guest in a foreign land dining at this restaurant: there's incredible attention to detail in everything from the tapestried chairs to the paintings of India and the traditional tandoori and curry dishes. Try the *tahli,* a daily special with six or seven curry, lamb, or chicken dishes, rice and naan, served in compartments on a silver platter. For large groups or those with heartier appetites, the Maharaja Menu offers a delirious smorgasbord of plates. ⊠ *2400 Wisconsin Ave. NW, Glover Park* ☎ *202/333–3120* ⊕ *www.heritageindiaofgeorgetown. com* ⌕ *Reservations essential* ▭ *AE, D, MC, V* ✛ *1:A2.*

$
MIDDLE EASTERN
✕ **Lebanese Taverna.** Arched ceilings, cedar panels etched with leaf patterns, woven rugs, and brass lighting fixtures give the Taverna a warm elegance. Start with an order of Arabic bread baked in a wood-burning oven. Lamb, beef, chicken, and seafood are either grilled on skewers, slow roasted, or smothered with a garlicky yogurt sauce. A group can make a meal of the meze platters—a mix of appetizers and sliced *shawarma* (spit-roasted lamb). The original location is in suburban Virginia, but this younger sibling has become better known. ⊠ *2641 Connecticut Ave. NW, Woodley Park* ☎ *202/265–8681* ⊕ *www.lebanesetaverna.com* ▭ *AE, MC, V* ⊘ *No lunch Sun.* Ⓜ *Woodley Park/Zoo* ✛ *1:D1.*

$$–$$$
NEW AMERICAN
✕ **New Heights.** This inviting restaurant has 11 large windows that overlook nearby Rock Creek Park. The sophisticated contemporary cooking blends bold world flavors into the traditional American dishes. Truffled potato-leek soup gets dolled up with a cheddar-cheese pierogi; king salmon wrapped in *katifi* (shredded wheat) is one of the more unusual entrées. Chocophiles will appreciate the chocolate mousse torte with strawberry coulis. ⊠ *2317 Calvert St. NW, Woodley Park* ☎ *202/234–4110* ⊕ *www.newheightsrestaurant.com* ⌕ *Reservations essential* ▭ *AE, D, DC, MC, V* ⊘ *Closed Mon. and Tues.* Ⓜ *Woodley Park/Zoo* ✛ *1:D1.*

$$–$$$
NEW AMERICAN
Fodor's Choice
★
✕ **Palena.** Chef Frank Ruta and pastry chef Ann Amernick met while working in the White House kitchens. At their contemporary American restaurant the French- and Italian-influenced menu changes seasonally. Among the can't-miss presentations are kabocha squash ravioli with goat cheese, poached scallops with roasted beets, and a venison chop with andouille sausage. Comforting desserts such as a tangy German apple cake or a chocolate torte are a perfect match for the earthy cooking.

■ TIP→ Tasting menus are $58 for three courses, $67 for four courses, and $76 for five courses. Reservations are not accepted for the equally fabulous lounge, where the inexpensive menu includes a cheeseburger with truffles, foie-gras terrine, and an extravagant platter of fries, onion rings, and paper-thin fried Meyer lemon slices. ✉ *3529 Connecticut Ave. NW, Cleveland Park* ☎ *202/537–9250* ⊕ *www.palenarestaurant. com* ⌖ *Reservations essential* ▭ *AE, D, MC, V* ⊘ *Closed Sun. and Mon. No lunch* Ⓜ *Cleveland Park* ✛ *1:D1.*

SUBURBAN MARYLAND

$$$

SEAFOOD

✕ **Bethesda Crab House.** This modest, noisy, ultracasual restaurant is the best place to enjoy one of the Chesapeake Bay area's great delicacies— blue crabs steamed with Old Bay seasoning. Order as many crabs as you want; when they're ready, they'll be dumped on your paper-covered table. That's your cue to pick up a mallet and knife and attack the crustaceans. (The waiters gladly give instructions.) Then settle back with a beer for some serious crab pickin'. The price varies with the time of year. It's a good idea to call in advance to reserve your crabs—the restaurant sometimes runs out. ✉ *4958 Bethesda Ave., Bethesda, MD* ☎ *301/652–3382* ▭ *MC, V* Ⓜ *Bethesda* ✛ *1:A1.*

SUBURBAN VIRGINIA

$$$

NEW AMERICAN

Fodor's Choice

★

✕ **2941 Restaurant.** Soaring ceilings, a woodsy lakeside location, and a koi pond make this one of the most striking dining rooms in the area. The playful cooking continually surprises, with plates like roasted veal tenderloin and sweetbreads with eggplant puree, truffled free-range chicken, a deconstructed "creamsicle" of orange sorbet and Tahitian vanilla ice cream, and little gifts from the kitchen like rainbow-hue house-made cotton candy. It's a family affair, too. The chef's father makes the artisanal breads that run from rosemary-olive to cherry-almond. You can order à la carte, go for the bargain pretheater menu (three courses for $45), or splurge on one of the tasting menus ranging from $75 to $110. ✉ *2941 Fairview Park Dr., Falls Church, VA* ☎ *703/270–1500* ⊕ *www.2941.com* ⌖ *Reservations essential* ▭ *AE, D, DC, MC, V* ⊘ *No lunch Sat.* ✛ *1:A6.*

$$

AMERICAN

✕ **Ashby Inn.** If there's a recipe for a perfect country inn, Jackie and Charles Leopold have it. Head an hour west from D.C., and your reward is extraordinary comfort food. Dishes are made with the freshest local ingredients and presented in an intimate setting. Try the arugula salad with just-picked greens from the inn's garden. The roasted chicken, the first item the Ashby ever offered, remains sublime. Sunday brunch is from noon to 2:30. ✉ *692 Federal St., Paris, VA* ☎ *540/592–3900* ⊕ *www.ashbyinn.com* ▭ *AE, MC, V* ⊘ *No lunch. No dinner Sun.– Tues.* ✛ *1:A6.*

$$

NEW AMERICAN

✕ **Carlyle Grand Café.** Whether you eat at the bustling bar or in the dining room upstairs, you'll find an imaginative, generous interpretation of Modern American cooking. Start with the blue-crab fritter or the house-made potato chips drizzled with blue cheese, then move on to entrées such as pecan-crusted trout, veal meat loaf, and roast pork tenderloin with a citrus glaze. The warm flourless chocolate–macadamia nut waffle with vanilla ice cream and hot fudge sauce has become a

6

local classic. You can even buy a loaf of the bread at the restaurant's own bakery, the Best Buns Bread Company, next door. ⊠ *4000 S. 28th St., Arlington, VA* ☎ *703/931–0777* ⊕ *www.greatamericanrestaurants. com/carlyle* ⊟ *AE, D, DC, MC, V* ✛ *1:A6.*

$$$ ✕ **Fyve Restaurant Lounge.** This formerly staid dining room in the Ritz-Carlton got a modern makeover to match the inventive cuisine stylings of new chef Amy Brandwein, who trained under Washington legend Roberto Donna. Warm tones of red and orange accentuate the sensuality of the Italian-inspired menu. Standout dishes include the grilled octopus salad studded with sun-dried tomatoes and cubes of Yukon Gold potatoes, and a lemon-roasted chicken that leaves a sweet kiss of citrus on your palate. "Amy's Purse," a fragrant bundle of cod in a tomato-cilantro broth served encased in cellophane, is another favorite. ⊠ *Ritz-Carlton, 1250 S. Hayes St., Pentagon City* ☎ *703/412–2760* ⊕ *www.fyverestaurant.com* ⊟ *AE, D, MC, V* ✛ *2:B6.*

NEW AMERICAN

$$$$ ✕ **Inn at Little Washington.** A 90-minute drive from the District takes you past hills and farms to this English country manor, where the service matches the setting. A seven-course dinner (without wine) is $138 Monday to Thursday, $148 on Friday and Sunday, and $168 on Saturday. After a first course of tiny canapés such as a mini-BLT on house-made bread, soup follows—perhaps chilled fruit or creamy leek. Braised duck and seared foie gras over watercress might come next, then squab over garlic polenta. Desserts, including the "palette" of pastel-hue sorbets, are fanciful, or choose the cheese plate, delivered on a life-size, mooing faux cow. ⊠ *Middle and Main Sts., Washington, VA* ☎ *540/675–3800* ⊕ *www.theinnatlittlewashington.com* ⌖ *Reservations essential* ⊟ *MC, V* ☾ *No Lunch. Closed Tues. in Jan.–Apr., June–Sept.* ✛ *2:A6.*

AMERICAN
Fodor's Choice
★

Dining and Lodging Atlas

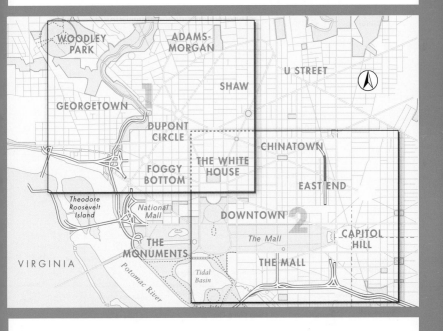

WOODLEY PARK

ADAMS-MORGAN

U STREET

SHAW

GEORGETOWN

DUPONT CIRCLE

CHINATOWN

FOGGY BOTTOM

THE WHITE HOUSE

EAST END

Theodore Roosevelt Island

National Mall

DOWNTOWN

2

CAPITOL HILL

THE MONUMENTS

The Mall

VIRGINIA

Potomac River

Tidal Basin

THE MALL

1

KEY	
☐	Hotels
▪	Restaurants
▪	Restaurant in Hotel
Ⓜ	Metro Station

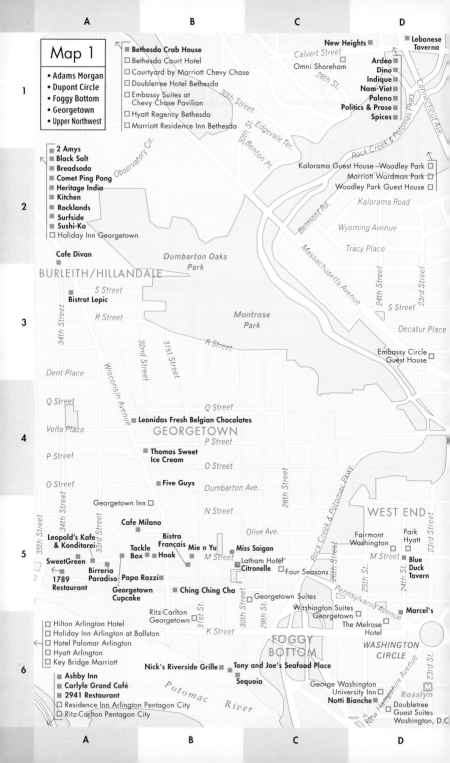

Map 1

- Adams Morgan
- Dupont Circle
- Foggy Bottom
- Georgetown
- Upper Northwest

A

- Bethesda Crab House
- Bethesda Court Hotel
- Courtyard by Marriott Chevy Chase
- Doubletree Hotel Bethesda
- Embassy Suites at Chevy Chase Pavilion
- Hyatt Regency Bethesda
- Marriott Residence Inn Bethesda

New Heights
Calvert Street
Omni Shoreham
Lebanese Taverna
Ardeo
Dino
Indique
Nam-Viet
Palena
Politics & Prose
Spices

- 2 Amys
- Black Salt
- Breadsoda
- Comet Ping Pong
- Heritage India
- Kitchen
- Rocklands
- Surfside
- Sushi-Ko
- Holiday Inn Georgetown

Kalorama Guest House –Woodley Park
Marriott Wardman Park
Woodley Park Guest House

Kalorama Road
Wyoming Avenue
Tracy Place

Cafe Divan

BURLEITH/HILLANDALE

S Street
Bistrot Lepic

R Street

Dumbarton Oaks Park

Montrose Park

R Street

S Street

Decatur Place

Dent Place

Q Street

Volta Place

P Street

O Street

Q Street

Leonidas Fresh Belgian Chocolates

GEORGETOWN

P Street

Thomas Sweet Ice Cream

O Street

Five Guys

Dumbarton Ave.

Embassy Circle Guest House

WEST END

Georgetown Inn

Cafe Milano

N Street

Olive Ave.

Fairmont Washington

Park Hyatt

Bistro Français

Leopold's Kafe & Konditorei

Tackle Box

Mie n Yu

Miss Saigon

M Street

Blue Duck Tavern

SweetGreen

Hook

Citronelle

Four Seasons

Birreria Paradiso

Papa Razzi

Latham Hotel

1789 Restaurant

Georgetown Cupcake

Ching Ching Cha

Georgetown Suites

Washington Suites Georgetown

Marcel's

Ritz-Carlton Georgetown

K Street

The Melrose Hotel

FOGGY BOTTOM

WASHINGTON CIRCLE

- Hilton Arlington Hotel
- Holiday Inn Arlington at Ballston
- Hotel Palomar Arlington
- Hyatt Arlington
- Key Bridge Marriott

Nick's Riverside Grille

Tony and Joe's Seafood Place

Sequoia

George Washington University Inn

Rosslyn

- Ashby Inn
- Carlyle Grand Café
- 2941 Restaurant
- Residence Inn Arlington Pentagon City
- Ritz-Carlton Pentagon City

Potomac River

Notti Bianche

Doubletree Guest Suites Washington, D.C

A **B** **C** **D**

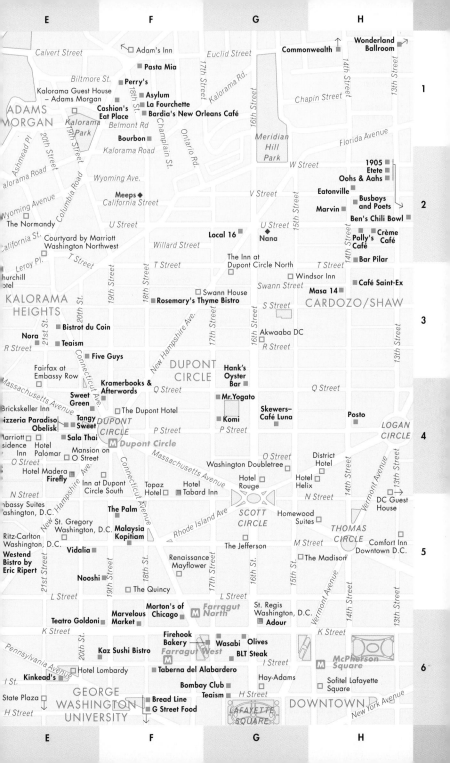

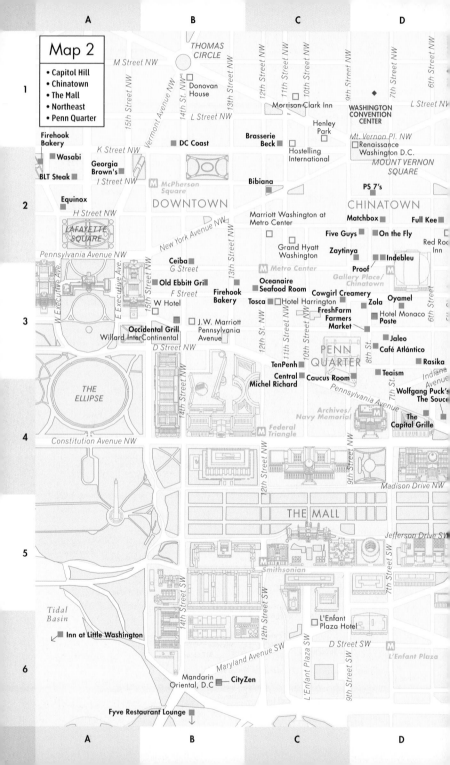

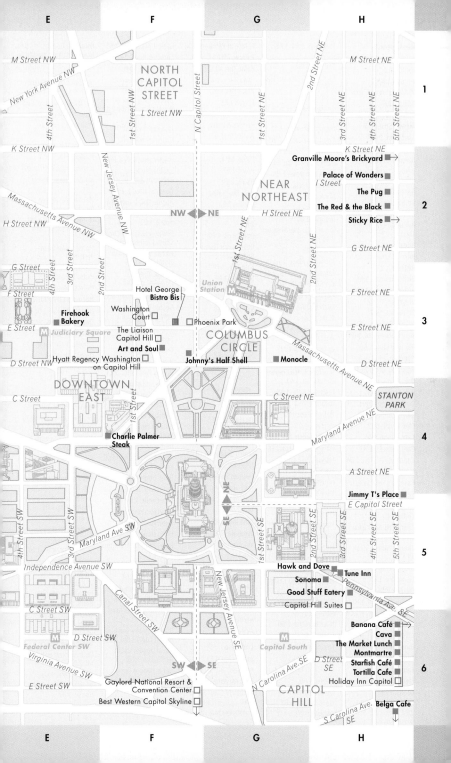

Where to Stay

WORD OF MOUTH

"I think Dupont Circle is a good idea because there are several hotels from which you could walk a very short distance to break-fast, or dinner, or just for coffee. It is, of course, very convenient to the Metro, but it's also easy to catch cabs between Dupont and the areas where museums are clustered."

—NewbE

THE SCENE

Updated by
Beth Kanter

D.C.'s transformation from stodgy Southern capital to bastion of culture and cool is well underway, and hotels here reflect the welcome change. Dignified lodgings fit for presidents and royalty share these pages with blingy boutique hotels straight out of New York or L.A.

This wave of renovation has led to a variety of options, so you'll do well to be choosy. Some hotels, like the Donavan House and Liaison Capitol Hill, or the newly refurbished The Jefferson, embrace the modern. Others, like the restored Fairfax at Embassy Row, gracefully combine historic character with modern amenities.

If you crave people watching, barhopping, and chic restaurants all within walking distance, try staying in Dupont Circle. Rooms here are as diverse as the people you'll see on the sidewalks.

If you are looking for more of an *American President* experience, book a room on Capitol Hill. The Hill will put you in filibuster distance of the Capitol, the National Mall with all its museums, and the Library of Congress. Tony Georgetown, with a renovated Four Seasons and a boutique-style Ritz-Carlton, is another option for an upscale experience.

Funky digs like Hotel Monaco in Penn Quarter put you near Chinatown, the International Spy Museum, high-end restaurants, and shopping. For a quieter stay, try Foggy Bottom, and for the best rates, head over the border to Bethesda, Maryland, or suburban Virginia. New water-taxi service from Old Town Alexandria will help make the trip across the Potomac more scenic, not to mention more fun.

Whichever neighborhood you unpack your suitcase in, remember that another one is never far away on the Metro. There are many appealing options in places you might not think to look. We've listed them in the pages that follow.

WHERE SHOULD I STAY?

	NEIGHBORHOOD VIBE	PROS	CONS
Adams Morgan	Diverse area with lively bar-and-club scene. The city's center of late-night activity, filled with students and young professionals.	Wide selection of restaurants, bars, and offbeat shopping options. Filled with 19th-century architecture. Stylish budget sleeps.	Some areas are dodgy after dark; it's a 15-minute walk to the Metro; street parking is in short supply. Few nearby monuments.
Capitol Hill	Charming residential blocks of Victorian row houses populated by members of Congress and their staffers.	Convenient to Union Station and the Capitol. Stylish (if not cheap) hotels. Fine assortment of restaurants and shops.	Some streets iffy at night; parking takes some work; hotels are pricey. Chock-full of tourists and high-priced hotels.
Downtown	This once-abandoned part of town is undergoing a renaissance. It's packed during the day but a little lonely at night.	Right in the heart of the Metro system; easy access to the White House. Large hotel selection.	Can feel desolate at night; few browse-worthy shops; daytime street parking near impossible.
Dupont Circle	D.C.'s most cosmopolitan neighborhood, filled with stylish bars, restaurants, and shops.	Modern design hotels … and lots of them; plentiful nightlife; easy Metro access.	Few budget options; limited street parking; very crowded in summer months.
Foggy Bottom	Charming residential and office area along Pennsylvania Avenue. Stately early-20th-century buildings.	Safe area; walking distance to Georgetown, State Department, and the Kennedy Center; good Metro access.	Paltry dining options and lots of traffic. Far from tourist attractions. Older hotels with few budget rates.
Georgetown	Wealthy neighborhood bordered by the Potomac and a world-class university. Filled with students and upscale shops and eateries.	Safe area. Historic charm on every tree-lined street. Wonderful walking paths along river.	Crowded; no nearby Metro access; lots of traffic. Lodging options are limited and tend to be expensive.
Southwest	The outer frontier of visitors' Washington, near the Smithsonian museums and the Mall.	Near the Mall; family-friendly hotels; easy Metro access; great river views.	Not much going on other than federal offices; may be too quiet for some travelers.
Upper Northwest	A pleasant residential neighborhood with a lively strip of good restaurants.	Safe and quiet; an easy walk to the zoo, Metro, and restaurants; street parking easier than Downtown.	A long ride to attractions other than the zoo; feels almost suburban. Few new hotels.

7

WHERE TO STAY PLANNER

Where Should We Stay?

With hundreds of D.C.-area hotels, it may seem like a daunting question. But fret not—our expert writers and editors have done most of the legwork. The 80-plus selections here represent the best this city has to offer—from the best budget motels to the sleekest designer hotels.

Scan "Best Bets" on the following pages for top recommendations by price and experience. Or find a review quickly in the listings. Search by neighborhood, then alphabetically. Happy hunting!

Hotel Extras

Hotels in the nation's capital work hard to provide extras as varied as their clientele. Almost all inside-the-Beltway properties have Wi-Fi, work desks, sleek gyms (or health-club passes), and morning coffee for lobbyists on the go. At family-friendly hotels you can often find swimming pools, zoo packages, bath toys, babysitting referrals, and kid-friendly fare on room-service and restaurant menus. Top hotels here offer everything from butler service to in-room spa treatments to evening canapés.

Need a Reservation?

With more than 92,000 guest rooms available in the area, you can usually find a place to stay—though it's always prudent to reserve. Hotels often fill up with conventioneers, politicians in transit, families, and, in spring, school groups. Hotel rooms in D.C. can be particularly hard to come by during the Cherry Blossom Festival in late March or early April, and also in May, when many graduate from college. Late October's Marine Corps Marathon also increases demand for rooms. **Destination DC** (☎ 800/422–8644 ⊕ www.washington.org) runs a reservation service. Many participating hotels are among the best in town.

Traveling with Kids

From the free Smithsonian museums on the Mall to the cuddly pandas at the National Zoo, D.C. is a very family-friendly town. Major convention hotels (and those on the waterfront) don't really cater to families, so we recommend looking Downtown, in Foggy Bottom, or in Upper Northwest, where many hotels offer special panda packages for the zoo bound. Also, the closer your hotel is to a Metro stop, the quicker you can get on the sightseeing trail. The Metro itself often ranks as a favorite attraction among the under-12 set. Consider a stay at an all-suites hotel. This will allow you to spread out and, if you prepare your meals in a kitchenette, to keep costs down. It gives the grown-ups the option of staying up past bedtime, too. A pool may well be essential for a stay with children, especially during D.C.'s notoriously humid summer months.

A number of well-known chains, including **Embassy Suites**, **Fairmont**, **Four Seasons**, **Ritz-Carlton**, and **St. Regis** also offer special programs for kids and usually have babysitting services. **Holiday Inns** allow kids (typically under 12) to eat free in their restaurants.

In the listings, look for the ☺, which indicates the property is particularly good for kids.

Facilities

We always list a property's facilities, but not whether you'll be charged extra to use them; when pricing accommodations, ask what's included. You can assume that all rooms have private baths, phones, TVs, and air-conditioning unless otherwise noted, and that all hotels operate on the European Plan (with no meals) unless we specify that they use the Continental Plan (CP, with a Continental breakfast), Breakfast Plan (BP, with a full-cooked breakfast), Modified American Plan (MAP, with breakfast and dinner), or the Full American Plan (FAP, with all meals).

Parking

Hotel parking fees range from free to $45 per night. This sometimes involves valet parking, with its additional gratuities. Street parking is free on Sunday and usually after 6:30 PM. But there are often far more cars searching than there are spaces available, particularly Downtown, in Georgetown, and in the upper Connecticut Avenue area.

During weekday rush hours, many streets are unavailable for parking; illegally parked cars are towed, and reclaiming a car is expensive and very inconvenient. *Read signs carefully*; some are confusing, and the ticket writers are quick.

Prices

If you're interested in visiting Washington at a calmer, less-expensive time—and if you can stand semitropical weather—come in August, during the congressional recess. Rates also drop in late December and January, except around an inauguration. Weekend, off-season, and special rates (such as AAA discounts and Web-only promotions) can also make rooms more affordable. A little bit of research can pay off in big savings.

WHAT IT COSTS					
	¢	$	$$	$$$	$$$$
FOR TWO PEOPLE	under $125	$125–$210	$211–$295	$296–$399	over $400

Prices are for a standard double room in high season, excluding room tax (14.5% in D.C., 12.5% in MD, and 10.15% in VA).

In This Chapter

7

BEST BETS FOR WASHINGTON, D.C. LODGING

Fodor's offers a selective listing of quality lodging experiences at every price range, from the city's best budget motel to its most sophisticated luxury hotel. Here are our top recommendations by price and experience. The very best properties—those that provide a particularly remarkable experience in a price range—are designated with a Fodor's Choice logo.

Fodor's Choice ★

Embassy Circle Guest House, p. 250

Four Seasons Hotel, p. 256

Hay-Adams Hotel, p. 240

Hotel George, p. 237

Hotel Madera, p. 251

Hotel Monaco, p. 243

Hotel Rouge, p. 251

Latham Hotel, p. 257

Mandarin Oriental Washington, D.C., p. 244

Omni Shoreham Hotel, p. 261

Ritz-Carlton Georgetown, p. 258

Sofitel Lafayette Square Washington, p. 247

St. Regis, p. 247

Swann House, p. 253

Best by Price

¢

Adam's Inn, p. 260

Hotel Tabard Inn, p. 252

Woodley Park, p. 260

$

Akwaaba DC, p. 248

George Washington University Inn, p. 255

Homewood Suites, p. 241

Latham Hotel, p. 257

Woodley Park Guest House, p 261

$$

DC GuestHouse, p. 239

Hotel Madera, p. 251

Hotel Monaco, p. 243

Swann House, p. 253

$$$

Hay-Adams Hotel, p. 240

Hotel Rouge, p. 251

Sofitel Lafayette Square Washington, p. 247

St. Gregory Hotel, p. 256

Topaz Hotel, p. 254

$$$$

Four Seasons, p. 256

Hotel George, p. 237

Hotel Palomar, p. 251

St. Regis, p. 247

Willard, p. 248

Best by Experience

BEST B&BS

DC GuestHouse, p. 239

Embassy Circle Guest House, p. 250

The Inn at Dupont Circle South, p. 252

Swann House, p. 253

Woodley Park Guest House, p. 261

BUSINESS TRAVEL

Grand Hyatt, p. 240

Park Hyatt, p. 258

Renaissance Washington, D.C., p. 246

St. Regis, p. 247

BEST CONCIERGE

Grand Hyatt, p. 240

The Jefferson, p. 243

St. Regis, p. 247

BEST DESIGN

Hotel George, p. 237

Hotel Monaco, p. 243

Hotel Palomar Arlington, p. 265

Hotel Rouge, p. 251

Ritz-Carlton Georgetown, p. 258

BEST SPA

Four Seasons, p. 256

Mandarin Oriental, p. 244

BEST POOL

Best Western Capitol Skyline, p. 259

Marriott Washington at Metro Center, p. 244

Omni Shoreham, p. 261

HOT SCENE

Donovan House, p. 240

The Dupont Hotel, p. 249

Hotel Madera, p. 251

Hotel Rouge, p. 251

Topaz Hotel, p. 254

W Hotel, p. 247

BEST FOR KIDS

Capitol Hill Suites, p. 237

Courtyard by Marriott Chevy Chase, p. 262

Fairmont Washington, p. 255

Four Seasons, p. 256

Homewood Suites, p. 241

Marriott Wardman Park, p. 261

Omni Shoreham, p. 261

MOST ROMANTIC

Fairmont Washington, p. 255

Hotel Monaco, p. 243

Hotel Rouge, p. 251

Swann House, p. 253

BEST VIEW

Hay-Adams Hotel, p. 240

JW Marriott Pennsylvania Avenue, p. 243

Key Bridge Marriott, p. 265

L'Enfant Plaza Hotel, p. 259

Mandarin Oriental, p. 244

Omni Shoreham, p. 261

Residence Inn Arlington Pentagon City, p. 265

BEST HOTEL GYM

Fairmont Washington, p. 255

Mandarin Oriental, p. 244

Renaissance Mayflower Hotel, p. 246

Ritz-Carlton Washington, DC, p. 255

Willard, p. 248

MOST ECO-FRIENDLY

Capitol Hill Suites, p. 237

Courtyard by Marriott Chevy Chase, p. 262

Embassy Suites at Chevy Chase Pavilion, p. 260

Hyatt Regency Washington on Capitol Hill, p. 238

Willard, p. 248

GRANDEST GRANDE DAMES

Hay-Adams Hotel, p. 240

The Jefferson, p. 243

Renaissance Mayflower Hotel, p. 246

St. Regis, p. 247

Willard, p. 248

BEST LOBBY

Mandarin Oriental, p. 244

Renaissance Mayflower Hotel, p. 246

Ritz-Carlton Georgetown, p. 258

St. Regis, p. 247

Willard, p. 248

PET-FRIENDLY

Hay-Adams Hotel, p. 240

Hotel Helix, p. 242

Hotel Rouge, p. 251

BEST FOR JOGGING BUFFS

Mandarin Oriental, p. 244

Marriott Wardman Park, p. 261

Omni Shoreham, p. 261

Ritz-Carlton Georgetown, p. 258

The Westin Alexandria, p. TK

BEST HOTELS WITH WASHINGTON-INSIDER BARS

Fairfax at Embassy Row, p. 250

Hay-Adams Hotel, p. 240

Renaissance Mayflower Hotel, p. 246

W Hotel, p. 247

BEST HOTELS FOR AFTERNOON TEA

The Henley Park Hotel, p. 241

The Jefferson, p. 243

Renaissance Mayflower Hotel, p. 246

Ritz-Carlton, Pentagon City, p. 266

BEST ALL-SUITES

Capitol Hill Suites, p. 237

Embassy Suites at Chevy Chase Pavilion, p. 260

State Plaza Hotel, p. 256

BEST OUTSIDE THE CITY LIMITS

Gaylord National Resort & Convention Center, p. TK

Hotel Palomar Arlington, p. 265

BEST-KEPT SECRETS

Akwaaba DC, p. 248

Embassy Circle Guest House, p. 250

Hotel Palomar Arlington, p. 265

Inn at Dupont Circle South, p. 252

BEST LOCATION

Grand Hyatt Washington, p. 240

Hotel Monaco, p. 243

BEST BOUTIQUE HOTELS

Hay-Adams, p. 240

Hotel George, p. 237

Hotel Monaco, p. 243

Topaz Hotel, p. 254

BEST SPLURGE

Hay-Adams, p. 240

The Jefferson, p. 243

Mandarin Oriental, p. 244

Ritz-Carlton Georgetown, p. 258

Sofitel Lafayette Square Washington, p. 247

St. Regis, p. 247

7

Hotel George

Hay-Adams Hotel

Hotel Monaco

Mandarin Oriental Washington, D.C.

Sofitel Lafayette Square Washington

St. Regis Washington, DC.

Embassy Row Guest House

Hotel Madera

Hotel Rouge

Swann House

Four Seasons Hotel

Latham Hotel

Ritz-Carlton Georgetown

Omni Shoreham Hotel

ADAMS MORGAN

$ **Kalorama Guest House—Adams Morgan.** Like its sister property in Woodley Park, this Adams Morgan location has been created out of early-20th-century Victorian town houses. The rooms, which vary in size, include 19th-century antiques and cozy furnishings. Some have shared baths, and only the suites offer phones and TVs. **Pros:** cozy alternative to a big hotel; walking distance to many restaurants. **Cons:** not all rooms have private baths; limited privacy. ✉ *1854 Mintwood Pl. NW, Adams Morgan* ☎ *202/667–6369* 🌐 *www.kaloramaguesthouse.com* *24 rooms, 9 with bath, 5 suites* *In-room: no phone (some), no TV (some). In-hotel: laundry facilities, Wi-Fi, parking (paid), no kids under 6, no-smoking rooms* *AE, D, DC, MC, V* *CP* Ⓜ *Woodley Park/Zoo* ✥ *1:E1.*

CAPITOL HILL

$$$ **Capitol Hill Suites.** Looking spiffy after a multimillion-dollar renovation, this is a great choice if you need some extra room to spread out. Suites are done in soothing earth tones and have large work desks, flat-screen TVs, and spacious closets. The hotel is extremely eco-friendly, doing everything from serving free-trade coffee in the lobby to using water-saving showerheads in every suite. All the appliances here from the boiler on up are high-efficiency models, and the hotel even runs an in-house paper recycling program. **Pros:** good for extended stays; free Internet access; close to Metro. **Cons:** limited street parking; wings are not connected. ✉ *200 C St. SE, Capitol Hill* ☎ *202/543–6000* 🌐 *www.capitolhillsuites.com* *152 suites* *In-room: safe, kitchen, refrigerator, DVD, Internet, Wi-Fi. In-hotel: gym, laundry service, Internet terminal, Wi-Fi, parking (paid), some pets allowed, no smoking rooms* *AE, D, DC, MC, V* *CP* Ⓜ *Capitol South* ✥ *2:H5.*

$$$$ Fodor's Choice ★ **Hotel George.** This hotel burst onto the scene in 1998, introducing the city to the concept of contemporary boutique lodging. More than a decade later, it still excels at providing a fun and funky alternative to the cookie-cutter chains. Portraits of America's first president by Andy Warhol protégé Steve Kaufman adorn public areas and add a pop of bright color to the mostly white public spaces. Guest rooms, done in cream and beige with cobalt-blue accents, have 300-count Egyptian cotton linens, marble-topped ergonomic desks, and expansive flat-screen TVs. Popular restaurant Bistro Bis is known for its contemporary French cuisine as well as its people watching. If you're driving a hybrid car you get a $10 discount off your parking bill. **Pros:** close to Union Station; popular restaurant; updated fitness center. **Cons:** small closets; some reports of street noise; ultra-modern feel not everyone's cup of tea. ✉ *15 E St. NW, Capitol Hill* ☎ *202/347–4200 or 800/576–8331* 🌐 *www.hotelgeorge.com* *139 rooms, 1 suite* *In-room: safe, DVD, Internet, Wi-Fi. In-hotel: restaurant, room service, bar, gym, laundry service, Wi-Fi, parking (paid), some pets allowed, no-smoking rooms* *AE, D, DC, MC, V* Ⓜ *Union Station* ✥ *2:F3.*

7

$$$-$$$$ 🖼 **Hyatt Regency Washington on Capitol Hill.** A favorite for political events, fund-raising dinners, and networking meetings, this property is a solid choice if you're planning on spending a lot of time on the Hill. Expect to find the newly renovated lobby abuzz with groups getting ready to participate in the political process. The Hyatt often serves as home base

> **GOING GREEN**
>
> The Hyatt Regency Washington is one of the city's most eco-friendly lodgings. It is one of only two hotels in town to have obtained Green Seal status, and even recycles the oil used in the kitchens.

for lobbying days, where organizations bring in busloads of people to meet with lawmakers. The hotel is within walking distance of Union Station, home to Amtrak, the Metro, shops, a food court, and restaurants. The recently expanded gift shop serves Starbucks coffee along with fresh pastries, bagels, and other treats. You can feel good about your carbon footprint when you sleep here. The hotel is one of the most environmentally friendly in the city, doing everything from pre-setting thermostats in guest rooms to utilizing earth-friendly cleaning products to monitoring its electrical use each day. ■TIP→ The Old Town Trolley has a stop right in front of the hotel and goes to the city's top tourist destinations. **Pros:** indoor pool; quick walk to Union Station; near the Capitol. **Cons:** busy; lots of groups; escalator in lobby. ⊠ *400 New Jersey Ave. NW, Capitol Hill* ☎ *202/737–1234 or 800/233–1234* ⊕ *www.hyattregencywashington. com* ⟿ *802 rooms, 32 suites* ⚬ *In-room: DVD (some), Internet, Wi-Fi. In-hotel: restaurant, room service, bar, pool, gym, laundry service, Wi-Fi, parking (paid), no-smoking rooms* ▭ *AE, D, DC, MC, V* Ⓜ *Union Station* ✛ *2:F3.*

$$$$ 🖼 **The Liaison Capitol Hill, An Affinia Hotel.** The Manhattan-based Affinia Hotel group is the latest urban hotel chain to stake its claim on Washington. The Liaison marries modern style with customized service elements, such as a pillow menu. The lobby gives off a private nightclub vibe and showcases a series of specially commissioned 6-foot monochromatic portraits of world leaders like Martin Luther King, Margaret Thatcher, and Gandhi. The space also houses the hotel's popular lounge, which buzzes into the early hours of the morning with political players and night owls alike. **Pros:** fantastic rooftop pool and deck; in-house Art and Soul restaurant is a choice dining destination; sidewalk patio for people-watching and summer cocktails. **Cons:** some street noise at night; no great room views; expensive parking. ⊠ *415 New Jersey Ave. NW, Capitol Hill* ☎ *202/638–1616 or 866/233–4642* ⊕ *www.affinia. com* ⟿ *343 rooms* ⚬ *In-room: safe, Internet, Wi-Fi. In-hotel: restaurant, room service, bar, pool, gym, laundry service, parking (paid), some pets allowed, no-smoking rooms* ▭ *AE, D, DC, MC, V* Ⓜ *Union Station* ✛ *2:F3.*

$$$$ 🖼 **Phoenix Park Hotel.** If you prefer to be near the Hill but not in a convention hotel, Phoenix Park may be for you. Guest rooms at this hotel named for a Dublin park boast comfy beds with 300-thread count Egyptian cotton sheets and equally soft Irish cotton bathrobes in the closets. The hotel is also across the street from Union Station, meaning

you have lots of dining choices. At the always-packed Dubliner Restaurant and Pub, which provides in-room dining, Irish entertainers perform nightly. **Pros:** perfect location; pleasant guest rooms. **Cons:** no swimming pool; small rooms. ⊠ *520 N. Capitol St. NW, Capitol Hill* ☎ *202/638–6900 or 800/824–5419* ⊕ *www.phoenixparkhotel.com* ⥽ *149 rooms, 6 suites* ♿ *In-room: safe, Internet, Wi-Fi . In-hotel: restaurant, room service, bar, gym, laundry service, Wi-Fi, parking (paid), no-smoking rooms* ☰ *AE, D, DC, MC, V* Ⓜ *Union Station* ⊹ *2:F3.*

$$$ 🏨 **Washington Court Hotel.** Marble stairs lead you up to a contemporary atrium lobby with a skylight, waterfall, and glass elevator. Each Deluxe room has a spacious work desk, a lounge chair and ottoman, and marble bathroom. The larger Executive King rooms offer expanded sitting areas with a pullout sofa bed. **Pros:** good location; Capitol views from many rooms. **Cons:** mixed service; expensive parking. ⊠ *525 New Jersey Ave. NW, Capitol Hill* ☎ *202/628–2100* ⊕ *www.washingtoncourthotel.com* ⥽ *252 rooms, 12 suites* ♿ *In-room: Internet. In-hotel: restaurant, room service, bar, gym, laundry service, parking (paid), no-smoking rooms* ☰ *AE, D, DC, MC, V* Ⓜ *Union Station* ⊹ *2:F3.*

DOWNTOWN

$ 🏨 **Comfort Inn Downtown D.C.** The recently renovated guest rooms here are clean, roomy and get a healthy dose of natural light. (Added bonus: the windows actually open.) Although the immediate area is mostly residential, a fair number of restaurants and clubs are a few blocks away, and there are a slew of takeout options that will deliver to the hotel. The Metro is about 15 minutes away on foot, and if you don't mind walking you can keep going for another 15 and hit the White House and the Mall. A deluxe Continental breakfast is served in the basement and includes eggs and waffles. **Pros:** light-filled guest rooms; fresh cookies at check-in; pleasant staff. **Cons:** some reports of street noise at night; walk to Metro; no restaurants or stores in immediate area. ⊠ *1201 13th St. NW, Downtown* ☎ *202/682–5300* ⊕ *www.choicehotels.com* ⥽ *100 rooms* ♿ *In-room: safe, Internet. In-hotel: gym, laundry facilities, laundry service, Internet terminal, Wi-Fi, parking (paid)* ☰ *AE, D, DC, MC, V* ⵔⵕ *CP* Ⓜ *McPherson Sq. 1:H5.*

$$–$$$ 🏨 **DC GuestHouse.** Grand and gorgeous, this double town house is yours to enjoy, along with an eclectic collection of African antiquities adorning sitting and guest rooms. There are original 1867 wood floors throughout; much of the rest has been salvaged from local antiques furnishers as this neighborhood has gentrified. Sleeping quarters are roomy, with satin coverlets, huge closets, high ceilings, and the same selective, just-so taste that blesses the sitting and dining rooms. Two of the rooms share a bath—they can be booked as a suite, or bathless for a lower price. ■ TIP➜ **Make sure to read the fine print on the strict cancellation policy: they charge a 10% fee if you cancel 15–30 days out and there is no refund if you cancel during the two weeks prior to your stay. Pros:** utterly charming host; terrific design and decor; full cooked breakfast in gorgeous dining room. **Cons:** small bathrooms; may be too personal for some. ⊠ *1337 10th St. NW, Downtown* ☎ *202/332–2502* ⊕ *www.*

7

dcguesthouse.com ⤻ *7 rooms, 5 with bath* ⚐ *In-room: DVD, Wi-Fi. In-hotel: Wi-Fi, parking (free), no kids under 12, no-smoking rooms* ▭ *AE, D, DC, MC, V* ⃝ *BP* Ⓜ *McPherson Sq.* ✛ *1:H4.*

$ ⌘ **The District Hotel.** Housed in creaky 1920s apartment building, the District Hotel gives off something of a Europe-on-$25-a-day vibe. It's small, dark, rundown in places, sees its fair share of students, and doesn't have much in the way of amenities. Still it's a bargain for the neighborhood. For under a $100 a night you can be Downtown and in walking distance of two Metro stations, the While House, restaurants, a grocery store, and lots of nightlife. Other bonuses include new flat-screen TVs in the tiny double standard rooms, free Wi-Fi access, and a light breakfast set up near the front desk in the mornings. **Pros:** cheap; good location; free Wi-Fi. **Cons:** shabby not chic; stairs to get into the building and then again into the lobby; little natural light. ⊠ *1440 Rhode Island Ave. NW, Downtown* ☎ *202/ 232–7800 or 800/350–5759* ⊕ *www.thedistricthotel.com* ⤻ *58 rooms* ⚐ *In-room: refrigerator (some), Wi-Fi. In-hotel: Internet terminal (fee), Wi-Fi, parking (paid)* ▭ *AE, D, DC, MC, V* ⃝ *CP* Ⓜ *McPherson Sq.* ✛ *1:H4.*

$ ⌘ **Donovan House.** You won't find anything remotely close to a colonial reproduction here. Complete with its hanging egg chairs, iPod docking stations, and circular showers, the Donovan House seems more Manhattan than Washington. The boutique-style hotel opened in 2008 and is already making a big splash. Guests tend to be as hip as the decor, often taking advantage of the nearby nightclubs. The hotel's restaurant Zentan serves global Asian cuisine and offers some favorites upstairs at the rooftop pool. **Pros:** modern design; rooftop pool; near clubs. **Cons:** smallish rooms; 10-minute walk to Metro. ⊠ *1155 14th St. NW, Downtown* ☎ *202/737–1200* ⊕ *www.thompsonhotels. com* ⤻ *193 rooms* ⚐ *In-room: safe, refrigerator, Internet, Wi-Fi. In-hotel: restaurant, room service, bar, pool, gym, laundry service, Wi-Fi, parking (paid), no smoking rooms* ▭ *AE, D, DC, MC, V* Ⓜ *McPherson Sq.* ✛ *2:B1.*

$$$ ⌘ **Grand Hyatt Washington.** In this high-rise hotel's airy atrium a player piano sits on a small island surrounded by a waterfall-fed blue lagoon. You can enter Metro Center, the hub of D.C.'s subway system, directly from the lobby. Cozy guest rooms have plush mattresses and thick down comforters, and marble baths are filled with Portico spa products. The hotel's sports bar is a good place to catch the game and a beer. **Pros:** great location for sightseeing and shopping; often has weekend deals. **Cons:** often filled with conventioneers; chain-hotel feel, service can be impersonal. ⊠ *1000 H St. NW, Downtown* ☎ *202/582–1234 or 800/233–1234* ⊕ *www.grandwashington.hyatt.com* ⤻ *851 rooms, 37 suites* ⚐ *In-room: Wi-Fi, refrigerator (some). In-hotel: 4 restaurants, room service, bars, pool, gym, laundry service, Wi-Fi, parking (paid), no-smoking rooms* ▭ *AE, D, DC, MC, V* Ⓜ *Metro Center* ✛ *2:C2.*

$$$ ⌘ **Hay-Adams Hotel.** It's no wonder that the Obamas chose this impres-
Fodor's Choice sive Washington landmark as their first Washington home as they got
★ ready to move into 1600 Pennsylvania Avenue. Less expensive guest rooms overlook the historic St. John's Episcopal Church and are equally

lovely. The Lafayette serves American fare and serves as the backdrop to many a Washington power lunch or dinner. The Off the Record bar downstairs lives up to its reputation as "the place to be seen but not heard." A new fitness center was recently opened at the hotel.

Pros: plush guest rooms; impeccable service; almost in the shadow of the White House. **Cons:** expensive; no pool. ⊠ *1 Lafayette Sq. NW, Downtown* ☎ *202/638–6600 or 800/424–5054* ⊕ *www.hayadams.com* ⇨ *145 rooms, 21 suites* ⟁ *In-room: safe, refrigerator (some), Wi-Fi. In-hotel: restaurant, room service, bar, laundry service, Wi-Fi, parking (paid), some pets allowed, no-smoking rooms* ☰ *AE, MC, V* Ⓜ *McPherson Sq. or Farragut N* ✛ *1:G6.*

$$$$ ▥ **Henley Park Hotel.** A Tudor-style building adorned with gargoyles, this National Historic Trust hotel has the cozy charm of an English country house. Rooms are charming, with nice touches like four-poster beds. There are also modern amenities like flat-screen TVs. ■**TIP**➔ **Afternoon tea is served at 4 PM in the handsome Wilkes room.** The highly acclaimed Coeur de Lion restaurant serves regional American dishes. **Pros:** historic building; privileges at nearby pool; frequent weekend specials. **Cons:** little parking; some street noise. ⊠ *926 Massachusetts Ave. NW, Downtown* ☎ *202/638–5200 or 800/222–8474* ⊕ *www.henleypark.com* ⇨ *83 rooms, 13 suites* ⟁ *In-room: safe, Wi-Fi. In-hotel: restaurant, bar, room service, laundry service, Wi-Fi, parking (paid), no-smoking rooms* ☰ *AE, D, DC, MC, V* Ⓜ *Metro Center* ✛ *2:C1.*

$ ▥ **Homewood Suites by Hilton, Washington.** The large family room-style
Ⓒ lobby here often is abuzz with people in suits preparing presentations and tourists resting up from the day. In the morning all guests can take advantage of the extensive breakfast buffet. The main room in the two-room suites (all were renovated in 2008) have pullout sofas, a work area that doubles as a table, and kitchens complete with microwaves, dishwashers and full-size refrigerators. If you drop off a list in the morning, hotel staff will do your grocery shopping for no additional fee. You can also buy ice cream, frozen dinners, and snacks at the little shop off the front desk and there is a complimentary dinner buffet Monday through Thursday. **Pros:** roomy suites; reduced weekend rates; good for families and extended stays. **Cons:** no pool; difficult street parking; 10 minutes to Metro. ⊠ *1475 Massachusetts Ave. NW, Downtown* ☎ *202/265–8000* ⊕ *www.homewoodsuites.com* ⇨ *175 suites* ⟁ *In-room: kitchen, refrigerator, Internet, Wi-Fi. In-hotel: gym, laundry facilities, laundry service, Internet terminal, Wi-Fi, parking (paid)* ☰ *AE, D, DC, MC, V* ❄⦿ *BP* Ⓜ *McPherson Sq.* ✛ *1:H5.*

¢ ▥ **Hostelling International–Washington, D.C.** This well-kept hostel has a living room with a big-screen TV and DVD player, a communal kitchen, a small gift shop, and Internet access. Rooms are generally dormitory-style, without private bathrooms, but families can have their own room if the hostel is not full. Towels and linens are included in the

7

rates. ■TIP➔ The maximum stay is 14 days, and reservations are highly recommended. College-age travelers predominate, and July and August are the busiest months. The facility uses earth-friendly paint, carpeting, and lightbulbs, and stocks its kitchen with reusable goods rather than paper and plastic ones. **Pros:** price can't be beat; free Wi-Fi, inexpensive breakfast. **Cons:** little privacy; crowded during college

WORD OF MOUTH

"The Hotel Harrington is cheap because it's an old tourist-class hotel that caters to tour and student groups. Rooms are small and bare bones, but the location is great for tourists."

—obxgirl

breaks, which makes getting a reservation difficult in summer. ✉ *1009 11th St. NW, Downtown* ☎ *202/737–2333 or 888/464–4872* ⊕ *www. hiwashingtondc.org* ⤸ *250 beds without bath* ♿ *In-room: no phone, no TV, Wi-Fi. In-hotel: laundry facilities, Wi-Fi, no-smoking rooms* ▭ *MC, V* Ⓜ *Metro Center* ✛ *2:C1.*

¢–$ 🏨 **Hotel Harrington.** One of Washington's oldest continuously operating hotels, the Harrington doesn't offer many frills, but it does have low prices and a location right in the center of everything. It's very popular with springtime high-school bus tours. The hotel offers free Wi-Fi. **Pros:** bargain prices; convenient location. **Cons:** no real amenities; shabby but not chic. ✉ *436 11th St. NW, Downtown* ☎ *202/628–8140 or 800/424–8532* ⊕ *www.hotel-harrington.com* ⤸ *245 rooms* ♿ *In-room: refrigerator (some), Wi-Fi. In-hotel: 3 restaurants, room service, bar, laundry facilities, Wi-Fi hotspot, parking (paid), some pets allowed, no-smoking rooms* ▭ *AE, D, DC, MC, V* Ⓜ *Metro Center* ✛ *2:C3.*

$$$ 🏨 **Hotel Helix.** In the Logan Circle neighborhood, the Helix combines a hip vibe with colorful hospitality. The theme here is fame, with blown-up photos of pop-culture icons ranging from Little Richard to Martin Luther King Jr. Some suites have bunk beds and flat-screen TVs. The minibar is stocked with fun extras like Pop Rocks candy. The Helix Lounge serves such American comfort food as its well-loved Helix burger. **Pros:** funky feel; good service; afternoon champagne. **Cons:** a schlep to the Metro; no pool; small gym. ✉ *1430 Rhode Island Ave. NW, Downtown* ☎ *202/462–9001 or 866/508–0658* ⊕ *www.hotelhelix. com* ⤸ *160 rooms, 18 suites* ♿ *In-room: safe, DVD, Wi-Fi. In-hotel: restaurant, room service, bar, gym, laundry service, Wi-Fi, parking (paid), some pets allowed, no-smoking rooms* ▭ *AE, D, DC, MC, V* Ⓜ *McPherson Sq.* ✛ *1:H4.*

$$$ 🏨 **Hotel Lombardy.** From the European antiques to the Oriental wool rugs to the original oil paintings, Hotel Lombardy has lots of charm. The 1926 art deco building, recognized by the National Trust for Historic Preservation, originally served as a luxury apartment house. Guest rooms feature plush bedding, work desks, and steel-and-chrome bathrooms. ■TIP➔ In summer, ask for free passes to the pool at the nearby Washington Plaza. **Pros:** homey rooms; beautiful lounge; three blocks from the White House. **Cons:** old-fashioned; expensive breakfast; on busy street. ✉ *2019 Pennsylvania Ave. NW, Downtown*

☏ *202/828–2600* ⊕ *www.hotellombardy.com* ⤳ *140 rooms 20 suites* ⚙ *In-room: kitchen, refrigerator, Internet. In-hotel: restaurant, room service, bar, gym, laundry service, parking (paid), no-smoking rooms* ▭ *AE, D, DC, MC, V* Ⓜ *Foggy Bottom-GWU* ✛ *1:E6.*

$$–$$$
Fodor's Choice
★

🛏 **Hotel Monaco.** Designed by Robert Mills (who also did the Washington Monument), the 1839 Tariff Building was one of the leading neoclassical buildings of its day. The brilliantly restored interior introduces a colorful, playful feel to the landmark edifice. Rooms have 15-foot vaulted ceilings, eclectic furnishings, and minibars with martini kits. If you wish, the staff will deliver companion goldfish to your room for the duration of your stay. The fashionable Poste Brasserie serves contemporary American cuisine, and the Verizon Center is right across the street. **Pros:** fun location next to Spy Museum; near great restaurants and shops; convenient to the Metro. **Cons:** noisy part of town; pricey; no pool. ✉ *700 F St. NW, Penn Quarter* ☏ *202/628–7177 or 877/202–5411* ⊕ *www.monaco-dc.com* ⤳ *167 rooms, 16 suites* ⚙ *In-room: safe, refrigerator, DVD, Wi-Fi. In-hotel: restaurant, room service, gym, laundry service, parking (paid), some pets allowed, no-smoking rooms* ▭ *AE, D, DC, MC, V* Ⓜ *Gallery Pl./Chinatown* ✛ *2:D3.*

$$$$
🛏 **The Jefferson.** For a moment, after the top hat–clad doorman ushers you into The Jefferson's exquisite marble lobby, you may think you stepped into a different stately residence down the street—at 1600 Pennsylvania Avenue. Every inch of this 1923 Beaux-Arts luxury hotel has been touched by its recent two-year-long restoration. The small historic hotel once again exudes refined elegance, from the intimate seating areas that take the place of a traditional check-in counter to the delicate blooms and glass atrium at The Greenhouse restaurant. Guest rooms have plush Porthault linens, Italian marble walk-in showers, and televisions recessed into the bathroom mirrors. The hotel's butlers even keep a supply of belts and dress shoes on hand. **Pros:** exquisite newly restored historic hotel; impeccable service; prestigious location. **Cons:** expensive; some rooms have views of other buildings; some street noise at night. ✉ *1200 16th St. NW, Downtown* ☏ *202/448–2300* ⊕ *www.jeffersondc.com* ⤳ *99 rooms, 20 suites* ⚙ *In-room: safe, kitchen (some), refrigerator (some), DVD (some), Internet, Wi-Fi. In-hotel: 2 restaurants, room service, bar, gym, spa, laundry service, Wi-Fi hotspot, parking (paid), some pets allowed, no-smoking rooms* ▭ *AE, D, DC, MC, V* Ⓜ *Farragut North* ✛ *1:G5.*

$$$$
🛏 **JW Marriott Pennsylvania Avenue.** From the location near the White House to the views from the top floors, it's hard to forget you are in the nation's capital when you stay here. Down in the lobby there is always lots of hustle and bustle as the many tourists and businesspeople who stay here get ready to take on Capitol Hill. **Pros:** in the heart of town; spiffy rooms; good views from top floors. **Cons:** very busy; expensive for what you get; chain-hotel feel. ✉ *1331 Pennsylvania Ave. NW, Downtown* ☏ *202/393–2000 or 800/393–2503* ⊕ *www.jwmarriottdc.com* ⤳ *729 rooms, 33 suites* ⚙ *In-room: safe, refrigerator, Wi-Fi. In-hotel: 2 restaurants, room service, bars, pool, gym, laundry service (fee), parking (paid), no-smoking room* ▭ *AE, D, DC, MC, V* Ⓜ *Metro Center* ✛ *2:B3.*

7

$$$ 🏨 **The Madison.** Luxury and meticulous service prevail at the stately Madison, which is why the signatures of presidents, prime ministers, sultans, and kings fill the guest register. Deceptively contemporary on the outside, the 15-story building is an elegant blend of Georgian, Federal, and American Empire styles. The M Street location puts you close to the White House, many monuments, and dozens of Downtown restaurants. A 2008 renovation bathed the guest rooms in soothing natural colors and gave them a more-contemporary feel. The plush bed linens and the heated towel racks are favorites with many regulars. **Pros:** twice-daily maid service; central location. **Cons:** pricey; no pool. ⊠ *1177 15th St. NW, Downtown* ☎ *202/862–1600 or 800/424–8577* ⤵ *311 rooms, 38 suites* ⌂ *In-room: safe, refrigerator (some), Internet. In-hotel: 2 restaurants, room service, bar, gym, spa, parking (paid), laundry service, some pets allowed* ⊟ *AE, DC, MC, V* Ⓜ *McPherson Sq.* ✦ *1:G5.*

> **GREEN POOL**
>
> The Marriott Washington at Metro Center recently switched to a saline swimming pool, an environmentally friendly alternative to pools treated with chlorine. Added bonus: no red eyes or green hair from dunking under.

$$$$ 🏨 **Mandarin Oriental Washington, D.C.** This hotel set a new standard of
Fodor's Choice sophisticated luxury and refined service. The expansive lobby's floor-
★ to-ceiling windows let you take in the grandeur of the Tidal Basin and the Jefferson Memorial. During cherry blossom season the Empress Lounge is among the most sought-after spots in town. Throughout the year, the gourmet CityZen is one of Washington's hottest restaurants. Asian accents and an impressive art collection are incorporated throughout the public areas and the guest rooms, which either overlook the waterfront or the Mall. The beds, dressed in imported Fili D'oro linens, will lull you to sleep and might very well make you want to ignore your wake-up call. The decadent spa is among the best around. **Pros:** decadent spa; beautiful views; best location for cherry-blossom viewing. **Cons:** expensive; a bit out of the way; few nearby dining options. ⊠ *1330 Maryland Ave. SW, Downtown* ☎ *202/554–8588 or 888/888–1778* ⊕ *www.mandarinoriental.com* ⤵ *400 rooms, 53 suites* ⌂ *In-room: safe, Internet, Wi-Fi. In-hotel: 2 restaurants, room service, bar, pool, gym, spa, laundry service, Wi-Fi, parking (paid), no-smoking rooms* ⊟ *AE, D, DC, MC, V* Ⓜ *Smithsonian* ✦ *2:B6.*

$$$–$$$$ 🏨 **Marriott Washington at Metro Center.** Near the White House, the MCI Center, and the Smithsonian museums, the Marriott has many virtues, including a marble lobby, original artwork, and the popular Metro Center Grille, Plaza Stop Café, and Regatta Raw Bar. Guest rooms have all the bells and whistles. The indoor pool and health club are among the best in town. **Pros:** great location; popular restaurants. **Cons:** busy location; big chain hotel. ⊠ *775 12th St. NW, Downtown* ☎ *202/737–2200 or 800/393–2100* ⊕ *www.marriott.com/wasmc* ⤵ *451 rooms, 2 suites* ⌂ *In-room: Wi-Fi. In-hotel: 2 restaurants, room service, bar, pool, gym, laundry service, Wi-Fi, parking (paid), no-smoking rooms* ⊟ *AE, D, DC, MC, V* Ⓜ *Metro Center* ✦ *2:C2.*

$$$$ ⊞ **Morrison-Clark Inn.** The elegant merging of two 1864 Victorian town houses, this inn (the only one in D.C. listed on the National Register of Historic Places) functioned as the Soldiers', Sailors', Marines', and Airmen's Club in the early 1900s. The antiques-filled public rooms have marble fireplaces, bay windows, 14-foot pier mirrors, and porch access, and one house has an ornate Chinese porch from 1917. Rooms have neoclassical, French country, or Victorian furnishings, and six have fireplaces. American cuisine with Southern and other regional accents is served at the inn's highly regarded restaurant, which has an outstanding wine selection. **Pros:** charming alternative to cookie-cutter hotels; historic feel throughout. **Cons:** some street noise; a long walk to Metro; not ideal for young children. ⊠ *1015 L St. NW, Downtown* ☎ *202/898–1200 or 800/332–7898* ⊕ *www.morrisonclark.com* ⮌ *54 rooms, 12 suites* ♿ *In-room: Wi-Fi. In-hotel: restaurant, room service, gym, laundry service, parking (paid), no-smoking rooms* ▭ *AE, D, DC, MC, V* ⦿⦿ *CP* Ⓜ *Metro Center* ✛ *2:C1.*

$–$$ ⊞ **The Quincy.** The black, white, and orange color scheme carries throughout the property, which now offers studio-style rooms with various-size kitchenettes. Kids—and the kid inside you—will get a kick out of the pay-per-play Nintendo games, while the many business travelers who pass through appreciate the large desks, laptop-size safes, and free Wi-Fi. Two different Metro stations—Farragut North and Farragut West—are a short walk from the front door, making it convenient to most of the city. Mackey's, the hotel's popular Irish pub, serves traditional Irish food and drink and gives off an everybody-knows-your-name kind of vibe. **Pros:** central location; convenient to Metro; affordable weekend rates. **Cons:** much of the area shuts down at end of the workday; no pool. ⊠ *1823 L St. NW, Downtown* ☎ *202/223–4320 or 800/424–2970* ⊕ *www.thequincy.com* ⮌ *78 rooms, 21 suites* ♿ *In-room: safe, kitchen, refrigerator, Wi-Fi. In-hotel: 2 restaurants, bar, room service, laundry facilities, Wi-Fi, parking (paid), no-smoking rooms* ▭ *AE, D, DC, MC, V* Ⓜ *Farragut N or Farragut W* ✛ *1:F5.*

$ ⊞ **Red Roof Inn, Downtown.** What makes this Red Roof different from others out there in Anytown, USA? Three words: location, location, location. This wallet conscious property puts you close to the heart of Penn Quarter. The Metro is a few blocks away as are the shops, restaurants, and clubs that have grown up as part of Chinatown's gentrification. (The hotel sits in a part of the area that has been more touched by urban blight than renovation so exercise a bit more caution at night.) Rooms are clean and serviceable but not fancy. The pub attached to the hotel serves meals and has something of a cult following among Guinness lovers. Its owners have gone to great lengths to install the proper taps and train its bartenders in the ways of the double pour. **Pros:** great location; good online deals; lots of restaurants and entertainment nearby. **Cons:** some Fodorites complain about street noise; few frills; church bells ring on the 5th Street side of the hotel from 7 AM to 7 PM. ⊠ *500 H St. NW, Penn Quarter/Chinatown* ☎ *202/289–5959* ⊕ *www.redroof.com* ⮌ *196 rooms* ♿ *In-room: safe, refrigerator (some), Wi-Fi. In-hotel: restaurant, laundry facilities, Wi-Fi, parking*

CLOSE UP

The Mayflower Hotel: Did You Know?

■ President Franklin D. Roosevelt wrote, "The only thing we have to fear is fear itself" in Room 776.

■ J. Edgar Hoover ate lunch at the Mayflower restaurant almost every weekday for 20 years. He almost always brought his own diet salad dressing.

■ Walt Disney once dined on the Mayflower's roof.

■ The state dinner celebrating the 1979 Arab-Israeli peace treaty was held here.

■ Winston Churchill sat for a portrait here.

■ Members of Congress interviewed Monica Lewinsky in the 10th-floor Presidential Suite while pursuing the impeachment of President Bill Clinton.

■ Former New York Governor Eliot Spitzer was allegedly visited by a high-priced call girl at his room here in 2008. The resulting scandal led to his resignation.

(paid), some pets allowed ⊟ *AE, D, DC, MC, V* ⓘⓄⓘ *EP* Ⓜ *Gallery Pl./ Chinatown* ✛ *2:D5.*

$$$$ 🏨 **Renaissance Mayflower Hotel.** The magnificent block-long lobby with its series of antique crystal chandeliers and gilded columns is a destination in itself. Guest rooms at this grande dame hotel, which opened its doors in 1925 for Calvin Coolidge's inauguration, are done in soothing yellows, green, tans, and blues. Town and Country, the hotel's inside-the-Beltway power bar, has been a place for political wheeling and dealing for nearly as long as the hotel. Sam the bartender mixes up 101 martinis to keep guests happily in the drink. Work off the booze and the crab cakes, a favorite on the menu at the hotel's elegant Café Promenade, in the spa-like fitness center. **Pros:** historic building; near dozens of restaurants; a few steps from Metro. **Cons:** rooms vary greatly in size; no pool. ⊠ *1127 Connecticut Ave. NW, Downtown* ☎ *202/347–3000 or 800/228–7697* ⊕ *www.marriott.com* 🛏 *657 rooms, 74 suites* ⚒ *In-room: Internet. In-hotel: restaurant, room service, bar, gym, laundry service, Wi-Fi, parking (paid), no-smoking rooms* ⊟ *AE, D, DC, MC, V* Ⓜ *Farragut N* ✛ *1:F5.*

$$–$$$ 🏨 **Renaissance Washington, D.C. Downtown Hotel.** Close to the Washington Convention Center and MCI Center, the Renaissance offers extensive business services and guest rooms with special mattresses and linens. The hotel includes a 10,000-square-foot fitness center and indoor lap pool. The casual restaurant, 15 Squares, serves regional American cuisine; the Presidents' Sports Bar is decorated with black-and-white photos of U.S. presidents at play; Starbuck's serves its signature brew in the lobby. **Pros:** convenient to convention center; near Metro. **Cons:** convention crowds; chain-hotel feel. ⊠ *999 9th St. NW, Downtown* ☎ *202/898– 9000 or 800/228–9898* ⊕ *www.marriott.com* 🛏 *775 rooms, 26 suites* ⚒ *In-hotel: 2 restaurants, room service, bar, pool, gym, laundry service,*

Wi-Fi, parking (paid), some pets allowed, no-smoking rooms ⊟ *AE, D, DC, MC, V* Ⓜ *Gallery Pl./Chinatown* ✛ *2:D2.*

$$$–$$$$ 🏨 **Sofitel Lafayette Square Washington.** The French could not have landed
Fodor's Choice a better location for the Sofitel, a minute's walk from the White House.
★ The boutique hotel has maintained the 1920s style of the original Shoreham Building, with an understated, sophisticated lobby and chic, though slightly small, guest rooms with beautiful marble bathrooms. The multilingual staff caters to Europeans and Americans. Cafe 15 serves artful French dishes under the direction of an award-winning chef. **Pros:** prestigious location; highly rated restaurant. **Cons:** lobby on the small side; expensive parking. ⊠ *806 15th St. NW, Downtown* ☎ *202/730–8800* ⊕ *www.sofitel.com* ⤳ *237 rooms, 16 suites* ♿ *In-room: safe, Wi-Fi. In-hotel: restaurant, room service, bar, gym, laundry service, Wi-Fi, parking (paid), some pets allowed, no-smoking rooms* ⊟ *AE, D, DC, MC, V* Ⓜ *McPherson Sq.* ✛ *1:H6.*

$$$$ 🏨 **St. Regis Washington, D.C.** Don't forget to admire the hand-painted
Fodor's Choice ceiling in the newly restored lobby of the St. Regis, a 1926 landmark
★ hotel that reopened in January 2008 after an extensive 16-month restoration. Pratesi linens line the beds, a 15-inch LCD TV is recessed behind the bathroom mirror in every guest room, and personal butlers now carry BlackBerrys, so while you're out you can e-mail requests like "Please pack my bags." Just two blocks from the White House, this Italian Renaissance–style hotel attracts a formal business crowd. If you check in with children, hotel staff will give them F.A.O. Schwarz teddy bears and bring kid-size robes to your room. The concierge also keeps a selection of toys and games on hand and can arrange babysitting. Newly opened Adour offers a contemporary French menu created by executive chef Julien Jouhannaud. **Pros:** close to White House; historic property; exceptional service. **Cons:** no pool; most rooms don't have great views; very expensive. ⊠ *923 16th St. NW, Downtown* ☎ *202/638–2626* ⊕ *www.stregis.com/washington* ⤳ *175 rooms, 25 suites* ♿ *In-room: safe, refrigerator (some), DVD, Internet, Wi-Fi. In hotel: restaurant, room service, bar, gym, spa, laundry service, Wi-Fi, parking (paid), some pets allowed, no smoking rooms* ⊟ *AE, D, DC, MC, V* Ⓜ *Farragut North* ✛ *1:G6.*

$$$$ 🏨 **W Washington, D.C.** From the DJ that spins tunes the living room–style lobby to the ultramodern room furnishings, this isn't your grandparents' hotel. The brand new W is the latest player to enter DC's growing contemporary hotel scene. It's nearly impossible to forget where you are: floor-to-ceiling windows in the J&G Steakhouse restaurant offer spectacular views of the Washington Monument and other iconic sites and, unless your last name is Obama, you pretty much aren't going to get a better look at the White House than from the outdoor rooftop bar lounge. **Pros:** new hip hotel; individualized and attentive service; fabulous location **Cons:** pricey; too modern for some; no pool. ⊠ *515 15th Street, NW, Downtown* ☎ *202/661–2400* ⊕ *www.starwoodhotels.com/whotels* ⤳ *317 rooms, 32 suites* ♿ *In-room: phone, safe, refrigerator (some), DVD (some), Internet, Wi-Fi. In-hotel: 1 restaurant, room service, 4 bars, gym, spa, laundry service, Internet terminal, Wi-Fi, parking*

7

(paid), some pets allowed, no-smoking rooms. ☰ *AE, D, DC, MC, V* Ⓜ *McPherson Sq.* ✛ *2:B3.*

$ ☷ **Washington Doubletree Hotel.** Just off Scott Circle, the Doubletree offers spacious, recently renovated guest rooms that have comfortable beds, well-equipped workstations, clock radios with MP3 players, and coffeemakers. An American bistro, 15 Ria, brings a New York sensibility to the hotel, which is only six blocks from the White House. **Pros:** child-friendly; good location; new fitness center. **Cons:** no pool; limited street parking. ✉ *1515 Rhode Island Ave. NW, Downtown* ☎ *202/232–7000 or 800/222–8733* ⊕ *www.washington.doubletree.com* ↳ *181 rooms, 39 suites* ⚒ *In-room: safe, Internet, refrigerator. In-hotel: restaurant, gym, Wi-Fi, parking (paid)* ☰ *AE, D, DC, MC, V* Ⓜ *Dupont Circle* ✛ *1:G4.*

WORD OF MOUTH

"The Willard and new W hotel are lovely and the location is great. Right next to the White House and an easy walk to all the museums/memorials on the National Mall."

—AGF324

$$$$ ☷ **Willard InterContinental.** This historic hotel has long been a favorite of American presidents and other newsmakers. Superb service and a wealth of amenities are hallmarks of the hotel, two blocks from the White House. The spectacular Beaux-Arts lobby showcases great columns, sparkling chandeliers, mosaic floors, and elaborate ceilings. Period detail is reflected in the rooms, which have Federal-style furniture and sleek marble bathrooms. The new French bistro–style restaurant Café du Parc serves three meals in a casual atmosphere. The Willard has opened its own history gallery, which chronicles the hotel's legendary past with photos, newspaper articles, and artifacts. **Pros:** luxurious historic hotel; great location; decadent spa. **Cons:** expensive; no pool. ✉ *1401 Pennsylvania Ave. NW, Downtown* ☎ *202/628–9100 or 800/827–1747* ⊕ *www.washington.interconti.com* ↳ *292 rooms, 40 suites* ⚒ *In-room: safe, DVD (some), Internet. In-hotel: 2 restaurants, room service, bar, gym, laundry service, Wi-Fi, parking (paid), some pets allowed, no-smoking rooms* ☰ *AE, D, DC, MC, V* Ⓜ *Metro Center* ✛ *2:B3.*

DUPONT CIRCLE

$–$$ ☷ **Akwaaba DC.** Celebrating African-American literary heritage in a guesthouse was the idea of Essence editor-turned-hotelier Monique Greenwood, and the result is D.C.'s best place to curl up with a good book. Rooms named for authors feature collections of their work, and individual decor meant to evoke their spirits. The Langston Hughes Suite channels its namesake's 1920s style with a massive antique writing desk, while Toni Morrison's love of Africa is reflected in fabrics and designs in the room that bears her name. The bright-red and glamorous Zora Neale Hurston room features a sexy two-person Jacuzzi tub. **Pros:** neighborhood location; nice breakfasts. **Cons:** smallish bathrooms. ✉ *1708 16th St. NW, Dupont Circle* ☎ *877/893–3233* ⊕ *www.akwaaba.com* ↳ *8 rooms, 1 apartment* ⚒ *In-room: refrigerator (some),*

Wi-Fi. In-hotel: Wi-Fi, no kids under 12, no-smoking rooms ≡ *AE, D, MC, V* ⊙ *BP* Ⓜ *Dupont Circle* ✛ *1:G3.*

$ 🏨 **Brickskeller Inn.** Run by the same family for 50 years, this 1912 building channels the spirit of an inexpensive European pension: shared baths, tacky linens, and some of the lowest prices in the neighborhood, if not the city. For some, shag carpeting may be unthinkable at any price, but if you're looking to save on lodging without skimping on location, look no further. The friendly owners are full of sightseeing tips—first stop, their downstairs bar and restaurant, which serves food until 1 AM. **Pros:** rock-bottom price; convenient location. **Cons:** shared bath; noise from bar downstairs. ⊠ *1523 22nd St. NW, Dupont Circle* ☎ *202/293–1885* ⊕ *www.lovethebeer.com* ⤴ *43 rooms, 2 with bath* ⚴ *In-room: no TV (some), no a/c (some). In-hotel: restaurant, bar, laundry facilities, no-smoking rooms* ≡ *AE, D, DC, MC, V* Ⓜ *Dupont Circle* ✛ *1:E4.*

$$ 🏨 **Churchill Hotel.** This historic Beaux-Arts hotel offers comfort and elegance near Dupont Circle. Spacious rooms have small work and sitting areas. The building's hilltop location means that many guest rooms have excellent views. The staff goes out of the way to be helpful, and complimentary coffee is offered in the lounge. **Pros:** friendly service; good-size rooms; frequent specials. **Cons:** far walk to Metro; uphill from Metro to hotel. ⊠ *1914 Connecticut Ave. NW, Dupont Circle* ☎ *202/797–2000 or 800/424–2464* ⊕ *www.thechurchillhotel.com* ⤴ *173 rooms, 83 suites* ⚴ *In-room: kitchen (some), Wi-Fi. In-hotel: Wi-Fi, restaurant, room service, bar, gym, laundry service, parking (paid)* ≡ *AE, D, DC, MC, V* Ⓜ *Dupont Circle* ✛ *1:D3.*

$$ 🏨 **Courtyard by Marriott Washington Northwest.** The Courtyard by Marriott is hiding something. The Connecticut Avenue hotel's secret is that some of its rooms have fantastic panoramic views of the city. The Washington Monument and other historic landmarks can be spotted from some of the south-facing rooms on higher floors. No matter which direction they face, all the guest rooms have the same floor-to-ceiling windows. The hotel recently underwent a small renovation and has standard Courtyard amenities like free breakfast and free Wi-Fi. **Pros:** great views from some rooms; good location; outdoor pool. **Cons:** chain-hotel feel with few unique touches; older hotel design. ⊠ *1900 Connecticut Ave. NW, Dupont Circle* ☎ *202/332–9300* ⊕ *www.marriott.com* ⤴ *147 rooms, 1 suite In-room: safe, refrigerator (some), Internet. In-hotel: bar, pool gym, Internet terminal, parking (paid), Wi-Fi hotspot, no-smoking rooms* ≡ *AE, D, DC, MC, V* ⊙ *BP* Ⓜ *Dupont Circle* ✛ *1:E2.*

$$–$$$ 🏨 **The Dupont Hotel.** The newly renovated Dupont Hotel has pulled off Mad Men chic without so much as a hint of kitsch. The small but comfortable guest rooms are outfitted with heated bathroom floors, flat-screen TVs and surprisingly effective noise-blocking windows. A $52 million renovation and rebranding effort has upgraded all the public areas and rooms. Even a new floor has been added: Level Nine, which is like a hotel within a hotel. Each of Level Nine's contemporary rooms boasts wood floors, high ceilings, balconies that overlook the city, twice-daily housekeeping service, and access to a library-style sitting

7

CLOSE UP

The Fairfax at Embassy Row: Did You Know?

The Fairfax at Embassy Row has a long connection to D.C. Here are a few fun facts about the historic property:

■ Al Gore lived here as a child (it was not a hotel at the time).

■ Hilary Clinton held press conferences here when she was running for president.

■ The Steinway piano in the lounge was a gift from the Kennedy family.

■ Nancy Reagan was a Jockey Club regular (she liked the corner table) and back in the day had a chicken salad named for her.

■ The Jockey Club opened for business in 1961 on the day John F. Kennedy took the presidential oath of office.

---

room with complimentary food, drink, and business amenities. The dark pub in the hotel's lobby has been replaced by a bright restaurant with a South Beach–style outdoor seating area overlooking the circle. **Pros:** right on Dupont Circle; newly renovated hotel; fabulous Level Nine concierge level. **Cons:** traffic and noise on Dupont Circle; guest rooms on the small side; limited closet space. ⊠ *1500 New Hampshire Ave. NW, Dupont Circle* ☎ *202/483–6000 or 800/423–6953* ⊕ *www. doylecollection.com/dupont* ⥵ *295 rooms, 32 suites* ⌂ *In-room: safe, kitchen (some), refrigerator (some), DVD (some), Internet (some), Wi-Fi. In-hotel: restaurant, room service, bar, gym, laundry service, Wi-Fi hotspot, parking (paid), no-smoking rooms* ⊟ *AE, D, DC, MC, V* ⏀⏀ Ⓜ *Dupont Circle* ✛ *1:F4.*

$–$$

Fodor's Choice

★

Embassy Circle Guest House. Owners Laura and Raymond Saba have lovingly restored this former embassy, transforming it into a warm and friendly home away from home. The charming pair like to introduce guests to each other during breakfast or at the evening wine-and-cheese reception, and are happy to make restaurant recommendations. Raymond loves to cook, and has been known to whip up something for his guests. Almost all of the impressive art displayed at the bed-and-breakfast was created by artists who were also guests at one time or another. Rooms are bright, with light wood floors and Oriental rugs. **Pros:** lovely hosts; personal service; good location. **Cons:** no bathtubs; too intimate for some. ⊠ *2224 R St. NW, Dupont Circle* ☎ *202/232–7744 or 877/232–7744* ⊕ *www.dcinns.com* ⥵ *11 rooms* ⌂ *In room: no TV, Wi-Fi. In hotel: laundry facilities, Wi-Fi, no smoking rooms* ⊟ *AE, D, MC, V* Ⓜ *Dupont Circle* ✛ *1:D3.*

$$–$$$

The Fairfax at Embassy Row. Two years and many millions of dollars turned what was once a perfectly lovely historic hotel into a wonderfully luxurious one. Gone are the English hunt club–themed rooms, the dark decor, and the Westin name. In its place are light-filled hallways, inviting bright guest rooms, and a new identity as an exclusive Luxury Collection member. Insanely soft bed lines, marble baths, decorator furnishings, more double rooms, and impeccable service make this hotel, which used to be Al Gore's childhood home, a good choice for business and leisure travelers alike. The old photos of Washington embassies and other landmarks that line the corridors pay tribute to the hotel's prestigious address and are worth checking out. The fabled Jockey Club, frequented by every first lady since Jackie Kennedy, reopened in 2008, much to the delight of Washington insiders. **Pros:** historic hotel; larger rooms; great location. **Cons:** no pool; challenging street parking. ⊠ *2100 Massachusetts Ave. NW, Dupont Circle* ☎ *202/293–2100 or 888/625–5144* ⊕ *www.fairfaxhoteldc.com* ⇨ *259 rooms, 27 suites* ⚴ *In-room: safe, Internet. In-hotel: 2 restaurants, room service, bar, gym, laundry service, parking (paid), some pets allowed* ▭ *AE, D, DC, MC, V* Ⓜ *Dupont Circle* ✛ *1:E4.*

$$–$$$
Fodor'sChoice
★
🔅 **Hotel Madera.** The unique Hotel Madera sits in a quiet part of town southwest of Dupont Circle. Innovative guest rooms with art-nouveau styling have high-tech touches. Extra-spacious "specialty rooms" have finer furnishings, although the bathrooms remain small. The adjoining Firefly Bistro has a sophisticated look and specializes in American comfort food. A tree hung with candles calls to mind the restaurant's name. ■ TIP→ Check in with a hybrid car and get a discount on parking. **Pros:** fun hotel; convenient location. **Cons:** no pool or gym; small bathrooms. ⊠ *1310 New Hampshire Ave. NW, Dupont Circle* ☎ *202/296–7600 or 800/430–1202* ⊕ *www.hotelmadera.com* ⇨ *82 rooms* ⚴ *In-room: safe, kitchen (some), refrigerator (some), DVD, Wi-Fi. In-hotel: restaurant, bar, parking (paid), some pets allowed, no-smoking rooms* ▭ *AE, D, DC, MC, V* Ⓜ *Dupont Circle* ✛ *1:E4.*

$$$$
🔅 **Hotel Palomar.** The Palomar is winning hearts and minds with space, style, and its hard-to-beat location. Guest rooms here are some of the largest in town, and are decorated with cool animal prints. (Think tiger-striped robes, crocodile-patterned carpets, and faux-lynx throws.) Plush purple and fuschia furnishings splash color on muted chocolate-beige rooms. Although bathrooms are surprisingly small, L'Occitane toiletries ease the blow; other up-to-the-minute details include laptop-size safes and iPod docking stations. **Pros:** spacious rooms; outdoor pool; good for pet owners. **Cons:** smallish baths; busy public areas not cozy for sitting. ⊠ *2121 P St. NW, Dupont Circle* ☎ *202/448–1800* ⊕ *www.hotelpalomar-dc.com* ⇨ *315 rooms, 20 suites* ⚴ *In-room: safe, refrigerator, DVD, Internet, Wi-Fi. In-hotel: restaurant, room service, bar, pool, gym, laundry service, parking (paid), some pets allowed, no-smoking rooms* ▭ *AE, D, DC, MC, V* Ⓜ *Dupont Circle* ✛ *1:E4.*

$$$
Fodor'sChoice
★
🔅 **Hotel Rouge.** This postmodern hotel bathed in red succeeds at bringing Florida's South Beach club scene to D.C. guest rooms. With specialty themes such as "chill or chow," the rooms are decorated with swanky eye-catching furniture. In the hip lobby lounge the bartenders are always busy concocting sweet new drinks. Bar Rouge, the cocktail lounge, attracts club-going denizens at all hours. **Pros:** great lounge scene; gay-friendly vibe; good location. **Cons:** no pool; the scene is not for everybody. ⊠ *1315 16th St. NW, Dupont Circle* ☎ *202/232–8000 or 800/738–1202* ⊕ *www.rougehotel.com* ⇨ *137 rooms* ⚴ *In-room:*

7

safe, kitchen (some), refrigerator (some), DVD. In-hotel: room service, bar, gym, Wi-Fi, parking (paid), some pets allowed, no-smoking rooms ⊟ *AE, D, DC, MC, V* Ⓜ *Dupont Circle* ✛ *1:G4.*

¢–$ **Hotel Tabard Inn.** Three Victorian town houses were consolidated to form the Tabard, one of the oldest hotels in D.C. Although the wooden floorboards creak and room sizes vary considerably (some share bathrooms), the dimly lighted hotel feels like an Old World inn, with alluring nooks and crannies inside and a brick-walled garden outside. The Tabard Inn's fireside bar may be one of the city's coziest winter retreats, and the restaurant remains a favorite among locals. Free passes are provided to the nearby YMCA, which has extensive fitness facilities. **Pros:** affordable choice; lots of character; Sunday-night jazz in the hotel lounge. **Cons:** some shared bathrooms; limited privacy, steps to climb. ✉ *1739 N St. NW, Dupont Circle* ☎ *202/785–1277* ⊕ *www.tabardinn.com* ⤳ *40 rooms, 25 with bath* ♿ *In-room: no TV (some), Wi-Fi. In-hotel: restaurant, bar, laundry facilities, Wi-Fi, some pets allowed, no-smoking rooms* ⊟ *AE, D, DC, MC, V* ⦿⃝*CP* Ⓜ *Dupont Circle* ✛ *1:F4.*

$ **The Inn at Dupont Circle North.** A more modern version of its sister property, the Inn at Dupont Circle South, this small hotel is a good choice if you want to be close to the restaurants and shops of Dupont Circle. Rooms have high-tech touches like flat-screen TVs and free Wi-Fi. Some have whirlpool tubs and working fireplaces. A full breakfast is served every morning. **Pros:** good location; breakfast included. **Cons:** not as charming as other bed-and-breakfasts; some shared baths; steps to climb. ✉ *1620 T St. NW, Dupont Circle* ☎ *202/467–6777 or 866/467–2100* ⊕ *www.thedupontcollection.com* ⤳ *7 rooms, 5 with bath* ♿ *In room: safe, refrigerator, Wi-Fi. In-hotel: laundry facilities, Wi-Fi, no-smoking rooms* ⊟ *AE, MC, V* Ⓜ *Dupont Circle* ✛ *1:G3.*

$–$$ **The Inn at Dupont Circle South.** This is the inn where everybody knows your name. Innkeeper Carolyn Torralba jokes that her guests are "her babies," and the personal attention shows: there are many repeat customers here. Most rooms have private baths; all have featherbeds and typical inn decor complete with doilies, bric-a-brac, and impressionist posters. Carolyn serves a hot breakfast in the parlor or on the sun porch. ■ **TIP→ The Nook Room is aptly named and budget-friendly at $95 per night. Pros:** personable innkeeper; across from Metro; children welcome; airport shuttle. **Cons:** creaking floors; steps to climb; not all rooms have private baths. ✉ *1312 19th St. NW, Dupont Circle* ☎ *202/467–6777 or 866/467–2100* ⊕ *thedupontcollection.com* ⤳ *8 rooms, 3 with shared bath* ♿ *In room: safe, refrigerator, Wi-Fi. In-hotel: laundry facilities, Wi-Fi, parking (paid), no-smoking rooms* ⊟ *AE, MC, V* ⦿⃝*BP* Ⓜ *Dupont Circle* ✛ *1:F4.*

$$$–$$$$ **Mansion on O Street.** Rock 'n' roll palace meets urban thrift shop in this oddball supper club-cum-guesthouse, a scramble of five side-by-side town houses crammed with art, junk, and everything in between. Nothing here suggests a hotel: from a two-story log-cabin suite with fish tanks and pony-skin chairs to the John Lennon–theme room with a signed guitar case and hologrammed bathroom floor, this is the most unusual sleep in town. Squander your evenings shooting pool in the

billiards room, or pick up one of the ubiquitous guitars and write a song about the place. Breakfast (included) is self-service in the giant, funky turquoise kitchen, and 24-hour room service is now available—just tell the chef what you are in the mood for and wait for the knock on your door. Watch for secret doorways, some left from when the Mansion was a dorm for Hoover's G-Men. **Pros:** one-of-a-kind; serious about privacy; glamorous common areas. **Cons:** layout makes for many dark rooms; eccentric staff and service; expensive. ⊠ *2020 O St. NW, Dupont Circle* ☎ *202/496–2020* ⊕ *www.omansion.com* 🛏 *18 rooms, 11 suites* △ *In-room: DVD (some), Wi-Fi. In-hotel: room service, bar, laundry service, Wi-Fi, parking (paid), no-smoking rooms* ☰ *AE, D, DC, MC, V* ⊙| *BP* Ⓜ *Dupont Circle* ✦ *1:E4.*

$$$ **Marriott Residence Inn.** It's remarkable that a commercial chain can feel so cozy, but this Residence Inn does just that by offering a small fireplace sitting room right off the lobby. The hotel has studios and one- and two-bedroom suites, excellent for business travelers or families. An evening reception (Monday through Thursday) is offered with complimentary snacks, and the bistro next door has an innovative bar with piano and cabaret-style singing on weekends and half-price wine nights on Monday and Tuesday. **Pros:** breakfast buffet; good choice for families. **Cons:** chain-hotel rooms; few unique touches. ⊠ *2120 P St. NW, Dupont Circle* ☎ *202/466–6800 or 800/331–3131* ⊕ *www.marriott.com/wasri* 🛏 *107 suites* △ *In-room: kitchen, Internet. In-hotel: restaurant, room service, gym, laundry facilities, Wi-Fi, parking (paid), no-smoking rooms* ☰ *AE, D, DC, MC, V* ⊙| *CP* Ⓜ *Dupont Circle* ✦ *1:E4.*

$$–$$$ **The Normandy.** Nestled on a residential street near Embassy Row, this quiet bed-and-breakfast–style hotel is walking distance to dozens of restaurants, shops, and bars without being on top of any of them. All of the cozy rooms were recently updated. Breakfast is served every morning in the pretty conservatory and in good weather can be enjoyed on the terrace. The staff bakes cookies each afternoon and hosts a weekly wine-and-cheese reception. In the summer guests can use the outdoor pool at the nearby Courtyard by Marriott. **Pros:** quiet location; close to restaurants and shops; charming inn-like hotel. **Cons:** no fitness center or pool on-site; a bit of a walk to the Metro. ⊠ *2118 Wyoming Ave. NW, Dupont Circle* ☎ *202/483–1350* ⊕ *www.doylecollection.com/ normandy* 🛏 *75 rooms* △ *In-room: safe, refrigerator, DVD (some), Wi-Fi . In-hotel: laundry service, Wi-Fi hotspot, parking (paid), some pets allowed, no-smoking rooms* ☰ *AE, D, DC, MC, V* ⊙| *CP* Ⓜ *Dupont Circle* ✦ *1:E2.*

$$–$$$ **Swann House.** From breakfast under the antique crystal chandelier to evening sherry by the fire, the days pass grandly in this romantic 1883 mansion. Equidistant from Dupont Circle's establishment scene and U Street's antiestablishment one, the location is convenient for much of D.C.'s nightlife. But like the local couples who come here for romantic weekends, you might be tempted to stay in, particularly if you've booked a room with a whirlpool tub or a two-person claw-foot tub. The Lighthouse Room, in one of the mansion's round turrets, is small, but three huge windows flood it with light, and there's an engaging view of

Fodor's Choice
★

7

the dog park across the street. A small swimming pool beckons in hot weather. **Pros:** perfect location; beautiful and lavish rooms; fireplaces in winter; a pool in summer. **Cons:** it is a bed-and-breakfast, so you're expected to mingle; cheaper rooms are small. ⊠ *1808 New Hampshire Ave. NW, Dupont Circle* ☎ *202/265–4414* ⊕ *www.swannhouse.com* �bed *9 rooms, 4 suites* ⚬ *In-room: DVD (some), Wi-Fi. In-hotel: pool, Wi-Fi, parking (paid), no kids under 12, no-smoking rooms* ☰ *AE, D, DC, MC, V* ⦿⦿ *CP* Ⓜ *Dupont Circle* ✛ *1:F3.*

$$$ 🛏 **Topaz Hotel.** A night at the Topaz is akin to a slumber party at a New Age dance club. The hotel's mystical theme is expressed through the colorful walls and art, allusions to different forms of enlightenment, and the fruity "power shots" served every morning. Creatively themed guest rooms may come with exercise equipment or yoga mats. The popular (and loud) Topaz Bar draws people from all over town. **Pros:** hybrid cars park free; good service; no cookie-cutter rooms. **Cons:** funky style not for everyone; no pool. ⊠ *1733 N St. NW, Dupont Circle* ☎ *202/393–3000 or 800/775–1202* ⊕ *www.topazhotel.com* ↬ *91 rooms, 8 suites* ⚬ *In-room: safe, DVD, Wi-Fi. In-hotel: bar, laundry service, Wi-Fi, parking (paid), some pets allowed, no-smoking rooms* ☰ *AE, D, DC, MC, V* Ⓜ *Dupont Circle* ✛ *1:F4.*

$–$$ 🛏 **Windsor Inn.** Near tree-lined New Hampshire Avenue, this bed-and-breakfast is in one of Washington's most attractive neighborhoods. The Phillips Collection and the restaurants and shops of Dupont Circle lie within six blocks. The three-story inn is actually two buildings, and neither has an elevator. Rooms are tastefully decorated, and most have showers only. There are some amenities expected of larger hotels, such as hair dryers and a morning newspaper. Three nights per week, sherry or wine is served in the downstairs lobby and a continental breakfast is out in the mornings. **Pros:** pleasant decor; pretty location; short walk to Metro. **Cons:** rooms on the small side; steps to climb; no pool. ⊠ *1842 16th St. NW, Dupont Circle* ☎ *202/667–0300 or 800/423–9111* ⊕ *www.hotelsdowntowndc.com* ↬ *36 rooms, 10 suites* ⚬ *In-room: refrigerator (some), Wi-Fi. In-hotel: Wi-Fi, no-smoking rooms* ☰ *AE, DC, MC, V* ⦿⦿ *CP* Ⓜ *Dupont Circle* ✛ *1:G3.*

FOGGY BOTTOM

$$–$$$ 🛏 **Doubletree Guest Suites Washington, D.C.** Among the row houses on this stretch of New Hampshire Avenue you might not realize at first how close you are to the Kennedy Center and Georgetown. This all-suites hotel has a tiny lobby, but its roomy one- and two-bedroom suites have full kitchens and living-dining areas with desks, dining tables, and sofa beds. The rooftop pool provides a place to relax after summertime sightseeing. You receive chocolate-chip cookies upon arrival. **Pros:** near Metro; quiet neighborhood; good online deals available. **Cons:** far from the museums; too quiet for some. ⊠ *801 New Hampshire Ave. NW, Foggy Bottom* ☎ *202/785–2000 or 800/222–8733* ⊕ *www.doubletree. com* ↬ *105 suites* ⚬ *In-room: kitchen, Wi-Fi. In-hotel: room service, pool, laundry facilities, laundry service, Wi-Fi, parking (paid), some pets*

allowed, no-smoking rooms ▭ *AE, D, DC, MC, V* Ⓜ *Foggy Bottom/ GWU* ✛ *1:D6.*

$$–$$$ 🏨 **Embassy Suites Washington, D.C.** Plants cascade over balconies beneath a skylight in this modern hotel's atrium, which is filled with classical columns, plaster lions, wrought-iron lanterns, waterfalls, and tall palms. Within walking distance of Georgetown and Dupont Circle, the suites here are suitable for both business travelers and families. Beverages are complimentary at the nightly manager's reception, and the rate includes cooked-to-order breakfast. There's a kids' corner with movies and games, and the Italian restaurant, Trattoria Nicola's, serves lunch and dinner. **Pros:** family-friendly; all suites; pool to keep the little ones—and sweaty tourists—happy. **Cons:** not a lot of character; museums not in walking distance. ✉ *1250 22nd St. NW, West End* ☎ *202/857–3388 or 800/362–2779* ⊕ *www.embassysuites.com* ⟿ *318 suites* ♿ *In-room: refrigerator, Wi-Fi. In-hotel: restaurant, room service, bar, pool, gym, laundry service, parking (paid), no-smoking rooms* ▭ *AE, D, DC, MC, V* ⊠|*BP* Ⓜ *Foggy Bottom/GWU or Dupont Circle* ✛ *1:D5.*

$$$$ 🏨 **Fairmont Washington.** The large glassed-in lobby and about a third of the bright, spacious rooms overlook a central courtyard and gardens. Rooms are comfortable, if not the city's most modern. The informal Juniper restaurant serves mid-Atlantic fare and has courtyard dining; there's a champagne brunch on Sunday in the Colonnade Room. ■ TIP→ The health club is one of the best in the city. Families have access to the pool, kids' menus and crayons in the restaurant, and a babysitting referral service. Family packages include things like a trip to visit the pandas at the National Zoo. **Pros:** fitness fanatics will love the health club; lots of kid-friendly features. **Cons:** pricey; far from most attractions. ✉ *2401 M St. NW, Foggy Bottom* ☎ *202/429–2400 or 866/540–4505* ⊕ *www.fairmont.com* ⟿ *406 rooms, 9 suites* ♿ *In-room: safe, Internet. In-hotel: restaurant, room service, bar, pool, gym, parking (paid), some pets allowed, no-smoking rooms* ▭ *AE, D, DC, MC, V* Ⓜ *Foggy Bottom/GWU* ✛ *1:D5.*

$ 🏨 **George Washington University Inn.** This boutique hotel is in a quiet neighborhood a few blocks from the Kennedy Center, the State Department, and George Washington University. Wrought-iron gates lead through a courtyard to the hotel's front entrance, where beveled-glass doors open onto a small lobby with a gray marble floor. Rooms, which vary in size and configuration, have colonial-style furniture and complimentary high-speed Internet access. Guests also receive free entry to the nearby Bally Total Fitness club. **Pros:** good price; close to Metro. **Cons:** not many amenities; far from museums. ✉ *824 New Hampshire Ave. NW, Foggy Bottom* ☎ *202/337–6620 or 800/426–4455* ⊕ *www. gwuinn.com* ⟿ *64 rooms, 31 suites* ♿ *In-room: safe, kitchen (some), refrigerator, Wi-Fi. In-hotel: restaurant, bar, laundry facilities, laundry service, parking (paid), no-smoking rooms* ▭ *AE, DC, MC, V* Ⓜ *Foggy Bottom/GWU* ✛ *1:D6.*

$$$$ 🏨 **Ritz-Carlton Washington, D.C.** Already one of the city's top hotels, the Ritz-Carlton got a $12 million face-lift in 2008, leaving the guest rooms, lobby, and lounges even more luxurious. Rooms are done in soothing pale yellow and moss-green, embracing a refined classic look that has

come to define the Ritz-Carlton. Beds are dressed in 400-thread-count Egyptian cotton linens and have earned the reputation as some of the most comfortable in town. The large marble tubs, separate showers, and Bulgari toiletries are similarly inviting. Impeccable service makes you feel pampered. The hotel's Westend Bistro by Eric Ripert serves American fare and has amassed a loyal following. **Pros:** attentive service; convenient to several parts of town. **Cons:** pricey room rates; expensive valet parking. ⊠ *1150 22nd St. NW, Foggy Bottom* ☎ *202/835–0500 or 800/241–3333* ⊕ *www.ritzcarlton.com/hotels/washington_dc* ⤳ *300 rooms, 32 suites* ♿ *In-room: safe, Internet, Wi-Fi. In-hotel: 2 restaurants, room service, bar, pool, gym, spa, laundry service, Wi-Fi, parking (paid), some pets allowed, no smoking rooms* ▭ *AE, D, DC, MC, V* Ⓜ *Foggy Bottom/GWU* ✛ *1:E5.*

$$$ 🛏 **St. Gregory Hotel.** The handsome St. Gregory caters to business and leisure travelers who appreciate spacious accommodations that include fully stocked kitchens. All rooms include turndown service, a newspaper, and shoe shine. The modern lobby, which has a sculpture of Marilyn Monroe, connects to the M Street Bar & Grill. **Pros:** big rooms; good for long-term stays. **Cons:** far from museums; area is sleepy at night. ⊠ *2033 M St. NW, West End* ☎ *202/530–3600 or 800/829–5034* ⊕ *www.capitolhotelswdc.com* ⤳ *54 rooms, 100 suites* ♿ *In-room: kitchen (some), refrigerator, Internet, Wi-Fi. In-hotel: restaurant, room service, gym, laundry service, parking (paid), no-smoking rooms* ▭ *AE, D, DC, MC, V* Ⓜ *Dupont Circle* ✛ *1:E5.*

$$$$ 🛏 **State Plaza Hotel.** No Washington hotel gets you quicker access to the State Department, which sits across the street. There's nothing distinguishing about the lobby, but the spacious suites have kitchenettes and lighted dressing tables, and the hotel staff is friendly and attentive. Guests receive a complimentary newspaper and a shoe shine. Nightly turndown service is provided. **Pros:** all suites; free Internet access; walk to Metro. **Cons:** far from museums; not a lot of character. ⊠ *2117 E St. NW, Foggy Bottom* ☎ *202/861–8200 or 800/424–2859* ⊕ *www.stateplaza.com* ⤳ *230 suites* ♿ *In-room: kitchen. In-hotel: restaurant, room service, gym, laundry service, parking (paid), no-smoking rooms* ▭ *AE, D, DC, MC, V* Ⓜ *Foggy Bottom/GWU* ✛ *1:E6.*

GEORGETOWN

$$$$
☾
Fodor'sChoice
★

🛏 **Four Seasons Hotel.** After a whopping $40 million renovation, the Four Seasons has reasserted its role as Washington's leading hotel. Impeccable service and a wealth of amenities have long made this a favorite with celebrities, hotel connoisseurs, and families. Luxurious, ultramodern rooms offer heavenly beds, flat-screen digital TVs with DVD players, and French limestone or marble baths with separate showers and sunken tubs. A 2,000-piece original art collection graces the walls, and a walk through the corridors seems like a visit to a wing of the National Gallery. The formal Seasons restaurant offers traditional dishes with an elegant twist, as well as a popular Sunday brunch. The sophisticated spa here is one of the best in town. **Pros:** edge of Georgetown makes for a fabulous location; lap-of-luxury feel; impeccable service. **Cons:**

expensive; challenging street parking; far from Metro. ✉ *2800 Pennsylvania Ave. NW, Georgetown* ☎ *202/342–0444 or 800/332–3442* ⊕ *www.fourseasons.com/washington* ↝ *160 rooms, 51 suites* ⟳ *In-room: Wi-Fi, safe, Internet. In-hotel: restaurant, room service, bar, pool, gym, children's programs (ages 5–16), parking (paid), some pets allowed, no-smoking rooms* ▭ *AE, D, DC, MC, V* Ⓜ *Foggy Bottom* ✛ *1:C5.*

$ 🔲 **Georgetown Inn.** Reminiscent of a gentleman's club, this Federal-style hotel seems like something from the 1700s. The quiet, spacious guest rooms are decorated in a colonial style. The redbrick hotel, in the heart of historic Georgetown, lies near shopping, dining, galleries, and theaters. The publike Daily Grill restaurant serves American cuisine. **Pros:** shoppers love the location; good price for the neighborhood; some nice views. **Cons:** a hike to Metro; congested area. ✉ *1310 Wisconsin Ave. NW, Georgetown* ☎ *202/333–8900 or 888/587–2388* ⊕ *www.georgetowncollection.com* ↝ *86 rooms, 10 suites* ⟳ *In-room: Wi-Fi. In-hotel: restaurant, room service, bar, gym, Wi-Fi, parking (paid), no smoking rooms* ▭ *AE, D, DC, MC, V* Ⓜ *Foggy Bottom* ✛ *1:B5.*

$–$$ 🔲 **Georgetown Suites.** If you consider standard hotel rooms cramped ☾ and overpriced, you'll find this establishment a welcome surprise. Consisting of two buildings a block apart in the heart of Georgetown, the hotel has suites of varying sizes. All have fully equipped kitchens and separate sitting rooms, and include free local calls and Continental breakfast. **Pros:** spacious rooms; good choice for a family that wants to spread out; perfect location. **Cons:** parking can be challenging; not a lot of character. ✉ *1111 30th St. NW, Georgetown* ☎ *202/298–7800 or 800/348–7203* ⊕ *www.georgetownsuites.com* ↝ *216 suites* ⟳ *In-room: kitchen, Wi-Fi. In-hotel: gym, laundry facilities, laundry service, Wi-Fi, parking (paid), no-smoking rooms* ▭ *AE, D, DC, MC, V* ⟆ *CP* Ⓜ *Foggy Bottom* ✛ *1:B5.*

$–$$ 🔲 **Holiday Inn Georgetown.** On the edge of Georgetown, this Holiday ☾ Inn is a short walk from Dumbarton Oaks, National Cathedral, and Georgetown University. Many guest rooms offer a scenic view of the Washington skyline. There's a free shuttle service to the Metro and a bus stop at the front door. ■ TIP→ Kids under 12 eat free, and rooms offer video games. **Pros:** quiet neighborhood; walk to restaurants; pretty pool. **Cons:** not near a Metro; far from Downtown. ✉ *2101 Wisconsin Ave. NW, Georgetown* ☎ *202/338–4600 or 877/863–4780* ⊕ *www.higeorgetown.com* ↝ *281 rooms, 4 suites* ⟳ *In-room: Wi-Fi. In-hotel: restaurant, room service, bar, pool, gym, laundry facilities, Wi-Fi, parking (paid), no-smoking rooms* ▭ *AE, D, DC, MC, V* Ⓜ *Foggy Bottom* ✛ *1:A2.*

$ 🔲 **Latham Hotel.** Many of the beautifully decorated rooms at this bou-
Fodor's Choice tique hotel offer treetop views of the Potomac River and the C&O ★ Canal. The polished-brass-and-glass lobby leads to Citronelle, one of the city's most acclaimed (and expensive) French restaurants—make reservations well before you arrive. You'll find a number of Washington's most illustrious personalities here for dinner, with many diplomats overnighting at the hotel. Be prepared for occasional street noise in some rooms, as the Latham lies on a fashionable avenue. **Pros:** fun location; lots of charm; great restaurant. **Cons:** street noise; busy area at night

and on weekends. ⌧ *3000 M St. NW, Georgetown* ☎ *202/726–5000 or 866/481–9126* ⊕ *www.thelatham.com* ⟿ *133 rooms, 9 suites* ⌂ *In-room: Wi-Fi. In-hotel: restaurant, room service, bar, pool, Wi-Fi, parking (paid), no-smoking rooms* ⊟ *AE, D, DC, MC, V* Ⓜ *Foggy Bottom* ✛ *1:B5.*

$$$ 🏨 **The Melrose Hotel.** At this European-style boutique hotel, the gracious rooms are done in a soothing palette of creams and blues. All have marble baths, and many have pullout sofa beds, making this hotel a good choice for families. Watercolors of local attractions were specially commissioned for the hotel. The lobby connects to the Landmark restaurant and intimate Library bar. Note to light sleepers: Rooms facing K Street are quieter. **Pros:** nice alternative to chain hotels; good location; walk to dining and shopping. **Cons:** street noise. ⌧ *2430 Pennsylvania Ave. NW, Georgetown* ☎ *202/955–6400 or 800/635–7673* ⊕ *www. melrosehoteldc.com* ⟿ *249 rooms, 34 suites* ⌂ *In-room: safe, Internet, Wi-Fi. In-hotel: restaurant, room service, bar, gym, laundry service, Wi-Fi, parking (paid), some pets allowed, no-smoking rooms* ⊟ *AE, D, DC, MC, V* ✛ *1:D6.*

$$$$ 🏨 **Park Hyatt.** A study in stylish neutrality, this hotel is all clean lines, natural wood, and sun-warmed glass. Minimalist rooms are enlivened by duck decoys and Shaker accents; delicate white linens make up wide, luxurious beds. Deluxe rooms are worth the extra cost, with separate living rooms and spacious, spa-style stone bathrooms equipped with massive showerheads. Free car service from the hotel is offered weekdays 7 AM to 11 PM. Downstairs, the Blue Duck Tavern is recommended. **Pros:** spacious rooms; good for entertaining; lull-you-to-sleep beds. **Cons:** expensive valet parking; not convenient to Metro. ⌧ *1201 24th St. NW, Georgetown* ☎ *202/789–1234* ⊕ *www.parkwashington. hyatt.com* ⟿ *196 rooms, 19 suites* ⌂ *In-room: safe, refrigerator (some), Internet, Wi-Fi. In-hotel: restaurant, room service, bar, pool, gym, laundry service, Wi-Fi, parking (paid), no-smoking rooms* ⊟ *AE, D, DC, MC, V* ✛ *1:D5.*

$$$$ 🏨 **Ritz-Carlton Georgetown.** An incinerator dating from the 1920s might
Fodor's Choice   seem the most unlikely of places for an upscale hotel, but spend five
★   minutes in the Ritz-Carlton Georgetown and you'll agree it works. A fire theme unites the intimate space, a complete departure from the chain's more traditional style. A large fireplace warms the private club-like lobby, and you can practically smell the embers burning as you pass through the exposed brick hallways. All the large and luxurious guest rooms have feather duvets, goose-down pillows, and marble baths. Upper-level suites facing the river boast some of the city's best views. The hotel's sexy Fahrenheit restaurant serves contemporary American cuisine. **Pros:** hot design; steps away from restaurants and shopping; refined service. **Cons:** far from the Metro; very expensive. ⌧ *3100 South St. NW, Georgetown* ☎ *202/912–4200* ⊕ *www.ritzcarlton.com/hotels/ georgetown* ⟿ *86 rooms, 29 suites* ⌂ *In-room: safe, DVD, Internet, Wi-Fi. In-hotel: restaurant, room service, bar, gym, spa, Wi-Fi, parking (paid), some pets allowed, no-smoking rooms* ⊟ *AE, D, DC, MC, V* ✛ *1:B6.*

$$–$$$ ⊞ **Washington Suites Georgetown.** Outside the center of Georgetown, this older all-suites accommodation offers families and long-term-stay travelers an alternative to standard hotel rooms. Each suite has a fully equipped kitchen, a small living and dining area, and a separate bedroom and bath. Fresh pastries, juices, and cereal are served each morning in the breakfast room. Many of the staff members have worked at the hotel for years and know regular guests by name. ■TIP→ **Stock your fridge at the Trader Joe's across the street. Pros:** friendly staff; good for long-term stays; excellent value. **Cons:** few frills; breakfast room can be crowded. ⊠ *2500 Pennsylvania Ave. NW, Georgetown* ☏ *202/333– 8060 or 877/736–2500* ⊕ *www.washingtonsuitesgeorgetown.com* ⇩ *124 suites* ⚐ *In-room: kitchen, Internet. In-hotel: gym, laundry facilities, parking (paid), no-smoking rooms* ⊟ *AE, D, DC, MC, V* ⊙| *CP* Ⓜ *Foggy Bottom* ✣ *1:D5.*

SOUTHWEST

$–$$ ⊞ **Best Western Capitol Skyline.** Who could believe that a Best Western, built in the 1960s would make a 21st-century comeback? Yet the Capitol Skyline has done just that. The hotel is a cool retro embodiment of its earlier heritage, with a gleaming lobby and inviting rooms done in red, white, and blue (some with views of the U.S. Capitol). Children staying here will enjoy the summertime pool, and the restaurant offers a kids' menu. The hotel lies in an area considered a last frontier in Washington's development, and you will need to wait for the hotel's free shuttle, hail a cab, or hop on the Metro to reach major tourist attractions. **Pros:** big outdoor pool; spacious rooms; good value. **Cons:** area sketchy at night; out-of-the-way location; restaurant has uneven food and slow service. ⊠ *10 I St. SW, Southwest* ☏ *202/488–7500 or 800/458–7500* ⊕ *www. capitolskyline.com* ⇩ *197 rooms, 6 suites* ⚐ *In-room: safe, Wi-Fi. In-hotel: restaurant, pool, laundry service, parking (paid), no-smoking rooms* ⊟ *AE, D, DC, MC, V* Ⓜ *Navy Yard* ✣ *2:F6.*

$–$$ ⊞ **Holiday Inn Capitol.** One block from the National Air and Space Museum, this family-friendly hotel has a great location for those bound for the Smithsonian museums. Rooms have comfortable beds, granite vanities in the bathrooms, coffeemakers, and hair dryers. The Downtown sightseeing trolley stops here, making getting around town a snap. Kids stay free, and those under 12 eat for free at Capitol Bistro. **Pros:** family-friendly; rooftop pool; close to museums. **Cons:** limited dining options nearby; not much going on in the neighborhood at night. ⊠ *550 C St. SW, Southwest* ☏ *202/479–4000* ⊕ *www.hicapitoldc.com* ⇩ *532 rooms, 13 suites* ⚐ *In-room: refrigerator, Wi-Fi. In-hotel: 2 restaurants, room service, bar, pool, gym, laundry facilities, laundry service, parking (paid), no-smoking rooms* ⊟ *AE, D, DC, MC, V* ⊙| *BP* Ⓜ *L'Enfant Plaza* ✣ *2:H6.*

$$–$$$ ⊞ **L'Enfant Plaza Hotel.** An oasis of calm above a Metro stop and a shopping mall, L'Enfant Plaza lies two blocks from the Smithsonian museums and has spectacular views of the river and the monuments. A heated rooftop pool is open year-round. Business travelers in particular take advantage of its proximity to several government agencies (USDA,

7

USPS, and DOT). All rooms have coffeemakers. A pet-friendly hotel, guest traveling with furry friends can request a pet bed. **Pros:** short walk to Smithsonian; good views from top floors. **Cons:** area is sleepy at night; not many nearby restaurants. ⊠ *480 L'Enfant Plaza SW, Southwest* ☎ *202/484–1000 or 800/635–5065* ⊕ *www.lenfantplazahotel.com* ⤶ *370 rooms, 102 suites* ⚐ *In-room: Wi-Fi. In-hotel: 3 restaurants, room service, bars, pool, gym, laundry service, Wi-Fi, parking (paid), some pets allowed, no-smoking rooms* ▭ *AE, D, DC, MC, V* Ⓜ *L'Enfant Plaza* ✛ *2:C6.*

UPPER NORTHWEST

¢–$ 📛 **Adam's Inn.** This cozy bed-and-breakfast spreads through three residential town houses near Adams Morgan, the zoo, and Dupont Circle. The Victorian-style rooms are small but comfortable. Many share baths, but those that do also have a sink in the room. A communal kitchen and limited garage parking are available. A two-night stay is required on weekends, but the hotel is flexible on that rule in the off-season. **Pros:** affordable rates; nearby Metro; lively neighborhood. **Cons:** some shared baths; steps to climb. ⊠ *1746 Lanier Pl. NW, Woodley Park* ☎ *202/745–3600 or 800/578–6807* ⊕ *www.adamsinn.com* ⤶ *26 rooms, 16 with bath* ⚐ *In-room: no phone, no TV. In-hotel: laundry facilities, parking (paid), no-smoking rooms* ▭ *AE, D, DC, MC, V* ⵏⵔⵍ *CP* Ⓜ *Woodley Park/Zoo* ✛ *1:F1.*

$–$$ 📛 **Embassy Suites at Chevy Chase Pavilion.** You can feel good about your
☁ carbon footprint as you enjoy the newly renovated suites at this green hotel. The hotel cut its energy usage by a third in 2007 and boasts efficient heating and cooling systems in every suite, Energy Star appliances, a saline pool, and even prints with soy-based ink. Families will love the free breakfast and afternoon reception, two-room suites, and being attached to two shopping malls complete with dining and movie theaters. You can hop on the Metro without ever stepping outside. **Pros:** eco- and family-friendly; close to Metro. **Cons:** lots of families; chain hotel. ⊠ *4300 Military Rd., Upper Northwest* ☎ *202/362–9300 or 800/760–6120* ⊕ *www.embassysuitesdcmetro.com* ⤶ *198 suites* ⚐ *In-room: refrigerator, Internet. In-hotel: room service, bar, pool, gym, laundry service, parking (paid), no-smoking rooms* ▭ *AE, D, DC, MC, V* ⵏⵔⵍ *BP* Ⓜ *Friendship Heights* ✛ *1:A1.*

¢ 📛 **Kalorama Guest House—Woodley Park.** Two elegantly restored Victorian town houses make for comfortable and convenient lodging near the National Cathedral. The cozy rooms, which have just been renovated, are furnished with 19th-century antiques and vary in size. Those in search of a television or a phone will need to visit one of the original house parlors, where sherry and tea are available around the clock. **Pros:** continental breakfast included; close to Metro; walk to some restaurants. **Cons:** limited privacy; no in-room phones; far from museums. ✉ *2700 Cathedral Ave. NW, Woodley Park* ☎ *202/328–0860 or 800/974–9101* ⊕ *www.kaloramaguesthouse.com* ↪ *18 rooms, 12 with bath; 3 suites* ♿ *In-room: no phone, no TV. In-hotel: laundry facilities, Wi-Fi, parking (paid), no kids under 6, no-smoking rooms* ▭ *AE, D, DC, MC, V* ⦾*CP* Ⓜ *Woodley Park/Zoo* ✛ *1:D2.*

$$$ 🏨 **Marriott Wardman Park.** You almost get the sense that you stepped
ⓒ   into a mini city when you first enter the Marriott Wardman Park. The hotel, housed in a hard-to-miss redbrick Victorian building behind the Woodley Park Metro, is massive. Many rooms recently benefited from a $100 million upgrade, leaving them with splashes of bright colors typical of many a Marriott these days. Rooms in the decidedly quieter 1918 Wardman Tower have not yet been renovated, but some will prefer its low-key vibe. The hotel's ground level has tons of seating, food choices, a full-service Starbucks, and lots of places to plug in. Kids will love the outdoor pool and the proximity to the pandas. **Pros:** on top of Metro; light-filled sundeck; pretty residential neighborhood with good restaurants. **Cons:** busy; loud; lines at restaurants when hotel is full. ✉ *2660 Woodley Rd. NW, Woodley Park* ☎ *202/328–2000 or 800/228–9290* ⊕ *www.marriott.com* ↪ *1,171 rooms, 145 suites* ♿ *In-room: safe, kitchen (some), refrigerator (some), Internet. In-hotel: 2 restaurants, room service, bars, pool, gym, spa, laundry service, Wi-Fi, parking (paid), some pets allowed, no-smoking rooms* ▭ *AE, D, DC, MC, V* Ⓜ *Woodley Park/Zoo* ✛ *1:D2.*

$$$–$$$$ 🏨 **Omni Shoreham Hotel.** This elegant hotel overlooking Rock Creek Park
ⓒ   has been lovingly tended and is aging gracefully. The light-filled guest
Fodor's Choice   rooms have a soothing garden palette and feature flat-screen TVs and
★   marble bathrooms. The vast art deco-and-Renaissance–style lobby welcomes visitors, who in the past have ranged from the Beatles to heads of state (the hotel has played host to inaugural balls since its 1930 opening). There is even a resident ghost said to haunt Suite 870. Families will love the larger-than-typical guest rooms, kiddie pool, bird-watching, bike rentals, and movie nights. ■TIP→ **Parents: Ask the concierge about story time and cuddles with the guide dog for the blind who trains at the hotel. Pros:** historic property; great pool and sundeck; good views from many rooms. **Cons:** not Downtown; big. ✉ *2500 Calvert St., NW, Woodley Park* ☎ *202/234–0700 or 800/834–6664* ⊕ *www.omnihotels. com* ↪ *818 rooms, 16 suites* ♿ *In-room: safe, refrigerator (some), DVD (some), Internet, Wi-Fi. In-hotel: restaurant, room service, bar, pool, gym, spa, bicycles, children's programs (ages 3–13), laundry service, Wi-Fi, parking (paid), some pets allowed, no-smoking rooms* ▭ *AE, D, DC, MC, V* Ⓜ *Woodley Park/Zoo* ✛ *1:C1.*

$–$$ 🏨 **Woodley Park Guest House.** This warm, peaceful bed-and-breakfast
on a quiet residential street lies near the entrance to the Metro nearest the zoo and close to Adams Morgan and Rock Creek Park. Antiques-filled rooms are individually decorated, and some have private baths. Conversation between guests is encouraged at the communal breakfast, which includes a fresh fruit salad, cereal, yogurt, and homemade

pastries. A two-night minimum stay is required, with few exceptions. **Pros:** close to Metro; near the zoo; breakfast included. **Cons:** Metro ride to Downtown; some shared baths; limited privacy. ☒ *2647 Woodley Rd. NW, Woodley Park* ☎ *202/667–0218 or 866/667–0218* ⊕ *www.dcinns.com* ↙ *16 rooms, 12 with bath* ☖ *In-room: no TV, Wi-Fi. In-hotel: laundry service, parking (paid), no kids under 12* ▭ *AE, D, MC, V* ⦿| *CP* Ⓜ *Wood-ley Park/Zoo* ✛ *1:D2.*

> ### WORD OF MOUTH
>
> "We have two kids and I'm done with hotels when we travel as a family. The site (⊕ www.vrbo.com) is all condo rentals directly from the owners.... We've had great luck with vrbo. The prices are usually MUCH less than a hotel and you get a kitchen and living room!"
>
> —kelliebellie

SUBURBAN MARYLAND

$–$$ 🖼 **Bethesda Court Hotel.** Bright burgundy awnings frame the entrance to this comfortable small hotel. Rooms have new down-filled bedding and updated bathrooms. The low-key hotel is two blocks from the Bethesda Metro and set back from busy Wisconsin Avenue. Nearby downtown Bethesda is home to restaurants, shops, and an independent movie theater. ■TIP→ Evening tea with cookies is complimentary, as are limousine service and shuttles to the National Institutes of Health. **Pros:** free Wi-Fi; close to Metro; basic Continental breakfast included. **Cons:** far from Downtown and major attractions; small rooms; no room service. ☒ *7740 Wisconsin Ave., Bethesda, MD* ☎ *301/656–2100* ⊕ *www.bethesdacourtwashdc.com* ↙ *74 rooms, 1 suite* ☖ *In-room: safe, refrigerator, Wi-Fi. In-hotel: gym, laundry facilities, Wi-Fi, parking (paid)* ▭ *AE, D, DC, MC, V* ⦿| *CP* Ⓜ *Bethesda.* ✛ *1:A1.*

$$ 🖼 **Courtyard by Marriott Chevy Chase.** Everything about the new Courtyard by Marriot Chevy Chase is bright and shiny. The sleek lobby features the chain's new interactive touch-screen "GoBoard" listing attractions, restaurants, and printable maps. Rooms are a good size and have high-tech amenities like free Wi-Fi and flat-screen TVs. Bonus for bikers: the hotel has a few bicycles (for kids and adults) that it lends guests for free on a first-come, first-served basis. **Pros:** new hotel; green initiatives at work throughout the hotel; close to Metro, restaurants, and shops; outdoor pool. **Cons:** not downtown. ☒ *5520 Wisconsin Ave., Chevy Chase* ☎ *301/656–1500* ⊕ *www.marriott.com* ↙ *225 rooms, 1 suite* ☖ *In-room: refrigerator, Internet, laundry. In-hotel: restaurant, gym, bicycles, laundry facilities, laundry service, Internet terminal, Wi-Fi hotspot, parking (paid), no-smoking rooms* ▭ *AE, D, DC, MC, V* ⦿| *BP* Ⓜ *Friendship Heights.* ✛ *1:A1.*

$$ 🖼 **Doubletree Hotel Bethesda.** The Doubletree has guest rooms that are larger than those at comparable hotels, with firm, comfortable beds, ample working space, and free morning newspaper delivery. The hotel caters to business travelers with a free shuttle to the nearby Metro, the National Institutes of Health, and the Naval Medical Center. **Pros:** rooftop pool; hypoallergenic rooms; good value. **Cons:** outside the city;

far from major attractions; a bit of a walk to Metro. ⊠ *8120 Wisconsin Ave., Bethesda, MD* ☎ *301/652–2000* ⊕ *www.doubletreebethesda.com* ⌁ *269 rooms, 7 suites* ⚬ *In-room: safe, Wi-Fi. In-hotel: restaurant, bar, pool, gym, laundry facilities, laundry service, parking (paid)* ⊟ *AE, D, DC, MC, V* Ⓜ *Bethesda.* ✛ *1:A1.*

$$$ 🖬 **Hyatt Regency Bethesda.** This hotel stands atop the Bethesda Metro station on Wisconsin Avenue, the main artery between Bethesda and Georgetown; Downtown Washington is a 15-minute Metro ride away. Well-equipped guest rooms have sleigh beds and mahogany furnishings, as well as large workstations for business travelers. They also include 32-inch TVs and marble baths. The rooftop fitness center and indoor pool are welcome retreats from a busy day in the city. **Pros:** at Metro; walk to dozens of restaurants; indoor pool. **Cons:** often crowded; noise from lobby. ⊠ *1 Bethesda Metro Center, 7400 block of Wisconsin Ave., Bethesda, MD* ☎ *301/657–1234 or 800/233–1234* ⊕ *www.bethesda. hyatt.com* ⌁ *391 rooms, 7 suites* ⚬ *In-room: Wi-Fi. In-hotel: 3 restaurants, room service, bars, pool, gym, laundry service, Wi-Fi, parking (paid)* ⊟ *AE, D, DC, MC, V* Ⓜ *Bethesda.* ✛ *1:A1.*

$$$ 🖬 **Marriott Residence Inn Bethesda Downtown.** In the heart of downtown Bethesda, this all-suites hotel caters primarily to business travelers who stay for several nights. If you're looking for an affordable home away from home, this is a sensible option. The comfortably (though slightly blandly) furnished one- and two-bedroom suites come with fully equipped kitchens with a standard-size refrigerator and dishwasher, plates, and utensils. ■TIP➔ The many complimentary services include grocery shopping, a breakfast buffet, and evening cocktail and dessert receptions. **Pros:** tons of restaurants within walking distance; rooftop pool; walk to Metro. **Cons:** far from monuments; chain-hotel feel. ⊠ *7335 Wisconsin Ave., Bethesda, MD* ☎ *301/718–0200 or 800/331–3131* ⊕ *www.residenceinnbethesdahotel.com* ⌁ *187 suites* ⚬ *In-room: kitchen, Internet. In-hotel: pool, gym, laundry facilities, parking (paid), no-smoking rooms* ⊟ *AE, D, DC, MC, V* ⧄ *BP* Ⓜ *Bethesda.* ✛ *1:A1.*

SUBURBAN VIRGINIA

$$$ 🖬 **Hilton Arlington Hotel.** Traveling Downtown is easy from this hotel just above a Metro stop. Guest rooms offer "serenity" beds, work desks, and comfy chairs, and the hotel's service is friendly and responsive. The hotel also has direct access via a covered skywalk to the Ballston Common Mall and National Science Foundation. The hotel now has a workout room on-site. **Pros:** easy Metro access; big rooms; online check-in. **Cons:** far from attractions; chain-hotel feel; no pool. ⊠ *950 N. Stafford St., Arlington, VA* ☎ *703/528–6000 or 800/445–8667* ⊕ *www. hiltonarlington.com* ⌁ *209 rooms, 5 suites* ⚬ *In-room: Wi-Fi. In-hotel: restaurant, bar, laundry service, Wi-Fi, parking (paid)* ⊟ *AE, D, DC, MC, V* Ⓜ *Ballston.* ✛ *1:A6.*

$–$$ 🖬 **Holiday Inn Arlington at Ballston.** You can get in and out of Washington quickly from this hotel three blocks from a Metro station. Especially comfortable for business travelers, rooms have spacious workspaces, plus tea/coffeemakers. Sightseers can take advantage of the hotel's

LODGING ALTERNATIVES

APARTMENT RENTALS

D.C. is a notoriously transient town, with people hopping on and off the campaign trail on a moment's notice often leaving their apartments in the sublets and long-term rental columns of local newspapers and Web sites. If you can't stomach the idea of another family vacation with you and the kids squeezed into a single hotel room with no kitchen, or if you are traveling with others, a furnished rental might be for you. Often these rentals wind up saving you money—especially on meals and snacks. Be warned, the allure of a full kitchen and room to spread out might get you hooked on apartment rentals for life. Here are some Web sites to help you find hotel alternatives, short-term apartment rentals, and apartment exchanges.

⊕ www.vrbo.com

⊕ www.washingtondc.craigslist.org

⊕ thehill.com/classifieds.html

⊕ www.militarybyowner.com

⊕ www.dcdigs.com

⊕ www.remington-dc.com

⊕ www.cyberrentals.com

⊕ www.thebrooklandinn.com

International Agents Hideaways International (✉ 767 Islington St., Portsmouth, NH ☎ 603/430-4433 or 800/843-4433 ⊕ www.hideaways. com), membership $185.

Rental Listings Washington Post (⊕ www.washingtonpost.com). **Washington CityPaper** (⊕ www. washingtoncitypaper.com).

BED-AND-BREAKFASTS

To find reasonably priced accommodations in small guesthouses and private homes, try **Bed and Breakfast Accommodations, Ltd.** (☎ 413/582-9888 or 877/893-3233 ⊕ www.bedandbreakfastdc.com) which is staffed weekdays 10-5. It handles about 45 different properties in the area.

HOME EXCHANGES

If you would like to exchange your home for someone else's, join a home-exchange organization, which will send you its updated listings of available exchanges for a year and include your own listing in at least one of them. It's up to you to make specific arrangements.

Exchange Clubs HomeLink International (☎ 813/975-9825 or 800/638-3841 ⊕ www.homelink. org) ; $80 for a listing published in a directory and on Web sites. **Intervac U.S.** (☎ 800/756-4663 ⊕ www. intervacus.com) ; $126 yearly for a listing, online access, and a catalog; $78.88 without catalog.

HOSTELS

No matter what your age, you can save on lodging costs by staying at hostels. **Hostelling International— USA** (✉ 8401 Colesville Rd., Suite 600, Silver Spring, MD ☎ 301/495- 1240 ⊕ www.hiusa.org) offers single-sex, dorm-style beds and, at many hostels, rooms for couples and family accommodations. Membership allows you to stay in HI-affiliated hostels at member rates; one-year membership is about $28 for adults, and hostels charge about $10-$30 per night. Members have priority if the hostel is full.

proximity to Arlington National Cemetery and the Iwo Jima and Downtown monuments and museums. Kids 12 and under eat free. **Pros:** free high-speed Internet access; free parking on Friday and Saturday nights; near the Metro. **Cons:** outside the city; typical chain-style guest rooms. ⊠ *4610 N. Fairfax Dr., Arlington, VA* ☎ *703/243–9800* ⊕ *www. hiarlington.com* ⥽ *221 rooms, 2 suites* ⌂ *In-room: Internet, Wi-Fi. In-hotel: restaurant, room service, bar, pool, gym, laundry facilities, Wi-Fi, parking (paid)* ▭ *AE, D, DC, MC, V* Ⓜ *Ballston.* ✛ *1:A6.*

$$$ 🔳 **Hotel Palomar Arlington.** From the mood lighting to the burnt-orange marble reception desk to the fantastically funky living room off the lobby, you might think you woke up in South Beach rather than Rosslyn. Complimentary coffee, tea, and newspapers are in the living room every morning, and all meals are served at the hotel's Italian restaurant, Domaso. The Metro is a short walk away. ■TIP➔ Stop by for the nightly "Wines Around the World" reception. **Pros:** sleek design; attention to detail; comfy beds. **Cons:** un-hip location; some noise from airport; no swimming pool. ⊠ *1121 N. 19th St., Rosslyn* ☎ *703/351–9170* ⊕ *www. hotelpalomar-arlington.com* ⥽ *142 rooms, 12 suites* ⌂ *In-room: safe, refrigerator, DVD, Internet, Wi-Fi. In-hotel: restaurant, gym, laundry services, Wi-Fi, parking (paid), some pets allowed, no-smoking rooms* ▭ *AE, D, DC, MC,V* Ⓜ *Rosslyn.* ✛ *1:A6.*

$$ 🔳 **Hyatt Arlington.** The renovations gods have recently kissed this Hyatt, leaving it a solid over-the-Potomac choice. Most guest rooms are large and modern and have comfy mattresses, flat-screen TVs, and large workstations. The hotel's restaurant, Cityhouse, serves classic American cuisine, and the lobby bar is a good place to relax with an early-evening martini or late-night drink. Jogging paths and golf courses can be found nearby. **Pros:** free Internet access; across from Metro. **Cons:** outside the city; dull neighborhood. ⊠ *1325 Wilson Blvd., Arlington, VA* ☎ *703/525–1234 or 800/908–4790* ⊕ *www.hyattarlington.com* ⥽ *317 rooms, 8 suites* ⌂ *In-room: Wi-Fi. In-hotel: restaurant, room service, bar, gym, laundry service, parking (paid)* ▭ *AE, D, DC, MC, V.* ✛ *1:A6.*

$$$ 🔳 **Key Bridge Marriott.** If you don't mind being across the Potomac, this ☾ hotel is a good choice. Guest rooms sparkle, and the views from the hotel's Potomac side are camera worthy. Although the property carries a Virginia zip code, you can walk over the Key Bridge into Georgetown, and the Rosslyn Metro is about four blocks away. Added bonus: one of the few hotels in town with an indoor-outdoor pool. **Pros:** good choice if traveling with kids; near the Metro. **Cons:** outside the city; area dull at night. ⊠ *1401 Lee Hwy., Arlington, VA* ☎ *703/524–6400 or 800/228–9290* ⊕ *www.marriott/waskb-key-bridge* ⥽ *568 rooms, 14 suites* ⌂ *In-room: safe, refrigerator (some). In-hotel: 2 restaurants, room service, bar, pool, gym, spa, laundry service, Wi-Fi, parking (paid), no-smoking rooms* ▭ *AE, D, DC, MC, V* Ⓜ *Rosslyn.* ✛ *1:A6.*

$$–$$$ 🔳 **Residence Inn Arlington Pentagon City.** The view across the Potomac of the D.C. skyline and the monuments is magnificent from this all-suites hotel. Adjacent to the Pentagon, the high-rise is two blocks from the Pentagon City Fashion Centre mall, which has a food court, shops, and a Metro stop. ■TIP➔ All suites include full kitchens with dishwashers,

ice makers, coffeemakers, toasters, dishes, and utensils. Complimentary services include grocery shopping, daily newspaper delivery, full breakfast, light dinner Monday to Wednesday, and movies, popcorn, and ice cream on Thursday evening. **Pros:** a plus for families; easy walk to Metro; airport shuttle. **Cons:** outside D.C.; neighborhood dead at night. ⊠ *550 Army Navy Dr., Arlington, VA* ☎ *703/413–6630 or 800/331–3131* ⊕ *www.marriott.com* ⇦ *299 suites* ⌂ *In-room: kitchen, Internet. In-hotel: pool, gym, laundry facilities, laundry service, Wi-Fi, parking (paid), some pets allowed (fee)* ⊟ *AE, D, DC, MC, V* ⊚| *BP* Ⓜ *Pentagon City.* ⊕ *1:A6.*

$$$$ ⛫ **Ritz-Carlton Pentagon City.** This Ritz has a more contemporary feel than one might traditionally associate with the luxury chain. The large guest rooms now shine in gold, yellow, and blue, and flat-screen TVs have been placed in all rooms. Attached to a shopping mall, this Ritz-Carlton is a quick cab ride from both Ronald Reagan National Airport and Downtown D.C. Afternoon tea remains popular. Metro can be accessed through the mall. **Pros:** indoor walk to Metro; lovely restaurant; indoor pool; airport shuttle. **Cons:** outside D.C.; slightly less ritzy than other Ritz properties. ⊠ *1250 S. Hayes St., Arlington, VA* ☎ *703/415–5000 or 800/241–3333* ⊕ *www.ritzcarlton.com* ⇦ *345 rooms, 21 suites* ⌂ *In-room: safe, Wi-Fi. In-hotel: restaurant, room service, bar, pool, gym, parking (paid)* ⊟ *AE, D, DC, MC, V* Ⓜ *Pentagon City.*

Nightlife

WORD OF MOUTH

"The 930 Club will have most of the popular touring bands. The Black Cat will get the slightly smaller ones. Rock and Roll Hotel and Velvet Lounge are definitely geared toward a younger crowd. The Birchmere is a sit-down dinner and concert hall—they get big names, though. And Iota is a bar that has shows . . . but it's clean and more upscale."

—GypsyHeart

NIGHTLIFE PLANNER

The Price of Admission

Most bars in D.C. have cover charges for bands and DJs, especially those performing on Friday and Saturday. Expect to pay from $10 to $20 for most dance clubs. Jazz and comedy clubs often have higher cover charges along with drink minimums.

Dress Code

Most bars and clubs require men to wear a shirt with a collar (polo shirts are fine) and dress shoes. No sneakers or Timberlands allowed. Jeans are acceptable if they are not torn or baggy. Shirts with logos are often not allowed. The code is less strict for women. "Dress to impress" or you won't get in.

Last Call

Last call in D.C. is 2 AM, and most bars and clubs close by 3 AM on the weekend and between midnight and 2 AM during the week. The exceptions are after-hours dance clubs and bars with kitchens that stay open late.

Five Great Nightlife Experiences

Café Saint-Ex: There's an upstairs and downstairs for your wild and mild sides.

Blues Alley: D.C.'s classiest jazz club is the place to enjoy outstanding performers and Cajun food in an intimate setting.

Indebleu: Located along the 7th Street arts corridor, this lounge has a hip vibe and an incredible menu.

Modern: Unlike many of its snootier neighbors, this Georgetown favorite offers a swank environment and great music without being pretentious.

The Birchmere: Go a little bit country or a little bit rock and roll at this Alexandria live-music venue with concerts from artists like Rosanne Cash and the Felice Brothers to Amadou & Mariam.

Where to Find What's Going On

To survey the local scene, consult Friday's "Weekend" section in the *Washington Post* and the free weekly *Washington CityPaper*. The free publications *Metro Weekly* and *Washington Blade* offer insights on gay and lesbian nightlife.

Local blog DCist (⊕ *www.dcist.com*) posts daily on D.C. events. It's a good idea to call clubs ahead of time, as last week's punk-rock party might be this week's merengue marathon.

Signs of Life in the Burbs

The city's suburbs have a nightlife of their own, in part thanks to Washington's Metro system, which runs until 3 AM on weekends. Near the Bethesda stop in downtown Bethesda, Maryland, there's a relaxed nightlife scene. In northern Virginia, to which droves of young people in search of cheaper rent have decamped, bars and clubs heat up the areas surrounding the Clarendon and Courthouse Metro stations.

ADAMS MORGAN
18th and Columbia is a nightlife nexus

U STREET CORRIDOR
live rock and jazz, hipster bars

Columbia Rd.

Florida Ave.

16th St.

Florida Ave.

New Hampshire Ave.

Vermont Ave.

Sheridan Circle

Massachusetts Ave.

Dupont Circle

Logan Circle

Rhode Island Ave.

GEORGETOWN
college kids and well-heeled grownups

Rock Creek

DUPONT CIRCLE
gay-friendly; trendy clubs

Scott Circle

M St.

Connecticut Ave.

Thomas Circle

M St.

Washington Circle

K St.

Whitehurst Fwy.

23rd St.

Pennsylvania Ave.

15th St.

14th St.

New York Ave.

FOGGY BOTTOM

Virginia Ave.

Theodore Roosevelt Island

DOWNTOWN
upscale drinking and dancing

Constitution Ave.

THE MALL

Reflecting Pool

THE MONUMENTS

Independence Ave.

Arlington Memorial Br.

CAPITOL HILL
casual bars where staffers unwind

Columbia Island

Tidal Basin

Potomac River

Francis Case Memorial Br.

Washington Canal

VIRGINIA

0	500 yards
0	500 meters

Updated by
Mitchell Tropin
and Cathy
Sharpe

From buttoned-down political appointees who've just arrived to laid-back folks who've lived here their whole lives, Washingtonians are always looking for a place to relax. And they have plenty of options when they head out for a night on the town. Most places are clustered in several key neighborhoods, making a night of barhopping relatively easy.

Georgetown's dozens of bars, nightclubs, and restaurants radiate from the intersection of Wisconsin and M streets. The crowds include older adults and college students. Georgetown is one of the safest neighborhoods in D.C., with a large police presence on weekends. Parking, however, is a scarce commodity, and there is no nearby Metro station. Taxis are often the best choice.

Georgetown may seem a little reserved to some. Those seeking a more diverse and less inhibited nightlife may prefer the 18th Street strip in Adams Morgan between Columbia Road and Kalorama Avenue, which offers a wide variety of places that feature hip-hop DJs, Latin music, and everything in between. If you're looking for offbeat spots that don't take themselves too seriously, you're in the right place. Getting there is easy, with three nearby Metro stops: Woodley Park/Adams Morgan (Red Line), Columbia Heights (Green and Yellow lines), and U Street/Cardozo (Green and Yellow lines). Taxis also are easy to find.

For serious dance action, head to the Northeast. Huge crowds and loud music ranging from hip-hop and Latin to techno and trance await you at the ever-popular warehouse-turned-mega clubs like Love and Ibiza. This is a rougher part of town, so be cautious. Make use of the premium parking—for about $20—that will put you close to the entrance. Even parking a few blocks away on neighborhood streets is risky at night. Taxis are another good option, as there is no nearby Metro. The U Street Corridor (U Street NW between 12th and 16th streets), once D.C.'s hippest neighborhood and a regular stop for jazz greats, is now undergoing a revival, with bars that appeal to all types. The U Street Corridor is accessible from two Metro stops: Columbia

Heights and U St./Cardozo, both on the Green and Yellow lines. Taxis also are easy to find.

The stretch of Pennsylvania Avenue between 2nd and 4th streets has a half-dozen Capitol Hill bars. And thanks to massive recent development, Penn Quarter is burgeoning with squeaky-clean new bars. You can take the Metro, exiting at the Archives/Navy Memorial/Penn Quarter station (Green and Yellow lines).

BARS AND LOUNGES

When it comes to the bar scene, Washington can feel like a college town—senators are even referred to as "junior" and "senior." Residents go out regularly, and they're served by a large number and wide variety of watering holes, most packed with people of all ages and interests. If you're into going out, you can find what you're looking for here.

CAPITOL HILL

★ **Dubliner.** A Washington institution that offers cozy paneled rooms, rich pints of Guinness, and nightly live Irish entertainment make this place popular among Capitol Hill staffers and Georgetown law students. It is located near Union Station. ⊠ *Phoenix Park Hotel, 520 N. Capitol St. NW, Capitol Hill* ☎ *202/737–3773* ⊕ *www.dublinerdc.com* Ⓜ *Union Station.*

Hawk and Dove. The regulars at this friendly bar—in the shadow of the Capitol—include politicos, lobbyists, and disgruntled interns. Conversation is usually about the political events of the day, although some just come to watch sports on the TVs above the bar. ⊠ *329 Pennsylvania Ave. SE, Capitol Hill* ☎ *202/543–3300* ⊕ *www.hawkanddoveonline. com* Ⓜ *Eastern Market.*

DOWNTOWN

Fadó Irish Pub. Built with authentic materials, dark and warm Fadó is really four pubs in one: the Library, the Victorian Pub, the Gaelic, and the Cottage. The pub's name comes from an old Irish expression meaning "long ago." Live Irish acoustic music is performed every Sunday afternoon, and there's live Celtic rock on Wednesday and Saturday nights. Monday night is quiz night. Fadó often pulls a crowd from the nearby Verizon Center. ⊠ *808 7th St. NW, Chinatown* ☎ *202/789–0066* ⊕ *www.fadoirishpub.com* Ⓜ *Gallery Pl./Chinatown.*

Gordon Biersch Brewery. This brewery-restaurant in the revived Chinatown neighborhood offers great pub food and lively crowds. Beer fans will savor the many German-style brews that are made according to the "Reinheitsgebot"—the German Purity Law of 1516. ⊠ *900 F St. NW, Chinatown* ☎ *202/783–5454* ⊕ *wwwgordonbiersch.com* Ⓜ *Gallery Pl./Chinatown.*

Fodor's Choice **Indebleu.** Dressed in vivid red and orange, this ultracool lounge has one
★ of the most popular bar menus in town. Not only does it include a large list of hot cocktails, it has the imagination to logically arrange them on a D.C. Metro map. This club has earned an international reputation, so expect crowds. ⊠ *707 G St. NW, Chinatown* ☎ *202/333–2538* ⊕ *www. bleu.com/indebleu* Ⓜ *Gallery Pl./Chinatown.*

8

★ **Shadow Room.** This highly popular club seems out of place on the K Street Corridor, which is better known as a location for lobbyists. The club attracts big crowds thanks to such top-of-the-line amenities as priority valet service and personalized waitstaff. The place also is well known for high-tech touches like text-messaging drink orders. Some may be turned off by the club's tough door policy. ⊠ *2131 K St. NW, Northwest* ☎ *202/887–1200* ⊕ *wwwshadowroom.com.* Ⓜ *Farragut West.*

GEORGETOWN

The center of Georgetown is a 15- or 20-minute walk from the nearest Metro (Foggy Bottom), but flagging down a cab is never a problem.

Degrees. Inside what was once the Georgetown Incinerator, this modern bar is a breath of fresh air in the neighborhood's rather monotone scene. With an extensive wine and cocktail selection behind the black granite bar and a hip, well-dressed set of patrons in front of it, Degrees exudes elegance from all corners. If there's too much attitude in the bar, head out to the hotel's lovely lobby and sit by the fireplace. ⊠ *Ritz-Carlton, 3100 South St. NW, Georgetown* ☎ *202/912–4100* ⊕ *www.ritzcarlton.com.*

★ **J Paul's.** This is a great neighborhood saloon and a terrific place to go for a beer and a game. The menu is extensive, but stick to the great hamburgers and seafood dishes. J Paul's attracts a diverse crowd from students to lobbyists and politicians. ⊠ *3218 M St. NW, Georgetown* ☎ *202/333–3450* ⊕ *j-pauls.capitalrestaurants.com.*

DUPONT CIRCLE

Brickskeller. Its selection of more than 1,000 varieties of beer from around the world secured a place for Brickskeller in the *Guinness World Records.* Other draws include the cozy, although slightly grungy, cellar location; the diverse clientele; the tasty burgers; and the adept servers, who actually have to attend "beer school" to land a job here. ⊠ *1523 22nd St. NW, Dupont Circle* ☎ *202/293–1885* ⊕ *www.lovethebeer.com* Ⓜ *Dupont Circle.*

Fodor'sChoice
★ **Eighteenth Street Lounge.** Home to Washington's chic set, ESL's unmarked visage might be intimidating, but this multilevel club's array of sofa-filled hardwood coves makes it seem like the city's chilliest house party. On the top floor of this former mansion jazz musicians often entertain. Fans of techno music flock here because it's the home of the ESL record label and the renowned musical duo Thievery Corporation. ■ **TIP→** The dress code here is strictly enforced by the doorman; no khakis, baseball caps, sneakers, or light-colored jeans. ⊠ *1212 18th St. NW, Dupont Circle* ☎ *202/466–3922* ⊕ *www.eighteenthstreetlounge.com* Ⓜ *Dupont Circle.*

Gazuza. This bar, whose name means "lust" in Castilian Spanish, draws an attractive local crowd that attempts to chat over the throbbing house music. The tiny interior, done in an aggressively modern style, fills up early, spilling patrons onto the spacious balcony, a prime people-watching spot. ⊠ *1629 Connecticut Ave. NW, Dupont Circle* ☎ *202/667–5500* ⊕ *www.latinconcepts.com/gazuza* Ⓜ *Dupont Circle.*

D.C.'S PARTY ANIMALS: INTERNS

GENERAL DESCRIPTION
Migratory species, aged 16 to 25, present in the region in great abundance in summer.

IDENTIFYING MARKS
Eager expression, hangover. Can be confused with law students, but interns are almost always spotted in groups of four or more, do not carry books, and wear badges marked INTERN—a dead giveaway. The male is nearly uniform in khakis, blazer, and tie. Female shows greater variety of plumage, but look for sundresses in spring and summer and pearls year-round.

DIET
A fairly regular daily diet of Starbucks in the morning, Chinese takeout at lunch, and pizza, burritos, and the like in the evening is enriched by great quantities of draft beer, often consumed by groups of interns, from pitchers.

HABITAT
During the day interns flock with other political species to the Capitol and White House, and are most easily spotted inside these buildings, Republican and Democratic subspecies sometimes intermingling. After hours, they congregate both at Hill bars like **Capital Lounge** (mostly Republicans) and the **Hawk and Dove** (mostly Democrats), and also farther afield, at **Third Edition** in Georgetown. On weekends, look for interns at **Open City** in Woodley Park, gathering in great numbers to feed on pancakes.

BEHAVIOR
When among their own, Washington interns are known for late-night parties and beer pong. In the presence of other political species (staffers, legislators), behavior is markedly more subdued. Interns are nearly always single while in Washington, and their mating rituals are particularly showy; coupling up between Republican and Democratic subspecies is not unusual, and occasional interns have been known to pair temporarily with legislators and others.

ADAMS MORGAN

Chief Ike's Mambo Room. This is a favorite spot for a friendly, laidback evening. Chief Ike's is known for attracting a wild and eccentric crowd—the drinks may not be anything special, but the person sitting next to you may very well be. There's plenty of room to hang out, chat, and sip a cool cocktail with dancing downstairs. You can't miss Chief Ike's gaudy entrance. ⊠ *1725 Columbia Rd. NW, Adams Morgan* ☎ *202/332–2211* ⊕ *www.chiefikesmamboroom.com* Ⓜ *Woodley Park/Zoo.*

Madam's Organ. Neon lights behind the bar, walls covered in kitsch, and works from local artists add to the gritty feel that infuses Madam's Organ. Its three levels play host to an eclectic clientele that shoots pool, listens to live music performed every night on the lower level, and soaks up rays on the roof deck. There are some who dislike Madam's Organ for its popularity, but, for most, it's a place that's hard not to like. ⊠ *2461 18th St. NW, Adams Morgan* ☎ *202/667–5370* ⊕ *www. madamsorgan.com* Ⓜ *Woodley Park/Zoo.*

Tryst. Bohemian and unpretentious, this coffeehouse-bar serves fancy sandwiches and exotic coffee creations. Comfy chairs and couches fill the big open space, where you can sit for hours sipping a cup of tea— or a martini, in the evening—while chatting or clacking away at your laptop. Tryst is best in the warm months, when the front windows swing open and the temperature matches the temperament. ⊠ *2459 18th St. NW, Adams Morgan* ☎ *202/232–5500* ⊕ *www.trystdc.com* Ⓜ *Woodley Park/Zoo.*

U STREET/CARDOZO

Café Saint-Ex. Themed after the life of Antoine de Saint-Exupéry, French pilot and author of *The Little Prince,* this bi-level bar has a split personality. The upstairs brasserie has pressed-tin ceilings and a propeller hanging over the polished wooden bar. Downstairs is the Gate 54 nightclub, designed to resemble an airplane hangar, with dropped corrugated-metal ceilings and backlit aerial photographs. The DJs draw twentysomethings nightly. ⊠ *1847 14th St. NW, Logan Circle* ☎ *202/265–7839* ⊕ *www.saint-ex.com* Ⓜ *U St./Cardozo.*

★ **Chi-Cha Lounge.** Insular groups of young professionals relax on sofas and armchairs in this hip hangout, while Latin jazz mingles with Peruvian and Bolivian folk music in the background and old movies run silently behind the bar. This lounge, modeled after an Ecuadorian hacienda, gets packed on weekends, so come early to get a coveted sofa along the back wall. Down the tasty tapas as you enjoy the namesake drink—think sangria with a bigger kick. For a price, you can smoke a hookah filled with imported honey-cured tobacco. ⊠ *1624 U St. NW, U Street Corridor* ☎ *202/234–8400* ⊕ *www.latinconcepts.com/chicha* Ⓜ *U St./Cardozo.*

Helix Lounge. Despite feeling like someone's lounged-out basement, Helix caters to a mixed, completely non-Hill crowd—an oddity in D.C. Locals, who sit on couches and overstuffed ottomans, sip specialty cocktails and chat among themselves. Most are well dressed, but it's definitely not a scene. ⊠ *Hotel Helix, 1430 Rhode Island Ave. NW, Logan Circle* ☎ *202/462–9001* ⊕ *www.hotelhelix.com/heldini* Ⓜ *U St./Cardozo.*

The Saloon. A classic watering hole, the Saloon has no TVs, no light beer, and no martinis. What you can find are locals engaged in conversation—a stated goal of the owner—and some of the world's best beers, including the rare Urbock 23, an Austrian beer that is rated one of the tastiest and strongest in the world, with 9.6% alcohol content (limit one per customer). ⊠ *1207 U St. NW, U Street Corridor* ☎ *202/462–2640* Ⓜ *U St./Cardozo.*

U-topia. A colorful and offbeat dining establishment, U-topia offers culinary flair in a room filled with art. Customers enjoy an eclectic menu that includes such diverse choices as Cajun jambalaya, Moroccan seasoned lamb couscous, and cumin chicken. Meanwhile, the music tends toward acoustic jazz featuring piano trios. A neighborhood hot spot, the place has grown with the neighborhood, catering to those who prefer a place where one can converse while listening to softer jazz. ⊠ *1418 U St. NW, U Street Corridor* ☎ *202/483–7669* ⊕ *www.utopiadc.com* Ⓜ *U St./Cardozo.*

D.C.'S PARTY ANIMALS: STAFFERS

GENERAL DESCRIPTION

Prolific species endemic to the Washington area; similar species are present in state capitals throughout the country, but the Washington staffer is notably more rapacious. Republican and Democratic subspecies are distinct; Senate, congressional, White House, and departmental varieties are less so, due in part to migration between offices every two to four years.

IDENTIFYING MARKS

BlackBerry; security badge, usually worn around neck; males tend toward dark suits but females are often seen in red. Republican subspecies tends to be heavier, and the males have extremely neat hair; Democratic subspecies is svelter and hairier in both sexes, but dress is less predictable. Both subspecies are distinguishable from lawyers only by badge.

DIET

The bulk of the staffer's diet is coffee, but it also consumes takeout and martinis. While staffers are technically omnivores, their actual intake depends on their environment and which other species are present. A staffer may eat lo mein with legislators or lobster with lobbyists, or both, in the same day.

HABITAT

Like other political species, staffers tend to stick close to the Capitol and White House during the day, although they can also be spotted at the **Union Pub** and the **Capital Grille** at lunchtime. After hours, the best places to watch Republican staffers are **Bullfeathers** and **Tortilla Coast**, both on the Hill. Democratic staffers are also present on the Hill at the **Hawk and Dove**, and farther afield, on V Street at **Busboys and Poets**. As populations of GOP and Democratic staffers shift, turf wars sometimes erupt; observe Democratic staffers moving in on Republican territory at the **Capital Lounge** on the Hill, and the reverse at **Stetson's**, in Adams Morgan.

BEHAVIOR

Remarkably intelligent and adaptable, staffers are some of Washington's most interesting species to observe. It is not uncommon to observe a staffer simultaneously sending e-mails on its BlackBerry, talking on a cell phone, and ordering in a restaurant or bar (the scientific name for this behavior is formulating policy). Staffers are gregarious among their own, but can become obsequious and competitive when in the presence of legislators.

8

SOUTHWEST/WATERFRONT

★ **Zanzibar on the Waterfront.** Featuring Caribbean- and African-influenced food, this addition to the traditional seafood restaurants on D.C.'s Southwest waterfront caters to well-dressed professionals. Live entertainment is offered as well as multiple dance floors. Zanzibar also schedules special events, such as performances by Jamaica's Elephant Man and R&B singer Melba Moore. ⊠ *700 Water St. SW, Waterfront* ☎ *202/554–9100* ⊕ *www.zanzibar-otw.com* Ⓜ *L'Enfant Plaza.*

VIRGINIA

Carpool. "Andy Warhol meets General Motors" is how one magazine described this former-garage-turned-bar. Enjoy a brew and food from a kitchen run by Rocklands, which makes some of the best barbecue in the area. Carpool, which serves a local clientele, has 12 pool tables, seven dartboards, and a cigar room with a walk-in humidor. ☒ *4000 Fairfax Dr., Arlington, VA* ☎ *703/532–7665* ⊕ *www.carpoolweb.com* Ⓜ *Ballston.*

Fishmarket. There's something different in just about every section of this multilevel, multiroom space, from a piano-bar crooner to a rag-time piano shouter and a guitar strummer. The thirty- and fortysome-thing crowd is boisterous. If you really like beer, order the largest size; it comes in a glass big enough to put your face in. ☒ *105 King St., Old Town Alexandria, VA* ☎ *703/836–5676* ⊕ *www.fishmarketva.com* Ⓜ *King St.*

Iota. With bands playing alt-country or stripped-down rock every night, the unpretentious, attentive crowds come mainly because they like good music. Expect to fight your way to the bar—the place gets crowded quickly. There's a cover that ranges from $5 to $17, depending on the act. ☒ *2832 Wilson Blvd., Arlington, VA* ☎ *703/522–8340* ⊕ *www.iotaclubandcafe.com* Ⓜ *Clarendon.*

State Theatre. This is the place to go to see famous bands from the past like Leon Russell, the Smithereens, and Jefferson Starship. You have the choice of sitting or standing in this renovated movie theater, which is about 10 mi south of D.C. ☒ *220 N. Washington St., Falls Church, VA* ☎ *703/237–0300* ⊕ *wwwthestatetheatre.com* Ⓜ *East Falls Church.*

GAY AND LESBIAN BARS

Washington's gay population has traditionally congregated in Dupont Circle, although things have changed. Gay clubs tended to be conserva-tive, playing down their presence. But today on the circle, shops, bars, and restaurants proudly fly the Gay Pride rainbow flag and there is a very gay-friendly vibe.

★ **Halo.** At this Logan Circle hangout you won't have to elbow for room or shout to be heard—a rarity in nearby gay bars. Sleek and stylish, the bar uses dramatic lighting to make the most of its tunnel-like space, where well-dressed men lounge on modern leather furniture. ☒ *1435 P St. NW, Logan Circle* ☎ *202/797–9730* ⊕ *www.halodc.com* Ⓜ *Dupont Circle.*

JR's Bar & Grill. On the 17th Street strip, JR's packs in a mostly male, mostly professional crowd. Patrons shoot pool, play video games, gaze at videos on the big screen, and chat with their neighbors. ☒ *1519 17th St. NW, Dupont Circle* ☎ *202/328–0090* ⊕ *www.jrswdc.com* Ⓜ *Dupont Circle.*

Phase One. An eclectic, mostly female clientele frequents this longtime neighborhood hangout. The small dance floor and pool tables in the back make it an intimate and comfortable spot, although sometimes the place gets very crowded. ☒ *525 8th St. SE, Capitol Hill* ☎ *202/544–6831* ⊕ *www.phase1dc.com* Ⓜ *Eastern Market.*

D.C.'S PARTY ANIMALS: LOBBYISTS

GENERAL DESCRIPTION

Though currently plentiful, the lobbyist is a threatened species in Washington. Ironically, recent legislation about and public awareness of the species have only deepened its endangerment.

IDENTIFYING MARKS

Lobbyists may look familiar to New Yorkers, due to their marked resemblance to investment bankers (the latter are extremely rare in Washington). Easy to identify by custom-made suits, stylish haircuts, and the occasional suspender or cigar (males only), they are distinguishable from lawyers by their habit of picking up the check.

DIET

Studies of lobbyists' expense reports indicate a particularly voracious appetite, heavy on red meat, sushi, and fine wine. It is interesting to note, however, that lobbyists take virtually all their meals in restaurants, and thus have a limited ability to find food on their own; without an expense account, the lobbyist may starve.

HABITAT

The lobbyist's habitat is shrinking rapidly, and is a source of some concern. Washington lobbyists are native only to K Street, but in recent years their normal range had extended to the Capitol, with a vast migratory range encompassing Scottish golf courses, Mississippi casinos, and the Mariana Islands. As pressure increases on the species, it is being driven back to K Street, but can still be reliably spotted at **Charlie Palmer, Capital Grille, La Colline, The Monocle,** and **The Capitol Hill Club.** Follow the sommelier.

BEHAVIOR

Lobbyists coexist symbiotically with legislators, each reliant on the other for protection and sustenance. Thus, the two species are often spotted together: the lobbyist feeding the legislator with food, trips, and campaign cash, the legislator reciprocating with spending bills. In such company, the lobbyist is at its most resplendent—charming and expansive. When alone or with members of their own species, however, lobbyists can be gruff and temperamental. Watch for them on cell phones in expensive restaurants.

8

MUSIC CLUBS

At the junction between the North, the South, and the Rust Belt, D.C. has become somewhat of a crossroads for folk, rock, and jazz acts. The high number of venues, sustained by a hard-working, hard-playing population, entices many of them to stay and play. Also, as the nation's capital D.C. often pulls the biggest acts for special events and celebrations. Stay tuned with the *Washington Post*, the *Washington Citypaper*, and *DCist* (⊕ *www.dcist.com*).

ACOUSTIC, FOLK, AND COUNTRY MUSIC CLUBS

Fodor's Choice
★
The Birchmere. A legend in the D.C. area, the Birchmere is one of the best places outside the Blue Ridge Mountains to hear acoustic folk, country, and bluegrass. Enthusiastic crowds have enjoyed performances by artists such as Mary Chapin Carpenter, Lyle Lovett, Leon Redbone, and Emmylou Harris. More

recently, the club has expanded its offerings to include jazz performers such as Diane Schuur and Al Jareau, and blues artists like Robert Cray and Buddy Guy. ⊠ *3701 Mt. Vernon Ave., Alexandria, VA* ☎ *703/549–7500* ⊕ *www.birchmere.com.*

Folklore Society of Greater Washington. At more than 200 events a year, the society presents folk and traditional musicians and dancers from all over the country. Venues around the D.C. area host events ranging from contra dancing to storytelling to open-mike singing. ☎ *202/546–2228* ⊕ *www.fsgw.org.*

JAZZ AND BLUES CLUBS

The **D.C. Blues Society** (⊕ *www.dcblues.org*) is a clearinghouse for information on upcoming shows, festivals, and jam sessions in the metropolitan area. It also publishes a monthly newsletter.

Fodor's Choice
★
Blues Alley. Head here for a classy evening in an intimate setting, complete with great music and outstanding New Orleans–style grub. The cover charge is typically $25 for well-known performers such as Mose Allison, and more for top acts like Wynton Marsalis. There is also a $10 food or drink minimum. ■ TIP➔ You can come for just the show, but those who enjoy a meal get better seats. ⊠ *1073 Wisconsin Ave. NW, near M St., Georgetown* ☎ *202/337–4141* ⊕ *www.bluesalley.com* Ⓜ *Foggy Bottom.*

Bohemian Caverns. The cramped stairway delivers you to a performance space designed to look like a cave, a complete and accurate renovation of the Crystal Caverns, once a mainstay of D.C.'s "Black Broadway" and the place to see Miles Davis and Charlie Parker. The club rightfully calls itself "the Sole Home for Soul Jazz." These days Friday and Saturday are given over to jazz; blues acts headline on Thursday; and open-mike night on Wednesday brings jazz-influenced poets to the stage. ⊠ *2001 11th St. NW, U Street Corridor* ☎ *202/299–0800* ⊕ *www.bohemiancaverns.com* Ⓜ *U St./Cardozo.*

Columbia Station. This unpretentious neighborhood bar attracts an eclectic crowd, many of whom were pulled in off the street by the good vibes emanating from this place. Amber lights and morphed musical instruments adorn the walls, and high-quality live local jazz and blues fills the air. The large, open windows up front keep the place cool in summer months. ⊠ *2325 18th St. NW, Adams Morgan* ☎ *202/462–6040* Ⓜ *Woodley Park/Zoo.*

★ **HR-57.** Named after a congressional resolution proclaiming jazz a "rare and valuable national treasure," HR-57 isn't just a club, it's a non-profit cultural center. It spotlights musicians based in the D.C. area, many of whom have national followings. Fried chicken and collard greens are on the menu; beer and wine are available, or bring your own bottle (corkage is $3 per person). ⊠ *1610 14th St. NW, Logan Circle* ☎ *202/667–3700* ⊕ *www.hr57.org* Ⓜ *U St./Cardozo.*

Mr. Henry's. This laid-back club is the last holdout of a once-thriving live-music scene on Capitol Hill. Roberta Flack got her start in the upstairs performance space, where a dozen or so tables are scattered around the wood-paneled room. There's never a cover. ⊠ *601 Pennsylvania Ave. SE, Capitol Hill* ☎ *202/546–8412* ⊕ *www.mrhenrysrestaurant.com* Ⓜ *Eastern Market.*

New Vegas Lounge. Dr. Blues doesn't allow any soft-jazz-bluesy-fusion in his house. Even during the weekly open-jam session at this longtime favorite, it's strictly no-nonsense wailing guitar rhythms by seasoned local players. ⊠ *1415 P St. NW, Dupont Circle* ☎ *202/483–3971* ⊕ *www.newvegasloungedc.com* Ⓜ *Dupont Circle.*

Takoma Station Tavern. Beside the subway stop that lends the place its name, the Takoma hosts such local favorites as Marshall Keys and Keith Killgo, with the occasional nationally known artist stopping by to jam. The jazz happy hours starting at 6:30 PM Thursday and Friday pack the joint. There's reggae on Saturday and comedy on Monday. Sneakers and athletic wear are not allowed. ⊠ *6914 4th St. NW, Takoma Park* ☎ *202/829–1999* ⊕ *www.takomastation.com* Ⓜ *Takoma.*

Twins Jazz. Twin sisters Kelly and Maze Tesfaye offer great jazz at their club on U Street. The club features some of D.C.'s strongest straight-ahead jazz players, as well as groups from as far away as New York. On the club's menu are tasty nachos, wings, and burgers. If you happen to be in Upper Northwest, visit the sisters' other club, Twins Lounge. ⊠ *1344 U St. NW, U Street Corridor* ☎ *202/234–0072* ⊕ *www.twinsjazz.com* Ⓜ *U St./Cardozo.*

ROCK AND POP CLUBS

Fodor's Choice
★ **Black Cat.** Come here to see the latest local bands as well as indie stars such as Neko Case, Modest Mouse, and Clinic. Dave Grohl, lead singer of the Foo Fighters, owns a stake in the club. The post-punk crowd whiles away the time in the Red Room, a side bar with pool tables, an eclectic jukebox, and no cover charge. The club also is home to Food for Thought, a legendary vegetarian café. ⊠ *1811 14th St. NW, U Street Corridor* ☎ *202/667–7960* ⊕ *www.blackcatdc.com* Ⓜ *U St./Cardozo.*

8

DC9. With live music seven days a week, this two-story rock club hosts up-and-coming indie rock bands and the occasional nationally known act. There's a narrow bar on the ground floor and a humongous concert space upstairs. ⊠ *1940 9th St. NW, U Street Corridor* ☎ *202/483–5000* ⊕ *www.dcnine.com* Ⓜ *U St./Cardozo.*

★ **9:30 Club.** When they come to town, the best indie performers, and a few of the bigger acts, play this large but cozy space wrapped by balconies on three sides. Recent acts have included current sensations as well as groups with a long history, such as the B-52s, Reconteurs, Lou Reed, Crowded House, and Joe Jackson. ■TIP➔ For the best seats, arrive at least an hour before the doors open, typically at 7:30. ⊠ *815 V St. NW, U Street Corridor* ☎ *202/265–0930* ⊕ *www.930.com* Ⓜ *U St./Cardozo.*

Rock and Roll Hotel. In the revived H Street Corridor, this venue offers some of the nation's best indie acts. Housed in a former funeral home, the multiple dance floors can get very crowded when well-known musicians perform. Live acts are in the main room and DJs spin on the second floor, called the Hotel Bar. Notable acts include the Walkmen, Andrew W.K., and Juliette and the Licks. ■TIP➔ Take the H Street Shuttle from the Gallery Place Metro stop. The shuttle is free, operating Sunday through Thursday from 5 PM–midnight and 5 PM–3 AM on Friday and Saturday. ⊠ *1353 H St. NE, H Street Corridor* ☎ *202/388–7625* ⊕ *www. rockandrollhoteldc.com* Ⓜ *Potomac Avenue.*

Velvet Lounge. Squeeze up the narrow stairway and check out the eclectic local and national bands that play at this unassuming neighborhood joint. Performers ranging from indie mainstays to acclaimed up-and-comers rock the house with psychobilly, alt-country, and indie pop. ⊠ *915 U St. NW, U Street Corridor* ☎ *202/462–3213* ⊕ *www. velvetloungedc.com* Ⓜ *U St./Cardozo.*

DANCE CLUBS

Washington's dance clubs seem constantly to be re-creating themselves. A club might offer heavy industrial music on Wednesday, host a largely gay clientele on Thursday, and thump to the sounds of '70s disco on Friday. Club-hoppers can choose from five hubs: Georgetown, Adams Morgan, Dupont Circle, U Street, and along 9th Street NW near Gallery Place Metro station.

Fur. This multilevel entertainment mecca offers a variety of electronic, Latin, and hip-hop music, with some nights devoted to a music specialty. The dance floor is massive, accommodating over 2,000 people with state-of-the-art sound and lighting systems. The club enforces its dress code, requiring shirts with collars and no sneakers or Timberlands. ⊠ *33 Patterson St. NE, Northeast* ☎ *202/842–3401* ⊕ *www.fur-nightclub.com* Ⓜ *New York Ave./Florida Ave./Gallaudet U.*

★ **Habana Village.** No matter what the temperature is outside, it's always balmy inside the unpretentious Habana Village. The tiny dance floors are packed nightly with couples moving to the latest live salsa and merengue tunes. When it's time to cool down, you can head to one of several lounges in this converted four-story town house and sip the house specialty: a mojito garnished with sugarcane. ⊠ *1834 Columbia*

D.C.'S PARTY ANIMALS: LEGISLATORS

GENERAL DESCRIPTION

The legislator's life cycle is one of migration, from its home state to Washington and back, during weekends, congressional recesses, and finally, election years. Natural selection has made it thus a particularly hardy and dynamic species; its struggles for dominance are among Washington's most dramatic and powerful.

IDENTIFYING MARKS

Prominent smile, entourage. Legislators are rarely alone, but outside the Capitol, seldom in the company of other legislators, preferring the company of staffers, lobbyists, and sometimes, interns. They often travel in black SUVs and tend to be hard to catch, but can sometimes be lured by cameras and microphones. The Senate variety is almost exclusively white and largely male; the House variety is more diverse and vocal.

DIET

While in Washington, legislators eat a rich diet of porterhouse steak, Chinese takeout, and French fries (N.B., some of the Republican subspecies prefer Freedom fries). But in election years a legislator's epic journey of campaign migration results in significant culinary hardship, and during this time many subsist on donuts and pie.

HABITAT

Observe legislators in the Capitol itself, and around the Hill and White House at TenPenh, Capital Grille, and The Caucus Room, as well as in Georgetown at Café Milano and Citronelle. On Friday afternoons and Monday mornings you may catch a glimpse of legislators migrating through Reagan National Airport. In election years their habitat changes dramatically, and while hard to find in Washington, they're easy to spot at county fairs and senior citizens' homes.

BEHAVIOR

This species is known for noisy and complex displays of principle, called speechifying. These displays are meant to simultaneously attract voters and intimidate competitors; occasionally, they also result in legislation.

8

Rd. NW, Adams Morgan ☎ 202/462–6310 ⊕ www.habanavillage.com Ⓜ Woodley Park/Zoo.

Ibiza. Ibiza remains one of D.C.'s most popular dance clubs. The club attracts a diverse crowd of mostly African-American and Hispanic young people, but everyone feels welcome. This is a great space, but only if you like your music loud. The place also gets very crowded, even with its cavernous space and seven bars. When you need a breath of fresh air, Ibiza has a rooftop deck—a rarity in D.C. ✉ 1222 1st St. NE., Northeast ☎ 202/234–9225 ⊕ www.ibizadc.com Ⓜ New York Ave.-Florida Ave.-Gallaudet.

★ **Love.** This four-story dance powerhouse looms over an industrial area far from Downtown. Elegant and minimalist, Love makes the most of its former warehouse home. The music changes from night to night, and from floor to floor, but you're sure to sample salsa, house, and trance. This wood-paneled club attracts a primarily upscale, but diverse clientele. Washington Wizards players and other celebrities are frequently

The Lowdown on Late-Night Eats

Top off a night of barhopping with a stop at one of these delicious late-night haunts.

ADAMS MORGAN

The menu at **Amsterdam Falafelshop** (✉ 2425 18th St. NW ☎ 202/234–1969 Ⓜ Woodley Park/Zoo, Adams Morgan) might consist of only three items—falafels in pita, Dutch-style french fries, and brownies—but the choices are far from limited. At this cash-only spot, choose from nearly 20 different garnishes and a variety of dipping sauces

As the bars clear out after last call, make your way off crowded and chaotic 18th Street and into the pleasantly low-key **El Tamarindo** (✉ 1785 Florida Ave. NW ☎ 202/238–3660 Ⓜ Dupont Circle) for cheap heaping portions of Mexican and Salvadoran cuisine. You can enjoy a full sit-down meal at 3 AM, including quesadillas, enchiladas, and Salvadoran-style *pupusas* (tortillas stuffed with cheese and other fillings).

DUPONT CIRCLE

It's not only the literati who flock to the charming **Kramerbooks & Afterwards** (✉ 1517 Connecticut Ave. NW ☎ 202/387–3825 Ⓜ Dupont Circle) for a book and brew. This all-inclusive bookstore, bar, and café is a popular after-hours destination attracting hip, young Washingtonians. Open 24 hours on Friday and Saturday, and late at night during the week, this is the perfect place to wind down after a long night. The dinner menu offers classic American dishes from bacon cheeseburgers to crab-cake sandwiches and decadent cakes and pies.

Once a popular gay hangout, **Annie's Paramount Steak House** (✉ 1609 17th St. NW ☎ 202/232–0395 Ⓜ Dupont Circle) now attracts a more varied crowd. Anyone who craves steak and eggs in the middle of the night will appreciate this reliable and relatively cheap steak house, open 24 hours on Friday and Saturday.

GEORGETOWN

After a night of hobnobbing with politicos, stop in at **Five Guys Famous Burger and Fries** (✉ 1335 Wisconsin Ave. NW ☎ 202/337–0400 Ⓜ Foggy Bottom). It's famous for a reason—their award-winning ground-beef burgers with all the fixings and crispy, twice-fried fries hit the spot. If you're going to fill up on the free peanuts, make sure to select the "little" burger, which is one patty instead of the usual two.

Amid all the hubbub of Georgetown's M Street is **Mon Cheri Café** (✉ 3015 M St. NW ☎ 202/338–2745 Ⓜ Foggy Bottom), a sandwich-to-go shop. What it lacks in ambience, it makes up for in the food. Serving everything from burgers to gyros to cheesesteaks, this unpretentious café is a nice departure from its somewhat haughty surroundings.

The name says it all at Georgetown's **Bistro Français** (✉ 3128 M St. NW ☎ 202/338–3830 Ⓜ Foggy Bottom), where you can expect straightforward French fare. Open until 3 AM Tuesday through Thursday and until 4 AM Friday through Sunday, this neighborhood landmark is where many local chefs relax when they're finished cooking.

—Carolyn Galgano

spotted in the VIP areas. Love also has occasional concerts from performers such as Wyclef Jean and Alicia Keys. ■TIP➔ Shuttle service is available from 18th and M streets, a boon, considering Love's isolated locale. ⊠ *1350 Okie St. NE, Northeast* ☎ *202/636–9030* ⊕ *www. lovetheclub.com.*

★ **Modern.** A small, underground club with lowered bar and high-backed booths, Modern is cozy and familiar. The DJs spin songs you know, from Madonna to Outkast, and the crowd dresses up to match the swank surroundings. ⊠ *3287 M St. NW, Georgetown* ☎ *202/338–7027* ⊕ *www.modern-dc.com.*

Ultrabar. Relatively intimate, this bar offers a fun and luxurious environment. The club offers the metallic interior of Croma, a VIP room, warm wood paneling in the Bedroom, and spectacular lasers on the Main Floor, with multiple dance floors featuring hip-hop, Latin, and international music. ⊠ *911 F St. NW, Downtown* ☎ *202/638–4663* ⊕ *www.ultrabardc.com* Ⓜ *Metro Center.*

GAY AND LESBIAN DANCE CLUBS

Apex. A legendary establishment just off P Street, Apex has undergone several name changes over the years. This hot spot for gay men offers a light show and a fog machine to add atmosphere to the dance floor. It's a bit easier to get a drink at the upstairs bar. A room in the back shows '80s music videos. There's less attitude here than at larger clubs. ⊠ *1415 22nd St. NW, Dupont Circle* ☎ *202/296–0505* ⊕ *www.apex-dc. com* Ⓜ *Dupont Circle.*

Cobalt. Stop for a martini in the swank second-floor 30 Degrees lounge before heading upstairs to the dance floor. The Tuesday night "Flashback" parties are always fun, although most of the songs are older than the twentysomethings who pack the place. Weekend parties are known to be wild. ⊠ *1639 R St. NW, Dupont Circle* ☎ *202/462–6569* ⊕ *www. cobaltdc.com* Ⓜ *Dupont Circle.*

Remington's. Country-western dancing is all the rage at this cavernous club on Capitol Hill. The upstairs lounge features karaoke, pool, and foosball. Dance lessons are offered on Monday and Wednesday from 8:30 to 9:30 PM. ⊠ *639 Pennsylvania Ave. SE, Capitol Hill* ☎ *202/543– 3113* ⊕ *www.remingtonswdc.com* Ⓜ *Eastern Market.*

Town. This club stands out by regularly hosting drag shows and cabaret performances. It even has its own dance troupe, X-faction, to get the crowd worked up. Located in the Shaw neighborhood—not known for gay clubs—the club attracts a varied audience of gay men and lesbians in a friendly environment. There are two adjacent parking lots—a plus in Washington. Since this is not the safest neighborhood, take a cab. ⊠ *2009 8th St. NW, Shaw* ☎ *202/234–8696* ⊕ *www. towndc.com* Ⓜ *Shaw-Howard U.*

COMEDY CLUBS

With perhaps the richest of all subjects to mine—the machinations of government and those who try to run it—D.C.'s political satirists thrive. Jon Stewart's a Johnny-come-lately in this town. Countless open-mike

8

nights in bars all over town even let Hill staffers lampoon themselves. But Washington is a one-horse town: few top stand-up acts visit, but those who do come to the Improv.

Capitol Steps. Putting the "mock" in democracy, the musical political satire of this group of current and former Hill staffers is presented in the amphitheater of the Trade Center every Friday and Saturday at 7:30 PM and occasionally at other spots around town. Tickets are available through Ticketmaster. ⊠ *Ronald Reagan Bldg. and International Trade Center, 1300 Pennsylvania Ave. NW, Downtown* ☎ *703/683–8330* ⊕ *www.capsteps.com* Ⓜ *Federal Triangle.*

Ⓒ **ComedySportz.** Located south of D.C. in the Ballston Common Mall, two teams of comedians compete in this skit-based improv competition Thursday, Friday, and Saturday nights. There is an early family show where no obscenities are allowed and a late-night adults-only show with more-mature material on Friday and Saturday. ⊠ *Ballston Common Mall, 4238 Wilson Blvd., Arlington, VA* ☎ *703/294–5233* ⊕ *www.cszdc.com* Ⓜ *Ballston.*

DC Improv. The Improv, as everyone calls it, offers a steady menu of well-known and promising stand-up headliners. Recent acts have included Kevin Nealon, Colin Quinn, and a bevy of funny amateurs. ⊠ *1140 Connecticut Ave. NW, Downtown* ☎ *202/296–7008* ⊕ *www.dcimprov.com* Ⓜ *Farragut N.*

The Performing Arts

WORD OF MOUTH

"I would take an 8- or 9-year-old to Ford's Theatre because it stimulates the imagination about Lincoln's assassination and about theater in the 19th Century."

—happytrailstoyou

PERFORMING ARTS PLANNER

Tickets: The Standard Sources

Tickets to most events are available by calling or visiting the venue's box office or through the following ticket agencies: **Ticketmaster** (☎ 202/397–7328, 703/573–7328, or 410/547–7328 ⊕ www.ticketmaster.com) sells tickets for events at most venues. You can buy by phone, on the Web, or in person at Macy's department stores and the D.C. Visitor Information Center. **Tickets.com** (☎ 800/955–5566 ⊕ www.tickets.com) takes online reservations for a number of events around town.

Tickets: On the Cheap

TICKETplace (✉ Old Post Office Pavilion, 407 7th St. NW, Downtown ☎ 202/842–5387 ⊕ www.ticketplace.org Ⓜ Archives/Navy Memorial)sells half-price, day-of-performance tickets for select shows. Hours are: Wednesday–Friday 11–6, Saturday 10–5, and Sunday noon–4. A 12% service charge is included in the ticket price.

Find Out What's Happening

To sift through the flurry of events, check out these resources:

The Greater Washington Cultural Alliance (⊕ www.cultural-alliance.org), which offers a one-stop shopping for arts and culture in the nation's capital

The daily "Guide to the Lively Arts" and the Friday "Weekend" sections in the *Washington Post*

The Thursday *Washington Times* "Washington Weekend" section

The free weekly *Washington CityPaper* (⊕ www.washingtoncitypaper.com), published on Thursday

The "City Lights" section in the monthly *Washingtonian* magazine

Online, the *Post* (⊕ www.washingtonpost.com/cityguide), *Times* (⊕ www.washingtontimes.com/activityguide), and *Washingtonian* (⊕ www.washingtonian.com/inwashington) all publish entertainment guides. DCist (⊕ www.dcist.com), a popular local blog, and Express Night Out (⊕ www.expressnightout.com) post daily on D.C. events.

Free Events

The abundance of freebies in Washington extends to the arts. Highlights among the no-charge events include:

The **Shakespeare Theatre Free for All,** a two-week run of performances every June

The Millennium Stage at the **Kennedy Center,** where there are free performances daily at 6 PM

The **National Cathedral,** which hosts frequent concerts

Screen on the Green, a showing of classic films on the Mall every Monday in July and August

The **National Academy of Sciences,** which shows off its acoustically advanced auditorium with concerts of chamber music on Sunday afternoons from fall through spring

The **Fort Dupont Summer Theater's** jazz series Saturday nights in July and August

Updated by Mitchell Tropin and Cathy Sharpe

In the past 40 years D.C. has gone from being a cultural desert to a thriving arts center. The arts scene has exploded to meet the demands of young professionals who flock here for opportunities in government. Visitors have the opportunity to view incredible theater, music, and dance in fresh, dynamic facilities. When you include the old steadfasts—the Kennedy Center, the Washington National Opera, and the National Theatre—it's clear that Washington's art scene is a major draw of talent on the East Coast. The opening of several new theaters has greatly increased the number of top-rate productions.

PERFORMANCE VENUES

Though most of the very best out-of-town performers flock to the Kennedy Center or the Verizon Center, Washington is also peppered with dozens of small and medium-size venues. Performance halls tend to showcase musicians, but there's no shortage of dance and theater troupes, or stand-up comedians. Don't go looking for a theater district: the venues are spread across town and in the Maryland and Virginia suburbs.

Atlas Performing Arts Center. Known as the "People's Kennedy Center," this relatively new performance venue is community-based, encompassing four theaters and three dance studios. Located in a restored historic movie theater, the Atlas is home to a diverse group of resident arts organizations, including theater troupes, dance companies, orchestras, and choral groups. Free nightly H Street shuttle service is available from the Gallery Place Metro stop. Parking is available on the street. ✉ *1333 H St. NE, Northeast* ☎ *202/399–7993* ⊕ *www.atlasarts.org.*

Five Great Arts Experiences

■ **Kennedy Center:** The gem of the D.C. arts scene, this is the one performance venue you might take with you if you were stranded on a desert isle.

■ **National Gallery of Art garden concerts:** These are classy events where you're actually encouraged to take off your shoes.

■ **Screen on the Green:** Not even your neighbor the lobbyist (or the neighborhood multiplex) has a screen this big.

■ **Shakespeare Theatre:** Among the top Shakespeare companies in the world, this troupe excels at both classical and contemporary interpretations.

■ **Woolly Mammoth:** This remarkable theater company stages some of the most creative and entertaining new plays from the nation's best playwrights.

Center for the Arts. This state-of-the-art performance complex on the suburban Virginia campus of George Mason University satisfies music, ballet, and drama patrons in its 1,900-seat concert hall, the 500-seat proscenium Harris Theater, and the intimate 150-seat black-box Theater of the First Amendment. The 9,500-seat Patriot Center, site of pop acts and sporting events, is also on campus. ⊠ *Rte. 123 and Braddock Rd., Fairfax, VA* ☎ *888/945–2468* ⊕ *www. gmu.edu/cfa.*

Clarice Smith Performing Arts Center at Maryland. The 17-acre center, on the College Park campus of the University of Maryland, presents a wide range of music, dance, and drama in half a dozen striking venues. Shuttle service to the center is available at the College Park Metro station during the academic year. ⊠ *University Blvd. and Stadium Dr., College Park, MD* ☎ *301/405–2787* ⊕ *www.claricesmithcenter.umd. edu* Ⓜ *College Park.*

DAR Constitution Hall. Acts ranging from Jamie Foxx to Clay Aiken to B. B. King perform at this 3,700-seat venue, one of Washington's grand old halls. ⊠ *1776 D St. NW, Downtown* ☎ *202/628–4780* ⊕ *www.dar. org/conthall* Ⓜ *Farragut West.*

Fodor's Choice ★ **John F. Kennedy Center for the Performing Arts.** On the bank of the Potomac River, the gem of the D.C. arts scene is home to the National Symphony Orchestra, the Washington Ballet, and the Washington National Opera. The best out-of-town acts perform at one of three performance spaces—the Concert Hall, the Opera House, or the Eisenhower Theater. Eclectic performers can be found at the Center's smaller venues, including the Terrace Theater, showcasing chamber groups and experimental works; the Theater Lab, home to cabaret-style performances like the audience-participation hit *Sheer Madness*; the KC Jazz Club; and a 320-seat family theater. But that's not all. On the Millennium Stage in the center's Grand Foyer you can catch free performances almost any day at 6 PM. ■TIP→ On performance days, a free shuttle bus runs between the Center and the Foggy Bottom/GWU Metro stop. ⊠ *New Hampshire Ave. and Rock Creek Pkwy. NW, Foggy Bottom* ☎ *202/467–4600 or*

800/444–1324 ⊕ *www.kennedy-center.org* Ⓜ *Foggy Bottom/GWU.*

Lisner Auditorium. A 1,500-seat theater on the campus of George Washington University in Downtown D.C., Lisner hosts pop, classical, and choral music shows, modern dance performances, and musical theater. ✉ *730 21st St. NW, Foggy Bottom* ☎ *202/994–6800* ⊕ *www.lisner.org* Ⓜ *Foggy Bottom/GWU.*

Fodor'sChoice ★ **Music Center at Strathmore.** Located 0.5 mi outside the Capital Beltway in North Bethesda, this concert hall receives praise for its acoustics and its audience-friendly design. Major national folk, blues, pop, jazz, Broadway, and classical artists perform here. The center is home to the Baltimore Symphony Orchestra and the National Philharmonic. More-intimate performances are held in the 100-seat Dorothy M. and Maurice C. Shapiro Music Room. ■TIP➔ Consider taking the Metro to Strathmore; the center is less than a block from the Grosvenor Metro station. ✉ *5301 Tuckerman La., North Bethesda* ☎ *301/581–5200* ⊕ *www.strathmore.org* Ⓜ *Grosvenor/Strathmore.*

★ **National Gallery of Art.** Since 1942 the National Gallery has offered a variety of music. On Friday from Memorial Day through Labor Day, local jazz groups perform from 5 to 9 PM to a packed crowd in the sculpture garden. Loyal listeners dip their weary feet in the fountain, sip sangria, and let their week wash away. From October to June free concerts by the National Gallery Orchestra and performances by visiting recitalists and ensembles are held in the West Building's West Garden Court on Sunday nights. Entry is first-come, first-served, with doors opening at 6 PM and concerts starting at 6:30 PM. ✉ *6th St. and Constitution Ave. NW, The Mall* ☎ *202/737–4215* ⊕ *www.nga.gov* Ⓜ *Archives/Navy Memorial.*

Fodor'sChoice ★ **Smithsonian Institution.** Jazz, musical theater, and popular standards are performed in the National Museum of American History. In the museum's third-floor Hall of Musical Instruments, musicians occasionally play period instruments from the museum's collection. The Smithsonian's annual Folklife Festival, held on the Mall, highlights the cuisine, crafts, and day-to-day life of several different cultures. (Texas, Wales, Haiti, and Bhutan are among the most recent ones to have been featured.) The Smithsonian Associates sponsor programs that offer everything from a cappella groups to Cajun zydeco bands; all events require tickets, and locations vary. ✉ *1000 Jefferson Dr. SW, The Mall* ☎ *202/357–2700, 202/633–1000 recording, 202/357–3030 Smithsonian Associates* ⊕ *www.si.edu* Ⓜ *Smithsonian.*

Verizon Center. In addition to being the home of the Washington Capitals hockey and Washington Wizards basketball teams, this 19,000-seat arena also plays host to D.C.'s biggest concerts, ice-skating events, and the circus. Parking can be a problem, but several Metro lines converge at an adjacent station. ✉ *601 F St. NW, Chinatown* ☎ *202/661–5000* ⊕ *www.verizoncenter.com* Ⓜ *Gallery Place/Chinatown.*

9

Wolf Trap National Park for the Performing Arts. Wolf Trap is the only national park dedicated to the performing arts. June through September, the massive, outdoor Filene Center hosts close to 100 performances, ranging from pop and jazz concerts to dance and musical theater productions. In summer, the National Symphony Orchestra is based here, and the Children's Theatre-in-the-Woods delivers 70 free performances. During the colder months the intimate, indoor Barns at Wolf Trap fill with the sounds of musicians playing folk, country, and chamber music, along with myriad other styles. The park is just off the Dulles Toll Road, about 20 mi from Downtown. ■TIP➜ When the Filene Center hosts an event, Metrorail operates a $3.10 (exact change is required) round-trip shuttle bus from the West Falls Church Metro station. The bus leaves 20 minutes after the show or no later than 11 pm, whether the show is over or not. ⊠ *1645 Trap Rd., Vienna, VA* ☎ *703/255–1900, 703/938–2404 Barns at Wolf Trap* ⊕ *www.wolftrap.org* Ⓜ *Vienna.*

MUSIC

With dozens of acoustically superior venues and majestic backdrops around town, D.C. sets a lofty stage for its musicians, who have the talent to match. Whether it's the four armed services bands marching in the footsteps of John Philip Sousa, opera singers performing under the direction of Plácido Domingo, or chamber players performing Renaissance pieces on period instruments, this city's musicians consistently lay down a fitting sound track.

CHAMBER MUSIC

Coolidge Auditorium at the Library of Congress. Over the past 81 years the Coolidge has hosted most of the 20th-century's greatest performers and composers, including Copland and Stravinsky. Today it draws musicians from all genres, including classical, jazz, and gospel, and it continues to wow audiences with its near-perfect acoustics and sightlines. Concert tickets are free, but must be ordered in advance through Ticketmaster. ⊠ *Library of Congress, Jefferson Bldg., 101 Independence Ave. SE, Capitol Hill* ☎ *800/551–7328* ⊕ *www.loc.gov* Ⓜ *Capitol South.*

Corcoran Gallery of Art. Hungary's Takács String Quartet and the Klavier Trio Amsterdam are among the chamber groups that have appeared in the Corcoran's Musical Evening Series, held one night each month from October to May and periodically in summer. On weekday afternoons the Corcoran hosts musicians playing jazz and other musical styles. ⊠ *500 17th St. NW, Downtown* ☎ *202/639–1700* ⊕ *www.corcoran. org* Ⓜ *Farragut W.*

Dumbarton Concerts. Dumbarton United Methodist Church, a fixture in Georgetown since 1772 (in its current location since 1850), sponsors this concert series, which has been host to musicians such as the American Chamber Players, the St. Petersburg String Quartet, and the Thibaud String Trio. ⊠ *Dumbarton United Methodist Church, 3133 Dumbarton Ave. NW, Georgetown* ☎ *202/965–2000* ⊕ *www. dumbartonconcerts.org* Ⓜ *Foggy Bottom.*

Folger Shakespeare Library. The library's internationally acclaimed resident chamber music ensemble, the Folger Consort, regularly presents medieval, Renaissance, and baroque pieces performed on period instruments. The season runs from October to May. ⊠ *201 E. Capitol St. SE, Capitol Hill* ☎ *202/544–7077* ⊕ *www.folger.edu* Ⓜ *Union Station or Capitol South.*

National Academy of Sciences. Free Sunday afternoon performances are given fall through spring in the academy's 670-seat auditorium. ⊠ *2100 C St. NW, Downtown* ☎ *202/334–2436* ⊕ *www.nationalacademies.org/arts* Ⓜ *Foggy Bottom/GWU.*

Phillips Collection. Duncan Phillips's mansion is more than an art museum. On Sunday afternoons from October through May, chamber groups from around the world perform in its long, dark-paneled Music Room. ■TIP➜ The free concerts begin at 4 PM; arrive early for decent seats. ⊠ *1600 21st St. NW, Dupont Circle* ☎ *202/387–2151* ⊕ *www.phillipscollection.org* Ⓜ *Dupont Circle.*

> **WORD OF MOUTH**
>
> "A concert at the National Cathedral is enthralling and magnificent. On the 4th of July we went to the organ concert there—it was spectacular (and free!) ... we also attended *The Messiah* last December, which was thrilling (but not free)."
>
> —vivi

CHORAL MUSIC

Basilica of the National Shrine of the Immaculate Conception. Choral and church groups occasionally perform at the largest Catholic church in the Americas. Every summer the Basilica offers organ recitals, featuring the Shrine's massive pipe organ. ⊠ *400 Michigan Ave. NE, Catholic University* ☎ *202/526–8300* ⊕ *www.nationalshrine.com* Ⓜ *Brookland/CUA.*

Choral Arts Society of Washington. From spring to fall the 200-voice Choral Arts Society choir performs a variety of classical pieces at the Kennedy Center. Three Christmas sing-alongs are scheduled each December, along with a popular tribute to Martin Luther King Jr. on his birthday. ☎ *202/244–3669* ⊕ *www.choralarts.org.*

Washington National Cathedral. Choral and church groups frequently perform in this grand church. Every month, usually toward the end of the month, organ recitals on the massive pipe organ are offered around 5:15. Admission is usually free. ⊠ *Massachusetts and Wisconsin Aves. NW, Cleveland Park* ☎ *202/537–6207* ⊕ *www.nationalcathedral.org* Ⓜ *Tenleytown/AU.*

OPERA

The *Washington Post* "Weekend" section is a good source for information on opera and classical performances.

In Series. Trademark cabaret, experimental chamber opera, and Spanish musical theater (also known as *zarzuela*) are among the hallmarks of this burgeoning nonprofit company, which performs at venues around the city. ☎ *202/518–0152* ⊕ *www.inseries.org.*

☾ **Opera Theatre of Northern Virginia.** Four times a year this company stages an opera at an Arlington community theater. The winter production is geared to young audiences. The productions are sung in English. ☎ *703/528–1433* ⊕ *www.novaopera.org.*

Fodor'sChoice   **Washington National Opera.** Under the directorship of Plácido Domingo,
★   the Washington National Opera presents eight operas in fall and spring at the Kennedy Center Opera House. The operas, presented in their original languages with English supertitles, are often sold out to subscribers, but returned tickets are available an hour before curtain time. ■TIP➔ **For standing-room tickets to each week's performances, inquire at the box office starting the preceding Saturday.** ☎ *202/295–2400 or 800/876–7372* ⊕ *www.dc-opera.org.*

ORCHESTRAS

Baltimore Symphony Orchestra. When the 2,000-seat Music Center at Strathmore opened in 2005, the world-renowned Baltimore Symphony Orchestra relocated to the Greater Washington area. The orchestra, under the leadership of Maestra Alsop, performs year-round at the center, a half mile outside the Beltway in North Bethesda. A Metro station is less than a block away. ⊠ *5301 Tuckerman La., North Bethesda* ☎ *877/276–1444* ⊕ *www.bsmusic.org* Ⓜ *Grosvenor/Strathmore.*

National Symphony Orchestra. Under the direction of Ivan Fischer, the NSO performs from September to June at the Kennedy Center Concert Hall. In summer the orchestra performs at Wolf Trap and gives free concerts at Rock Creek Park's Carter Barron Amphitheatre. On Memorial and Labor Day weekends and July 4 the orchestra performs on the West Lawn of the Capitol. ⊠ *New Hampshire Ave. and Rock Creek Pkwy. NW, Foggy Bottom* ☎ *202/462–4600* ⊕ *www.kennedy-center.org/nso.*

PERFORMANCE SERIES

Armed Forces Concert Series. A Washington tradition, bands from the four branches of the armed services perform June to August on Monday, Tuesday, Wednesday, and Friday evenings on the East Terrace of the Capitol. Other performances take place at 8 PM from June to August, on Tuesday, Thursday, Friday, and Sunday nights at the **Sylvan Theater** (⊠ *Washington Monument grounds, 14th St. and Constitution Ave., The Mall* ☎ *202/426–6841* Ⓜ *Smithsonian*). Concerts usually include marches, patriotic numbers, and some classical music. The Air Force celebrity series features popular artists such as Earl Klugh and Keiko Matsui on Sunday in February and March at DAR Constitutional Hall. ☎ *202/767–5658 Air Force, 703/696–3718 Army, 202/433–4011 Marines, 202/433–2525 Navy.*

Carter Barron Amphitheatre. On Saturday and Sunday nights from June to September this 3,750-seat outdoor theater hosts pop, jazz, gospel, and rhythm-and-blues artists such as Chick Corea and Nancy Wilson. The National Symphony Orchestra also performs here, and for two weeks the Shakespeare Theatre presents a free play. ⊠ *Rock Creek Park, 4850 Colorado Ave. NW, Upper Northwest* ☎ *202/426–0486* ⊕ *www.nps. gov/rocr/planyourvisit/cbarron.htm.*

Fort Dupont Summer Theater. The National Park Service presents national and international jazz artists at 8 PM on Saturday evenings from July to August at the outdoor Fort Dupont Summer Theater. Wynton Marsalis, Shirley Horne, and Ramsey Lewis are among the artists who have performed free concerts here. ⊠ *Minnesota Ave. and Randall Circle SE, Southeast* ☎ *202/426–5961* ⊕ *www.nps.gov/fodu.*

Institute of Musical Traditions. Emerging, near-famous, and celebrated folk performers such as Si Kahn, John McCutcheon, and the Kennedys perform at the Institute's concerts, most often held at the St. Mark Presbyterian Church in Rockville, a 30-minute drive from Washington. ⊠ *10701 Old Georgetown Rd., Rockville, MD* ☎ *301/754–3611* ⊕ *www.imtfolk.org.*

Washington Performing Arts Society. One of the city's oldest arts organizations, this nonprofit stages high-quality classical music, jazz, gospel, modern dance, and performance art in halls around the city. Past artists include the Alvin Ailey American Dance Theater, Yo-Yo Ma, the Chieftains, Sweet Honey in the Rock, and Cecilia Bartoli. ☎ *202/833–9800* ⊕ *www.wpas.org.*

THEATER AND PERFORMANCE ART

Perhaps as a counterbalance to all the political theater in town, D.C.'s playhouses, large and small, have grown into a force to be reckoned with over the past few years. Nearly every major theater in town has recently renovated its performance spaces or is in the process of doing so, and new small theaters are popping up all the time. As if all that weren't enough, D.C. often hosts some of the best touring companies from the East Coast and beyond.

9

LARGE THEATERS

★ **Arena Stage.** The first regional theater company to win a Tony Award, Arena Stage performs innovative American theater, reviving some classic plays and showcasing the country's best new writers. Arena is currently staging most of its productions in its temporary home in the Crystal Forum, a 400-seat venue located a few miles south of Washington in Crystal City, Virginia. Arena expects to move into a new $120 million home in fall 2010. Located near the waterfront in Southeast Washington, the theater's expanded space will feature three different stages: a theater in the round seating 650, a modified thrust stage theater seating 514, and "Cradle," a new 200-seat black-box theater for experimental productions. Arena's new home will stand out architecturally with a high glass curtain surrounding a campus that incorporates the three theaters, expanded lobbies, cafés, and offices. ⊠ *1800 S. Bell St., Crystal City* ☎ *202/488–3300* ⊕ *www.arenastage.org* Ⓜ *Crystal City.*

☾ **Ford's Theatre.** Looking much as it did when President Lincoln was shot at a performance of *Our American Cousin,* Ford's primarily hosts musicals, most with family appeal. Dickens's *A Christmas Carol* is staged every year. The historic theater, maintained by the National Park Service, is now more audience-friendly, thanks to an $8.5 million renovation that included replacing hard wooden chairs with more-comfortable padded seats, new restrooms, improved lighting and sound, and the building's first elevator. Tours of the theater and a renovated museum are available for free, but timed entry tickets are required. ⊠ *511 10th St. NW, Downtown* ☎ *202/426–6925* ⊕ *www.fordstheatre. org* Ⓜ *Metro Center.*

Lincoln Theatre. Once the host of such notable black performers as Cab Calloway, Lena Horne, and Duke Ellington, the 1,250-seat Lincoln is part of the revitalized and lively U Street Corridor. It presents movies, comedy shows, and musical performers such as Harry Belafonte, the Count Basie Orchestra, and the Harlem Boys and Girls Choir. ⊠ *1215 U St. NW, U Street Corridor* ☎ *202/328–6000* ⊕ *www.thelincolntheatre. org* Ⓜ *U St./Cardozo.*

☺ **National Theatre.** Though rebuilt several times, the National Theatre has operated in the same location since 1835. It now hosts touring Broadway shows, such as *Spamalot* and *Movin' Out.* ■**TIP**➜ **From September through April, look for free children's shows Saturday morning and free Monday night shows that may include Asian dance, performance art, and a cappella cabarets.** ⊠ *1321 Pennsylvania Ave. NW, Downtown* ☎ *202/783–3372* ⊕ *www.nationaltheatre.org* Ⓜ *Metro Center.*

Fodor'sChoice **Shakespeare Theatre.** This acclaimed troupe, known as one of the world's
★ three great Shakespearean companies, crafts fantastically staged and acted performances of works by Shakespeare and his contemporaries. The theater has undergone an amazing transformation. Complementing the existing stage in the Lansburgh Theatre is the Sidney Harman Hall, which opened in October 2007. The new stage provides a 21st-century, state-of-the-art, mid-size venue for an outstanding variety of performances, from Shakespeare's *Julius Caesar* to the hilarious *Abridged History of America*. For two weeks in late spring they perform Shakespeare for free at Carter Barron Amphitheatre. ⊠ *450 7th St. NW, Downtown* ☎ *202/547–1122* ⊕ *www.shakespearedc.org* Ⓜ *Gallery Pl./Chinatown or Archives/Navy Memorial.*

Warner Theatre. One of Washington's grand theaters, the Warner hosts road shows, dance recitals, pop music, and the occasional comedy acts in its majestic art deco performance space. ⊠ *513 13th St. NW, Downtown* ☎ *202/783–4000* ⊕ *www.warnertheatre.com* Ⓜ *Metro Center.*

SMALL THEATERS AND COMPANIES

Often performing in churches and other less-than-ideal settings, Washington's small companies present drama that can be every bit as enthralling as—and often more daring than—that offered by their blockbuster counterparts. No matter the size, all companies in town compete fiercely for the Helen Hayes Award, Washington's version of the Tony.

American Century Theatre. Devoted to staging overlooked or forgotten classic American plays, American Century has staged performances of Kurt Vonnegut's *Happy Birthday, Wanda June*, Orson Wells's *Moby*

Dick Rehearsed, and even a rare Mel Brooks production, *Archy and Mehitabel.* ✉ *2700 Lang St., Arlington VA* ☎ *703/998–4555* ⊕ *www. americancentury.org.*

District of Columbia Arts Center. Known by area artists as DCAC, this cross-genre space shows changing exhibits in its gallery and presents avant-garde performance art, improv, and experimental plays in its tiny black-box theater. ✉ *2438 18th St. NW, Adams Morgan* ☎ *202/462– 7833* ⊕ *www.dcartscenter.org.*

Folger Shakespeare Library. The library's theater, a 250-seat re-creation of the inn-yard theaters with seating in the balcony popular in Shakespeare's time, hosts three to four productions a year of Shakespeare or Shakespeare-influenced works. Though the stage is a throwback, the sharp acting and staging certainly push the envelope. ✉ *201 E. Capitol St. SE, Capitol Hill* ☎ *202/544–7077* ⊕ *www.folger.edu* Ⓜ *Union Station or Capitol S.*

Gala Hispanic Theatre. This company attracts outstanding Hispanic actors from around the world, performing works by such leading dramatists as Federico García Lorca and Mario Vargas Llosa. Plays are presented in English or in Spanish with instant English translations supplied through earphones. The company performs in the newly renovated Tivoli Theatre in Columbia Heights, a hot spot for Latino culture and cuisine. ✉ *Tivoli Sq., 3333 14th St. NW, 14th and Park Rd., Columbia Heights* ☎ *202/234–7174* ⊕ *www.galatheatre.org* Ⓜ *Columbia Heights.*

↻ **Glen Echo Park.** The National Park Service has transformed this former amusement park into a thriving arts center. Every weekend the Adventure Theater puts on traditional plays and musicals aimed at children ages four and up. Families can spread out on carpeted steps. At the Puppet Company Playhouse skilled puppeteers perform classic stories Wednesday through Sunday. ✉ *7300 MacArthur Blvd., Glen Echo, MD* ☎ *301/634–2222, 301/320–5331 Adventure Theater, 301/320–6668 Puppet Co.* ⊕ *www.glenechopark.org.*

↻ **Imagination Stage.** Shows like Roald Dahl's classic story *The BFG*, and original fare such as Karen Zacarias and Deborah Wicks LaPuma's *Cinderella Likes Rice and Beans* are produced here for children ages four and up. The state-of-the-art center in Bethesda includes two theaters and a digital media studio. Make reservations in advance. ✉ *4908 Auburn Ave., Bethesda, MD* ☎ *301/961–6060* ⊕ *www.imaginationstage.org.*

Rorschach Theatre. A newcomer on the D.C. theater scene, Rorschach stages some of the most creative plays in Washington, featuring intimate and passionate performances. The company offers lesser-known works by such playwrights as Pulitzer Prize–winning Tony Kusher and Russia's Mikhail Bulgakov, as well as stage adaptations of literary classics such as *Lord of the Flies.* The theater, which lacks a permanent home, currently presents its plays in Georgetown University's Davis Performing Arts Center. ✉ *1421 Columbia Rd., Columbia Heights* ☎ *202/452– 5538* ⊕ *www.rorschachtheatre.com* Ⓜ *Columbia Heights.*

Round House Theatre. Each season on its Main Stage in Bethesda, Round House presents an eclectic body of work ranging from world premieres to great 20th-century works to contemporary adaptations of the classics. Round House's 150-seat black-box stage, home to more-experimental works, is in Silver Spring, adjacent to the American Film Institute Silver Theater. ✉ *4545 East–West Hwy., Bethesda, MD* ☎ *240/644–1099* ⊕ *www.round-house.org* Ⓜ *Bethesda* ✉ *8641 Colesville Rd., Silver Spring, MD* ☎ *240/644–1099* Ⓜ *Silver Spring.*

Signature Theatre. Led by artistic director Eric Schaeffer, Signature has earned national acclaim for its presentation of contemporary plays and groundbreaking American musicals, especially those of Stephen Sondheim. The company performs in a dramatic new facility in Arlington, Virginia, with two performance spaces, the 299-seat MAX and the 99-seat ARK. ✉ *2800 S. Stafford St., Arlington, VA* ☎ *703/820–9771* ⊕ *www.signature-theatre.org.*

★ **Studio Theatre.** One of the busiest groups in the city, this independent company produces an eclectic season of classic and offbeat plays in four spaces: the original Mead and Milton theaters, the newer 200-seat Metheny Theatre, and the experimental Stage 4. The theater is part of the revitalized 14th Street Corridor. ✉ *1333 P St. NW, Dupont Circle* ☎ *202/332–3300* ⊕ *www.studiotheatre.org* Ⓜ *Dupont Circle.*

Theater J. In recent years Theater J has emerged as one of the country's most distinctive and progressive Jewish performance venues, offering an ambitious range of programming that includes work by noted playwrights, directors, designers, and actors. Performances take place in the Aaron and Cecile Goldman Theater at the D.C. Jewish Community Center. ✉ *1529 16th St. NW, Downtown* ☎ *202/518–9400* ⊕ *www. theaterj.org* Ⓜ *Dupont Circle.*

Washington Stage Guild. This company performs neglected classics and foreign plays at its new beautiful and intimate venue, offering lesser-known works by Oscar Wilde and George Bernard Shaw, such as *Don Juan in Hell* and *Lord Arthur Savile's Crime.* The Guild also stages selections from the Lady Gregory plays, hilarious slices of Irish life that presage Yeats and Beckett. George Bernard Shaw is a specialty. ✉ *E St. and 8th Ave. NW, Penn Quarter* ☎ *240/582–0050* ⊕ *www.stageguild. org* Ⓜ *Gallery Pl./Chinatown or Archives/Navy Memorial.*

Fodor'sChoice
★ **Woolly Mammoth.** Unusual avant-garde shows with edgy staging and solid acting have earned Woolly Mammoth top reviews and favorable comparisons to Chicago's Steppenwolf. The troupe's talent is accentuated by its modern 265-seat theater in Penn Quarter near the Verizon Center. ✉ *641 D St. NW, Downtown* ☎ *202/393–3939* ⊕ *www.woollymammoth.net* Ⓜ *Gallery Pl./Chinatown or Archives/Navy Memorial.*

DANCE

The solid performances of the Washington Ballet, generally considered one of the better troupes in the United States, and those of smaller companies around town are complemented by frequent visits from some of the world's best companies, including the Kirov Ballet and the Alvin Ailey American Dance Theater. Washington is also host to many festivals, and dance is often highlighted. The traditional Japanese dance featured during the Cherry Blossom Festival and the varied styles that come to town during the Smithsonian Folklife Festival are particular treats.

Dance Place. This studio theater showcases the best local dance talent in an assortment of modern and ethnic shows; performances take place most weekends. It also conducts dance classes daily. The company's home is in Northeast Washington near Catholic University, quite close to the Metro. ✉ *3225 8th St. NE, Catholic University* ☎ *202/269–1600* ⊕ *www.danceplace.org* Ⓜ *Catholic University.*

Joy of Motion. Several area troupes perform in the studio's Jack Guidone Theatre, located in Northwest Washington. Joy of Motion includes the resident Dana Tai Soon Burgess & Company (modern), CrossCurrents Dance Company (contemporary), and Silk Road Dance Company (traditional Middle Eastern and Central Asian). ✉ *5207 Wisconsin Ave. NW, Friendship Heights* ☎ *202/276–2599* ⊕ *www.joyofmotion.org* Ⓜ *Friendship Heights.*

★ **Washington Ballet.** Between September and May this company presents classical and contemporary ballets, including works by choreographers such as George Balanchine, Choo-San Goh, and artistic director Septime Webre. Its main shows are mounted at the Kennedy Center. Each December the Washington Ballet performs *The Nutcracker* at the Warner Theatre. ☎ *202/362–3606* ⊕ *www.washingtonballet.org.*

FILM

D.C.'s countless foundations, embassies, national museums, and institutions offer the visiting cinephile an unexpected side benefit—quirky, long-forgotten, seldom-seen, and arcane films on as many topics as there are special interests.

The most common venues are listed below; more-limited engagements are listed in the *Washington CityPaper* or the *Washington Post.* Those looking for selections a little less obscure will likely find what they're looking for in D.C.'s many repertory, independent, and first-run theaters.

Fodor's Choice
★ **American Film Institute Silver Theatre and Cultural Center.** This state-of-the-art center for film is a restoration of architect John Eberson's art deco Silver Theatre, built in 1938. The AFI hosts film retrospectives, festivals, and tributes celebrating artists from Jeanne Moreau to Russell Crowe. The AFI Silver also hosts the annual Silver Docs festival, which features some of the world's best documentaries and appearances by some of the greatest filmmakers, such as Martin Scorsese. ✉ *8633 Colesville Rd., Silver Spring, MD* ☎ *301/495–6700* ⊕ *www.afi.com/silver* Ⓜ *Silver Spring.*

Arlington Cinema 'N' Drafthouse. The rules are relaxed at this second-run theater, where you can enjoy beer and nosh, like pizza and buffalo wings, while you watch yesterday's blockbuster. Most matinee and early shows don't allow smoking. The drafthouse also features stand-up comics, who perform on the old movie theater's stage. ■TIP→ Minors (under 21) must be accompanied by a parent or guardian. ✉ *2903 Columbia Pike, Arlington, VA* ☎ *703/486–2345* ⊕ *www.arlingtondrafthouse.com.*

Filmfest DC. An annual citywide festival of international cinema, the D.C. International Film Festival, or Filmfest, takes place in late April or early May at venues throughout the city. ☎ *202/628–3456* ⊕ *www. filmfestdc.org.*

9

Hirshhorn Museum and Sculpture Garden. Avant-garde and experimental first-run documentaries, features, and short films are frequently screened here for free. ⊠ *Independence Ave. and 7th St. SW, The Mall* ☎ *202/357–2700* ⊕ *www.hirshhorn.si.edu* Ⓜ *Smithsonian or L'Enfant Plaza.*

Landmark's E Street Cinema. Specializing in independent, foreign, and documentary films, this theater has been warmly welcomed by D.C. movie lovers both for its selection and state-of-the-art facilities. It has an impressive concession stand, stocked to please the gourmand, the health-conscious, and those who just want a jumbo box of Milk Duds. ⊠ *555 11th St. NW, Downtown* ☎ *202/452–7672* ⊕ *www.landmarktheatres. com* Ⓜ *Metro Center.*

Loews Cineplex Uptown 1. Featuring the largest movie screen in town, the Uptown is a true movie palace with art deco flourishes; a wonderful balcony; and—in one happy concession to modernity—crystal-clear Dolby sound. It's home to Washington's biggest movie premieres. ⊠ *3426 Connecticut Ave. NW, Cleveland Park* ☎ *202/966–5400* Ⓜ *Cleveland Park.*

National Archives. Historical films, usually documentaries, are shown here daily. Screenings range from the 1942 documentary by Robert Flaherty on the plight of migrant workers to archival footage of Charles Lindbergh's solo flight from New York to Paris. ⊠ *Constitution Ave. between 7th and 9th Sts. NW, The Mall* ☎ *202/501–5000* ⊕ *www. archives.gov* Ⓜ *Archives/Navy Memorial.*

National Gallery of Art, East Building. Free classic and international films, often complementing the exhibits, are shown in this museum's large auditorium. Pick up a film calendar at the museum or online. ⊠ *Constitution Ave. between 3rd and 4th Sts. NW, The Mall* ☎ *202/842–6799* ⊕ *www.nga.gov* Ⓜ *Archives/Navy Memorial.*

National Geographic Society. Documentary films with a scientific, geographic, or anthropological focus are shown regularly at National Geographic's Grosvenor Auditorium. ⊠ *1600 M St., Dupont Circle* ☎ *202/857–7700* ⊕ *www.nationalgeographic.com/nglive/washington* Ⓜ *Farragut N.*

★ **Screen on the Green.** Every July and August this weekly series of classic films turns the Mall into an open-air cinema. People arrive as early as 5 PM to picnic, socialize, and reserve a spot. The show starts at dusk. ⊠ *The Mall at 7th St.* ☎ *877/262–5866* Ⓜ *Smithsonian.*

Sports and the Outdoors

WORD OF MOUTH

"Generally speaking the zoo is a better option early in the day when the animals are more active and the kids are less likely to moan about walking. It's hilly in places."

—obxgirl

SPORTS AND THE OUTDOORS PLANNER

Where the Pros Play

If you're going to a pro sports event, chances are you'll be headed to one of four venues. The perennially popular Redskins play football in the Maryland suburbs at FedEx Field (⊠ Arena Dr., Landover, MD). The Redskins' home is the largest stadium in the National Football League, seating 91,000. Check the Washington Post want ads and Craig's List for tickets. Parking is a hassle, so arrive several hours early if you don't want to miss the kickoff.

Robert F. Kennedy Stadium (⊠ 2400 E. Capitol St. NE, at 22nd St. Ⓜ Stadium), the Redskins' former residence on Capitol Hill, is now home to Major League Soccer's D.C. United.

D.C.'s baseball team, the Nationals, play in the new spacious state-of-the-art **Nationals Park** (⊠ 1500 S. Capitol St., SE Ⓜ Navy Yard), on the Anacostia waterfront in Southwest Washington.

Verizon Center (⊠ 601 F St. NW, between 6th and 7th Sts., Ⓜ Gallery Place/Chinatown) hosts many sporting events, including hockey, basketball, and figure skating.

Five Great Outdoor Experiences

Last chance to see the giant pandas: Washington's love affair with the pandas at the National Zoo will end sometime in 2010. Take the opportunity to see the District's most beloved residents, Mei Xiang, Tian Tian, and Tai Shan.

Picture-postcard motivation: Run or bike with Washington's monuments as a unique background.

Bird-watching on Theodore Roosevelt Island: Take in the spectacular scenery at the wildlife sanctuary.

One of Washington's loveliest places for a stroll: Walk through Dumbarton Oaks' many acres of distinctive gardens modeled after classic French, English, and Italian landscapes.

A new perspective on the cherry trees: Take a leisurely trip in a paddleboat around the Tidal Basin, surrounded by the famous blossoms in spring.

Washington for Every Season

With every change of the seasons, D.C. offers new pleasures for sports and outdoor enthusiasts:

In **winter** you can have an old-fashioned afternoon of ice-skating and hot chocolate in the National Gallery's sculpture garden, or go to the Verizon Center to see the Wizards play basketball or the Capitals play hockey.

Come **spring** the city emerges from the cold with activities everywhere. Runners become a common sight on the Mall, and boating is available nearby.

In **summer** baseball fans head to new Nationals Park to see the Nationals play, and Washington Redskins fans check out their favorite football stars at training camp in Ashburn, Virginia.

When **fall** arrives the seasonal colors of the trees in Rock Creek Park are a spectacular sight for bikers, hikers, and runners. Tickets to see the Redskins at FedEx Field are some of the city's most prized commodities.

Updated by
Mitchell Tropin
and Cathy
Sharpe

Washingtonians are an active bunch and the city provides a fantastic recreational backyard, with dozens of beautiful open spaces. The city's residents take full advantage of it, exploring by bike, running amid the monuments, and even sailing up the Potomac. They're also passionate about their local teams—especially the Redskins, whose games are sold out year after year.

Visitors to Washington can enjoy a host of outdoor attractions. Rock Creek Park is one of the city's treasures, with miles of wooded trails and paths for bikers, runners, and walkers that extend to almost every part of the city. The National Mall connects the Lincoln Memorial and the Capitol building. With the monuments as a backdrop, you can ride a bike or take a jog. Around the Tidal Basin, see the Jefferson Memorial from a paddleboat or run alongside the Potomac River. Theodore Roosevelt Island, a wildlife sanctuary that deserves to be better known, has several paths for hiking and enjoyable spots for a picnic.

10

PARKS AND NATURE

Washington is more than marble and limestone buildings. The city is blessed with numerous parks and outdoor attractions that provide a break from the museums and government facilities. Rock Creek Park extends through much of the city; there may just be an entrance to the park nearby your hotel. Other outdoor attractions, such as the Tidal Basin, Potomac Park, and Constitution Gardens, offer a chance to see nature, combined with the beauty of nearby waterways and the majesty of the city's most beloved monuments, such as the Vietnam Memorial, World War II Memorial, and the FDR Memorial.

ANIMALS

National Aquarium. The aquarium has an incongruous location inside the lower level of the Commerce Department Building, near the massive Ronald Reagan Building. Established in 1873, it's the country's oldest public aquarium, with more than 1,200 fish and other creatures—such as eels, sharks, and alligators—representing 270 species of fresh- and saltwater life. Operated by a nonprofit organization, without the benefit of large federal funding, the exhibits look somewhat dated, but the easy-to-view tanks, accessible touching pool (with crabs and sea urchins), low admission fee (only $3 for children), and absence of crowds make this a good outing with small children. The Aquarium's cafeteria is also a great place to stop for a snack. ■TIP➔ The aquarium does not accept credit cards, so be sure to have cash or a check handy. ⊠ *14th St. and Constitution Ave. NW, East End* ☎ *202/482–2825* ⊕ *www.nationalaquarium.com* ⊠ *$7* ☺ *Daily 9–5, last admission at 4:30; sharks fed Mon., Wed., and Sat. at 2; piranhas fed Tues., Thurs., and Sun. at 2* Ⓜ *Federal Triangle.*

National Zoo.
Fodor's Choice
★
Since 2000 the zoo's most famous residents have been the giant pandas Tian Tian and Mei Xiang. The excitement surrounding the pandas was heightened when Tai Shan, the National Zoo's first panda cub, was born in 2005. Tai is only the third panda born in the United States. However, Tai returned to China in February 2010, and the 10-year agreement that brought Tian Tian and Mei Xiang to Washington ends in December 2010. At this writing the National Zoo was in talks with Chinese officials regarding the pandas' future, and it is possible they will return to China. Check with the zoo's Web site before you go; you can also sign up for panda e-mail alerts on the zoo's Web site. Even if you miss the pandas, the zoo is still well worth the visit. It continues to add exciting new exhibits, such as the Asia trail that features: sloth bears, fishing cats, red pandas, a Japanese giant salamander, clouded leopards, and other Asian species.

Carved out of Rock Creek Park, the National Zoo contains 2,000 animals, representing 400 species. The zoo is a series of rolling, wooded hills that complement the many innovative compounds showing animals in their native settings. Step inside the Great Flight Cage to observe the free flight of many species of birds; this walk-in aviary is open from May to October (the birds are moved indoors during the colder months). Between 10 and 2 each day you can catch the orangutan population traveling on the "O Line," a series of cables and towers near the Great Ape House that allows the primates to swing hand over hand about 35 feet over your head. One of the more unusual and impressive exhibits is Amazonia, an amazingly authentic reproduction of a South American rain-forest ecosystem. You feel as if you are deep inside a steamy jungle, with monkeys leaping overhead and noisy birds flying from branch to branch. Part of the Smithsonian Institution, the National Zoo was created by an Act of Congress in 1889, and the 163-acre park was designed by landscape architect Frederick Law Olmsted, who also designed the U.S. Capitol grounds and New York's Central Park. Before the zoo opened in 1890, live animals used as taxidermists' models were kept on the Mall. ⊠ *3001 Connecticut Ave. NW, Woodley Park* ☎ *202/673–4800 or 202/673–4717* ⊕ *www.si.edu/natzoo* ☒ *Free, parking $16* ♢ *May–mid-Sept., daily 6 AM–8 PM; mid-Sept.–Apr., daily 6–6. Zoo buildings open at 10 and close before zoo closes* Ⓜ *Cleveland Park or Woodley Park/Zoo.*

GARDENS

Constitution Gardens. Many ideas were proposed to develop this 50-acre site near the Reflecting Pool and the Vietnam Veterans Memorial. It once held "temporary" buildings erected by the Navy before World War I and not removed until after World War II. President Nixon is said to have favored something resembling Copenhagen's Tivoli Gardens. The final design was plainer, with paths winding through groves of trees and, on the lake, a tiny island paying tribute to the signers of the Declaration of Independence, their signatures carved into a low stone wall. In 1986 President Reagan proclaimed the gardens a living legacy to the Constitution; in that spirit, a naturalization ceremony for new citizens now takes place here each year. ⊠ *Constitution Ave. between 17th and 23rd Sts. NW, White House area* ⊕ *www.nps.gov/coga* Ⓜ *Foggy Bottom.*

QUICK BITES | At the circular snack bar just west of the Constitution Gardens lake, you can get hot dogs, potato chips, candy bars, soft drinks, and beer at prices lower than those charged by most street vendors.

Fodor'sChoice ★ **Dumbarton Oaks.** One of the loveliest places for a stroll in Washington is Dumbarton Oaks, the acres of enchanting gardens adjoining Dumbarton House in Georgetown. Planned by noted landscape architect Beatrix Farrand, the gardens incorporate elements of traditional English, Italian, and French styles such as a formal rose garden, an English country garden, and an orangery (circa 1810). A full-time crew of a dozen gardeners toils to maintain the stunning collection of terraces, geometric gardens, tree-shaded brick walks, fountains, arbors, and pools. Plenty of well-positioned benches make this a good place for resting weary feet, too. You enter the gardens at 31st and R streets. **Dumbarton House** houses world-renowned collections of Byzantine and pre-Columbian art. ⊠ *1703 32nd St. NW, Georgetown* ☎ *202/339–6401 or 202/339–6400* ⊕ *www.doaks.org* ☒ *Gardens: Apr.–Oct. $8, Nov.–Mar. free* ♢ *Gardens: Apr.–Oct., Tues.–Sun. 2–6; Nov.–Mar., Tues.–Sun. 2–5.*

★ **Hillwood Estate, Museum and Gardens.** Cereal heiress Marjorie Merriweather Post purchased the 25-acre Hillwood Estate in 1955. Post devoted as much attention to her gardens as she did to the 40-room Georgian mansion: you can wander through 13 acres of them, including a Japanese rock and waterfall garden, a manicured formal French garden, a rose garden, Mediterranean fountains, and a greenhouse full of orchids. The "Lunar Lawn," where she threw garden parties that were the most coveted invitation in Washington society, is planted with dogwood, magnolia, cherry, and plum trees, as well as azaleas, camellias, lilacs, tulips, and pansies. The estate is best reached by taxi or car (parking is available on the grounds). It's a 20- to 30-minute walk from the Metro. ⊠ *4155 Linnean Ave. NW, Northwest* ☎ *202/686–5807 or 202/686–8500* ⊕ *www.*

10

hillwoodmuseum.org ⌖ *House and grounds $12* ☉ *Feb.–Dec., Tues.–Sat. 10–5* Ⓜ *Van Ness/UDC.*

Kenilworth Aquatic Gardens. Exotic water lilies, lotuses, hyacinths, and other water-loving plants thrive in this 14-acre sanctuary of quiet ponds and marshy flats. The gardens' wetland animals include turtles, frogs, beavers, spring azure butterflies, and some 40 species of birds. ■TIP→ In July nearly everything blossoms; early morning is the best time to visit, when day-bloomers are just opening and night-bloomers have yet to close. The nearest Metro stop is a 15-minute walk away. ⌖ *Anacostia Ave. and Douglas St. NE, Anacostia* ☎ *202/426–6905* ⊕ *www.nps.gov/keaq* ⌖ *Free* ☉ *Gardens and visitor center, daily 7–4; garden tours daily at 9, 10, and 11* Ⓜ *Deanwood.*

Tudor Place. A little more than a block from Dumbarton Oaks in Georgetown is this little-known gem, the former home of Martha Washington's granddaughter. The house has 5.5 acres of gardens that offer impressive replications of Federal-period gardens and include 19th-century specimen trees and boxwoods from Mount Vernon. Make time for a one-hour tour of the house itself, which features many rare possessions of George and Martha Washington. ⌖ *1644 31st Pl. NW, Georgetown* ☎ *202/965–0400* ⊕ *www.tudorplace.org* ⌖ *$8, garden $3* ☉ *House tours: Tues.–Sat. on the hr 10–3; Sun. on the hr noon–3. Garden: Mon.–Sat. 10–4, Sun. noon–4. Closed Jan.* Ⓜ *Woodley Park or Dupont Circle.*

☺ **United States Botanic Garden.** Established by Congress in 1820, this is the oldest botanic garden in North America. The garden conservatory sits at the foot of Capitol Hill, in the shadow of the Capitol building. It offers an escape from the stone and marble federal office buildings that surround it; inside are exotic rain-forest species, desert flora, and trees from all parts of the world. A special treat is the extensive collection of rare and unusual orchids. Walkways suspended 24 feet above the ground provide a fascinating view of the plants. A relatively new addition is the National Garden, opened in 2006, which emphasizes educational exhibits. The garden features the Rose Garden, Butterfly Garden, Lawn Terrace, First Ladies' Water Garden, and Regional Garden. ⌖ *1st St. and Maryland Ave. SW, Capitol Hill* ☎ *202/225–8333* ⊕ *www.usbg.gov* ⌖ *Free* ☉ *Daily 10–5; National Garden closes at 7* Ⓜ *Federal Center SW.*

Fodor's Choice ★ **United States National Arboretum.** During azalea season (mid-April through May) this 446-acre oasis is a blaze of color. In early summer, clematis, peonies, rhododendrons, and roses bloom. At any time of year the 22 original Corinthian columns from the U.S. Capitol, re-erected here in 1990, are striking. For a soothing, relaxing walk, visit the Cryptomeria Walk and Japanese Stroll Garden, which are part of the Bonsai and

Penjing Museum. On weekends a tram tours the arboretum's curving roadways at 10:30, 11:30, 1, 2, 3, and 4; tickets are $4. The **National Herb Garden** and the **National Bonsai Collection** are also here. ⊠ *3501 New York Ave. NE, Northeast* ☎ *202/245–2726* ⊕ *www.usna. usda.gov* ✉ *Free* ⊗ *Arboretum and herb garden daily 8–5, bonsai collection daily 10–4* Ⓜ *Weekends only, Union Station, then X6 bus (runs every 40 mins); weekdays, Stadium/Armory, then B2 bus to Bladensburg Rd. and R St.*

> **WORD OF MOUTH**
>
> "I guess the question is whether the point is just to see cherry trees, or to see a larger context. The Arboreteum is lovely (but not easy to get to if you don't know D.C.) but the Tidal Basin has the advantage, of well, being the Tidal Basin and on the Mall. The cherry trees are part of a larger experience visually. The Arboreteum will be much less crowded."   —MikeT

PARKS

C&O Canal. This waterway kept Georgetown open to shipping after its harbor had filled with silt. George Washington was one of the first to advance the idea of a canal linking the Potomac with the Ohio River across the Appalachians. Work started on the Chesapeake & Ohio Canal in 1828, and when it opened in 1850 its 74 locks linked Georgetown with Cumberland, Maryland, 184.5 mi to the northwest (still short of its intended destination). Lumber, coal, iron, wheat, and flour moved up and down the canal, but it was never as successful as its planners had hoped it would be. Many of the bridges spanning the canal in Georgetown were too low to allow anything other than fully loaded barges to pass underneath, and competition from the Baltimore & Ohio Railroad eventually spelled an end to profitability. Today the canal is part of the National Park System; walkers follow the towpath once used by mules, while canoeists paddle the canal's calm waters.

You can glide into history aboard a mule-drawn **canal boat ride.** The National Park service provides the hour-long rides from about mid-April through late October; tickets cost $5 and are available across the canal, next to the Foundry Building. The schedule varies by season, with limited rides in spring and fall. In summer the boats run at least twice a day from Wednesday through Sunday. Call the visitor center for the exact schedule on the day of your visit. Canal-boat rides also depart from the Great Falls Tavern visitor center in Maryland. ⇨ *For more information on the Great Falls segment of the park, see Chapter 12, "Side Trips."* ⊠ *Georgetown Canal Visitor Center, 1057 Thomas Jefferson St. NW, Georgetown* ☎ *202/653–5190* ⊕ *www.nps.gov/choh* ⊗ *Apr.–Oct., Wed.–Sun. 9–4:30; Nov.–Mar., weekends 10–4, staffing permitting.*

East Potomac Park. This 328-acre finger of land extends from the Tidal Basin between the Washington Channel to the east and the Potomac River to the west. There are playgrounds, picnic tables, tennis courts, swimming pools, a driving range, two 9-hole golf courses, miniature golf, and an 18-hole golf course. Double-blossoming cherry trees line Ohio Drive and bloom about two weeks after the single-blossoming variety that attracts throngs to the Tidal Basin each spring. ⊠ *Maine Ave. SW heading west, or Ohio Dr. heading south, follow signs carefully; Ohio Dr. closed to traffic on summer weekends and holidays 3* PM–6 AM ☎ *202/619–7222* ⊕ *www. npca.org/parks* Ⓜ *Smithsonian.*

Pershing Park. A quiet, sunken garden honors General John J. "Black Jack" Pershing, the first to hold the title General of the Armies, a rank Congress created in 1919 to recognize his military achievements. Engravings on the stone walls recount pivotal campaigns from World War I, when Pershing commanded the American expeditionary force and conducted other military exploits. Ice-skaters glide on the square pool here in winter. ⊠ *15th St. and Pennsylvania Ave., White House area* Ⓜ *McPherson Sq.*

WORD OF MOUTH

"My suggestions would be to spend time in Rock Creek Park, the canal area in Georgetown, as well as possibly Dumbarton Oaks in Georgetown, and/or Hillwood Estate which is on the edge of Rock Creek Park, both of which have pretty grounds."

—Cicerone

 ☺ **Rock Creek Park.** The 1,800 acres surrounding Rock Creek have provided a cool oasis for D.C. residents ever since Congress set them aside for recreational use in 1890. Bicycle routes and hiking and equestrian trails wind through the groves of dogwoods, beeches, oaks, and cedars, and 30 picnic areas are scattered about. Rangers at the **Nature Center and Planetarium** (⊠ *South of Military Rd., 5200 Glover Rd. NW, Northwest* ☎ *202/426–6829*) introduce visitors to the park and keep track of daily events; guided nature walks leave from the center weekends at 2. The center and planetarium are open Wednesday through Sunday from 9 to 5. The renovated 19th-century **Klingle Mansion** (⊠ *3545 Williamsburg La. NW, Northwest* Ⓜ *Cleveland Park*) is used as the National Park Service's Rock Creek headquarters. Also in distant areas of the park are Fort Reno, Fort Bayard, Fort Stevens, and Fort DeRussy, remnants of the original ring of forts that guarded Washington during the Civil War, and the Rock Creek Park Golf Course, an 18-hole public course. Landscape architect Horace Peaslee created oft-overlooked **Meridian Hill Park** (⊠ *16th and Euclid Sts., Adams Morgan* Ⓜ *U Street/Cardozo*), a noncontiguous section of Rock Creek Park, after a 1917 study of the parks of Europe. As a result, it contains elements of parks in France (a long, straight mall bordered with plants), Italy (terraces and wall fountains), and Switzerland (a lower-level reflecting pool based on one in Zurich). It's also unofficially known as Malcolm X Park in honor of the civil rights leader. Drug activity once made it unwise to visit Meridian Hill alone; it's somewhat safer now, but avoid it after dark.

 ☺ **Tidal Basin.** This placid pond was part of the Potomac until 1882, when portions of the river were filled in to improve navigation and create additional parkland. At the **boathouse** (☎ *202/479–2426* ⊕ *www. tidalbasinpaddleboats.com*) on the northeast bank of the Tidal Basin you can rent paddleboats during the warmer months. Rental cost is $10 per hour for a two-person boat, $18 per hour for a four-person boat. The boathouse is open from mid-March through October from 10 to 6.

10

Two grotesque sculpted heads on the sides of the Inlet Bridge can be seen as you walk along the sidewalk that hugs the basin. The inside walls of the bridge also feature two other interesting sculptures: bronze, human-headed fish that spout water from their mouths. The bridge was refurbished in the 1980s at the same time the chief of the park, Jack Fish, was retiring. Sculptor Constantine Sephralis played a little joke: these fish heads are actually Fish's head.

Once you cross the bridge, continue along the Tidal Basin to the right. This route is especially scenic when the **cherry trees** are in bloom. The first batch of these trees arrived from Japan in 1909. The trees were infected with insects and fungus, however, and the Department of Agriculture ordered them destroyed. A diplomatic crisis was averted when the United States politely asked the Japanese for another batch, and in 1912 First Lady Helen Taft planted the first tree. The second was planted by the wife of the Japanese ambassador, Viscountess Chinda. About 200 of the original trees still grow near the Tidal Basin. (These cherry trees are the single-flowering Akebeno and Yoshino variety. Double-blossom Fugenzo and Kwanzan trees grow in East Potomac Park and flower about two weeks after their more famous cousins.)

The trees are now the centerpiece of Washington's two-week **Cherry Blossom Festival,** held each spring since 1935. The festivities are kicked off by the lighting of a ceremonial Japanese lantern that rests on the north shore of the Tidal Basin, not far from where the first tree was planted. The once-simple celebration has grown over the years to include concerts, martial-arts demonstrations, and a parade. Park-service experts try their best to predict exactly when the buds will pop. The trees are usually in bloom for about 10–12 days in late March or early April. When winter refuses to release its grip, the parade and festival are held anyway, without the presence of blossoms, no matter how inclement the weather. And when the weather complies and the blossoms are at their peak at the time of the festivities, Washington rejoices. ⊠ *Bordered by Independence and Maine Aves., The Mall* Ⓜ *Smithsonian.*

West Potomac Park. Between the Potomac and the Tidal Basin, West Potomac Park is best known for its flowering cherry trees, which bloom for two weeks in late March or early April. During the rest of the year, West Potomac Park is just a nice place to relax, play ball, or admire the views at the Tidal Basin.

PARTICIPATION SPORTS

Washington is well designed for outdoor sports, with numerous places to play, run, and ride. When the weather is good, it seems like all of Washington is out riding a bike, playing softball and volleyball, jogging past monuments, or taking a relaxing stroll. Many of the favorite locations for participation sports are in the shadow of D.C.'s most famous spots, such as Capitol Hill and the White House.

Hop on two wheels to give your feet a break and explore the monuments by bike.

BICYCLING

The numerous trails in the District and its surrounding areas are well maintained and clearly marked.

For scenery, you can't beat the **C&O Canal Towpath** (⊕ *www.nps.gov/ choh*), which starts in Georgetown and runs along the C&O Canal into Maryland. You could pedal to the end of the canal, nearly 200 mi away in Cumberland, Maryland, but most cyclists stop at Great Falls, 13 mi from where the canal starts. The occasionally bumpy towpath, made of gravel and packed earth, passes through wooded areas of the C&O Canal National Historical Park. You can see 19th-century locks from the canal's working days, and if you're particularly lucky, you may catch a glimpse of mules pulling a canal barge. The barges now take passengers, not cargo.

Suited for bicyclists, walkers, rollerbladers, and strollers, the paved **Capital Crescent Trail** (☎ *202/234–4874 Capital Crescent Coalition*) stretches along the old Georgetown Branch, a B&O Railroad line that was completed in 1910 and was in operation until 1985. The 7.5-mi route's first leg runs from Georgetown near Key Bridge to central Bethesda at Bethesda and Woodmont avenues. At Bethesda and Woodmont the trail heads through a well-lighted tunnel near the heart of Bethesda's lively business area and continues into Silver Spring. The 3.5-mi stretch from Bethesda to Silver Spring is gravel. The Georgetown Branch Trail, as this section is officially named, connects with the Rock Creek Trail, which goes to Rockville in the north and Memorial Bridge past the Washington Monument in the south. On weekends when the weather's nice, all sections of the trails are crowded.

Cyclists interested in serious training might try the 3-mi loop around the golf course in **East Potomac Park** (☏ *202/485–9874 National Park Service*) at Hains Point, the southern area of the park (entry is near the Jefferson Memorial). It's a favorite training course for dedicated local racers and would-be triathletes.

Each day bicyclists cruise the **Mall** amid the endless throngs of runners, walkers, and tourists. There's relatively little car traffic, and bikers can take in some of Washington's landmarks, such as the Washington Monument, the Reflecting Pool, the Vietnam Memorial, and some of the city's more interesting architecture, such as the Smithsonian Castle and the Hirshhorn, the "Doughnut on the Mall."

BIKING THE MALL

A pleasant loop route begins at the Lincoln Memorial, going north past the Washington Monument, and turning around at the Tidal Basin. Along the way are small fountains and parks for taking a break and getting a drink of water.

Mount Vernon Trail, across the Potomac in Virginia, has two sections. The northern part, closest to D.C. proper, is 3.5 mi long and begins near the causeway across the river from the Kennedy Center that heads to Theodore Roosevelt Island (⇨ *See Hiking*). It then passes Ronald Reagan National Airport and continues on to Old Town Alexandria. This section has slight slopes and almost no interruptions for traffic, making it a delightful, but challenging, biking route. Even relatively inexperienced bikers enjoy the trail, which provides wonderful views of the Potomac. To access the trail from the District, take the Theodore Roosevelt Bridge or the Rochambeau Memorial Bridge, also known as the 14th Street Bridge. South of the airport, the trail runs down to the Washington Marina. The final mile of the trail's northern section meanders through protected wetlands before ending in the heart of Old Town Alexandria. The trail's 9-mi southern section extends along the Potomac from Alexandria to Mount Vernon.

Rock Creek Park covers an area from the edge of Georgetown to Montgomery County, Maryland. The bike path there is asphalt and has a few challenging hills, but it's mostly flat. You can bike several miles without having to stop for cars (the roadway is closed entirely to cars on weekends). The two separate northern parts of the trail, which begin in Bethesda and Silver Spring, merge around the Washington, D.C., line. Many bikers gather at this point and follow the trail on a path that goes past the Washington Zoo and eventually runs toward the Lincoln Memorial and Kennedy Center. Fifteen miles of dirt trails are also in the park; these are best for hiking.

INFORMATION

Washington Area Bicyclist Association (✉ *1803 Connecticut Ave., 3rd fl., Northwest* ☏ *202/518–0524* ⊕ *www.waba.org*).

RENTALS AND TOURS

Better Bikes Inc. (✉ *1902 16th St. NW at New Hampshire Ave., Adams Morgan* ☏ *202/293–2080* ⊕ *www.betterbikesinc.com*) offers free delivery of rental bikes—mountain, hybrid, kids', and bikes with baby buggies from $38 to $48 per day—to most local hotels. Rentals include helmets, backpacks, locks, and tips on where to bike. Reservations are required.

Big Wheel Bikes, near the C&O Canal Towpath, rents multispeed bikes for $25 per day and $15 for three hours. Tandem bikes, kids' bikes, and bikes with baby carriers are also available. A second location is near the Capital Crescent Trail. There's also an Alexandria branch if you want to ride the Mount Vernon Trail. ⊠ *1034 33rd St. NW, Georgetown* ☎ *202/337–0254* ⊕ *www.bigwheelbikes.com* ⊠ *3119 Lee Hwy., Arlington, VA* ☎ *301/652–0192* ⊠ *2 Prince St., Alexandria, VA* ☎ *703/739–2300.*

Bike and Roll (☎ *202/966–8662* ⊕ *www.bikethesites.com*) is a tour company that offers three-hour, 4- to 8-mi guided tours of Downtown Washington. Formerly known as Bike the Sites, the company offers tours that range in cost from $32 to $45, and bike rental is included. Advance reservations are required. Tours start from the Mall.

The Boathouse at Fletcher's Cove (⊠ *4940 Canal Rd., at Reservoir Rd., Foxhall* ☎ *202/244–0461* ⊕ *www.fletcherscove.com*), next to the C&O Towpath and Capital Crescent Trail, rents fixed-gear bikes for $6 per hour and $25 per day.

Thompson's Boat Center (⊠ *2900 Virginia Ave. NW, Foggy Bottom* ☎ *202/333–4861 or 202/333-9543* Ⓜ *Foggy Bottom/GWU*) allows easy access to the Rock Creek Trail and the C&O Towpath and is close to the monuments. Adult single-speed bikes are $4 per hour and $15 per day. Multispeed cruiser bikes are $8 per hour and $25 per day. Rentals are on a first-come, first-served basis.

BOATING AND SAILING

Canoeing, sailing, and powerboating are popular in the Washington, D.C., area. Several places rent boats along the **Potomac River** north and south of the city. You can dip your paddle just about anywhere along the river—go canoeing in the C&O Canal, sailing in the widening river south of Alexandria, or even kayaking in the raging rapids at Great Falls, a 30-minute drive from the capital.

RENTALS

Belle Haven Marina (⊠ *George Washington Pkwy., Alexandria, VA* ☎ *703/768–0018* ⊕ *www.saildc.com*), south of Reagan National Airport and Old Town Alexandria, rents two types of sailboats: Sunfish are $30 for two hours during the week and $35 for two hours on the weekend; Flying Scots are $46 for two hours during the week and $54 for two hours during the weekend. Canoes, jon boats, and kayaks are available for rent at $20 for two hours. Rentals are available from April to October.

The Boathouse at Fletcher's Cove (⊠ *4940 Canal Rd., at Reservoir Rd., Foxhall* ☎ *202/244–0461* ⊕ *www.fletcherscove.com*), just north of Georgetown, rents 17-foot rowboats for $11 per hour and $20 per day. Canoes are available for rent at $11 per hour and $22 per day. Single kayaks are $8 per hour and $24 per day, while double kayaks are $15 per hour and $35 per day.

10

Thompson's Boat Center (✉ *2900 Virginia Ave. NW, Foggy Bottom* ☎ *202/333–4861or 202/333-9543* ⊕ *www.thompsonboatcenter.com* Ⓜ *Foggy Bottom/GWU 1*) is near Georgetown and Theodore Roosevelt Island. The center rents canoes for $8 per hour and $22 per day. Single kayaks are $8 per hour and $24 per day, and double kayaks are $10 per hour and $30 per day. Rowing sculls are also available, but you must demonstrate prior experience and a suitably high skill level.

Tidal Basin (✉ *Bordered by Independence Ave. and Maine Ave., The Mall* ☎ *202/479–2426* ⊕ *www.tidalbasinpeddleboats.com* Ⓜ *Farragut W*), in front of the Jefferson Memorial, rents paddleboats beginning in mid-March and usually ending in October. The entrance is at 1501 Maine Avenue SW, on the east side of the Tidal Basin. You can rent two-passenger boats at $10 per hour and four-passenger boats at $18 per hour.

HIKING

Hikes and nature walks are listed in the Friday "Weekend" section of the *Washington Post*. Several area organizations sponsor outings, and most are guided. The **Potomac-Appalachian Trail Club** (✉ *118 Park St. SE, Vienna, VA* ☎ *703/242–0965* ⊕ *potomacappalachian.org*) sponsors hikes—usually free—on trails from Pennsylvania to Virginia, including the C&O Canal and the Appalachian Trail. The **Sierra Club** (☎ *202/547–2326* ⊕ *www.sierrapotomac.org*) has many regional outings; call for details. The **Billy Goat Trail** (✉ *MacArthur Blvd., Potomac, MD* ☎ *301/413–0720* ⊕ *www.nps.gov/choh*) has some outstanding views of the wilder parts of the Potomac. This challenging 2-mi trail, which starts and ends at the C&O Canal Towpath below Great Falls, has some steep downhills and climbs.

Fodor's Choice ★ **Theodore Roosevelt Island** (✉ *Turkey Run Park, George Washington Memorial Pkwy., McLean, VA* ☎ *703/289-2552 or 703/289-2550* ⊕ *www.nps.gov/this*), designed as a memorial to the environmentally minded president, is a wildlife sanctuary off the George Washington Parkway on the Virginia side of the city—close to Foggy Bottom, Georgetown, East Potomac Park, and the area near the Kennedy Center. The island can be reached by car by taking the Theodore Roosevelt Bridge or I–66. Hikers and bicyclists can easily reach it by taking the 14th Street Bridge. Many birds and other animals live in the island's marsh and forests.

A self-guided nature trail winds through **Woodend** (✉ *8940 Jones Mill Rd., Chevy Chase, MD* ☎ *301/652–9188, 301/652–1088 for recent bird sightings* ⊕ *www.audubonnaturalist.org*), a verdant 40-acre estate, and around the suburban Maryland headquarters of the local **Audubon Naturalist Society**. The estate was designed in the 1920s by Jefferson Memorial architect John Russell Pope, and has a mansion, also called Woodend, on its grounds. You're never far from the trill of birdsong here, as the Audubon Society has turned the place into something of a private nature preserve, forbidding the use of toxic chemicals and leaving some areas in a wild, natural state. Programs include wildlife identification walks, environmental education programs, and a weekly

Saturday bird walk September through June. A bookstore stocks titles on conservation, ecology, and birds. The grounds are open daily sunrise to sunset, and admission is free.

A 1,460-acre refuge in Alexandria, **Huntley Meadows Park** (⊠ *3701 Lockheed Blvd., Alexandria, VA* ☏ *703/768–2525* ⊕ *www.fairfaxcounty. gov/parks/huntley*) is made for birders. You can spot more than 200 species—from ospreys to owls, egrets, and ibis. Much of the park is wetlands, a favorite of aquatic species. A boardwalk circles through a marsh, enabling you to spot beaver lodges, and 4 mi of trails wend through the park, making it likely you'll see deer, muskrats, and river otters as well. The park is usually open daily dawn to dusk.

ICE-SKATING

Area rinks typically charge from $6.50 to $7 for a two-hour session. Skate rentals, available at all the rinks listed, are usually around $2.50 to $3. Some rinks charge a small fee for renting a locker.

The **National Gallery of Art Ice Rink** (⊠ *Constitution Ave. NW, between 7th and 9th Sts., Downtown* ☏ *202/289–3361* Ⓜ *Archives/Navy Memorial*) is surrounded by the gallery's Sculpture Garden. The art deco design of the rink makes it one of the most popular outdoor winter sites in Washington. In spring the rink becomes a fountain.

Fodor'sChoice
★ The prime location of the **Pershing Park Ice Rink** (⊠ *Pennsylvania Ave. and 14th St. NW, Downtown* ☏ *202/737–6938* ⊕ *www.pershingparkicerink. com* Ⓜ *Metro Center*), a few blocks from the White House, major hotels, and a Metro station, makes this rink one of the most convenient spots in Washington for outdoor skating.

RUNNING

Running is one of the best ways to see the city, and several scenic trails wend through Downtown Washington and nearby northern Virginia. It can be dangerous to run at night on the trails, although the streets are fairly well lighted. Even in daylight, it's best to run in pairs when venturing beyond public areas or heavily used sections of trails.

The 89-mi-long **C&O Canal Towpath** (⊕ *www.nps.gov/choh*) in the C&O National Historical Park is a favorite of runners and cyclists. The path is mostly gravel and dirt, making it easy on knees and feet. The most popular loop, which goes from a point just north of the Key Bridge in Georgetown to the Boat House at Fletcher's Cove, is about 4 mi round-trip.

Fodor'sChoice
★ The most popular running route in Washington is the 4.5-mi loop on the **Mall** around the Capitol and past the Smithsonian museums, the Washington Monument, the Reflecting Pool, and the Lincoln Memorial. At any time of day hundreds of runners, speed walkers, bicyclists, and tourists make their way along the gravel pathways. For a longer run, veer south of the Mall on either side of the Tidal Basin and head for the Jefferson Memorial and East Potomac Park, the site of many races.

10

Across the Potomac in Virginia is the **Mount Vernon Trail**. The 3.5-mi northern section begins near the pedestrian causeway leading to Theodore Roosevelt Island (directly across the river from the Kennedy Center) and goes past Ronald Reagan National Airport and on to Old Town Alexandria. You can get to the trail from the District by crossing either the Theodore Roosevelt Bridge at the Lincoln Memorial or the Rochambeau Memorial Bridge at the Jefferson Memorial. South of the airport, the trail runs down to the Washington Marina. The 9-mi southern section leads to Mount Vernon.

Rock Creek Park has 15 mi of trails, a bicycle path, a bridle path, picnic groves, playgrounds, and the boulder-strewn rolling stream that gives it its name. The creek isn't safe or pleasant for swimming. Starting one block south of the corner of P and 22nd streets on the edge of Georgetown, Rock Creek Park runs all the way to Montgomery County, Maryland. The most popular run in the park is a trail along the creek from Georgetown to the National Zoo: about a 4-mi loop. In summer there's considerable shade, and there are water fountains and an exercise station along the way. The roadway is closed to traffic on weekends.

INFORMATION AND ORGANIZATIONS

Group runs and weekend races around Washington are listed in the Friday "Weekend" section of the *Washington Post*. You can also check the Thursday calendar of events in the *Washington Times*. Comprehensive listings of running and walking events are posted online by the *Washington Running Report* (⊕ *www.runwashington.com*) and *racePacket* (⊕ *www.racepacket.com*).

Tuesday and Thursday evenings at 6:30 PM you can join the **Capitol Hill Runners** (☎ *301/283–0821*) on a 6- to 8-mi run, which begins at the Reflecting Pool at the base of the Capitol's west side. Most Sunday mornings the **Fleet Feet Sports Shop** (✉ *1841 Columbia Rd. NW, Adams Morgan* ☎ *202/387–3888* Ⓜ *Woodley Park/Zoo*) sponsors informal runs through Rock Creek Park and other areas. The shop's owner and father of the city's mayor Phil Fenty leads the runs. The courses change at Phil's discretion and usually go from 5 to 7 mi. Call the **Road Runners Club of America Hotline** (☎ *703/525–3890*) for general information about running and racing in the area.

SPECTATOR SPORTS

BASEBALL

Major League Baseball has returned to D.C., where the **Washington Nationals** (✉ *1500 S. Capitol St. SE* ☎ *202/675–6287* ⊕ *washingtonnationals.mlb.com* Ⓜ *Navy Yard*) of the National League play in their new spectacular home, Nationals Park. Tickets range from $5 to $325. The $5 tickets are only available on game day at the park box office. Individual game tickets may be purchased at the park or through the team's Web site. ■TIP➔ The Metro is a hassle-free and inexpensive way to get to the ballpark. The closest and most convenient stop is the Navy Yard on the Green Line. Parking is very scarce.

BASKETBALL

There are several top-flight college basketball teams here. Of the Division I men's college basketball teams in the area, the most prominent are the **Georgetown University Hoyas** (⊕ *guhoyas.collegesports.com*), former NCAA national champions. The Hoyas became a national basketball powerhouse under their coach John Thompson III. Most home games are played at the **Verizon Center** (✉ *601 F St. NW, between 6th and 7th Sts., Downtown* ☎ *202/628–3200, 202/432–7328 box office* ⊕ *www.verizoncenter.com* Ⓜ *Gallery Pl./Chinatown*).

The WNBA's **Washington Mystics** (✉ *6th and F Sts., Downtown* ☎ *202/432–7328* ⊕ *www.wnba.com/mystics* Ⓜ *Gallery Pl./Chinatown*) play at the Verizon Center in Downtown Washington. The Mystics perennially lead the WNBA in attendance, despite a losing record. The games are loud, boisterous events. Ticket prices range from $17 to $70, with courtside tickets for $125. You can buy tickets at the Verizon Center box office or through Ticketmaster. The women's basketball season runs from late May to August.

The NBA's **Washington Wizards** (✉ *6th and F Sts., Downtown* ☎ *202/432–7328* ⊕ *www.nba.com/wizards* Ⓜ *Gallery Pl./Chinatown*) play from October to April at the Verizon Center and feature superstar Gilbert Arenas. Tickets for individual games cost $40 to $850. The team also offers $10 seats in the upper level and courtside seats for a whopping $2,500. Buy tickets from the Verizon Center box office or from Ticketmaster.

FOOTBALL

The **Washington Redskins** (☎ *301/276–6000 FedEx Field stadium* ⊕ *www.redskins.com*) has become one of the top 3 most valuable franchises in the NFL based on its 1983, '88, and '92 Super Bowl wins. As a result, diehard fans snap up season tickets year after year. Even though FedEx Field is the largest football stadium in the NFL with 91,000 seats, individual game day tickets can be hard to come by if the team is enjoying a strong season. Your best bet is to check out StubHub (⊕ *www.stubhub*), the official ticket marketplace of the Redskins. Tickets can range anywhere from $75 to $1,200, depending on the match up. ■ TIP➡ **Game tickets can be difficult to get, but fans can see the players up close and for free at training camp, held in August.** The Redskins invite the public to attend their training camp in Ashburn, in nearby Loudoun County, Virginia. Camp begins in late July and continues through mid-August. The practices typically last from 90 minutes to two hours. Fans can bring their own chairs, and the players are usually available after practice to sign autographs. Call ahead to make sure the practices are open that day. A practice schedule is on the team's Web site.

HOCKEY

★ One of pro hockey's top teams, the **Washington Capitals** (✉ *6th and F Sts., Downtown* ☎ *202/432–7328* ⊕ *www.washingtoncaps.com* Ⓜ *Gallery Pl./Chinatown*) play home games October through April at the Verizon

Center and feature one of hockey's superstars, Alex Ovechkin. Seats on the main level range from $75 to $300, and those in the upper deck range from $35 to $60. Tickets can be purchased at the Verizon Center box office or from Ticketmaster.

SOCCER

Fodor's Choice
★

D.C. United (✉ *Robert F. Kennedy Stadium, 2400 E. Capitol St. SE, Capitol Hill* ☎ *202/547–3134* ⊕ *www.dcunited.com* Ⓜ *Stadium*) is one of the best Major League soccer (U.S. pro soccer) teams. International matches, including some World Cup preliminaries, are often played on RFK Stadium's grass field, dedicated exclusively to soccer play. Games are April through September. You can buy tickets, which generally cost $25–$65, with discounts for groups, at the RFK Stadium ticket office, or through the team's Web site, which offers special youth pricing.

Shopping

WORD OF MOUTH

"If you do have a day to just "wander," Georgetown is the place. There are lots of chain stores on M Street but if you walk up Wisconsin Ave. on little side streets, you will find antiques and boutique shops unique to D.C."

—309pbg

SHOPPING PLANNER

Beat the Heat

D.C.'s summertime humidity can take the starch out of any shopper. When it's sticky out, head to Georgetown, where stores are tightly packed and waterfront breezes drift up the side streets, and Dupont Circle, where you can duck inside for an iced coffee or ice cream between gallery stops.

Gallery Hopping

Washington has three main gallery districts—Downtown, Dupont Circle, and Georgetown—though small galleries can be found all over in converted houses and storefronts. Whatever their location, many keep unusual hours and close entirely on Sunday and Monday. The *Washington Post* "Weekend" section and *Washington CityPaper* (published on Thursday) are excellent sources of information on current exhibits and hours.

Hours

Store hours vary greatly. In general, Georgetown stores are open late and on Sunday; stores Downtown that cater to office workers close at 6 PM and may not open at all on weekends. Some stores extend their hours on Thursday.

Getting Around

Georgetown is a neighborhood the Metro doesn't reach, so you can walk, drive (though parking is a challenge), take a taxi, or hop on the D.C. Circulator bus (the Georgetown-Union Station loop traverses the shopping strips on M Street and Wisconsin Avenue). Some locations in Friendship Heights on Connecticut Avenue are most easily reached by car.

Historic Walks

Shopping is the perfect way to acquaint yourself with some of D.C.'s historic neighborhoods. A quick diversion down a side street in Georgetown reveals the neighborhood's historic charm and current glamour. Peer around a corner in Dupont or Capitol Hill to see a true D.C. architecture classic—the row house. Wandering Downtown you are sure to bump into one of the nation's great neoclassical structures, whether it is the White House or the historic Hotel Monaco.

How to Save Money

If you're willing to dig a bit, D.C. can be a savvy shopper's dream. Upscale consignment stores like Secondi in Dupont Circle and discount outlets like Loehmann's in Friendship Heights provide an alternative to the surrounding luxury retail. Secondhand bookstores in Dupont and Georgetown provide hours of browsing and buying at welcoming prices.

Where to Find Unique Gifts

Museum shops are the best places to find unusual items, like the astronaut food on sale at the Air and Space Museum. Downtown galleries sell distinctive modern design gifts. Eastern Market and the surrounding Capitol Hill neighborhood offer local wares, including jewelry, political books, and even hot sauce.

**FRIENDSHIP HEIGHTS/
WISCONSIN AVENUE**
luxury & discount
retailers in a
suburban strip

**ADAMS
MORGAN**
eclectic bohemian
rummaging

**U STREET
CORRIDOR**
small vintage, urban
boutiques & chic home
design stores

GEORGETOWN
retail chains,
antiques & galleries,
endless hours of
cruising

DUPONT CIRCLE
books, coffee,
galleries, perfect
on the weekends

DOWNTOWN
modern home
furnishings &
specialty items

**EASTERN
MARKET**
local weekend market
& neighborhood
stores for unique
gifts

Columbia Rd.

Florida Ave.

16th St.

Florida Ave.

New Hampshire Ave.

Vermont Ave.

Sheridan
Circle

Massachusetts Ave.

Dupont
Circle

Logan
Circle

Rhode Island Ave.

Rock Creek

Connecticut Ave.

Scott
Circle

M St.

Thomas
Circle

M St.

Whitehurst Fwy.

Washington
Circle

K St.

New York Ave.

Pennsylvania Ave.

23rd St.

**FOGGY
BOTTOM**

15th St.

14th St.

Theodore
Roosevelt
Island

Virginia Ave.

Constitution Ave.

THE MALL

Independence Ave.

Reflecting Pool

**THE
MONUMENTS**

Arlington Memorial
Br.

Columbia
Island

Tidal Basin

Francis Case

Memorial Br.

Washington
Canal

Potomac River

⚓

0   500 yards

0   500 meters

VIRGINIA

Updated by Kathryn McKay and Cathy Sharpe

African masks that could have inspired Picasso; kitchenware as objets d'art; bargains on Christian Dior, Hugo Boss, and Burberry; paisley scarves from India; American and European antiques; books of every description; handicrafts from almost two dozen Native American tribes; music boxes by the thousands; busts of U.S. presidents; textiles by the armful; fine leather goods—all this and more can be found in the nation's capital.

Many of the smaller one-of-a-kind shops have survived urban renewal, the number of designer boutiques is on the rise, and interesting specialty shops and new shopping areas are springing up all over town. Weekdays, Downtown street vendors offer a funky mix of jewelry; brightly patterned ties; buyer-beware watches; sunglasses; and African-inspired clothing, accessories, and art. Discriminating shoppers will find satisfaction at upscale malls on the city's outskirts. Of course, T-shirts and Capitol City souvenirs are always in plentiful supply, especially on the streets ringing the Mall.

ADAMS MORGAN

Scattered among the dozens of Latin, Ethiopian, and international restaurants in this most bohemian of Washington neighborhoods are a score of eccentric shops. If quality is what you seek, Adams Morgan and nearby Woodley Park can be a minefield; tread cautiously. Still, for the bargain hunter it's great fun. ■ TIP➔ **If bound for a specific shop, you may wish to call ahead to verify hours.** Adams Morganites are often not clock-watchers, although you can be sure an afternoon stroll on the weekend will yield a few hours of great browsing. The evening hours bring scores of revelers to the row, so plan to go before dark unless you want to couple your shopping with a party pit stop.

How to get there is another question. Though the Woodley Park/Zoo/ Adams Morgan Metro stop is technically closer to the 18th Street strip (where the interesting shops are), getting off here means that you will have to walk over the bridge on Calvert Street. Five minutes longer, the walk from the Dupont Circle Metro stop is more scenic; you cruise north on 18th Street through tree-lined streets of row houses and embassies. You can also easily catch Metrobus 42 or a cab from Dupont to Adams Morgan. ⊠ *18th St. NW between Florida Ave. and Columbia Ave., Adams Morgan* Ⓜ *Woodley Park/Zoo/Adams Morgan or Dupont Circle.*

QUICK BITES

Tryst Coffeehouse. Relax with a latte on one of the couches or cushiony chairs at this neighborhood hangout. They have a surprisingly large menu that includes sandwiches, bagels, pastries, and alcoholic drinks in addition to their coffee selections. Free Wi-Fi is an added bonus. ⊠ *2459 18th St. NW, Adams Morgan* ☎ *202/232–5500* ⊕ *www.trystdc.com.* Ⓜ *Dupont Circle.*

SPECIALTY STORES

BOOKS **Idle Time Books.** This multilevel used-book store sells "rare to medium rare" books with plenty of meaty titles in all genres, especially out-of-print literature. ⊠ *2467 18th St. NW, Adams Morgan* ☎ *202/232–4774* ⊕ *www.idletimebooks.com* Ⓜ *Woodley Park/Zoo.*

CHOCOLATE **biagio.** For chocoholics, this is one-stop shopping. The shop will feed your passions, with offerings both foreign (Valrhona from France) and domestic (MarieBelle from New York and Vosges Haut Chocolat from Chicago). Selections from D.C.-area chocolatiers make for tasty souvenirs. ⊠ *1904 18th St. NW, Adams Morgan* ☎ *202/328–1506* ⊕ *www.biagiochocolate.com* ⊗ *Closed Mon.* Ⓜ *Dupont Circle.*

CRAFTS AND GIFTS **Toro Mata.** Stunning black-and-white pottery from the Peruvian town of Chulucana is a specialty of this gallery; they directly represent six different artisans living and working there. The walls of the gallery are lined with elegant handcrafted wood mirrors, colorful original paintings, alpaca apparel, and other imported Andean crafts. ⊠ *2410 18th St. NW, Adams Morgan* ☎ *202/232–3890* ⊕ *www.toromata.com* ⊗ *Closed Mon.* Ⓜ *Woodley Park/Zoo.*

HOME FURNISHINGS **Skynear and Company.** The owners of this extravagant shop travel the world to find the unusual, and their journeys have netted rich textiles, furniture, and home accessories. A staff of interior designers is on hand to help you identify and sort through the collection of treasures. ⊠ *2122 18th St. NW, Adams Morgan* ☎ *202/797–7160* ⊕ *www.skynearonline.com* Ⓜ *Woodley Park/Zoo.*

MEN'S AND WOMEN'S CLOTHING **Kobos.** All the traditional and contemporary ethnic clothing and accessories at this neighborhood staple were imported from West Africa. ⊠ *2444 18th St. NW, Adams Morgan* ☎ *202/332–9580* ⊕ *www.kobosclothiers.com* Ⓜ *Woodley Park/Zoo.*

Meeps Fashionette. Catering to fans of shabby-chic and campy glamour, this shop at the bottom of the Adams Morgan strip stocks a wide selection of vintage clothes and costumes for women and men from the '40s through the '80s. There's also an expanding selection of new, original designs by local talent. ⊠ *2104 18th St. NW, Adams Morgan* ☎ *202/265–6546* ⊕ *www.meepsDC.com* Ⓜ *Dupont Circle.*

FIVE GREAT SHOPPING EXPERIENCES

Après Peau, Downtown: "Monu-mint" chocolate bar, anyone? Washington-themed products sit alongside luscious lotions and creams at this marvelously minimalist shop.

Kramerbooks & Afterwords, Dupont Circle: Meeting up at Kramerbooks for a lazy Sunday afternoon of brunch and shopping is a quintessential D.C. experience.

Eastern Market: Artists, musicians, farmers, and more make this beautifully restored market a feast for the senses. Most vendors accept only cash, but ATMs are nearby.

Urban Chic, Georgetown: Searching for somewhere to begin in chockablock Georgetown? Look no further.

Nana, U Street: Fashion is fun again at Nana, where the designers are up-and-coming and the knowledgeable staff is refreshingly attitude-free.

Shake Your Booty. Trend-conscious Washingtoniennes come here for funky and affordable clothing, belts, jewelry, and bags. ⊠ *2206 18th St. NW, Adams Morgan* ☎ *202/518–8205* Ⓜ *Woodley Park/Zoo.*

SHOES **Fleet Feet Sports Shop.** The expert staff at this friendly shop will assess your feet and your training schedule before recommending the perfect pair of new running shoes. Shoes, apparel, and accessories for running, swimming, soccer, and cycling crowd the small space, where you might just bump into Mayor Adrian Fenty (his brother and sister-in-law own the shop). ⊠ *1841 Columbia Rd. NW, Adams Morgan* ☎ *202/387–3888* ⊕ *www.fleetfeetdc.com* Ⓜ *Woodley Park/Zoo.*

CAPITOL HILL–EASTERN MARKET

As the Capitol Hill area has become gentrified, unique shops and boutiques have sprung up, many clustered around the redbrick Eastern Market. Inside are produce and meat counters, plus the Market Five art gallery. ■TIP➜ The flea market, held on weekends outdoors, presents nostalgia and local crafts by the crateful. There's also a farmers' market on Saturday. Along 7th Street you can find a number of small shops selling such specialties as art books, handwoven rugs, and antiques. Cross Pennsylvania Avenue and head south on 8th Street for historic Barracks Row. Shops, bars, and restaurants inhabit the charming row houses leading toward the Anacostia River. The other shopping lure on the Hill is Union Station, D.C.'s gorgeous train station. Beautifully restored, it now houses both mall shops and Amtrak and commuter trains.

Keep in mind that Union Station and Eastern Market are on opposite sides of the Hill. The Eastern Market Metro stop is the midpoint between the Eastern Market strip and Barracks Row; Union Station is several blocks away. You can certainly walk to Union Station from the Eastern Market stop, but it might be taxing after the time already spent on your feet in the shops. ⊠ *7th and C Sts. SE, Capitol Hill* Ⓜ *Eastern Market or Union Station.*

11

The Market Lunch. Locals line up for pancakes, especially the blueberry buckwheat, and fried fish at this greasy grill next to the fish counter in Eastern Market's food bazaar. Try their specialty, crab-cake sandwiches, on Sunday. ⊠ *North corner of Eastern Market, 225 7th St. SE, Capitol Hill* ☎ *202/547–8444* ⊘ *Closed Mon.* Ⓜ *Eastern Market.*

A MARKET AND A MALL

Eastern Market. Vibrantly colored produce and flowers; freshly caught fish; fragrant cheeses; and tempting sweets are sold by independent vendors at Eastern Market, which first opened its doors in 1873. On weekends a flea market and an arts-and-crafts market add to the fun. The redbrick building was gutted by fire in April 2007. A $22 million reconstruction has not only made the market more structurally sound, but has restored it to its original Victorian grandeur. Now it is a vibrant and lively gathering place complete with entertainment, art showings, and a pottery studio. ⊠ *7th St. and North Carolina Ave. SE, Capitol Hill* ⊕ *www.easternmarketdc.com* ⊘ *Closed Mon.* Ⓜ *Eastern Market.*

Union Station. Resplendent with marble floors and vaulted ceilings, Union Station is a shopping mall as well as a train station. Upscale retailers include such familiar chains as L'Occitane, White House/Black Market, and Godiva, as well as a bookstore, a movie theater, fine restaurants, and a food court. The east hall is filled with vendors of expensive domestic and international wares who sell from open stalls. Making History sells a more eclectic selection of souvenirs than you'll find in most gift shops. ■TIP➔ There's a tiny outpost of Vacarro's Italian Pastry Shop in the food court. The cannoli and biscotti are to die for. The Christmas season brings lights, a train display, and seasonal gift shops to Union Station. ⊠ *50 Massachusetts Ave. NE, Capitol Hill* ☎ *202/289–1908* ⊕ *www.unionstationdc.com* Ⓜ *Union Station.*

SPECIALTY STORES

BOOKS **Capitol Hill Books.** Pop into this three-story maze of used books to browse through a wonderful collection of out-of-print history books, political and fiction writings, and modern first editions. ⊠ *657 C St. SE, Capitol Hill* ☎ *202/544–1621* ⊕ *www.capitolhillbooks-dc.com* Ⓜ *Eastern Market.*

☺ **Fairy Godmother.** This specialty store, which opened in 1984, features books for children, from infants through teens, in English, Spanish, and French. It also sells puppets, toys, craft sets, and CDs. ⊠ *319 7th St. SE, Capitol Hill* ☎ *202/547–5474* Ⓜ *Eastern Market.*

CHILDREN'S
CLOTHING **Dawn Price Baby.** The infant and toddler clothing at this friendly row-house boutique has been carefully selected with an eye for super-comfortable

☺ fabrics and distinct designs. The shop also stocks toys, gifts, cribs, bedding, and bibs for baby Democrats and Republicans. There's a second location in Georgetown. ⊠ *325 7th St. SE, Capitol Hill* ☎ *202/543–2920* ⊕ *www.dawnpricebaby.com* ⊘ *Closed Mon.* Ⓜ *Eastern Market.*

CRAFTS
AND GIFTS **Homebody.** Original artwork, contemporary rugs, delicious-smelling candles, modern kitchen items, and an eclectic mix of jewelry, bags,
Fodor's Choice and wallets crowd this sophisticated and irreverent boutique. ⊠ *715*
★ *8th St. SE, Capitol Hill* ☎ *202/544–8445* ⊕ *www.homebodydc.com* ⊘ *Closed Mon.* Ⓜ *Eastern Market.*

The Village Gallery. This collection of artsy gifts and women's clothing is found in a welcoming house and garden. The upstairs gallery showcases a permanent exhibit of work by D.C. painter Alan Braley, along with a changing roster of local, American, and international artists. ✉ *705 North Carolina Ave. SE, Capitol Hill* ☎ *202/546–3040* ⊕ *www.thevillageoncapitolhill.com* ⊗ *Closed Mon. and Tues.* Ⓜ *Eastern Market.*

SPLENDID SHOE STORES
■ Church's, Downtown
■ Fleet Feet, Adams Morgan
■ Sassanova, Georgetown

Woven History/Silk Road. Landmarks in this bohemian neighborhood, these connected stores sell handmade treasures from small villages around the world. Silk Road sells home furnishings, gifts, clothing, rugs, and accessories made in Asian mountain communities. Woven History's rugs are made the old-fashioned way, with vegetable dyes and hand-spun wool. ✉ *311–315 7th St. SE, Capitol Hill* ☎ *202/543–1705* ⊕ *www.wovenhistory.com* ⊗ *Closed Mon.* Ⓜ *Eastern Market.*

WOMEN'S CLOTHING **Forecast.** If you like classic, contemporary styles, Forecast should be in your future. It sells silk and wool-blend sweaters in solid, muted tones for women seeking elegant but practical clothing from brands like Yansi Fugel. The housewares and gifts selection on the first floor is colorful and of high quality. ✉ *218 7th St. SE, Capitol Hill* ☎ *202/547–7337* ⊗ *Closed Mon.* Ⓜ *Eastern Market.*

DOWNTOWN

Downtown D.C. is spread out and sprinkled with federal buildings and museums. Shopping options run the gamut, from the Gallery Place shopping center to small art galleries and bookstores. Gallery Place houses familiar chain stores like Urban Outfitters, Bed, Bath & Beyond, Ann Taylor Loft, and Aveda; it also has a movie theater and a bowling alley. Other big names in the Downtown area include Macy's and chain stores like H&M and Banana Republic. With its many offices, Downtown tends to shut down at 5 PM sharp, with the exception of the department stores and larger chain stores. A jolly happy-hour crowd springs up after working hours and families and fans fill the streets during weekend sporting events. The revitalized Penn Quarter has some of the best restaurants in town peppered among its galleries and specialty stores.

The worthwhile shops are not concentrated in one area, however. The Gallery Place Metro stop provides the most central starting point—you can walk south to the galleries and design shops, or west toward Metro Center and Farragut North, though this trek is only for the ambitious. Although Gallery Place is a nightlife hot spot, Metro Center and the Farragut area are largely silent after working hours. ✉ *North of Pennsylvania Ave. between 7th and 18th Sts., up to Connecticut Ave. below L St., Downtown* Ⓜ *Archives/Navy Memorial, Farragut N and W, Gallery Pl., McPherson Sq., or Metro Center.*

11

CLOSE UP

D.C.'s Museum Shops

Would someone in your life love a replica of the Hope diamond? It's waiting for you at the gift shop in the National Museum of Natural History. With a wide range of merchandise and price points, from inexpensive postcards to pricey pottery, museum gift shops allow you the flexibility to bring home a small memento of your visit to the nation's capital or to invest in a piece of American art or history. Museum gift shops offer everything from period jewelry reproductions to science kits for kids, not to mention prints and postcards of the masterpiece paintings in the permanent collections. If you don't want to carry around multiple shopping bags, rest assured that most of the items in museum shops can be purchased off the museum's Web site once you return home. Prices are no higher than you'd find in comparable stores. Another bonus: you won't pay tax on anything purchased in a public museum.

SPECIALTY STORES

CRAFTS AND GIFTS

Après Peau. Exclusive Washington-themed note cards, coasters, and chocolates sell alongside jewelry, perfume, and lotions in this bright and airy gift shop owned by local dermatologist Tina Alster. ✉ *1430 K St. NW, Downtown* ☎ *202/783–0022* ⊕ *www.aprespeau.com* ☾ *Closed weekends* Ⓜ *Farragut N.*

Fahrney's. What began in 1929 as a repair shop and a pen bar—a place to fill your fountain pen before setting out for work—is now a wonderland for anyone who loves a good writing instrument. You'll find pens in silver, gold, and lacquer by the world's leading manufacturers. ✉ *1317 F St. NW, Downtown* ☎ *202/628–9525* ⊕ *www.fahrneyspens.com* ☾ *Closed Sun.* Ⓜ *Metro Center.*

Indian Craft Shop. Jewelry, pottery, sand paintings, weavings, and baskets from more than 45 Native American tribes, including Navajo, Pueblo, Zuni, Cherokee, Lakota, and Seminole, are at your fingertips here—as long as you have a photo ID to enter the federal building. Items range from inexpensive jewelry (as little as $5) on up to collector-quality art pieces (more than $1,000). ✉ *U.S. Department of the Interior, 1849 C St. NW, Room 1023, Downtown* ☎ *202/208–4056* ⊕ *www.indiancraftshop.com* ☾ *Closed weekends, except 3rd Sat. of each month* Ⓜ *Farragut W or Farragut N.*

Music Box Center. Listen to a total of 500 melodies on more than 1,500 music boxes at this exquisite—and unusual—store. One irresistible item: the Harry Potter music box that plays "That's What Friends Are For." ✉ *1920 I St. NW, Downtown* ☎ *202/783–9399* ☾ *Closed Sun.* Ⓜ *Farragut W.*

FOOD AND WINE

Fodor'sChoice ★

Cowgirl Creamery. A California original, this self-titled "cheese shop" has an educated staff that can help you find the perfect block (through many taste tests) as well as a matching wine or olive spread. Their artisan cheeses hail from the Bay area, from local cheese makers, and from points beyond. ✉ *919 F St. NW, Downtown* ☎ *202/393–6880* ⊕ *www.cowgirlcreamery.com* ☾ *Closed Sun.* Ⓜ *Gallery Pl.*

SPAS AND BEAUTY SALONS

Andre Chreky. Housed in an elegantly renovated Victorian town house, this salon offers complete services—hair, nails, facials, waxing, massage, and makeup. And because it's a favorite of the Washington elite, you might just overhear a tidbit or two on who's going to what black-tie function with whom. Adjacent whirlpool pedicure chairs allow two friends to get pampered simultaneously. ⊠ *1604 K St. NW, Downtown* ☎ *202/293–9393* ⊕ *www.andrechreky.com* Ⓜ *Farragut N.*

The Grooming Lounge. Most spas are geared to women, but guys are pampered here. You can find old-fashioned hot-lather shaves, haircuts, and business manicures and pedicures—everything a man needs to look terrific. The hair- and skin-care products—from Clarins, American Crew, and Acqua di Parma, to name just a few—are worth a visit even if you don't have time for a service. ⊠ *1745 L St. NW, Downtown* ☎ *202/466–8900* ⊕ *www.groominglounge.com* Ⓜ *Farragut N.*

WOMEN'S CLOTHING

Fodor's Choice

★

Coup de Foudre. All of the upscale lingerie in this inviting, elegant boutique hails from France. Coup de Foudre—which translates to "love at first sight"—specializes in friendly, personalized bra fittings. ⊠ *1008 E St. NW, Downtown* ☎ *202/393–0878* ⊕ *www.coupdefoudrelingerie. com* ☽ *Closed Sun.* Ⓜ *Metro Center.*

Rizik Bros. This tony, patrician Washington institution offers designer women's clothing and expert advice. The sales staff will help find just the right style from the store's inventory, which is particularly strong in formal dresses. Take the elevator up from the northwest corner of Connecticut Avenue and L Street. ⊠ *1100 Connecticut Ave. NW, Downtown* ☎ *202/223–4050* ⊕ *www.riziks.com* Ⓜ *Farragut N.*

DUPONT CIRCLE

You might call Dupont Circle a younger, less staid version of Georgetown—almost as pricey but with more apartment buildings than houses. Its many restaurants, offbeat shops, and specialty book and record stores give it a cosmopolitan air. The street scene here is more urban than Georgetown's, with bike messengers and chess aficionados filling up the park. The Sunday farmers' market is a popular destination for organic food, fresh cheese, homemade soap, and hand-spun wool. To the south of Dupont Circle proper are several boutiques and familiar retail stores close to the Farragut and Farragut North Metro stops. Burberry and Thomas Pink both have stores in this area of Dupont. ⊠ *Connecticut Ave. between M and S Sts. Dupont Circle* Ⓜ *Dupont Circle.*

QUICK BITES

Kramerbooks & Afterwords. Serving brunch in the morning, snacks in the afternoon, cocktails in the evening, and coffee all day long, Kramer's is the perfect spot for a break. Try to snag an outside table, drop your shopping bags, and watch the world go by. "Sharezies," appetizers served on tiered plates are perfect for, well, sharing. ⊠ *1517 Connecticut Ave. NW, Dupont Circle* ☎ *202/387–1400* ⊕ *www.kramers.com* Ⓜ *Dupont Circle.*

11

SPECIALTY STORES

ANTIQUES
AND COL-
LECTIBLES

Geoffrey Diner Gallery. A must for hard-core antiques shoppers on the hunt for 19th-, 20th-, and 21st-century wares, this store sells Tiffany lamps and Arts and Crafts pieces from pivotal designers from Europe and the United States. It's open Saturday and by appointment only. ✉ *1730 21st St. NW, Dupont Circle* ☎ *202/483–5005* ⊕ *www.dinergallery.com* ☼ *Closed Sun.–Fri.* Ⓜ *Dupont Circle.*

Burton Marinkovich Fine Art. You know you've reached this gallery when you spot the small front yard with two modern abstract sculptures (they're by Lesley Dill and Leonard Cave). The gallery has works on paper by modern and contemporary masters, including Ross Bleckner, Richard Diebenkorn, David Hockney, Kandinsky, Matisse, Miró, Motherwell, Picasso, and others. Rare modern illustrated books and British linocuts from the Grosvenor School are also specialties. ✉ *1506 21st St. NW, Dupont Circle* ☎ *202/296–6563* ⊕ *www.burtonmarinkovich.com* ☼ *Closed Sun. and Mon.* Ⓜ *Dupont Circle.*

Fodor's Choice
★

Hemphill Fine Arts. This spacious gem of a contemporary gallery shows established artists in all mediums such as Jacob Kainen and William Christenberry as well as emerging ones like Colby Caldwell. ✉ *1515 14th St. NW, 3rd fl., Logan Circle* ☎ *202/234–5601* ⊕ *www.hemphillfinearts.com* ☼ *Closed Sun. and Mon.* Ⓜ *Dupont Circle.*

Irvine Contemporary. This bright and open gallery space showcases emerging regional and international artists. Noteworthy names include Teo Gonzalez, Paul D. Miller (DJ Spooky), James Marshall (Dalek), and Shepard Fairey. ✉ *1412 14th St. NW, Dupont Circle* ☎ *202/332–8767* ⊕ *www.irvinecontemporary.com* ☼ *Closed Sun. and Mon.* Ⓜ *Dupont Circle.*

BOOKS
Fodor's Choice
★

Kramerbooks & Afterwords. One of Washington's best-loved independents, this cozy shop has a choice selection of fiction and nonfiction. Open 24 hours on Friday and Saturday, it's a convenient meeting place. Kramerbooks shares space with a café that has late-night dining and live music from Wednesday to Saturday. ■ TIP→ There's a computer with free Internet access available in the bar. ✉ *1517 Connecticut Ave. NW, Dupont Circle* ☎ *202/387–1400* ⊕ *www.kramers.com* Ⓜ *Dupont Circle.*

★

Second Story Books. A used-books and -records emporium that stays open late, Second Story may lead bibliophiles to browse for hours. ✉ *2000 P St. NW, Dupont Circle* ☎ *202/659–8884* ⊕ *www.secondstorybooks.com* Ⓜ *Dupont Circle.*

CHILDREN'S
CLOTHING
★

Kid's Closet. If filling a little one's closet is on your list, stop here for high-quality contemporary infant and children's clothing and toys. Open since 1982, the shop carries sizes 0–7 for boys and 0–16 for girls. ✉ *1226 Connecticut Ave. NW, Dupont Circle* ☎ *202/429–9247* ⊕ *www.kidsclosetdc.com* ☼ *Closed Sun.* Ⓜ *Dupont Circle.*

CRAFTS
AND GIFTS

Beadazzled. A rainbow of ready-to-string beads fills the cases at this appealing shop. They also stock jewelry as well as books on crafts history and techniques. Check their Web site for a class schedule. ✉ *1507 Connecticut Ave. NW, Dupont Circle* ☎ *202/265–2323* ⊕ *www.beadazzled.net* Ⓜ *Dupont Circle.*

The Chocolate Moose. This store is simple, sheer fun for adults and kids alike. Looking for clacking, windup teeth? You can find them here, along with unusual greeting cards, strange boxer shorts, and unique

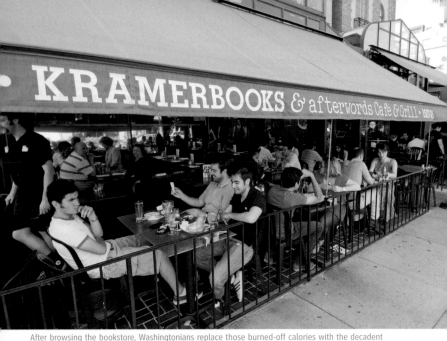

After browsing the bookstore, Washingtonians replace those burned-off calories with the decadent Dysfunctional Family Sundae at Kramerbooks & Afterwords.

handcrafts. If playing with all those fun toys makes you hungry, you can pick up a select line of premium European chocolates. ✉ *1743 L St. NW, Dupont Circle* ☎ *202/463–0992* ⊕ *www.chocolatemoosedc.com* ⊙ *Closed Sun.* Ⓜ *Farragut N.*

The Written Word. Not just a stationery store, the Written Word is more like a tribute to paper. In addition to a wide variety of handmade papers, there are journals, photo albums, and scrapbooks—all made out of unusual papers, as well as unique greeting cards. It's also one of the few places in D.C. that offer custom letterpress printing. ✉ *1427 P St. NW, Dupont Circle* ☎ *202/223–1400* ⊕ *www.writtenwordstudio.com* Ⓜ *Dupont Circle.*

HOME FURNISHINGS

Reincarnations. Reincarnations is a neighborhood favorite. It's hard to pinpoint one style that dominates—trendy, antique, funky—so everyone can find something to like. ✉ *1401 14th St. NW, Logan Circle* ☎ *202/319–1606* ⊕ *www.reincarnationsfurnishings.com* Ⓜ *Dupont Circle.*

Tabletop. Evoking a museum gift shop, this two-story row house is a delightful place to find bags by Swedish designer Lotta Jansdotter, Marimekko accessories, and Daphne Olive jewelry, as well as modern furniture, pillows, and rugs. ✉ *1608 20th St. NW, Dupont Circle* ☎ *202/387–7117* ⊕ *www.tabletopdc.com* Ⓜ *Dupont Circle.*

JEWELRY

Pampillonia Jewelers. Here you can find traditional designs in 18-karat gold and platinum as well as eye-catching contemporary designs. The shop also carries estate and antique jewelry and makes repairs. The selection for men is particularly good. ✉ *1213 Connecticut Ave. NW, Farragut Sq.* ☎ *202/628–6305* ⊕ *www.pampillonia.com* ⊙ *Closed Sun. and Sat. May–Sept.* Ⓜ *Farragut N.*

Tiny Jewel Box. Despite its name, this venerable D.C. favorite contains six floors of precious and semiprecious wares, including unique gifts, home accessories, vintage pieces, and works by well-known designers. ✉ *1147 Connecticut Ave. NW, Farragut Sq.* ☎ *202/393–2747* ⊕ *www.tinyjewelbox.com* ⊙ *Closed Sun.* Ⓜ *Farragut N.*

KITCHENWARE

Coffee and the Works. Coffee and tea lovers head to this charmingly cluttered shop for high-end kitchen gadgets, magnets, colorful ceramic pots, mugs with mammals and sea monsters in the bottom, and other accessories, as well as the beans and leaves themselves. ✉ *1627 Connecticut Ave. NW, Dupont Circle* ☎ *202/483–8050* Ⓜ *Dupont Circle.*

OPEN HOUSE FOR ART

On the "First Friday" of every month, the streets of Dupont Circle fill with wine-and-cheese-loving gallery hoppers, who are there to attend the joint open houses held by almost 20 galleries. Check out **The Galleries of Dupont Circle** (⊕ *www.dupontcirclegalleries.com*) for information on all events.

MEN'S CLOTHING

J. Press. Like its flagship store, founded in Connecticut in 1902 as a custom shop for Yale University, this Washington outlet is resolutely traditional: Shetland and Irish wool sport coats are a specialty. ✉ *1801 L St. NW, Farragut Sq.* ☎ *202/857–0120* ⊕ *www.jpressonline.com* ⊙ *Closed Sun.* Ⓜ *Farragut N.*

WOMEN'S CLOTHING

Fodor'sChoice ★

Betsy Fisher. Catering to women of all ages and sizes in search of contemporary and trendy styles, this store stocks one-of-a-kind accessories, clothes, shoes, and jewelry by well-known designers like Diane Von Furstenberg. A small selection of up-and-coming designs is also available. ✉ *1224 Connecticut Ave. NW, Dupont Circle* ☎ *202/785–1975* ⊕ *www.betsyfisher.com* Ⓜ *Dupont Circle.*

Fodor'sChoice ★

Secondi. One of the city's finest consignment shops, Secondi carries a well-chosen selection of women's designer and casual clothing, accessories, and shoes. The brands carried include Marc Jacobs, Louis Vuitton, Donna Karan, Prada, and Ann Taylor. ✉ *1702 Connecticut Ave. NW, 2nd fl., Dupont Circle* ☎ *202/667–1122* ⊕ *www.secondi.com* Ⓜ *Dupont Circle.*

Terra. This popular shop changed from selling eclectic gifts to focus on women's clothing from jeans to little black dresses. Brands include Carmen Marcvalvo, Pink Tartan, Robert Rodreguez, and Black Halo. ✉ *1706 Connecticut Ave. NW, Dupont Circle* ☎ *202/232–8581* ⊕ *www.shopterradc.com* Ⓜ *Dupont Circle.*

GEORGETOWN

Although Georgetown is not on a Metro line and street parking is nonexistent, people still flock here, keeping it D.C.'s favorite shopping area. This is also the capital's center for famous residents, as well as being a hot spot for restaurants, bars, and nightclubs.

National chains and designer shops now stand side by side with the specialty shops that first gave the district its allure, but the historic neighborhood is still charming and its street scene lively. In addition to housing tony antiques, elegant crafts, and high-style shoe and clothing boutiques, Georgetown offers wares that attract local college students and young people: books, music, and fashions from familiar names such as Banana Republic, BCBG, Betsey Johnson, Kate Spade, and Urban Outfitters. Most stores lie east and west on M Street and to the north on Wisconsin Avenue. The intersection of M and Wisconsin is the nexus for chain stores and big-name designer shops. The farther you venture in any direction from this intersection, the more eclectic and interesting the shops become. Some of the big-name stores are worth a look for their architecture alone; several shops blend traditional Georgetown town-house exteriors with airy modern showroom interiors.

Shopping in Georgetown can be expensive, but you don't have to add expensive parking lot fees to your total bill. The nearest Metro, Foggy Bottom/GWU, is a 10- to 15-minute walk from the shops. ∎TIP➔ The D.C. Circulator is your best bet for getting into and out of Georgetown, especially if it's hot or if you are laden down with many purchases. This $1 bus runs along M Street and up Wisconsin, passing the major shopping strips. ✉ *Intersection of Wisconsin Ave. and M St., Georgetown* Ⓜ *Foggy Bottom/GWU.*

QUICK BITES

DolceZZa. The handmade gelato and sorbet at this all-white storefront are divine, especially during the heat of summer. The flavors, such as coconut con dulce de leche, are endlessly inventive. Strawberry-, peach-, apple-, and clementine-flavored sorbets are available seasonally. Espresso and churros will warm winter afternoons. ✉ *1560 Wisconsin Ave. NW, Georgetown* ☎ *202/333–4646* ⊕ *www.dolcezzagelato.com* Ⓜ *Foggy Bottom/GWU.*

MALL

Shops at Georgetown Park. Near the hub of the Georgetown shopping district is this posh tri-level mall, which looks like a Victorian ice-cream parlor inside. The pricey clothing and accessory boutiques and the ubiquitous chain stores draw international visitors in droves. Next door is a branch of the Dean & Deluca gourmet grocery and café. ✉ *3222 M St. NW, Georgetown* ☎ *202/298–5577* ⊕ *www.shopsatgeorgetownpark. com* Ⓜ *Foggy Bottom/GWU.*

SPECIALTY STORES

ANTIQUES AND COLLECTIBLES

Cherub Antiques Gallery & Michael Getz Antiques. Two dealers have shared this Victorian row house since 1983. Michael Getz Antiques carries fireplace equipment and silver. Cherub Antiques Gallery specializes in art nouveau and art deco. A glass case by the door holds a collection of more than 100 cocktail shakers, including Prohibition-era pieces disguised as penguins, roosters, and dumbbells. ✉ *2918 M St. NW, Georgetown* ☎ *202/337–2224 Cherub Gallery, 202/338–3811 Michael Getz Antiques* Ⓜ *Foggy Bottom/GWU.*

Fodor's Choice ★

Jean Pierre Antiques. Very Georgetown, but fairly close to Dupont Circle, this gorgeous shop sells antique furniture and gifts from France, Germany, Sweden, and Italy. ✉ *2601 and 2603 P St. NW, Georgetown* ☎ *202/337–1731* ⊕ *www.jeanpierreantiques.com* Ⓜ *Dupont Circle.*

Marston Luce. House and garden accessories are in the mix here, but the emphasis is on 18th- and 19th-century French country furniture discovered by the owner on yearly buying trips in Europe. They also carry Scandinavian painted furniture. ⊠ *1651 Wisconsin Ave. NW, Georgetown* ☎ *202/333–6800* ⊕ *www.marstonluce.com* ⊗ *Closed Sun.* Ⓜ *Foggy Bottom/GWU.*

Opportunity Shop of the Christ Child Society. This Georgetown landmark, staffed by volunteers, sells fine jewelry, antiques, crystal, silver, and porcelain on consignment. Prices are moderate, and profits go to a good cause—the Christ Child Society, which provides for the needs of local children and young mothers. ⊠ *1427 Wisconsin Ave. NW, Georgetown* ☎ *202/333–6635* ⊕ *www.christchilddc.org* Ⓜ *Foggy Bottom/GWU.*

ART GALLERIES   Many of Georgetown's galleries are on side streets. Their holdings are primarily work by established artists.

Addison Ripley. This well-respected gallery exhibits contemporary work by national and local artists, including painters Manon Cleary and Wolf Kahn and photographer Frank Hallam Day. ⊠ *1670 Wisconsin Ave. NW, Georgetown* ☎ *202/338–5180* ⊕ *www.addisonripleyfineart.com* ⊗ *Closed Sun. and Mon.* Ⓜ *Foggy Bottom/GWU.*

Appalachian Spring. The glossy wooden jewelry boxes displayed here are treasures in their own right. Traditional and contemporary American-made crafts—including art glass, pottery, jewelry, and toys—fill this lovely shop. There's also an outpost in Union Station. ⊠ *1415 Wisconsin Ave. NW, Georgetown* ☎ *202/337–5780* ⊕ *www.appalachianspring. com* ⊠ *Union Station, East Hall, 50 Massachusetts Ave. NE, Capitol Hill* ☎ *202/682–0505* Ⓜ *Union Station.*

Galleries 1054. Several distinct galleries live under one roof at this location. **cross mackenzie ceramic art** (☎ *202/333–7970*) features vibrant and unusual contemporary ceramic pieces. **Parish** (☎ *202/944–2310*) features contemporary work in all mediums by primarily African-American artists. **Alla Rogers** (☎ *202/333–8595*) has contemporary Eastern European, Russian, and American art and photography. ⊠ *1054 31st St. NW, Georgetown* ⊗ *Closed Sun. and Mon.* Ⓜ *Foggy Bottom/GWU.*

BOOKS   **Bartleby's Books.** Surround yourself with rare and precious books in this antiquarian bookstore. The Americana collection—organized by state—is particularly browsable; you might just find an unexpected souvenir from home. ⊠ *1132 29th St. NW, Georgetown* ☎ *202/298–0486* ⊕ *www.bartlebysbooks.com* ⊗ *Closed Sun. and Mon.*

Bridge Street Books. This charming independent store focuses on politics, history, philosophy, poetry, literature, film, and Judaica. ⊠ *2814 Pennsylvania Ave. NW, Georgetown* ☎ *202/965–5200* ⊕ *www. bridgestreetbooks.com* Ⓜ *Foggy Bottom/GWU.*

CHILDREN'S   **Piccolo Piggies.** Chock-full of fun and educational toys as well as clas-
CLOTHING   sic layette and children's clothing (up to size 14 for girls and 10 for boys), this warm store is a pleasure to browse through—even if you're a bit over the age limit. ⊠ *1533 Wisconsin Ave. NW, Georgetown* ☎ *202/333–0123* ⊕ *www.piccolo-piggies.com.*

Yiro. One hundred percent organic, Yiro clothing (newborn to 10 years) is produced without chemicals and is colored only with natural dyes (and yes, the outfits are soft and attractive). A baby registry will help you pick the perfect gift for the environmentally conscious mom. Its sister store, **Tugooh Toys** (⊠ *1319 Wisconsin Ave. NW, Georgetown*

☏ 202/338–9476) sells eco-friendly toys. ✉ *1419 Wisconsin Ave. NW, Georgetown* ☏ *202/333–0032* ⊕ *www.yirostores.com*

HOME FURNISHINGS
Fodor's Choice
★

A Mano. The store's name is Italian for "by hand," and it lives up to its name, stocking colorful hand-painted ceramics, hand-dyed tablecloths, blown-glass stemware, and other home and garden accessories by Italian and French artisans. There are even adorable kids' gifts. Items are now also available in their online catalog. ✉ *1677 Wisconsin Ave. NW, Georgetown* ☏ *202/298–7200* ⊕ *www.amano.bz.*

Theodore's. A Washington institution, Theodore's is the place to visit for ultramod housewares, from stylish furniture to accessories, leather, and upholstery that make a statement. There's an excellent selection of wall-storage units for almost all tastes. ✉ *2233 Wisconsin Ave. NW, Georgetown* ☏ *202/333–2300* ⊕ *www.theodores.com.*

MEN'S AND WOMEN'S CLOTHING
Commander Salamander. Open since 1979, this funky outpost sells clothes for punks, goths, and ravers. Retro aficionados will also find clothing and accessories for their wardrobes. Sifting through the assortment of leather, chains, toys, and candy-color makeup is as much entertainment as it is shopping. ✉ *1420 Wisconsin Ave. NW, Georgetown* ☏ *202/337–2265* Ⓜ *Foggy Bottom/GWU.*

relish. In fashionable Cady's Alley, this dramatic space holds an expanding men and women's collection handpicked seasonally by the owner. Modern, elegant, and practical selections include European classics and well-tailored modern designers, such as Narciso Rodriguez and Dries Van Noten. ✉ *3312 Cady's Alley NW, Georgetown* ☏ *202/333–5343* ⊕ *www.relishdc.com* ☽ *Closed Sun.* Ⓜ *Foggy Bottom/GWU.*

SHOES
Fodor's Choice
★

Hu's Shoes. This cutting-edge shoe store would shine in Paris, Tokyo, or New York. Luckily for us, it brings ballet flats, heels, and boots from designers like Chloé, Maison Martin Margiela, Proenza Schouler, and Sonia Rykiel right here to Georgetown. ✉ *3005 M St. NW, Georgetown* ☏ *202/342–0202* ⊕ *www.hushoes.com* Ⓜ *Foggy Bottom/GWU.*

Sassanova. There are high-end shoes in this girly shop for every occasion—be it a walk on the beach or through a boardroom. Brands carried include the latest from Emma Hope and Sigerson Morrison. Jewelry, bags, and shoes for kids round out the selection. ✉ *1641 Wisconsin Ave. NW, Georgetown* ☏ *202/471–4400* ⊕ *www.sassanova.com.*

SPAS AND BEAUTY SALONS
Fodor's Choice
★

Blue Mercury. Hard-to-find skin-care lines—Laura Mercier, Trish McEvoy, are just two—are what set this homegrown, now national, chain apart. The retail space up front sells soaps, lotions, perfumes, cosmetics, and skin- and hair-care products. Behind the glass door is the "skin gym," where you can treat yourself to facials, waxing, massage, and oxygen treatments. ✉ *3059 M St. NW, Georgetown* ☏ *202/965–1300* ⊕ *www.bluemercury.com* Ⓜ *Foggy Bottom/GWU* ✉ *1619 Connecticut Ave. NW, Dupont Circle* ☏ *202/462–1300* Ⓜ *Dupont Circle.*

WOMEN'S CLOTHING
The Phoenix. Here you can find contemporary clothing in natural fibers by designers such as Eileen Fisher and Flax, as well as jewelry and fine- and folk-art pieces from Mexico. ✉ *1514 Wisconsin Ave. NW, Georgetown* ☏ *202/338–4404* ⊕ *www.thephoenixdc.com.*

Urban Chic. It's hard to imagine a fashionista who wouldn't find something here—whether she could afford it might be another story. Gorgeous suits,

DID YOU KNOW?

Georgetown, one of D.C.'s oldest and storied neighborhoods, is a great spot for political celebrity sightings. Heavyweights like Senator John Kerry, political pundit George Stephanopoulos, and Bob Woodard live here.

jeans, cocktail dresses, and accessories from Catherine Malandrino, Ella Moss, Rebecca Taylor, and Susana Monaco are to be had. The handbags are a highlight. ⌧ *1626 Wisconsin Ave. NW, Georgetown* ☎ *202/338–5398* ⊕ *www.urbanchiconline.com.*

Wink. While the clientele and styles skew toward the young and trendy, women of all ages shop in this subterranean space for coveted jeans and colorful, sparkly tops, dresses, and jewelry. Theory, Fighting Eel, and Rebecca Taylor are among the labels carried. ⌧ *3109 M St. NW, Georgetown* ☎ *202/338–9465* ⊕ *www.shopwinkdc.com* Ⓜ *Foggy Bottom/GWU.*

ALL AMERICAN GIFTS
■ Appalachian Spring, Georgetown
■ Bartleby's Books, Georgetown
■ Cowgirl Creamery, Downtown
■ GoodWood, U Street Corridor

U STREET CORRIDOR

In the 1930s and '40s U Street was known for its classy theaters and jazz clubs. After decades of decline following the 1968 riots, the neighborhood has been revitalized. The area has gentrified at lightning speed, but has retained a diverse mix of multiethnic young professionals and older, working-class African-Americans. At night the neighborhood's club, bar, and restaurant scene comes alive. During the day the street scene is more laid-back, with more locals than tourists occupying the distinctive shops. ■TIP➔ On the third Thursday of each month, the area shops stay open late to offer light refreshments and special deals for the fun "Shopper Socials." ⌧ *U St. between 12th and 17th Sts., U Street Corridor* Ⓜ *U St./Cardozo.*

QUICK BITES

Love Café. The sister store to the CakeLove bakery across the street, this is a casual community hot spot. The buttercream cupcakes are incredibly sweet, and the rosy atmosphere warms you on the inside. ⌧ *1501 U St. NW, U Street Corridor* ☎ *202/265–9800* ⊕ *www.cakelove.com* Ⓜ *U St./Cardozo.*

SPECIALTY STORES

ANTIQUES AND COLLECTIBLES

GoodWood. This friendly shop sells vintage and antique wood furniture, including wonderful 19th-century American pieces, along with stained glass, mirrors, and other decorative items—even a small but gorgeous collection of estate jewelry. ⌧ *1428 U St. NW, U Street Corridor* ☎ *202/986–3640* ⊕ *www.goodwooddc.com* ☉ *Closed Mon.–Wed.* Ⓜ *U St./Cardozo.*

Millennium. This eclectic shop sells what it calls "20th-century antiques," a unique blend of high-end vintage midcentury modern furniture and decorative art. ⌧ *1528 U St. NW, downstairs, U Street Corridor* ☎ *202/483–1218* ☉ *Closed Mon.–Wed.* Ⓜ *U St./Cardozo.*

HOME FURNISHINGS

Go Mama Go! This colorful, inviting store makes you feel as if you're wandering through the stalls of a global marketplace. African, Asian, and Latin home furnishings and unique gifts dominate the wares. ⌧ *1809 14th St. NW, U Street Corridor* ☎ *202/299–0850* ⊕ *www.gomamago.com* Ⓜ *U St./Cardozo.*

Habitat. This store sells artist-made jewelry and well-chosen desk sets, lamps, and tabletop items. ✉ *1512 U St. NW, U Street Corridor* ☎ *202/518–7222* ⊕ *www. habitatstyle.com* Ⓜ *U St./Cardozo.*

┌─────────────────────────┐
FASHIONS FOR HER

■ Betsy Fisher, Dupont Circle

■ Coup de Foudre, Downtown

■ Nana, U Street Corridor

■ relish, Georgetown
└─────────────────────────┘

Miss Pixie's Furnishings and Whatnot. The well-chosen collectibles—handpicked by Miss Pixie herself—include gorgeous textiles, antique home furnishings, lamps and mirrors, glass- and silverware, and hardwood bed frames. The reasonable prices will grab your attention, as will the location, an old car-dealer showroom. ✉ *1626 14th St, NW, Logan Circle* ☎ *202/232–8171* ⊕ *www.misspixies.com* ☉ *Closed Mon. and Tues.* Ⓜ *U St./Cordozo or Dupont Circle.*

Muléh. Exquisite contemporary Indonesian and Filipino home furnishings and trendy clothes from L.A. and New York fill this expansive showroom. The furniture pieces, which are the primary focus of the store, are made from fine organic materials. It's sort of like wandering through a luxury resort in Southeast Asia and finding a fabulous clothing boutique tucked in the back. ✉ *1831 14th St. NW, U Street Corridor* ☎ *202/667–3440* ⊕ *www.muleh.com* ☉ *Closed Mon.* Ⓜ *U St./Cardozo.*

Zawadi. The name means "gift" in Swahili, but you may want to buy the beautiful African art, textiles, home accessories, and jewelry for yourself. ✉ *1524 U St. NW, U Street Corridor* ☎ *202/232–2214* ⊕ *www. zawadidc.com* Ⓜ *U St./Cardozo.*

WOMEN'S CLOTHING

Fodor'sChoice ★

Nana. A hip and friendly staff is one of the reasons why D.C. women love this store. Another is the stock of both new and vintage women's clothes at affordable prices, plus handmade jewelry and cool handbags. ✉ *1528 U St. NW, upstairs, U Street Corridor* ☎ *202/667–6955* ⊕ *www.nanadc.com* Ⓜ *U St./Cardozo.*

FRIENDSHIP HEIGHTS

The major thoroughfare Wisconsin Avenue runs northwest through the city from Georgetown toward Maryland. It crosses the border in the midst of the Friendship Heights shopping district, which is also near Chevy Chase. Other neighborhoods in the District yield more interesting finds and more enjoyable shopping and sightseeing, but it's hard to beat Friendship Heights for sheer convenience and selection. Bloomingdale's is the latest addition to the upscale lineup, which includes Barneys CO-OP, Neiman Marcus, and Saks Fifth Avenue. Stand-alone designer stores like Jimmy Choo, Louis Vuitton, Christian Dior, and Cartier up the luxury quotient. Filene's Basement, Loehmann's, and T.J. Maxx hawk the designer names at much lower prices. Lord & Taylor and chains like the Gap, Ann Taylor Loft, and Williams Sonoma occupy the middle ground.

Tightly packed into a few blocks, the big-name area is self-explanatory. However, there are also a few local gems in the surrounding neighborhood. ✉ *Wisconsin Ave. between Jenifer St. NW and Western Ave., Friendship Heights.*

SPECIALTY STORES

BOOKS **Politics and Prose.** The calendar of this legendary independent is jam-packed with author events and signings, and their tables are endlessly browsable. There's a coffee shop downstairs where you can debate the issues of the day. The nearest Metro is 15 minutes away. ⊠ *5015 Connecticut Ave. NW, Friendship Heights* ☎ *202/364–1919* ⊕ *www.politics-prose.com* Ⓜ *Friendship Heights.*

FOOD AND WINE **Calvert Woodley Liquors.** This liquor store carries not only an excellent selection of wine and hard liquor, but also many kinds of cheese and other picnic and cocktail-party fare, as well as the legendary H&H bagels from New York. Its international offerings have made it a favorite pantry for embassy parties. ⊠ *4339 Connecticut Ave. NW, Tenleytown* ☎ *202/966–4400* ⊕ *www.calvertwoodley.com* ☾ *Closed Sun.* Ⓜ *Van Ness/UDC.*

Rodman's Discount Foods and Drugstore. The rare store that carries wine, cheese, and space heaters, Rodman's is a fascinating hybrid of Kmart and Dean & Deluca. The appliances are downstairs, the imported peppers and chocolates upstairs. ⊠ *5100 Wisconsin Ave. NW, Friendship Heights* ☎ *202/363–3466* ⊕ *www.rodmans.com* Ⓜ *Friendship Heights.*

GIFTS **Periwinkle Inc.** Warm and welcoming, Periwinkle offers a panoply of gift options: boutique chocolates, cases of nutty and gummy treats, handmade jewelry, Stonewall Kitchen snacks, hand-designed wrapping paper, scented bath products, printed note cards, and Voluspa candles. ⊠ *3815 Livingston St. NW, Friendship Heights* ☎ *202/364–3076* Ⓜ *Friendship Heights.*

WOMEN'S CLOTHING **Sahba.** This avant-garde women's clothing boutique stocks an expertly selected cache of J Brand jeans, Rick Owens tops, and Ann Demeulemeester clothing, shoes, and accessories. ⊠ *5300 Wisconsin Ave. NW, Friendship Heights* ☎ *202/966–5080* Ⓜ *Friendship Heights.*

Side Trips

WORD OF MOUTH

"A favorite with families of all ages has been Mount Vernon, which is a beautiful drive south of Washington. It has been updated and the interactive museums are really cool."

—tlangenbach

WELCOME TO SIDE TRIPS

TOP REASONS TO GO

★ **Walk in Washington's Shadow:** The minute you step onto the grounds of Mount Vernon, you'll be transported back in time to colonial America.

★ **Colonial Meets Bohemian:** Delve into colonial history in Old Town Alexandria, then fast-forward to the 21st century with funky shops, artist's galleries, hot restaurants, boutiques, and bars. Don't miss Alexandria's farmers' market, held every Saturday, year-round, from 5:30 to 10:30 am. Believe it or not, it has been around for more than 250 years.

★ **Take a Hike:** Great Falls Park and the C&O Canal offer dozens of hiking and walking trails. Or, you can enjoy the views while biking along the area's excellent bike paths. Reward yourself with a picnic along the water. An eagle sighting is an added bonus.

★ **Feeling Crabby?:** Head east to Annapolis on the Chesapeake Bay and feast on a Maryland specialty: blue crabs by the bushel (the bib is optional).

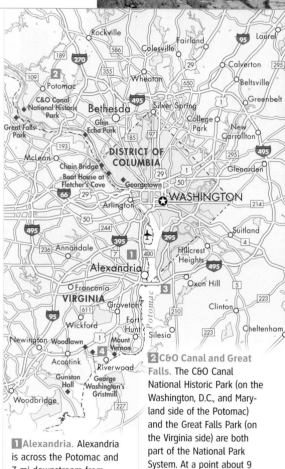

1 **Alexandria.** Alexandria is across the Potomac and 7 mi downstream from Washington. As a commercial port, it competed with Georgetown in the days before Washington was a city. It's now a big small town loaded with historic homes, shops, and restaurants.

2 **C&O Canal and Great Falls.** The C&O Canal National Historic Park (on the Washington, D.C., and Maryland side of the Potomac) and the Great Falls Park (on the Virginia side) are both part of the National Park System. At a point about 9 mi west of the District line, the two parks face each other. It's here that the steep, jagged falls of the Potomac roar into a narrow gorge, providing one of the most spectacular scenic attractions in the East. Hiking, canoeing, bicycling, and fishing are popular in the parks.

Opposite: Great Falls Park,
Left: United States Naval Academy.
Annapolis, Maryland.

12

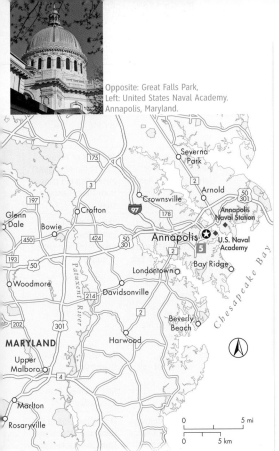

5 **Annapolis, Maryland.**
Maryland's capital is a
popular destination for
seafood lovers and boating
fans. Warm, sunny days
bring many boats to the
City Dock, where they're
moored against a back-
ground of waterfront shops
and restaurants. The city has
one of the country's largest
assemblages of 18th-cen-
tury architecture. Its nautical
reputation is enhanced by
the presence of the U.S.
Naval Academy.

GETTING ORIENTED

There's no question that
Washington, D.C., has
enough sights, sounds, and
experiences to keep you
busy for a week or more
without seeing everything
on your itinerary. The five
destinations highlighted
here help enrich your
experience whether you're
a history buff, foodie, outdoor enthusiast, or boater.
With just a bit of planning,
any one of these trips can
be done in a day or even
an afternoon. Follow the
locals' example and escape
the heat of the capital with
a trip to the countryside.

3 **National Harbor.** Just
15 minutes from Washing-
ton, D.C., along the Potomac
River in Maryland is the
National Harbor urban-
waterfront community. Here
you'll find dozens of shops,
commercial and residen-
tial buildings, restaurants,
and hotels. Special events
are held regularly and the
National Children's Museum
is scheduled to open here
in 2013.

4 **Mount Vernon, Woodlawn, and Gunston Hall.**
Three splendid examples
of plantation architecture
remain on the Virginia side
of the Potomac, 16 mi south
of D.C. Mount Vernon, the
most-visited historic house
in America, was the home
of George Washington;
Woodlawn was the estate
of Washington's step-granddaughter; and Gunston Hall
was the residence of George
Mason, a patriot and author
of the document on which
the Bill of Rights was based.

SIDE TRIPS PLANNER

Kid Tips

It's summer, it's hot, your kids have had enough history and are ready for some splash time: check out **Cameron Run Regional Park** in Alexandria, with its Great Waves Waterpark boasting a wave pool, four-story waterslide, and kiddie pool.

No matter the ages of your children, the **C&O Canal** affords dozens of family-friendly activities, from the mule-drawn boat rides and ranger-led hikes to your own bike, canoe, or picnic adventure.

While adults enjoy tours of **Mt. Vernon**, kids under 10 may get bored. Instead explore the outbuildings and gardens, including a 4-acre farm where docents demonstrate everything from smoking hogs to milling corn.

If you have tots three and under, the **Chesapeake Children's Museum** in Annapolis has lots of hands-on activities to keep them busy. There's an arts-and-crafts center, dress-up area, climbable 10-foot boat, and aquariums.

Check out the **U.S. Naval Academy**, with two kid faves just across from the visitor center: a midcentury jet and six-man submarine from the 1950s.

TO GET TO...	BY CAR:	BY METRO OR BUS:
Alexandria	George Washington Memorial Pkwy. or Jefferson Davis Hwy. (Rte. 1) south from Arlington (20 mins)	The Blue or Yellow Line to the King Street Metro stop (25 mins from Metro Center stop)
C&O Canal	Canal Rd. or MacArthur Blvd. from Georgetown (15 mins) or the Beltway to Exit 41 from D.C.; follow signs to Carderock (20 mins)	The D.C. Circulator Union Station-Georgetown route and get off at stop #35 (15 mins)
Great Falls	Rte. 193 (Exit 13 off the Beltway) to Rte. 738 (25 mins)	No Metro or bus
National Harbor	I-295 South to National Harbor exit (15–30 mins)	The Green Line to the Branch Ave. Metro stop. Then take bus NH1 (20 mins from Branch Ave. stop)
Mount Vernon	Exit 1 off the Beltway; follow signs to George Washington Memorial Pkwy. southbound (30 mins)	The Yellow Line to the Huntington Metro stop. From there, take Fairfax County Connector Bus 101, 151, or 152 (45–50 mins)
Woodlawn	Rte. 1 southwest to the second Rte. 235 intersection; entrance is on the right at the traffic light (40 mins)	Bus 151, 152, or 171 from Huntington Metro station (45–50 mins)
Gunston Hall	Rte. 1 south to Rte. 242; turn left and go 3.5 mi to entrance (30 mins)	No Metro or bus
Annapolis	U.S. 50 east to the Rowe Blvd. Exit (35–45 mins, except during weekday rush hour when it will take twice as long)	Amtrak from Union Station to BWI; MTA Light Rail from BWI to Patapsco Light Rail Station; transfer to Bus #14 (2 hrs)

12

Updated by
Cathy Sharpe

Within an hour of D.C. are getaway destinations connected to the nation's first president, naval history, colonial events, and the Civil War. Alexandria was once a bustling colonial port, and Old Town preserves this flavor with its cobblestone streets, taverns, and waterfront. Cycle 7 mi downriver along the banks of the Potomac to get here, or hop on the Metro for a quick 30-minute ride.

For another active trip into the past, walk or bike along the 13-mi path that parallels a section of the Chesapeake & Ohio (C&O) Canal, past Glen Echo Park, to Great Falls Tavern on the Maryland side of the Potomac. This is one of Washington's favorite nearby destinations for weekend hiking. Mount Vernon, George Washington's plantation, is a mere 16 mi from D.C. on the Virginia side of the Potomac. Make a day of it, and visit the two other interesting plantation homes—Woodlawn and Gunston Hall—that are nearby.

Another option is to get out on the water—either at the nearby National Harbor, or in Annapolis, a major center for boating and home to the U.S. Naval Academy. Feast on the Chesapeake Bay's famous crabs, then watch the midshipmen parade on campus at the academy.

ALEXANDRIA, VIRGINIA

A short drive (or bike ride) from Washington, Alexandria provides a welcome break from the monuments and hustle and bustle of the District. Here you encounter America's colonial heritage. Founded in 1749 by Scottish merchants eager to capitalize on the booming tobacco trade, Alexandria became one of the most important colonial ports. Alexandria has been associated with the most significant personages of the colonial, Revolutionary, and Civil War periods. In Old Town this colorful past is revived through restored 18th- and 19th-century homes, churches, and taverns; on the cobbled streets; and on the revitalized waterfront, where clipper ships docked and artisans displayed

their wares. Alexandria also has a wide variety of small to medium-size restaurants and pubs, plus a wealth of boutiques and antiques dealers vying for your time and money.

GETTING HERE AND AROUND

Take either the George Washington Memorial Parkway or Jefferson Davis Highway (Route 1) south from Arlington to reach Alexandria. ■TIP→ Stop at the Alexandria Convention & Visitors Association in Ramsay House (221 King Street) for a 24-hour free parking permit good at any two-hour metered spot. You can get one even if you're visiting from elsewhere in Virginia.

The King Street Metro stop (about 25 minutes from Metro Center) is right next to the Masonic Memorial and a 10-block walk on King Street from the center of Old Town. ■TIP→ On Saturday from 10 AM to midnight and on Sunday from 11 to 7 (even later in spring and summer), there's a free Dash About shuttle between the King Street station and Market Square near Ramsay House.

ESSENTIALS

Visitor Information Alexandria Convention & Visitors Association (☎ 703/746–3301 or 800/388–9119 ⊕ www.visitalexandriava.com).

EXPLORING

TOP ATTRACTIONS

⓫ **Alexandria Black History Museum.** A
★ museum, reading room, and park
comprise this 9-acre site that pays
tribute to the African-American
experience. The museum incorporates the Robert H. Robinson
Library, a building constructed in
the wake of a landmark 1939 sit-
in protesting the segregation of
Alexandria libraries. It recounts
the history of African-Americans
in Alexandria and Virginia from
1749 to the present. The federal
census of 1790 recorded 52 free
blacks living in the city, and Alexandria had two of the busiest slave
markets in the South. Adjacent to
the museum is the Watson Reading
Room, filled with historical documents and videos highlighting the

history and culture of African-Americans. Volunteers are on hand to
help visitors with research. You'll also want to stroll through Heritage
Park, which includes a 19th-century cemetery, sculptures commemorating the contributions of African-Americans to Alexandria, and a
wetland area that is home to beavers, mallards, and turtles. ✉ *902
Wythe St., Old Town* ☎ *703/838–4356* ⊕ *oha.alexandriava.gov/bhrc*
💲*$2* ⊙ *Tues.–Sat. 10–4.*

❹ **Athenaeum.** One of the most noteworthy structures in Alexandria, the
Athenaeum is a striking, reddish-brown Greek Revival edifice at the
corner of Prince and Lee streets. It was built as a bank in the 1850s, and
is now home to the Northern Virginia Fine Arts Association. The vol-
unteer-staffed gallery showing changing art exhibits is open Thursday,
Friday, and Sunday from noon to 4 and Saturday from 1 to 4. ✉ *201
Prince St., Old Town* ☎ *703/548–0035* ⊕ *www.nvfaa.org.*

❼ **Carlyle House Historic Park.** The grandest of Alexandria's older houses,
Carlyle House was patterned after a Scottish country manor house.
Scottish merchant John Carlyle completed the structure in 1753. This
was General Edward Braddock's headquarters, and the place where he
met with five royal governors in 1755 to plan the strategy and funding
of the early campaigns of the French and Indian War. ✉ *121 N. Fairfax
St., Old Town* ☎ *703/549–2997* ⊕ *www.nvrpa.org/parks/carlylehouse*
💲*$5* ⊙ *Tues.–Sat. 10–4, Sun. noon–4, guided tours every ½ hr, last
tours begin at 4.*

⓮ **Friendship Fire House.** Alexandria's showcase firehouse, home to the area's
☾ first volunteer fire company beginning in 1774, is outfitted in typical
19th-century firefighting fashion. Artifacts include leather water buckets, axes, and hand- and steam-powered pumpers. ✉ *107 S. Alfred St.,*

Old Town ☎ *703/838–3891* 🌐 *oha.alexandriava.gov/friendship* 🎟 *$2* ⏲ *Fri. and Sat. 10–4, Sun. 1–4.*

CAPITAL FACTS

George Washington went to birthday celebrations in the ballroom at the Gadsby Tavern.

8 **Gadsby's Tavern Museum.** This museum is housed in the old City Tavern and Hotel, which was a center of political and social life in the late 18th century. A tour takes you through the taproom, dining room, assembly room, ballroom, and communal bedrooms. Friday-evening tours visit the same rooms but are led by a costumed guide using a lantern. There also are a number of special events that vary from month to month, including "Tea with Martha Washington," lectures, and programs for children and families like "Swordsmen's Rendezvous." Check the Web site for a calendar of events. ✉ *134 N. Royal St., Old Town* ☎ *703/838–4242* 🌐 *oha.alexandriava.gov/gadsby* 🎟 *$5, $2 children 11–17, lantern tours $5* ⏲ *Nov.–Mar., Wed.–Sat. 11–4, Sun. 1–4, last tour at 3:45; Apr.–Oct., Tues.–Sat. 10–5, Sun. and Mon. 1–5, last tour at 4:45; tours 15 mins before and after the hr. Lantern tours June–Aug., Fri. 7–10.*

15 **George Washington Masonic National Memorial.** Alexandria, like Washington, has no tall buildings, so the spire of this memorial dominates the surroundings. The building fronts King and Duke streets, Alexandria's major east–west arteries; from the ninth-floor observation deck you get a spectacular view of Alexandria, with Washington in the distance. (Note: you cannot go above the mezzanine except on the guided tour.) The building contains furnishings from the first Masonic lodge in Alexandria, of which George Washington was a member; he became a Mason in 1753 and was a Worshipful Master, a high rank, at the same time he served as president. ✉ *101 Callahan Dr., Old Town* ☎ *703/683–2007* 🌐 *www.gwmemorial.org* 🎟 *Free* ⏲ *Apr.–Sept. Mon.–Sat. 9–4, Sun. noon–4; Oct.–Mar. Mon.–Sat. 10–4, Sun. noon–4; 50-min guided tours of building and observation deck daily at 10, 11:30, 1:30, and 3.*

1 **Ramsay House.** The best place to start a tour of Alexandria's Old Town is at the **Alexandria Visitors Center,** in Ramsay House, a re-creation of the home of the town's founder, a merchant and first lord mayor, William Ramsay. The structure is believed to be on the site of the oldest house in Alexandria. Travel counselors here provide brochures and maps for self-guided walking tours; tour companies give guided walking tours that leave from here. Ticket prices vary, though most are about $10. Call ahead to get guided tour times. **■ TIP→ They can also give you a 24-hour permit for free parking at any two-hour metered spot, even if you're visiting from elsewhere in Virginia.** ✉ *221 King St., Old Town* ☎ *703/838–4200 or 800/388–9119* 🌐 *www.visitalexandriava.com* ⏲ *Daily 9–8.*

6 ★ **Torpedo Factory Art Center.** Torpedoes were manufactured here by the U.S. Navy during World Wars I and II. Now the building houses the studios and workshops of about 85 artists and artisans, and has become one of Alexandria's most popular attractions. You can view the workshops of printmakers, jewelry makers, sculptors, painters, and potters, and most of the art and the crafts are for sale. On the second Thursday of every

month the building hosts an Art Night, in which visitors can tour galleries, meet artists, and enjoy refreshments. The Torpedo Factory also houses the **Alexandria Archaeology Museum** (☎ 703/838–4399 ⊕ *oha. alexandriava.gov/archaeology*), a city-operated research facility devoted to urban archaeology and conservation. Artifacts from excavations in Alexandria are on display here. Admission is free; hours are

WORD OF MOUTH

"Old Town Alexandria is its own interesting experience of shops, restaurants, and galleries. Although it's a little distant from downtown D.C., the King St. Metro is walkably close."

—Cassandra

Tuesday through Friday 10–3, Saturday 10–5, and Sunday 1–5. ⊠ *105 N. Union St., Old Town* ☎ *703/838–4565* ⊕ *www.torpedofactory.org* ⊠ *Free* ⊘ *Daily 10–6; galleries open until 9 on Thurs.*

WORTH NOTING

⑩ **Boyhood Home of Robert E. Lee.** The childhood home of the Commander in Chief of the Confederate forces of Virginia, Robert E. Lee, is a fine example of a 19th-century town house with Federal architecture. It's now a private home and is not open to visitors. Some of the furnishings, however, are displayed at the Lyceum. You can visit the Web site for a virtual tour. ⊠ *607 Oronoco St., Old Town* ⊕ *www.leeboyhoodhome.com.*

⑯ **Cameron Run Regional Park.** Alexandria's largest park features a Great Waves Waterpark, miniature golf course, batting cages, 2-acre lake for shore fishing, and grassy areas. On hot summer days, expect crowds at Great Waves with its wave pool, four-story slides, toddler pool with bubblers and waterfall, snack bar, and ice-cream shop. ⊠ *4001 Eisenhower Ave., Seminary Hill* ☎ *703/960–0767* ⊕ *www.nvrpa.org/parks/cameronrun* ⊠ *Great Waves: $10.95–$15; additional fees for miniature golf and batting cages* ⊘ *Great Waves: Memorial weekend 11–7; May 29–June 17, Fri. 1–7, weekends 11–7; June 18–Sept. 7, daily 11–7; schedule varies for miniature golf and batting cages.*

❺ **Captain's Row.** Many of Alexandria's sea captains once lived on this block. The cobblestones in the street were allegedly laid by Hessian mercenaries who had fought for the British during the Revolution and were held in Alexandria as prisoners of war. ⊠ *Prince St. between Lee and Union Sts., Old Town.*

⑫ **Christ Church.** Both Washington and Lee were pewholders in this Episcopal church. (Washington paid 36 pounds and 10 shillings—a lot of money in those days—for Pew 60.) Built in 1773, Christ Church is a good example of Georgian church architecture. It has a fine Palladian window, an interior balcony, and an English wrought-brass-and-crystal chandelier. Docents give tours during visiting hours. ⊠ *118 N. Washington St., Old Town* ☎ *703/549–1450* ⊕ *www.historicchristchurch.org* ⊠ *Free, $5 donation suggested* ⊘ *Mon.–Sat. 9–4, Sun. 2–4:30.*

❾ **Lee-Fendall House Museum.** The short block of Alexandria's Oronoco Street between Washington and St. Asaph streets is the site of two Lee-owned houses. One is the Lee-Fendall House, the home of several illustrious members of the Lee family, and the other is the boyhood home of Robert E. Lee. The house and its furnishings are those of a Lee home of the 1850–70 period. United Mine Workers leader John Lewis lived here from 1937 until his death in 1969. ⊠ *614 Oronoco St., Old Town* ☏ *703/548–1789* ⊕ *www.leefendallhouse.org* ⊡ *$5* ⊘ *Wed.– Sat. 10–4, Sun. 1–4; tours every hr, last tour begins at 3; sometimes closed weekends.*

⑬ Lyceum. Built in 1839, the Lyceum has served as a library, a Civil War hospital, a residence, and an office building. It now houses two galleries with exhibits on the history of Alexandria, a third gallery with changing exhibits, and a gift shop. Some travel information for the entire state is also available here. ⊠ *201 S. Washington St., Old Town* ☏ *703/838–4994* ⊕ *oha.alexandriava.gov/lyceum* ⊡ *$2* ⊘ *Mon.–Sat. 10–5, Sun. 1–5.*

❸ Old Presbyterian Meeting House. Built in 1774, the Old Presbyterian Meeting House was Presbyterian Alexandria's gathering place, not a "church," because the only "church" was the Church of England. Scottish patriots met there during the Revolution. Eulogies for George Washington were delivered here on December 29, 1799. In a corner of the churchyard is the tomb of an unknown soldier of the American Revolution. ⊠ *321 S. Fairfax St., Old Town* ☏ *703/549–6670* ⊕ *www. opmh.org* ⊡ *Free* ⊘ *Sanctuary weekdays 8:30–4; key available at church office at 316 S. Royal St.; Sun. services Sept.–June at 8:30 and 11; July and Aug. at 10.*

❷ Stabler-Leadbeater Apothecary. Once patronized by George Washington and the Lee family, Alexandria's Stabler-Leadbeater Apothecary is the third-oldest apothecary in the country (the oldest is reputedly in Bethlehem, Pennsylvania). Some believe that it was here, on October 17, 1859, that Lt. Col. Robert E. Lee received orders to lead Marines from the Washington Barracks to suppress John Brown's insurrection at Harper's Ferry (then part of Virginia). The shop now houses a small museum of 18th-, 19th-, and 20th-century apothecary artifacts, including one of the finest collections of apothecary bottles in the country (more than 800 bottles in all). The apothecary remained in business until 1932. ⊠ *105–107 S. Fairfax St., Old Town* ☏ *703/838–3852* ⊕ *www. apothecarymuseum.org* ⊡ *$5* ⊘ *Apr.–Oct., Tues.–Sat. 10–5, Sun. and Mon. 1–5; Nov.–Mar., Wed.–Sat. 11–4, Sun. 1–4, by guided tour only, tours 15 mins before and after the hr.*

WHERE TO EAT

$$$

AMERICAN

Fodor's Choice

★

✕ **Restaurant Eve.** Diners who visit star chef Cathal Armstrong's understated restaurant in charming Old Town pick between sitting in the bistro or the chef's tasting room. Comfortably contemporary in shades of pale moss and cinnamon, the bistro is known for plates such as bacon, egg, and cheese salad and pork-belly confit. Glossy wood floors and buttercup-yellow couches set the scene in the more intimate, expensive tasting room, where a five-course meal is $110 and a nine-course meal $150 per person. Here, look for the distinctive lobster crème brûlée, butter-poached halibut with leek cream, and fried apple with ricotta tart. Even a Bloody Mary gets new life here, with lemongrass and chilies.

King Street is the heart of historic Old Town Alexandria, Virginia, with lively restaurants and shops.

✉ *110 S. Pitt St., Old Town* ☎ *703/706–0450* ⊕ *www.restauranteve. com* 🖃 *AE, D, MC, V* ☺ *Closed Sun. No lunch Sat.* Ⓜ *King St.*

¢–$ ✗ **Rocklands.** This homegrown barbecue stop is known for its flavorful

BARBECUE pork ribs smoked over hickory and red oak. Sides like silky corn pud-

☺ ding, rich mac 'n' cheese, and crunchy slaw are as good as the meats, which cover everything from beef brisket and chopped pork barbecue to chicken and fish. Come early for dinner: they close at 8 PM daily. This outpost of the local chain caters to a sit-down, family crowd. ✉ *25 S. Quaker La., Old Town* ☎ *703/778–9663* ⊕ *www.rocklands. com* 🖃 *AE, MC, V.*

WHERE TO STAY

$$–$$$ 🏨 **Embassy Suites Old Town Alexandria.** Adjacent to Alexandria's land-

☺ mark George Washington Masonic Temple, this all-suites hotel sits across the street from the Metro station and around the corner from the Amtrak station. A free shuttle is available to transport you to the scenic Alexandria riverfront, which has shops and restaurants. The cooked-to-order breakfast is complimentary, as is the cocktail reception every evening. There's also a playroom for children. **Pros:** large rooms; across from Metro station. **Cons:** outside city; small pool which is often crowded; popular with school groups. ✉ *1900 Diagonal Rd., Old Town* ☎ *703/684–5900 or 800/362–2779* ⊕ *www.embassysuites.com* ⤺ *268 suites* ⌂ *In-room: kitchen (some), refrigerator, Wi-Fi. In-hotel: Wi-Fi, restaurant, pool, gym, laundry facilities, laundry service, parking (paid)* 🖃 *AE, D, DC, MC, V* ⎮◎⎮ *BP* Ⓜ *King Street.*

$$–$$$ **☵ Hotel Monaco Alexandria.** When you walk into Old Town's Hotel Monaco you might feel bad for those poor souls who made reservations elsewhere. But don't worry, the Adriatic blue walls, European and Moroccan travel props, and the cheerful and committed staff will cheer you up in no time. Inviting guest rooms pick up on this hotel's theme of "history" with fun details like faux snakeskin walls and chairs done in upholstery with the image of a local vintage map. While the Old Town location puts you outside the District, this historic neighborhood holds its own. Stroll down to the water and admire the D.C. view. ■TIP➔ Water bowls runneth over at the hotel's doggie happy hour on Tuesday and Thursday nights in summer. **Pros:** restaurant gets great reviews; bend-over-backwards attitude toward service; near many restaurants, shops, and sights; airport shuttle. **Cons:** not in D.C.; long walk to Metro. ⊠ 489 King St., Old Town ☎ 703/549–6080 ⊕ www.monaco-alexandria.com ⟳ 231 rooms, 10 suites ⚅ In room: safe, kitchen (some), refrigerator, DVD, Internet, Wi-Fi. In-hotel: restaurant, room service, pool, gym, laundry service, Wi-Fi, parking (paid), some pets allowed, no-smoking rooms ⊟ AE, D, DC, MC, V.

$$–$$$

Fodor's Choice

★

☵ Morrison House. The interesting architecture, parquet floors, crystal chandeliers, decorative fireplaces, and furnishings of Morrison House are so faithful to the Federal period (1790–1820) that it's often mistaken for a renovation rather than a structure built from scratch in 1985. The elegant hotel blends Early American charm with modern conveniences. Rooms are individually furnished, and some offer decorative fireplaces and four-poster beds. The popular Elysium Restaurant serves contemporary American cuisine. The hotel sits in the heart of Old Town Alexandria, eight blocks from the train and Metro stations. **Pros:** attentive staff; great piano bar; lots of charm. **Cons:** outside the city; no pool. ⊠ 116 S. Alfred St.,Old Town ☎ 703/838–8000 or 866/834–6628 ⊕ www.morrisonhouse.com ⟳ 45 rooms, 3 suites ⚅ In-room: Wi-Fi. In-hotel: Wi-Fi, restaurant, room service, bar, parking (paid) ⊟ AE, DC, MC, V Ⓜ King St.

$$$–$$$$ **☵ The Westin Alexandria.** The staff seems genuinely happy to see you come through the door at this brand-new hotel plopped down in a recently developed section of Old Town. Done in blues, wood tones, and imported Jerusalem stone, the lobby and public areas have something of a Frank Lloyd Wright feel, while the rooms offer standard Westin features like flat-screen TVs. It's a good option to get more for your travel dollar if you don't need or want to be in D.C., but it will take you around 25 minutes to get downtown by Metro, and the closest stop is about four blocks away. **Pros:** rooms have pretty views; close to airport and Metro. **Cons:** outside the city; half-hour walk to waterfront. ⊠ 400 Courthouse Sq., Old Town ☎ 703/253–8600 ⊕ www.westin.com/alexandria ⟳ 309 rooms, 10 suites ⚅ In-room: safe, refrigerator (some), Wi-Fi. In-hotel: restaurant, room service, bar, children's programs (ages 4–12), pool, gym, laundry service, Wi-Fi, parking (paid), some pets allowed, no-smoking rooms ⊟ AE, D, DC, MC, V.

C&O CANAL AND GREAT FALLS PARKS

In the 18th and early 19th centuries the Potomac River was the main transportation route between Cumberland, Maryland, one of the most important ports on the nation's frontier, and the seaports of the Chesapeake Bay. Coal, tobacco, grain, whiskey, furs, iron ore, and timber were sent down the Potomac to Georgetown and Alexandria, which served as major distribution points for both domestic and international markets.

Although it was a vital link with the country's western territories, the Potomac had some drawbacks as a commercial waterway: rapids and waterfalls along the 185 mi between Cumberland and Washington originally made it impossible for traders to travel the entire distance by boat. Just a few miles upstream from Washington the Potomac cascades through two such barriers: the breathtakingly beautiful Great Falls and the less dramatic but equally impassable Little Falls.

To help traders move goods between the eastern markets and the western frontier more efficiently, 18th-century engineers proposed that a canal with a series of elevator locks be constructed parallel to the river. George Washington founded a company to build the canal, and in 1802 (after his death) the firm opened the Patowmack Canal on the Virginia side of the river.

In 1828 construction of the Chesapeake & Ohio Canal began on the opposite side of the Potomac River. It eventually stretched from downtown Washington to Cumberland, Maryland. However, by the time it had opened, newer technology was starting to make canals obsolete. The Baltimore & Ohio Railroad, whose construction began the same day as the C&O, finally put the canal out of business in 1924.

C&O CANAL NATIONAL HISTORIC PARK, MARYLAND

Extends 13 mi west from Georgetown, including Great Falls Tavern.

C&O Canal National Historic Park originates in Georgetown and encloses a 184.5-mi towpath that ends in Cumberland, Maryland. This relic of America's canal-building era and a few structures are still there. Construction along the Maryland bank began in 1828, using the principles of the Erie Canal in New York. When construction ended in 1850, canals stretched from downtown Washington to Cumberland through 74 locks. The original plan to extend a canal to the Ohio River was superseded by the success of the Baltimore & Ohio (B&O) Railroad, which eventually put the canal out of business.

Construction of the C&O Canal and the B&O Railroad began on the same day, July 4, 1828. Initially, the C&O provided an economical and practical way for traders to move goods through the Washington area to the lower Chesapeake. During the mid-19th century, boats carried as much as a million tons of merchandise a year. But the C&O Canal suffered a flood in late spring 1889 and couldn't recover from the financial disaster that ensued. Ownership then shifted to the B&O Railroad, the canal's largest stockholder, and operation continued until 1924, when another flood ended traffic. The railroad transferred ownership of the canal to the federal government in 1938 to settle a $2 million debt.

In the 1950s a proposal to build a highway over the canal near Washington was thwarted by residents of the Palisades (between Georgetown and Glen Echo) and others concerned with the canal's history and legacy. Since 1971 the canal has been a national park, providing a window into the past and a marvelous place to enjoy the outdoors.

> **DID YOU KNOW?**
>
> The public restroom at the intersection of 17th Street and Constitution Avenue was originally a lock house of an earlier canal through Washington.

GETTING HERE AND AROUND

C&O Canal National Historic Park is along the Maryland side of the Potomac and is accessible by taking Canal Road or MacArthur Boulevard from Georgetown or by taking Exit 41 off the Beltway and then following the signs to Carderock. There are several roadside stops accessible from the southbound lanes of Canal Road where you can park and visit restored canal locks and lock houses.

BIKING, BOATING, HIKING, AND FISHING

The C&O Canal National Historic Park and its towpath are favorites of walkers, joggers, bikers, and canoeists. The path has a slight grade, which makes for a leisurely ride or hike. Most recreational bikers consider the 13 mi from Georgetown to Great Falls Tavern an easy ride; you need to carry your bike for only one short stretch of rocky ground near Great Falls. You can also take a bike path that parallels MacArthur Boulevard and runs from Georgetown to Great Falls Tavern. Storm damage has left parts of the canal dry, but many segments remain intact and navigable by canoe.

The Boat House at Fletcher's Cove, on the D.C. side of the Potomac, rents rowboats, canoes, and bicycles and sells tackle, snack foods, and D.C. fishing licenses. Here you can catch shad, perch, catfish, striped bass, and other freshwater species. Canoeing is allowed on the canal and, weather permitting, on the Potomac. There's a large picnic area along the riverbank. ⊠ *4940 Canal Rd., at Reservoir Rd., Georgetown* ☎ *202/244–0461* ⊕ *www.fletcherscove.com* ⊙ *Mar.–Nov., daily 7–7.*

The towpath along the canal in **Georgetown** passes remnants of that area's industrial past, such as the Godey Lime Kilns near the mouth of Rock Creek, as well as the fronts of numerous houses that date from 1810. At the Foundry Mall you can start a tour of the area on foot, by bike, or by mule-drawn boat.

At the **Georgetown Visitor Center,** National Park Service rangers and volunteers offer themed canal-boat rides and walking tours in spring, summer, and fall. The schedule of programs is published in a quarterly visitor guide available at the park. Or, you can call the day before you plan to visit to get the exact schedule. In winter the center is only open on weekends. Rangers are always on hand when the center is open to provide maps, information on what you can do that day, and canal history. ⊠ *1057 Thomas Jefferson St. NW, Georgetown* ☎ *202/653–5190* ⊕ *www.nps.gov/choh* ⊙ *Apr.–Oct., Wed.–Sun. 9–4:30; Nov.–Mar., weekends 10–4, staffing permitting.*

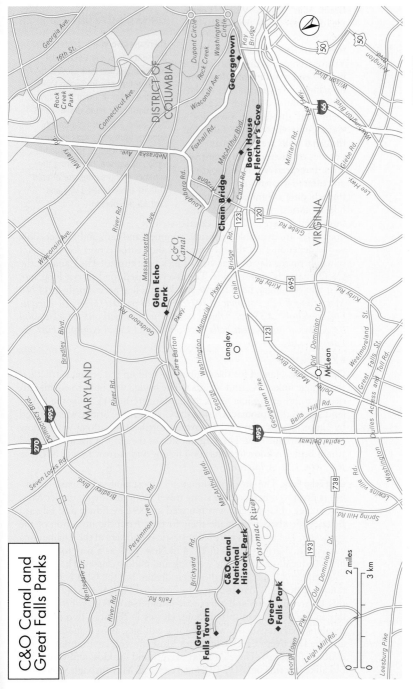

12

C&O Canal and
Great Falls Parks

Great Falls Tavern Visitor Center. Headquarters for the Palisades area of C&O Canal National Historic Park, the Great Falls Tavern Visitor Center has displays of canal history and photographs that show how high the river can rise. A platform on Olmsted Island, accessible from near the tavern, provides a spectacular view of the falls. On the canal walls are grooves worn by decades of friction from boat towlines. Interpretive ranger programs are offered year-round (in winter the schedule is limited), including hikes, nature walks, demonstrations, and lectures. Themed canal-boat rides are available in spring, summer, and fall, and the schedule varies depending on the month. Call the visitor center for the exact schedule on the day of your visit or pick up a copy of The Canaller, the C&O quarterly visitor guide. The tavern ceased food service long ago, so if you're hungry, head for the snack bar a few paces north. ⊠ *11710 MacArthur Blvd., Potomac* ☏ *301/299–3613 or 301/767–3714* ⊕ *www. nps.gov/choh* ✆ *$5 per vehicle, $3 per person without vehicle; good for 3 days at both Great Falls Park and C&O Canal National Historic Park* ☉ *Daily 9–4:45.*

> ## CANAL BOAT RIDES
>
> There are two visitor centers in the sections of the C&O Canal National Historic Park closest to Washington: one in Georgetown and the other at Great Falls Tavern. Both offer mule-drawn canal-boat rides Wednesday through Sunday, from early April through the end of October. The schedule varies by season, but during the summer months rides are offered at least three times a day and cost $5 per person.

EXPLORING

Chain Bridge. Named for the chains that held up the original structure, this bridge links D.C. and Virginia. The bridge was built to enable cattlemen to bring Virginia herds to the slaughterhouses along the Maryland side of the Potomac. During the Civil War the bridge was guarded by Union troops stationed at earthen fortifications along what's now Potomac Avenue NW. The Virginia side of the river in the area around Chain Bridge is known for its good fishing and narrow rapids. ⊠ *Glebe Rd., Rte. 120, Arlington.*

Glen Echo Park. The site of Washington's oldest amusement park (1911–68) is preserved here, as is a stone tower from the town's earlier days. The village of Glen Echo was founded in 1891 by Edwin and Edward Baltzley, brothers who made their fortune from the invention of the eggbeater. The brothers were enthusiastic supporters of the Chautauqua movement, a group begun in 1874 in New York as a way to promote liberal education among the working and middle classes. The brothers sold land and houses to further their dream, but the Glen Echo Chautauqua lasted only one season. The National Park Service administers this 10-acre property and offers year-round dances Friday through Sunday in the 1933 Spanish Ballroom, classes in the arts, two children's theaters, two art galleries with ongoing exhibits, artist demonstrations, and the Discovery Creek Children's Museum with environmental education workshops. There's a great playground for kids, and young and old alike can ride on a 1921 Dentzel carousel May through September.

The Glen Echo Park Partnership for Arts and Culture has a monthly calendar on its Web site ⊕ *www.glenechopark.org* that lists everything from art classes and performances to holiday workshops and artist showings. ⊠ *7300 MacArthur Blvd. NW, Glen Echo* ☎ *301/320–1400 park ranger office, 301/634–2222 events hotline* ⊕ *www.nps.gov/glec* ⊡ *Park free, carousel ride $1, Discovery Creek Museum $5, cost varies for dances and theater performances.*

GREAT FALLS PARK, VIRGINIA

23 mi northwest of Georgetown.

Part of the National Park System, Great Falls Park is on the Virginia side of the Potomac, across the river from C&O Canal National Historic Park.

GETTING HERE AND AROUND

To reach Great Falls Park, take the scenic and winding Route 193 (Exit 13 off Route 495, the Beltway) to Route 738 (Old Dominion Drive), and follow the signs. It takes about 25 minutes to drive to the park from the Beltway.

ESSENTIALS

Visitor Informaton **National Park Service** (⊠ *Georgetown Visitor Center, 1057 Thomas Jefferson St. NW, Georgetown* ☎ *202/653–5190* ⊕ *www.nps.gov/choh*).

EXPLORING

Great Falls Park. This park's 800 acres are a favorite place for outings. The steep, jagged falls roar into the narrow Mather Gorge—a spectacular scene. There are stunning views of the Potomac here, and a marker shows the river's high-water marks. The site, overlooking the falls, had an amusement park built by the railroad that operated from Georgetown, Rosslyn, and stations between during the early 1900s. Fifteen miles of trails lead past the old Patowmack Canal and among the boulders along the edge of the falls. You can fish (a Virginia or Maryland license is required for anglers 16 and older), climb rocks (climbers must register at the visitor center beforehand), or—if you're an experienced boater with your own equipment—go white-water kayaking (*below* the falls only). However, you can't camp overnight, drink alcoholic beverages, or wade or swim in the park. As is true all along this stretch of the river, the currents are deadly. Despite frequent signs and warnings, there are occasionally those who dare the water and drown.

A tour of the **Great Falls Park Visitor Center and Museum** takes 30 minutes. ■**TIP→** Staff members also conduct park walks year-round; the visitor-center tour and guided park walks are included in the price of admission. You're encouraged to take self-guided tours along well-marked trails, including one that follows the route of the old Patowmack Canal; the visitor center provides maps for the various trails. ⊠ *9200 Old Dominion Dr., McLean, VA* ☎ *703/285–2966 or 703/285–2965* ⊕ *www.nps. gov/grfa* ⊡ *$5 per vehicle, $3 per person without vehicle; good for 3 days at both Great Falls Park and C&O Canal National Historic Park; annual park pass $20* ⊘ *7* AM*–dark; visitor center mid-Oct.–mid-Mar., daily 10–4; mid-Mar.–mid-Oct., weekdays 10–5, weekends 10–6; hrs subject to change.*

NATIONAL HARBOR

12 mi south of downtown Washington, D.C., 2 mi west of Oxon Hill.

The National Harbor sprawls across 300 acres of the previously abandoned banks of the Potomac River across from Old Town Alexandria. Although it is still in development and construction is to be expected, the location already offers world-class accommodations, dining, and water-taxi tours to other hot spots on the Potomac.

GETTING HERE AND AROUND

The easiest way to reach National Harbor is by car via Interstate 295, Interstate 95, or Interstate 495. Water taxis from Old Town Alexandria or Georgetown are also convenient. Once in National Harbor, all you need to get around is a good pair of shoes.

ESSENTIALS

Visitor Information **National Harbor Marina Office** (⊠ *163 Waterfront St., National Harbor* ☎ *301/749–1582* ⊕ *www.nationalharbor.com*).

EXPLORING

American Market. Shop for local produce at this upscale outdoor market, which also features crafts such as hand-sewn dolls, hot glass jewelry, and folk-art prints. Pick up pecan butter tarts or applesauce sweet breads to appease your sweet tooth. ⊠ *137 National Plaza, across from the Gaylord National Resort* ⊕ *www.americanmarketnh.com* ⊙ *Memorial Day–mid.–Oct., Sat. 9–2.*

Art Whino. This exhibition showcases a collection of 133 artists specializing in pop-surrealism, lowbrow, and urban contemporary art. ⊠ *173 Waterfront St.* ☎ *301/567–8210* ⊕ *www.artwhino.com* ⊙ *Sun. and Mon. noon–6, Tues.–Sat. 10 AM–10 PM.*

Fodor's Choice **The Awakening.** This sculpture depicts a 100-foot giant struggling to ★ free himself from the earth. The display is actually five separate pieces buried in the ground, and was created by J. Seward Johnson. Its original location was at Hains Point in Alexandria, but it moved to National Harbor in 2008. ⊠ *National Plaza* ◺ *Free.*

Potomac Riverboat Company. Jump aboard a cruise ship from National Harbor's dock for a water tour of Mount Vernon, Alexandria, Georgetown, or the monuments of Washington. The ferry to Mount Vernon includes admission to the grounds. The company also operates hourly water taxis across the Potomac to the dock in Alexandria, where National Harbor's visitors can find even more shopping and dining options. On Thursday evenings, dogs can join their owners for a tour of Alexandria's seaport. ⊠ *Commercial Pier* ☎ *703/548–9000 or 877/511–2628* ⊕ *www.potomacriverboatco.com* ◺ *Taxis and tours $9–$38* ⊙ *Call ahead for hrs.*

WHERE TO EAT AND STAY

$$–$$$ ╳ **Moon Bay Coastal Cuisine.** Meander through the Gaylord National's SEAFOOD 18-story atrium, across a small wooden bridge, and straight into a historic Chesapeake fish market with bare wooden walls and a high ceiling exposing vents. Although it may look drab at first sight, Moon

12

Bay Coastal Cuisine serves upscale seafood dishes and boasts a topflight wine cave. Start off with the chopped salad or a selection of unique sushi and sashimi creations. Entrée options include pan-seared scallops served on a truffled potato plank and smothered in creamed corn with bacon. If you're up for a culinary challenge, order the crispy striped bass which comes whole with stone-ground cheddar grits. Moon Bay also offers a few non-seafood options, such as the cherry-maple-glazed pork loin. ✉ *201 Waterfront St.* ☎ *301/965–2000* 🞜 *AE, D, DC, MC, V.*

$$$$
AMERICAN
Fodor's Choice
★

✕ **Old Hickory Steakhouse.** The signature restaurant of the Gaylord National Resort, Old Hickory serves prime cuts of meat in an elegant setting. It's perfect for a romantic evening with the sun setting over the harbor or for an expense-account evening of cocktails and fine cigars out on the terrace. Order filet mignon or a 24-ounce porterhouse with four sauce choices, including béarnaise, bordelaise, green peppercorn, and bleu cheese; try the slightly crispy truffle fries on the side and you won't be disappointed. Old Hickory also has its own full-time Maître d'Fromage who presents guests with artisanal cheese from around the world. Fish and chicken options are available, but the real draw is the expensive steak. ✉ *201 Waterfront St.* ☎ *301/965–4000* 🧥 *Jacket required* 🞜 *AE, D, DC, MC, V.*

$$$$
🏨 **Gaylord National Resort & Convention Center.** The $800 million Gaylord National Resort & Convention Center is larger than life (and everything else around it). Guests at the 2,000-room resort can dine, shop, get pampered, and even go clubbing without ever leaving the property, which anchors the newly developed National Harbor waterfront in Prince George's County, Maryland. About a 25-minute ride to the National Mall, the Gaylord is shaping up to be a fun alternative for the D.C.-bound who don't mind commuting to museums and monuments. Room balconies opening on to the 230-foot-high glass atrium are a good place to watch the nightly dancing fountain show in the massive lobby below. **Pros:** 30-foot-wide media wall in the National Pastime Sports Bar and Grill; waterfront location. **Cons:** cab, car, or public bus necessary to get downtown; might be a bit too big for some; area still in development. ✉ *201 Waterfront St.* ☎ *301/965–2000 or 301/965–2001* ⊕ *www.gaylordnational.com* ⊏ *2,000 rooms* 🛏 *In-room: safe, kitchen (some), refrigerator, DVD (some), Wi-Fi. In-hotel: 4 restaurants, bars, pool, gym, spa, laundry service, Wi-Fi hotspot, parking (paid), no-smoking rooms* 🞜 *AE, D, DC, MC, V.*

MOUNT VERNON, WOODLAWN, AND GUNSTON HALL

Long before Washington, D.C., was planned, the shores of the Potomac had been divided into plantations by wealthy traders and gentleman farmers. Most traces of the colonial era were obliterated as the capital grew in the 19th century, but several splendid examples of plantation architecture remain on the Virginia side of the Potomac, 15 mi or so south of D.C. In one day you can easily visit three such mansions: Mount Vernon, the home of George Washington and one of the most popular sites in the area; Woodlawn, the estate of Washington's step-granddaughter; and Gunston Hall, the home of George Mason, author of the document that inspired the Bill of Rights. On hillsides overlooking the river, these estates offer magnificent vistas and make a bygone era vivid.

MOUNT VERNON, VIRGINIA

16 mi southeast of Washington, D.C., 8 mi south of Alexandria, VA.

Mount Vernon and the surrounding lands had been in the Washington family for nearly 90 years by the time George inherited it all in 1761. Before taking command of the Continental Army, Washington was a yeoman farmer managing the 8,000-acre plantation, of which more than 3,000 acres were under cultivation. He also oversaw the transformation of the main house from an ordinary farm dwelling into what was, for the time, a grand mansion.

GETTING HERE AND AROUND

To reach Mount Vernon by car from the Capital Beltway (Route 495), take Exit 1 and follow the signs to George Washington Memorial Parkway southbound. Mount Vernon is about 8.5 mi south. From downtown Washington, cross into Arlington on Key Bridge, Memorial Bridge, or the 14th Street Bridge and drive south on the George Washington Memorial Parkway past Ronald Reagan National Airport through Alexandria straight to Mount Vernon. The trip from D.C. takes about a half hour.

Getting to Mount Vernon by public transportation requires that you take both the Metro and a bus. Begin by taking the Yellow Line train to the Huntington Metro station. From here, take Fairfax County Connector Bus 101, 151, or 152 ($1.35 cash or $1.25 with SmarTrip card). Buses of each route leave about once an hour—more often during rush hour—and operate weekdays from about 4:30 AM to 9:15 PM, weekends from about 6:30 AM to 7 PM.

TOURS

BOAT TOURS The *Spirit of Mount Vernon* makes a pleasant trip from Washington down the Potomac to Mount Vernon from mid-March through mid-October. Boarding begins at 8:15 for the narrated cruise down the Potomac River. Once you arrive at Mount Vernon, you'll have more than three hours to tour the estate before reboarding at 1:30. Tickets cost $42 and include discounted admission to the estate.

BUS TOURS Gray Line runs four-hour trips to Mount Vernon (with a stop in Alexandria), departing daily at 8 AM from Union Station. A ticket is $55 and includes admission to the mansion and grounds. There's also a seasonal Mount Vernon-by-candlelight tour that departs at 5:30 on selected Friday and Saturday evenings in November and December for $50.

Tourmobile offers five-hour trips to Mount Vernon June 15 through Labor Day, departing from Arlington National Cemetery daily at 11 AM. Purchase tickets the same day of your tour, beginning at 8 AM at Arlington; the $30 ticket includes admission to the mansion. Advance reservations are not accepted and there is limited seating.

12

ESSENTIALS

Boat Information Spirit of Mount Vernon (⊠ *Pier 4, 6th and Water Sts. SW, Southeast, Washington, DC* ☎ *866/302–2469 boat reservations* ⊕ *www. spiritcruises.com*).

Bus Information Fairfax County Connector (☎ *703/339–7200* ⊕ *www.fairfax-connector.com*).

Bus Tour Information Gray Line (☎ *800/862–1400* ⊕ *www.graylinedc.com*).
Tourmobile (☎ *202/554–5100* ⊕ *www.tourmobile.com*).

EXPLORING

Mount Vernon. The estate's state-of-the-art Orientation Center and Museum and Education Center are not to be missed. George Washington comes to life through interactive displays, life-size models, action-adventure movies, short educational videos, and more than 500 artifacts on display for the first time. Perhaps the most awe-inspiring artifact is the terra-cotta bust of Washington that is believed to be the most accurate depiction of this great leader. And, since it was installed at his actual height, it almost seems to come to life. Other artifacts of note: Washington's sword, shoe and knee buckles, and his last will and testament. The 20-minute mini-epic film shown in the Orientation Center reenacts the pivotal moment in our country's history when Washington crossed the Delaware River. There's also a scale replica of the mansion and an incredible stained-glass window that depicts momentous times in Washington's life.

The red-roof house is elegant though understated, with a yellow pine exterior that's been painted and coated with layers of sand to resemble white-stone blocks. The first-floor rooms are quite ornate, especially the large formal dining room, with a molded ceiling decorated with agricultural motifs. Throughout the house are other smaller symbols of the owner's eminence, such as a key to the main portal of the Bastille—presented to Washington by the Marquis de Lafayette—and Washington's presidential chair. When you step into Washington's private sanctuary, the first-floor study, you can't help but imagine him sitting at his desk, reading overseer's reports, making entries in his diary, or referencing one of his 884 books that are displayed in the glass-enclosed bookshelves. As you tour the mansion, guides are stationed throughout the house to describe the furnishings and answer questions.

You can stroll around 45 of the estate's 500 acres. In addition to the mansion, highlights include four gardens with heirloom plants

> **THE VIEW OUT BACK**
>
> Beneath a 90-foot portico is George Washington's contribution to architecture and the real treasure of Mount Vernon: the home's dramatic riverside porch. The porch overlooks an expanse of lawn that slopes down to the Potomac. In springtime the view of the river (a mile wide where it passes the plantation) is framed by redbud and dogwood blossoms. United States Navy and Coast Guard ships salute ("render honors") when passing the house during daylight hours. Foreign naval vessels often salute, too.

Fodor's Choice
★

United States Navy and Coast Guard ships salute (render honors) when passing Mount Vernon during daylight hours.

dating to the 1700s and 13 trees that were planted by George Washington, slave quarters, smokehouse, kitchen, carriage house, greenhouse, and, down the hill toward the boat landing, the tomb of George and Martha Washington. There's also a pioneer farmer site: a 4-acre hands-on exhibit with a reconstruction of George Washington's 16-sided treading barn as its centerpiece. ■TIP→ Among the souvenirs sold at the plantation are stripling boxwoods that began life as clippings from bushes planted in 1798, the year before Washington died. A tour of the house and grounds takes about four hours. Private evening candlelight tours of the mansion with staff dressed in 18th-century costumes can be arranged. Throughout the year special events are held at the estate including festivals, holiday celebrations, walking tours, craft fairs, and children's storytelling sessions. Check the Web site when planning your visit.

MARTHA WASHINGTON: HOT OR NOT?

As hard as it may be to believe from the portraits of her in history books, Martha Washington was a hottie. Far from the frumpy, heavy-set woman we know as the first first lady, Martha wore sequined purple high heels on her wedding day, read romance novels, and had many admirers, not to mention a previous husband. A team of forensic anthropologists used a 1796 portrait of Mrs. Washington to digitally create an image of what she might have looked like in her 20s. The image inspired Michael Deas to create a portrait of the young first lady, which now hangs in the Education building at Mount Vernon.

George Washington's Distillery & Gristmill, located 3 mi from Mount Vernon on Route 235, is open daily April–October. During the guided tours, led by historic interpreters, you can meet an 18th-century miller, watch the water-powered wheel grind grain into flour just as it did 220 years ago, and learn techniques of distilling using five of the original copper stills. Tickets can be purchased either at the distillery and gristmill itself or at Mount Vernon's Main Gate. ⊠ *Southern end of George Washington Pkwy., Mount Vernon, VA* ☎ *703/780–2000* ⊕ *www.mountvernon.org* 🖾 *$15, gristmill $4, combination ticket $17* ☾ *Apr.–Oct., daily 10–5.*

BIKING

An asphalt bicycle path leads from the Virginia side of Key Bridge (across from Georgetown), past Ronald Reagan National Airport, and through Alexandria all the way to Mount Vernon. Bikers in moderately good condition can make the 16-mi trip in less than two hours. You can rent bicycles at several locations in Washington.

A great place to rent a bike is the Washington Sailing Marina (☎ *703/548–9027* ⊕ *www.washingtonsailingmarina.com)*, which is beside the Mount Vernon Bike Trail just past the airport. A 12-mi ride south will take you right up to the front doors of Mount Vernon. Cruiser bikes rent for $8 per hour or $25 per day. The marina is open 9–5 daily.

WOODLAWN, VIRGINIA

3 mi west of Mount Vernon, 15 mi south of Washington, D.C.

Woodlawn was once part of the Mount Vernon estate. From here you can still see traces of the bowling green that fronted Washington's home.

GETTING HERE AND AROUND

To drive to Woodlawn, travel southwest on Route 1 to the second Route 235 intersection (the first leads to Mount Vernon). The entrance to Woodlawn is on the right at the traffic light. From Mount Vernon, travel northwest on Route 235 to the Route 1 intersection; Woodlawn is straight ahead through the intersection.

To use public transportation, take Bus 151, 152, or 171 ($1.35 cash or $1.25 with SmarTrip card) from Huntington Metro station. Route 171 begins earlier and runs later than the other two buses and well beyond Woodlawn operating hours. Buses returning to the station have the same numbers but are marked HUNTINGTON.

ESSENTIALS

Bus Information Fairfax County Connector (☎ *703/339–7200* ⊕ *www. fairfaxconnector.com).*

EXPLORING

Woodlawn. This house was built for Washington's step-granddaughter, Nelly Custis, who married his favorite nephew, Lawrence Lewis. (Lewis had come to Mount Vernon from Fredericksburg to help Uncle George manage his five farms.) The Lewises' home, completed in 1805, was designed by Dr. William Thornton, a physician and amateur architect

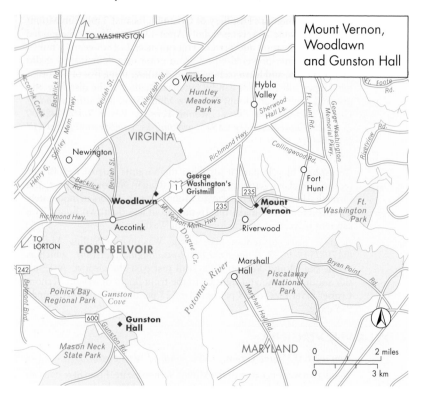

Mount Vernon,
Woodlawn
and Gunston Hall

from the West Indies who drew up the original plans for the U.S. Capitol. Like Mount Vernon, the Woodlawn house is constructed of native materials, including the clay for its bricks and the yellow pine used throughout its interior. ■TIP→ Built on a site selected by George Washington, the house has commanding views of the surrounding countryside and the Potomac River beyond. In the tradition of Southern riverfront mansions, Woodlawn has a central hallway that provides a cool refuge in summer. At one corner of the passage is a bust of George Washington set on a pedestal so the crown of the head is at 6 feet, 2 inches—Washington's actual height.

Woodlawn was once a plantation where more than 100 people, most of them slaves, lived and worked. As plantation owners, the Lewises lived in luxury. Docents talk about how the family entertained and how the slaves grew produce and prepared these lavish meals as well as their own. As intimates of the Washingtons' household, the Lewises displayed a collection of objects in honor of their illustrious benefactor. Many Washington family items are on display today. In 1957 the property was acquired by the National Trust for Historic Preservation, which had been operating it as a museum since 1951.

Also on the grounds of Woodlawn is the **Pope-Leighey House** (⊕ *www. popeleighey1940.org*). Frank Lloyd Wright designed his Usonian houses like this one as a means of providing affordable housing for people of modest means. It was built in 1940 and moved here from Falls Church, Virginia, in 1964. ✉ *9000 Richmond Hwy., Mount Vernon, VA* ☎ *703/780–4000* ⊕ *www.woodlawn1805.org* 🖻 *$8.50 for either Woodlawn or Pope-Leighey House, combination ticket $15* ⊘ *Mar.– Dec., Thurs.–Mon. 10–5; limited guided tours in Mar. because of annual needlework show; tours leave every ½ hr; last tour at 4.*

GUNSTON HALL, VIRGINIA

12 mi south of Woodlawn, 25 mi south of Washington, D.C.

Gunston Hall Plantation, down the Potomac from Mount Vernon, was the home of another important George: George Mason.

GETTING HERE AND AROUND

You'll have to use a car to get to Gunston Hall, because there is no bus stop within walking distance. Travel south on Route 1, 9 mi past Woodlawn to Route 242; turn left there and go 3.5 mi to the plantation entrance.

EXPLORING

Gunston Hall. Gentleman farmer George Mason was a colonel of the Fairfax militia and author of the Virginia Declaration of Rights, the model for the U.S. Bill of Rights, which called for freedom of the press, tolerance of religion, and other fundamental democratic principles. Mason was a framer of the Constitution but refused to sign the final document because it didn't stop the importation of slaves, adequately restrain the powers of the federal government, or include a bill of rights. Mason's objections spurred the movement for the inclusion of the Bill of Rights into the Constitution.

Mason's home was built circa 1755. ■TIP➡ The Georgian-style mansion has some of the finest hand-carved ornamented interiors in the country. It's the handiwork of the 18th-century's foremost architect, William Buckland, who also designed the Hammond-Harwood and Chase-Lloyd houses in Annapolis. Gunston Hall is built of brick, black walnut, and yellow pine. The style of the time demanded symmetry in all structures, which explains the false door set into one side of the center hallway. The house's interior, which has carved woodwork in styles from Chinese to Gothic, has been meticulously restored, with paints made from the original formulas and carefully carved replacements for the intricate mahogany medallions in the moldings. Restored outbuildings include a kitchen, dairy, laundry, and smokehouse. A schoolhouse has also been reconstructed.

The formal gardens, under excavation by a team of archaeologists, are famous for their boxwoods—some now 12 feet high—thought to have been planted during George Mason's time, making them among the oldest in the country. The Potomac is visible past the expansive deer park. Also on the grounds is an active farmyard with livestock and crop species; special programs, such as history lectures and hearth-cooking demonstrations, are offered throughout the year. ■TIP➡ A tour of Gunston Hall takes at least 45 minutes; tours begin at the visitor center, which includes a museum and gift shop. ✉ *10709 Gunston Rd., Mason Neck, VA* ☎ *703/550–9220* ⊕ *www.gunstonhall.org* 🎟 *$9* ⊙ *Daily 9:30–5; tours every half hour.*

ANNAPOLIS, MARYLAND

Although it has long since been overtaken by Baltimore as the major Maryland port, Annapolis is still a popular destination for pleasure boating. On warm, sunny days the waters off City Dock become center stage for an amateur show of powerboaters maneuvering through the heavy traffic. Annapolis's enduring nautical reputation derives largely from the presence of the U.S. Naval Academy: its midshipmen throng the city streets in white uniforms in summer and in navy blue in winter.

Annapolis also has a wealth of 18th-century architecture, including more surviving colonial buildings than any other place in the country. Maryland is the only state in which the homes of all its signers of the Declaration of Independence still stand. The houses are all in Annapolis, and you can tour two of the four—the homes of Samuel Chase and William Paca. Although chain stores and eateries are encroaching upon the old parts of town, the legacy of the historic buildings endures.

This history began in 1649, when a group of Puritan settlers moved from Virginia to a spot at the mouth of the Severn River, where they established a community called Providence. Lord Baltimore, who held the royal charter to settle Maryland, named the area around this town Anne Arundel County, after his wife. In 1684 Anne Arundel Town was established across from Providence on the Severn's south side. Ten years later, Anne Arundel Town became the capital of Maryland and was renamed Annapolis, for Princess Anne, who later became queen. It received its city charter in 1708 and became a major port, particularly for the export of tobacco. In 1774 patriots here matched their Boston counterparts (who had thrown their famous tea party the year before) by burning the *Peggy Stewart*, a ship loaded with taxed tea. Annapolis later served as the nation's first peacetime capital (1783–84).

GETTING HERE AND AROUND

The drive (east on U.S. 50 to the Rowe Boulevard exit) normally takes 35–45 minutes from Washington. During rush hour (weekdays 3:30–6:30 PM), however, it takes about twice as long. Also beware of Navy football Saturdays.

Parking spots on Annapolis's historic downtown streets are scarce, but there are some parking meters for $1 an hour (maximum two hours). You can park on residential streets free where allowable. You can pay $5 ($10 for recreational vehicles) to park at the Navy–Marine Corps Stadium (to the right of Rowe Boulevard as you enter town from Route 50), and ride a free Annapolis Transit shuttle bus downtown. Annapolis Transit also offers free shuttle transportation within the Historic Area. There are three parking garages in the downtown area with a $10 per day maximum; Sunday mornings from 6 AM to 1 PM parking is free.

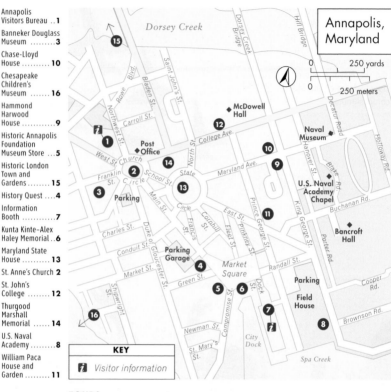

TOURS

BOAT TOURS Watermark Cruises runs boat tours that last from 40 minutes to 7½ hours and go as far as St. Michaels on the Eastern Shore, where you'll find a maritime museum, yachts, dining, and boutiques. Prices range from $12 to $70. Schooner *Woodwind* has two-hour sailing cruises aboard a 74-foot wooden staysail schooner up to four times daily (depending on season), except Monday, when, May 14–Labor Day, there's a sunset sailing only. Trips begin at $34.

BUS TOURS Discover Annapolis Tours leads one-hour or 40-minute narrated minibus tours ($18 or $14) that introduce the history and architecture of Annapolis. Tours leave from the visitor center or History Quest daily April through November and most weekends December through March.

WALKING TOURS The Historic Annapolis Foundation rents four self-guided walking tours that use audiotapes and maps: "Annapolis Highlights," "African-American Annapolis," "Rebels to Statesmen: Revolution in Annapolis," and "A City Divided–Annapolis During the Civil War." The cost for each is $10, and tickets can be purchased online or in person at History Quest. The Foundation's Web site lists several guided tours that are available year-round including carriage rides, trolley tours, and walkabouts with costumed guides.

ESSENTIALS

Boat Tour Information Schooner *Woodwind* (✉ *80 Compromise St., departs from Annapolis Marriott Hotel, Historic Area* ☎ *410/263–7837* ⊕ *www. schoonerwoodwind.com*). **Watermark Cruises** (✉ *City Dock, Historic Area, Box 3350* ☎ *410/268–7601 or 800/569–9622* ⊕ *www.watermarkcruises.com*).

Bus Tour Information Discover Annapolis Tours (☎ *410/626–6000* ⊕ *www. discover-annapolis.com*).

Walking Tour Information Historic Annapolis Foundation (✉ *99 Main St., Historic Area* ☎ *410/267–6656* ⊕ *www.annapolis.org*).

EXPLORING

TOP ATTRACTIONS

❶ **Annapolis & Anne Arundel County Conference & Visitors Bureau.** Start your visit at Annapolis's main visitor center. Here you can pick up maps and brochures or begin a guided tour. ✉ *26 West St., Historic Area* ☎ *410/280–0445 or 888/302–2852* ⊕ *www.visitannapolis.org* ☾ *Daily 9–5.*

❾ **Hammond-Harwood House.** Ninety percent of this 1774 home is origi-
★ nal. A fine example of colonial five-part Georgian architecture (a single block with two connecting rooms and wings on each side), the
Hammond-Harwood House is the only verifiable full-scale example of
William Buckland's work. It was also his final project, as he died the
year the house was completed. Exquisite moldings, cornices, and other
carvings appear throughout (note especially the garlands of roses above
the front doorway). The house was meant to be a wedding present from
Matthias Hammond, a planter and revolutionary, to his fiancée, who
jilted him before the house was finished. Hammond died a bachelor
in 1784. The Harwoods took over the house toward the turn of the
19th century. Today it's furnished with 18th-century pieces, and the
garden's plants also are reflective of the period. ■TIP➜ **Tours leave at
the top of the hour and are approximately 40 minutes; the last tour begins
at 4.** ✉ *19 Maryland Ave., Historic Area* ☎ *410/263–4683* ⊕ *www.
hammondharwoodhouse.org* ◈ *$6* ☾ *Apr.–Oct., Tues.–Sun. noon–5;
Nov.–Mar. open for group tours, special events, and select weekends
only; check ahead for opening times.*

❺ **Historic Annapolis Foundation Museum Store.** The Historic Annapolis Foundation operates its museum store in a warehouse that held supplies for
the Continental Army during the Revolutionary War. Here you can
shop, check out a diorama of the city's 18th-century waterfront, and
rent taped narrations for walking tours. ✉ *77 Main St., Historic Area*
☎ *410/268–5576* ⊕ *www.annapolis.org* ◈ *Free* ☾ *Mon.–Thurs. 10–6,
Fri. and Sat. 10–8, Sun. 11–6.*

⓯ **Historic London Town and Gardens.** This National Historic Landmark on
the South River is a short car ride from Annapolis. The 17th-century
tobacco port of London was made up of 40 dwellings, shops, and taverns; one of its landmarks was a magnificent three-story waterfront brick
house built by William Brown circa 1760 as an upscale tavern. London
disappeared in the late 18th century; its buildings were abandoned and
left to decay. It's now the site of an ongoing archaeological excavation.

In May, July, and September you can join in on an occasional dig day (call for schedule). Docents conduct 45- to 60-minute Historic Area tours; allow more time to wander the grounds, which include 8 acres of beautiful ornamental and woodland gardens. House tours leave on the hour (the last is at 3). Garden tours are self-guided. ⊠ *839 London-town Rd., Edgewater* ☎ *410/222–1919* ⊕ *www.historiclondontown. com* ⊠ *$10* ☉ *Mar.–Dec., Wed.–Sat. 10–4, Sun. noon–4.*

❹ History Quest. Historic Annapolis Foundation also operates this site, a three-story warehouse built in 1791 following a fire the preceding year that destroyed an entire block near City Dock. It's now an orientation center, with displays of Annapolis history, including photos of archaeological finds from the site that date back to the 17th century. Guided tours leave from here, and you can rent taped narrations for self-guided walking tours. ⊠ *99 Main St., Historic Area* ☎ *410/268–5576* ⊕ *www. annapolis.org* ⊠ *Free* ☉ *Sat. 9:30–7, Sun.–Fri. 9:30–5:30. Variable extended hrs in summer.*

❼ Information Booth. From April to October the information booth on City Dock, adjacent to the harbormaster's office, is open and stocked with maps and brochures. ⊠ *Dock St. parking lot, Historic Area* ☎ *410/280–0445.*

❻ Kunta Kinte–Alex Haley Memorial. A series of plaques along the waterfront recounting the story of African-Americans in Maryland leads to a sculpture group depicting the famed author reading to a group of children. Beside the statue, a stone with three plaques commemorates the 1767 arrival of the African slave immortalized in Alex Haley's *Roots.* ⊠ *Market Sq.* ⊕ *www.kintehaley.org.*

⓭ Maryland State House. Completed in 1780, the State House has the nation's largest wooden dome and is the oldest state capitol in continuous legislative use; it's also the only one in which the U.S. Congress has sat (1783–84). It was here that General George Washington resigned as commander in chief of the Continental Army and where the Treaty of Paris was ratified, ending the Revolutionary War. Both events took place in the Old Senate Chamber, which is filled with intricate woodwork (attributed to colonial architect William Buckland) featuring the ubiquitous tobacco motif. Also decorating this room is Charles Willson Peale's painting *Washington at the Battle of Yorktown,* a masterpiece by the Revolutionary War period's finest portrait artist. The Maryland Senate and House now hold their sessions in two other chambers in the building. Also on the grounds is the oldest public building in Maryland, the tiny redbrick Treasury, built in 1735. ■TIP→ Note that you must have a photo ID to enter the State House. ⊠ *State Circle, Historic Area* ☎ *410/974–3400* ⊕ *www.msa.md.gov/msa/stagser/s1259/131/html/ tours.html* ⊠ *Free* ☉ *Public areas weekdays 9–5, weekends 10–4; ½-hr tour usually at 11 and 3.*

❽ U.S. Naval Academy. Probably the most interesting and important site in Annapolis, the Naval Academy runs along the Severn River and abuts downtown Annapolis. Men and women enter from every part of the United States and many foreign countries to undergo rigorous study in subjects that range from literature to navigation to nuclear engineering.

Fodor'sChoice
★

12

The academy, established in 1845 on the site of a U.S. Army fort, occupies 329 waterfront acres. The centerpiece of the campus is the bright copper-clad dome of the interdenominational **U.S. Naval Academy Chapel** (☉ *Mon.–Sat. 9–4, Sun. 1–4*).

On the grounds, midshipmen (the term used for women as well as men) go to classes, conduct military drills, and practice for or compete in intercollegiate and intramural sports. **Bancroft Hall,** closed to the public, is one of the largest dormitories in the world—it houses the entire 4,200-member Brigade of Midshipmen. The **Statue of Tecumseh,** in front of Bancroft Hall, is a bronze replica of the USS *Delaware*'s wooden figurehead, "Tamanend." It's decorated by midshipmen for athletic events; during exams students pitch pennies into his quiver of arrows for luck. If you're there weekdays at noon in fair weather, you might see midshipmen muster outside Bancroft Hall for inspection and then march to lunch to the music of the Drum and Bugle Corps.

Adjoining Halsey Field House is the **USNA Armel-Leftwich Visitor Center** (⊠ *52 King George St., Historic Area* ☎ *410/293–8687*), which has exhibits of midshipman life, including a mock-up of a midshipman's room, and the *Freedom 7* space capsule flown by astronaut Alan Shepard, an academy graduate. Walking tours of the Naval Academy led by licensed guides leave from here. You must have a photo ID to be admitted through the academy's gates, and only cars with Department of Defense registration may enter the grounds. ⊕ *www.navyonline.com* 🎫 *Grounds tour $9* ☉ *USNA Armel-Leftwich Visitor Center: Mar.–Dec., daily 9–5; Jan. and Feb., daily 9–4. Guided walking tours generally leave Mon.–Sat. 10–3 and Sun. 12:30–3; call ahead to confirm tour times.*

⓫ ★ **William Paca House and Garden.** Paca (pronounced *Pay*-cuh) was a signer of the Declaration of Independence and a Maryland governor from 1782 to 1785. His house was completed in 1765, and its original garden was finished in 1772. Inside, the collection of American, English, and continental European artifacts and paintings is displayed in the same manner it might have been while the Paca family was in residence. The paint schemes and architectural details of the period between 1765 and 1780 have also been re-created. The adjacent 2-acre garden provides a longer perspective on the back of the house, plus worthwhile sights of its own: upper terraces, a Chinese-style bridge, a pond, a wilderness area, and formal arrangements of 18th-century heirloom plants. An inn, Carvel Hall, once stood in the gardens. After the inn was demolished in 1965, it took eight years to rebuild the gardens. ■TIP➜ You can take a self-guided tour of the garden, but to see the house you must go on the 45-minute docent-led tour, which leaves every hour at half past. The last tour leaves 1½ hours before closing. ⊠ *186 Prince George St., Historic Area* ☎ *800/603–4020 or 410/267–7619* ⊕ *www.annapolis.org* 🎫 *House and garden $8* ☉ *Apr.–Dec., Mon.–Sat. 10–5, Sun. noon–5; Feb. and Mar., Sat. 10–5, Sun. noon–5.*

WORTH NOTING

③ Banneker-Douglass Museum. This former church has changing exhibits, lectures, films, and literature about the African-American experience in Maryland. The church plays host to performances, lectures, and educational programs, and the addition houses both permanent and changing exhibits. Audio and visual presentations and hands-on exhibits make the museum engaging for kids, while also bringing home the hardships of slave life. It's named for Frederick Douglass, the 19th-century abolitionist, and Benjamin Banneker, a Maryland astronomer, surveyor, and mathematician who helped Pierre-Charles L'Enfant survey what would become Washington, D.C. ⊠ *84 Franklin St., Historic Area* ☎ *410/216–6180* ⊕ *www.bdmuseum.com* ☒ *Free* ☉ *Tues.–Sat. 10–4.*

QUICK BITES

The reconstructed **Market House Pavilion** (⊠ *City Dock, Historic Area*) is a collection of about 13 food stalls in the center of Market Square. Most are national chains that sell baked goods, fast food, and seafood. There's no seating, but you can stand and eat at a few counters. Another option is to picnic anywhere on the dock.

⑩ Chase-Lloyd House. Built by the prominent colonial architect William Buckland, the Chase-Lloyd House was begun in 1769 by Samuel Chase, a signer of the Declaration of Independence and future Supreme Court justice. Five years later the tobacco planter and revolutionary Edward Lloyd IV completed the work. The first floor is open to the public, and contains some impressive sections of Buckland's handiwork, including a parlor mantelpiece with tobacco leaves carved into the marble. (Buckland was famous for his interior woodwork; you can see more of it in the Hammond-Harwood House across the street and in George Mason's Gunston Hall in Mason Neck, Virginia.) The house, furnished with a mixture of 18th-, 19th-, and 20th-century pieces, has a staircase that parts dramatically around an arched triple window. For more than 100 years the house has served as a home for older women, who live upstairs. ⊠ *22 Maryland Ave., Historic Area* ☎ *410/263–2723* ☒ *$2* ☉ *Mar.–Dec., Tues.–Sat. 2–4.*

⑯ Chesapeake Children's Museum. Designed for preschool and early elementary aged children, the museum has indoor exhibits and outdoor gardens complete with nature trails and an underground railroad trail with posts explaining how slaves used nature in their quest for freedom. There are dress up areas, an arts-and-crafts station with recyclable materials, a 10-foot climbable boat, and a South American village setting, among other interactive exhibits. The museum is on Spa Creek, a five-minute drive from Annapolis' Historic Area. Check the Web site for special events and their monthly free admission deal. ⊠ *25 Silopanna Rd., Truxton Heights* ☎ *410/990–1993* ⊕ *www.theccm.org* ☒ *$3* ☉ *Thurs.–Tues. 10–4; Wed. only open to groups of 10 or more.*

12

FIRST AFRICAN-AMERICAN GRADUATE

In 1949 a man by the name of Wesley Brown made history as the U.S. Naval Academy's first African-American graduate. Five others had tried before him but were forced out by intense racism and violence. Brown also suffered greatly in his years at the academy. A group of upperclassmen tried to force him out by piling him up with unwarranted demerits and ensuring he was snubbed by his peers, but Brown never gave up. A veteran of World War II and the Korean and Vietnam wars, Brown served another 20 years in the Navy as a lieutenant commander in the Civil Engineering Corps before retiring in 1969. In 2008 the Naval Academy unveiled its $50 million Wesley Brown Field House, a state-of-the-art gymnasium that overlooks the Severn River—a fitting tribute to a man who is credited with not only helping to improve the Navy, but also the country. Today nearly one-fourth of the student body is comprised of minorities. To read more about Brown's fascinating story, check out *Breaking the Color Barrier,* by historian Robert J. Schneller Jr.

➋ **St. Anne's Church.** St. Anne's Episcopal parish was founded in 1692; King William III donated the Communion silver. The first St. Anne's Church, built in 1704, was torn down in 1775. The second, consecrated in 1792, burned down in 1858. Parts of the walls survived and were incorporated into the present structure, finished the following year. The churchyard contains the grave of the last colonial governor, Sir Robert Eden. ✉ *Church Circle, Historic Area* ☎ *410/267–9333* ⊕ *www.stannes-annapolis.org* ⊿ *Free* ☉ *Weekdays 6–6, Sat. 6–2; services on Sun., call for times.*

⑫ **St. John's College.** Since 1937 St. John's has been best known as the birthplace of the Great Books curriculum, which includes reading the works of great authors from Homer to Faulkner and beyond (it's also the alma mater of Francis Scott Key, lyricist of "The Star Spangled Banner"). All students at the college follow the same curriculum for four years, and classes are conducted as discussions rather than lectures. Climb the gradual slope of the long, brick-paved path to the impressive golden cupola of **McDowell Hall,** the third-oldest academic building in the country, just as St. John's is the third-oldest college in the country (after Harvard and William and Mary). St. John's grounds once held the last living Liberty Tree, under which the Sons of Liberty convened to hear patriots plan the revolution against England. Damaged in a 1999 hurricane, the 400-year-old tree was removed; its progeny stands to the left of McDowell Hall. The **Elizabeth Myers Mitchell Art Gallery** (☎ *410/626–2556*), on the east side of Mellon Hall, presents exhibits and special programs that relate to the fine arts. On King George Street is the **Carroll-Barrister House,** now the college admissions office. The house was built in 1722 at Main and Conduit streets and was moved onto campus in 1955. Charles Carroll (not the signer of the Declaration of Independence but his cousin), who helped draft Maryland's Declaration of Rights, was born here. ✉ *60 College Ave., at St. John's St., Historic Area* ☎ *410/263–2371* ⊕ *www.sjca.edu.*

⓮ Thurgood Marshall Memorial. Born in Baltimore, Thurgood Marshall (1908–93) was the first African-American Supreme Court justice and was one of the 20th century's foremost leaders in the struggle for equal rights under the law. Marshall won the decision in 1954's *Brown v. Board of Education,* in which the Supreme Court overturned the doctrine of "separate but equal." Marshall was appointed United States Solicitor General in 1965 and to the Supreme Court in 1967 by President Lyndon B. Johnson. The 8-foot statue depicts Marshall as a young lawyer. ⊠ *Lawyer's Mall, Rowe Blvd. and College Ave., Historic Area.*

WHERE TO EAT

In the beginning, there was crab: crab cakes, crab soup, whole crabs to crack. This Chesapeake Bay specialty is still found in abundance, but Annapolis has broadened its horizons to include eateries—many in the Historic District—that offer many sorts of cuisines. Ask for a restaurant guide at the visitor center.

HISTORIC AREA

$$–$$$ ✕ **Café Normandie.** Wood beams, skylights, and a four-sided fireplace
FRENCH   make this petite French restaurant homey. Out of the open kitchen comes an astonishingly good French onion soup, made daily from scratch. Bouillabaisse, puffy omelets, crepes, and seafood dishes are other specialties. The restaurant's breakfast, served only on weekends, includes poached eggs in ratatouille, eggs Benedict, seafood omelets, and crepes, waffles, and croissants. ⊠ *185 Main St., Historic Area* ☎ *410/263–3382* ▭ *AE, D, DC, MC, V.*

¢–$ ✕ **Chick and Ruth's Delly.** Deli sandwiches (named for local politicos),
AMERICAN burgers, subs, milk shakes, and other ice-cream concoctions are the bill of fare at this very busy counter-and-booth institution. Built in 1899, the edifice was a sandwich shop when Baltimoreans Chick and Ruth Levitt purchased it in 1965. They also ran a little boardinghouse with 12 rooms and only two bathrooms above the deli. It was renovated after a fire and became the Scotlaur Inn. ⊠ *165 Main St. Historic Area* ☎ *410/269–6737* ⊕ *www.chickandruths.com* ▭ *No credit cards.*

$–$$ ✕ **Joss Café & Sushi Bar.** It's small, noisy, and crowded, and you'll prob-
JAPANESE ably have to wait in line for a table at this sushi joint, but as Joss's fans will tell you, it's worth it. Aside from the incredibly fresh sushi, the tempuras are light and crisp, and the chicken katsu and beef teriyaki are tender and delicious. There's a good wine list, but a cold Kirin beer often hits the spot. ⊠ *195 Main St., Historic Area* ☎ *410/263–4688* ⊕ *www. josscafe-sushibar.com* ⩲ *Reservations not accepted* ▭ *AE, MC, V.*

¢–$ ✕ **Lemongrass.** What's not to love about a place that consistently serves
THAI   incredibly fresh and innovative Thai food at affordable prices? Sure it can get pretty busy on weekends and the noise level can be high, but the soothing colors and artwork that grace the walls help create a comfortable dining experience. Try the lettuce wraps with crispy ginger fish, followed by the lemongrass shrimp special and you won't be disappointed. ⊠ *167 West St., Historic Area* ☎ *410/280–0086* ⊕ *www. lemongrassannapolis.com* ▭ *AE, MC, V.*

$$–$$$
SEAFOOD

✕**Middleton Tavern.** Horatio Middleton began operating this "inn for seafaring men" in 1750; Washington, Jefferson, and Franklin were among its patrons. Today two fireplaces, wood floors, paneled walls, and a nautical theme make it cozy. Seafood tops the menu; the Maryland crab soup and pan-seared

12

Chesapeake Bay rockfish are standouts. Try the tavern's own Middleton Ale, perhaps during happy hour or during a weekend blues session in the upstairs piano bar. Brunch is served on weekends, and you can dine outdoors in good weather. At times this place can get very crowded. ⊠ *City Dock at Randall St., Historic Area* ☎ *410/263–3323* ⊕ *www. middletontavern.com* ⊟ *AE, D, DC, MC, V.*

$$
AMERICAN

✕**Rams Head Tavern.** Tour the tiny Fordham Brewing Company, housed inside this English-style pub. Then settle in for better-than-usual tavern fare (locals swear by the burgers), including spicy shrimp salad, crab cakes, and beer-battered shrimp, as well as more than 100 beers—30 on tap—from around the world. Brunch is served on Sunday. Nationally known folk, rock, jazz, country, and bluegrass artists perform at the Rams Head Tavern on Stage, a separate theater serving drinks and meals. ⊠ *33 West St., Historic Area* ☎ *410/268–4545* ⊕ *www. ramsheadtavern.com* ⊟ *AE, D, DC, MC, V.*

$$$–$$$$
SEAFOOD

✕**Treaty of Paris Restaurant.** This is where Benjamin Franklin, John Adams, and John Jay celebrated the end of the American Revolution, and 225 years later you can celebrate as they did at this handsome restaurant decorated with period reproduction furniture and fabrics. For dinner you can select from a variety of continental dishes, fine steaks, or seafood. Sunday brunch is legendary, with buffet and carving stations laden with fresh fruit, omelets, crepes, pastries, and seafood filling the entire dining room. ⊠ *Maryland Inn, 58 State Circle, Historic Area* ☎ *410/263–2641* ⊟ *AE, D, DC, MC, V.*

AROUND ANNAPOLIS

$–$$
CAFÉ

✕**49 West Coffeehouse and Gallery.** This is the kind of spot you might wish was in your neighborhood—a cozy place for hanging out with friends while listening to talented musicians. In what was once a hardware store, one interior wall is exposed brick and another has art for sale by local artists. This tiny, eclectic, casual eatery serves wines, microbrewed beer, and mixed drinks as well as meals. Cover charges begin at $6. ⊠ *49 West St., West Side* ☎ *410/626–9796* ⊕ *www.49westcoffeehouse. com* ⊟ *AE, DC, MC, V.*

$$–$$$
SEAFOOD

✕**Cantler's Riverside Inn.** Boat owners tie up at the dock of this local institution, which opened in 1974. Inside, there are wooden blinds and floors, and nautical artifacts laminated beneath tabletops. Food is served on disposable dinnerware atop butcher paper, which makes it that much easier to get down and dirty cracking open and diving into just-steamed Chesapeake blue crabs. Outdoor dining is available seasonally. Cantler's serves other seafood dishes, but the crabs are the best.

✉ *458 Forest Beach Rd., Mill Creek* ☎ *410/757–1311* ⊕ *www.cantlers. com* ▭ *AE, D, DC, MC, V.*

$$$
AMERICAN

✕ **Carrol's Creek.** Walk, catch a water taxi from City Dock, or drive over the Spa Creek drawbridge to this local favorite in Eastport. Whether you dine indoors or out, the view of historic Annapolis and its harbor is spectacular. The all-you-can-eat Sunday brunch ($22) is worth checking out, as are the seafood specialties. Any of the entrées, including the herb-encrusted rockfish fillet ($29) or macadamia-encrusted mahi-mahi ($24), can be turned into a four-course meal, with the addition of soup, salad, and dessert for $14 more. ✉ *410 Severn Ave., Eastport* ☎ *410/263–8102* ⊕ *www.carrolscreek.com* ▭ *AE, D, DC, MC, V.*

$$$–$$$$
SEAFOOD

✕ **O'Leary's Seafood Restaurant.** Locals flock to this casually elegant restaurant on the water when they want to wow out-of-town guests with fantastic seafood. For starters, try the lobster cappuccino, seared calamari, or crispy Virginia oysters. The seared rockfish with shell beans and melted leeks or the prosciutto-wrapped tuna are just two of the seasonal specialties. Gracious and attentive service, a nice wine list, and a room decorated with mustard-color walls and photos of old Annapolis make this one of the city's top dining spots. ✉ *310 3rd St., Eastport* ☎ *410/263–0884* ⊕ *www.olearysseafood.com* ♨ *Reservations essential* ▭ *AE, D, DC, MC, V.*

WHERE TO STAY

There are many places to stay near the heart of the city, as well as area bed-and-breakfasts and chain motels a few miles outside town. Prices vary considerably. They rise astronomically when the Maryland legislature is in session and for "Commissioning Week" at the Naval Academy (late May). A unique "Crabtown" option is Boat & Breakfasts, in which you sleep, eat, and cruise on a yacht or schooner. Be sure to book ahead, and be aware that this is not for the faint of purse. Contact the visitor center for information.

Two reservation services operate in Annapolis. **Annapolis Accommodations** (✉ *41 Maryland Ave., Historic Area* ☎ *410/263–3262* ⊕ *www. stayannapolis.com*) specializes in medium- to long-term rentals. Their office is open 9–5 weekdays. **Annapolis Bed & Breakfast Association** (⊕ *www.annapolisbandb.com*) books lodging in 13 bed-and-breakfasts in the old section of town, which has many restaurants and shops, and in Eastport.

HISTORIC AREA

$–$$

⊞ **Governor Calvert House.** This home facing the State House was built in 1727 and lived in by two former Maryland governors. During its 1984 expansion workers discovered a hypocaust (central heating system) in the basement: you can view it through a section of the floor. Rooms in the historic section are furnished with period antiques; newer rooms have period reproductions. This is a no-smoking property. **Pros:** historic charm; great location; wonderful views of State House or Colonial Gardens from rooms. **Cons:** some of the rooms, especially in the historic section, are small. ✉ *58 State Circle, Historic Area* ☎ *410/263–2641 or 800/847–8882* ⊕ *www.historicinnsofannapolis.com* ⬐ *54 rooms*

In-room: Wi-Fi. In-hotel: laundry service, parking (paid) ⊟ AE, D, DC, MC, V.

$–$$ **Maryland Inn.** If walls could talk, imagine what you'd hear as you walk through the halls at this elegant inn. Eleven delegates of the 1786 U.S. Congress stayed here, and legend has it that Benjamin Franklin and John Adams enjoyed a libation or two every so often at the inn's tavern. Many of the guest rooms date back to the Revolutionary War era (the wooden porches and marble-tile lobby are Victorian). Mahogany furniture and a velvet wing chair rest on aqua carpeting in the guest rooms, which also have floral wallpaper and draperies and many antique furnishings. This is one of the three Historic Inns of Annapolis; register at the Governor Calvert House. **Pros:** historic charm; great location. **Cons:** check-in is at the Governor Calvert House; some rooms are small. ⊠ 16 Church Circle, entrance on Main St., Historic Area ☎ 410/263–2641 or 800/847–8882 ⊕ www.historicinnsofannapolis.com ⟿ 39 rooms, 5 suites In-room: kitchen (some), Wi-Fi. In-hotel: restaurant, bar, laundry service, parking (paid) ⊟ AE, D, DC, MC, V.

$–$$ **Robert Johnson House.** One of the three Historic Inns of Annapolis, this hotel is actually three cleverly integrated 18th-century houses that overlook the State House and Governor's Mansion. Some guest rooms are furnished with 19th-century antiques and four-poster beds; others are furnished with reproductions. Register at the Governor Calvert House. This is a no-smoking property. **Pros:** historic charm; great location overlooking State House and Governor's Mansion; beautiful antique furnishings. **Cons:** check-in is at the Governor Calvert House; some rooms are small. ⊠ 23 State Circle, Historic Area ☎ 410/263–2641 or 800/847–8882 ⊕ www.historicinnsofannapolis.com ⟿ 26 rooms In-room: Wi-Fi. In-hotel: laundry service, parking (paid) ⊟ AE, D, DC, MC, V.

¢–$ **Scotlaur Inn.** You'll feel like a member of the family when you walk into this friendly bed-and-breakfast in the heart of the Historic District. On the two floors above Chick and Ruth's Delly (named after the parents of the owner, Ted Levitt), you'll find 10 rooms papered in pastel colonial prints with simple, but very comfortable furnishings. The beds are topped with fluffy comforters, teddy bears, and lots of pillows. Chandeliers in each room and marble floors in the private bathrooms bring this place a long way from its first days as a boardinghouse. Check-in and breakfast are in the deli downstairs. **Pros:** old-fashioned charm at a great price; within walking distance of all major sites; breakfast included. **Cons:** rooms are small; minimum stay on weekends. ⊠ 165 Main St., Historic Area ☎ 410/268–5665 ⊕ www.scotlaurinn.com ⟿ 10 rooms In-hotel: Wi-Fi, restaurant ⊟ MC, V ⦿| BP.

WEST SIDE

$$$–$$$$ **Annapolis Marriott Waterfront.** You can practically fish from your room at the city's only waterfront hotel. Rooms are designed in warm earth-tone colors and have balconies over the water or large windows with views of the harbor or the Historic District. A handful of rooms even have two-person whirlpool tubs in the bedroom. Pusser's, the outdoor bar by the harbor's edge, is popular in nice weather. Prices vary considerably depending upon the time of year and day of the week. **Pros:** views; waterfront location; rooms with whirlpool tubs; free bike rentals; free

newspaper delivery; 74-foot schooners docked on property offer harbor cruises. **Cons:** pricey during the summer months; rooms overlooking entrance are noisy. ⊠ *80 Compromise St., West Side* ☎ *410/268-7555 or 800/336-0072* ⊕ *www.annapolismarriott.com* ↝ *150 rooms* ⚼ *In-room: Wi-Fi. In-hotel: restaurant, bars, gym, concierge, laundry service, parking (paid), no-smoking rooms* ⊟ *AE, D, DC, MC, V.*

AROUND ANNAPOLIS

$–$$ 🖼 **Hampton Inn and Suites.** There's a fireplace, coffee bar, and pool table (upstairs) in the two-floor lobby of this hotel, which is minutes from historic Annapolis. Rooms are traditional, and the apartment-style suites have fully equipped kitchens. A free hot breakfast is served daily in the lobby. **Pros:** suites are ideal for families; comfortable beds; nice breakfasts. **Cons:** no shuttle service provided to Historic Area. ⊠ *124 Womack Dr., Parole* ☎ *410/571-0200* ⊕ *www.hamptoninn.com* ↝ *86 rooms, 31 suites* ⚼ *In-room: kitchen (some), microwaves, refrigerators, Internet. In-hotel: pool, gym, laundry facilities, laundry service, public Wi-Fi* ⊟ *AE, D, DC, MC, V* ⵑ◯ⵑ *CP.*

$–$$ 🖼 **Westin Annapolis.** The newest addition to the Annapolis hotel scene, this contemporary beauty, with a brick exterior, Palladian-style windows, and columned portico, is located about a mile from the Maryland State House. Part of a planned development that will include low-rise office and condominium buildings, a retail complex and a performing-arts center, the property already includes a Morton's Steakhouse, Starbuck's, and the upscale Azure Restaurant and Lounge. The lobby is serene, with marble floors, abstract art, floor-to-ceiling windows, and modern furniture in greens, blues, and browns. **Pros:** new hotel; free bikes for guests; great restaurants; beds are incredibly comfortable; heated indoor pool; dog beds available. **Cons:** a bit of a walk to Historic Area; charge of $9.95 per day for in-room Wi-Fi; parking costs $10 per day for self or $23 for valet. ⊠ *100 Westgate Cir., Uptown* ☎ *410/972-4300 or 888/627-8994* ⊕ *www.starwood.com/westin* ↝ *225 rooms* ⚼ *In-room: Wi-Fi. In-hotel: 2 restaurants, room service, pool, gym, spa, parking (paid), some pets allowed, no-smoking rooms* ⊟ *AE, D, DC, MC, V.*

Travel Smart Washington, D.C.

WORD OF MOUTH

"If you're flying into one of the airports around D.C., pick up a free *Washington Flyer* magazine that are in stands at various places throughout. They have a fantastic map of the metro D.C. area in the back. It also has a map of the Metro system. Tear those pages out and carry them around with you."

—MyownHeroine

"The Five Guys (best burgers ever) at National Airport is open early and has breakfast sandwiches and their superior burgers I think starting at 6:00 AM. Yum. (Yes, the burgers are so good I will eat one at 6:00 AM.)"

— BlueSwimmer

www.fodors.com/community

GETTING HERE AND AROUND

Although it may not appear so at first glance, there's a system to addresses in D.C., albeit one that's a bit confusing for newcomers. The city is divided into the four quadrants of a compass (NW, NE, SE, SW), with the U.S. Capitol at the center. Because the Capitol doesn't sit in the exact center of the city, Northwest is the largest quadrant. Northwest also has most of the important landmarks, although Northeast and Southwest have their fair share. The boundaries are North Capitol Street, East Capitol Street, South Capitol Street, and the National Mall.

If someone tells you to meet them at 6th and G, ask them to specify the quadrant, because there are actually four different 6th and G intersections (one per quadrant). Within each quadrant, numbered streets run north to south, and lettered streets run east to west (the letter J was omitted to avoid confusion with the letter I). The streets form a fairly simple grid—for instance, 900 G Street NW is the intersection of 9th and G streets in the NW quadrant of the city. Likewise, if you count the letters of the alphabet, skipping J, you can get a good approximation of an address for a numbered street. For instance, 1600 16th Street NW is close to Q Street, Q being the 16th letter of the alphabet if you skip J.

As if all this weren't confusing enough, Major Pierre L'Enfant, the Frenchman who originally designed the city, threw in diagonal avenues recalling those of Paris. Most of D.C.'s avenues are named after U.S. states. You can find addresses on avenues the same way you find those on numbered streets, so 1200 Connecticut Avenue NW is close to M Street, because M is the 12th letter of the alphabet when you skip J.

❚ AIR TRAVEL

A flight to D.C. from New York takes a little less than an hour. It's about 1½ hours from Chicago, 3 hours from Denver or Dallas, and 5 hours from San Francisco. Passengers flying from London should expect a trip of about 6 hours. From Sydney it's an 18-hour flight.

Airline Contacts AirTran (☎ 800/825-8538 ⊕ www.airtran.com). **American Airlines/ American Eagle** (☎ 800/433-7300 ⊕ www. aa.com). **Continental Airlines** (☎ 800/523-3273 ⊕ www.continental.com). **Delta Airlines** (☎ 800/221-1212 ⊕ www.delta.com). **jetBlue** (☎ 800/538-2583 ⊕ www.jetblue.com). **Southwest Airlines** (☎ 800/435-9792 ⊕ www. southwest.com). **United Airlines** (☎ 800/864-8331 ⊕ www.united.com). **US Airways** (☎ 800/428-4322 ⊕ www.usairways.com).

Airlines and Airports Airline and Airport Links.com (⊕ www.airlineandairportlinks.com).

Airline Security Issues Transportation Security Administration (⊕ www.tsa.gov).

Air Travel Resources in Washington, D.C. U.S. Department of Transportation Aviation Consumer Protection Division (☎ 202/366-2220 ⊕ http://airconsumer.ost.dot.gov).

AIRPORTS

The major gateways to D.C. are **Ronald Reagan Washington National Airport (DCA)** in Virginia, 4 mi south of Downtown Washington; **Dulles International Airport (IAD)**, 26 mi west of Washington, D.C.; and **Baltimore/Washington International–Thurgood Marshall Airport (BWI)** in Maryland, about 30 mi to the northeast.

Reagan National Airport is closest to Downtown D.C., and has a Metro stop in the terminal. East Coast shuttles and shorter flights tend to fly in and out of this airport. However, the Mid-Atlantic region is prone to quirky weather that can snarl air traffic, especially at Reagan National.

Dulles is configured primarily for long-haul flights. BWI offers blended service, with its many gates for no-frills Southwest Air, as well as international flights. Although the Metro doesn't serve Dulles and BWI, there is affordable and convenient public transportation to and from each airport. Prices vary between each of the three area airports, so be sure to compare fares before booking your flights.

■ **TIP→** Long layovers don't have to be only about sitting around or shopping. These days they can be about burning off vacation calories. Check out ⊕ www.airportgyms.com for lists of health clubs that are in or near many U.S. and Canadian airports.

Airport Information Baltimore/Washington International-Thurgood Marshall Airport (BWI ☎ 410/859–7100 ⊕ www.bwiairport. com). Dulles International Airport (IAD ☎ 703/572–2700 ⊕ www.metwashairports. com/Dulles). Ronald Reagan Washington National Airport (DCA ☎ 703/417–8000 ⊕ www.metwashairports.com/National).

GROUND TRANSPORTATION: REAGAN NATIONAL (DCA)

By Car: Take the George Washington Memorial Parkway north for approximately 1 mi. Exit on I–395 North; bear left onto US-1 North toward Downtown. For the city center, turn left on Madison Drive NW and turn right on 15th Street NW. The drive takes 20–30 minutes, depending on traffic and your destination.

By Metro: The Metro station is within easy walking distance of Terminals B and C, and a free airport bus shuttles between the station and Terminal A. The Metro ride Downtown takes about 20 minutes and costs about $1.35, depending on the time of day and your final destination.

By Shuttle: SuperShuttle, a fleet of bright blue vans, will take you to any hotel or residence in the city. The length of the ride varies, depending on traffic and the number of stops. The approximately 20-minute ride from Reagan National to Downtown averages $14.

TAXI TIP

If you plan to take a cab from Reagan National Airport, note that a $1.75 surcharge is added to the fare. There are additional charges for baggage handling by the driver, luggage pieces in the trunk, and more than one passenger. Be aware that unscrupulous cabbies prey on out-of-towners. If the fare seems astronomical, get the driver's name and cab number and threaten to call the D.C. Taxicab Commission.

By Taxi: Expect to pay $10–$15 to get from National to Downtown.

Contacts SuperShuttle (☎ 800/258–3826 or 202/296–6662 ⊕ www.supershuttle.com). **Washington Metropolitan Area Transit Authority** (☎ 202/637–7000, 202/638–3780 TTY ⊕ www.wmata.com).

GROUND TRANSPORTATION: BALTIMORE/WASHINGTON INTERNATIONAL (BWI)

By Car: Exit BWI and follow I-95 West. Take Exit 2B to MD-295 South for 24 mi; exit on US-50 West toward Washington. Continue on New York Avenue for about 3 mi; continue on Mount Vernon Place NW for 2 mi. Continue on Massachusetts Avenue NW; turn left on Vermont Avenue NW at Thomas Circle. Turn right on K Street NW; take a left on 17th Street NW and you're now basically in the city center. Distance is about 34 mi and should take 50–60 minutes.

By Public Transit: Amtrak and Maryland Rail Commuter Service (MARC) trains run between BWI and Washington, D.C.'s Union Station from around 6 AM to 10 PM. The cost of the 30-minute ride is $9–$44 on Amtrak and $6 on MARC, which runs only on weekdays. A free shuttle bus transports passengers between airline terminals and the train station (which is in a distant parking lot).

Washington Metropolitan Area Transit Authority (WMATA) operates express bus service (Bus B30) between BWI and the Greenbelt Metro station. Buses run between 6 AM and 10 PM. The fare is $3.10.

By Shuttle: SuperShuttle will take you to any hotel or residence in the city. The ride from BWI, which takes approximately 60 minutes, averages $37.

By Taxi: The fare from BWI is about $90.

Contacts Amtrak (📞 800/872-7245 ⊕ www. amtrak.com). Maryland Rail Commuter Service (📞 410/539-5000, 410/539-3497 TTY, 866/743-3682 ⊕ www.mtamaryland.com). SuperShuttle (📞 800/258-3826 or 202/296-6662 ⊕ www.supershuttle.com). Washington Metropolitan Area Transit Authority (📞 202/637-7000, 202/638-3780 TTY ⊕ www. wmata.com).

GROUND TRANSPORTATION: DULLES (IAD)

By Car: From Dulles Airport, exit onto Dulles Airport Access Road and follow this for 14 mi; merge onto VA-267 East. Merge onto I–66 East; follow this for approximately 6 mi and exit to the left on E Street Expressway. Take the ramp to E Street NW. Total distance from the airport to Downtown is about 27 mi and should take about 45 minutes.

By Public Transit: Washington Flyer links Dulles International Airport and the West Falls Church Metro station. The 20-minute ride is $10 one-way and $18 round-trip for adults, free for children under six. Buses run every half hour from 5:45 AM to 10:15 PM. All coaches are accessible to those in wheelchairs. Fares may be paid with cash or credit card at the ticket counter near Door 4 at the Arrivals/Baggage Claim Level. Board the bus just outside the door.

The Washington Metropolitan Area Transit Authority (WMATA) operates express bus service between Dulles and several stops in Downtown D.C., including the L'Enfant Plaza Metro station. Bus 5A, which costs $3.10, runs every hour between 5:30 AM and 11:30 PM. Make sure to have the exact fare, as drivers cannot make change. Or, you can buy a rechargeable SmarTrip card that you can use while in D.C.

By Shuttle: The roughly 45-minute ride from Dulles on the SuperShuttle runs $29.

By Taxi: The fare from Dulles is about $50–$60.

Contacts SuperShuttle (📞 800/258-3826 or 202/296-6662 ⊕ www.supershuttle.com). Washington Flyer (📞 888/927-4359 ⊕ www. washfly.com). Washington Metropolitan Area Transit Authority (📞 202/637-7000, 202/638-3780 TTY ⊕ www.wmata.com).

▮ BUS TRAVEL

REGIONAL BUSES

Several bus lines run between China-town in New York City and Chinatown in Washington, D.C., including BOLT-BUS, Megabus, Today's Bus, Tripper Bus, and Vamoose. All the buses are clean, the service satisfactory and the price can't be beat. Believe it or not, with advance planning, you might be able to get a round-trip ticket for just $2. Several of the bus lines offer power outlets, Wi-Fi, and a frequent-rider loyalty program. GotoBus, is an online booking agent that sells bus tickets and tours offered by several bus lines. It's a fast and easy way to compare prices.

Information BOLTBUS (✉ 11th and G St. NW 📞 877/265-8287 ⊕ www.boltbus.com). GotoBus.com (📞 202/408-8200 ⊕ wwwgotobus.com). Megabus (✉ Parking lot H, opposite 10th St. NW 📞 877/462-6342 ⊕ www.megabus.com). Today's Bus (✉ 715 H St. NW 📞 202/408-8200 ⊕ www.todaysbus. com). Tripper Bus (📞 877/826-3874 ⊕ www. tripperbus.com). Vamoose (✉ 610 I St. NW 📞 877/393-2828 ⊕ www.vamoosebus.com).

CITY BUSES

Most of the sightseeing neighborhoods (the Mall, Capitol Hill, Downtown, Dupont Circle) are near Metro rail stations, but a few (Georgetown, Adams Morgan) are more easily reached by the red, white, and blue buses operated by the Washington Metropolitan Area Transit Authority. The No. 42 bus travels from the Dupont Circle

Metro stop to and through Adams Morgan. Georgetown is a hike from the closest Metro rail station, but you can take a Georgetown Metro Connection shuttle to any Metrobus stop from the Foggy Bottom or Dupont Circle Metro stations in D.C. or the Rosslyn Metro station in Virginia. The D.C. Circulator is another option for getting around the city; it has five routes and charges $1. The Convention Center–Southwest Waterfront, Union Station–Navy Yard via Capitol Hill, and Woodley Park–Adams Morgan–McPherson Square Metro routes cut a path from north to south; the Georgetown–Union Station route goes east to west; operating on weekends only, is the Smithsonian–National Gallery Loop, which circles the National Mall.

Complete bus and Metro maps for the metropolitan D.C. area, which note museums, monuments, theaters, and parks, can be picked up free of charge at the Metro Center sales office.

FARES AND TRANSFERS

All regular buses within the District are $1.35; express buses, which make fewer stops, are $3.10. For every adult ticket purchased, two children under the age of four travel free. Children five and older pay the regular fare. You'll save 10¢ by using a SmarTrip card, a plastic card that holds any fare amount. The fare is deducted as you board the bus. You'll also be able to transfer bus-to-bus for free within a three-hour period with this card.

To transfer Metro-to-bus, take a pass from the rail-to-bus-transfer machine in the Metro station after you go through the turnstile and before you board your train. When you board the bus, you'll pay a transfer charge (45¢ on regular Metrobus routes and $2.20 on express routes). There are no bus-to-Metro transfers.

D.C. Circulator passengers can pay cash when boarding (exact change only) or use Metro Farecards, SmarTrip cards, and all-day passes. Tickets also may be purchased at fare meters or multispace parking meters on the sidewalk near Circulator stops. Machines accept change or credit cards and make change. You only have to wait about 5–10 minutes at any of the stops for the next bus.

PAYMENT AND PASSES

Buses require exact change in bills, coins, or both. You can eliminate the exact-change hassle by purchasing a seven-day bus Metrobus pass for $11, or better yet, the rechargeable SmarTrip card at the Metro Center sales office, open weekdays from 7:30 AM to 6:30 PM. The SmarTrip card can be used on the bus and rail systems. You can also order Metrobus passes and SmarTrip online with a credit card. There's no charge for shipping and handling, but there is a $5 fee for SmarTrip. Metrobus passes and/or SmarTrip are mailed within two days of your order via first-class mail.

Information D.C. Circulator (☎ 202/962–1423 ⊕ www.dccirculator.com). **Metro Center sales office** (✉ 12th and F Sts. NW ☎ No phone). **Washington Metropolitan Area Transit Authority** (☎ 202/637–7000, 202/638–3780 TTY ⊕ www.wmata.com).

■ CAR TRAVEL

A car is often a drawback in Washington, D.C. Traffic is horrendous, especially at rush hour, and driving is often confusing, with many lanes and some entire streets changing direction suddenly during rush hour. Even longtime residents carry maps in their cars to help navigate confusing traffic circles and randomly arranged one-way streets. Most traffic lights stand at the side of intersections (instead of hanging suspended over them), and the streets are dotted with giant potholes. The city's most popular sights are within a short walk of a Metro station anyway, so it's best to leave your car at the hotel. Touring by car is a good idea only for visiting sights in Maryland or Virginia.

Zipcar has been around for a few years now and seems to be growing in popularity. You can rent a car for a couple of hours or a couple of days. Gas, insurance, parking, and satellite radio are included. It's not cheap; $7 an hour or $69 a day, plus a $25 application fee and $50 annual fee, but it may be worth it for the hassle-free convenience. Once you sign up either online or over the phone, a wireless signal is sent to the car, which is parked nearby. When you get to your car, you get in and go. You then simply return the car to the same location.

Information zipcar (☎ 866/494–7227 ⊕ www.zipcar.com).

GASOLINE

Gas tends to be slightly higher in the District than it is in Maryland or Virginia. As a rule, gas stations are hard to find in the District, especially around Pennsylvania Avenue and the National Mall. Your best bets are a BP station at the corner of 18th and S streets NW, the Mobil station at the corner of 15th and U streets NW, the Exxon station at 2150 M Street NW, and the Mobil station at the corner of 22nd and P streets NW.

LAY OF THE LAND

Interstate 95 skirts D.C. as part of the Beltway, the six- to eight-lane highway that encircles the city. The eastern half of the Beltway is labeled both I–95 and I–495; the western half is just I–495. If you're coming from the south, take I–95 to I–395 and cross the 14th Street Bridge to 14th Street in the District. From the north, stay on I–95 South. Take the exit to Washington, which will place you onto the Baltimore–Washington (B-W) Parkway heading south. The B-W Parkway will turn into New York Avenue, taking you into Downtown Washington, D.C.

Interstate 66 approaches the city from the southwest. You can get Downtown by taking I–66 across the Theodore Roosevelt Bridge to Constitution Avenue.

Interstate 270 approaches Washington, D.C., from the northwest before hitting I–495. To reach Downtown, take I–495 East to Connecticut Avenue South, toward Chevy Chase.

PARKING

Parking in D.C. is an adventure; the police are quick to tow away or immobilize with a boot any vehicle parked illegally. If you find you've been towed from a city street, call ☎ 202/727–5000 or log on to ⊕ www.dmv.washingtondc.gov. Be sure you know the license-plate number, make, model, and color of the car before you call.

Most of the outlying, suburban Metro stations have parking lots, though these fill quickly with city-bound commuters. If you plan to park in one of these lots, arrive early.

Private parking lots Downtown often charge around $5 an hour and $25 a day. There's free, three-hour parking around the Mall on Jefferson and Madison drives, though these spots are almost always filled. There is no parking near the Lincoln or Roosevelt memorials. The closest free parking is in three lots in East Potomac Park, south of the 14th Street Bridge.

RENTAL CARS

If you're staying in D.C., there really is no need to rent a car. Public transportation in the city is convenient and affordable, to say nothing of the fact that driving in Washington, D.C., is not for the faint of heart.

Many families visiting D.C. find it much more affordable to stay in a hotel in Virginia or Maryland. If you choose to stay outside of District, check when you're making your reservations whether the hotel is within walking distance of a Metro station or offers shuttle transportation to D.C. If neither is the case, then you'll need to rent a car.

Daily rental rates in Washington, D.C., begin at about $40 during the week and about $22 on weekends for an economy car with air-conditioning, automatic transmission, and unlimited mileage. This does not include airport facility fees or the tax on car rentals.

In Washington, D.C., many agencies require you to be at least 25 to rent a car. However, employees of major corporations and military or government personnel on official business may be able to rent a car even if they're under age 25.

ROADSIDE EMERGENCIES

Dial 911 to report accidents on the road and to reach police, the highway patrol, or the fire department. For police non-emergencies, dial 311.

Emergency Services U.S. Park Police (☎ 202/619-7300).

RULES OF THE ROAD

In D.C. you may turn right at a red light after stopping if there's no oncoming traffic. When in doubt, wait for the green. Be alert for one-way streets, "no left turn" intersections, and blocks closed to car traffic. The use of handheld mobile phones while operating a vehicle is illegal in Washington, D.C. Drivers can also be cited for "failure to pay full time and attention while operating a motor vehicle."

Radar detectors are illegal in Washington, D.C., and Virginia.

During rush hour (6–9 AM and 4–7 PM), HOV (high-occupancy vehicle) lanes on I–395 and I–95 are reserved for cars with three or more people. All the lanes of I–66 inside the Beltway are reserved for cars carrying two or more during rush hour, as are some of the lanes on the Dulles Toll Road and on I–270.

Always strap children under a year old or under 20 pounds into approved rear-facing child-safety seats in the backseat. In Washington, D.C., children weighing 20–40 pounds must also ride in a car seat in the back, although it may face the front. Children cannot sit in the front seat of a car until they are at least four years old and weigh more than 80 pounds.

▮ METRO TRAVEL

The Metro, which opened in 1976, is one of the country's cleanest, most efficient, and safest subway systems. It begins operation at 5 AM on weekdays and 7 AM on weekends. The Metro closes on weekdays at midnight and weekends at 3 AM. Don't get to the station at the last minute, as trains from the ends of the lines depart before the official closing time. During the weekday peak periods (5–9:30 AM and 3–7 PM), trains come along every three to six minutes. At other times and on weekends and holidays, trains run about every 12–15 minutes. Lighted displays at the platforms show estimated arrival and departure times of trains, as well as the number of cars available. Eating, drinking, smoking, and littering in stations and on the trains are strictly prohibited.

FARES

The Metro's base fare is $1.65; the actual price you pay depends on the time of day and the distance traveled, which means you might end up paying $4.50 if you're traveling to a distant station at rush hour. Up to two children under age five ride free when accompanied by a paying passenger.

PAYMENT AND PASSES

Buy your ticket at the Farecard machines; they accept coins and crisp $1, $5, $10, or $20 bills. If the machine spits your bill back out at you, try folding and unfolding it lengthwise before asking someone for help. Some newer machines will also accept credit cards. You can buy one-day passes for $7.80 and seven-day passes for $39. Locals use the SmarTrip card, a plastic card that can hold any fare amount and can be used throughout the Metro, bus, and parking system. The cost of each ride is deducted as you enter the subway. Buy passes or SmarTrip cards at the Metro Center sales office or online.

Insert your Farecard into the turnstile to enter the platform. Make sure you hang on to the card—you need it to exit at your destination.

Metro Information Washington Metropolitan Area Transit Authority (*WMATA ⊠ 12th and F Sts. NW, sales center* ☎ *202/637-7000, 202/638-3780 TTY, 202/962-1195 lost and found* ⊕ *www.wmata.com*).

▌ TAXI TRAVEL

You can hail a taxi on the street just about anywhere in the city, and they tend to congregate around major hotels. If you find yourself on a quiet street in a residential area, either walk to a busier street or phone for a taxi. Although it depends on your location and the time of day, a taxi ought to arrive in 10 to 15 minutes. There are a number of different cab companies in the city, and as a result, D.C. cabs do not have a uniform appearance (unlike New York's yellow cabs, for example). And you may find yourself in a taxi that's older and a bit rundown.

Most District cab drivers are independent operators and may ignore a potential passenger. Cabbies are also known for refusing to pick up passengers after learning of their destination, and the D.C. government rarely enforces the taxi laws that require drivers who are free to either pick up passengers or display an off-duty sign. If after several minutes you haven't been able to get a cab, your best bet is to find the nearest Metro station and take the subway or walk to a nearby hotel and get a cab there.

FARES

After 70 years of a zone system, taxis in the District are now on time and distance meters. The base rate for the first one-sixth mi is $3. Each additional one-sixth mi and each minute stopped or traveling at less than 10 mph. is 25¢. There is a $2 surcharge per piece of large luggage in the trunk and a 50¢ per bag handling charge. There is a $2 surcharge for radio dispatch and $1.50 for each additional person. During D.C.-declared snow emergencies, there is an additional 25% surcharge. The maximum fare for trips starting and ending in the District is $19 plus applicable surcharges.

Maryland and Virginia taxis also have meters. These taxis can take you into or out of D.C., but are not allowed to take you between points in D.C.

Taxi Companies **Diamond** (☎ 202/387–6200). **Mayflower** (☎ 202/783–1111). **Yellow** (☎ 202/544–1212).

▌ TRAIN TRAVEL

More than 80 trains a day arrive at Washington, D.C.'s, Union Station. Amtrak's regular service runs from D.C. to New York in 3¼–3¾ hours and from D.C. to Boston in 7¾–8 hours. Acela, Amtrak's high-speed service, travels from D.C. to New York in 2¾–3 hours and from D.C. to Boston in 6½ hours.

Two commuter lines—Maryland Rail Commuter Service (MARC) and Virginia Railway Express (VRE)—run to the nearby suburbs. They're cheaper than Amtrak, but they don't run on weekends.

Amtrak tickets and reservations are available at Amtrak stations, by telephone, through travel agents, or online. Amtrak schedule and fare information can be found at Union Station as well as online.

Amtrak has both reserved and unreserved trains available. If you plan to travel during peak times, such as a Friday night or near a holiday, you'll need to get a reservation and a ticket in advance. Some trains at nonpeak times are unreserved, with seats assigned on a first-come, first-served basis.

Information **Amtrak** (☎ 800/872–7245 ⊕ www.amtrak.com). **Maryland Rail Commuter Service** (MARC ☎ 800/325–7245 ⊕ www.mtamaryland.com). **Union Station** (✉ 50 Massachusetts Ave. NE ☎ 202/371–9441 ⊕ www.unionstationdc.com). **Virginia Railway Express** (VRE ☎ 703/684–1001 ⊕ www.vre.org).

ESSENTIALS

▌ BUSINESS SERVICES AND FACILITIES

Imagine two Washington monuments laid end to end, and you will have an idea about the size of the Washington Convention Center, the District's largest building. Recognized nationally for its architectural design, the center also has a $4 million art collection featuring 120 sculptures, oil paintings, and photos from artists around the world.

Should you find yourself in need of business services while in D.C., Capital Business Center at the Convention Center, and FedEx Kinko's, across the street from the Convention Center, provide everything from photocopying and digital printing to shipping–receiving packages. In addition, several companies offer translation and interpretation services, including Capital Communications Group, Comprehensive Language Center, and MFM Conference Interpretation. Capital Communications Group also offers multilingual city tours.

Business Services Capital Business Center (✉ 801 Mt. Vernon Pl. NW ☎ 202/249–3969 ⊕ www.capitalbusinesscenter.com). **FedEx Kinko's** (✉ 800 K St. NW ☎ 202/487–6150 or 888/231–9867 ⊕ www.fedex.com).

Convention Center Washington Convention Center (✉ 801 Mt. Vernon Pl. NW ☎ 202/249–3000 or 800/368–9000 ⊕ www.dcconvention.com).

Translation Services Capital Communications Group (☎ 202/349–1444 ⊕ www.capcomgroup.com). **Comprehensive Language Center** (☎ 703/247–0700 or 800/634–5764 ⊕ www.comprehensivelc.com). **MFM Conference Interpretation** (☎ 703/440–5061 or 800/814–6548 wwww.mfmgroup.com).

▌ COMMUNICATIONS

INTERNET

If you're planning on bringing your laptop with you to D.C., you will have no problem checking e-mail or connecting to the Internet. Most of the major hotels offer high-speed access in rooms and/or lobbies and business centers.

In addition, dozens of D.C. area restaurants and coffee shops provide free wireless broadband Internet service, including branches of Così all over town. The Martin Luther King Jr. Memorial Public Library and 21 other branches of the D.C. Library System offer Wi-Fi access free of charge to all library visitors. At Kramerbooks & Afterwords Café you can check your e-mail for free on the computer located at the full-service bar.

Contacts Così (⊕ www.getcosi.com). **Cybercafes** (⊕ www.cybercafes.com). **Kramerbooks & Afterwords Café** (✉ 1517 Connecticut Ave. NW ☎ 202/387–1400 ⊕ www.kramers.com). **Martin Luther King Jr. Memorial Library** (✉ 900 G St. NW ☎ 202/727–1111 ⊕ www.dclibrary.org).

▌ HOURS OF OPERATION

If you're getting around on the Metro, remember that from Sunday through Thursday the Metro closes at midnight, and on Friday and Saturday nights it stops running at 3 AM. Give yourself enough time to get to the station, because at many stations the last trains leave earlier than the closing times. If it's a holiday, be sure to check the schedule before you leave the station, as trains may be running on a different timetable. Bars and nightclubs close at 2 AM on weekdays and 3 AM on weekends.

▮ MONEY

Washington is an expensive city, comparable to New York. On the other hand, many attractions, including most of the museums, are free.

ITEM	AVERAGE COST
Cup of Coffee	$1 at a diner, $4 at an upscale café
Glass of Wine	$7–$10 and up
Pint of Beer	$5–$7
Sandwich	$5–$7
One-Mile Taxi Ride in Capital City	$5–$10
Museum Admission	Usually free

Prices throughout this guide are given for adults. Substantially reduced fees are almost always available for children, students, and senior citizens.

CREDIT CARDS

Throughout this guide, the following abbreviations are used: **AE**, American Express; **D**, Discover; **DC**, Diners Club; **MC**, MasterCard; and **V**, Visa.

▮ PACKING

Walk along the National Mall or in Downtown and you can encounter people wearing everything from three-piece suits to shorts and T-shirts. Business attire in D.C. tends to be fairly conservative; it's around the campuses of Georgetown and American University where you can find more-eclectic dressing. But D.C. is also understood to be a major year-round tourism destination, so the key is to dress comfortably and for the weather.

In fall, temperatures hover around the 50s and 60s, but it can get cooler, so pants, long-sleeve shirts, and a coat are appropriate. Winter is relatively mild in the D.C. area, with temperatures ranging from the 20s at night to the 40s and 50s and lately even the 60s during the day.

There are usually one or two major snowstorms and an occasional ice storm. Pack clothes that can be layered and bring a warm coat.

D.C. in spring is gorgeous, with lots of sun, an occasional rainstorm, and temperatures ranging from the 40s to 60s. Pack light sweaters, pants, and a lightweight coat. Summer is muggy and hot, with temperatures in the 80s and 90s and high humidity. Expect an evening thundershower or two. Plan on wearing cool, breathable fabrics like cotton, and bring a sweater for overly air-conditioned buildings.

Most important, D.C. is a walking town. Distances, especially on the Mall, are long. Whatever the reason for your visit, wear comfortable shoes.

▮ RESTROOMS

Restrooms are found in all the city's museums and galleries. Most are accessible to people in wheelchairs, and many are equipped with changing tables for babies. Locating a restroom is often difficult when you're strolling along the Mall. There are facilities at the Washington Monument, the Lincoln Memorial, the Jefferson Memorial, and Constitution Gardens, near the Vietnam Veterans Memorial, but these are not always as clean as they should be. A better option is to step inside one of the museums along the Mall.

Restrooms are available in restaurants, hotels, and department stores. Unlike in many other cities, these businesses are usually happy to help out those in need. There's one state-of-the-art public restroom in the Huntington Station on the Metro. All other stations have restrooms available in cases of emergency. You should ask one of the uniformed attendants in the kiosks.

Find a Loo The Bathroom Diaries (⊕ *www. thebathroomdiaries.com*).

▐ SAFETY

Washington, D.C., is a fairly safe city, but as with any major metropolitan area it's best to be alert and aware. Be aware of your surroundings before you use an ATM, especially one that is outdoors. Move on to a different machine if you notice people loitering nearby. Pickpocketing and other petty crimes are rare in D.C., but they do occur, especially in markets and other crowded areas. Keep an eye on purses and backpacks.

Panhandlers can be aggressive, and may respond with verbal insults, but otherwise are usually harmless. If someone threatens you with violence, it's best to hand over your money and seek help from police later.

The Metro is quite safe, with few incidents reported each year. Buses are also safe, but be aware that a few petty crimes have occurred at bus stops. Stick to those along busy streets.

The only scam you'll encounter in D.C. is an elaborate story from a panhandler. To evoke sympathy, a well-dressed panhandler may pretend to have lost his wallet and need money to get home, or a woman may say she needs cab fare to take a sick child to the hospital. A simple "I'm sorry" is usually enough to send them on their way.

▐TIP→ Distribute your cash, credit cards, IDs, and other valuables between a deep front pocket, an inside jacket or vest pocket, and a hidden money pouch. Don't reach for the money pouch once you're in public.

▐ TAXES

Washington has the region's highest hotel tax, a whopping 14.5%. Maryland and Virginia have no state hotel tax, but charge sales tax. Individual counties add their own hotel taxes, which range from 5% to 10%.

Sales tax is 5.75% in D.C., 6% in Maryland, and 4% plus local amounts in Virginia.

▐ TIME

Washington, D.C., is in the Eastern time zone. It's 3 hours ahead of Los Angeles, 1 hour ahead of Chicago, 5 hours behind London, and 15 hours behind Sydney.

Time Zones Timeanddate.com (⊕ *www.timeanddate.com/worldclock*).

▐ TIPPING

TIPPING GUIDES FOR WASHINGTON D.C.	
Bartender	$1–$5 per round of drinks, depending on the number of drinks
Bellhop	$1–$5 per bag, depending on the level of the hotel
Hotel Concierge	$5 or more, depending on the service
Hotel Doorman	$1–$5 for help with bags or hailing a cab
Hotel Maid	$2–$5 a day (either daily or at the end of your stay, in cash)
Hotel Room Service Waiter	$1–$2 per delivery, even if a service charge has been added
Porter at Airport or Train Station	$1 per bag
Skycap at Airport	$1–$3 per bag checked
Taxi Driver	15%, but round up the fare to the next dollar amount
Tour Guide	10% of the cost of the tour
Valet Parking Attendant	$2–$5, each time your car is brought to you
Waiter	15%–20%, with 20% being the norm at high-end restaurants; nothing additional if a service charge is added to the bill
Spa Personnel	15%–20% of the cost of your service
Restroom Attendants	$1 or small change
Coat Check	$1–$2 per coat

▌TOURS

GUIDED TOURS

Collette Vacations, in partnership with Smithsonian Journeys Travel Adventures, has a five-day "Spirit of Washington, D.C." tour that includes guided tours of the Freer Gallery, National Gallery of Art, and National Museum of the American Indian led by Smithsonian historians; a tour of the Library of Congress; and a narrated coach tour of the city's monuments and memorials, including a visit to Arlington National Cemetery. Globus has two itineraries that include two nights in D.C.: "Patriot's Passage" and "America's Historic East," eight-day tours of Washington, D.C. and Philadelphia. Both trips include a half-day guided city tour and free time, followed by an illumination tour of the monuments. Mayflower Tours offers a seven-day "Washington, D.C. and Williamsburg" tour that includes four nights in D.C. with visits to the U.S. Capitol, two Smithsonian museums, The Newseum, Arlington Cemetery, and monuments, as well as stops at Mount Vernon and Jamestown. Tauck Travel also has a "Williamsburg and Washington, D.C." itinerary, which includes two nights in D.C. WorldStrides, which specializes in educational student travel, has 10 "Discover D.C." programs that are designed to enrich the study of U.S. history and government.

Recommended Companies Collette Vacations (☎ 800/340–5158 ⊕ www. collettevacations.com). **Globus** (☎ 866/755–8581 ⊕ www.globusjourneys.com). **Mayflower Tours** (☎ 800/323–7604 ⊕ www. mayflowertours.com). **Tauck** (☎ 800/788–7885 ⊕ www.tauck.com). **WorldStrides** (☎ 800/468–5899 ⊕ www.worldstrides.com).

SPECIAL-INTEREST TOURS

Elderhostel offers several guided tours for older adults that provide fascinating in-depth looks into the history and beauty of D.C. The nonprofit educational travel organization has been leading all-inclusive learning adventures around the world for more than 20 years. In addition to the programs listed here, Elderhostel also has several other world studies and history programs in D.C. All Elderhostel programs include accommodations, meals, and in-town transportation.

Presented in conjunction with the Close Up Foundation, the nation's largest non-profit citizenship education organization, "Monumental D.C." is a four-night program that includes seminars on many of the figures memorialized on and near the National Mall. Prices start at about $980 per person.

"Spies, Lies and Intelligence: The Shadowy World of International Espionage" is a fascinating exploration of the country's intelligence operation. Retired CIA agents share secrets of high-profile spying cases on this three-night trip that costs about $689 per person. Highlights include visits to the International Spy Museum and the NSA Cryptologic Museum.

"Discover Washington, D.C.: Our Nation's Capital" enables participants to learn more about our nation's cultural and political foundations through presentations at memorials and museums, visits to historical neighborhoods, meetings and seminars with Washington policy makers, and an evening at the theater. This five-night program starts at about $1,118 per person.

Contact Elderhostel (☎ 800/454–5768 ⊕ www.elderhostel.org).

DAY TOURS AND GUIDES

We recommend any of the tours offered by the Smithsonian Associates Program, A Tour de Force, and Anecdotal History Tours of D.C. For price and convenience, you can't beat the Old Town Trolley Tours or Tourmobile buses, which take you to all the major historical and cultural landmarks in the city. What's great about those tours is that you can get on and off as you please and stay as long as you like at any spot; you can reboard for free all day long.

From April through October, Washington Walks has two-hour guided tours that are interesting and, at $10 per person, affordable. From February to November, join a free tour of the monuments and memorials with DC by Foot. If it's too hot to walk, hop onboard Capitol River Cruises for a look at the city from the water.

For families we recommend the bike or Segway tours, the DC Duck tour (younger kids will get a kick out of the quackers that are given to all riders), a mule-drawn barge ride on the C&O Canal, the Bureau of Engraving and Printing tour, and any of Natalie Zanin's historic strolls, especially the Ghost Story Tour of Washington. Traveling on your own? Check out the six-hour D.C. Party Shuttle Tour.

BICYCLE TOURS

Bike the Sites Tours has knowledgeable guides leading daily excursions past dozens of Washington, D.C., landmarks. All tours start at the Old Post Office Pavilion. Bicycles, helmets, snacks, and water bottles are included in the rates, which start at $40. Their Capital Sites and Monuments night tours cost $45 and there's even a Blossoms by Bike tour for $32 during the annual Cherry Blossom Festival. The Adventure Cycling Association, a national organization promoting bicycle travel, recommends tours around the region.

Contacts Adventure Cycling Association (☏ 800/755–2453 ⊕ www.adventurecycling. org). Bike the Sites Tours (☏ 202/842–2453 ⊕ www.bikethesites.com).

BOAT TOURS

During one-hour rides on mule-drawn barges on the C&O Canal, costumed guides and volunteers explain the waterway's history. The barge rides, which cost $5 and are run by the National Park Service, depart from its visitor center Wednesday through Sunday from April through October.

Capitol River Cruises offers 45-minute sightseeing tours aboard the *Nightingale* and *Nightingale II*, Great Lakes boats from the 1950s. Beverages and light snacks are available. Hourly cruises depart from Washington Harbour noon to 9 PM April to October. Prices are $13 for adults and $6 for children 3 to 12.

Several swanky cruises depart from the waterfront in Southwest D.C. The *Odyssey III*, specially built to fit under the Potomac's bridges, departs from the Gangplank Marina at 6th and Water streets SW. Tickets are approximately $49 for the weekday lunch cruise, $63 for the weekend brunch cruise, and $93–$110 for the daily dinner cruise. As the prices suggest, this is an elegant affair; jackets are requested for men at dinner. The sleek *Spirit of Washington* offers lunch and dinner cruises that range from $39 to $86. Odyssey and Spirit, as well as a handful of other companies offer sightseeing boat tours from the new National Harbour on the banks of the Potomac River in Maryland. Located just minutes from D.C., National Harbour is opening in stages with a convention center, hotels, shops, restaurants, and condominiums.

Departing from Alexandria, the glass-enclosed *Dandy* and *Nina's Dandy* cruise up the Potomac year-round to Georgetown, taking you past many of D.C.'s monuments. Lunch cruises cost $45 Monday through Friday and $50 on Saturday. A Sunday champagne brunch cruise costs $55. Boarding for these cruises starts at 11 AM. Depending on the day, dinner cruises start boarding at 6 or 6:30 PM and cost $86 Sunday through Friday and $96 on Saturday. The *Dandy* and *Nina's Dandy* also offer special holiday cruises.

From mid-March through October, DC Ducks offers 90-minute tours in funky converted World War II amphibious vehicles. After an hour-long road tour of landlocked sights, the tour moves to the water, where for 30 minutes you get a boat's-eye view of the city. Tours depart from Union Station and cost $28.80 for adults and $14.40 for children ages 4–12; seating is on a first-come, first-served basis.

Contacts C&O Canal Barges (⊠ *Canal Visitor Center, 1057 Thomas Jefferson St. NW, Georgetown* ☎ *202/653–5190* ⊕ *www.nps.gov/choh*). **Capitol River Cruises** (⊠ *31st and K Sts. NW, Georgetown* ☎ *301/460–7447 or 800/405–5511* ⊕ *www.capitolrivercruises.com*). **Dandy Cruises** (⊠ *Prince St. between Duke and King Sts., Alexandria, VA* ☎ *703/683–6076* ⊕ *www. dandydinnerboat.com*). **DC Ducks** (⊠ *50 Massachusetts Ave. NE, Union Station* ☎ *202/832–9800* ⊕ *www.dcducks.com*). **Odyssey III** (⊠ *600 Water St. SW, D.C. Waterfront* ☎ *202/488–6010 or 800/946–7245* ⊕ *www.odysseycruises.com*). **Spirit of Washington** (⊠ *Pier 4, 6th and Water Sts. SW, D.C. Waterfront* ☎ *202/554–8013 or 866/211–3811* ⊕ *www.spiritcruises.com*).

BUS TOURS

All About Town has half-day, all-day, two-day, and twilight bus tours to get acquainted with the city. Tours leave from various Downtown locations. An all-day tour costs $50–$62, half-day and twilight tours cost $36–$46.

Gray Line's eight-hour "D.C. in a Day" tour stops at the White House Visitor Center, U.S. Capitol, World War II Memorial, and Smithsonian Museums. The cost is $55 for adults and $30 for children ages 3–11. Another all-day tour, "Mt. Vernon/ Arlington Cemetery" includes visits to George Washington's home, Old Town Alexandria, Tomb of the Unknowns Soldier, and the Iwo Jima, Pentagon, Air Force, and Jefferson memorials. It is priced at $70 for adults and $45 for children. There's also a 2½-hour tour on Tuesday and Saturday mornings presented in conjunction with the International Spy Museum that showcases more than 25 sites used by infamous spies. Included in the cost of $75 per person is same-day admission to the museum.

Gross National Product's Scandal Tours, led by members of the GNP comedy troupe, last 1½ hours and cover scandals from George Washington to George W. Bush. The tours, held on Saturday from April through August at 1 PM, cost $30 per person; reservations are required.

On Location Tours has a 2½-hour tour that visits more than 30 locations used in the filming of movies and TV shows, including *No Way Out*, *The Exorcist*, *Wedding Crashers*, *All the President's Men*, *West Wing*, and *24*, among others. Tours are offered Saturday beginning at 10 AM and cost $34 (plus $2 ticket fee) per person.

Washington D.C. Party Shuttle Tours offers a daily six-hour "D.C. It All" tour, where you hop on and off with the guide at 12 locations. The cost is $60 for adults and $45 for children under 12. Their three-hour "D.C. The Lights" nightlife tour costs $40 per person.

Contacts All About Town (☎ *301/856–5556* ⊕ *www.allabouttown.com*). **Gray Line** (☎ *301/386–8300 or 800/862–1400* ⊕ *www. graylinedc.com*). **Gross National Product** (☎ *202/783–7212* ⊕ *www.gnpcomedy. com*). **On Location Tours** (☎ *212/209–3370* ⊕ *www.screentours.com*). **Washington D.C. Party Shuttle** (☎ *202/756–1983* ⊕ *www. washingtondcpartyshuttle.com*).

ORIENTATION TOURS

Old Town Trolley Tours, orange-and-green motorized trolleys, take in the main Downtown sights and also head into Georgetown and the upper Northwest in a speedy two hours if you ride straight through. However, you can hop on and off as many times as you like, taking your time at the stops you choose. Tickets are $32 for adults. Tourmobile buses, authorized by the National Park Service, operate in a similar fashion, making 25 stops at historic sites between the Capitol and Arlington National Cemetery. Tickets, available at kiosks at Arlington National Cemetery, Union Station, and the Washington Monument, are $27 for adults. Tickets for just Arlington National Cemetery are $7.50 for adults. Tourmobile also offers three seasonal tours including a "Twilight Ride Through History Tour," "Mt. Vernon Tour," and "Frederick Douglass Tour."

Contacts **Old Town Trolley Tours**
(☎ 202/832–9800 ⊕ www.historictours.com).
Tourmobile (☎ 202/554–5100 or 888/868–
7707 ⊕ www.tourmobile.com).

PRIVATE GUIDES

A Tour de Force has limo tours of historic
homes, diplomatic buildings, and "the
best little museums in Washington." Tours
are led by Jeanne Fogle, a local historian.
In business since 1964, the Guide Service
of Washington puts together half-day
and full-day tours of D.C. sights, including some off the beaten path. Nationally
known photographer Sonny Odom offers
custom tours for shutterbugs at $50/hour,
with a four-hour minimum.

Contacts **A Tour de Force** (✉ Box 2782,
Washington, DC ☎ 703/525–2948 ⊕ www.
atourdeforce.com). **Guide Service of Washington** (✉ 734 15th St. NW, Suite 701, Washington, DC 20005 ☎ 202/628–2842 ⊕ www.
dctourguides.com). **Sonny Odom** (✉ 2420 F
S. Walter Reed Dr., Arlington, VA 22206
☎ 703/379–1633 ⊕ www.sonnyodom.com).

SEGWAY AND SCOOTER TOURS

Rest your feet and glide by the monuments, museums, and major attractions
aboard a Segway. Guided tours usually
last about two hours. D.C. city ordinance
requires that riders be at least 16 years
old; some tour companies have weight
restrictions of around 265 pounds. Tours
cost around $65–$70 per person and are
limited to 6 to 10 people.

City Scooter Tours rents scooters and
wheelchairs for self-guided tours. Three-
day rental prices start at $175 for scooters
and $165 for wheelchairs.

Contacts **Capital Segway** (☎ 202/682–
1980 ⊕ www.capitalsegway.com). **City
Segway Tours** (☎ 877/734–8687 ⊕ www.
citysegwaytours.com). **City Scooter Tours**
(☎ 888/441–7575 ⊕ www.cityscootertours.
com). **Segs in the City** (☎ 800/734–7393
⊕ www.segsinthecity.net).

WORD OF MOUTH

"Take advantage of the free docent-led
tours of the museums and other places,
such as the Library of Congress. The
docents are very knowledgeable and make
your visit so much more enjoyable than a
quick run through the building."

—Devonmci

GOVERNMENT BUILDING TOURS

Special tours of government buildings
with heavy security, including the White
House and the Capitol, can be arranged
through your representative or senator's
office. Limited numbers of these so-called
VIP tickets are available, so plan up to six
months in advance of your trip. Govern-
mental buildings close to visitors when the
Department of Homeland Security issues
a high alert, so call ahead.

Don't miss the stunning Capitol Visitor
Center which opened in 2008. Before your
tour of the Capitol, you can watch orientation films, view historical documents
from the Library of Congress and the
National Archives, learn about the history
of democracy through interactive touch-
screen displays, walk alongside statues of
notable historical figures, and see models
of the Capitol and the Dome. The center,
which also features a gift shop and cafeteria, is open daily from 8:30 AM to 4:30 PM.
To avoid delays, order Capitol tour tickets online (if you haven't reserved through
your House or Senate member). There
will be a few same-day passes available
at the kiosk outside the Capitol and at the
information desks in the Center's Emancipation Hall. The Bureau of Engraving
and Printing has fascinating tours that
begin every 15 minutes from 9 to 10:45
and 12:30 to 2 on weekdays (as well as 2
to 3:45 and 5 to 7 in summer). The free
tours are popular. During the peak season from March through August, tickets
are given out on a first-come, first-served
basis at the ticket booth on Raoul Wallenberg Place (formerly 15th Street). The

booth opens at 8 AM and closes as soon as all tickets have been handed out; lines form early and tickets go quickly, usually by 9 AM. From September through February, tickets are not required; you line up at the Visitor's Entrance on 14th Street.

Foreign dignitaries are received at the Department of State's lavish Diplomatic Reception Rooms, but everyone else can get a peek on weekdays on 45-minute tours that begin at 9:30, 10:30, and 2:45. This is a fine-arts tour and not recommended for children under 12. Reservations are required and should be made at least three months in advance, either online or by phone.

Contacts Bureau of Engraving and Printing (✉ *14th and C Sts. SW* ☎ *202/874–2330 or 866/874–2330* ⊕ *www.moneyfactory.com/ locations*). **Department of State** (✉ *2201 C St. NW* ☎ *202/647–3241, 202/736–4474 TDD* ⊕ *www.state.gov/www/about_state/diprooms/ tour.html*). **United States Capitol Visitor Center** (☎ *202/226–8000* ⊕ *www.visitthecapitol. gov*). **White House Visitor Center** (✉ *15th and E Sts. NW* ☎ *202/456–7041* ⊕ *www. whitehouse.gov/about/tours_and_events/*).

MEDIA TOURS

A much-used tool for spreading the word about democracy in foreign lands is the Voice of America. You can tour its headquarters on weekdays at noon and 3 PM. Reservations are recommended and can be made either online or by phone.

National Public Radio leads tours of its broadcast facilities on Tuesday and Thursday at 11 AM. Call four weeks ahead to reserve a spot. Want to know what goes on in the newsroom of the *Washington Post*? You can arrange a tour by calling in advance. Guided tours for groups of 10 to 25 are also offered at the Post's printing plants in Maryland (Tuesday, 10 and 11 AM) and Virginia (Thursday, 10 and 11 AM). Reservations are required and must be made in writing up to four weeks in advance.

Contacts National Public Radio (✉ *635 Massachusetts Ave. NW, Washington, DC*

☎ *202/513–3232* ⊕ *www.npr.org/about/place*). **Voice of America** (✉ *330 Independence Ave. SW* ☎ *202/203–4990* ⊕ *www.voa.gov*). **The *Washington Post*** (✉ *1150 15th St. NW, Downtown* ☎ *202/334–7969* ⊕ *www.washpost. com/community/you/index.shtml*).

WALKING TOURS

Guided walks around Washington, D.C., and nearby communities are routinely offered by the Smithsonian Associates Program; advance tickets are required. Tour D.C. specializes in private group walking tours of Georgetown and Dupont Circle, covering topics such as the Civil War, the Underground Railroad, and Kennedy's Georgetown. Anecdotal History Tours leads tours in Georgetown, Adams Morgan, and Capitol Hill, as well as tours of the theater where Lincoln was shot and the homes of former presidents.

DC by Foot offers free tours (the guides work for tips, which makes them lively and entertaining) to the major memorials and monuments. The 1½-hour tours are available March through November; days and times vary by season. Look out for the guides in blue T-shirts and orange caps at the start of the tour on the north corner of 15th Street and Constitution Ave. NW; the tours end at the Lincoln Memorial.

Washington Walks has a wide range of tours, including "I've Got a Secret" featuring Washington, D.C. lore, "Moveable Feast: A Taste of D.C.," a walking snack-a-thon through Downtown, "The Most Haunted Houses," a look at the city's most ghost-filled residences, and "Before Harlem There Was U St.," a walk along Washington's "Black Broadway." Each tour costs just $10 per person.

The nonprofit group Cultural Tourism DC leads guided walking tours that cover the history and architecture of neighborhoods from the southwest waterfront to points much farther north: Or, if you'd prefer to explore neighborhoods on your own, their Web site features seven self-guided walking tours, all of which are highlighted with historic markers. You also can check out other cultural events, many free, happening around the city on the Cultural Tourism DC Web site. Spies of Washington Walking Tour, led by a retired Air Force officer and former president of the National Military Intelligence Association, visits sites in Washington associated with espionage over the past 200 years. The approximately two-hour tours cost $12 per person.

Step back in time on one of Natalie Zanin's interactive theatrical tours to learn about Washington, D.C., during the Civil War, WW II, or the '60s. Or you can sign up for a Ghost Story Tour, on which Zanin dresses as Dolly Madison's ghost and shares stories of hauntings around the city, including Lafayette Square Park, where Edgar Allan Poe's spirit is said to wander. Tours cost $10 for adults and $5 for children. UC Tours encourages visitors to stroll, strut, and stride on walking adventures including "Black Georgetown Re-Visited, "The Avenue of Latin Liberators," "Heroes on the Hill," and "Uptown on U Street," among others. The cost is $10 for adults and $5 for children.

One of the more popular tours in the city is the U.S. National Arboretum's Full Moon Hike offered about three times a month, excluding July and August. It's a brisk 5-mi walk through the grounds and hills by the Anacostia River, which afford beautiful views of the city at night. It costs $19/person and registration is required.

Contacts Anecdotal History Tours (☎ 301/294-9514 ⊕ www.dcsightseeing. com). Cultural Tourism DC (☎ 202/661-7581 ⊕ www.culturaltourismdc.org). DC by Foot (☎ 571/431-7543 ⊕ www.dcbyfoot.com). Natalie Zanin's Historic Strolls (☎ 301/588-9255 ⊕ www.historicstrolls.com). Smithsonian Associates Program (☎ 202/357-3030 ⊕ www.smithsonianassociates.org). Spies of Washington Walking Tours (☎ 703/569-1875 ⊕ www.spiesofwashingtontour.com). Tour D.C. (☎ 301/588-8999 ⊕ www.tourdc.com) . UC Tours (☎ 202/526-3384 ⊕ www.uctours.com) U.S. National Arboretum Full Moon Hike (☎ 202/245-4521 ⊕ www.usna.

usda.gov/Education/events.html). Washington Walks (☎ 202/484-1865 ⊕ www.washingtonwalks.com).

▌ VISITOR INFORMATION

You can gather information about the city before your trip and stop in at the D.C. Visitor Information Center when you arrive. The center is located in the Ronald Reagan Building and International Trade Center, two blocks from the National Mall and one block from the White House Visitor Center.

Because it's a government office building, you can enter only after flashing your ID and passing through a metal detector. While there you can pick up maps, guides, and brochures, watch a brief film highlighting the city's must-see sights, and speak with staff members. There are also interactive touch-screen kiosks with maps and other information on D.C.

The Washington, DC Convention and Tourism Corporation's free, 108-page publication titled *The Official Visitors' Guide* is full of sightseeing tips, maps, and contacts. You can order a copy online or by phone, or pick one up in their office.

The most popular sights in D.C. are run by either the National Park Service (NPS) or the Smithsonian, both of which have recorded information about locations and hours of operation.

Events and Attractions National Park Service (☎ 202/619-7275 "Dial-a-Park" ⊕ www.nps.gov). Smithsonian (☎ 202/633-1000, 202/633-5285 TTY ⊕ www.si.edu). White House Visitor Center (☎ 202/208-1631 ⊕ www.nps.gov/whho).

Information Center D.C. Visitor Information Center (✉ 1213 K St. NW, Washington, DC ☎ 866/324-7386 or 202/289-8317 ⊕ www.dcchamber.org).

State Information State of Maryland (☎ 866/639-3526 ⊕ www.mdisfun.org). Virginia Tourism Corporation (☎ 804/786-2051 or 800/847-4882 ⊕ www.virginia.org).

FOR INTERNATIONAL TRAVELERS

CURRENCY

The dollar is the basic unit of U.S. currency. It has 100 cents. Coins are the penny (1¢); the nickel (5¢), dime (10¢), quarter (25¢), half-dollar (50¢), and the rare golden $1 coin and rarer silver $1. Bills are denominated $1, $5, $10, $20, $50, and $100, all mostly green and identical in size; designs and background tints vary. A $2 bill exists but is extremely rare.

CUSTOMS

Information **U.S. Customs and Border Protection** (⊕ *www.cbp.gov*).

DRIVING

Driving in the United States is on the right. Speed limits are posted in miles per hour (usually between 55 mph and 70 mph). Most states require front-seat passengers to wear seat belts; children should be in the back seat and buckled up. In major cities, rush hours are 7 to 10 AM and 4 to 7 PM. Some freeways have high-occupancy vehicle (HOV) lanes, ordinarily marked with a diamond, for cars carrying two people or more.

Highways are well paved. Interstates—limited-access, multilane highways designated with an "I–" before the number—are fastest. Interstates with three-digit numbers circle urban areas, which may also have other expressways, freeways, and parkways. Limited-access highways sometimes have tolls.

Gas stations are plentiful, except in rural areas. Most stay open late (some 24 hours). Along larger highways, roadside stops with restrooms, fast-food restaurants, and sundries stores are well spaced. State police and tow trucks patrol major highways. If your car breaks down, pull onto the shoulder and wait, or have passengers wait while you walk to a roadside emergency phone (most states). On a cell phone, dial *55.

ELECTRICITY

The U.S. standard is AC, 110 volts/60 cycles. Plugs have two flat pins set parallel to each other.

EMBASSIES

Contacts Australia (☏ *202/797–3000* ⊕ *www.austemb.org*). **Canada** (☏ *202/682–1740* ⊕ *www.canadianembassy.org*). **UK** (☏ *202/588–7800* ⊕ *www.britainusa.com*).

EMERGENCIES

For police, fire, or ambulance, dial 911 (0 in rural areas).

HOLIDAYS

New Year's Day (Jan. 1); Martin Luther King Day (3rd Mon. in Jan.); Presidents' Day (3rd Mon. in Feb.); Memorial Day (last Mon. in May); Independence Day (July 4); Labor Day (1st Mon. in Sept.); Columbus Day (2nd Mon. in Oct.); Thanksgiving Day (4th Thurs. in Nov.); Christmas Eve and Christmas Day (Dec. 24 and 25); and New Year's Eve (Dec. 31).

MAIL

You can buy stamps and send letters and parcels in post offices. Stamp-dispensing machines can occasionally be found in airports, bus and train stations, convenience stores, and in ATMs. U.S. mailboxes are stout, dark-blue steel bins; pickup schedules are posted inside the bin (pull the handle). Mail parcels over a pound at a post office.

A first-class letter weighing 1 ounce or less costs 44¢; each additional ounce costs 17¢. Postcards cost 28¢. Postcards or 1-ounce airmail letters to most countries cost 98¢; postcards or 1-ounce letters to Canada cost 75¢ or to Mexico cost 79¢.

To receive mail on the road, have it sent c/o General Delivery to your destination's main post office. You must pick up mail in person within 30 days with a driver's license or passport for identification.

Contacts **DHL** (☎ *800/225–5345* ⊕ *www. dhl.com*). **FedEx** (☎ *800/463–3339* ⊕ *www. fedex.com*). **Mail Boxes, Etc./The UPS Store** (☎ *800/789–4623* ⊕ *www.mbe.com*). **USPS** (⊕ *www.usps.com*).

PASSPORTS AND VISAS
Visitor visas aren't necessary for citizens of Australia, Canada, the United Kingdom, or most citizens of EU countries coming for tourism and staying for under 90 days. A visa is $100, and waiting time can be substantial. Apply for a visa at the U.S. consulate in your place of residence.

Visa Information**Destination USA** (⊕ *www. unitedstatesvisas.gov*).

PHONES
Numbers consist of a three-digit area code and a seven-digit local number. Within many local calling areas, dial just seven digits. In Washington, D.C., the area code is 202; surrounding areas use 703 or 301. In others, dial "1" first and all 10 digits; this is true for calling toll-free numbers—prefixed by "800," "888," "866," and "877." Dial "1" before "900" numbers, too, but know they're very expensive.

For international calls, dial "011," the country code, and the number. For help, dial "0" and ask for an overseas operator. Most phone books list country codes and U.S. area codes. The country code for Australia is 61, for New Zealand 64, for the United Kingdom 44. Calling Canada is the same as calling within the United States (country code: 1).

For operator assistance, dial "0." For directory assistance, call 555–1212 or 411 (free at many public phones). To call "collect" (reverse charges), dial "0" instead of "1" before the 10-digit number.

Instructions are generally posted on pay phones. Usually you insert coins in a slot (usually 25¢–50¢ for local calls) and wait for a steady tone before dialing. On long-distance calls the operator tells you how much to insert; prepaid phone cards, widely available, can be used from any phone. Follow the directions to activate the card, then dial your number.

CELL PHONES
The United States has several GSM (Global System for Mobile Communications) networks, so multiband mobiles from most countries (except for Japan) work here. It's almost impossible to buy just a pay-as-you-go mobile SIM card in the U.S.—needed to avoid roaming charges—but cell phones with pay-as-you-go plans are available for well under $100. AT&T (GoPhone) and Virgin Mobile have the cheapest with national coverage.

Contacts **AT&T** (☎ *888/333–6651* ⊕ *www. cingular.com*). **Virgin Mobile** (☎ *No phone* ⊕ *www.wireless.att.com*).

Tourist Information **Washington, DC Convention and Tourism Corporation** (⊠ *901 7th St., NW, 4th fl., Washington, DC* 🕾 *202/789–7000 or 800/422–8644* ⊕ *www. washington.org*).

ALL ABOUT WASHINGTON, D.C.

The **Smithsonian Web site** (⊕ *www.si.edu*) is a good place to start planning a trip to the Mall and its museums. You can check out the exhibitions and events that will be held during your visit.

Cultural Tourism D.C. (⊕ *www.cultural-tourismdc.org*) is a nonprofit coalition whose mission is to highlight the city's arts and heritage. Their Web site is loaded with great information about sights, special events, and neighborhoods, including self-guided walking tours.

Billing itself as D.C.'s online community for the Web, **dcregistry.com** (⊕ *www. dcregistry.com*) lists more than 4,000 home pages with everything from arts and entertainment to real estate. There are discussion forums and a chat room, too.

Downtown D.C. Business Improvement District (⊕ *www.downtowndc.org*) is a nonprofit that oversees the 140-block area from the White House to the U.S. Capital. The Web site has special events, shopping, and dining listings and information about the wonderful red, white, and blue uniformed D.C. SAMs. In spring and summer, SAMs (which stands for safety, administration, and maintenance) are available to help visitors with directions, information, and emergencies. You'll spot their hospitality kiosks near Metro stops and major attractions.

Gay and Lesbian In addition to news and features, *Metro Weekly* (⊕ www.metroweekly. com) has a guide to bars and clubs, including a calendar of events.

Kids and Families **washingtonfamily. com** (⊕ www.washingtonfamily.com) features a "Best for Families" as voted on by area families. Families may also want to check out **washingtonparent.com** (⊕ www. washingtonparent.com) and **washingtond-ckids.com** (⊕ www.washingtondckids.com)

for kid-friendly hotels, activities, and special events.

News and Happenings The Web site of the *Washington Post* (⊕ www.washingtonpost. com) has a fairly comprehensive listing of what's going on around town. Also check out the site of *Washington CityPaper* (⊕ www. washingtoncitypaper.com), a free weekly newspaper. The *Washingtonian* (⊕ www. washingtonian.com) is a monthly magazine. For personalized e-mails of things to do, member reviews, and listings of half-price show and event tickets in D.C. and other major cities nationwide, register for free at ⊕ www. goldstarevents.com, an online entertainment company. The Cultural Alliance of Greater Washington (⊕ www.ticketplace.org) also has an online listing of half-price tickets to theater, dance, music, and opera performances.

Safety Transportation Security Administration (*TSA* ⊕ www.tsa.gov).

INDEX

PHOTO CREDITS

1, Fristle/Flickr. 2, Stuart Pearce/age fotostock. 5, JTB Photo/Japan Travel Bureau/photolibrary.com. **Chapter 1: Experience Washington:** 8-9, Hemis/Alamy. 10, Destination DC. 11 (left), Smiley Man with a Hat/Flickr. 11 (right), DymphieH/Flickr. 14, AgnosticPreachersKid/wikipedia.org. 15 (left), Molas/Flickr. 15 (right), Architect of the Capitol/wikipedia.org. 16 (left), graham s. klotz/Shutterstock. 16 (top center), S.Borisov/Shutterstock. 16 (top right), Kevin D. Oliver/Shutterstock. 16 (bottom right), Wadester16/wikipedia.org. 17 (left), alykat/wikipedia.org. 17 (top center), taylorandayumi/Flickr. 17 (top right), Jeremy R. Smith Sr./Shutterstock. 17 (bottom right), Kropotov Andrey/Shutterstock. 18, George Allen Penton/Shutterstock. 19 (left), LWPhotography/Shutterstock. 19 (right), Nickomargolies/wikipedia.org. 20 and 21, Destination DC. 22, DC St. Patrick's Day Parade Photographers. 23, Zhong Chen/Shutterstock. 24, National Cherry Blossom Festival. 27 (left), John Keith/Shutterstock. 27 (right), Ben Schumin/wikipedia.org. 30, Destination DC. **Chapter 2: Neighborhoods:** 31, ctankcycles/Flickr. 32, John Keith/Shutterstock. 33, PHOTOTAKE Inc./Alamy. 34, National Capital Planning Commission. 35 (top), POPPERFOTO/Alamy. 35 (center), Tramonto/age fotostock. 35 (bottom), Yoke Mc/Joacim Osterstam/wikipedia.org. 36 (#3), Dennis MacDonald/age fotostock. 36 (#1), Douglas Litchfield/Shutterstock. 36 (#11), Chuck Pefley/Alamy. 37 (#5), Smithsonian Institution. 37 (#9), P_R_/Flickr. 37 (#2), Sandra Baker/Alamy. 37 (#12), Stock Connection Distribution/Alamy. 37 (#7), Franko Khoury National Museum of African Art/ Smithsonian Institution. 37 (#8), Gordon Logue/Shutterstock. 37 (#4), David R. Frazier Photolibrary, Inc./Alamy. 37 (#13), United States Holocaust Memorial Museum. 38, Smithsonian Institution. 40 (top), DC St. Patrick's Day Parade Photographers. 40 (2nd from top), National Cherry Blossom Festival. 40 (3rd from top), William S. Kuta/Alamy. 40 (4th from top), San Rostro/age fotostock. 40 (bottom), Visions of America, LLC/Alamy. 41, Lee Foster/Alamy. 42, PHC C.M. Fitzpatrick/United States Department of Defense/wikipedia.org. 43, Wiskerke/Alamy. 45, Corcoran Gallery of Art. 47, Jake McGuire/Destination DC. 48, Brent Bergherm / age fotostock. 50, Jake McGuire/Destination DC. 53, Andreas Praefcke/wikipedia.org. 54, vittorio sciosia/age fotostock. 55, Jim West/Alamy. 57, Ilene MacDonald/Alamy. 59, Timothy Hursley/National Portrait Gallery and Smithsonian American Art Museum, Smithsonian Institution. 60, Kord.com/age fotostock. 63, vittorio sciosia/age fotostock. 65, Bill Helsel/Alamy. 66, Rudy Sulgan/age fotostock. 68, LOOK Die Bildagentur der Fotografen GmbH/Alamy. 70, Art Kowalsky/Alamy. 71, PCL/Alamy. 73, Destination DC. 76, Carrie Garcia/Alamy. 77, Susan Isakson/Alamy. 79, Poldavo (Alex)/Flickr. 81, NCinDC/Flickr. 83, G. Byron Peck/City Arts Inc. 84, Destination DC. 86, SUNNYphotography.com/Alamy. 89, Asiir/wikipedia.org. 90, thomwatson/Flickr. **Chapter 3: Museums:** 91, William S. Kuta/Alamy. 93, Alfred Wekelo/Shutterstock. 94, Corcoran Gallery of Art. 95, Richard T. Nowitz/age foto-stock. 96, Gryffindor/wikipedia.org. 97, Prakash Patel. 98 and 99, Eric Long/NASM, National Air and Space Museum, Smithsonian Institution. 100 (top left), NASA/wikipedia.org. 100 (top right), Son of Groucho/Flickr. 100 (bottom), Henristosch/wikipedia.org. 101 (top left), cliff1066/Flickr. 101 (top left center), dbking/Flickr. 101 (top right center), Eric Long/NASM, National Air and Space Museum, Smithsonian Institution. 101 (top right and bottom), Mr. T in DC/Flickr. 102-103, JTB Photo/Japan Travel Bureau/photolibrary.com. 104 (top left), Eric Long/NASM, National Air and Space Museum, Smithsonian Institution. 104 (top right), cliff1066/Flickr. 104 (bottom), by Mr. T in DC/Flickr. 105 (top), Pete Markham/Flickr. 105 (bottom), Jeffrey Johnson/Flickr. 106, Lisa Nipp for DELL. 107, Dennis MacDonald/age fotostock. 108, vittorio sciosia/age fotostock. 109, Dennis MacDonald/age foto-stock. 110, Lee Foster/Alamy. 111, Alvaro Leiva/age fotostock. 112, Chris Greenberg/Getty Images/Newscom. 113, Andre Jenny/Alamy. 114, Robert C Lautman. 115, William S. Kuta/Alamy. 116, Robin Weiner/U.S. Newswire. 117, United States Holocaust Memorial Museum. **Chapter 4: Monuments & Memorials:** 129, Graham De'ath/Shutterstock. 132, Hisham Ibrahim/age fotostock. 133, SuperStock/age fotostock. 134, Condor 36/Shutterstock. 135 (top left), Scott S. Warren/Aurora Photos. 135 (bottom left), Dennis Brack/Aurora Photos. 135 (right), vario images GmbH & Co.KG/Alamy. 136, Jeremy R. Smith Sr/Shutterstock. 138 (top left), Ken Hackett/Alamy. 138 (top right), Rough Guides/Alamy. 138 (bottom), National Archives and Records Administration. 139 (top left), William S. Kuta/Alamy. 139 (top right), Chris A Crumley/Alamy. 139 (bottom), Jeremy R. Smith/Shutterstock. 140, Robert J. Bennett/age fotostock. 141, vittorio sciosia/age fotostock. 142, Bruno Perousse/age fotostock. 143, Martin Luther King, Jr. National Memorial Project Foundation, Inc. 144, Kanwarjit Singh Boparai/Shutterstock. 145, idesygn/Shutterstock. 146, John Keith/Shutterstock. 147, S.Borisov/Shutterstock. 148, Visions of America, LLC/Alamy. **Chapter 5: Official Washington:** 151, Gary Blakeley/Shutterstock. 154, Architect of the Capitol/wikipedia.org. 155 (left), Bartomeu Amengual/age fotostock. 155 (top right), kimberlyfaye/Flickr. 155 (bottom right), SuperStock. 156 (top left and bottom left), Library of Congress Prints & Photographs Division. 156 (top right), Classic Vision/age fotostock. 156 (bottom right), Prints and Photographs Division Library of Congress. 157 (left), Architect of the Capitol. 157 (top right), José Fuste Raga/age fotostock. 157 (bottom), Architect of the Capitol/wikipedia.org. 158, U.S. Capitol Visitor Center. 159 (left), Wadester/wikipedia.org. 159 (right), wikipedia.org. 160 (left), MShades/Flickr. 160 (right), Architect of the Capitol/wikipedia.org. 162 (left), U.S. Senate, 110th Congress, Senate Photo Studio/wikipedia.org. 162 (top right), DCstockphoto.com/Alamy. 162 (center right), SCPhotos/Alamy. 162 (bottom right), United States Congress/wikipedia.org. 163, Dennis MacDonald/age fotostock. 164, Alvaro Leiva/age fotostock. 168, Ng Wei Keong/Shutterstock. 171, Robert Byrd/Shutterstock. 173, TIMOTHY A. CLARY/AFP/Getty Images/Newscom. 174 (top left and bottom left), Library of Congress Prints and Photographs Division. 174 (right) and 175 (top left), Bettmann/CORBIS. 175 (bottom left), wikipedia.org. 175 (right), Hunter Kahn/wikipedia.org. 176 (left), (c) 1924, The Washington Post. Reprinted with Permission. 176 (right), Matthew Brady/wikipedia.org. **Chapter 6: Where to Eat:** 177, Clay McLachlan/Aurora Photos. 178 and 182, Rasika. 183, Michael J. Colella. 184, Belga Café. 185 (top), Nayashkova Olga/Shutterstock. 185 (bottom), Anosmia/Flickr. 186, Ceiba. 187 (top), Monkey Business Images/Shutterstock. 187 (bottom), Lourdes Delgado. 188, 1789 Restaurant. 189 (top), Brasserie Beck. 189 (bottom), Leonidas. 190, Michael Matsil. 191 (top), James Ostrand/iStockphoto. 191 (bottom), Abdullah Pope. 192, Vegetate. 193 (top), Monkey Business Images/Shutterstock. 193 (bottom), Vegetate. 194, Allison Dinner. 195 (top), Graca Victoria/Shutterstock. 195 (bottom), Joe Gough/Shutterstock. **Chapter 7: Where to Stay:** 227, Bruce Buck. 228, George Apostolidis/Mandarin Oriental. 234 (top), David Phelps Photography/Kimpton Hotels & Restaurants. 234 (center left), The Hay-Adams. 234 (center right), David Phelps Photography/Kimpton Hotels & Restaurants. 234 (bottom left), George Apostolidis/Mandarin Oriental. 234 (bottom right), Sofitel Lafayette Square Washington DC. 235 (top), Bruce Buck. 235 (center left), Jumping Rocks Inc. 235 (center right and bottom left), David Phelps Photography/Kimpton Hotels & Restaurants. 235 (bottom right), Jumping Rocks Photography. 236 (top), Four Seasons Hotels and Resorts. 236 (center left), The Latham Hotel, Washington DC. 236 (center right), The Ritz-Carlton Company, L.L.C.. 236 (bottom), Omni Shoreham Hotel. **Chapter 8: Nightlife:** 267, Rough Guides/Alamy. 270, dk/Alamy. **Chapter 9: The Performing Arts:** 285, Bob Llewellyn/FOLIO Inc. 287, Karin Cooper. **Chapter 10: Sports & the Outdoors:** 299, Krista Rossow/age fotostock. 301, Visions of America, LLC/Alamy. 305, Anosmia/Flickr. 308-309, sneakerdog/Flickr. 311, William S. Kuta/Alamy. **Chapter 11: Shopping:** 319, Alex Segre/Alamy. 322, Michael J. Hipple/age fotostock. 330, Lee Foster/Alamy. 335, Alex Segre/Alamy. **Chapter 12: Side Trips:** 339, Olga Bogatyrenko/iStockphoto. 340, rpongsaj/Flickr. 341, 2265524729/Shutterstock. 343, Anton Albert/Shutterstock. 349, Krista Rossow/age fotostock. 360, Jeff Greenberg/age fotostock. 365, vittorio sciosia/age fotostock.

ABOUT OUR WRITERS

Beth Kanter is a feature writer who has spent the better part of the last two decades living in and writing about Washington, D.C. Her work has appeared in a variety of magazines, newspapers, and electronic publications including *Wondertime*, *Parents*, *American Baby*, *Shape*, vtravelled.com, the *Chicago Tribune* and *Pages*. She is also the author of the book *Day Trips from Washington, D.C.* Beth updated the Where to Stay chapter. You can visit her Web site at www.bethkanter.com.

Cathy Sharpe, a freelance writer with more than 20 years of experience in travel, has lived in the Maryland suburbs of Washington since 1998. She loves seeing the metro area's wonders through the eyes of her four children.

Elana Schor was bit by the Washington bug at age eight, when she first applied to become a Capitol tour guide. She still delights in showing D.C. newbies the ropes as a correspondent for Streetsblog Capitol Hill and restaurant reviewer for The Hill newspaper. She updated the Where to Eat chapter. She has also covered the capital for *Talking Points Memo* and *The Guardian* newspaper.